ESTATE PLANNING & TAXATION OF CAPITAL HANDBOOK

2nd edition

David Bertram

CLAYFIELD PROFESSIONAL GUIDANCE LTD

PEARSON EDUCATION LIMITED

Head Office:
Edinburgh Gate
Harlow CM20 2JE
Tel: +44 (0)1279 623623
Fax: +44 (0)1279 431059

London Office:
128 Long Acre, London WC2E 9AN
Tel: +44 (0) 207 447 2000
Fax: +44 (0) 207 240 5771

Websites: www.business-minds.com
www.pearsoned-ema.com

This edition first published in Great Britain in 2000

ISBN 0 273 65045 9

British Library Cataloguing in Publication Data
A CIP catalogue record for this book can be obtained
from the British Library

Typeset by M Rules
Printed and bound in Great Britain by Biddles Ltd, Guildford and King's Lynn

*The Publishers' policy is to use paper manufactured
from sustainable forests.*

CONTENTS

ABBREVIATIONS

ACT	advance corporation tax
APR	agricultural property relief
ATA	Agricultural Tenancies Act
BPR	business property relief
CCAB	Consultative Committee of the Accountancy Bodies
CGT	capital gains tax
CTO	Capital Taxes Office
ESC	extra-statutory concession
FA	Finance Act
GWR	gift with reservation
ICAEW	Institute of Chartered Accountants in England and Wales
IHTA	Inheritance Tax Act
IRPR	Inland Revenue Press Release
LPA	Law of Property Act
QCB	Qualifying Corporate Bond
SP	Statement of Practice
SVD	Shares Valuation Division
TA 1988	Income and Corporation Taxes Act 1988
TCGA 1992	Taxation of Chargeable Gains Act 1992

GLOSSARY

Appropriate person In relation to **qualifying investments** comprised in a person's estate immediately before death, the person liable for IHT attributable to the value of those investments or, if there is more than one such person, and one of them is in fact paying the IHT, that person.

In relation to any **interest in land** comprised in a person's estate immediately before death, the person liable for IHT attributable to the value of that interest or, if there is more than one such person, and one of them is in fact paying the IHT, that person.

Arm's length transaction A transaction where all the facts and circumstances are such as might have been expected if the parties to it had been independent persons dealing at arm's length (ie dealing with each other in a normal commercial manner unaffected by any special relationship between them).

Ascertained residue Property which, having ceased to be held by the deceased's personal representatives, is held as part of the deceased's estate residue.

Associated operations Any two or more operations of any kind, being:
(1) operations which affect the same property, or one of which affects some property and the other(s) of which affect property which represents, whether directly or indirectly, that property, or income arising from that property, or any property representing accumulations of any such income, or
(2) any two operations of which one is effected with reference to the other, or with a view to enabling the other to be effected or facilitating its being effected, and any further operation having a like relation to any of those two, and so on,

whether those operations are effected by the same person or different persons, and whether or not they are simultaneous; 'operation' includes an omission.

Bank:
(1) the Bank of England (TA 1988, s 840A(1)(a), applied by IHTA 1984, s 157(6));
(2) an institution authorised under the Banking Act 1987 (TA 1988, s 840A(1)(b));
(3) a **relevant European authorised institution** (TA 1988, s 840A(1)(c), applied by IHTA 1984, s 157(6)); or
(4) a relevant international organisation which is designated as a bank for the purposes of that provision by an order made by the Treasury (TA 1988, s 840A(1)(d), applied by IHTA 1984, s 157(6)).

Barrister This includes a member of the Faculty of Advocates.

Capital payment In relation to TCGA 1992, ss 86A–97:
(1) any payment which is not chargeable to income tax on the recipient or, in the case of a recipient who is neither resident nor ordinarily resident in the UK, any payment received otherwise than as income, but
(2) not a payment under a transaction entered into at arm's length if it is received on or after 19 March 1991.

Charges on residue   In relation to the estate of a deceased person, the following liabilities, properly payable thereout and interest payable in respect of them:
(1)   funeral, testamentary and administration expenses and debts (TA 1988, s 701(6)(a)), and
(2)   general legacies, demonstrative legacies, annuities and any sum payable out of residue to which a person is entitled under the law of intestacy of any part of the UK or any other country (s 701(6)(b)), and
(3)   any other liabilities of his personal representatives (s 701(6)(c)).

Close company   A company under the control of five or fewer persons, or under the control of its directors. A person or group of persons 'controls' a company if they are able to exercise control, directly or indirectly, over its affairs by owning the greater part of share capital, voting capital, or other capital giving entitlement to more than half of the assets on a winding-up. For the purposes of this book, a 'close company' is a company which is (or would be if UK-resident) a close company under TA 1988, ss 414–417 (which contain the full definition of 'close company').

Commercial association of companies   A company together with such of its associated companies (under TA 1988, s 416) as carry on businesses which are of such a nature that their businesses taken together may be reasonably considered to make up a single composite undertaking.

Conditionally exempt transfer   A lifetime transfer of, for example:
(1)   an historic house, a work of art, etc to the extent that the value transferred is so designated, following a claim to that effect, by the Treasury (under IHTA 1984, s 31);
(2)   an area of land which in the Treasury's opinion is essential for the protection of the character and amenities of a building of outstanding historic or architectural interest
See further Chapter 4.

Defined assets   All assets which constitute settled property of the settlement immediately before the trustees of a settlement become at any time ('the relevant time') neither resident nor ordinarily resident in the UK, and therefore outside the normal scope of CGT. If immediately after the relevant time the trustees carry on a trade in the UK through a branch or agency, and any assets are situated in the UK which are either used in, or for the purposes of, the trade or used or held for the purposes of the branch or agency, those assets are not defined assets. Also, assets are not defined assets if they are of a description specified in any double taxation relief arrangements, and, if the trustees were to dispose of them immediately before the relevant time, the trustees would not be liable in the UK to CGT on gains on the disposal.

Defined person   The settlor; his spouse; any child (or stepchild) of the settlor or of his spouse; the spouse of any such child (or stepchild); any grandchild of the settlor or of his spouse; the spouse of any such grandchild; a company controlled (under TA 1988, s 416) but without attributing shares to an associate who is not a participator (as defined in TA 1988, s 417(1)) by any of the foregoing persons; a company associated with such a company (under s 416) but without attributing shares to an associate who is not a participator (as defined in s 417(1)). Here 'child' includes a stepchild and 'grandchild' means a child of a child.

Derived property   In relation to any property, income from that property or any other property directly or indirectly representing proceeds of, or of income from, that property or income therefrom.

Disabled person   A person who is:
(1)   by reason of mental disorder (within the meaning of the Mental Health Act 1983) incapable of administering his property or managing his affairs, or
(2)   in receipt of an attendance allowance under s 64 of either the Social Security Contributions and Benefits Act 1992 or the Social Security Contributions and Benefits (Northern Ireland) Act 1992, s 64, or
(3)   in receipt of a disability living allowance under s 71 of either the Social Security Contributions and Benefits Act 1992 or the Social Security Contributions and Benefits (Northern Ireland) Act 1992 by being entitled to the care component at the highest or middle rate.

Disposition   This includes a disposition effected by **associated operations**.

Disposition-maker   A person or other entity who makes a disposition for the care or upkeep of another in the event of his death.

Eligible beneficiary   Under TCGA 1992, Sched A1, para 7 in relation to an asset comprised in a **settlement** and a certain time, any individual having at that time a **relevant interest in possession** under the settlement in either:
(1)   the whole of the settled property; or
(2)   a part of the settled property that is or includes that asset.

Enjoyment   Possession of an asset (usually land) without contested claims from third parties.

Estate duty   This includes estate duty under the law of Northern Ireland.

Exempt beneficiary   A beneficiary who receives an **exempt gift**.

Exempt body   A charity, political party or other body within IHTA 1984, ss 23–25 or the trustees of a settlement in relation to which a Treasury direction has been made under IHTA 1984, Sched 4, para 1.

Exempt gift   A gift is exempt under the following situations:
- transfers between spouses (IHTA 1984, s 18)
- gifts to charities (IHTA 1984, s 23)
- gifts to political parties (IHTA 1984, s 24)
- gifts to registered housing associations (IHTA 1984, s 24A)
- gifts for national purposes (IHTA 1984, s 25)
- PETs of property subsequently held for national purposes (IHTA 1984, s 26A)
- transfers to maintenance funds for historic buildings (IHTA 1984, s 27)
- transfers to employee trusts (IHTA 1984, s 28).

Where a transfer is exempt only up to a certain limit, it is exempt for so much of the gift as is within that limit (currently, none of the above exemptions has a limit – other than transfers between spouses where the transferee is non-domiciled).

51 per cent subsidiary   Generally, a company of another company under TCGA 1992, Sched A1, para 22(1) if and so long as more than 50 per cent of its ordinary share capital is owned directly or indirectly by that other company.

FOTRA securities   Government securities which are 'free of tax' in the hand of individuals who are neither resident nor domiciled in the UK.

Full-time working officer or employee   In relation to any company, an individual who under TCGA 1992, Sched A1, para 22(1):
(1)   is an officer or employee of that company or of that company and one or more other companies with which that company has a relevant connection; and
(2)   is required in that capacity to devote substantially the whole of his time to the service of that company, or to the service of those companies taken together.

Here, one company has a relevant connection with another at any time when they are both members of the same group of companies or of the same commercial association of companies.

In relation to one or more companies for the purposes of retirement relief, any officer or employee who is required to devote substantially the whole of his time to the service of that company, or those companies taken together, in a managerial or technical capacity. See generally Chapter 25.

Funds in court   These comprise:
   (1)   money in the Supreme Court, in county courts and statutory deposits (under the Administration of Justice Act 1982, s 40); and
   (2)   money in the Supreme Court of Judicature of Northern Ireland and in a county court in Northern Ireland.

Garden   In relation to a **permitted area**, an enclosed piece of ground devoted to the cultivation of flowers, fruit or vegetables. See Chapter 22.

Gift   In relation to any transfer of value, a gift is the benefit of any disposition or rule of law by which, on the making of the transfer, any property becomes (or would but for any abatement become) the property of any person or applicable for any purpose.

Government department   This includes a Northern Ireland department.

Grounds   In relation to a **permitted area**, an enclosed land surrounding or attached to a dwelling-house or other building serving chiefly for ornament or recreation (dictionary definition). See Chapter 22.

Group of companies   For the purposes of this book, a company which has one or more 51 per cent subsidiaries, together with those subsidiaries.

Heritable security   Any security capable of being constituted over any **interest in land** by disposition or assignation of that interest in security of any debt and of being recorded in the General Register of Sasines.

Holding company   A parent company whose business (disregarding any trade carried on by it) consists wholly or mainly of the holding of shares in one or more companies which are its 51 per cent subsidiaries.

Incumbrance   This includes any **heritable security**, or other debt or payment secured upon heritage.

Inland Revenue charge   A charge imposed under IHTA 1984, s 237.

Interest in possession   Although not defined by the legislation, a person with an interest in possession of settled property is treated as beneficially entitled to the underlying property. By contrast, if there is 'no interest in possession', a special IHT charging regime applies. See generally **16.2**.

Interests in a company   See **Rights and interests in a company**.

Interest in land   This does not include any estate, interest or right by way of mortgage or other security.

Land   This does not include any **estate**, interest or right by way of **mortgage** or other security.

Legatee   Any person taking under a testamentary disposition or on an intestacy or partial intestacy, whether beneficially or as trustee, and a person taking under a *donatio mortis causa* is treated (except under TCGA 1992, s 62) as a legatee and his acquisition as made at the time of the donor's death. Under TCGA 1992, property taken under a testamentary disposition or on an intestacy or partial intestacy includes any asset appropriated by the personal representatives in or towards satisfaction of a pecuniary legacy or any other interest or share in the property devolving under the disposition or intestacy. A legatee also includes a person who acquires assets as a result of appointment or appropriation by the deceased's personal representatives, where the recipient's consent is required to the appropriation (CCAB, June 1967),

Market-maker A person who holds himself out at all normal times in compliance with the rules of The Stock Exchange as willing to buy and sell securities, stocks or shares at a price specified by him, and is recognised as doing so by the Council of The Stock Exchange.

Material transaction A transaction by way of gift or otherwise.

Minority participator A participator of the transferor company who is not, and is not a person connected with, a participator of the principal company of the group or of any of the principal company's participators.

Mortgage This includes a **heritable security** and a security constituted over any interest in movable property.

Mutual company:
  (1) a mutual insurance company (under the Insurance Companies Act 1982, s 96(1)) (ie any insurance company carrying on a business without having a share capital); or
  (2) a company of another description carrying on a business on a mutual basis.

New tenant Either:
  (a) the person(s) identified in a **notice of intention to retire in favour of a new tenant** as the person(s) who it is desired should become the tenant of the property to which that notice relates; or
  (b) the survivor(s) of the person(s) so identified, whether alone or with any other person(s).

Newspaper holding company A company which has:
  (1) as its only or principal asset shares in a newspaper publishing company, and
  (2) powers of voting on all or most questions affecting the publishing company as a whole which if exercised would yield a majority of the votes capable of being exercised on them.

Newspaper publishing company A company whose business consists wholly or mainly in the publication of newspapers in the UK.

Notice of intention to retire in favour of a new tenant In the case of any property, a notice or other written intimation given to the landlord by the tenant, or (in the case of a joint tenancy or tenancy in common) all of the tenants, of the property indicating, in whatever terms, his or their wish that one or more persons identified in the notice or intimation should become the tenant of the property.

Occupation Possession of land.

Ordinary shares Shares which carry either a right to dividends not restricted to dividends at a fixed rate, or a right to conversion into shares carrying such a right.

Overseas territory Any country or territory outside the UK.

Owned directly or indirectly As regards ownership by a company under TA 1988, s 838, beneficially owned, whether directly (or partly directly) or through (or partly through) another company or other companies. The amount of ordinary share capital of one company owned by a second company through another is determined in the following way. Where there are a number of companies, and the first directly owns ordinary share capital of the second and the second directly owns ordinary share capital of the third, then the first is deemed to own ordinary share capital of the third through the second, and, if the third directly owns ordinary share capital of a fourth, the first is deemed to own ordinary share capital of the fourth through the second and third, and the second is deemed to own ordinary share capital of the fourth through the third, and so on.

A chain of three or more companies where each directly owns the next companies ordinary share capital is called a **series**.

Participator In relation to any company, any person who is (or would be if the company were UK-resident) a participator in that company (under TA 1988, s 417(1)), but not including a person who would only be such a participator because of being a loan creditor. A participator in a company which is not a close company is construed to include a person who would be a participator in the company if it were a close company. See also **Minority participator**.

Pension A gratuity and any sum payable on or in respect of death, and a return of contributions with or without interest thereon or any other addition thereto.

Permitted area In general, an area (inclusive of the site of a dwelling-house) of half a hectare (approximately $1^1/_4$ acres). See Chapter 22.

Personal company In relation to an individual, any company the voting rights in which are exercisable, as to not less than 5 per cent, by that individual. See Chapter 25.

Personal representatives This includes any person by whom or on whose behalf an application for a grant of administration or for the resealing of a grant made outside the UK is made.

Preference shares Shares which do not carry any right to dividends other than dividends at a rate per cent of the nominal value of the shares which is fixed, and which carry rights in respect of dividends and capital which are comparable with those general for fixed-dividend shares listed in the Official List of The Stock Exchange (TA 1988, s 210(4)).

Property This includes rights and interests of any description.

Purchaser A purchaser in good faith for consideration in money or money's worth other than a nominal consideration. This includes a lessee, mortgagee or other person who for such consideration acquires an interest in a property.

Qualifying interest in possession An **interest in possession** to which an individual (or eg a company or partnership) is beneficially entitled under IHTA 1984, s 59. In the case of a company, this applies where its business consists wholly or mainly in the acquisition of interests in **settled property**, and the company has acquired the interest for full consideration in money or money's worth from an individual who was beneficially entitled to it. Where such acquisition was before 14 March 1975, the condition that its business consists wholly or mainly in the acquisition of interests in settled property is treated as satisfied if that was its business at the time of the acquisition; that condition need not be satisfied if the company is a suitably authorised insurance company.

Qualifying investments Shares or securities which are quoted at the date of death, holdings in a unit trust which at that date is an authorised unit trust (under TA 1988, s 468) and shares in any common investment fund established under the Administration of Justice Act 1965, s 1. Shares or securities which are comprised in a person's estate immediately before death and for which listing on a recognised stock exchange or dealing on the USM/AIM is suspended at that time are qualifying investments if they are again so listed or dealt in when they are sold or exchanged.

Qualifying property Land of any description, wherever situated; shares or securities; or a business or an interest in a business.

Qualifying sale A sale in which:

(1) the vendors are either the persons in whom property vested immediately after death or the deceased's personal representatives;

(2) is at arm's length for a price freely negotiated at the time of sale and is not made in conjunction with a sale of any of **related property** taken into account or any of the property which was also comprised in the estate but has not at any time since the death been vested in the vendors;

(3) no person concerned as vendor (or as having an interest in the proceeds of sale) is the same as or connected with any person concerned as purchaser (or as having an interest in the purchase); and

(4) neither the vendors nor any other person having an interest in the proceeds of sale obtain in connection with the sale a right to acquire the property sold or any interest in or created out of it.

Quoted shares and securities   Shares and securities listed on a recognised stock exchange or dealt in on the USM/AIM.

Related property   Property comprised in a person's estate which:

(1) is comprised in his spouse's estate; or

(2) it is or has within the preceding five years been:

    (a) (as a result of a transfer by him or his spouse) the property of a charity, or held on trust for charitable purposes only (IHTA 1984, s 23); or

    (b) (as a result of a gift by him or his spouse) the property of a political party (IHTA 1984, s 24), of a housing association (IHTA 1984, s 24A), for national purposes (IHTA 1984, s 25), or for the public benefit.

Relevant European authorised institution   An institution within the meaning of the Banking Co-ordination (Second Council Directive) Regulations 1992 (TA 1988, s 840A(2)(a), applied by IHTA 1984, s 157(6)); and in relation to which the requirements of the Banking Co-ordination (Second Council Directive) Regulations 1992, Sched 2, para 1 have been complied with in relation to its establishment of a branch (TA 1988, s 840A(2)(b), applied by IHTA 1984, s 157(6)).

Relevant event   In relation to any property, a chargeable transfer of which the whole or part of the value transferred is attributable to the property's value, and anything which would otherwise be such a chargeable transfer.

Relevant interest in possession   In relation to property comprised in a settlement, any interest in possession under that settlement other than:

(i) a right under that settlement to receive an annuity; or

(ii) a fixed-term entitlement.

Here, 'fixed-term entitlement', in relation to property comprised in a settlement, means any interest under that settlement which is limited to a term that is fixed and is not a term at the end of which the person with that interest will become entitled to the property.

Relevant international organisation   An international organisation of which the UK is a member (TA 1988, s 840A(3), applied by IHTA 1984, s 157(6)).

Relevant proportion   In relation to **qualifying investments** to which a claim relates, the proportion by which a loss on sale is reduced.

Retiring tenant's tenancy   The tenancy of the person(s) giving the **notice of intention to retire in favour of a new tenant**.

Reversionary interest   A future interest under a settlement, whether vested or contingent, including an interest expectant on the termination of an **interest in possession** which is deemed to subsist in part of any property; in relation to Scotland, it includes an interest in the fee of property subject to a proper life-rent.

Rights and interests in a company   These include rights and interests in the company's assets available for distribution among **participators** in the event of a winding-up or in any other circumstances (IHTA 1984, s 102(2)).

Sale price   In relation to a specific investment, the price for which the investment was sold by the **appropriate person** or, if it is greater, the best consideration which could reasonably have been obtained for the specific investment at the time of the sale.

In relation to **interest in land**, the price for which it is sold or, if greater, the best consideration that could reasonably have been obtained for it at the time of the sale.

Sale value   In relation to **qualifying investments**, the value at which they were sold.

In relation to **interest in land**, its sale price as increased or reduced.

Series, a   In relation to ordinary share capital **owned directly or indirectly** by a chain of companies, in any series:

(1)   a company which owns ordinary share capital of another company through the remainder is referred to as the 'first owner';

(2)   that other company the ordinary share capital of which is so owned is referred to as 'the last owned company';

(3)   the remainder, if one only, is referred to as 'an intermediary' and, if more than one, are referred to as 'a chain of intermediaries'.

A company in a series which directly owns ordinary share capital of another company in the series is referred to as 'an owner'.

Settlement   Any disposition of property, whether effected by instrument, by parol or by operation of law, whereby the property is, for the time being (IHTA 1984, s 43(2)):

(1)   held in trust for persons in succession or for any person subject to a contingency; or

(2)   held by trustees to accumulate the property's income or to make payments out of that income at the discretion of the trustees, or some other person, with or without power to accumulate surplus income; or

(3)   charged or burdened (otherwise than for full consideration in money or money's worth) with the payment of any annuity, etc for a life or other limited or terminable period;

or would be so held or charged or burdened if the disposition was regulated by UK (or equivalent foreign) law.

In relation to Scotland, 'settlement' also includes (IHTA 1984, s 43(4)):

(1)   an entail;

(2)   any deed by which an annuity is charged on, or on the rents of, any property (the property being treated as that comprised in the settlement); and

(3)   any deed creating or reserving a proper life-rent of any property whether heritable or moveable (the property from time to time subject to the proper life-rent being treated as that comprised in the settlement).

Here, 'deed' includes any disposition, arrangement, contract, resolution, instrument or writing.

Settlor   In relation to a **settlement**, any person by whom the settlement was made directly or indirectly (IHTA 1984, s 44(1)), including in particular any person who has provided funds directly or indirectly for the settlement or has made a reciprocal arrangement with any other person for that other person to make the settlement.

Where more than one person is a settlor in relation to a **settlement**, and the circumstances so require, special rules for settlements apply as if the settled property were comprised in separate settlements (IHTA 1984, s 44(2)).

Specific disposition   A specific devise or bequest made by a testator, including the disposition of personal chattels made by the Administration of Estates Act 1925, s 46 of and any disposition having, whether by virtue of any enactment or otherwise, under the law of another country an effect similar to that of a specific devise or bequest under the law of England and Wales (TA 1988, s 701(5)). Real estate included (either by a specific or general description) in a residuary gift made by the will of a testator is deemed to be a part of the residue of his estate and not to be the subject of a specific disposition.

Specific gift   Any gift other than a gift of residue or of a share in residue.

Subsidiary   A company is a subsidiary of another company (its **holding company**) if the holding company:

(1)   holds a majority of the voting rights in it (Companies Act 1985, s 736(1)(a)), or

(2)   is a member of it and has the right to appoint or remove a majority of its board of directors (s 736(1)(b)), or

(3)   is a member of it and controls alone, under an agreement with other shareholders or members, a majority of the voting rights in it, or if it is a subsidiary of a company which is itself a subsidiary of that other company (s 736(1)(c)).

Tenant's retirement in favour of a new tenant   Either:

(a)   the assignment, or (in Scotland) assignation, of the retiring tenant's tenancy to the new tenant in circumstances such that the tenancy is or becomes binding on the landlord and the new tenant as landlord and tenant respectively; or

(b)   the grant of a tenancy of the property which is the subject of the retiring tenant's tenancy, or of any property comprising the whole or part of that property, to the new tenant and the acceptance of that tenancy by him; in Scotland, 'grant' and 'acceptance' respectively include the deemed grant, and the deemed acceptance, of a tenancy under or by virtue of any enactment.

Transferee   The person whose property the **qualifying property** became on a transfer or, where on the transfer the qualifying property became comprised in a **settlement** in which no **qualifying interest in possession** (under the no interest in possession regime under IHTA 1984, ss 58–85) subsists, the settlement trustees.

Trade   Under TCGA 1992, Sched A1, para 22(1), anything which is a trade, profession or vocation, as defined for income tax purposes, and is conducted on a commercial basis and with a view to the realisation of profits. See Chapter 25.

Trading company   Under TCGA 1992, Sched A1, para 22(1), a company which is either:

(1)   a company existing wholly for the purpose of carrying on one or more trades; or

(2)   a company that would so exist apart from any incidental purposes which have no substantial effect on the extent of the company's activities.

See Chapter 25.

Trading group   A group of companies the activities of which taken together do not, or not to any substantial extent, include activities carried on otherwise than in the course of, or for the purposes of, a **trade**. See Chapter 25.

Transaction This includes, under TCGA 1992, Sched A1, para 22(1), any agreement, arrangement or understanding, whether or not legally enforceable, and a series of transactions.

Trustee Where there would be no trustees, the persons in whose name the settled property or its management is for the time being vested (IHTA 1984, s 45).

UK trust territory A territory administered by the UK government under the United Nations' trusteeship system.

Unadministered estate All the property for the time being held by the deceased's personal representatives, excluding property devolving on them otherwise than as assets for the payment of debts and excluding property that is the subject of a specific disposition, and making due allowance for outstanding charges on residue and for any adjustments between capital and income remaining to be made in due course of administration.

Unquoted shares or securities Shares or securities not listed on a recognised stock exchange nor dealt in on the USM/AIM.

Value on death In relation to **qualifying investments**, their probate value.

In relation to **interest in land** comprised in a person's estate immediately before death, the value which otherwise (and apart from related property sales under IHTA 1984, s 176) would be its value as part of that estate for IHT purposes.

KEY CHANGES DUE TO
FA 1999 AND FA 2000

Capital gains tax

- Simpler calculation of CGT liability of individuals.
- Improved taper relief on disposal of business property; business property now includes shareholdings over 5 per cent (was 25 per cent); maximum taper relief on disposals of business property achieved after four years (but no 'bonus year').
- Changes to holdover relief on gifts of business property.

Taxation of trusts

- CGT anti-avoidance rules for trustees disposals of settled property:
  — Deemed disposal of underlying assets.
  — Special rules for transfers linked to trustee borrowing ('flip-flops').
  — Attribution of gains to beneficiaries.
  — Restriction of set-off of trust losses.

Inheritance tax

- Restrictions on gifts with reservation of land (following decision in *Ingram & Palmer-Tomkinson (Lady Ingram's Executors) v CIR*).

PREFACE

My aim in writing this handbook has been to provide both the professional and non-professional reader with a thorough understanding of the framework of the law and practice of the taxation relating to the making of gifts and passing on of assets by way of inheritance. The taxes covered are Capital Gains Tax, Inheritance Tax, and insofar as it is relevant to gifts, Stamp Duty.

Since the coming to power of the New Labour government, in May 1997, sweeping changes have been made to Capital Gains Tax.

Thus, a new five year (in place of the previous three year) rule now applies for individuals who dispose of assets during a period of temporary non-residence.

Indexation relief ceases to run beyond 5 April 1998, for disposals by individuals (although it continues to run for companies). Along with the 'freezing' of indexation, the requirement to pool shares etc no longer applies for acquisitions after 5 April 1998. However existing pools (now referred to as 'section 104 pools') remain. The identification rules for share disposals after 5 April 1998 are (1) with acquisitions on the same day; (2) with acquisitions in the following 30 days on a first in/first out basis (effectively preventing any advantage from 'bed and breakfasting'); (3) with earlier acquisitions (but after 5 April 1998) on a last in/first out basis; (4) with the 'section 104 pool'; (5) with the pre-6 April 1982 pool; and (6) with acquisitions prior to 6 April 1965.

In place of indexation, taper relief is introduced, whereby the amount of the gain which is chargeable to tax is reduced according to the length of time the asset has been held after 5 April 1998. The taper is increased arithmetically over ten years from 7.5 per cent (after one year) to 75 per cent (after ten years) for business assets, and from 5 per cent (after three years) to 40 per cent (after ten years) for non-business assets. Where an asset is held at 17 March 1998, an extra complete year of ownership is attributed to that asset. Retirement relief is being phased down over a five year period from 1999/2000 until it is finally abolished entirely for disposals after 5 April 2003.

Reinvestment relief is abolished for disposals after 5 April 1998, however, elements of the relief are absorbed into EIS deferral relief.

From 6 April 1998, gains realised by all UK resident trusts and by the personal representatives of deceased persons are now subject to a 34 per cent rate of Capital Gains Tax (whereas, previously, this rate applied only to discretionary and accumulation trusts). Also, a new harsher Capital Gains Tax regime applies to non-UK resident trusts.

By comparison, the changes made to Inheritance Tax are comparatively minor. The rules for conditional exemption for heritage assets are strengthened, and the procedures for surrender of assets in lieu of Inheritance Tax are simplified. Also the exemption for gifts and bequests to approved non-profit-making bodies is withdrawn (this also applies for Capital Gains Tax). The rules for lifetime gifts, where the donor reserves or receives a material benefit from the gifted asset, are extended following the House of Lords decision in the *Ingram* case. The probability is that further changes will create a somewhat harsher climate for Inheritance Tax planning.

I have tried to make this handbook 'accessible', whilst providing a comprehensive coverage of the relevant legislation. The text seeks to present the legislation in a logical order, so as to provide an ideal source of reference to the non-specialist practitioner and an invaluable guide for non-professionals. Worked examples illustrate the practical application of legislation, tax calculations and the effect of allowances and reliefs. Wherever possible, I have tried to avoid legal phraseology, and have sought to explain the statutes and relevant case law in clear and simple language. However, I believe it is essential to be familiar with the law itself. Accordingly, statutory references have been included to enable the appropriate legislation, or case report to be turned to for further research. It must be stressed that this handbook can deal only with principles, and specific advice taking account of the facts and circumstances of the particular case should be sought.

Throughout the text, there are comments about the practical implications of the law, including pointers to tax planning opportunities and of pitfalls to avoid. However, the final chapter comprises a summary of tax planning ideas and points to watch.

I am indebted to the editorial staff at Pearson Education for all their help and advice in bringing this project to fruition, through extremely tight deadlines.

This handbook incorporates recent tax legislation (including FA 1999 and FA 2000) and relevant case law up to 31 July 2000. The law is stated as applied for 2000/01 unless the context otherwise requires.

David Bertram

Other titles in the Allied Dunbar Handbook series

TAX HANDBOOK 2000/2001

Whether you are a financial adviser, accountant, solicitor, company secretary, finance director or private individual who wants to find out about your own tax situation, this thorough guide has to be your first choice for shrewd advice and tax saving hints. Fully revised and updated, this edition incorporates all the latest changes following the Finance Act 2000. It offers sound advice on how to cope with self assessment, as well as offering detailed information on the complete range of taxes including CGT, VAT, stamp duty, inheritance tax, life assurance and national insurance.

INVESTMENT & SAVINGS 2000/2001

The *Allied Dunbar Investment & Savings Handbook* guides you through the complexities surrounding the abundance of financial products available, so that you can make informed choices for your investment strategy. Completely up to date with the latest legislation (it features changes resulting from the Spring 2000 budget and the Finance Act 2000), it highlights the significant changes in the law and how they will impact on your investments and savings.

RETIREMENT PLANNING (7th edition)

The *Allied Dunbar Retirement Planning Handbook* is an essential addition to your bookshelf. It ensures that you are fully aware of long and short term investment opportunities and examines the options available for improving retirement prospects.

EXPATRIATE TAX & INVESTMENT (7th edition)

'Expat's bible' – *What Investment*   'An absolute must' – *Money Magazine*

Written by experts, the *Allied Dunbar Expatriate Tax & Investment Handbook* gives you comprehensive coverage of every aspect of expatriate tax and investment, from the effect of the single currency to advice on working abroad. It is the essential guide for expatriates wishing to manage their financial affairs to their greatest possible advantage.

PENSIONS (7th edition)

This is the complete guide for business owners, company directors, the self employed and professional pension planners. It gives you a detailed investigation of all the choices available for successful pension planning.

--- AVAILABLE SOON ---

BUSINESS TAX & LAW (3rd edition)

With detailed information and astute advice, the *Allied Dunbar Business Tax & Law Handbook* makes business planning easier. It details the important taxation and legal considerations that affect a business; and considers both the legal environment in which businesses operate and the taxation obligations which must be met.

**For further information contact your local bookseller,
telephone Pearson Education Ltd on 01704 50 80 80
or e-mail at customer.orders@pearsoned-ema.com**

1

AN INTRODUCTION TO IHT

1.1 MAIN CHARGING AND RELIEF PROVISIONS

1.1.1 Charge on transfers
(IHTA 1984, s 1)

The basis of IHT is that it is charged on value transferred by chargeable transfers.

1.1.2 Chargeable transfers and exempt transfers
(IHTA 1984, s 2)

A chargeable transfer is a transfer of value made by an individual, but which is not an exempt transfer (IHTA 1984, ss 18–29A, 30–35). A number of dispositions (listed below) are eliminated as not being transfers of value, provided that the relevant conditions are met:

- not intended to confer gratuitous benefit (IHTA 1984, s 10);
- for maintenance of the family (IHTA 1984, s 11);
- allowable for income tax or conferring retirement benefits (IHTA 1984, s 12);
- by close companies for the benefit of employees (IHTA 1984, s 13);
- waiver of remuneration (IHTA 1984, s 14);
- waiver of dividends (IHTA 1984, s 15);
- grant of tenancies of agricultural property for full consideration (IHTA 1984, s 16);
- changes in distribution of deceased's estate (IHTA 1984, s 17), ie
  - (i) alteration of dispositions taking effect on death (IHTA 1984, ss 17(a) and 142(1));
  - (ii) a transfer made in compliance with the testator's request (IHTA 1984, ss 17(b) and 143);
  - (iii) an election by a surviving spouse, in an intestacy, to take a capital sum instead of a life interest under the Administration of Estates Act 1925, s 47A (IHTA 1984, s 17(c));
  - (iv) the renunciation, in Scotland, of a claim to legitim within two years (longer at the Revenue's discretion) of attaining the age of 18 (IHTA 1984, ss 17(d) and 147(6));

- distributions from property settled by will (IHTA 1984, s 144);
- redemption of surviving spouse's life interest (IHTA 1984, s 145);
- inheritance (Provision for Family and Dependants) Act 1975 (IHTA 1984, s 146);
- chargeable transfer becoming voidable by enactment or rule of law (IHTA 1984, s 150);
- settled property entering a maintenance fund (IHTA 1984, s 57A).

A transfer of value by an individual may be exempt only to a limited extent. In such a case, the whole of the transfer is an exempt transfer if the value transferred is within that limit. In other cases, the transfer of value may be partly within and partly outside that limit. This means that the chargeable transfer is only so much of the value as exceeds that limit.

It may be that an individual makes a transfer of value, which is exempt only to a limited extent. In such a case, if all the value transferred by it is within the limit, it is an exempt transfer. But where the value transferred is partly within and partly outside the limit, there is a chargeable transfer of whatever value is outside the limit, and an exempt transfer of whatever value is within the limit. This could happen, for example, where a gift in excess of £55,000 is made to a non-UK domiciled spouse (IHTA 1984, s 18(2)), or if a gift is made in excess of the annual exemption (IHTA 1984, s 19(1)).

In general, references to chargeable transfers, to their making or to the values transferred by them are taken to include exit charges relating to 'no interest in possession' trusts (IHTA 1984, ss 2(3), 58–78, 80–85). There are, however, a number of exceptions to this general rule which are dealt with elsewhere in this book.

A number of extra-statutory concessionary practices are applicable:

- IHT is not claimed on death of a nominal owner of property of Roman Catholic religious communities (ESC F2);
- works of art temporarily in the UK (eg for cleaning, exhibition, etc) are not liable to IHT if otherwise they would not be (ESC F7);
- where a person died before 12 March 1952 and his estate was wholly exempted (by FA 1894, s 8(1)) from estate duty as the property of a common seaman, marine or soldier who died in the service of the Crown and under his will he left a limited interest to someone who dies after 12 March 1975, no IHT is charged on any property exempted on the original death which passes under the terms of the will on the termination of the limited interest (ESC F13);
- the Revenue confirmed (see SP/E14) that there is no liability to IHT on winnings by a football pool or similar syndicate (eg National Lottery).

In the case of syndicate winnings, however, the winnings must be paid out under the terms of an agreement drawn up before the win. If winnings are paid out, under a pre-existing and enforceable arrangement, among the members of a syndicate in proportion to the share of the stake money each has provided, then each member of the syndicate receives what already belongs to him or her. There is therefore no 'gift' or 'chargeable transfer' by the person who, on behalf of the members, receives the winnings from the promoter. It would be wise to record in a written, signed and dated statement, the existence and terms of the agreement between them. If, following a win the terms of such an agreement are varied or part of the winnings are distributed to persons who are not members of the syndicate, an IHT liability may arise.

1.1.3 Transfers of value
(IHTA 1984, s 3)

A transfer of value is a disposition, made by a 'transferor', as a result of which the value of his estate, immediately after the disposition, is less than it would be if the disposition had not been made. The amount by which his estate is reduced is the measure of the value transferred. This is also referred to as the 'loss to donor' principle, and is one of the basic principles of IHT.

Example

> A shareholder holds 51 per cent of the share capital of an unquoted company. He makes a gift of 2 per cent of the shares so that he is left with 49 per cent. The measure of the amount transferred is the difference between the value of the 51 per cent holding before the transfer, and that of the 49 per cent transfer thereafter. The value of the 2 per cent holding in isolation is not relevant for IHT purposes. This value is, however, the measure taken for CGT and stamp duty purposes.

However, no account is taken of 'excluded property' which leaves a person's estate as a result of a disposition.

Where the value of a person's estate is diminished and that of another person's estate, or of settled property in which there is 'no interest in possession', is increased by his *omission* to exercise a right, he is treated as having made a disposition at the time when he could have exercised the right. However, this does not apply if he can show that the omission was not deliberate. An example of a chargeable transfer arising from a failure or omission to exercise a right would be if a shareholder does not subscribe to a favourable rights issue in an unquoted company, while other shareholders exercise their rights, as this would in effect decrease his proportionate holding, and increase theirs. The effect of this failure is that the value of his estate has decreased, while the estates of the other shareholders has increased, thus giving rise to a *de facto* transfer of value. Sections 80–98 of and Sched 5 to TCGA 1992 contain rules for capital gains of certain offshore trusts. In such cases, the settlor has a right under TCGA 1992, Sched 5, para 6 to reimbursement of tax paid. If a settlor does not pursue his statutory right to reimbursement, the failure to exercise this right may give rise to an IHT claim, to which the usual rules for lifetime transfers would apply. The drop in value in the settlor's estate occurs when the right to reimbursement expires. The duration of the settlor's right to reimbursement is governed by the Limitation Act, which prescribes a six-year limit (unless the settlor indicates to the trustees before the expiration of this period that he does not intend to exercise his right to reimbursement, at which point the right expires). The six-year period begins when the settlor pays the IHT (see SP5/92 and ICAEW guidance note TAX 20/92).

Many pension scheme benefits are written under trust on terms which provide that the pension continues to be for the policyholder and the death benefit is assigned, normally to members of the family. Once the retirement benefit is taken, the death benefit lapses. It is a common feature of these schemes that, from a specified age, the policyholder can elect to take the retirement benefit. There are cases where policyholders do not elect to do so at the specified age and have still not done so when they die (so that the death benefit becomes payable). The CTO takes the view that, in certain circumstances, such failure to exercise that right before death can give rise to a lifetime charge to IHT. Such claims as do arise are likely to be limited to retirement annuity contracts or personal pension schemes. Only exceptionally would claims involve occupational pension schemes. The CTO will consider raising a claim only in cases where there is evidence that the policyholder's intention, in failing to take up retirement benefits, was to increase the estate of someone else (ie the beneficiaries) rather than to benefit himself. Thus, they look closely at certain pension arrangements where, for example, the policyholder became aware that he was suffering from a terminal illness, or was in such poor health that his life was uninsurable. If, at or after that time, the policyholder took out a new policy and assigned the death benefit on trust, or assigned on trust the death benefit of an existing policy, or paid further contributions to a single premium policy or enhanced contributions to a regular premium policy where the death benefit had been previously assigned on trust, or deferred the date for taking retirement benefits, it would be difficult to argue that the policyholder's actions were intended to make provision for his own retirement given the prospect of an early death.

However, the CTO does not pursue such a claim where the death benefit is paid to the policyholder's spouse and/or dependants. In addition, a claim is not normally pursued where the policyholder survives for two years or more after making any of these arrangements. The CTO will adopt a similar approach in cases involving personal pension schemes set up under deed poll under the Superannuation Funds Office or Integrated Model rules, or buy-out policies under trust, approved under TA 1988, s 591(2)(g) (commonly known as 'section 32 policies' after the original legislation) (see Tax Bulletin 2 (February 1992)).

There are a number of instances where a transfer of value is deemed to be made. However, some deemed transfers may be eligible for exemption.

1.1.4 Potentially exempt transfers (PETs)
(IHTA 1984, s 3A)

Most lifetime transfers are either exempt transfers (IHTA 1984, ss 18–29A) or PETs (IHTA 1984, s 3A). PETs comprise gifts:

- which are made outright by an individual and which would otherwise be chargeable transfers;
- to the extent that they are either to another individual or into an accumulation and maintenance trust, or a trust for a disabled person;
- to 'interest in possession trusts'.

The first of these categories refers to a transfer of value, as a gift to another individual, to the extent that the value transferred is attributable to property which, because of the transfer, becomes comprised in the estate of that other individual or, to the extent that, because of the transfer, the estate of that other individual is increased. This would exclude, for example, payment of school fees by a grandparent if the payment is made direct to the school, or payment by a settlor of premiums on a life policy.

The second category refers to a transfer of value, as a gift into an accumulation and maintenance trust (IHTA 1984, s 71), to the extent that the value transferred is attributable to property which, because of the transfer, becomes settled property. A gift into a disabled trust (IHTA 1984, s 89) likewise becomes settled property.

The third category comprises gifts to 'interest in possession trusts' on the basis that the life tenant is deemed to own the underlying assets (IHTA 1984, s 49).

There is, however, a variety of situations (identified at appropriate points in this work) where it is provided that a disposition (or transfer of value) of a particular description are stated not to be PETs.

A PET which is made seven years or more before the transferor's death becomes an exempt transfer, while those that fall within the seven year period become chargeable transfers. It is assumed, during the period beginning on the date a PET is made and ending immediately before the seventh anniversary or, if it is earlier, the transferor's death, that the transfer will prove to be an exempt transfer.

In any circumstance whereby IHT is to be charged as if a transfer of value had been made, that transfer is taken to be other than a PET. This does not apply where the charge concerned arises under IHTA 1984, s 52 (charge on termination of interest in possession). In other words, only actual, and not deemed, transfers qualify as PETs. If no property changes hands, the PET is limited to the increase in the value of the donee's estate.

A sliding scale of IHT applies to gifts more than three years before death (IHTA 1984, s 7(4)). It is not necessary to submit an account when a PET is made (*Law Society's Gazette*, 2 November 1988; 14 December 1988).

1.1.5 Transfers on death

(IHTA 1984, s 4)

On death a person is charged to IHT as if, immediately before his death, he had made a transfer of value equal to that of all of the assets comprised in his death estate, including PETs made within seven years preceding death (IHTA 1984 s 3A(4)). Where it cannot be known which of two or more persons who have died (eg in a road accident) survived the other or others they are assumed to have died at the same instant.

Although the requirement is to take the value of all of the assets comprised in the deceased's estate immediately before his death, in determining that value changes in its value which have occurred because of the death are taken into account as if they had occurred before the death (eg a life policy maturing is valued as the amount of proceeds received) (IHTA 1984, s 171(1)). The change can be an addition to the property comprised in the estate or an increase or decrease of the value of any property so comprised (IHTA 1984, s 171(2)). However, this does not apply to a decrease resulting from an alteration (or extinguishment) in so much of a close company's share or loan capital as does not consist of quoted shares or quoted securities (IHTA 1984, s 98(1)(a), (2)) or an alteration (or extinguishment) in any rights attaching to unquoted shares in or unquoted debentures of a close company (IHTA 1984, s 98(1)(b)). In this context no account is taken of changes in value arising on the termination on the death of, or the passing of, any interest by survivorship (IHTA 1984, s 171(2)).

The deceased's estate is also deemed to include the value of gifts made by the deceased during his lifetime, but in which he has reserved a benefit (FA 1986, s 102). These are known as 'gifts with reservation' (GWRs). Also included is the value of an absolute interest in settled property in which he was the life tenant (ie in which he had an interest in possession) (IHTA 1984, s 49(1)). This does not apply if the settled property reverts to the settlor (or to his spouse) and was not for a consideration in money or money's worth, or following the transfer of a reversionary interest after 9 March 1981.

Under the old estate duty rules, if a surviving spouse was left a life interest in an estate there was no further estate duty payable on the death of surviving spouse. Under IHT, however, an IHT charge arises on the subsequent death, but would be exempt on the first death (IHTA 1984, s 18). In such cases, where estate duty was paid on the first death (before 14 November 1974) there is no IHT charge on the surviving spouse's death (IHTA 1984, Sched 6, para 2). The trustees of such a settlement should follow a policy of investing in assets that are expected to appreciate.

1.1.6 Meaning of 'estate'

(IHTA 1984, s 5)

'Estate' is construed in accordance with IHTA 1984, s 5:

(1) A person's estate is the aggregate of all the property to which he is beneficially entitled. However, for IHT purposes, his estate immediately before his death does not include 'excluded property'. This includes settled property in which he has an interest in possession. However, certain reversionary interest may be excluded property (IHTA 1984, s 48).

(2) A person who has a general power which enables him, or would if he were *sui juris* enables him, to dispose of or to charge money on any property other than settled property, is treated as beneficially entitled to the property or money. For this purpose 'general power' means a power or authority enabling the person by whom it is exercisable to appoint or dispose of property as he thinks fit (see *Estate and Gift Duty Commissioners v Fiji Resorts Ltd* [1982] STC 871, PC).

(3) In determining the value of a person's estate his liabilities at that time are taken into account, only insofar as there is a specific provision to do so. The liabilities which can be taken into account in determining the value of a transferor's estate immediately after a transfer of value include his liability for IHT on the value transferred, but not his liability (if any) for any other tax or duty (eg CGT or stamp duty) resulting from the transfer. Except for a liability imposed by law, a liability incurred by a transferor is taken into account only to the extent that it was incurred for a consideration in money or money's worth.

(4) An interest (whether in possession or not) in any settled property where the person entitled to that interest acquires a reversionary interest expectant (whether immediately or not) on that interest. However, the disposition by which the interest was acquired does not qualify as a disposition not intended to confer gratuitous benefit (IHTA 1984, ss 10(1), 55(2)).

This is one of the key concepts of IHT because of the 'loss to donor' principle which underlies the tax:

- during life, the value transferred is the amount by which the transferor's estate is reduced by that transfer (IHTA 1984, s 3(1));
- on death, a person is treated as having made a transfer of value equal to the value of his estate immediately before his death (IHTA 1984, s 4(1)).

A person's estate for IHT purposes comprises the aggregate of all property (including rights and interests of any description) to which he is beneficially entitled (IHTA 1984, s 272):

- a person's estate immediately before his death does not include 'excluded property';
- a person who is beneficially entitled to an interest in possession in settled property is treated as beneficially entitled to that property (IHTA 1984, s 49(1));
- property over which a person has a 'general power' is included;
- gifts made by a deceased in which he had reserved a benefit (GWRs) are included (FA 1986, s 102);

7

- a person's liabilities are taken into account in determining the value of his estate.

A person who has a 'general power' which enables him to dispose of, or to charge money on, any property other than settled property is treated as beneficially entitled to the property or money. For this purpose 'general power' means a power or authority enabling the person by whom it is exercisable to appoint or dispose of property as he thinks fit (see also *Estate and Gift Duty Commissioners v Fiji Resorts Ltd* [1982] STC 871, PC).

In determining the value of a person's estate his liabilities at that time are taken into account, only insofar as there is a specific provision to do so. The liabilities which can be taken into account in determining the value of a transferor's estate immediately after a transfer of value include his liability for IHT on the value transferred but not his liability (if any) for any other tax or duty (eg CGT or stamp duty) resulting from the transfer. Except for a liability imposed by law, a liability incurred by a transferor is taken into account only to the extent that it was incurred for a consideration in money or money's worth.

1.1.7 Other liabilities which are deductible

Subject to satisfying certain conditions, the following liabilities can be deducted in arriving at the value of a person's estate:

- funeral expenses, including the tombstone and reasonable mourning expenses (IHTA 1984, s 172; SP 7/87; ESC F1);
- an allowance against the value of property situated outside the UK of up to 5 per cent for the added expense of administering or realising that property (IHTA 1984, s 173); this covers additional costs of resealing a grant of probate etc, obtaining the relevant tax clearance, but not substantive expenses (eg tax liabilities);
- previously undischarged tax liabilities (if paid out of the estate) (IHTA 1984, s 174), including income tax liabilities arising on deemed disposals on death for:
  (i) offshore income gains (TA 1988, ss 757–764, Scheds 27, 28); and
  (ii) deep discount securities (TA 1988, s 57, Sched 4);
- IHT liabilities outstanding from a previous transfer, but if the tax is not eventually paid out of the estate, an adjustment must be made;
- any liability to make future payments or transfers of assets (IHTA 1984, ss 175, 262);
- a charge on a property, so far as possible, from the value of that property, so that only the net value is brought into account; liabilities to non-residents are deducted, so far as possible, from the value of property outside the UK, unless it is intended that the debt be discharged in the UK, or if it is charged on UK property;

- certain debts and incumbrances, but subject to abatement if, in determining the value of a person's estate immediately before his death, account would otherwise be taken of a liability consisting of a debt incurred, or an incumbrance created by a disposition made, by him to an extent proportionate to the value of any of the consideration given for the debt or incumbrance which consisted of property derived from the deceased; or consideration (not being property derived from the deceased) given by any person who was at any time entitled to, or amongst whose resources there was at any time included, any property derived from the deceased (FA 1986, s 103).

In determining the value of a person's estate immediately before his death, no account is taken (IHTA 1984, s 5) of any liability arising under or in connection with a life insurance policy made after 30 June 1986 unless the whole of the sums assured under that policy form part of that person's estate immediately before his death (FA 1986, s 103).

Reimbursement
(IHTA 1984, s 162)

A liability for which there is a right of reimbursement is taken into account only to the extent that reimbursement cannot reasonably be expected to be obtained. However, a liability which will be discharged after the time at which it is to be taken into account is valued as at that time. But, in determining the value of a person's estate immediately after a transfer of value, his IHT liability is computed without any allowance for the fact that the IHT is not immediately due, and as if any tax recovered otherwise from the transferor (or in certain cases his spouse) were paid in discharge of a liability for which the transferor had a right of reimbursement (IHTA 1984, s 203(1)).

Charge on specific property
(IHTA 1984, s 162)

A charge on any property is taken so far as possible as reducing the value of property concerned. A liability to a non-resident is deducted so far as possible from property outside the UK, unless it is to be discharged in the UK or charged against UK property.

Property transferred and lent back
(FA 1986, s 103)

Debts are subject to abatement, if the loan is received from a person to whom the deceased had given property, to the extent that the consideration given for the debt comprises such property.

Property transferred – different property lent back
(FA 1986, s 103(2), (3))

No abatement is given if the consideration given for the debt does not consist of property derived from the deceased and lent back, but instead consists of some other consideration given by a person, whose resources have included any property derived from the deceased. 'Property derived from the deceased' means, property comprised in a disposition, in whatever form, made by the deceased. Such dispositions may be alone or in concert, or by arrangement with other persons, or represented any of the subject matter of such a disposition, whether directly or indirectly, and whether by means of one or more intermediate dispositions.

Neither 'transfer of value' nor 'associated operations'
(FA 1986, s 103)

If the disposition was not a transfer of value, and was not part of associated operations which include a disposition by the deceased (alone or in concert, or by arrangement with any other person) otherwise than for full consideration in money or money's worth paid to the deceased for his own use or benefit, or a disposition by any other person which reduces the value of the property of the deceased, the disposition is left out of account.

Money paid by the deceased
(FA 1986, s 103)

If, prior to his death, money or money's worth was paid by the deceased in satisfaction or discharge of a debt to which an abatement would have applied on his death had the debt not already been satisfied or discharged, or in reduction of a debt for which an abatement was applied on his death, the deceased is treated as if, at the time of the payment, he had made a PET if the donor dies within seven years of the repayment.

Life insurance
(FA 1986, s 103)

In determining the value of a death estate, a liability arising in connection with a life insurance policy made after 30 June 1986, can be deducted only if the policy proceeds form part of the estate.

Formality

Where a loan is made between individuals, the CTO will not accept that the loan has been waived and the lender's estate reduced unless the waiver was effected by deed (*Law Society's Gazette*, 18 December 1991).

1.1.8 Excluded property
(IHTA 1984, s 6)

The following property is likely to qualify as excluded property, in which case it is not included in a person's estate:

- property situated outside the UK, if the owner is non-UK-domiciled (IHTA 1984, s 6(1));
- FOTRA securities if they are held in trust and the person concerned holds a qualifying interest in possession (see IHTA 1984, ss 48(4), 59);
- certain property held by persons domiciled in the Channel Islands or in the Isle of Man, eg:
  (i) war savings certificates,
  (ii) National Savings certificates (including Ulster savings certificates),
  (iii) premium savings bonds,
  (iv) deposits with the National Savings Bank or with a trustee savings bank,
  (v) a certified contractual savings scheme (TA 1988, s 326),
  (iv) emoluments and property of visiting forces (IHTA 1984, s 155);
- reversionary interests unless purchased by the deceased, or if the deceased (or his spouse) was the settlor (IHTA 1984, s 48(1));
- property comprised in a settlement situated outside the UK (but not a reversionary interest in the settlement), unless the settlor was UK-domiciled when the settlement was made (IHTA 1984, s 48(3)(a));
- property held in a settlement in which a person holds an interest in possession, and which is otherwise subject to an IHT charge when that interest comes to an end, if the property is excluded property (IHTA 1984, s 53(1)).

1.1.9 Property 'left out of account'

The property set out below is 'left out of account' in determining the value of a person's estate on death. Although no IHT is charged on the property it is not exempt, and since it remains in the death estate it can have an effect on the value of other property:

- PETs (IHTA 1984, s 3A) unless they become chargeable transfers on the donor's death within seven years, or seven years pass and they become exempt;
- an interest in possession held by the deceased, but which reverts to the settlor during his lifetime (IHTA 1984, s 54(1));
- an interest in possession held by the deceased, but to which the settlor's spouse (or widow or widower if the settlor died less than two years earlier) becomes entitled to the settled property and is UK-domiciled (IHTA 1984, s 54(2));

- under the terms of a settlement, remuneration for a trustee's services to an interest in possession in property comprised in the settlement, to the extent that it represents reasonable remuneration (IHTA 1984, s 90);
- where an election has been made for the value of trees and underwood to be left out of account until felled (IHTA 1984, s 125);
- certain income rights:
  (i) under pensions paid to non-UK resident persons (TA 1988, s 615(3); IHTA 1984, s 151(1)),
  (ii) under exempt approved schemes or statutory schemes (TA 1988, ss 590–612),
  (iii) under approved retirement annuities and other approved contracts (TA 1988, ss 620, 621; IHTA 1984, s 151(1)),
  (iv) under approved personal pension schemes (TA 1988, ss 630–655),
  (v) under pensions for service for certain ex-colonial territories (IHTA 1984, s 153(1));
- qualifying foreign currency bank accounts of persons not domiciled, resident or ordinarily resident in the UK (IHTA 1984, s 157(1), (2));
- the interest of a tenant in an unexpired portion of a lease for a fixed term of agricultural property in Scotland to the extent of any value associated with any prospect of renewal of the lease by tacit relocation (IHTA 1984, s 177(1)); it is a requirement that the deceased must have been tenant of the property in question continuously for a period of at least two years immediately preceding his death or had become tenant by succession (IHTA 1984, s 177(3));
- the interest of a tenant of agricultural property in Scotland, being an interest which is held by virtue of tacit relocation, and acquired on the death by a new tenant, to the extent of the interest's value (IHTA 1984, s 177(2)); the IHTA 1984, s 177(3) requirement applies (see above), and the value to be left out of account does not include the value of any rights to compensation in respect of tenant's improvements (IHTA 1984, s 177(4));
- where the surviving spouse exemption applied under the old estate duty rules (IHTA 1984, Sched 6, para 2).

1.1.10 Not part of his estate

The following property is 'not part of his estate':

- Where it cannot be known which of two or more persons who have died survived the other or others they are assumed to have died at the same instant (IHTA 1984, s 4(2)). The effect of this is that the estates immediately before the death of any them does not include property that they would have inherited from the others;
- An interest (whether in possession or not) in any settled property where the person entitled to that interest acquires a reversionary interest

expectant (whether immediately or not) on that interest (IHTA 1984, s 55(1)). However, the disposition by which the interest was acquired does not qualify as a disposition not intended to confer gratuitous benefit (IHTA 1984, ss 10(1), 55(2)).

- Where under approved personal pension arrangements (TA 1988, ss 630–655; IHTA 1984, s 152(a)), or under a contract or trust scheme approved by the Revenue (TA 1984, s 620 or 621) or (before 6 April under FA 1956, s 22 (IHTA 1984, s 152(b)), an annuity becomes payable on a person's death to a widow, widower or dependant of that person, and under the terms of the contract or scheme a sum of money might at his option have become payable instead to his personal representatives, he is not treated as having been beneficially entitled to that sum (IHTA 1984, s 152). This overrides the general rule, in IHTA 1984, s 5(2), that a person who has a general power which enables him to dispose of, or to charge money on, any property other than settled property is treated as beneficially entitled to the property or money.

- References to property to which a person is beneficially entitled does not include property to which a person is entitled as a corporation sole (eg property held by the Archbishop of Canterbury because of his office) (IHTA 1984, s 271). This definition specifically excludes the application of IHTA 1984, s 59 which defines a qualifying interest in possession as one to which an individual is beneficially entitled.

1.1.11 Dispositions that are not transfers of value

There are number of dispositions that are not treated as transfers of value, and which are therefore ignored for the purposes of IHT:

- dispositions not intended to confer gratuitous benefit (IHTA 1984, s 10);
- dispositions for maintenance of family (IHTA 1984, s 11);
- dispositions allowable for income tax or conferring retirement benefits (IHTA 1984, s 12);
- dispositions by close companies for the benefit of employees (IHTA 1984, s 13);
- waiver of remuneration (IHTA 1984, s 14);
- waiver of dividends (IHTA 1984, s 15);
- grants of tenancies of agricultural property (IHTA 1984, s 16);
- changes in distribution of deceased's estate (IHTA 1984, s 17).

1.1.12 Transfers exempt for lifetime transfers

The following transfers are exempt for lifetime transfers:

- annual exemption of £3,000 (IHTA 1984, s 19);
- small gifts not exceeding £250 (IHTA 1984, s 20);

- normal expenditure out of income (IHTA 1984, s 21);
- gifts in consideration of marriage (IHTA 1984, s 22).

1.1.13 Transfers exempt for lifetime transfers and on death

The following transfers of value are exempt on both lifetime transfers and on death:

- transfers between spouses (IHTA 1984, s 18);
- gifts to charities (IHTA 1984, s 23);
- gifts to political parties (IHTA 1984, s 24);
- gifts to housing associations (IHTA 1984, s 24A);
- gifts for national purposes (IHTA 1984, s 25);
- gifts for public benefit, prior to 17 March 1998 (IHTA 1984, s 26);
- PETs of property subsequently held for national purposes, etc (IHTA 1984, s 26A);
- maintenance funds for historic buildings (IHTA 1984, s 27);
- employee trusts (IHTA 1988, s 28).

1.1.14 Conditionally exempt transfers

Certain property, if so designated by the Treasury, may be conditionally exempt (IHTA 1984, ss 30–35).

1.1.15 Transfers exempt to limited extent

Certain transfers of value are exempt only to a limited extent:

- a gift in excess of £55,000 to a spouse who is not UK-domiciled (IHTA 1984, s 18(2)); or
- a gift in excess of the annual exemption (IHTA 1984, s 19(1)).

1.1.16 Exemptions only available for death transfers

Certain exemptions (eg death on active service (IHTA 1984, s 154)) are only available in respect of death transfers.

1.1.17 Rights and properties outside the scope of IHT

There are certain rights and properties which are entirely outside the scope of IHT:

- rights conferred by the Wellington Museum Act 1947, s 3 (Apsley House) (IHTA 1984, s 156(a));
- property held on trust under the Chevening Estate Act 1959 (Chevening House) (IHTA 1984, s 156(b)); and
- property covered by certain local or private Acts of Parliament.

1.1.18 Relief by reduction in value

Relief is available by means of a percentage reduction (of 100 or 50 per cent) in the value comprised in a person's estate on death, or in a lifetime chargeable transfer so as the value is attributable to:

- relevant business property (IHTA 1984, ss 103–114); or
- the agricultural value of agricultural property (IHTA 1984, ss 115–124B).

1.1.19 Adjustments

Adjustments can be made to the value of the deceased's estate to take account of the following matters:

- Actual (lower) sale proceeds can be substituted in place of probate valuation for 'related property' sold within three years of death by an arm's length sale freely negotiated and not in conjunction with the sale of any other related property (IHTA 1984, s 176). However, this does not apply to shares in a close company where the value thereof has been reduced by more than 5 per cent as a result of alteration to share or loan capital.
- Certain adjustments can be made to take account of the prospect of renewal of Scottish agricultural leases (IHTA 1984, s 177).

Adjustments can be made to take account of losses (compared with probate) realised on quoted shares sold within 12 months of death (IHTA 1984, ss 178–189).

1.1.20 Substitutions

Actual (higher or lower) sale proceeds can be substituted in place of probate valuation for land sold within three years of death (IHTA 1984, ss 190–198). The sale proceeds must differ from probate by more than 5 per cent of probate value, or £1,000 (whichever is the lesser amount). The revised value also applies for CGT (thereby reducing the amount of the gain) (TCGA 1992, s 274). If the sale value is higher than probate, but no IHT is paid, a claim would eliminate the gain. However, it is possible that the Revenue may refuse such claims on the basis that there is no 'appropriate person'.

1.1.21 Application to 'no interest in possession' trusts

Unless the context otherwise requires, references to chargeable transfers, to their making, or to the values transferred by them, include taxable occasions under the 'no interest in possession' trust regime (IHTA 1984, ss 2(3), 58–78, 80–85). This is because a chargeable transfer is a transfer of value made by an individual other than an exempt transfer. The general provisions in IHTA 1984 which apply to transfers of value as opposed to chargeable

15

transfers (in particular the exemptions) are not relevant to 'no interest in possession' trusts, which have their own separate scheme of exemptions.

Woodlands relief is available only in relation to a transfer of value on death and is inapplicable to 'no interest in possession' trusts (TA 1982, ss 125–130).

The main provisions of IHTA 1984 which do not relate exclusively to settled property, but which are capable of applying to 'no interest in possession' trusts are:

- business property relief (IHTA 1984, ss 103–114)
- agricultural property relief (IHTA 1984, ss 115–124B)
- relief for successive charges (IHTA 1984, s 141)
- orders under the Inheritance (Provision for Family and Dependants) Act 1975 (IHTA 1984, s 146)
- voidable transfers (IHTA 1984, s 150)
- double taxation relief (IHTA 1984, ss 158–159)
- reduction of valuation for CGT paid (IHTA 1984, s 165)
- valuation of life policies (IHTA 1984, s 167)
- liability (IHTA 1984, ss 201, 204, 212)
- administration and collection (IHTA 1984, s 216(1)(c))
- payment of IHT by instalments (IHTA 1984, ss 227–228)
- occasions of IHT charge affecting more than one property (IHTA 1984, s 265) and
- occasions of IHT charge made on the same day (IHTA 1984, s 266).

1.2 COMPLETION OF GIFT

The general rule is that a transfer is deemed made when the gift is complete, and there has been a shift of value from one estate to another. The legal requirements that must be fulfilled to ensure such a shift vary depending on the gift's subject matter. Usually, all the requirements relating to the type of asset must be satisfied by the donor before the gift becomes effective, and the transferor has done all that is necessary to divest himself of ownership (eg signed a stock transfer form and delivered scrip). The rules for particular types of asset are summarised below.

Freehold or leasehold land is gifted on the conveyance or assignment under seal or declaration of trust evidenced in writing. Choses in possession (eg motor cars, furniture) are gifted when the appropriate formalities are completed (eg the execution of a deed, declaration of trust or actual or constructive delivery). Choses in action (eg shares and insurance policies) are normally gifted on the completion of the appropriate transfer or assignment although negotiable instruments are transferable by delivery; a transfer of shares is not complete until all the requirements of the company's articles have been complied with or the individual has complied with them to the best of his powers (*Re Rose, Rose & others v CIR* [1952]

1 All ER 1217). In this case the gift was held to be complete, even though he had not been registered as a member.

Interests under trusts are gifted when the necessary formalities have been completed. A disposition of an equitable interest must be in writing (*Grey & another v CIR* [1960] AC 1); an oral agreement is not sufficient (*Oughtred v CIR* [1959] 3 All ER 623). For the position of when trustees make an appointment which is in part in breach of trust until a later date see *Stenhouse's Trustees v Lord Advocate* [1984] STC 195, CS.

Cheques are gifted on payment, and not when the cheque is received (ie the gift remains incomplete until the cheque is cleared by the paying bank; see *Re Owen, Owen v CIR* [1949] 1 All ER 901). Insurance policies (eg where written to benefit a person other than the person insured or paying the premiums) are treated as made when one party has unconditionally accepted an offer (or counter-offer) from the other party and has notified the other party accordingly (IRPR, 18 March 1986).

An omission to exercise a right (unless not deliberate) is treated as made at the time, or latest time, the right could have been exercised (IHTA 1984, s 3(3)).

1.3 RATES OF TAX ON CHARGEABLE TRANSFERS
(IHTA 1984, s 7)

The IHT charged on the value transferred by a chargeable transfer made by any transferor is charged at the following rates (IHTA 1984, s 7(1)):

- if the transfer is the first chargeable transfer made by that transferor in the period of seven years ending with the date of the transfer, at the rate or rates applicable to that value under the table set out below (for transfers after 5 April 1999 and 5 April 2000 respectively):

After	Portion of value		Rate of tax
	Lower limit	Upper limit	
	(£)	(£)	%
5 April 1999	–	231,000	Nil
	231,000	–	40
5 April 2000	–	234,000	–
	234,000	–	40

- in any other case, at the rate applicable under the Table in IHTA 1984, Sched 1 to such part of the cumulative total of:
  (i)   that value, and
  (ii) the values transferred by previous chargeable transfers made by him in the period of seven years ending with the date of the transfer, as is the highest part of that aggregate and is equal to that value;

- the IHT charged on the value transferred by a chargeable transfer made during the lifetime of the transferor is charged at one-half of the rate applying on death (ie currently at $\frac{1}{2} \times 40\% = 20\%$);
- this does not apply to a chargeable transfer made within seven years before the death of the transferor; for a chargeable transfer made within that period but more than three years before the death, the IHT charged on the value transferred is charged at the following percentages of the rate applicable under the Table (ie currently at 40 per cent).

Period between transfer and death	% of rate
3–4 years	80
4–5 years	60
5–6 years	40
6–7 years	20

- if, in the case of a chargeable transfer made before the transferor's death, the IHT which would fall to be charged as above is less than the IHT which would have been chargeable on a lifetime transfer if the transferor had not died within the seven-year period beginning with the date of the transfer, the lower rate does not apply to that that transfer;
- a special IHT regime applies to settlements with 'no interests in possession' (IHTA 1984, ss 58–85);
- a form of taper relief is available where a person's estate has been by reference to settled property in which he has an interest, and within five years passes the property on by way of a chargeable transfer or on his death (IHTA 1984, s 141); the relief is given as a percentage of the IHT charged on the first transfer, on so much of the value transferred by the first transfer as is attributable to the increase in the estate of the person concerned:

Period between transfer and death	% of rate
0–1 year	100
1–2 years	80
2–3 years	60
3–4 years	40
over 4 years	20

Where the *transferor* pays the IHT arising on a lifetime transfer, the reduction in his estate includes payment of IHT and it is necessary to 'gross-up' the 'net' value of the transfer at the appropriate rate.

IHT is charged on certain lifetime transfers by reference to the *cumulative* value of chargeable transfers previously made and still within date.

2

DISPOSITIONS THAT ARE NOT TRANSFERS OF VALUE

There are a number of dispositions that are not treated as transfers of value, and which are therefore ignored for IHT purposes.

2.1 DISPOSITIONS NOT INTENDED TO CONFER GRATUITOUS BENEFIT
(IHTA 1984, s 10)

A disposition (including a deemed disposition arising on a failure or omission to exercise a right (IHTA 1984, s 3(3)) is not a transfer of value if it is shown that it is not (and is not made in a transaction) intended to confer any gratuitous benefit on any person. For this purpose a transaction may be a single transaction, or may include a series of transactions and any associated operations. It must also be shown that it is made in a transaction at arm's length between unconnected persons. If that is not the case, alternatively it must be shown that the transaction is such as might be expected to be made in an arm's length transaction between unconnected persons. This does not apply to a sale of unquoted shares or unquoted debentures unless it is shown that the sale is at a price (or at a price such as might be expected to be) freely negotiated at the time of the sale (see *CIR v Spencer-Nairn* [1991] STC 60, CS).

For a benefit to be gratuitous, it must also be shown that there was gratuitous intent (see *Macpherson v CIR* [1987] STC 73). Two estate duty cases show that there can be no gratuitous benefit where a transaction is carried out for full consideration.

The first is *A-G v Boden and another* [1912] 1 KB 539. A father was in partnership with his two sons. However, he was not required to devote as much time to the business as his sons. On his death, his share of the partnership was split equally between his sons, subject to their paying to his estate the value of his share excluding any amount for goodwill. It was held that the sons' obligations under the partnership deed constituted full consideration for the deceased's share of the goodwill.

In the second case, *A-G v Ralli and others* (1936) 15 ATC 523, KB, the deceased had been a partner in a banking partnership, holding large reserves for the partnership business. The partnership deed provided that each partner's share in the reserves accrued to the remaining partners on his death or retirement. It was held that estate duty was not payable on the deceased's interest in the reserves. There was no gift but merely an ordinary commercial transaction for full consideration.

Problems can arise with partnership assurance policies unless they meet the conditions set out in ESC F10. The concession states that a partnership assurance scheme whereby each partner effects a policy on his own life in trust for the other partners is not a settlement for IHT purposes if the following conditions are fulfilled:

(i) the premiums paid on the policy fall within IHTA 1984, s 10 (exemption for dispositions not intended to confer a gratuitous benefit on any person);
(ii) the policy was effected prior to 15 September 1976 and has not been varied on or after that date (the exercise of a power of appointment under a 'discretionary' trust policy is not regarded as a variation);
(iii) the trusts are governed by English or Scottish law, provided that in the latter case the policy does not directly or indirectly involve a partnership itself as a separate persona.

2.2 DISPOSITIONS FOR MAINTENANCE OF FAMILY
(IHTA 1984, s 11)

A disposition is not a transfer of value if it is made by one party to a marriage in favour of the other or of a child of either party and is for the maintenance of the other party. Similarly, a disposition is not a transfer of value if it is made by one party to a marriage in favour of a child of either party and is for the child's maintenance, education or training for a period ending not later than the tax year in which he attains age 18 or, after attaining that age, ceases to undergo full-time education or training. Furthermore, a disposition is not a transfer of value if it is made in favour of a child who is not in the care of a parent of his, and is for his maintenance, education or training for a period ending not later than the tax year in which he attains age 18, or after attaining that age he ceases to undergo full-time education or training. Note, however, that this latter condition applies only if, before attaining age 18, the child was for substantial periods in the care of the disposition maker.

'Marriage', in relation to a disposition made on the dissolution or annulment of a marriage, and in relation to a second disposition varying the first, includes a former marriage. 'Child' includes a stepchild and an adopted child; 'parent' is construed accordingly.

A disposition is not a transfer of value if it is made in favour of a disposition-maker's illegitimate child and is for the child's maintenance, education or training (see above).

A disposition is not a transfer of value if it is made in favour of a disposition-maker's dependent relative and is a reasonable provision for his care or maintenance. A 'dependent relative' is a person's or his spouse's relative who is:

(1) incapacitated by old age or infirmity, or
(2) his or his spouse's mother who is
   • widowed, or
   • living apart from her husband, or
   • a single woman in consequence of dissolution or annulment of marriage.

A disposition by a person in favour of his unmarried mother (so far as it represents a reasonable provision for her care or maintenance) qualifies for exemption if she is incapacitated by old age or infirmity. By concession (ESC F12) such a disposition is also treated as exempt if the person's mother is not incapacitated but is genuinely financially dependent on him.

Where a disposition satisfies the above conditions to a limited extent only, whatever satisfies them and whatever does not satisfy them are treated as separate dispositions. The transfer of an interest in possession for these purposes does not give rise to a charge on the termination of that interest (IHTA 1984, ss 51, 52).

2.3 DISPOSITIONS ALLOWABLE FOR INCOME TAX OR CONFERRING RETIREMENT BENEFITS
(IHTA 1984, s 12)

A disposition made by any person is not a transfer of value if it is allowable in computing that person's profits or gains for income or corporation tax purposes or would be so allowable if those profits or gains were sufficient and fell to be so computed. There are some payments which are not deductible for income or corporation tax purposes (eg entertainment expenses or payments for capital assets). Technically, such payments could be transfers of value. However, in most cases it is possible to show that no gratuitous benefit is intended.

Specifically, a disposition made by any person is not a transfer of value if it falls into either of the following categories:

(i) it is a contribution to an approved occupational pension scheme (TA 1988, ss 590–612) and provides benefits for service which is or includes service as an employee (TA 1988, s 612(1)) of that person; or
(ii) it is made so as to provide benefits on or after retirement for a person not connected with him who is or has been in his employ, or benefits on or after that person's death for his widow or dependants;
(iii) it is a contribution under approved personal pension arrangements (TA 1988, ss 630–655) entered into by a disposition-maker's employee.

Also, the disposition must not result in the recipient receiving benefits which, having regard to their form and amount, are greater than what could be provided under an approved scheme. Dispositions of the kinds described in (i) and (ii) above in respect of service by the same person are regarded as satisfying the conditions only to the extent to which the benefits they provide, taken in aggregate, do not exceed what could be provided by a disposition.

The right to occupy a dwelling rent free or at a rent less than might be expected to be obtained in an arm's length transaction between unconnected persons is regarded as equivalent to a pension at a rate equal to the rent or to the additional rent that might be expected.

Where a disposition satisfies these conditions to a limited extent only, whatever satisfies them and whatever does not satisfy them are treated as separate dispositions.

2.4 DISPOSITIONS BY CLOSE COMPANIES FOR EMPLOYEES' BENEFIT
(IHTA 1984, s 13)

A disposition of property made to trustees by a close company whereby the property is held on trust (IHTA 1984, s 86(1)) is not a transfer of value if the persons for whose benefit the trust permits the property to be applied include all or most of the persons employed by or holding office with the company, or any one or more subsidiaries of the company. SP/E11, issued on 1 December 1976, clarifies the application of this provision where employees of a subsidiary company are included in the trust. The Revenue considers it as requiring that where the trust is to benefit such employees, those eligible to benefit must include all or most of the subsidiary's *and* the holding company's employees and officers taken as a single class.

Therefore, it would be possible to exclude all of the officers and employees of the holding company without losing the exemption if they comprised only a minority of the combined class. However, the exemption is not available for a contribution to a fund for the sole benefit of the employees of a small subsidiary, since it is easy to create such a situation artificially to benefit a favoured group of a officeholders or employees. But even where the participators outnumber the other employees, the exemption is not irretrievably lost. The requirement to exclude participators and those connected with them from benefit is modified by limiting the meaning of 'a participator' to a person having a substantial stake in the assets being transferred and makes an exception in favour of income benefits. Thus for employees who are major participators, or for their relatives, an exempt transfer could be made if the trust provides only for income benefits and the eventual disposal of the capital away from the participators and their families. This restriction does not affect the exemptions offered by IHTA 1984, s 86 from IHT charges during the continuance of a trust for employees which meets the conditions.

The treatment such dispositions as not being transfers of value does not apply if the trust permits any of the property to be applied at any time within a period (whether defined by a date or in some other way) or later for the benefit of:

(1) a person who is a participator in the company making the disposition, or

(2) any other person who is a participator in any close company that has made a disposition whereby property became comprised in the same settlement, being a disposition which would otherwise have been a transfer of value, or

(3) any other person who has been a participator in any such company at any time after, or during the ten years prior to, the disposition made by that company, or

(4) any person who is connected with any such person.

Such participators do not include any participator who is not beneficially entitled to, or to rights entitling him to, acquire 5 per cent or more of, or of any class of the shares comprised in, its issued share capital, and on a winding-up of the company would not be entitled to 5 per cent or more of its assets. In determining whether the trust permits property to be applied in these ways, no account is taken of any power to make a payment which is the income of any person for any income tax purposes, or would be the income for any of those purposes of a person not resident in the UK if he were so resident. Nor is any account taken, if the trust is of an approved profit-sharing scheme (IHTA 1984, Sched 9), of any power to appropriate shares in accordance with the scheme. Finally, if the trusts are those of an approved employee share ownership plan (FA 2000, s 47 and Sched 8), no account is taken of any power to appropriate or to acquire shares on behalf of individuals under the plan.

The trust(s) of the settlement (ie for the employees' benefit) must meet the following description:

(1) the trust by which settled property is held, either indefinitely or until the end of a period (whether defined by a date or in some other way) must not permit any of the settled property to be applied otherwise than for the benefit (IHTA 1984, s 86(1)) of:

   (a) persons of a class defined by reference to employment in a particular trade or profession, or employment by, or office with, a body carrying on a trade, profession or undertaking (s 86(1)(a)), or

   (b) persons of a class defined by reference to marriage or relationship to, or dependence on, such persons (s 86(1)(b)),

   (c) charitable purposes (s 86(2));

(2) where any class is defined by reference to employment by or office with

a particular body, the class must comprise all or most of the persons employed by or holding office with the body concerned (s 86(3)(a), or the trust in which the settled property is held is of an approved profit-sharing scheme under TA 1988, Sched 9 (s 86(3)(b))).

Such transactions do not give rise to any CGT liability (TCGA 1992, s 239).

2.5 WAIVER OF REMUNERATION
(IHTA 1984, s 14)

The waiver or repayment of remuneration is not a transfer of value if, apart from the waiver or repayment, that amount would be assessable to income tax under Schedule E. It is a requirement that the employer's accounts should be adjusted to ensure that the amount waived is brought into account for income or corporation tax purposes. In the absence of consideration, the document should be executed under seal.

2.6 WAIVER OF DIVIDENDS
(IHTA 1984, s 15)

A waiver of a dividend on shares of a company within 12 months before any right to the dividend has accrued is not a transfer of value. In the absence of consideration, the document should be executed under seal.

2.7 GRANT OF AGRICULTURAL PROPERTY TENANCIES
(IHTA 1984, s 16)

The grant of a tenancy of agricultural property in the UK, the Channel Islands or the Isle of Man for agricultural use is not a transfer of value by the grantor if he makes it for full consideration in money or money's worth. For this purpose 'agricultural property' is agricultural land or pasture and includes woodland and any building used in connection with the intensive rearing of livestock or fish if the woodland or building is occupied with agricultural land or pasture and the occupation is ancillary to that of the agricultural land or pasture. This includes cottages, farm buildings and farmhouses, together with the land occupied with them, as are of a character appropriate to the property (IHTA 1984, s 115(2), applied by IHTA 1984, s 16(2)). The breeding, rearing and grazing of horses on a stud farm is taken to be agriculture and any buildings used in connection with those activities to be farm buildings (IHTA 1984, s 115(4), applied by s 16(2)). The agricultural value of any agricultural property is that which would be its value if it were subject to a perpetual covenant prohibiting its use otherwise than as agricultural property (IHTA 1984, s 115(3), applied by s 16(2)).

2.8 CHANGES IN DISTRIBUTION OF DECEASED'S ESTATE, ETC
(IHTA 1984, s 17)

None of the following is transfer of value:

(1) a variation or disclaimer under IHTA 1984, s 142(1);
(2) a transfer made in compliance with the testator's request under IHTA 1984, s 143;
(3) an election by a surviving spouse, in an intestacy, to take a capital sum instead of a life interest under the Administration of Estates Act 1925, s 47A; and
(4) the renunciation, in Scotland, of a claim to legitim within two years (longer at the Revenue's discretion) of attaining age 18.

3

EXEMPT TRANSFERS

3.1 LIFETIME GIFTS ONLY

3.1.1 Annual £3,000 exemption
(IHTA 1984, s 19)

Transfers of value are exempt to the extent that they do not exceed a limit per tax year of £3,000 (not grossed up). Any excess over £3,000 which is not covered by any other exemption is a chargeable transfer. A shortfall below £3,000 can be carried forward and added to the annual £3,000 exemption for the next following year *only*, available *after* the £3,000 exemption for that year.

Where transfers are made on different days, the excess over £3,000 is attributed to later gifts before earlier transfers. Where transfers are made on the same day, the excess over £3,000 is attributed in proportion to their respective values.

Initially, PETs are left out of account as it was intended that the annual £3,000 exemption be applied first against transfers which are not PETs, and then against PETs which subsequently become chargeable. It appears that this legislation is defective, as IHTA 1984, s 3A defines a PET as one which would be chargeable; as a result, the exemption must be applied in date order (Booklet IHT1 (1991), para 5.16).

This is not one of the cases to which is applied the overriding rule that transfers of value include events on the happening of which IHT is chargeable as if a transfer of value had been made (ie deemed disposals). This is, however, subject to further modifications in the case of settled property (IHTA 1984, s 57) and charges on participators in close companies) (IHTA 1984, s 94(5)).

The annual exemption does not apply to deemed dispositions such as settlements or death (other than termination of a life interest). Separate annual exemptions are available to both husband and wife. The exemption does not prevent CGT gift relief from applying (TCGA 1992, s 260).

3.1.2 Small gifts exemption
(IHTA 1984, s 20)

Gifts not exceeding £250 in each tax year per recipient (not grossed up) are exempt. This is not one of the cases to which is applied the overriding rule regarding deemed disposals (see **3.1.1**). The GWR rules also do not apply (FA 1986, s 102(5)(b)). Where a transfer of value involves a loan, whether of money or of property, the transfer is deemed to be an outright gift (IHTA 1984, s 29(3)).

3.1.3 **Normal expenditure out of income**
(IHTA 1984, s 21)

A transfer of value is an exempt transfer if is shown to be made as part of the transferor's normal expenditure taking one tax year with another (ie having made all transfers of value forming part of normal expenditure, the transferor is left with sufficient income to maintain his usual standard of living). This also applies where the transfer value involves a loan of money or of property. Regrettably, the legislation does not give a clear definition of 'income' for this purpose. The Revenue takes the view that it has to be interpreted in accordance with normal accountancy rules, taking income net of tax (letter from the Revenue, *Law Society's Gazette*, 9 June 1976).

Suppose that a married woman receives income in her own right. If she makes no contribution towards household and living expenses, could it be said that the whole of her income was available for normal expenditure transfers? Or could income be directed to a separate bank account from which the normal expenditure transfers are made? It is thought that a transfer would be considered to be a normal expenditure transfer if it is made three times and there is evidence of an intention of continuing to make similar transfers. If payments are under contract (eg premiums under a life assurance policy), it is probable that they will be treated as normal from the outset.

A payment of an insurance policy premium on the transferor's life, or a gift to fund the payment of such a premium, is not treated as part of normal expenditure if, when the insurance was made *or at any earlier or later time*, an annuity was purchased on his life. This does not apply if it can be shown that the purchase of the annuity, and the making or any variation of the insurance (or prior insurance for which it has been substituted), are not associated operations (IHTA 1984, s 268)). It must be shown that both the insurance policy and the annuity are taken out on normal terms. This may be easier to demonstrate if they are taken out with different companies. The capital element of a purchased life annuity is not income for this purpose.

This is not one of the cases to which is applied the overriding rule regarding deemed disposals (see **3.1.1**).

A possible use of the exemption for normal expenditure transfers is the payment, by means of annual gifts, of life insurance premiums on the transferor's own or his spouse's life, but in favour of children or grandchildren, to meet IHT liabilities. Cash payments may qualify as normal expenditure transfers. However, the payments should be regular in timing and amount (*Nadin v CIR* (1997) SWTI 202, SpC 112). On the other hand, in a case where a life tenant directed the payment of surplus trust income to her children, payments of amounts differing widely from year to year were accepted as normal expenditure transfers (*Bennett and others v CIR* [1995] STC 54).

3.1.4 Exemption for marriage gifts
(IHTA 1984, s 22)

Gifts in consideration of marriage are exempt to the extent that the values transferred by any one transferor in respect of a particular marriage do not exceed the amounts described below (not grossed-up). The following gifts are within the scope of this exemption:

(1) up to £5,000 by a parent of the bride or groom:
    (a) if the gift is an outright gift to a child (who is a party to the marriage) of the transferor;
    (b) if the transferor is a parent of either the bride or groom and the gift either is made outright to either party or is a gift in settlement;
(2) up to £2,500 by a grandparent, etc of the bride or groom:
    (a) if the gift is an outright gift to a child, grandchild etc (who is a party to the marriage) of the transferor;
    (b) if the transferor is a grandparent etc of either party and the gift either is made outright to either party, or is a gift in settlement;
(3) up to £2,500 by the bride to the groom or vice versa, if the transferor is a party to the marriage and the gift is made outright to the other party or is a gift in settlement; and
(4) up to £1,000 in any other case.

Note that 'child' includes an illegitimate child, an adopted child and a stepchild; parent, descendant and ancestor are construed accordingly. Note also that persons who are legitimated by the marriage, or who are adopted by husband and wife jointly, are included among the issue of the marriage.

The exemption applies to outright gifts to a child or grandchild of the transferor. An outright gift must be to a party to the marriage. The gift may be made via a PET.

For a disposition in consideration of a marriage (made otherwise than by outright gift) the present or future beneficiaries must comprise:

(1) parties to the marriage, children of the marriage, or a spouse of such children;
(2) persons becoming entitled on the failure of trusts for such children under which trust property would vest indefeasibly on the attainment of a specified age or either on the attainment of such an age or on some earlier event, or persons becoming entitled on the failure of any limitation in tail;
(3) a subsequent spouse of a party to the marriage, or any children or spouse of such children of a subsequent marriage;
(4) persons becoming entitled under protective trusts; and

(5) the trustees of the settlement (to the extent of reasonable remuneration).

Gifts must be in contemplation of a particular marriage which has been arranged and should be made before the marriage, or under an enforceable agreement made before the marriage. The exemption can apply to termination of an interest in possession as a result of which trust property is transferred absolutely to or resettled for the parties to the marriage. This is not one of the cases to which is applied the overriding rule regarding deemed disposals (see **3.1.1**). Where a transfer of value involves a loan, whether of money or of property, the transfer is deemed to be an outright gift (IHTA 1984, s 29(3)). The gifts with reservation rules (see **7**) do not apply (FA 1986, s 102(5)(c)). Marriage gifts can be made by means of a PET.

3.2 LIFETIME GIFTS AND TRANSFERS ON DEATH

3.2.1 Gifts between spouses
(IHTA 1984, s 18)

Transfers between spouses are exempt if both are UK-domiciled, or if both are non-domiciled, or if the transferee is UK-domiciled. This does not apply, if a reversionary interest in settled property is acquired by the donee spouse for money or money's worth, to the property when it falls into possession on the termination of the immediate prior interest. There is, however, exemption for an interest under a settlement created before 16 April 1976. Nor does it apply if property is given in consideration for the transfer of a reversionary interest in settled property which under IHTA 1984, s 55 does not form part of the acquirer's estate. There is an exemption for reversionary interests acquired before 10 March 1981.

If the transferor spouse is UK-domiciled, but the transferee spouse is non-domiciled, the exemption is only £55,000 (not grossed-up), applied to the cumulative total of such gifts. Gifts in excess of this £55,000 threshold may be PETs.

The exemption for intra-spouse transfers does not, however, apply if the testamentary or other disposition by which it is given takes effect on the subsequent termination of any interest or period. But the exemption is nonetheless available where the gift is made to a spouse on condition that he survives the other spouse for a specified period. Nor does the exemption apply where the gift depends upon a condition which is not satisfied within 12 months after the transfer.

Care should be taken here. Suppose that a disposition takes effect (in possession) only after a stated period, or on the termination of a prior interest, but subject to the proviso that this does not apply if the period relates only to surviving the other spouse for a stated period. The exemption could be lost by granting prior powers of maintenance, or occupation of property, with the residue ultimately passing to the spouse or to a charity. A further problem may arise with particular reference to a disposition which is subject to these conditions. They are also referred to in relation to gifts to charities (IHTA 1984, s 23), to political parties (s 24), to housing associations (s 24A) and for national purposes (s 25), with the additional condition that the exemption is not available if the testamentary or other disposition by which it is given is defeasible. It is not clear whether this refers only to conditions precedent (eg a contingent gift which does not vest until the condition is satisfied), and not to conditions subsequent such as a defeasible interest where there is immediate vesting but subsequently on breach of a condition the property is taken away.

Where a transfer of value involves a loan, whether of money or of property, the borrower's estate is deemed to be increased by an amount equal to the value transferred, but attribution rules do not apply (IHTA 1984, s 29(2)).

CGT disposals between husband and wife living together are on a no gain/no loss basis (TCGA 1992, s 58).

Great care is needed to avoid falling foul of the rules for 'associated operations' (IHTA 1984, s 268); the rules for 'related property' (s 161); and the application of the doctrine in *Furniss v Dawson* [1984] STC 153.

The gifts with reservation rules (see **7**) do not apply to exempt spouse transfers (FA 1986, s 102(5)(a)).

3.2.2 Gifts to charities
(IHTA 1984, s 23)

Transfers of value to charities are exempt without monetary limit. However, the exemption does not apply to property if the disposition by which it is given takes effect on the termination, after the transfer of value, of any interest or period; or if it depends upon a condition which is not satisfied within 12 months after the transfer; or is defeasible. For this purpose any disposition which has not been defeated within 12 months after the transfer of value and is not defeasible thereafter is treated as never having been defeasible (irrespective of whether it was capable of being defeated before that time).

The exemption does not apply to property which is an interest in other property if it is a lesser interest than the donor's (12 months after the transfer of value), or the property is given for a limited period. Nor does it apply if the property is land or buildings and is subject to the donor's right of occupation rent free or at low rent, or the property (not being land) is subject to an interest reserved or created by the donor other than for full consideration, or the property (not being land) is subject to an interest which does not substantially affect the enjoyment of the property by the donee (to be decided in all cases 12 months after the transfer of value).

The exemption does not apply to property if it may cease to be held for charitable purposes etc.

Where the value transferred (ie the loss to transferor's estate as a result of the disposition) exceeds the value of the gift in the hands of a charity, the Revenue takes the view that the exemption extends to the whole value transferred (SP/E13).

Beware that property may be valued as related property (see IHTA 1984 s 161) if it is, or has been, within the previous five years, the property of a trust, or trust for charitable purposes only, and became so on a transfer of value made by the individual concerned or his spouse and was then exempt to the extent that the value then transferred was attributable to the property (s 161(2)(b)(i)).

For CGT, there is no chargeable gain on a gift or on a sale below the base cost of an asset; however, consideration in excess of allowable cost will give rise to a partial gain (TCGA 1992, s 257(2)).

The gifts with reservation rules (see **7**) do not apply to gifts to charities (FA 1986, s 102(5)(d)).

3.2.3 Gifts to political parties
(IHTA 1984, s 24)

Transfers of value to qualifying political parties are exempt without limit. 'Qualifying political parties' are defined by reference to voting criteria at the last General Election. This test is satisfied if two MPs of the party were elected, or one MP was elected and not less than 150,000 votes overall were cast for the overall number of candidates for the party. However, the exemption does not apply to property if the disposition by which it is given takes effect on the termination, after the transfer of value, of any interest or period (IHTA 1984, s 23(2)(a), applied by IHTA 1984, s 24(3)); or if it depends upon a condition which is not satisfied within 12 months after the transfer (s 23(2)(b), applied by s 24(3)); or is defeasible (s 23(2)(c), applied by s 24(3)). For this purpose any disposition which has not been defeated within 12 months after the transfer of value and is not defeasible thereafter is treated as never having been defeasible (irrespective of whether it was capable of being defeated before that time).

The exemption does not apply to property which is an interest in other property if it is a lesser interest than the donor's 12 months after the transfer of value (IHTA 1984, s 23(3)(a), applied by s 24(3)), or the property is given for a limited period (s 23(3)(b), applied by s 24(3)).

It does not apply if the property is land or buildings and is subject to the donor's right of occupation rent free or at low rent, the property (not being land) is subject to an interest reserved (s 23(4)(a), applied by s 24(3)) or created by the donor other than for full consideration (s 23(4)(b)(i), applied by s 24(3)), or the property (not being land) is subject to an interest which does not substantially affect the enjoyment of the property by the donee (s 23(4)(b)(ii), applied by s 24(3)) (to be decided in all cases 12 months after the transfer of value). Nor does it apply to property if it may cease to be held for political party purposes etc.

Where the value transferred (ie the loss to transferor's estate as a result of the disposition) exceeds the value of the gift in the hands of the political party, the Revenue takes the view that the exemption extends to the whole value transferred (SP/E13).

Beware that property may be valued as related property (IHTA 1984, s 161) if the property is, or has been, within the previous five years, the property of a political party, and became so on a transfer of value made by the individual concerned or his spouse and was then exempt to the extent that the value then transferred was attributable to the property (s 161(2)(b)(ii)).

For CGT, there is no chargeable gain on a gift or on a sale below the base cost of an asset. However, consideration in excess of allowable cost will give rise to a partial gain (TCGA 1992, s 260(2)).

The gifts with reservation rules (see 7) do not apply to gifts to political parties (FA 1986, s 102(5)(e)).

3.2.4 Gifts to housing associations
(IHTA 1984, s 24A)

Transfers of value, comprising land, to registered housing associations are exempt without limit. However, the exemption does not apply to property if the disposition by which it is given takes effect on the termination, after the transfer of value, of any interest or period (IHTA 1984, s 23(2)(a), applied by s 24A(3)); or if it depends upon a condition which is not satisfied within 12 months after the transfer (s 23(2)(b), applied by s 24A(3)); or is defeasible (s 23(2)(c), applied by s 24A(3)). For this purpose any disposition which has not been defeated within 12 months after the transfer of value and is not defeasible thereafter is treated as never having been defeasible (irrespective of whether it was capable of being defeated before that time).

The exemption does not apply to property which is an interest in other property if it is a lesser interest than the donor's 12 months after the transfer of value (s 23(3)(a), applied by s 24A(3)), or the property is given for a limited period (s 23(3)(b), applied by s 24A(3)).

It does not apply if the property is land or buildings and is subject to the donor's right of occupation rent free or at low rent, the property (not being land) is subject to an interest reserved (s 23(4)(a), applied by s 24A(3)), or created by the donor other than for full consideration (s 23(4)(b)(i), applied by s 24A(3)), or, the property (not being land) is subject to an interest which does not substantially affect the enjoyment of the property by the donee (s 23(4)(b)(ii), applied by s 24A(3)) (to be decided in all cases 12 months after the transfer of value). Nor does it apply to property if it may cease to be held for the purposes of a housing association etc.

Beware that property may be valued as related property (IHTA 1984, s 161) if it is, or has been, within the previous five years, the property of a registered housing association, and became so on a transfer of value made by the individual concerned or his spouse and was then exempt to the extent that the value then transferred was attributable to the property (s 161(2)(b)(ii)).

For CGT, there is no chargeable gain on a gift or on a sale below the base cost of an asset; however, consideration in excess of allowable cost will give rise to a partial gain (TCGA 1992, s 259(2)).

The gifts with reservation rules (see 7) do not apply to gifts to registered housing associations (FA 1986, s 102(5)(ee)).

3.2.5 Gifts for national purposes
(IHTA 1984, s 25)

A transfer of value is exempt to the extent that the value transferred by it is attributable to property which becomes the property of a national purposes body (IHTA 1984, Sched 3 – see the list at the back of the book). However, the exemption does not apply to property if the disposition by which it is given takes effect on the termination, after the transfer of value, of any interest or period (IHTA 1984, s 23(2)(a), applied by s 25(2)); or if it depends upon a condition which is not satisfied within 12 months after the transfer (s 23(2)(b), applied by s 25(2)); or is defeasible (s 23(2)(c), applied by s 25(2)). For this purpose any disposition which has not been defeated within 12 months after the transfer of value and is not defeasible thereafter is treated as never having been defeasible (irrespective of whether it was capable of being defeated before that time).

The exemption does not apply to property which is an interest in other property if it is a lesser interest than the donor's 12 months after the transfer of value (s 23(3)(a), applied by s 25(2)), or the property is given for a limited period (s 23(3)(b), applied by s 25(2)).

It does not apply if the property is land or buildings and is subject to the donor's right of occupation rent free or at low rent, the property (not being land) is subject to an interest reserved (s 23(4)(a), applied by s 25(2)), or created by the donor other than for full consideration (s 23(4)(b)(i), applied by s 25(2)), or the property (not being land) is subject to an interest which does not substantially affect the enjoyment of the property by the donee (s 23(4)(b)(ii), applied by s 25(2)) (to be decided in all cases 12 months after the transfer of value). Nor does it apply to property if it may cease to be held for for national purposes etc.

The exemption extends to the whole of the value transferred (ie loss to donor's estate) and not, if less, the value of the property in the hands of the national purposes body (SP/E13).

Where a transfer of value involves a loan, whether of money or of property, the rules as described for charities apply with necessary modifications (IHTA 1984, s 29(5)). The value transferred is treated as attributable to the property of which the borrower is allowed the use (s 29(5)(a)), and that property is treated as given to, or as becoming the property of, the borrower unless the use allowed includes use for purposes other than charitable purposes or those of a political party, a national purposes body or, where it is land, of a registered housing association. The exclusion of the exemption, as described above, does not apply.

Beware that property may be valued as related property (IHTA 1984, s 161) if it is, or has been, within the previous five years, the property of a registered housing association, and became so on a transfer of value made by the individual concerned or his spouse and was then exempt to the extent that the value then transferred was attributable to the property (s 161(2)(b)(ii)).

For CGT, there is no chargeable gain on a gift or on a sale below the base cost of an asset. However, consideration in excess of allowable cost will give rise to a partial gain (TCGA 1992, s 258(2)).

The gifts with reservation rules (see **7**) do not apply to gifts to national purpose bodies (FA 1986, s 102(5)(f)).

The tax position of gifts to the arts and sales of artistic objects was set out in a press release issued in March 1977 by the then Department of Education and Science. The Office of Arts and Libraries has produced leaflets which summarise and illustrate the benefits of the tax reliefs and provide guidance on the administrative procedures involved in particular circumstances. These are:

- Works of Art: A Basic Guide to Capital Taxation and the National Heritage (1982)
- Works of Art: Guidelines on in situ offers in lieu of capital taxation (April 1984)
- Works of Art: Private Treaty Sales (November 1986).

In addition the Revenue revise each quarter the Register of Conditionally Exempt Works of Art.

3.2.6 PETs of property subsequently held for national purposes
(IHTA 1984, s 26A)

A PET which (otherwise) would become a chargeable transfer is exempt to the extent of value attributable to property which is or could be designated by the Treasury (under IHTA 1984, s 31(1) – see below), and which between the date of transfer and the transferor's death has been sold by private treaty or otherwise to a 'national purpose' body (s 26A(a) – see above), or accepted in lieu of tax (IHTA 1984, ss 26A(b), 230).

3.2.7 Maintenance funds for historic buildings, etc
(IHTA 1984, s 27)

A transfer of value is an exempt transfer to the extent that at the time of the transfer or subsequently it is comprised in a settlement for which the

Treasury has given a direction, eg in relation to historic buildings (under IHTA 1984, Sched 4, para 1). A claim for a direction after the time of the transfer must be made within two years thereafter (or longer at the Revenue's discretion).

However, the exemption does not apply to property if the disposition by which it is given takes effect on the termination, after the transfer of value, of any interest or period (IHTA 1984, s 23(2)(a), applied by s 27(2)); or if it depends upon a condition which is not satisfied within 12 months after the transfer (s 23(2)(b), applied by s 27(2)); or is defeasible (s 23(2)(c), applied by s 27(2)). For this purpose, any disposition which has not been defeated within 12 months after the transfer of value and is not defeasible thereafter is treated as never having been defeasible (irrespective of whether it was capable of being defeated before that time).

The exemption does not apply to property which is an interest in other property if it is a lesser interest than the donor's 12 months after the transfer of value (s 23(3)(a), applied by s 27(2)), or the property is given for a limited period (s 23(3)(b), applied by s 27(2)).

For CGT, there is no chargeable gain on a gift or on a sale below the base cost of an asset; however, consideration in excess of allowable cost will give rise to a partial gain (TCGA 1992, s 257(2)).

The gifts with reservation rules (see **7**) do not apply to gifts to maintenance funds for historic buildings (FA 1986, s 102(5)(h)).

3.2.8 Employee trusts
(IHTA 1984, s 28)

A transfer of value made by an individual who is beneficially entitled to shares in a company is an exempt transfer to the extent that the value transferred is attributable to shares in or securities of the company which become comprised in a settlement if:

(1) the trusts of the settlement are for the benefit of employees (IHTA 1984, s 86(1)), and

(2) the beneficiaries comprise all or most of the persons employed by or holding office with the company.

This does not apply if the trusts permit any of the settled property to be applied at any time (either indefinitely or until the end of a period, whether defined by a date or in some other way) for the benefit of the participators described at **2.4**.

The exemption does not apply unless, at the date of the transfer, or within one year thereafter, both the following conditions are satisfied:

(1) the trustees:
    (a) hold more than one-half of the ordinary shares in the company, and

   (b)   have powers of voting on all questions affecting the company as a whole which if exercised would constitute a majority of the votes available;

(2) there are no provisions in any agreement or instrument affecting the company's constitution or management or its shares or securities whereby the voting condition could be altered without the trustees' consent.

Where the company has shares or securities of any class giving powers of voting limited to either or both of

(1) the question of winding up the company, and

(2) any question primarily affecting shares or securities of that class,

questions affecting the company as a whole comprise all such questions except any in relation to which those powers are capable of being exercised.

The trusts of the settlement must meet the description outlined in **2.4**.

The gifts with reservation rules (see **7**) do not apply to gifts to employee trusts (FA 1986, s 102(5)(i)).

3.2.9 Loans – modifications of exemptions
(IHTA 1984, s 29)

If or to the extent that a transfer of value is a disposition whereby the use of money or other property is allowed by one person to a 'borrower', the various exemptions described above apply with the following modifications.

For the purposes of exempt transfers for between spouses (IHTA 1984, s 18), the borrower's estate is increased by an amount equal to the value transferred. Under that exemption, a transfer of value is exempt to the extent that the value is attributable to property which becomes comprised in the transferor's spouse's estate or, so far as the value transferred is not so attributable, to the extent that that estate is increased. In the general application of the exemption, it is provided that this does not apply to property if the testamentary or other disposition by which it is given:

(1) takes effect on the termination after the transfer of value of any interest or period (but this is not applied by reason only that the property is given to a spouse only if he survives the other spouse for a specified period), or

(2) depends on a condition which is not satisfied within 12 months after the transfer.

This disapplication is specifically overridden.

For the exemptions for small gifts (IHTA 1984, s 20) and gifts in consideration of marriage (s 22), the transfer of value is treated as made by an outright gift.

For the exemption for normal expenditure out of income (s 21), it must be shown (in place of the conditions normally applying) that:

(1) the transfer was a normal one on the transferor's part, and
(2) after allowing for all transfers of value forming part of his normal expenditure, the transferor is left with sufficient income to maintain his usual standard of living.

For exemptions for gifts to charities, to political parties, to housing associations and for national purposes, the value transferred is attributed to the property of which the borrower is allowed the use, and that property is treated as given to, or as becoming the property of, the borrower unless the use allowed includes use for purposes other than charitable, or political party, national or (where it is land) housing association purposes.

3.3 EXEMPTIONS ONLY AVAILABLE ON DEATH TRANSFERS
(IHTA 1984, s 154)

No IHT is paid on the death estate of a person who dies whilst on active service. This is discussed in detail at **14.4**.

3.4 ABATEMENT OF EXEMPTION WHERE CLAIM SETTLED OUT OF BENEFICIARY'S RESOURCES
(IHTA 1984, s 29A)

A special rule applies where a transfer of value made on the death is by an exempt gift, and the exempt beneficiary settles a claim made against the deceased's estate out of his own property. The special rule does not apply to any claim against the deceased's estate in so much of any liability, as is required under the IHT legislation, to be taken into account in determining the value of the transfer.

The IHT rules are applied to the transfer as if an amount of the 'relevant value', equal to the amount by which the value of the exempt beneficiary's estate immediately after the disposition is reduced, were attributable to a specific gift made by a chargeable transfer to the exempt beneficiary (instead of being attributable to a gift made by an exempt transfer). In this context, 'the relevant value' in relation to a transfer of value is so much of the value transferred as is attributable to the gift concerned.

It has to be assumed that the gifts are made by chargeable transfers and bear their own IHT (IHTA 1984, s 38(1)(a), (b), applied by s 29A(3)). Alternatively, where that amount exceeds the relevant value, the whole of the relevant value is taken into account.

In determining the value of the exempt beneficiary's estate for these purposes, no deduction is made in relation to the claim. Also, if the disposition referred to constitutes a transfer of value, then no account is taken of any liability of the beneficiary for any IHT on the value transferred; business property relief (IHTA 1984, s 104) and agricultural property relief (s 116) are disregarded.

3.5 CONDITIONAL EXEMPTION

Conditional exemption is available on lifetime gifts of historic houses, works of art etc, subject to Treasury consent, undertakings and monitoring (IHTA 1984, ss 30–35 – see Chapter 4). There are equivalent provisions for CGT (TCGA 1992, ss 258, 260).

4

CONDITIONAL EXEMPTION

4.1 CONDITIONALLY EXEMPT TRANSFERS
(IHTA 1984, s 30)

A transfer of value comprising an historic house, a work of art, etc can be a conditionally exempt transfer to the extent that the value transferred is so designated, following a claim to that effect, by the Treasury (IHTA 1984, s 31). Designation is only given subject to such undertaking, as the Treasury thinks appropriate in the circumstances of the case. This can also apply to an area of land which, in the Treasury's opinion, is essential for the protection of the character and amenities of a building for the preservation of which special steps should, in its opinion, be taken by reason of its outstanding historic or architectural interest. Conditional exemption cannot be granted, except in the case of a transfer on death (IHTA 1984, s 4), unless:

(1) the transferor or his spouse or both of them were beneficially entitled to the property throughout the six years ending with the transfer, or
(2) the transferor acquired the property by a transfer on a death which was itself a conditionally exempt transfer of the property.

Whether a transfer is a PET (IHTA 1984, s 3A) is decided without reference to the rules for conditional exemption.

Conditional exemption must be claimed within two years after the date of the transfer of value, or in the case of a claim regarding a PET, the date of death, or (in either case) within a longer period at the Revenue's discretion. Conditional exemption does not apply to a PET to the extent that the value transferred by it is attributable to property which has been disposed of by sale during the period beginning with the transfer date and ending with the transferor's death.

Conditional exemption does not apply to exempt transfers between spouses (IHTA 1984, s 18) or gifts to charities (s 23). For CGT, such transfers are deemed to be made for a consideration on a no gain/no loss basis (TCGA 1984, s 257(1)(b)).

4.2 DESIGNATION AND UNDERTAKINGS

The Treasury may designate any of the following:

(1) Any relevant object which appears to be pre-eminent for its national (ie UK) scientific, historic or artistic interest. In determining its pre-eminence, regard is had to any significant association of the object with a particular place. A 'relevant object' is:
    (a) a picture, print, book, manuscript, work of art or scientific object, or
    (b) any such object that does not yield income.

(2) Any collection or group of relevant objects which, taken as a whole, appears to be pre-eminent for its national scientific, historic or artistic interest. In determining its pre-eminence, regard is had to any significant association of the collection or group with a particular place.

(3) Any land which in the Treasury's opinion is of outstanding scenic, historic or scientific interest.

(4) Any building for the preservation of which special steps should in the Treasury's opinion be taken by reason of its outstanding historic or architectural interest.

(5) Any area of land which in the Treasury's opinion is essential to protect the character and amenities of such a building.

(6) Any object which in the Treasury's opinion is historically associated with such a building.

Where the transfer of value in such claim is a PET which (apart from IHTA 1984, s 30) has proved to be a chargeable transfer, the question whether any property is appropriate for designation is determined by reference to circumstances existing after the transferor's death. Where it is a PET which has proved to be a chargeable transfer, and at the time of the transferor's death an undertaking given under IHTA 1984, Sched 4, para 3(3) (maintenance funds for historic buildings) or under TCGA 1992, s 258 (exemption from CGT for gifts of works of art) is in force for any property to which the value transferred is attributable, that undertaking is treated as one given under IHTA 1984, s 30.

For property within (1) or (2) above, the requisite undertaking is that, until the person beneficially entitled to the property dies or the property is disposed of, whether by sale, gift or otherwise, the property is kept permanently in the UK and will not leave it temporarily except for a Treasury-approved purpose and period. An undertaking is also required that such steps as are agreed between the Treasury and the person giving the undertaking will be taken for the property's preservation and for securing reasonable public access to it. If, on a claim, the Treasury agrees that any documents which are designated, under (1) or (2) above, contain information which for personal or other reasons ought to be treated as confidential, it may exclude those documents, in whole or in part, from so much of the undertaking as relates to public access.

In the case of property within (3)–(6), above, the requisite undertaking is that, until the person beneficially entitled to the property dies or the property is disposed of, whether by sale, gift or otherwise, such steps as are agreed between the Treasury and the person giving the undertaking will be taken:

(1) in the case of land of outstanding scenic, historic or scientific interest which is being farmed, for its maintenance and the preservation of its character, and

(2) in the case of any other property, for its maintenance, repair and preservation and, if it is an object which in the Treasury's opinion is historically associated with such a building, for keeping it associated with the building concerned.

The undertaking must also ensure reasonable public access.

An additional undertaking is required in the case of an area of land under item (4) above. The property subject to this undertaking is not only the building for which such protection of character and amenities the relevant land is considered to be essential. It may also include any other area of land regarded as essential and which either lies between or is physically closely connected with the relevant land and the building. Thus, until the person beneficially entitled to these other areas of land dies, or it is disposed of by sale, gift or otherwise, specified steps will be taken for its maintenance, repair and preservation and for securing reasonable public access. If an undertaking is required for these other areas of land for the maintenance, etc, it is required notwithstanding that some other undertaking for its maintenance, etc is also in place.

It is for the person seeking the designation of relevant land to secure that any required undertaking is given.

The steps agreed for securing reasonable public access must ensure that it is not confined to access only where a prior appointment has been made.

A *Hansard* written answer given on 9 February 1987 dealt with the question of publicity for conditionally exempt landscape schemes. Publicity about public access to heritage property which has been conditionally exempted from IHT is incorporated in the management agreement terms negotiated to give effect to the preservation and public access undertakings that are required as a precondition of exemption. Outstanding chattels apart (for which different arrangements apply), these normally comprise some or all of the following, under which the owner should:

(a) inform the British Tourist Authority, the Scottish Tourist Board and the Highlands and Islands Development Board in Scotland of the opening arrangements and subsequent changes;

(b) advertise the opening arrangements in one or more suitable publications with national circulation;

(c) display a notice outside the property giving details of the opening arrangements;

(d) agree that the advisory body or bodies (or its or their agents), which confirmed the property's eligible quality and with whom the detailed management agreement terms were negotiated, can divulge the access arrangements to anyone who enquires about them;

(e) agree to such other publicity as any advisory body considers to be appropriate, which could include displaying a notice in some public place in the locality (eg post office, library, tourist office or town hall) or in a local preservation society's newsletter.

The management agreement would also normally provide scope for additional measures to be agreed, if appropriate, between the owner and any advisory body at a later stage.

Subject to the exclusion of access to any documents which contain confidential information (IHTA 1984, s 31(3)), where any steps in an undertaking include steps for securing reasonable public access, the steps that may be agreed and set out in that undertaking may also include steps involving the publication of:

(1) the terms of any undertaking given with respect to the property; or
(2) any other information relating to the property which would otherwise be treated as confidential.

In the IHT rules, any reference to an undertaking for public access is construed as so much of any undertaking for which taking of steps involving any such publication is necessary.

Where different persons are entitled (either beneficially or otherwise) to different properties being farmed, separate undertakings for each property's maintenance, etc are given by such persons as the Treasury thinks appropriate in the circumstances.

The Office of Arts and Libraries has produced leaflets which summarise and illustrate the benefits of the IHT reliefs and provide guidance on the administrative procedures involved in particular circumstances. These are listed at the end of **3.2.5**.

4.3 CHARGEABLE EVENTS
(IHTA 1984, s 32)

Where there has been a conditionally exempt transfer of any property, IHT is charged on the first occurrence after the transfer (or, if the transfer was a PET, after the transferor's death) of a chargeable event in relation to the property. If the Treasury is satisfied that at any time an undertaking given in relation to a property (IHTA 1984, s 30 or 31) has not been observed in a material respect, such failure gives rise to a chargeable event on the property.

If the person beneficially entitled to the property dies or the property is disposed of by sale, gift or otherwise, the death or disposal is a chargeable event on the property. However, a death or disposal is not a chargeable event if the deceased's personal representatives (or, in the case of settled property, the trustees or the person next entitled) within three years of the death make or, as the case may be, the disposal is:

(1) a disposal of the property by sale by private treaty to a national heritage body (IHTA 1984, Sched 3), or a disposal of it to such a body otherwise than by sale, or

(2) the surrender of the property in lieu of payment of IHT (IHTA 1984, s 230).

A death or disposal of the property otherwise than by sale is not a chargeable event if the transfer of value made on the death or the disposal is itself a conditionally exempt transfer. Nor is it a chargeable event if the required undertakings under IHTA 1984, s 31 are given.

4.4 ASSOCIATED PROPERTIES
(IHTA 1984, s 31)

Associated properties comprise buildings of outstanding historic or architectural interest for which special steps should, in the Treasury's opinion, be taken (as above), areas of land essential for protecting such buildings' character and amenities, and objects historically associated with such buildings. Where there has been a conditionally exempt transfer of any property, IHT is charged on the first occurrence after the transfer (or, if the transfer was a PET, after the transferor's death) of a chargeable event in relation to it.

If the Treasury is satisfied that an undertaking (under IHTA 1984, s 30 or 32A) for the maintenance, etc or keeping of any of the associated properties has not been observed in a material respect, there is a chargeable event on the whole of each of the associated properties of which there has been a conditionally exempt transfer.

If the person beneficially entitled to property dies or property is disposed of by sale, gift or otherwise, then, if the property is one of the associated properties and an undertaking for its maintenance, etc or keeping has been given, the death or disposal is a chargeable event on the whole of each of the associated conditionally exempt transfer properties.

The death of a person beneficially entitled to, or the disposal of, property is not a chargeable event if the deceased's personal representatives (or, in the case of settled property, the trustees or the person next entitled) within three years of the death make or, as the case may be, the disposal is:

(1) a disposal of the property concerned by sale by private treaty to a national purposes body (IHTA 1984, Sched 3), or to such a body otherwise than by sale, or

(2) the surrender of the property in lieu of payment of IHT (IHTA 1984, s 230).

If it is a part disposal, that does not make the event non-chargeable so far as concerns property other than that disposed of unless the requisite undertakings are given. In this context a 'part disposal' is a disposal which does not consist of or include the whole of each property which is one of the associated properties and of which there has been a conditionally exempt transfer.

Where, after there has been such a disposal, a person beneficially entitled to the property dies or the property is disposed of, the death or disposal is not a chargeable event unless there has again been a conditionally exempt transfer of the property after such disposal.

The death of a person beneficially entitled to property or the disposal of property otherwise than by sale is not a chargeable event if the transfer of value made on the death or the disposal is itself a conditionally exempt transfer. Nor is it a chargeable event if the required undertakings are given.

If the whole or part of any property is disposed of by sale and the required undertakings are given, the disposal is a chargeable event only so far as concerns the whole or part actually disposed of (if it is otherwise a chargeable event).

There may be some relief even if the Treasury is satisfied that there has been a failure to observe an undertaking for the property's maintenance, etc or keeping, or there is a disposal of part only of one of the associated properties. If the entity consisting of the associated properties has not been materially affected by the failure or disposal, the Treasury may direct that it is a chargeable event only in relation to the property or the part directly affected by the failure or disposal.

4.5 AMOUNT OF IHT CHARGE ON CHARGEABLE EVENT
(IHTA 1984, s 33)

IHT (under IHTA 1984, s 32 or 32A) is charged on an amount equal to the property's value at the time of the chargeable event. Where, because the property was partly exempt under IHTA 1984, s 18 (transfers between spouses) or s 23 (gifts to charities), the conditionally exempt transfer extended only to part of the property, its value is proportionately reduced. The rate at which IHT is charged depends upon whether the relevant person is alive or dead.

(1) If the relevant person is alive, IHT is charged at one-half of the full rate (ie 20 per cent) (IHTA 1984, s 7(2)).

(2) If the relevant person is dead, IHT is charged at the full rate (ie 40 per cent); However, if the transfer was a PET (IHTA 1984, s 3A) the full rate is abated (under s 7) if the death occurs more than three years before, but less than seven years before the death. This does not apply to gifts with reservation, as these are already deemed to be part of the deceased's estate (FA 1986, s 102(3)).

In both cases the application of this rate is subject to the total cumulative chargeable transfers exceeding the nil rate threshold (currently £223,000); the latter case assumes that the value deemed to be transferred by the chargeable event would have applied to the highest part of that value.

The property's value at the time of the chargeable event is taken to be equal to the sale proceeds where the chargeable event is a disposal on sale and the sale was not intended to confer any gratuitous benefit on any person, and was a transaction either

(a) at arm's length, or
(b) such as might be expected to be made at arm's length

between unconnected persons. Sale proceeds are taken to be the net proceeds (*Tyser v A-G* [1938] Ch 426).

The relevant person in relation to a chargeable event in respect of any property must be identified. The relevant person is one who made:

(1) if there has been only one conditionally exempt transfer of the property before the event, that transfer;
(2) if there have been two or more such transfers and the last was before, or only one of them was within, the 30-year period ending with the event, the last of those transfers; or
(3) if there have been two or more such transfers within that 30-year period, whichever of those transfers the Revenue may select.

The conditionally exempt transfers taken into account for this purpose do not include transfers made:

(1) before any previous chargeable event on the same property, or
(2) apart from a disposal made by the deceased's personal representatives within three years of the death by private treaty or otherwise than by a sale to a national purposes body, or surrender of the property in lieu of payment of IHT (IHTA 1984, s 230), either
    (a) before any event, or
    (b) where associated property has been disposed of before any event which would have been such a chargeable event (IHTA 1984, ss 32A(5), 33(6)).

Where after a conditionally exempt transfer of any property there is a chargeable transfer which is wholly or partly attributable to it, any IHT charged on its attributable value is allowed as a credit. If the chargeable transfer is a chargeable event, the credit is given against the IHT chargeable by reference to that event. If the chargeable transfer is not a chargeable event, the credit is given against the IHT chargeable on the next chargeable event on the property.

Where after a conditionally exempt transfer there is a PET, and the value transferred is wholly or partly attributable to that property, the IHT charged is allowed as a credit against any IHT which may become chargeable, by reason of the PET proving to be a chargeable transfer, on the attributed value. This applies in two situations:

(1) where the PET is a chargeable event in relation to the property;
(2) where after the PET, but before the PET transferor's death, a chargeable event occurs on the property.

4.6 REINSTATEMENT OF TRANSFEROR'S CUMULATIVE TOTAL
(IHTA 1984, s 34)

Where IHT is chargeable (IHTA 1984, s 32 or 32A) on a chargeable event in respect of any property (here referred to as 'the relevant event'), the IHT rate or rates applicable to any subsequent chargeable transfer made by the person who made the last conditionally exempt transfer of the property before the relevant event is determined as if the amount on which IHT has become chargeable were value transferred by a chargeable transfer made by him at the time of the relevant event.

However, where the person who made the last conditionally exempt transfer before the relevant event is dead, and is, for the purposes of the IHT charge on a chargeable event, the relevant person in relation to a subsequent chargeable event, the value transferred on his death is increased by the amount on which IHT has become chargeable on the relevant event.

A modification to the general rule applies in the following circumstances:

(1) the person who made the last conditionally exempt transfer before the relevant event is not the relevant person for the purposes of the IHT charge on chargeable events (IHTA 1984, s 33) in relation to that event, and
(2) at the time of that event or within the previous five years the property is or has been comprised in a settlement made not more than 30 years before that event, and
(3) a person who is the settlor in relation to the settlement has made a conditionally exempt transfer of the property within those 30 years.

Where IHT becomes chargeable on the relevant event, the IHT rate or rates applicable to any subsequent chargeable transfer made by the settlor who made a conditionally exempt transfer within 30 years is determined as if the amount on which IHT has become chargeable were value transferred by a chargeable transfer made by him at the time of the relevant event (IHTA 1984, s 34(1), as amended by IHTA 1984, s 34(3)). However, where the settlor who made a conditionally exempt transfer within 30 years is dead (s 34(2)(a), as amended by s 34(3)) and is, for the purposes of the IHT charge on a chargeable event, the relevant person in relation to a subsequent chargeable event (s 34(2)(b), as amended by s 34(3)), the value transferred on his death is increased by the amount on which IHT has become chargeable on the relevant event.

Where the settlor has made a conditionally exempt transfer of the property within 30 years, the conditionally exempt transfers to be taken into account in relation to the relevant event do not include transfers made before any previous chargeable event on the same property or before any event which (except under IHTA 1984, s 32(4)) would have been such a chargeable event, or associated property has been disposed of before any event which, apart from a disposal made by the deceased's personal representatives within three years of the death by private treaty or otherwise than by a sale to a national purposes body, or surrender of the property in lieu of payment of IHT (IHTA 1984, s 230), would have been such a chargeable event (ss 32A(5), 34(4)).

4.7 CONDITIONAL EXEMPTION ON DEATH BEFORE 7 APRIL 1976
(IHTA 1984, s 35, Sched 5)

Section 35 of and Sched 5 to IHTA 1984 provide continuity for conditional exemption from estate duty granted prior to 7 April 1976.

4.8 VARIATION OF UNDERTAKINGS

An undertaking given as described above (IHTA 1984, s 30, 32 or 32A or Sched 5, para 5) may be varied from time to time by agreement between the Revenue and the person bound by the undertaking. A Special Commissioner may direct that the undertaking is to have effect from a date specified by him as if the proposed variation had been agreed to by the person so bound where he is satisfied that:

(a) the Revenue has made a proposal for variation to the person bound by the undertaking;
(b) that person has failed to agree to the proposal within six months after the date on which it was made; and
(c) it is just and reasonable, in all the circumstances, to require the proposed variation to be made.

The date specified by the Special Commissioner must not be less than 60 days after the date of his direction. A direction does not, however, apply if, before the date specified by the Special Commissioner, a variation different from that to which the direction relates is agreed between the Revenue and the person bound.

5

ALLOCATION OF EXEMPTIONS

5.1 INTRODUCTION
(IHTA 1984, ss 36, 42)

Problems of allocation can arise if any one or more of the exemptions listed below apply in relation to a transfer of value but the transfer is not wholly exempt. An example of the sort of situation covered here is where a surviving spouse is left a share of the residue, whilst the rest of the residue is left to a chargeable beneficiary. The exemptions are:

- transfers between spouses (IHTA 1984, s 18)
- gifts to charities (s 23)
- gifts to political parties (s 24)
- gifts to registered housing associations (s 24A)
- gifts for national purposes (s 25)
- PETs of property subsequently held for national purposes (s 26A)
- maintenance funds for historic buildings (s 27) and
- conditionally exempt transfers (s 30)

Any question of the extent to which a transfer of value is exempt or, where it is exempt up to a limit, how an excess over the limit is to be attributed to the gifts concerned is determined as described below. The allocation of the IHT burden is also dealt with.

In the context of the allocation rules, a gift bears its own IHT if the IHT attributable to it falls on the person who becomes entitled to the property given or (as the case may be) is payable out of property applicable for the purposes for which it was given.

Where the whole or part of the value transferred is attributable to property which is the subject of two or more gifts, and the gifts' aggregate value is less than that (or that part) transferred, then the value of each gift is taken to be the relevant proportion of the value (or that part of it) transferred. The relevant proportion in relation to any gift is the proportion which the value of the property given bears to the aggregate.

Where, on a person's death, legal rights under Scottish law are claimed by a person so entitled, they are treated as a specific gift which bears its own

IHT; in determining the value of such legal rights, any IHT payable on the deceased's estate is left out of account.

Certain conditions must be satisfied if a deed of variation is to be brought within these rules (see **13.2.1** and **13.2.5**).

5.2 ABATEMENT OF GIFTS
(IHTA 1984, s 37)

If a gift would be abated owing to an insufficiency of assets and without regard to any IHT chargeable, it is treated under the rules for the allocation of exemptions as so abated. Where the value attributable to specific gifts exceeds the value transferred, the gifts are treated as reduced to the extent necessary to reduce their value to that of the value transferred. The reduction is made in the order in which, under the terms of the relevant disposition or any rule of law, it would fall to be made on a distribution of assets.

5.3 ATTRIBUTION OF VALUE TO SPECIFIC GIFTS
(IHTA 1984, ss 38, 39)

Such part of the value transferred is attributable to specific gifts as corresponds to their value. However, if or to the extent that they are not gifts for which, or they are outside the limit up to which, the transfer is exempt and do not bear their own IHT, the amount corresponding to their value is that arrived at as follows.

Where any question arises over which of two or more specific gifts are outside the limit up to which a transfer is exempt, or over the extent to which a specific gift is outside that limit, the excess is attributed to gifts not bearing their own IHT before being attributed to gifts which do. The excess is attributed to gifts in proportion to their values.

Where the only gifts for which the transfer is or might be chargeable are specific gifts which do not bear their own IHT, the amount corresponding to their value is the aggregate of their value. The amount of IHT is that which would be chargeable if the value transferred equalled that aggregate.

Where the specific gifts not bearing their own IHT are not the only gifts for which the transfer is or might be chargeable, the amount corresponding to their value is such amount as, after deduction of IHT at the assumed rate (calculated as below), would be equal to the sum of their value. For this purpose the assumed rate is that found by dividing the assumed amount of IHT (see below) by that part of the value transferred with respect to which the transfer would be chargeable on the hypothesis that:

(1) the amount corresponding to the value of specific gifts not bearing their own IHT is equal to their aggregate, and

(2) the parts of the value transferred attributable to specific gifts and to gifts of residue or shares in residue are determined accordingly.

The assumed amount of IHT is the amount that would be charged on the value transferred on the above hypothesis.

Any transferor liability which is not to be taken into account as being one incurred otherwise than for a consideration in money or money's worth (IHTA 1984, s 5(5)), or an abated debt or incumbrance under FA 1986, s 103, is treated as a specific gift.

Only such part of the value transferred is attributed to gifts of or shares in residue as is not attributed to specific gifts as above.

Example

George died on 3 August 2000, leaving an estate of £610,000. His will provided for pecuniary legacies free of IHT to his son, Paul, of £200,000 and to his nephew, John, of £50,000. The residue was left equally to his daughter, Mary, and his widow, Patricia, subject to the proviso that Mary's share of residue is to bear its own IHT. There were no lifetime transfers except to utilise the IHT annual exemptions. The nil rate band is currently £234,000.

Step 1: Calculate the notional tax on the IHT-free legacies assuming that they were the only transfers.

	£	£
Legacies (free of IHT)	250,000	
Nil rate band	234,000	234,000
Net of IHT transfers	16,000	
Gross equivalent × 100/60		26,667
Notional gross value free of IHT legacies		260,667
Legacies free of IHT		250,000
		10,667

Step 2: Calculate the residue

	£	£
Gross estate	610,000	
Notional gross value free of IHT legacies	260,667	260,667
Residue	349,333	
Patricia's share (½ of residue) (exempt)	174,667	
Mary's share (½ of residue)	174,666	174,666
Chargeable notional transfers on first grossing		435,333

Step 3: Calculate IHT on chargeable notional transfers on first grossing

	£
Chargeable notional transfers on first grossing	435,333
Nil rate band	234,000
	201,333
IHT at 40%	80,533

The estate rate for regrossing is $(80,533/435,333) \times 100 = 18.499\%$
Free of IHT legacies regrossed to $250,000 \times (100/81.501) = £306,745$

Step 4: Calculate the final estate rate

	£	£
Gross estate (as before)	610,000	
Free of IHT legacies re grossed	306,745	306,745
Revised residue	303,255	
Patricia's share (½ of residue) (exempt)	151,628	
Mary's share (½ of residue)	151,627	151,627
Liable to IHT		458,372
Nil rate band		234,000
		224,372
IHT at 40%		89,749

The final estate rate of $(89,749/458,372) \times 100 = 19.580\%$

	£	£
Gross estate		610,000
Legacies: Paul	200,000	
John	50,000	
	250,000	
Inheritance tax on notional figure of £306,745 at 19.580% (final estate rate)	60,061	310,061
Residue left		299,939
Mary's legacy (½ of residue)		149,970
Inheritance tax on notional figure of £151,627 at 19.580%		29,889
		120,081
Patricia's legacy (½ of residue) (exempt)		149,969

Reconciliation

	£
Paul (son)	200,000
John (nephew)	50,000
Mary (daughter)	120,081
Patricia (widow)	149,969
IHT (£60,061 + £29,889)	89,950
	610,000

5.4 ATTRIBUTION IN CASES OF BUSINESS OR AGRICULTURAL RELIEF
(IHTA 1984, s 39A)

The attribution rules are modified where any part of the value transferred is attributable to the value of relevant business property, or to agricultural value of agricultural property. In such cases, for the purpose of attributing the value transferred (as reduced by business property relief (BPR (see **8** below); IHTA 1984, s 104) or agricultural property relief (APR (see Chapter 9 below); IHTA 1984, s 116)), to specific gifts and gifts of residue or shares of residue, the value of any specific gifts of relevant business property or agricultural property is taken to be their value as reduced by percentage of the relevant relief. The value of other specific gifts is the 'appropriate fraction' of their value. This is a fraction of which:

(1) the numerator is the difference between the value transferred and the value, as reduced by BPR or APR, and

(2) the denominator is the difference between the 'unreduced value transferred' and the value, before the reduction by BPR or APR, of any such gifts.

The 'unreduced value transferred' is the amount which would be the value transferred but for the reduction required to give effect to BPR or APR. Such part of the value transferred is attributable to specific gifts (as reduced by BPR or APR, or the 'appropriate fraction' of their value) as corresponds to their value; but if or to the extent that they are not gifts for which, or are outside the limit up to which, the transfer is exempt and do not bear their own IHT, the amount corresponding to their value is that arrived at as follows.

Where any question arises over which of two or more specific gifts (as reduced by BPR or APR, or the appropriate fraction) are outside the limit up to which a transfer is exempt or over the extent to which a specific gift so reduced is outside that limit, the excess is attributed to gifts not bearing their own IHT before being attributed to those bearing which bear it, and the excess is attributed to gifts in proportion to their values.

Where the only gifts for which the transfer is or might be chargeable are specific gifts (as reduced by BPR or APR, or the appropriate fraction) which do not bear their own IHT, the amount corresponding to their value is the aggregate of their value, as applied by IHTA 1984, s 39A(5). The amount of IHT is that which would be chargeable if the value transferred equalled that aggregate.

Where the specific gifts (as reduced) not bearing their own IHT are not the only gifts for which the transfer is or might be chargeable, the amount corresponding to their value is such amount as, after deduction of IHT at the assumed rate (calculated as below), would be equal to the sum of the value of those gifts.

For this purpose the assumed rate is that found by dividing the assumed amount of IHT (see below) by that part of the value transferred with respect to which the transfer would be chargeable on the hypothesis that:

(1) the amount corresponding to the value of specific gifts (as reduced by BPR or APR) not bearing their own IHT is equal to the aggregate, and

(2) the parts of the value transferred attributable to specific gifts (as reduced by BPR or APR) and to gifts of residue or shares in residue are determined accordingly.

The assumed amount of IHT is the amount that would be charged on the value transferred on the above hypothesis.

Any transferor liability which is not to be taken into account as being one incurred otherwise than for a consideration in money or money's worth (IHTA 1984, s 5(5)), or an abated debt or incumbrance under FA 1986, s 103, is treated as a specific gift.

The value of a specific gift of relevant business or agricultural property does not include the value of any other gift payable out of that property. That other gift is not itself to be treated as a specific gift of relevant business or agricultural property.

Example

Henry died on 27 August 2000. His estate comprised the following assets:

	Gross (£)	After reliefs (£)
Business property eligible for 100% relief	400,000	Nil
Agricultural property eligible for 100% relief	800,000	Nil
Business property eligible for 50% relief	200,000	100,000
Other estate	800,000	800,000
	2,200,000	900,000

In his will Henry left:
   A legacy of £500,000 to his widow.
   The Business property eligible for 50% relief to his daughter.
   One-third of the residue to each of his three sons.
All of the bequests are to bear their own tax.

Step 1: Attribute value to specific gifts qualifying for APR, or BPR after deducting reliefs at appropriate rates.

	£
Gift to daughter	£100,000

Step 2: Attribute value to specific gifts of other property reduced by the appropriate fraction.

Legacy to widow £500,000

Appropriate fraction:

$$\frac{(900,000 - 100,000)}{2,200,000 - 200,000} + \frac{800,000}{2,000,000} \times 500,000 = \qquad 200,000$$

Step 3: Calculate amount attributable to residue: 600,000

Total chargeable estate   900,000

5.5 GIFTS MADE SEPARATELY OUT OF DIFFERENT FUNDS
(IHTA 1984, s 40)

Where gifts on a transfer of value take effect separately out of different funds, allocation of exemption rules are applied separately to them, with the necessary adjustments of the values and amounts. The rate of IHT used for 'grossing up' should be calculated separately for each fund (*Law Society Gazette*, 9 March 1990).

5.6 BURDEN OF IHT
(IHTA 1984, s 41)

Notwithstanding the terms of any disposition:

(1) none of the IHT on the value transferred falls on any specific gift if or to the extent that the transfer is exempt with respect to the gift, and

(2) none of the IHT attributable to the property's value comprised in residue falls on any gift of a share of residue if or to the extent that the transfer is exempt with respect to the gift.

Where there are charitable and non-charitable beneficiaries, and those beneficiaries are to benefit equally, the non-charitable beneficiaries receive grossed up shares (*Re Benham's Will Trusts: Lockhart v Harker, Read and the Royal National Lifeboat Institution* [1995] STC 210, ChD).

6

EXCLUDED PROPERTY

6.1 SIGNIFICANCE OF 'EXCLUDED PROPERTY'
(IHTA 1984, s 6)

A transfer of value does not take account of the value of any excluded property ceasing to form part of a person's estate as a result of a disposition (IHTA 1984, s 3(1)(2)). A person's estate immediately before his death (on which IHT is payable) does not include excluded property. If the excluded property is settled property, the termination of an interest in possession in it is not taxable (IHTA 1984, s 5(1)). Nor is it relevant property for the purposes of the rules for no interest in possession trusts (IHTA 1984, ss 53(1), 58(1)).

6.2 PROPERTY ABROAD

6.2.1 Held by individuals

Property situated outside the UK (including property which is so deemed by DTR agreements) is excluded property if the beneficial owner is non-UK domiciled (IHTA 1984, ss 6(1), 158(1)).

A person may be treated as UK-domiciled (IHTA 1984, s 267):

(1) if UK-domiciled at any time within three prior years (IHTA 1984, s 267(1)(a)); and
(2) if resident in the UK for 17 out of 20 tax years (s 267(1)(b)).

6.2.2 Held by trusts

Settled property (including a reversionary interest which is itself settled property) situated outside the UK is excluded property if the settlor was domiciled outside the UK when the settlement was made (IHTA 1984, s 48(3)(b)). The special provisions relating to domicile do not apply to property in a settlement before 10 December 1974 (ss 48(3), 267(3)).

Property is regarded as becoming comprised in a settlement when it (or other property which it represents) is introduced by the settlor (see SP/E9).

The status of excluded property is determined immediately before vesting (*von Ernst and others v CIR* [1980] STC 111, CA).

6.3 'FOTRA' SECURITIES

6.3.1 Held by individuals

Certain gilt-edged securities issued as 'free of tax' in the hands of persons not ordinarily resident nor domiciled in the UK (FOTRA) and beneficially owned by such persons are excluded property if, in general, they are not settled property. The special provisions relating to domicile do not apply (IHTA 1984, s 267(2)).

6.3.2 Held by settlements

Such securities held as settled property are excluded property if a person not ordinarily resident nor domiciled in the UK is entitled to a qualifying interest in possession in them (IHTA 1984, s 48(4)(a)). If such securities are settled property in which there is no qualifying interest in possession and all known persons for whose benefit the settled property or income from it has been or might be applied or who are or might become beneficially entitled to an interest in possession in it are neither domiciled nor ordinarily resident in the UK they are classed as excluded property (s 48(4)(b); *Montague Trust Co (Jersey) Ltd and others v CIR* [1989] STC 477).

If property ceases to be comprised in one settlement and becomes comprised in another (without any person in the meantime having become entitled to the property – and not merely to an interest in possession in it), the property in the second settlement is only excluded property if these requirements are satisfied by both settlements (s 48(5)).

6.3.3 Held by companies

If a close company is the person entitled, the participators in the company are treated as being entitled to the interest *pro rata* their respective rights and interests in the company (IHTA 1984, s 101(1)).

6.4 OVERSEAS PENSIONS: APPLICATION ON DEATH
(IHTA 1984, s 153)

In the case of transfers on death only, any pension receivable from a fund set up under the Government of India Act 1935, s 273 or a corresponding fund under the Overseas Pensions Act 1973, s 2 and funds relating to various former colonial countries or territories:

(1) constitute property situated outside the UK and are excluded property if the pensioner is domiciled overseas, and

(2) are left out in determining the value of a person's death estate.

See **14.3.3** for further discussion.

6.5 PERSONS DOMICILED IN THE ISLANDS: NATIONAL SAVINGS PRODUCTS
(IHTA 1984, s 6)

The following, if held by persons domiciled in the Channel Islands or the Isle of Man, are excluded property under TA 1988, s 326:

- war savings certificates
- National Savings certificates (including Ulster savings certificates)
- premium savings bonds
- deposits with the National Savings bank or a trustee savings bank
- a certified contractual savings scheme.

The special provisions relating to domicile do not apply (IHTA 1984, s 267(2)).

6.6 VISITING FORCES

6.6.1 Emoluments and chattels
(IHTA 1984, s 155)

Emoluments paid by the government of a country designated by Order in Council to a member of a visiting force of that country (including the member of a civilian component) are excluded property provided that member is not a British citizen, a British Dependent Territories citizen, or a British overseas citizen. Any tangible movable property in the UK solely because of that member's presence is also excluded. See further **14.4.2.**

6.6.2 Status
(IHTA 1984, s 155)

A period during which any such person is in the UK by reason solely of his being such a member is not treated for IHT purposes as a period of residence in the UK or as creating a change of residence or domicile.

6.7 SPECIAL DISCRETIONARY TRUSTS: CALCULATION OF EXIT CHARGE
(IHTA 1984, s 65)

Where IHT is charged when property leaves certain trusts, no account is taken of any quarter throughout which it was excluded property when determining the appropriate IHT rate (IHTA 1984, s 65):

(1) temporary charitable trusts (s 70(7));
(2) accumulation and maintenance trusts (s 71(5));
(3) employee trusts (s 72(5));
(4) pre-1978 protective trusts (s 73(3)); and
(5) pre-1981 trusts for disabled persons (s 74(3)).

6.8 REVERSIONARY INTERESTS

6.8.1 Excluded property
(IHTA 1984, s 48)

In general, a reversionary interest is excluded property. Where property, but not a reversionary interest in property, is situated abroad and is comprised in a settlement, then (IHTA 1984, s 6(1)):

(1) if the settlor was UK-domiciled when the settlement was made, and
(2) the reversionary interest is excluded property,
   a reversionary interest is excluded property, unless:

(a) it has been acquired by a person currently or previously entitled thereto for money or money's worth;
(b) for settlements made after 16 April 1976, but before 10 March 1981, the settlor or his spouse is entitled thereto;
(c) for settlements made after 10 March 1981, the settlor or his spouse is (or has been) entitled thereto;
(d) it is an interest expectant upon the determination of a lease of property for life unless granted for full consideration, or which subsequently becomes a lease at rack rent.

If a reversionary interest falls into one of these exceptions it may still be excluded property in certain circumstances if it is situated outside the UK.

Where more than one person is the settlor and the circumstances so require, the above provisions apply as if the settled property were comprised in separate settlements (IHTA 1984, s 44(2)).

6.8.2 Not excluded property
(IHTA 1984, s 48)

A reversionary interest is not excluded property if:

(1) it has at any time been acquired (by a person currently, or by a person previously, entitled to it) for a consideration in money or money's worth; or

(2) it is an interest expectant on the determination of a lease (which is treated as a settlement because the lease is for life or lives, or for a period ascertainable only by reference to death, or which is terminable on, or at a date ascertainable only by reference to, a death), and was not granted for full consideration in money or money's worth (where a lease, not granted at a rack rent, is at any time to become a lease at an increased rent, it is treated as terminable at that time); or

(3) for a settlement made after 15 April 1976, it is one to which either the settlor or his spouse is (or, for a reversionary interest acquired after 9 March 1981, has been) beneficially entitled.

6.9 SITUS

6.9.1 No specific rules

There no specific rules under IHT for determining whether property is situated in the UK, and the general law situs rules apply.

6.9.2 Application of general law

The following fall under the application of general law in establishing any IHT liability:

(1) Registered securities are regarded as situated where they are registered unless transferable in more than one country, in which case they are situate in the country in which they would be likely to be dealt with in the ordinary course of affairs (*R v Williams and another* [1942] AC 541, PC; *Ontario Treasurer v Aberdein* [1947] AC 24, PC; *Standard Chartered Bank Ltd v CIR* [1978] STC 272, ChD).

(2) Renounceable letters of allotment of shares in UK private companies have been held to be situated in the UK (*Young and another v Phillips* (1984) 58 TC 232, ChD).

(3) Bearer securities are situate in the country in which the certificate of title is kept (*Winans and another v A-G (No 2)* [1910] AC 27, HL). But for Eurobonds held through Euroclear, it is the location of the broker.

(4) Movable property is held to be situated where the property is physically situated.

(5) Freehold and leasehold land is also situate where the property is physically situated.

(6) Ships are held to be situated where registered, unless within UK national or territorial waters when this is displaced by the actual situs (*Trustees Executors & Agency Co Ltd v CIR* [1973] 1 All ER 563, ChD).

(7) Simple contract debts are generally situated where the debtor resides (*Kwok Chi Leung Karl (Executor of Lamson Kwok) v Commissioners of Estate Duty* [1988] STC 728 PC). If there is more than one country of residence the terms of the contract may serve to localise the debt (*New York Life Insurance Co v Public Trustee* [1924] 40 TLR 430, CA).

(8) Specialty debts (ie under seal) are situated where the bond or specialty is kept (*Royal Trust Co v Alberta Attorney General* [1929] TLR 25, PC).

(9) A debt owed by a bank (eg a bank account) is situated at the branch where it is primarily recoverable (*R v Lovitt* [1912] AC 212).

(10) A judgment debt is situated where the judgment is recorded.

(11) A work of art normally kept overseas becomes liable to IHT on the owner's death solely because it is physically situated in the UK at the relevant date. The liability is waived if the work was brought into the UK solely for public exhibition, cleaning or restoration (ESC F7). If the work of art is held by a discretionary trust (or other no interest in possession trust), the ten-year anniversary charge is similarly waived (IHTA 1984, s 64; ESC F7).

(12) A double taxation agreement may determine where property is to be treated as situated for IHT purposes (IHTA 1984, s 158(1)).

(13) Securities issued by the Inter-American Development Bank are treated as situated outside the UK (FA 1976, s 131).

(14) Securities issued by certain international organisations may be designated by the Treasury as being situated outside the UK for IHT purposes.

7

DISPOSITIONS – GIFTS WITH RESERVATION

7.1 THE BASIC RULES
(FA 1986, s 102)

IHT is charged on the property comprised in a gift with reservation (GWR) as if it still formed part of the donor's estate on his death. This is so even if the gift took place more than seven years before the donor's death.

The GWR rules apply where an individual disposes of any property by way of gift and either:

(1) possession and enjoyment of the property is not *bona fide* assumed by the donee at or before the beginning of the relevant period; or

(2) at any time in the relevant period the property is not enjoyed to the entire, or virtually the entire, exclusion of the donor and of any benefit to him by contract or otherwise.

Here 'the relevant period' is a period ending on the date of the donor's death and beginning seven years before that date or, if it is later, on the date of the gift. While either of the above conditions applies, the property is referred to (in relation to the gift and the donor) as property subject to a reservation.

The GWR rules do not apply if or to the extent that the disposal of property by way of gift is an exempt transfer, ie:

- transfers between spouses (IHTA 1984, s 18)
- small gifts (s 20)
- gifts in consideration of marriage (s 22)
- gifts to charities (s 23)
- gifts to political parties (s 24)
- gifts to housing associations (s 24A)
- gifts for national purposes, etc. (s 25)
- maintenance funds for historic buildings (s 27) and
- employee trusts (s 28).

The GWR rules do not apply if such disposal is made under the terms of an insurance policy issued before 18 March 1986 unless the policy is varied on or after that date so as to increase the benefits secured or to extend its term.

For this purpose, any change in the terms made under an option or other power conferred by the policy is deemed to be a variation of the policy. If a policy so issued confers an option or other power under which benefits and premiums may be increased to take account of increases in the retail prices index (under IHTA 1984, s 8(3)) or any similar index specified in the policy, then, to the extent that the right to exercise that option or power would have been lost if it had not been exercised on or before 1 August 1986, the exercise before that date is disregarded.

7.2 SPECIAL CASES

Further provisions, set out in FA 1986, Sched 20, deal with the application of the GWR rules. These are applied by reference to a material date. There are two situations:

(1) if, immediately before the donor's death, there is any of his property which is subject to a reservation then, to the extent that it would not otherwise form part of his estate immediately before his death, it is treated for IHT purposes as property to which he was beneficially entitled immediately before his death, and the material date is the donor's death;

(2) if, at a time before the end of the relevant period, any property ceases to be subject to a reservation, the donor is treated for IHT purposes as having at that time made a disposition of the property under a PET, and the material date is that on which the property ceases to be subject to a reservation.

7.2.1 Substitutions and accretions
(FA 1986, Sched 20, paras 2, 3)

Where there has been a gift, but before the material date the donee ceases to possess and enjoy the gifted property (or any part of it), Sched 20 applies as if any property which is substituted for all or part of the substituted property is treated as all or part of the original gift. However, if the disposed gift becomes settled property, or is exchanged in money of any currency, this does not apply. Property received by the donee in substitution of all or part of the original gift includes any benefit by way of sale, exchange or other disposition; any benefit received by way of satisfaction or redemption of a debt or security; and any property acquired under a right to acquire property.

Where, at a time before the material date, the donee makes a gift of property out of the original gift given to the him, or otherwise voluntarily divests himself of any such property otherwise than for a consideration in money or money's worth not less than the value of the property at that time, then, unless he does so in the donor's favour, he is treated as continuing to have the possession and enjoyment of that property. Here, a disposition made by the donee by agreement is not deemed to be made voluntarily if it is made to any authority who is or could be authorised to acquire the property compulsorily. A donee is treated as divesting himself, voluntarily and without consideration, of any interest in property which merges or is extinguished in another interest held or acquired by him in the same property.

If a gift is made up of company shares or debentures, and the donee is issued with further shares in or debentures of the same or another company, or is granted a right to acquire more, the additional shares and debentures are treated as additional to the original gift. This does not apply, however, if the further or acquired shares or debentures are in exchange for the original gift. 'Issue' includes by way of the donee having been a shareholder or a debenture holder, an offer or invitation made to him as (or as once) being a holder, and any preference given to him as a holder.

Here, the value of any consideration under the right to acquire property or the issue of shares and debentures in money or money's worth given by the donee is allowed as a deduction in valuing the property comprised in the gift at any time after the consideration is given. However, if any part (not being a sum of money) of that consideration consists of property comprised in the same or another gift from the donor and treated for IHT purposes as forming part of the donor's estate immediately before his death or as being attributable to the value transferred by a PET made by him, no deduction is made in relation to it. There is left out of account so much (if any) of the consideration for, or for the grant of any right to be issued with, any shares in or debentures of a company as consists in the capitalisation of that company's reserves, or in the retention by that company, by way of set-off or otherwise, of any property distributable by it, or is otherwise provided directly or indirectly out of the assets or at the expense of that or any associated company. Two companies are deemed to be associated if one has control of the other or if another person has control of both.

7.2.2 Donee predeceasing the material date
(FA 1986, Sched 20, para 4)

Where there is a disposal by way of gift and the donee dies before the material date, the above rules are applied as if:

(1) he had not died and the acts of his personal representatives were his acts; and
(2) property taken by any person under his testamentary dispositions or his intestacy (or partial intestacy) were taken under a gift made by him at the time of his death.

7.2.3 Settled gifts
(FA 1986, Sched 20, para 5)

Where there is a disposal by way of gift and the property comprised in the gift becomes settled property as a result, the rules for substitutions and accretions and where the donee predeceases the material date do not apply. Instead, the rules described below are applied as if such property consisted of the property comprised in the settlement on the material date, except insofar as that property neither is, nor represents, nor is derived from, property originally comprised in the gift.

If the settlement comes to an end at some time before the material date for all or any of the property which, if the donor had died immediately before that time, would be treated as comprised in the gift:

(1) the property in question, other than property to which the donor then becomes absolutely and beneficially entitled in possession, and

(2) any consideration (not consisting of rights under the settlement) given by the donor for any of the property to which he so becomes entitled

are treated as comprised in the gift (in addition to any other property so comprised).

Where property comprised in a gift does not become settled property as a result of the gift, but is before the material date settled by the donee, these provisions are applied to property comprised in the settlement as if the settlement had been made by the gift. For this purpose, property which becomes settled property under any testamentary disposition of the donee or on his (partial) intestacy is treated as settled by him. Where property comprised in a gift becomes settled property either by virtue of the gift or as mentioned above, any property which, on the material date, is comprised in the settlement and is derived, directly or indirectly, from a loan made by the donor to the settlement trustees is treated as derived from property originally comprised in the gift.

Where, under any trust or power relating to settled property, income arising from that property after the material date is accumulated, the accumulations are not treated as derived from that property.

7.2.4 Exclusion of benefit
(FA 1986, Sched 20, paras 6, 7)

In determining whether any property which is disposed of by way of gift is enjoyed to the (virtually) entire exclusion of the donor and of any benefit to him by contract or otherwise:

(1) in the case of property which is an interest in land or a chattel (or in Scotland a corporeal moveable), retention or assumption by the donor of actual occupation of the land, actual enjoyment of an incorporeal right over the land, or actual possession of the chattel is disregarded if it is for full consideration in money or money's worth;

(2) in the case of property which is an interest in land, any occupation by the donor of the whole or any part of the land shall be disregarded if:

   (a) it results from a change in the donor's circumstances since the time of the gift, being a change which was unforeseen at that time and was not brought about by the donor to receive the benefit of this provision; and

(b) it occurs at a time when the donor has become unable to maintain himself through old age, infirmity or otherwise; and

(c) it represents a reasonable provision by the donee for the care and maintenance of the donor; and

(d) the donee is a relative of the donor or his spouse;

(3) a benefit which the donor obtained by virtue of any associated operations (IHTA 1984, s 268) of which the disposal by way of gift is one treated as a benefit to him by contract or otherwise.

Any question whether any property comprised in a gift was at any time enjoyed to the (virtually) entire exclusion of the donor and of any benefit to him is (so far as that question depends upon the identity of the property) determined by reference to the property which is at that time treated as comprised in the gift.

Where arrangements are entered into under which:

(1) there is a disposal by way of gift which consists of or includes, or is made in connection with, an insurance policy on the donor's life or of his spouse's or on their joint lives, and

(2) the benefits which will or may accrue to the donee as a result of the gift vary by reference to benefits accruing to the donor or his spouse (or both of them) under that or another policy (whether issued before or at the same time),

the property comprised in the gift is treated as not enjoyed to the donor's (virtually) entire exclusion. Here, the reference to a policy on the joint lives of the donor and his spouse includes a policy on their joint lives and on the survivor's life; the reference to benefits accruing to the donor or his spouse (or both of them) includes benefits which accrue as a result of the exercise of rights conferred on either or both of them.

As noted above, the GWR provisions do not apply where an interest in land is given away and the donor pays full consideration for future use of the property. While the Revenue takes the view that such full consideration is required throughout the relevant period – and therefore considers that the rent paid should be reviewed at appropriate intervals to reflect market change – it does recognise that there is no single value at which consideration can be fixed as 'full'. Rather, it accepts that what constitutes full consideration in any case lies within a range of values reflecting normal valuation tolerances, and that any amount within that range can be accepted as satisfying the test (*Tax Bulletin* 9 (November 1993)).

7.2.5 **Agricultural and business property**
(FA 1986, Sched 20, para 8)

The rule set out below applies where there is a disposal by way of gift of property which, in relation to the donor, is at that time:

- a relevant business property (IHTA 1984, s 105), or
- an agricultural property (s 115), or
- shares or securities (s 122(1)) (agricultural property of companies),

and that property is subject to a reservation. In such event, any question whether, on the material transfer of value:

(1) any shares or securities fall within IHTA 1984, s 105(1)(b), (bb) or (cc) (certain shares or securities qualifying for relief) is determined as if the shares or securities were owned by the donor and had been owned by him since the disposal by way of gift; and

(2) relief is available by way of BPR or APR (see Chapters 8 and 9 respectively) is determined as if, so far as it is attributable to the property comprised in the gift, that transfer were a transfer of value by the donee.

In determining whether, on the transfer of value which the donee is assumed to make, the minimum period of ownership or occupation requirement is fulfilled:

(1) ownership by the donor prior to the disposal by way of gift is treated as ownership by the donee; and

(2) occupation by the donor prior to the disposal and any occupation by him after it is treated as occupation by the donee.

Where the property disposed of by gift consists of shares or securities, APR is available not on the material transfer of value unless:

(1) such relief applied in relation to the value transferred by the disposal, and

(2) throughout the period beginning with the disposal and ending on the material date, the shares or securities are owned by the donee.

For the purpose only of determining whether, on the transfer of value which the donee is assumed to make, the special requirements relating to the agricultural property of companies (IHTA 1984, s 123(1)) are fulfilled, it is assumed that the requirements as to the ownership of the shares or securities is fulfilled.

Here, 'the material transfer of value' means, as the case may require, the transfer of value:

(1) on the donor's death (IHTA 1984, s 4); or

(2) when any property ceases to be subject to a reservation, and the donor is treated for IHT purposes as having at that time made a disposition of the property under a PET (FA 1986, s 102(4)).

If the donee dies before the material transfer of value then, as respects any time after his death, any reference to the donee is construed as being to his personal representatives or, as the case may require, the person (if any) by whom the property, shares or securities concerned were taken under a testamentary disposition made by the donee or under his (partial) intestacy.

7.3 NOT ENJOYED TO DONOR'S (VIRTUALLY) ENTIRE EXCLUSION

A gift is regarded as one with reservation if:

(1) the donee does not take possession and enjoyment of the property at the date of the gift or seven years before the donor's death, if later; or

(2) at any time in the seven years prior to the donor's death, but after the date of the gift, the property is not enjoyed to the exclusion or to virtually the entire exclusion of the donor.

The Revenue has published its 'Interpretation of the *de minimis* rule' (*Tax Bulletin* 9 (November 1993)). It points out that the word 'virtually' in the *de minimis* rule is not defined and the statute does not give any express guidance about its meaning. However, the *Shorter Oxford English Dictionary* defines it as, among other things, 'to all intents' and 'as good as'.

The Revenue's interpretation of 'virtually to the entire exclusion' is that it covers cases in which the benefit to the donor is insignificant in relation to the gifted property.

Each case turns on its own unique circumstances and the questions are likely to be of fact and degree. But the Revenue does not interpret the *de minimis* rule in such a way that donors are unreasonably prevented from having limited access to property they have given away and a measure of flexibility is adopted in applying the test.

The Revenue gives some examples of situations in which it considers the *de minimis* rule permits limited benefit to the donor without bringing the GWR provisions into play:

(1) a house which becomes the donee's residence but where the donor subsequently stays or visits as follows:

(a) stays, in the donee's absence, for not more than two weeks each year;

(b) stays with the donee for less than one month each year;

(c) social visits, excluding overnight stays, made by a donor as the donee's guest to a house which he had given away (the extent of the social visits should be no greater than the visits which the donor might be expected to make to the donee's house in the absence of any gift);

(d) a temporary stay for some short-term purpose in a house the donor had previously given away, eg

      (i)   while the donor convalesces after medical treatment,

     (ii) while the donor looks after a donee convalescing after medical treatment, or

   (iii) while the donor's own home is being redecorated;

(2) visits to a house for domestic reasons, eg baby-sitting by the donor for the donee's children;

(3) a house together with a library of books which the donor visits less than five times in any year to consult or borrow a book;

(4) a motor car which the donee uses to give occasional (ie less than three times a month) lifts to the donor;

(5) land which the donor uses to walk his dogs or for horseriding provided this does not restrict the donee's use of the land.

It follows that if the benefit to the donor is, or becomes, more significant, the GWR provisions are likely to apply. Examples of this include gifts of:

(1) a house in which the donor then stays most weekends, or for a month or more each year;

(2) a second or holiday home which the donor and the donee both then use on an occasional basis;

(3) a house with a library in which the donor continues to keep his own books, or which the donor uses on a regular basis (eg because it is necessary for his work);

(4) a motor car which the donee uses every day to take the donor to work.

7.4 TERMINATION OF RESERVED BENEFITS AND ANNUAL EXEMPTION

Where a reservation ceases, the donor is treated as having made a PET at that time. In that event the PET is only taxable if the donor dies within the next seven years but the value of the PET cannot be reduced by any available annual exemption (IHTA 1984, s 19).

A typical outright gift to an individual of an amount exceeding the available annual exemption is partly exempt, with the balance above that exemption being a PET. But a PET itself cannot qualify for the annual exemption. The reason is that a PET is a transfer which, but for IHTA 1984, s 3A, would be an immediately chargeable transfer. By definition, a chargeable transfer is a transfer of value which is not exempt (see IHTA 1984, s 2(1)). So a PET cannot be an exempt transfer at the time it is made. The PET escapes an IHT charge if the donor survives the statutory period after making it.

The annual exemption is not necessarily lost. For example, suppose a donor made a gift of his home in August 1997 but continues to reside there. In May 1998 he finally leaves the gifted house and the reservation ceases. In October 1998 he makes a gift into a discretionary trust (an immediately chargeable transfer). He is treated as making a PET of his residence in May 1998, but the annual £3,000 exemption does not reduce its value. However, the exemption *is* available for setting off against the immediately chargeable transfer in October 1998, and so is any unused exemption carried forward from the previous year (*Tax Bulletin* 9 (November 1993)).

7.5 CHANGE OF CIRCUMSTANCES

If, owing to a change of circumstances which was unforeseen and not brought about by the donor himself, the donor returns to occupy part of a property previously given away, the gift of that property does not become a gift with reservation provided:

(1) the donor has become unable to maintain himself through old age, infirmity or otherwise;
(2) the offer of accommodation 'represents a reasonable provision by the donee for the care and maintenance of the donor'; and
(3) the donee is a relative of the donor or his spouse.

7.6 GIFT OF PART OR GIFT WITH RESERVATION OVER WHOLE

It is often difficult to distinguish between making a gift with reservation and giving away a part only of what one possesses. In *Munro v Stamp Duty Commrs of NSW [1934] AC 61, PC* it was held that arrangements made between a donee and a third party to give the donor a benefit were caught, whereas the retention of rights under a contract which was separate from the gift and made before it were not. This gave rise to the 'shearing' or to 'carve-out' scheme, whereby a gift of land which was already subject to a lease was not a GWR because the lease was not part of the gift. On the other hand, a gift of land which was subject to an agreement for a lease back, whether created at the same time, or later, was a GWR. The reasoning being that the gift comprised the grant of the whole, subject to something reserved out of it, as contrasted with a gift of a partial interest leaving something retained in the hands of the grantor (*Nichols v CIR* [1975] STC 278, CA).

The most recent case is *Ingram and Palmer-Tomkinson (Lady Ingram's Executors) v CIR* [1999] STC 37, HL. Lady Ingram transferred a property to the solicitor, who held the property as her nominee. He then executed a lease in favour of Lady Ingram giving her a rent free lease for 20 years. The land subject to the lease was transferred to a family trust. The executors' appeal was allowed. 'Although (FA 1986 s 102) does not allow a donor to have his cake and eat it, there is nothing to stop him from carefully dividing the cake, eating part and having the rest.' It is thus important to define precisely what interests are being given away, and those that are being retained. In this case the gift was the capital value of land after deduction of a leasehold interest. Although an owner of property cannot grant a lease to himself (*Rye v Rye* [1962] AC 496), in English law a trustee is not an agent for his beneficiary. The position is different in Scotland where a nominee cannot create an effective lease in favour of his principal, and a person cannot create a lease in favour of himself (*Kidrummy (Jersey) LTD v VIR* [1990] STC 657, CS).

As they apply to gifts of land, the GWR rules are extended where:

(1) the gift is made after 8 March 1999;
(2) the donor retains a right to continue to occupy the land or enjoy a right in relation thereto for less than full consideration;
(3) the gift is made within seven years after the interest which gives the continued right of occupation, etc. is created.

The extended GWR rules do not apply where:

(1) the gift is covered by an exemption from IHT;
(2) the benefit to the donor is negligible from the donee's point of view;
(3) the donor pays full consideration for the benefit;
(4) the donor's occupation is forced upon him due to an unexpected hardship arising after the gift.

7.7 RECEIPT OF BENEFIT

A gift may become one with reservation if, at any time in the period beginning with the later of the date the gift was made and seven years before the donor's death and ending with his death, the donor enjoyed a benefit from the property. A gift that was originally subject to a reservation may become a gift not subject to reservation if the donor ceases to enjoy any benefit from it.

The Revenue has made a number of other points, including:

(1) The fact that a benefit is reserved for the donor's spouse does not make the gift a GWR (eg there is no objection to a wife being a potential beneficiary under a discretionary trust established by her husband). However, the Revenue will want to be satisfied that the wife is not being used to channel benefits back to her husband (in other words, that there is not a GWR by associated operations) (IHTA 1984, s 268).
(2) A settlor does not make a GWR of the property he has settled merely by being appointed a trustee of the settlement. He should not however be paid (or be entitled to any remuneration) for acting as a trustee (*Oakes v NSW Stamp Duty Commrs* [1954] AC 57).

7.8 SETTLEMENT ON SELF

If an individual settles property on himself for life, with remainder to (say) his children, that property is on general principles counted as part of his taxable estate when he dies (IHTA 1984, s 49(1)). The Revenue's statement means that an individual may safely settle property on (say) his children for life, remainder to his grandchildren, with a reversion to himself should all his children and grandchildren pre-decease him.

7.9 EFFECTIVE DATE FOR VALUATION

Finally, the basic point should be re-emphasised that any property given away subject to reservation is taxed as if it remained part of the donor's estate at his death. This means that the property is to be valued at the time the donor dies, and not at the time the gift was made.

8

BUSINESS PROPERTY RELIEF

8.1 SCOPE: NATURE OF BUSINESS PROPERTY RELIEF
(IHTA 1984, ss 103–105)

To the extent that any value transferred is attributable to the value of relevant business property, such value is reduced by business property relief (BPR) at either 100 (for property within IHTA 1984, s 105(1)(a), (b) or (bb)) or 50 per cent (for other property). The relief is given before IHT is calculated, and before any grossing-up on the basis that the donor pays the IHT. This also includes the periodic and exit charges on transfers of value by no interest in possession trusts (IHTA 1984, ss 58–78, 80–85). It is also available on shares, securities and debentures in a company the business of which is that of a holding company of subsidiaries which are themselves not excluded.

Businesses carried on in the course of trades, professions or vocations are eligible for BPR, but not businesses carried on otherwise than for gain. It is not available if the business comprises:

(1) dealing in securities, stocks or shares;
(2) dealing in land or buildings; or
(3) making or holding investments.

This restriction does not apply if the business is wholly a market-maker or is a discount house and (in either case) is carried on in the UK.

Where at the date of a transfer a company holds funds on short-term deposit pending reinvestment in qualifying business premises, BPR is available (*Brown's Exor's v CIR* (1996) SSCD 277, SpC 83). The letting of industrial business units (*Martin & Horsfall (Moore's Executors) v CIR* (1995) SSCD 5, SpCS 2) and the letting of flats on shorthold tenancies (*Burkinyoung's Exor v CIR* (1995) SSCD 29, SpC 3) have been held not to qualify for BPR. However, the Special Commissioners decided that the owner of a business property who was actively involved in its management was entitled to claim BPR (*Taxation* 3 May 1990). In that case, a life tenant of settled land, who had used that land in his farming and forestry business, died. Although the land itself was not relevant business property, the life interest in the land was an asset used in the business. The asset had to be valued as if the deceased was beneficially entitled to the land itself, and therefore qualified for BPR (*Fetherstonhaugh and others v CIR* [1984] STC 261, CA).

BPR is not available to a transfer of value made after a winding-up order has been made, or a resolution for voluntary winding-up passed, unless it is for part of a reconstruction or amalgamation which is either the purpose of the winding-up or takes place within 12 months after the transfer of value.

Assets eligible for agricultural relief do not also qualify for BPR (IHTA 1984, s 114(1)). However, any agricultural assets (such as stock, plant or the development value of land) not qualifying for relief under the agricultural property relief provisions may well qualify for BPR (IHTA 1984, s 116).

Where the asset is woodlands, and the value transferred (to the extent that it comprises business property) is reduced because of sales of trees or underwood, BPR is available only on the reduced value (IHTA 1984, ss 114(2), 129). BPR is given before IHT is calculated, and before any grossing-up on the basis that the donor pays the IHT.

Companies are treated as quoted if their shares are dealt in on The Stock Exchange (IHTA 1984, s 272). Shares dealt in on the Alternative Investment Market (AIM) count as unquoted for this purpose. A company need not be incorporated in the UK.

8.2 RELEVANT BUSINESS PROPERTY

8.2.1 Applicable rate of BPR

For property consisting of a business or an interest in a business, the BPR rate is 100 per cent (IHTA 1984, s 105(1)(a)).

For securities of an *unquoted* (ie not listed) trading company (or the holding company of an unquoted trading group) which, alone or with other such securities owned by the transferor and any unquoted shares so owned, gave him in excess of 50 per cent voting control immediately before the transfer, the rate is 100 per cent (IHTA 1984, s 105(1)(b), (1ZA), (2), (4)(b)). However, 100 per cent relief is not available if a related property relief *claim* (sales from death estate within three years) has been made and the 50+ per cent holding is exceeded only by the inclusion of the related property (ss 105(2), 176).

For shares in an unquoted trading company or the unquoted holding company of a trading group, the rate is 100 per cent (s 105(1)(bb)). Where shares, etc are held by a settlement, the trustees' voting powers are deemed to be given to the person beneficially entitled in possession to the shares, etc (s 103(1)(b)). The relief is only available where the transferor has owned the relevant business property throughout two years prior to the transfer (s 106). Prior periods of ownership by a spouse can be aggregated for this test (s 108), even through successive intra-spouse transfers (provided either the earlier or the later transfer was a death transfer – s 109(1)(b)). The replacement property restriction does not apply (s 107(4)).

For shares, etc in a *quoted* trading company (or the holding company of a quoted trading group) which, alone or with other shares etc owned by the transferor, gave 50+ per cent voting control immediately before the transfer, the rate is 100 per cent (IHTA 1984, s 105(1)(cc), (4)(a)). The relief is not available if a related property relief *claim* (sales from death estate within three years) has been made and the 50+ per cent holding is exceeded only by the inclusion of the related property (ss 105(2)(b), 176). The replacement property restriction does not apply (s 107(4)).

Land, buildings, plant or machinery used by a trading company (or the holding company of a trading group) where the transferor had control immediately before the transfer attracts 50 per cent relief (IHTA 1984, s 105(1)(d)). For land, buildings, plant or machinery used by a partnership of which, immediately before the transfer, the transferor was a partner, the rate is 50 per cent (s 105(1)(e)). Land, etc is not eligible for BPR unless the business, or the transferor's interest therein, or the shares, etc of a company carrying on the business were themselves qualified as business property (s 105(6)).

Note that where the agricultural value of land takes account of the value of milk quotas, APR (see Chapter 9) is given on that value. If the milk quota is valued separately, it is eligible for BPR (*Tax Bulletin* 6 (February 1993)).

8.2.2 Ownership of property
(IHTA 1984, ss 106, 107)

In general, to qualify for BPR the individual or trustees must have owned the business property for at least two years. Replacement property may qualify if the property transferred and the property which it replaced were together owned for at least two of the five years preceding the transfer, and both qualified as business property. However, BPR is limited to such amount as would have been available had the replacement not been made, unless the change results from the formation, alteration or dissolution of a partnership, or the incorporation of a business into a company controlled by its former owners.

The replacement property rule does not apply where the shares transferred were acquired as a result of a reorganisation, reconstruction or amalgamation such that the new shares etc are equated for CGT purposes with the original shares (TCGA 1992, ss 126–136).

A period of ownership of a farming business which is replaced by non-agricultural business property is counted towards the minimum period of ownership applied to the replacement property (*Tax Bulletin* 14 (December 1994)).

8.2.3 Successions
(IHTA, s 108)

In applying the period of ownership test and the rules for replacement property, where the transferor became entitled to the property on another person's death, a legatee is deemed to have owned and occupied property (provided that he does subsequently occupy it) from the date of death.

Where an individual inherits business property from his spouse, or vice versa, the inheritor can claim that the deceased spouse's period of ownership should count towards the inheritor's two-year qualifying period for BPR. This only applies where one spouse has inherited the other's shares, not where one spouse makes a lifetime gift to the other.

8.2.4 Successive transfers
(IHTA 1984, s 109)

Business property which would have been eligible for BPR were it not for the minimum occupation and ownership conditions remains eligible if the following conditions are met:

(1) the value transferred by the earlier transfer was eligible for BPR (or would have been available if then in force);
(2) the property which, in relation to the earlier transfer, was or would have been eligible for BPR became, through the earlier transfer, the transferor's property in relation to the subsequent transfer, and at that time is occupied for agricultural purposes by the transferor or his personal representatives;
(3) the property or any property directly replacing it would have been eligible for BPR on the subsequent transfer; where, under the earlier transfer, the amount of the value transferred which was attributable to the property was part only of its value, a like part only of the value which otherwise would fall to be reduced by BPR is similarly so reduced;
(4) either the earlier or the subsequent transfer was made on the transferor's death.

If property which meets the above conditions is replaced, the amount of BPR is limited to such amount as would have been available had the replacement not been made, unless the change results from the formation, alteration or dissolution of a partnership.

8.3 VALUATION

8.3.1 How a business is valued for BPR
(IHTA 1984, s 110)

The value of a business or of an interest in a business is taken to be its net value. The net value is the value of the assets used in the business (including goodwill) reduced by the aggregate amount of any liabilities incurred for business purposes. Only those assets or liabilities which are relevant to the net value of the entire business are taken into account. See **8.2.1** in relation to milk quotas.

8.3.2 Exclusion of shares in companies with non-qualifying businesses
(IHTA 1984, s 111)

A special rule applies if a company is a member of a group and the business of any other member of the group comprises:

(1) dealing in securities, stocks or shares (otherwise than as a market-maker or discount house);
(2) dealing in land or buildings;
(3) making or holding investments (otherwise than as a holding company of companies which are not themselves within the above categories); or
(4) holding of land or buildings wholly or mainly occupied by group members whose businesses do not fall within the above categories.

The value of shares, etc of the company are calculated on the basis that the other company is not a member of the group.

8.3.3 Liabilities
(IHTA 1984, s 162)

A liability for which there is a right of reimbursement is taken into account only insofar as such reimbursement is considered unlikely to be made. If a liability falls to be discharged after the time when it is to be taken into account, its value is taken as at the time of the gift or death. In computing the value of the transferor's estate immediately after a transfer of value, no account is taken of the fact that the IHT will not be due immediately, and as if any IHT is recovered otherwise than from the transferor or his spouse (IHTA 1984, s 203(1)).

A liability which is an encumbrance on any property is, so far as possible, taken to reduce the value of that property. Equally, the value of any loan is deductible if secured on business assets, even if the amount borrowed was not spent on business purchases. Where a loan was made by a non-UK resident but is neither to be discharged in the UK nor an encumbrance on property in the UK, it is primarily taken to reduce the value of property outside the UK.

8.4 NOT ALL ASSETS QUALIFY

8.4.1 Exclusion of value of excepted assets
(IHTA 1984, s 112)

Such part of a transfer of value of relevant business property as is attributable to 'excepted assets' is left out of account. Excepted assets are those which are not:

(1) used wholly or mainly for business purposes and have been so used for the last two years of the relevant period (here, the relevant period, in relation to any asset, is that immediately preceding the transfer of value during which the asset (or, if the relevant business property is an interest in a business, a corresponding interest in the asset) was owned by the transferor or, if the business concerned is that of a company, was owned by that or any other company which immediately before the transfer was a member of the same group);

(2) required for the future business use unless the asset is used or required for the future use of another member of the same group of companies otherwise than for an excluded purpose.

Where a company has subsidiary companies, it is necessary to look at the group situation. Shares in subsidiaries may have to be treated as excepted assets if the subsidiaries are investment companies (but not otherwise).

An asset which is land, buildings, plant or machinery used by a trading company (or the holding company of a trading group) where the transferor had control immediately before the transfer is not an 'excepted asset', unless it:

- was so used for the two years preceding the transfer, or
- replaced another asset and together such assets were so used for two years in aggregate.

This condition is treated as satisfied if the asset (or it and the asset(s) replaced by it) was or were so used throughout the period between the earlier and the subsequent transfer (or throughout the part of that period during which it or they were owned by the transferor or his spouse). Where such use is only partial, each part is treated as a separate asset. Assets used wholly or mainly for the transferor's personal benefit cannot be business assets for BPR.

8.4.2 Contracts for sale
(IHTA 1984, s 113)

BPR is not due if a binding contract for sale exists at the time the property is transferred. There are two exceptions where the property is:

(1) a business or interest in a business and the sale is to a company which is to carry on the business and is made in consideration wholly or mainly of shares in or securities of that company, or

(2) shares in or securities of a company and the sale is made for the purpose of reconstruction or amalgamation.

Thus, if the terms of a partnership deed or shareholders agreement are such that the executors of a deceased partner or shareholder *must* sell his interest in the firm or company to the surviving partners or shareholders, no BPR is due. The Revenue has confirmed, in SP 12/80, that the relief is due if the survivors' merely have an *option* to buy the deceased's interest.

8.4.3 Assets owned by partners rather than firm

BPR is available at the rate of 50 per cent where the partner personally owns assets which are used in the partnership business. Bringing the property into the partnership (perhaps with an appropriate adjustment to the profit-sharing ratios) increases BPR to 100 per cent.

8.5 VOTING CONTROL
(IHTA 1984, s 269)

For certain purposes it is necessary that the shares should give the transferor voting control. This includes shares attributed under the related property rules (IHTA 1984, s 161), and held by trustees of a settlement in which he has an interest in possession. The control test is based exclusively on voting control, so that even if the donor's shares do not carry a right to the majority of dividends or of any surplus in a winding-up, the test may be satisfied. This is overridden if the shares give limited voting rights in relation to such matters. Where a company has shares or securities of any class giving powers of voting limited to either or both of:

(1) the question of winding-up the company, and

(2) any question primarily affecting shares or securities of that class,

all questions affecting the company as a whole have effect except any in relation to which those powers are capable of being exercised.

In a recent case where 24 per cent of shares were held by the four-year-old grandson of the deceased who held 45 per cent, the deceased was held to not have control as IHTA, s 269(1) deals with voting control, not the capabilities of the shareholders in whose name the shares are registered (*Walding and others (Walding's Exor's) v CIR* (1995) *The Times*, 28 November, ChD).

8.6 PETs AND BUSINESS PROPERTY RELIEF

8.6.1 Effect of later events
(IHTA 1984, s 113A)

If a PET subsequently becomes a chargeable transfer which would other-wise be eligible to BPR, it will not qualify unless further conditions are met. If these conditions are satisfied only for part of the original property, only a proportionate part of so much of the value transferred as is attributable to the original property is reduced to give effect to BPR. Where:

(1) the value of a chargeable transfer (other than a PET) is reduced by BPR, and
(2) the transfer is within seven years prior to the transferor's death

then, unless the further conditions are met, the additional IHT charged by reason of the transferor's death is calculated without BPR. The conditions which must be met, if BPR is to apply, are as follows:

(1) The original property must have been owned by the transferee through-out the period from the date of the chargeable transfer to the transferor's death.
(2) The original property comprised shares etc either quoted at the time of the chargeable transfer or comprised in a 50+ per cent control holding, and remained unquoted throughout the period from the date of the chargeable transfer to the transferor's death.
(3) In relation to a notional transfer made by the transferee immediately before the transferor's death, would, were it not for the two-year own-ership requirement, have qualified for BPR.

If the transferee died before the transferor, the date of the transferee's death is taken in place of the date of the transferor's death. Shares owned by the transferee immediately before the death in question, which:

(1) for CGT, are identified with the original property under the amalga-mation and reconstruction rules (TCGA 1992, ss 126–36), or
(2) were issued in consideration for the incorporation of a business

are treated as though they were the original property. The reduction of value to give effect to BPR is in any determination of whether there is a potentially exempt or chargeable transfer in any case.

Here, 'the original property' is the property which was relevant business property in relation to the chargeable transfer, and 'the transferee' is the person whose property the original property became on that chargeable transfer or, where on the transfer the original property became or remained settled property in which no qualifying interest in possession subsists, the trustees of the settlement.

In this case, a 'qualifying interest in possession' is, in certain circumstances, an interest in possession to which a company is beneficially entitled. This applies where:

(1) the business of the company consists wholly or mainly in the acquisition of interests in settled property, and
(2) the company has acquired the interest for full consideration in money or money's worth from an individual who was beneficially entitled to it.

Where such acquisition was before 14 March 1975, condition (1) above is treated as satisfied if that was the company's business at the time of acquisition. However, this condition need not be satisfied if the company is a suitably authorised insurance company.

8.6.2 Application of replacement property rules
(IHTA 1995, s 113B)

The replacement property rules in modified form apply if:

(1) the transferee has disposed of the original property before the transferor's death, and
(2) the whole of the consideration therefor has been applied to the purchase of the replacement property.

The modified rules do not apply unless:

(1) the replacement property was acquired, or a binding contract entered into, within three years (or longer at the Revenue's discretion) after the disposal of the original property (where a binding contract for the sale of property has been entered into at any time prior to the actual disposal, the disposal is deemed to take place at the date of the contract);
(2) the disposal and acquisition are both made at arm's length or at arm's length price.

If the above conditions are met, the conditions which must be met if BPR is to apply are deemed to be satisfied in relation to the original property, subject to three further tests:

(1) the replacement property is owned by the transferee immediately before the transferor's death, and
(2) throughout the period from the date of the chargeable transfer and ending with the transferor's death (disregarding any gap between disposal and acquisition) either the original or the replacement property was owned by the transferee, and
(3) in relation to a notional transfer made by the transferee immediately before the transferor's death, would, were it not for the two-year ownership requirement, have qualified for BPR.

If the transferee died before the transferor, the date of the transferee's death is taken in place of the date of the transferor's death.

The replacement property rule does not apply where shares are transferred which were acquired as a result of a reorganisation, reconstruction or amalgamation such that the new shares etc are equated for CGT purposes with the original shares (TCGA 1992, ss 126–136).

8.7 WHERE BOTH BUSINESS AND AGRICULTURAL RELIEFS COULD APPLY

The IHT legislation provides relief for transfers of agricultural property (see **9**) and business property. The Revenue gave its views, in *Tax Bulletin* 14 (December 1994), on the availability of relief:

(1) where agricultural property is replaced by business property (or vice versa) shortly before the owner's death; and

(2) on the donor's death, where the donee of a PET of agricultural property has sold it and reinvested the proceeds in a non-agricultural business (or vice versa).

BPR and APR reduce the value of relevant business or agricultural property by either 50 or 100 per cent. The rate of relief depends on the nature of the property and interest held.

The qualifying conditions for the relief include requirements of a minimum period of ownership and, in the case of agricultural property, of occupation of the property for agricultural purposes immediately before the transfer. If, and to the extent that, the same property may qualify for relief as both agricultural and business property, double relief is prevented.

There are also rules which allow for the sale and replacement of qualifying property. The replacement qualifies only if it, and the original qualifying property, have together been owned (and, in the case of agricultural property, occupied) for a combined minimum period.

In the Revenue's view, where agricultural property which is a farming business is replaced by non-agricultural business property, the period of ownership of the original property is relevant for applying the minimum ownership condition to the replacement property. BPR is available on the replacement if all the conditions for that relief are satisfied. Where non-agricultural business property is replaced by a farming business, and the latter is not eligible for APR (see **9**), BPR is not excluded if the conditions for that relief are satisfied.

There could be cases where, for example, agricultural land is not part of a farming business, so any replacement could only qualify for BPR if it satisfied the minimum ownership conditions in its own right. However, the Revenue's experience suggests such cases are likely to be exceptional.

Where the donee of a PET of a farming business sells the business, and replaces it with a non-agricultural business, the effect is to deny APR on the value transferred by the PET. Consequently, BPR is not excluded if the conditions for that relief are satisfied. In the reverse situation, the farming business acquired by the donee can be 'relevant business property' for BPR.

8.8 PROPERTY SUBJECT TO GIFT WITH RESERVATION
(FA 1986, s 102)

In general, a gift is regarded as a GWR if the donee does not take possession and enjoyment of the property within the relevant period beginning seven years prior to the donor's death, or if later at the date of the gift, or if, at any time in the relevant period the property is not enjoyed by the donee to the donor's (virtually) entire exclusion (see 7). If property is subject to a GWR, it remains in the donor's estate for IHT purposes, even though it is actually owned by the donee.

If, at a time before the end of the relevant period, any property ceases to be property subject to a reservation, the donor is treated as having at that time made a disposition of the property under a PET. Remember, however, that on the donor's death BPR may still be due (IHTA 1984, s 103).

9

AGRICULTURAL PROPERTY RELIEF

9.1 SCOPE

9.1.1 Nature of agricultural property relief
(IHTA 1984, s 115)

References to a transfer of value include an occasion on which IHT is chargeable under the no interest in possession regime (except for the exemption from the ten-yearly charge (IHTA 1984, s 79)). References to the value transferred by a transfer of value include the amount on which IHT is then chargeable, and those to the transferor include the trustees of the settlement concerned. This therefore includes the periodic and exit charges on transfers of value by no interest in possession trusts (IHTA 1984, ss 58–78, 80–85).

'Agricultural property' comprises the following:

(1) Bare agricultural land and pasture without buildings.
(2) Woodlands only if their occupation is ancillary to the occupation of agricultural land or pasture.
(3) Buildings used in the intensive rearing of livestock or fish provided that their occupation is ancillary to the occupation of the agricultural land or pasture.
(4) Such cottages, farm buildings and farmhouses (together with the land occupied with them) as are of a character appropriate to the property, but not a substantial farmhouse on 2.5 acres since it is not agricultural land and pasture (*Starke and another (Brown's Exor's) v CIR* [1994] STC 295).

With regard to items (1) and (3) above, horses are not 'livestock' and grazing by horses would only qualify if the horses were connected with agriculture (*Wheatley's Executors v CIR* [1998] SSCD 60, SpC 149). However, land and buildings used for breeding and rearing of horses at stud farms (including related grazing) does qualify (*Hansard*, 2 November 1983).

A farmhouse which had been unoccupied for a number of years was held not to be agricultural property (*Harrolds Exor's v CIR* (1996) 000071 SSCD 195, SpC). If a transfer of agricultural property includes a cottage occupied by a retired farm employee or his widow(er), the conditions concerning occupation for agricultural purposes is deemed satisfied if the occupier is a statutorily protected tenant or the occupation is under a lease granted to the employee for life (of self or surviving spouse) as part of the employment contract for agricultural purposes (ESC F16).

Agricultural property relief (APR) applies only to agricultural property in the UK, the Channel Islands and the Isle of Man including short rotation coppice (FA 1995, s 154(2), (3), (5)) and land in habitat schemes (IHTA 1984, s 124C). The agricultural value of any agricultural property is the value which would be its value if it were subject to a perpetual covenant prohibiting its use otherwise than as agricultural property. APR is not due on the other assets of a farming business, although they would normally qualify for BPR.

9.1.2 Land in habitat schemes
(IHTA 1984, s 124C)

The scope of APR is extended, for transfers of value from 26 November 1996, to cover land assets dedicated under habitat schemes for the protection of the environment and preservation of the countryside. This extension also applies to transfers of value made before 26 November 1996, for any IHT charge or extra IHT charge which arises because of an event occurring from 26 November 1996 (eg on death within seven years of a gift).

The habitat schemes' purpose is to provide a boost to environmental protection by ensuring that owners dedicating their assets under those schemes do not as a result lose any entitlement to APR. Some of the schemes, which usually run for up to ten years, allow land to be used for agriculture but in ways that are ecologically benign. Land dedicated under such schemes can qualify for APR relief and is not covered by the amended provision. Other schemes require land to be taken out of farming altogether for 20 years. If land is in a habitat scheme:

(1) the land is regarded as agricultural land;
(2) the land's management in accordance with the scheme's requirements is regarded as agriculture; and
(3) buildings used in connection with such management are regarded as farm buildings.

Land is regarded as being in a habitat scheme if:

(1) an application for aid, under the enactments listed below, has been accepted in relation to the land; and
(2) the undertakings to which the acceptance relates have not been terminated by
  (a) the expiry of the period to which they relate; or
  (b) being treated as terminated.

The enactments referred to in (1) above are:

- The Habitat (Water Fringe) Regulations 1994 (SI No 1291), reg 3(1)
- The Habitat (Former Set-Aside Land) Regulations 1994 (SI No 1292)
- The Habitat (Salt-Marsh) Regulations 1994 (SI No 1293)
- The Habitats (Scotland) Regulations 1994 (SI No 2710) (if undertakings are given under reg 3(2)(a))
- The Habitat Improvement Regulations (Northern Ireland) 1995 (SR(NI) No 134) (if an undertaking in respect of the land is given under reg 3(1)(a))
- Other enactments as added by Treasury order.

9.2 RELEVANT AGRICULTURAL PROPERTY

9.2.1 Applicable rate of APR
(IHTA 1984, s 116)

To the extent that the value transferred by a transfer of value is attributable to the value of relevant agricultural property, such value is reduced by APR at either 100 or 50 per cent (dependent upon the nature of the asset).

For an interest of a transferor (whether alone or as joint tenants, or tenants in common) which carries the right to vacant possession, or the right to obtain it in the next 12 months, the rate is 100 per cent (IHTA 1984, s 116(2)(a), (6)). The same rate applies for an interest of a transferor which does not carry the right to vacant possession, or the right to obtain it in the next 12 months (ie tenanted property) (s 116(2)(c), (5A)–(5E)). This condition is regarded as satisfied where the transferor's interest in the property either:

(1) carries a right to vacant possession within 24 months of the transfer date, or
(2) is, notwithstanding the tenancy terms, valued at an amount broadly equivalent to the property's vacant possession (ESC F17).

A transferor who beneficially owned his interest prior to 10 March 1981 and would have been entitled on a transfer and claim on 9 March 1981 to APR under the old rules to full relief (restriction for land in excess of £250,000 or 1,000 acres not applying) is entitled to a rate of 100 per cent (s 116(2)(b), (3)(a), (5)). The transferor's interest must not, at any time since 10 March 1981, have carried a right to vacant possession within the following 12 months, or fail to do so because of a deliberate act or omission by the transferor (s 116(3)(b)).

Where the transferor beneficially owned his interest prior to 10 March 1981 but would not have been entitled on a transfer and claim on 9 March 1981 to APR under the old rules to full relief (restriction for land in excess of £250,000 or 1,000 acres applying), the rate is 50 per cent (s 116(2)(b), (4), (5)).

A transfer of shares in a company to the extent of value attributable to agricultural property and giving the transferor 50+ per cent voting control of the company immediately prior to the transfer attracts a rate of 100 per cent (ss 122(1)(a), (b), (3)(a), 116). APR is not available if a related property relief claim (sales from death estate within three years) has been made and the 50+ per cent holding is exceeded only by the inclusion of the related property (ss 122(2)(a), (b), 176).

Where, in consequence of the death on or after 1 September 1995 of the tenant or the last surviving tenant of any property, the tenancy:

(1) becomes vested in a person beneficially entitled under the deceased tenant's will or other testamentary writing or on his intestacy, and

(2) is or becomes binding on the landlord and that person as landlord and tenant respectively,

the transferor's interest in the property immediately before the transfer does not carry the right either to vacant possession or to obtain it within the next 12 months, because the property is let on a tenancy beginning on the date of the death. Also, where in consequence of such death on or after 1 September 1995, a tenancy of the property or of any property comprising the whole or part of it:

(1) is obtained by a person under or by virtue of an enactment, or

(2) is granted to a person in circumstances such that he is already entitled under or by virtue of an enactment to obtain such a tenancy, but one which takes effect on a later date, or

(3) is granted to a person who is or has become the only or only remaining applicant, or the only or only remaining person eligible to apply, under a particular enactment for such a tenancy in the particular case,

again the transferor's interest in the property immediately before the transfer does not carry the right either to vacant possession or to obtain it within the next 12 months. This does not apply to property in Scotland.

If, in a case where the transferor dies on or after 1 September 1995,

(1) the tenant of any property has, before the death, given notice of intention to retire in favour of a new tenant, and

(2) the tenant's retirement in favour of the new tenant takes place after the death but not more than 30 months after the giving of the notice,

again the transferor's interest does not carry the right either to vacant possession or to obtain it within the next 12 months, because the tenancy granted or assigned to the new tenant had been a tenancy beginning immediately before the transfer of value which the transferor is treated (under IHTA 1984, s 4(1)) as making immediately before his death.

The definitions of 'new tenant', 'notice of intention to retire in favour of a new tenant', 'retiring tenant's tenancy' and 'tenant's retirement in favour of a new tenant' are given in the Glossary.

Under APR, the interest of one of two or more joint tenants or tenants in common (or, in Scotland, joint owners or owners in common) is taken to carry the right either to vacant possession or to obtain it within the next 12 months if the interests of all of them together carry that right. The Revenue has confirmed (ESC F17) that the 12-month condition is satisfied on a transfer of tenanted agricultural land where the transferor's interest in the property either carries a right to vacant possession within 24 months of the transfer date, or is, notwithstanding the tenancy terms, valued at an amount broadly equivalent to the vacant possession value of the property. Here, the value transferred by a transfer of value is calculated as that on which no IHT is chargeable.

An article entitled 'IHT: relief for tenanted agricultural land' (*Tax Bulletin* 18 (August 1995)) has clarified certain aspects. Section 155 of FA 1995 increased the IHT relief rate for transfers of tenanted agricultural land from 50 to 100 per cent. The full relief applies to transfers, made on or after 1 September 1995, of agricultural land which is let on a tenancy starting on or after that date.

The purpose of the full relief was to boost the previous Government's reforms of the law on agricultural tenancies, now contained in the Agricultural Tenancies Act (ATA) 1995, which applies to England and Wales, but not to Northern Ireland or Scotland.

The Revenue has received enquiries on whether the increased relief only applies where the tenancy in question is within the ATA 1995 provisions. Its response is that APR applies to all agricultural tenancies, throughout the UK, starting on or after 1 September 1995, provided that all the statutory conditions for relief are met. In particular, a tenancy starting on or after that date by reason of statutory succession to an existing tenancy is not excluded from the full relief.

The grant of tenancy of agricultural property for agricultural purposes usually means that the land's market value goes down, even though a market rent is charged. However, the grant of a lease of agricultural property in the UK, the Channel Islands or the Isle of Man is not a transfer of value unless the rent payable is less than the market rent (IHTA 1984, s 16).

9.2.2 Occupation and ownership of land
(IHTA 1984, ss 118, 119)

Occupation

APR is available where agricultural property has been occupied by the transferor for two years for agricultural purposes. Occupation by a partnership is treated as occupation by each partner. Occupation by a company which is controlled by the transferor is treated as occupation by the transferor.

Where a transferor has sold one farm and buys another, the replacement farm qualifies for APR provided the transferor has occupied one or other of the two farms for periods aggregating two years in the last five. The amount of APR is limited to such amount as would have been available had the replacement not been made, unless the change results from the formation, alteration or dissolution of a partnership.

Ownership

APR is also available where agricultural property has been owned by the transferor for seven years and occupied by him or by another person for agricultural purposes. Occupation by a partnership is treated as occupation by each partner. Occupation by a company which is controlled by the transferor is treated as occupation by the transferor.

Where a transferor has sold one farm and buys another, the replacement farm qualifies for APR provided the transferor occupied one or other of the two farms for periods aggregating seven years in the last ten. In this event, the amount of APR is limited to such amount as would have been available had the replacement not been made, unless the change results from the formation, alteration or dissolution of a partnership.

9.2.3 Occupation and ownership of land by company
(IHTA 1984, ss 118, 123)

Occupation

APR is available where agricultural property has been occupied, for agricultural purposes, for two years by a company of which the transferor has had control for two years prior to the transfer. The relief is available where a company occupied agricultural property which it has sold and replaced. The new property qualifies for APR provided the company has occupied the two properties for two of the last five years. The amount of APR is limited to such amount as would have been available had the replacement not been made.

Ownership

APR is also available where agricultural property has been owned for seven years by a company controlled by the transferor for seven years and which has been occupied, for agricultural purposes, by the company or by another person for seven years prior to the transfer. The relief is available where a company owned agricultural property which it sold and replaced. The new property qualifies for agricultural property relief provided the company owned the two properties which were occupied by the company or by another person for seven out of the ten years prior to the transfer. The amount of APR is limited to such amount as would have been available had the replacement not been made.

APR is available where shares etc owned by the transferor at the transfer replaced other eligible property (eg on incorporation or amalgamation) and conditions for combined period ownership are met.

A company is treated as having occupied agricultural property at any time when it was occupied by a person who subsequently controls 50+ per cent of the company.

9.2.4 Successions
(IHTA 1984, s 120)

In applying the period of ownership and of occupation tests, a legatee is deemed to have owned and occupied property (provided that he does subsequently occupy it) from the date of death.

Where an individual inherits agricultural property from his spouse, or vice versa, the inheritor can claim that the deceased spouse's period of ownership should count towards the inheritor's two-year qualifying period. This only applies where one spouse has *inherited* the other's shares, not where one spouse makes a lifetime gift to the other.

Where the transferor spouse became entitled to his interest on the death of a spouse after 9 March 1981:

(1) he is deemed, for the purpose of ascertaining APR entitlement of 100 per cent, to have been beneficially entitled thereto for any period during which the spouse was beneficially entitled to it;

(2) the condition that the transferor owned his interest prior to 10 March 1981 and would have been entitled on a transfer on 9 March 1981 to 50 per cent APR under the old rules (up to £250,000 or 1,000 acres) must have been satisfied by the deceased spouse;

(3) the condition that the transferor's interest did not, at any time since 10 March 1981, carry a right to vacant possession within the following 12 months, and did not fail to do so because of a deliberate act or omission by the transferor, must have been satisfied by both the deceased and the continuing spouse.

9.2.5 Successive transfers
(IHTA 1984, s 121)

Agricultural property which would have been eligible for APR were it not for the minimum occupation and ownership conditions remains eligible if the following conditions are met:

(1) the value transferred by the earlier transfer was eligible for APR (or would have been available if then in force);

(2) the property which, in relation to the earlier transfer, was or would have been eligible for APR became, through the earlier transfer, the transferor's property in relation to the subsequent transfer, and at that

time is occupied for agricultural purposes by the transferor or his personal representatives;

(3) the property or any property directly replacing it would, were it not for the minimum occupation and ownership conditions, have been eligible for APR on the subsequent transfer; where, under the earlier transfer, the amount of the value transferred was part only of its value, a like part only of the value which otherwise would fall to be reduced by virtue of APR is so reduced;

(4) either the earlier transfer, or the subsequent transfer was made on the transferor's death.

If property which meets the above conditions is replaced, the APR amount is limited to what would have been available had the replacement not been made, unless the change results from the formation, alteration or dissolution of a partnership.

Example

Giles died on 24 June 2000. He left his farm, which he had owned and occupied for over ten years, to his son, John, who commenced to farm on 25 December 2000, following release by Giles's personal representatives. John died on 28 February 2001.

APR is available on John's death. This is because, even though John's period of occupancy has been so short, he acquired on Giles's death, at which time Giles satisfied the test. John must be the occupier (not a landlord) but only at the time of his death (or transfer).

9.3 VALUATION

9.3.1 Liabilities

Where a loan is secured against agricultural property, APR is calculated on the net value after taking the loan into account (IHTA 1984, s 162(4)), whether or not the loan was taken out to meet farming or personal expenditure.

9.3.2 Farm cottages
(IHTA 1984, s 169)

In determining the value of agricultural property which includes agricultural tied cottages (IHTA 1984, s 169), by concession (ESC F16) no account is taken of any increase in value attributable to the fact that such cottages are suitable as residences for persons other than agricultural workers.

9.4 CONTRACTS FOR SALE
(IHTA 1984, s 124)

In general, no APR is due if a binding contract for sale exists at the time agricultural property is transferred (IHTA 1984, s 124(1)). Thus, if the terms of a partnership deed or shareholder's agreement are such that the executors of a deceased partner or shareholder must sell his interest to the surviving partners or shareholders, no APR is due. The relief is due, however, if the survivors merely have an option to buy the deceased's interest (SP 12/80).

APR is available if there is a binding contract for sale where the consideration is the issue of shares which will give the transferor control of the company where the sale is part of a reconstruction or amalgamation.

9.5 PETS AND AGRICULTURAL PROPERTY RELIEF
(IHTA 1984, s 124A)

If a PET subsequently becomes a chargeable transfer which would otherwise be eligible to APR, it will not qualify unless further conditions are met. If these conditions are satisfied only for part of the original property, then only a proportionate part of so much of the value transferred as is attributable to the original property is reduced by APR.

Where the value of a chargeable transfer (other than a PET) is reduced by APR, and the transfer is within seven years prior the transferor's death then, unless the further conditions are met, the additional IHT charged by reason of the transferor's death is calculated without APR. If these conditions are satisfied only for part of the original property, the additional IHT is calculated as if only a proportionate part of so much of the value transferred as was attributable to the original property had been reduced by APR.

The conditions which must be met if APR is to apply are:

(1) the original property must have been owned by the transferee throughout the period from the date of the chargeable transfer to the transferor's death and not at the time of the death subject to a binding contract for sale;

(2) the original property comprised shares etc in a company to the extent of value attributable to agricultural property and giving the transferors 50+ per cent voting control of the company immediately prior to the transfer;

(3) the original property is agricultural property immediately before the transferor's death and has been occupied by the transferee or by another person for agricultural purposes throughout the period from the date of the chargeable transfer to the transferor's death.

If the transferee died before the transferor, the date of the transferee's death is taken in place of the date of the transferor's death. Where shares were owned by the transferee immediately before the death in question and such shares are, for CGT, identified with the original property under the amalgamation and reconstruction rules (TCGA 1992, ss 126–136), and were issued in consideration for the incorporation of an agricultural business, the transferee's period of ownership is deemed to include his period of ownership of the shares. The reduction, by way of APR, of value transferred is disregarded in any determination, in this context, of whether there is a PET or chargeable transfer in any case.

Here, 'the original property' means the property which, in relation to the chargeable transfers concerned, was either agricultural property to which APR applied or shares or securities of a company owning agricultural property. 'The transferee' is the person whose property the original property became on that chargeable transfer or, where on the transfer the original property became or remained settled property in which there is no qualifying interest in possession (IHTA 1984, ss 58–85), the trustees of the settlement (IHTA 1984, s 124A(8)).

9.6 APPLICATION OF REPLACEMENT PROPERTY RULES
(IHTA 1984, s 124B)

The replacement property rules set out in **8.6.2** apply if the transferee has disposed of the original property before the transferor's death, and the whole of the consideration therefor has been applied to the purchase of the replacement property.

9.7 WHERE BOTH BUSINESS AND AGRICULTURAL RELIEFS COULD APPLY
(IHTA 1984, s 114)

See **8.7** for details of where both BPR and APR could apply to the same property.

9.8 PROPERTY SUBJECT TO GIFT WITH RESERVATION (GWR)
(FA 1986, s 102)

The GWR rules are the same as for BPR; see **8.8**. See also **7** generally on GWRs.

10

WOODLANDS RELIEF

10.1 NATURE OF THE RELIEF
(IHTA 1984, s 125)

Woodlands relief is available if part of a person's death estate comprises the value of land in the UK (but not the Channel Islands or the Isle of Man) on which trees or underwood are growing and which is not agricultural property or short rotation coppice, but which is treated as being agricultural property (IHTA 1984, s 115; FA 1995 s 154(2), (3), (5)). It must also be shown that he was beneficially entitled to the land throughout five years ending with his death, or that he became beneficially entitled to the land by gift or inheritance. If these conditions are met, and an election is made:

(1) the value of the trees and underwood are left out of the death estate, but
(2) IHT will arise on their subsequent sale (or of an interest therein).

This election must be made within two years of the death (or longer at the Revenue's discretion).

10.2 IHT CHARGE ON DISPOSAL OF TREES AND UNDERWOOD
(IHTA 1984, s 126)

Where, following an election, the value of trees and underwood has been left out of the death estate and, subsequently, the trees or underwood (with or without the land on which they were growing) are disposed of then, if the disposal occurs before any of that land is transferred on the death of any other person, IHT is charged. This IHT charge does not apply if the disposal is made from one spouse to the other. Once IHT has been charged on the disposal of trees or underwood it cannot be charged again by reference to the same death on a further disposal of the same trees or underwood.

10.2.1 Amount subject to charge
(IHTA 1984, s 127)

IHT is charged on the net proceeds of a sale for full consideration in money or money's worth, or on the net value of the trees or underwood in any other case (after deduction in either case of any expenses allowable for IHT and not allowable for income tax purposes).

The expenses allowable for IHT are those incurred in:

(1) disposing of the trees or underwood;
(2) replanting within three years (or longer at the Revenue's discretion) to replace the trees or underwood;
(3) replanting to replace the trees or underwood previously disposed of, insofar as not allowable on the previous disposal; and
(4) the amount left out of the death estate (ie the value of trees or underwood at that time), whereas the amount on which IHT is subsequently charged is calculated by adding to the death estate the proceeds of sale, or value of the trees or underwood on disposal. This is likely to give rise, ultimately, to a larger IHT liability; however, it also means that there are funds from which to meet it.

If, at the date of death the trees or underwood would have qualified for BPR (HTA 1984, ss 103–114), a 50 per cent reduction is made from net proceeds or net value when computing the IHT iability on their disposal.

Where possible BPR, at 100 per cent for commercial woodlands (IHTA 1984, s 105(1)), should be taken in preference to the postponement of IHT until a subsequent sale.

10.2.2 Rate of charge to IHT
(IHTA 1984, ss 128, 129)

The IHT charge on the subsequent sale of trees or underwood is computed at the rate in force at the date of death, taking the additional amount on which IHT is to be charged as 'top slice'. If the later disposal is itself a chargeable transfer, the value of the trees or underwood for the later disposal is reduced by IHT paid at the date of death.

Example

Guthrie died on 15 May 2000. He had made no lifetime transfers within the seven years before death and (ignoring BPR) left the following estate:

	£	£
Sundry assets	352,000	352,000
Value of trees and underwood	70,000	
	422,000	
		352,000
Election made so IHT payable at death:		
at 0% on	234,000	Nil
at 40% on	118,000	47,200
	352,000	
		47,200

On 14 March 2010 (after allowing for selling and replanting expenses) the trees and underwood were sold for: 180,000
Other assets at death 352,000
532,000

Election made so IHT payable on sale of timber:		
at 0% on	234,000	Nil
at 40% on	298,000	119,200
	532,000	119,200

IHT payable on death		47,200
IHT payable on sale of timber		72,000
		119,200

If no claim were made, inheritance tax on death would have been:		
at 0% on	234,000	Nil
at 40% on	188,000	75,200
	422,000	75,200

IHT payable on death		75,200
IHT payable on sale of timber		Nil
		75,200

What has to be weighed up is whether it is worth paying, overall, an additional IHT liability of (119,200 – 75,200) = £44,000 when the timber has been sold and the cash readily available, or paying IHT in full at the date of death albeit on a lower value. However the initial payment towards the ultimately larger IHT liability overall is, if an election is made, reduced by (75,200 – 47,200) = £28,000. Whether to take the election option and postpone part of the IHT until the actual disposal of the timber is largely a question of cashflow. It is also appropriate to take into account the instalments payments option (IHTA 1984, s 229).

11

CLOSE COMPANIES

Definitions for 'close company', 'participator', subsidiary' etc are given in the Glossary at the front of this book.

11.1 QUALIFYING INTEREST IN POSSESSION
(IHTA 1984, s 59)

A 'qualifying interest in possession' in certain circumstances is an interest in possession to which a company is beneficially entitled (IHTA 1984, s 59(1)). This applies where:

(1) the company's business consists wholly or mainly in the acquisition of interests in settled property (s 59(2)(a)), and
(2) the company has acquired the interest for full consideration in money or money's worth from an individual who was beneficially entitled to it (s 59(2)(b)).

Where such acquisition under (2) above was before 14 March 1975, the condition outlined in (1) above is treated as satisfied if that was the company's business at the time of acquisition (s 59(3)(a)); that condition need not be satisfied if the company is a suitably authorised insurance company (s 59(3)(b)).

11.2 TRANSFERS BY CLOSE COMPANIES

11.2.1 Charge on participators
(IHTA 1984, s 94)

Where a close company makes a transfer of value, IHT is charged as if each individual to whom an amount is apportioned had made a transfer of value of such amount as, after any deduction of IHT, would be equal to the amount so apportioned, less any amount by which the value of his estate is more than it would be but for the company's transfer. For this purpose, his estate is treated as not including any rights or interests in the company.

The value transferred is apportioned among the participators according to their respective rights and interests in the company immediately before the transfer, and any amount so apportioned to a close company is further apportioned among its participators, and so on. So much of that value as is attributable to any payment or transfer of assets to any person which falls to be taken into account in computing that person's profits, gains or losses for income or corporation tax purposes (or would fall to be so taken into account but for TA 1988, s 208 (UK company distributions not generally chargeable to corporation tax)) is not apportioned. Furthermore, if any amount which would otherwise be apportioned to a non-UK domiciled individual is attributable to the value of any property outside the UK, that amount is not apportioned.

In determining whether a disposition made by a close company is a transfer of value or what value is transferred by such a transfer, no account is taken of the surrender by the company, under TA 1988, s 240 (set-off of company's surplus ACT against subsidiary's liability to corporation tax) or s 402 (surrender of relief between members of groups and consortia), of any relief or of the benefit of any amount of ACT paid by it.

If the amount apportioned to a person is 5 per cent or less of the value transferred, IHT otherwise chargeable thereon is left out of account in determining, in relation to any time after the company's transfer, what previous transfers of value he has made.

In relation to the annual exemption (IHTA 1984, s 19), references to transfers of value made by a transferor and to the values transferred by them are treated as including apportionments made to a person and to the amounts for the IHT on which (if charged) he would be liable.

11.2.2 Participator in two companies
(IHTA 1984, s 95)

A further computation is required where the value of a company's estate ('the transferee company') is increased as the result of a transfer of value made by another close company ('the transferor company'), and an individual to whom part of the value transferred is apportioned (under IHTA 1984, s 94) has an interest in the transferee company (or in a company which is a participator of the transferee company, or any of its participators, and so on). The further computation applies to the computation of the amount to be offset, that is to say the amount by which the value of his estate is more than it would be but for the transfer.

In a case where the further computation is required, the increase in the value of the transferee company's estate is taken to be such part of the value transferred as accounts for the increase, and the increase so computed is apportioned among the transferee company's participators according to their respective rights and interests in the company immediately before the transfer (and, where necessary, further apportioned among their participators, and so on). The amount so apportioned to the individual is taken as the amount to be offset.

11.2.3 Preference shares disregarded
(IHTA 1984, s 96)

Where part of a close company's share capital consists of preference shares and a transfer of value made by that or any other close company has only a small effect on the value of those shares (compared with its effect on the value of other parts of the company's share capital), the preference shares are left out of account in determining the participators' respective rights and interests for the purposes of IHTA 1984, s 94 (charge on participators) and s 95 (participator in two companies).

11.2.4 Transfers within a group, etc
(IHTA 1984, s 97)

The rights and interests of the minority participators are left out of account in determining the transferor company's participators' respective rights and interests for apportioning the value transferred (IHTA 1984, s 94). This applies where a close company ('the transferor company') is a member, but not the principal company, of a group and:

(1) a disposal by the transferor company of any asset is a disposal on a no gain/no loss basis (TCGA 1992, s 171(1)) and is also a transfer of value, and

(2) the transfer of value has only a small effect on the value of the minority participators' rights and interests in that company compared with its effect on the value of the other participators' rights and interests.

SP E15, issued in March 1975, clarifies the position concerning dividend payments and transfers of assets from a subsidiary company to a parent or sister company. In the Revenue's view, the effect is that a dividend paid by a subsidiary company to its parent is not a transfer of value. Nor does the Revenue feel that it can justifiably treat a transfer of assets between a wholly owned subsidiary and its parent or between two wholly owned subsidiaries as a transfer of value.

11.3 EFFECT OF ALTERATIONS OF CAPITAL, ETC
(IHTA 1984, s 98)

An alteration (or extinguishment) in so much of a close company's share or loan capital as does not consist of quoted shares or quoted securities, or an alteration (or extinguishment) in any rights attaching to unquoted shares in or unquoted debentures of a close company is treated as having been made by a disposition made at that time by the participators. This applies whether or not it would otherwise be so treated, and is not taken to have affected the value immediately before that time of the unquoted shares or debentures. This deemed disposition is taken to be a chargeable transfer, and not a PET.

The Revenue has been advised that an alteration of rights occurs when deferred shares come to rank equally with another class of shares. Accordingly, claims for IHT will be raised where deferred shares, issued after 5 August 1991, subsequently come to rank equally, or become merged, with shares of another class (*Law Society's Gazette*, 11 September 1991).

11.4 SETTLED PROPERTY

11.4.1 Transfers where participators are trustees
(IHTA 1984, s 99)

Where any part of a close company's transfer of value is apportioned to a trustee of a settlement (IHTA 1984, s 94), then:

(1) if a qualifying interest in possession subsists in the settled property, a part of that interest corresponding to such part of the property as is of a value equal to that so apportioned less the amount specified in **11.2.1** is treated for the purposes of IHTA 1984, ss 49–57A (interests in possession and reversionary interests) as having come to an end on the making of the transfer; and

(2) if no qualifying interest in possession subsists in the settled property, IHTA 1984, ss 58–85 apply as if on the making of the transfer the trustee had made a disposition as a result of which the settled property's value had been reduced by an amount equal to the part so apportioned less the amount specified in **11.2.1**. Where a qualifying interest in possession relates to part only of the settled property, these rules apply with necessary adjustments of the values and amounts referred to.

The charge on trustee participators is as set out in **11.2.1**. Where the trustee particpator participates in two companies (see **11.2.2**), the following procedure applies:

(1) the increase in the value of the transferee company's estate is taken to be such part of the value transferred as accounts for the increase (IHTA 1984, s 95(2)(a)), and

(2) the increase so computed is apportioned among the transferee company's participators according to their respective rights and interests in the company immediately before the transfer (and, where necessary, further apportioned among their participators, and so on) (s 95(2)(b)), and the amount so apportioned to a trustee of a settlement is taken to be the amount to be offset.

11.4.2 Alterations of capital, etc where participators are trustees
(IHTA 1984, s 100)

A further rule applies where (under IHTA 1984, s 98), an alteration (or extinguishment) in a close company's share or loan capital, or of any rights attaching to shares in or debentures of a close company, is treated as a disposition made by the participators, and:

(1) a person is a participator in his capacity as trustee of a settlement, and
(2) the disposition would, if the trustee were beneficially entitled to the settled property, be a transfer of value made by him, and
(3) at the time of the alteration (or extinguishment) an individual is beneficially entitled to an interest in possession in the whole or part of so much of the settled property as consists of unquoted shares in or unquoted securities of the close company.

Where this rule applies, such part of the individual's interest is treated for the purposes of IHTA 1984, ss 49–57A (interests in possession and reversionary interests) as having come to an end at the time of the alteration as corresponds to the decrease of the value of the property in which the interest subsists caused by the alteration (or extinguishment) (IHTA 1984, s 100(2)).

11.4.3 Companies' interests in settled property
(IHTA 1984, s 101)

If a close company is entitled to an interest in possession in settled property, the company's participators are treated for IHT purposes (except IHTA 1984, s 55 (reversionary interest acquired by a beneficiary)) as being entitled to that interest according to their respective rights and interests in the company. Where such participators include the trustees of a settlement, and a person is beneficially entitled to an interest in possession in the whole or part of the settled property by virtue of which the trustees are participators, that person is treated as beneficially entitled to the whole or a corresponding part of the interest to which the trustees would otherwise be treated as entitled.

In *CIR v Brandenburg* [1982] STC 555, ChD, the taxpayer, who was resident and domiciled in the UK, transferred assets to her non-resident, non-domiciled daughter using a scheme involving exempt government securities and a settlement on a non-resident close company which was 100 per cent beneficially owned by her. At one stage the company had an interest in possession in the exempt securities which it assigned to the daughter. The Revenue issued a notice of determination on the basis that tax was chargeable as if the taxpayer had made a direct gift to her daughter. The taxpayer appealed, contending that the property which had been transferred qualified as excluded property. This contention was rejected, and it was held that, under IHTA 1984, s 101(1), the taxpayer was treated as the person entitled to the interest in possession and the securities were thus not excluded property.

In *Powell-Cotton v CIR* [1992] STC 625, ChD, a life interest in a settlement was sold in consideration for shares in a close company. The question at issue was whether the subsequent transfer of shares by way of gift was a disposal of an interest in possession in settled property. An individual had, in 1941, sold his life interest under a settlement to a close company. The consideration was £25,000, which was to be paid by 25,000 £1 shares in the company. In1964, he reacquired his life interest in part of the settled property from the company. The balance of his interest in the settled property remained vested in the company. The company was therefore entitled to an interest in possession in that part. In 1982 the individual transferred 2,999 of his shares to a charity by way of gift. Immediately before the transfer, he held 8,993 of the 46,000 shares in the company. He was therefore treated by (IHTA 1984, s 101(1)), as having been entitled to 8,993/46,000 of the interest in possession in the part of the settled property retained by the company. Following the transfer, he was treated as being entitled to 5,994/46,000 of the interest in possession. The Revenue issued a notice of determination on the basis that he had made a transfer of value equal to 2,999/8,993 × 8,993/46,000 of the settled property vested in the company. The taxpayer appealed, contending:

(1) that no part of the interest in possession had come to an end (under IHTA 1984, s 52(1)), and there was therefore no disposal within s 51(1), and

(2) in the alternative that any transfer of value was exempt as it was attributable to property given to a charity (under IHTA 1984, s 23(1)).

The appeal was unsuccessful. The provisions of s 101(1) require the interest in possession held by a close company to be treated as vested in the participators in that company. Accordingly, on the disposal of the shares, part of the taxpayer's interest in possession had come to an end (under s 52(1)). The corollary of s 101(1) was that the company could not be treated as having an interest in possession in the settled property, since that would be inconsistent with the beneficial ownership attributed to the participator, and the company's right to the income of the retained part therefore had to be disregarded. Furthermore, the effect of s 56(3) is that the deemed transfer of part of the settled property is not exempted by s 23(1).

12

TRANSFERS WITHIN SEVEN YEARS OF DEATH WHERE PET PROPERTY VALUE DECREASED

12.1 THE RELIEF
(IHTA 1984, s 131)

Where a transfer of value occurred in the seven-year period before death and the property value at the date either of death or of sale (if it has been sold) is less than the value at the date of the transfer, a claim can be made for the IHT or additional IHT payable by the donee, to be calculated as if the value transferred were the lower amount. A claim of reduced value can be made (within the six-year time limit) under three circumstances where the transferor dies within seven years of the transfer, i.e. where:

(1) an IHT charge arises on the PET-transferred value; and
(2) an additional IHT charge arises (under IHTA 1984, s 7(4)) on the value transferred by any other chargeable transfer; and
(3) in either (1) or (2) above, all or part of the transferred value is attributable to the transferred property which:
- on the date of death, is the transferee's or his spouse's possession; or
- before the date of death, was sold by the transferee or his spouse by a qualifying sale.

A 'qualifying sale' under these circumstances is one which is made at arm's length at a freely negotiated price. The sale must be between unconnected persons. There must be no conditions which allow the property to fall back into the seller's hands, or for the seller to maintain an interest in it.

If the transferred property's market value at the time of the chargeable transfer exceeds its market value on the relevant date, and a claim is made by a person liable to pay all or part of the (additional) IHT, the IHT is calculated as if the value transferred were reduced by the excess amount. Where the value transferred which is attributable to the transferred property's value (or agricultural value) is reduced by BPR or APR, the reduced value becomes the transferred property's actual market value.

This rule applies to PETs on becoming chargeable. It also applies to other previously chargeable transfers where additional IHT may be payable.

12.2 WASTING ASSETS
(IHTA 1984, s 132)

The relief is not available for a wasting asset which is tangible immovable property. 'Wasting assets' are defined as those with a predicted useful life of less than 50 years; plant and machinery are deemed always to be wasting assets.

12.3 SHARES OR SECURITIES – CAPITAL RECEIPTS
(IHTA 1984, s 133)

For transferred property which consists of shares or securities, for which at any time before the date of death or qualifying sale the transferee or his spouse becomes entitled to a capital payment in relation to them, for s 131 relief purposes the transferred property's market value on that date is (except where otherwise it reflects a right to the payment) increased by an amount equal to the payment.

If at any time before that date the transferee or his spouse receives or becomes entitled to receive a provisional allotment of shares or securities and disposes of the rights, the amount of the consideration for the disposal is treated for s 131 relief purposes as a capital payment. Here, a 'capital payment' means any money or money's worth which does not constitute income for income tax purposes.

12.4 PAYMENTS OF CALLS
(IHTA 1984, s 134)

The market value of transferred property of shares or securities for which, at any time before the relevant date, the transferee or his spouse become liable to make a payment under a call is (except where otherwise it reflects the liability) reduced by an amount equal to the payment.

12.5 REORGANISATION OF SHARE CAPITAL, ETC
(IHTA 1984, s 135)

The rule described below applies to transferred property of shares or securities for which before the relevant date there is a transaction under TCGA 1992, s 127 (equation of new shares or securities with original shareholding) or to which TCGA 1992 would apply but for TCGA 1992, s 134 (compensation stock):

(i)   a reorganisation as defined by TCGA 1992, s 126(1);
(ii)   the conversion of securities as defined by TCGA 1992, s 132 (equation of converted securities and new holding);

(iii) the issue by one company of shares or securities in exchange for shares or securities in another under TCGA 1992, s 135, where such exchange occurs to obtain a holding more than 25 per cent of or, as part of a general offer, the greater part of the ordinary share capital, and the transaction is for bona fide commercial reasons and not for the avoidance of CGT or corporation tax); or

(iv) the issue by a company of shares or securities under reconstruction or amalgamation involving securities (TCGA 1992, s 136), and the transaction is for bona fide commercial reasons and not for the avoidance of CGT or corporation tax; or

(v) any transaction relating to a unit trust scheme which corresponds to any of the above transactions and to which TCGA 1992, s 127 (equation of new shares or securities with original shareholding) applies under TCGA 1992 (application to unit trusts).

'Original shares or securities' are shares or securities held before, and concerned in, the reorganisation; a 'new holding' is in relation to any original shares or securities, the shares or securities in and debentures of the company which as a result of the reorganisation represent the original shares or securities (including such, if any, as remain) (TCGA 1992, s 126(1)). Where this rule applies, the original shares or securities and the new holding are treated as the same property for the relief purposes (IHTA 1984, ss 131, 135(3)).

Where this rule applies and as part of, or in connection with, the transaction concerned the transferee or his spouse becomes liable to give any consideration for all or part of the new holding, then for s 131 relief purposes the shares' or securities' market value on the relevant date is (except where otherwise it reflects the liability) reduced by an amount equal to that consideration. For this purpose, the following are not treated as such consideration:

(1) any surrender, cancellation or other alteration of any of the original shares or securities or of the rights attached thereto, or

(2) any consideration consisting of any application, in paying up the new holding or any part of it, of the company's assets or of any dividend or other distribution declared out of those assets but not made.

12.6 TRANSACTIONS OF CLOSE COMPANIES
(IHTA 1984, s 136)

A special rule applies where the transferred property consists of shares or securities in a close company (see **11**) for which, at any time after the chargeable transfer and before the relevant date, there is a relevant transaction. For this purpose a 'relevant transaction' is where the company makes:

(1) a transfer of value or an alteration in so much of its share or loan capital as does not consist of quoted shares or securities; or

(2) an alteration in any rights attaching to
  - unquoted shares or securities in, or
  - unquoted debentures of

the company, but which does not give rise to an adjustment.

Where this rule applies, the shares', securities' or debentures' market value on the relevant date is for s 131 relief purposes increased by an amount equal to the difference between:

(1) the transferred property's market value at the time of the chargeable transfer, and

(2) what that value would have been had the relevant transaction occurred before, and not after, that time.

Where a company makes a transfer which in turn increases the value of the transferor's or his UK-domiciled spouse's estate by any amount, the increase provided for above is reduced by that amount.

Where the transferred property's market value at the time of the chargeable transfer is less than it would have been as above, then, instead of providing for an increase, it provides for the market value on the relevant date to be reduced to what it would have been had the relevant transaction not occurred.

12.7 INTERESTS IN LAND
(IHTA 1984, s 137)

An 'interest in land' does not include any estate, interest or right by way of mortgage or other security. Where the transferred property is an interest in land in relation to which the conditions set out below are not satisfied, the transferred property's market value on the relevant date for s 131 relief purposes is increased by an amount equal to the difference between:

(1) the interest's market value, and

(2) what that market value would have been if the circumstances prevailing on the relevant date and by reason of which the conditions described below are not satisfied had prevailed

at the time of the chargeable transfer. The conditions are that:

(1) the interest was the same in all respects, and

(2) the land in which the interest subsists was in the same state

and in both cases with the same incidents at the time of the chargeable transfer and on the relevant date.

If after the date of the chargeable transfer but before the relevant date compensation becomes payable under any enactment to the transferee or his spouse, because

- of the imposition of a restriction on the land's use or development, or
- the interest's value is reduced for any other reason,

the imposition of the restriction or the other cause of the reduction in value is ignored for the above purposes, but the interest's market value on the relevant date is increased by an amount equal to that of the compensation.

Where the interest's market value at the time of the chargeable transfer is less than it would have been if the circumstances prevailing on the relevant date and by reason of which the conditions are not satisfied had prevailed at the time of the chargeable transfer, then, instead of providing for an increase, it provides for the market value on the relevant date to be reduced to what it would have been had the change in circumstances by reason of which the conditions are not satisfied not occurred.

12.8 LEASES
(IHTA 1984, s 138)

Where the transferred property is a lessee's interest under a lease the duration of which at the time of the chargeable transfer does not exceed 50 years, then for s 131 relief purposes the interest's market value on the relevant date is increased by an amount equal to the appropriate fraction of that market value at the time of the chargeable transfer. The appropriate fraction is:

$$\frac{P(1) - P(2)}{P(1)}$$

where $P(1) =$ the appropriate percentage from the curved line depreciation table for a premium on leases at the date of the gift *inter vivos*, and

$P(2) =$ the percentage at the date of sale or death.

These percentages are derived from the table in TCGA 1992, Sched 8, para 1, which is set out in Table 15.1 (see under **15.4.5**).

12.9 OTHER PROPERTY
(IHTA 1984, s 139)

Where the transferred property is neither shares, securities or debentures nor an interest in land and the condition below is not satisfied in relation to it, the property's market value on the relevant date is for s 131 relief purposes taken to be increased by an amount equal to the difference between:

(1) the property's market value, and
(2) what that value would have been had the circumstances prevailing at the relevant date and by reason of which the condition is not satisfied prevailed

at the time of the chargeable transfer. The condition is that the transferred property was the same in all respects at the time of the chargeable transfer and on the relevant date.

Where the transferred property's market value at the time of the chargeable transfer is less than it would have been as mentioned above, the rule applies as if, instead of providing for an increase, it provided for the market value on the relevant date to be reduced to what it would have been if the property had remained the same in all respects as it was at the time of the chargeable transfer.

If the transferred property is neither shares, securities or debentures nor an interest in land, and during the period between the time of chargeable transfer and the relevant date benefits in money or money's worth are derived from it which exceed a reasonable return on its market value at the time of the chargeable transfer, then:

(1) any effect of the benefits on the transferred property is ignored, but
(2) the transferred property's market value on the relevant date is taken for s 131 relief purposes to be increased by an amount equal to such excess.

12.10 MARKET VALUE
(IHTA 1984, s 140)

The market value at any time of any property is the price which the property might reasonably be expected to fetch if sold in the open market at that time. However, two assumptions are made:

(1) that the price is not assumed to be reduced on the ground that the whole property is on the market at one and the same time, and
(2) that, in the case of unquoted shares or securities, there is available to any prospective purchaser of the shares or securities all the information which a prudent prospective purchaser might reasonably require if he were proposing to purchase them from a willing vendor by private treaty and at arm's length.

(See generally **15**.)

13

CHANGES IN DISTRIBUTION OF DECEASED'S ESTATE

13.1 SCOPE

Under various provisions (listed below), it is possible, in effect, to reorganise and redirect dispositions contained in a person's will or under the law of intestacy. A number of conditions must be satisfied. Furthermore, these alterations are themselves eliminated as not being transfers of value:

- alteration of dispositions taking effect on death (IHTA 1984, s 142);
- a transfer made in compliance with the testator's request (s 143);
- distributions from property settled by will (s 144);
- an election by a surviving spouse, in an intestacy, to take a capital sum instead of a life interest under the Administration of Estates Act 1925, s 47A (s 145);
- the Inheritance (Provision for Family and Dependants) Act 1975 (s 146);
- the renunciation, in Scotland, of a claim to legitim within two years (longer at the Revenue's discretion) of attaining age 18 (s 147).

13.2 ALTERATION OF DISPOSITIONS TAKING EFFECT ON DEATH
(IHTA 1984, s 142)

13.2.1 Deeds of variation

Dispositions taking effect on death can be varied by a deed of variation made by any person who benefits or would benefit under the dispositions. IHTA 1984 is then applied as if the variation had been effected by the deceased or the disclaimed benefit had never been conferred, and the property concerned falls into the estate's residue. It is not possible to make a valid disclaimer where, since the death, a benefit has been derived from the property. A disclaimer normally comprises the whole interest, but a partial disclaimer of a legacy is permissible if the will includes a power to this effect.

Where such a deed is entered into within a two-year period after a person's death:

(1) any of the dispositions (whether effected by will, under intestacy or otherwise) of the property comprised in an individual's estate immediately before his death are varied, or

(2) the benefit conferred by any of those dispositions is disclaimed.

This does not apply to a variation unless an election to that effect is made by written notice given to the Revenue within six months after the date of the instrument (or longer at the Revenue's discretion), by the person(s) making the instrument and, where the variation results in additional IHT being payable, the personal representatives. However, personal representatives may decline to join in an election only if no, or insufficient, assets are held by them in that capacity for discharging any additional IHT.

The right to vary dispositions taking effect on death does not apply to a variation or disclaimer made for any consideration in money or money's worth other than consideration consisting of the making, in relation to another of the dispositions, of a variation or disclaimer.

Where a variation results in property being held in trust for a person for a period ending not more than two years after the death, IHTA 1984 applies as if the disposition that takes effect at the end of the period had had effect from the beginning of it. However, this does not affect any distribution or application of property occurring before that disposition takes effect. In Scotland, property which is subject to a proper life-rent is deemed to be held in trust for the life-renter.

For these purposes the property comprised in a person's estate includes any excluded property, but not any property to which he is treated as entitled as the beneficiary of an interest in possession trust (IHTA 1984, s 49(1) – see **16.2**) or by a GWR (FA 1986, s 102 – see generally **7**).

An election can be made whether or not the administration of the estate is complete or the property concerned has been distributed in accordance with the original dispositions.

In Scotland, there are certain circumstances in which a residuary legatee can make a partial disclaimer. Where this is possible, the Revenue accepts that the provisions of IHTA 1984, s 142, which deal with disclaimers, apply (SP E18, 8 June 1978).

13.2.2 **Death of original beneficiary**

An item in the *Tax Bulletin* 15 (February 1995) dealt with variation of inheritances following the death of an original beneficiary within the statutory two-year period. As explained above, for IHTA 1984, s 142 to apply, the beneficiaries under the dispositions affected by the variation must join in a written election to the Revenue. However, a question arose on how this requirement should be interpreted when one of the beneficiaries dies before a variation is made. The Revenue view is that the legal personal representatives of a beneficiary (the second deceased) may enter into a variation and sign an election. If the variation will reduce the entitlements of the beneficiaries of the second deceased then they, as well as the second deceased's legal personal representatives, must agree to the variation. The Revenue will require evidence of the second deceased's beneficiaries' consent to the variation. If they are not themselves parties to the variation, other written evidence of their consent will be sought.

13.2.3 Jointly held assets

The question of whether these rules apply to a variation of the deceased's interest in jointly held assets, which passed on the death to the surviving joint owner(s), has also been dealt with by the Revenue. Suppose, for example, the family home was owned by a mother and her son as beneficial joint tenants and, on the mother's death, her interest passed by survivorship to the son who then became the property's sole owner. It has been suggested that, in this example, the son cannot for IHT purposes vary his inheritance by redirecting it to his children.

The Revenue has confirmed that it does not share this view. The IHT rules apply not only to dispositions and inheritances arising under a will or the law of intestacy, but also to those effected 'otherwise'. In the Revenue's view, the words 'or otherwise' bring within the rules the automatic inheritance of a deceased owner's interest in jointly held assets by the surviving joint owner(s). (See *Tax Bulletin* 19 (October 1995).)

13.2.4 Waiver of loan

In the *Law Society's Gazette*, 18 December 1991, it was reported that the Capital Taxes Office would not accept that a loan made between individuals has been waived by the lender, so the lender's estate is reduced for IHT purposes by the amount of the loan released – unless the waiver was effected by deed. However, in the Law Society's Revenue Law Committee's opinion, letters and circumstantial evidence clearly indicating an intention to absolve the beneficiary of the loan from any liability to repay should be insufficient. The Revenue has quoted in support of its contention that a waiver is ineffective unless made by deed (*Pinnell* (1602) 5 Co Rep 117a; *Edwards v Walters* (1896) 2 Ch D 157, CA). In the Revenue Law Committee's view, although the Revenue's contention is not unassailable, unless and until the contention is confirmed or rejected by judicial authority, it must be prudent to advise that any IHT planning strategy involving the making of a loan, and subsequent waiver, should be effected by deed in order to ensure the lender's estate is reduced accordingly. For alterations of dispositions taking effect on death, IHTA 1984, s 142 does not require execution of a deed, but simply 'an instrument in writing', though in practice, as a prudent precaution, a deed is normally used.

13.2.5 Number and alteration of deeds of variation

In *Russell and another v CIR* [1988] STC 195, ChD it was confirmed that only one variation can be made within these provisions. It may, however, be possible to obtain a court order to rectify a defective deed of variation. In *Lake v Lake and others* [1989] STC 865, ChD, a testator died in November 1986, and a deed of variation was executed three months later by his widow and the trustees. Unfortunately, the solicitors drew up the deed incorrectly, which resulted in increased IHT. A second deed was executed to correct the error, but, following *Russell and another* above, the Revenue determined the liability in accordance with the original deed. On application to the High Court, the widow sought an order for the rectification of the original deed in accordance with the trustees' intentions. This was granted, on the finding that it was clear that the original deed did not carry out the parties' intentions, and that this did not present an obstacle to rectification.

Similarly, in *Seymour and another v Seymour* [1989] BTC 8043, ChD, a solicitor inserted a figure of £50,000 in a deed of variation instead of the £250,000 which the parties had intended. The High Court granted an application for rectification of the error. *Matthews v Martin and others* [1991] BTC 8048, ChD applied *Lake* and *Seymour*. A widow agreed with her children that their father's estate should be distributed in a manner different from that laid down in the Intestacy Rules. The deed was executed within two years of the deceased's death, as required by IHTA 1984, s 142, but it contained errors of which the parties only became aware after the expiry of the two-year period. The Chancery Division granted the application for retrospective rectification of the deed. The deed was clearly defective and did not reflect the parties' agreement and understanding. It did not matter, in this context, that the sole purpose of rectification was the obtaining of a fiscal advantage.

On a rather wider anti-avoidance point, the Revenue rejected a composite transaction in *Countess Fitzwilliam and others v CIR* [1993] STC 502, HL.

Another matter dealt with in the *Tax Bulletin* 15 (February 1995) concerns the application, or otherwise, in the context of IHT, of *Marshall v Kerr* [1994] STC 638, HL. In brief, in June 1994, the House of Lords was concerned with TCGA 1992, s 62 which applies where there is a variation and election, and concluded that TCGA 1992, s 62 did not mean that the variation of the terms of a deceased person's will was to be treated for all CGT purposes as made by the deceased. In response to the question of whether variations which meet the conditions in IHTA 1984, s 142 will still be treated for IHT purposes as made by the deceased and not by the beneficiary or beneficiaries, the Revenue has stated its view that, as the relevant IHT legislation differs from the CGT provisions which were considered in *Marshall v Kerr*, that decision has no application to IHT. Variations which meet all the statutory conditions will continue to be treated for IHT purposes as having been made by the deceased.

Where a person becomes entitled to an interest in settled property but disclaims the interest then, if the disclaimer is not made for a consideration in money or money's worth, he is treated for IHT purposes as if he had not become entitled to it (IHTA 1984, s 93).

13.2.6 Effect of variations for CGT purposes
(TCGA 1992, s 62(6)–(9))

For CGT, the position is similar, though not identical, to IHT. Any of the dispositions (whether effected by will, intestacy or otherwise) of the property of which the deceased was competent to dispose can be varied, or the benefit conferred by any of those dispositions can be disclaimed, by an instrument in writing made by any person who benefits or would benefit under the dispositions. The variation or disclaimer is not itself a disposal for CGT purposes. Matters then proceed as if the variation had been effected by the deceased or the disclaimed benefit had never been conferred.

The variation or disclaimer must be made within two years following the death. However, it is not valid for CGT purposes unless the person(s) making the instrument so elect by notice given to the Revenue within six months after the date of the instrument (or such longer time as the Revenue may allow). The claim can be made whether or not the administration of the estate is complete or the property has been distributed in accordance with the original dispositions.

For TCGA 1992, s 62 to apply with regard to the *Tax Bulletin* 15 (February 1995) article (death of original beneficiary), the Revenue view as for IHTA 1984, s 142 applies (see **13.2.2**). Note also that the Revenue view (*Tax Bulletin* 19 (October 1995)) regarding jointly owned assets also applies to CGT as it does for IHT (see **13.2.3**).

A claim is not possible where a variation or disclaimer is made for any consideration in money or money's worth other than consideration consisting of the making of a variation or disclaimer in respect of another of the dispositions.

In *Marshall v Kerr* [1994] STC 638, HL, Mrs K's father-in-law (B) died in 1977; he was classed as resident and ordinarily resident in Jersey. Half of B's personal estate was bequeathed to Mrs K, a UK resident. A deed of family arrangement was entered into in 1978 by which she settled her share of the estate on Jersey trustees, to be held on discretionary trusts for herself and her family. Administration of the estate was not completed until 1979; at no time were the assets vested in Mrs K. Later, the settlement trustees made capital payments to Mrs K. Assessments were under what is now TCGA 1992, ss 87–98 (attribution of gains to beneficiaries of non-resident settlements). Mrs K's appeal was on the basis that under TCGA 1992, s 62(6), B should be deemed to be the settlor of the trusts. Therefore, the argument proceeded, since he had been neither resident nor ordinarily resident in the UK, there was no CGT liability.

The House of Lords rejected this contention on the footing that the arrangement did not settle any specific assets comprised in the estate, but settled the legatee's half-share in the residuary estate, which had not by then been constituted. The property settled by Mrs K as legatee was a separate chose in action (ie her right to have the estate of the deceased duly administered). Where, as here, a legatee varied her entitlement under a will by means of a family arrangement, the making of the variation was not a disposal in itself. However, s 62(6) does not have the further effect of treating the assets vested in the legatee as acquired from the deceased at the date of death. As a result, the legatee was the settlor of the arrangement for the purposes of TCGA 1992, s 87 (attribution of gains to beneficiaries).

13.2.7 Effect of variations for income tax purposes

A variation or disclaimer is not valid for income tax purposes for any period prior to the making of the deed.

13.3 COMPLIANCE WITH TESTATOR'S REQUEST
(IHTA 1984, s 143)

Where a testator bequeaths a property by will to a legatee, but expresses a wish that the property should be transferred by the legatee to other persons, and the legatee transfers any of the property in accordance with that wish within two years after the testator's death, the property is treated for IHT purposes as if the property transferred had been bequeathed by the will direct to the transferee.

13.4 DISTRIBUTION ETC FROM PROPERTY SETTLED BY WILL
(IHTA 1984, s 144)

The rules described below apply where property comprised in a person's estate immediately before his death is settled by his will and, within two years after his death and before any interest in possession has subsisted in the property, on the happening of either of the following events:

(1) an event on which IHT would be charged, except by IHTA 1984, s 64 (exit charges on 'no interest in possession' trusts) or s 79 (failure of exemption from ten-yearly charge on 'no interest in possession' trusts) occurs, in which case IHT is not charged, under the provision in question, on that event, or

(2) an event on which IHT would be so chargeable but for IHTA 1984, s 75 (property becoming subject to employee trusts) or s 76 (property

becoming held for charitable purposes) or Sched 4, para 16(1) (property becoming comprised in maintenance funds).

In every case in which this rule applies in relation to an event, IHTA 1984 is applied as if the will had provided that on the testator's death the property should be held as it is held after the event.

Customarily, this is achieved where a testator settles property on a discretionary will trust. Then, before there is any interest in possession in the property, the trustees make a capital distribution, or some other event occurs within two years of the death, there is no IHT liability as a result of such transaction. Such a transaction would otherwise have given rise to IHT under the regime for settlements with no interest in possession (IHTA 1984, ss 58–85). Instead, IHT is payable as if the distribution or event had been provided for in the will.

In *Frankland v CIR* [1997] STC 1450, CA, a married woman died, leaving property on discretionary trusts for her husband's and children's benefit. Later, the property was transferred to a trust. The trust income was to be paid to the husband for the duration of his life. The intention was to benefit from the spouse exemption (under IHTA 1984, s 18(1)), thus avoiding the charge to tax which would otherwise have been payable. The Revenue issued a determination on the basis that the spouse exemption did not apply because the transfer was not made by the deceased. The trustee appealed on the basis that the effect of IHTA 1984, s 144 was that the husband's interest in possession should be deemed to have arisen under the deceased's will.

The Court of Appeal rejected this argument and held that s 144 did not apply. The effect of s 65(4) (no exit charge under 'no interest in possession' regime in the quarter after the commencement of a settlement, or after a ten-yearly charge) was that, since the later transfer took place within three months of the death, that transfer itself was not an event which gave rise to IHT, and s 144 only applies where there was an event on which tax would otherwise be chargeable. As a result, the transfer could not be treated as having been made by the deceased, and the spouse exemption did not apply.

For IHT and for CGT (under TCGA 1992, s 62(6)–(9)), this provision is a very flexible way of bequeathing an estate where it is not clear, when the will is made, what would be the most beneficial and desirable manner of making the distribution. This is commonly referred to as a 'discretionary will'.

13.5 REDEMPTION OF SURVIVING SPOUSE'S LIFE INTEREST
(IHTA 1984, s 145)

Where an election is made by a surviving spouse under the Administration of Estates Act 1925, s 47A, IHTA 1984 is applied as if the surviving spouse, instead of being entitled to the life interest, had been entitled to a sum equal to the capital value there mentioned.

13.6 INHERITANCE (PROVISION FOR FAMILY AND DEPENDANTS) ACT 1975
(IHTA 1984, s 146)

Where an order is made under the Inheritance (Provision for Family and Dependants) Act 1975, s 2 in relation to any property forming part of the deceased's net estate, then, without prejudice to s 19(1) of the 1975 Act the property is, for IHT purposes, treated as if it had on his death devolved subject to the provisions of the order.

Where an order is made under s 10 of the 1975 Act requiring a person to provide any money or other property by reason of a disposition made by the deceased, then:

(1) if that disposition was a chargeable transfer and the deceased's personal representatives make a claim for the purpose, IHT (and interest thereon) paid or payable on the value transferred by that chargeable transfer (whether or not by the claimants) is repaid to them by the Revenue or, as the case may be, is not payable, and

   (a) IHT (and interest thereon) repaid is included in the deceased's estate for transfer of value purposes made by him on his death; and IHT (and interest thereon) repaid form part of the deceased's net estate for the purposes of the Inheritance (Provision for Family and Dependants) Act 1975;

   (b) the IHT rate(s) (and interest thereon) applicable to the transfer of value made by the deceased on his death are determined as if the values previously transferred by chargeable transfers made by him were reduced by that value;

(2) the money or property is included in the deceased's estate for the purpose of the transfer of value made by him on his death.

Where the money or other property ordered to be provided under s 10 of the 1975 Act is less than the maximum thereby permitted, this rule is applied to such part of the value there mentioned as is appropriate.

The adjustment, in consequence of this rule, or of s 19(1) of the 1975 Act, of the IHT payable in relation to the transfer of value made by the deceased on his death does not affect the amount:

(1) of any deduction to be made under s 8 of the 1975 Act in relation to the IHT borne by the person mentioned in s 8(3) of that Act, or

(2) of IHT to which regard is to be had under s 9(2) of the 1975 Act;

and where a person is ordered under the 1975 Act to make a payment or transfer property by reason of his holding property treated as part of the deceased's net estate under ss 8 or 9 and IHT borne by him is taken into account for the purposes of the order, any repayment of that IHT is made to the deceased's personal representatives and not to him.

Anything which is done in compliance with an order under the 1975 Act or occurs on such an order coming into force, and which would otherwise constitute an occasion on which IHT is chargeable under the no interest in possession regime (other than IHTA 1984, s 79 (failure of exemption from ten-yearly charge)) does not constitute such an occasion. Where such an order provides for property to be settled or for the variation of a settlement, and otherwise IHT would be charged under IHTA 1984, s 52(1) (charge on termination of interest in possession on the coming into force of the order), s 52(1) does not apply.

Where an order is made staying or dismissing proceedings under the 1975 Act on terms set out in or scheduled to the order, IHTA 1984, s 146 has effect as if any of those terms which could have been included in an order under s 2 or 10 of the 1975 Act were provisions of such an order.

Here, any reference to, or to any provision of, the 1975 Act includes a reference to, or to the corresponding provision of, the Inheritance (Provision for Family and Dependants) (Northern Ireland) Order 1979.

13.7 SCOTLAND: LEGITIM
(IHTA 1984, s 147)

Where a testator dies leaving a surviving spouse and a person under age 18 entitled to claim legitim, and provision is made in his will or other testamentary document for a disposition to his spouse which, if it could take effect, would leave insufficient property in the estate to satisfy the entitlement of that person in respect of legitim, the following rules apply.

IHT is charged at the testator's death as if the disposition to the spouse did not include any amount in respect of legitim. However, if within two years of his attaining age 18 or such longer period as the Revenue may permit, the person(s) concerned renounce their claim to legitim, IHT is repaid to the estate calculated on the basis that the disposition to the spouse did include the amount renounced. Where this applies in relation to any estate, the Revenue may repay IHT and interest thereon, without time limit, notwithstanding the general six-year limit on such repayments (IHTA 1984, s 241).

The testator's executors or judicial factor may elect that this does not apply. Instead IHT is charged at the testator's death as if the disposition to the spouse had taken effect. However, where the person concerned claims legitim within two years of his attaining age 18 or such longer period as the Revenue may permit, IHT is charged on the amount so claimed calculated on the basis that the legitim fund had been paid out in full at the testator's death (excluding any part of the fund renounced before any claim has been made) and the IHT chargeable thereon had been apportioned rateably among the persons entitled to claim legitim (excluding any who have renounced). Where the testator's executors or judicial factor decide to make an election they (or he) must give notice to the Revenue within two years from the date of death or such longer period as the Revenue may permit.

Where this applies in relation to any estate then, notwithstanding anything in IHTA 1984, s 239 (certificate of discharge), a certificate of discharge may be given in respect of the whole estate and, notwithstanding anything in s 240 (adjustments for underpayments), the giving of the certificate does not preclude the Revenue from claiming IHT and interest thereon without time limit.

Where a person dies before attaining age 18 or before making a renunciation, these rules apply in relation to that person's executors or judicial factor as they would have applied had that person attained age 18. The date of death is substituted for the date on which a person attained that age. Where the executors or factor renounce a claim to legitim under these circumstances, the amount renounced is not treated as part of that person's estate.

14

SUCCESSIVE CHARGES, VOIDABLE TRANSFERS, PENSIONS AND OTHER MISCELLANEOUS MATTERS

14.1 SUCCESSIVE CHARGES
(IHTA 1984, s 141)

A form of taper relief is available where the value of a person's estate was increased by a 'first chargeable transfer' made not more than five years before his death, or before a 'later (lifetime) chargeable transfer' for which the conditions outlined below are satisfied. A reduced amount of IHT is chargeable on the value transferred by the transfer made on death or on the later (lifetime) chargeable transfer as described below. The conditions are that:

(1) the value transferred by the later transfer is determined by reference to the value of settled property in which the transferor has an interest in possession;

(2) the value transferred by the first transfer was also determined by reference to the value of that property; and

(3) the first transfer either was or included the making of the settlement or was made after the making of the settlement.

The amount of the reduction is a percentage of the IHT charged on so much of the first value transferred as is attributable to the increase in the estate:

Period between transfer and death	% of rate
0–1 years	100
1–2 years	80
2–3 years	60
3–4 years	40
over 4 years	20

Where there is more than one later transfer, the reduction is given only for the earliest of them, unless the reduction is less than the whole of the IHT charged; in that case, a further reduction can be made on subsequent transfers (in chronological order) until reductions representing the whole of that IHT have been made.

In determining whether or to what extent the value of the transferor's estate was increased by a chargeable transfer, any excluded property consisting of a reversionary interest to which he became entitled on the occurrence or before the chargeable transfer is disregarded. Where the estate's value was increased in consequence of a gift *inter vivos*, or a disposition or determination of a beneficial interest in possession in property comprised in a settlement, and IHT under FA 1975, s 22(5) was payable on a subsequent death by reason of the gift or interest, this rule applies as if the increase had been by the chargeable transfer made on death.

14.2 VOIDABLE TRANSFERS
(IHTA 1984, s 150)

If it is shown that the whole or any part of a chargeable transfer has by any enactment or rule of law been set aside as voidable or otherwise defeasible, IHT (or interest thereon) paid or payable by the claimant (in relation to that transfer or any other chargeable transfer made before the claim) that would not have been payable had the relevant transfer been void *ab initio* can, on a claim, be repaid to him by the Revenue or not be payable. The IHT rate applicable to any chargeable transfer made after that claim is determined as if that transfer, or that part of it, had been void *ab initio*.

14.3 PENSION SCHEMES

14.3.1 Treatment of pension rights
(IHTA 1984, s 151)

The rule described below applies to:

(1) any fund to which TA 1988, s 615(3) (no deduction of income tax from annuity paid to person not resident in UK) applies;
(2) any scheme approved under TA 1988, s 620 or 621 (retirement annuities);
(3) any exempt approved scheme or statutory scheme as defined in TA 1988, ss 590–612;
(4) any other sponsored superannuation scheme under TA 1988, s 624; and
(5) approved personal pension arrangements (TA 1988, ss 630–655).

There is left out of account in determining the estate's value immediately before death an interest in, or under, a fund or scheme which comes to an end on death if the interest is:

(1) or is a right to, a pension or annuity, and
(2) not one resulting (whether under the instrument establishing the fund or

scheme or otherwise) from the application of any benefit provided under the fund or scheme otherwise than by way of a pension or annuity.

Sections 49–53 of IHTA 1984 (treatment of interests in possession) do not apply in relation to an interest satisfying these conditions.

Where a benefit has become payable under a fund or scheme to which this rule applies, and the benefit becomes comprised in a settlement made by a person other than the person entitled it, the settlement is treated as made by the person so entitled.

SP E3 (issued in September 1975) clarifies the IHT liability of benefits payable under pension schemes, as follows. Generally, no liability to IHT arises on benefits payable on death under a normal pension scheme (but see below for exceptions). Nor does a charge to IHT arise on payments made by superannuation scheme trustees within IHTA 1984, s 151 in direct exercise of a discretion to pay a lump sum death benefit to any one or more of a member's dependants. It is not considered that, pending the exercise of the discretion, the benefit should normally be regarded as property comprised in a settlement so as to bring it within the scope of the settled property provisions. The s 151 protection does not, though, extend further if the trustees themselves then settle the property so paid.

Benefits *are* liable to IHT if:

(1) they form part of the freely disposable property passing under will or intestacy; this applies only if the executors or administrators have a legally enforceable claim to the benefits: if they were payable to them only at the (for example) pension fund trustees' discretion they are not liable to IHT;

(2) the deceased had the power, immediately before his death, to nominate or appoint the benefits to any person, including dependants.

In these cases the benefits should be included in the personal representatives' account (ie the schedule of the deceased's assets) which must be completed when applying for a grant of probate or letters of administration. The IHT (if any) which is assessed on the personal representatives' account must be paid before the grant can be obtained.

On some events other than death, information should be given to the appropriate CTO:

(1) payment of contributions to a scheme which has not been approved for income tax purposes;

(2) making an irrevocable nomination or disposal of a benefit by a member in his lifetime (otherwise than in favour of a spouse) which reduces his estate's value (eg the surrender of part of the pension or lump sum benefit in exchange for a pension for the life of another).

If IHT proves to be payable, the CTO will communicate with the persons liable to pay the tax.

In SP10/86 (issued on 9 July 1986), the Revenue confirmed its previous practice of not charging IHT on death benefits payable from tax-approved occupational pension and retirement annuity schemes under discretionary trusts. It also confirmed that the practice extends to IHT under the GWR rules and to tax under the ordinary IHT rules.

The Revenue published correspondence with The National Association of Pension Funds, including a note prepared, at the NAPF's request, primarily to enable pension scheme administrators to answer enquiries about the IHT liability of benefits payable under such schemes. Generally, no IHT liability arises over benefits payable on death under a normal pension scheme except in the circumstances explained below. However, such benefits *are* liable to IHT as set out above. Likewise, the events other than death outlined above which the CTO should be informed of also apply.

Correspondence in 1991 between the CTO and the Association of British Insurers concerned the possible application of IHTA 1984, s 3(3) to retirement benefits. The CTO's conclusion is that while a claim under s 3(3) may be appropriate in particular limited circumstances, genuine pension arrangements should not be affected. The purpose in the CTO letter is to:

(1) to clarify the basis for the claim and the very limited circumstances in which one might be raised;
(2) provide reassurance that fears of wider repercussions are misplaced; and so
(3) remove uncertainty as far as possible about what the CTO approach will be.

Scope for a claim
(IHTA 1984, s 3(3))

The vast majority of policyholders exercise their right to take an annuity during their lifetime or survive to the age beyond which deferment cannot be made. All these cases fall outside the scope of the potential claim. The field is further restricted in practice to those policyholders whose chargeable estate exceeds the IHT threshold.

The CTO would generally expect any claims that do arise to be limited to retirement annuity contracts or personal pension schemes. Only exceptionally would claims involve occupational pension schemes. There is no question of a claim being raised in cases of genuine pensions arrangements (ie where it is clear that the policyholder's primary intention is to provide for his own retirement benefits).

The CTO would consider raising a claim in such cases as remain only where there is *prima facie* evidence that the policyholder's intention in failing to take up retirement benefits was to increase somebody else's estate (ie his beneficiaries) rather than to benefit himself. The CTO look closely at pensions arrangements where the policyholder became aware that he was suffering from a terminal illness or was in such poor health that his life was uninsurable and at or after that time the policyholder:

(1) took out a new policy and assigned the death benefit on trust; or

(2) assigned on trust the death benefit of an existing policy; or

(3) paid further contributions to a single premium policy or enhanced contributions to a regular premium policy where the death benefit had been previously assigned on trust; or

(4) deferred the date for taking retirement benefits.

In these circumstances it would be difficult to argue that the policyholder's actions were intended to make provision for his own retirement given the prospect of an early death. Even then the CTO would not pursue the claim where the death benefit was paid to the policyholder's spouse and/or dependants (ie any individuals financially dependent on the policyholder). In addition, a claim would not normally be pursued where the policyholder survived for two years or more after making any of these arrangements, but the CTO reserves the right to examine each case individually.

For the avoidance of doubt, the CTO adopts a similar approach in cases involving:

(1) personal pension schemes set up under deed poll under the Superannuation Funds Office or Integrated Model rules; or

(2) buy-out policies under trust, approved under TA 1988, s 591(2)(g) (commonly known as 'Section 32 policies' after the original legislation).

(*Tax Bulletin* 2 (February 1992), p 12; see also ICAEW TR 854.)

14.3.2 Cash options
(IHTA 1984, s 152)

Where, under:

(1) approved personal pension arrangements (TA 1984, ss 630–655), or

(2) a Revenue approved contract or trust scheme (TA 1984, s 620 or 621 or, before 6 April 1970, FA 1956, s 22),

an annuity becomes payable on a person's death to the widow(er) or a dependant, and under the terms of the contract or scheme a sum of money might at his option have become payable instead to his personal representatives, he is not treated as having been beneficially entitled to that sum. This overrides the general rule, in IHTA 1984, s 5(2), that a person who has a general power which enables, or would if he were *sui juris* enable, him to dispose of, or to charge money on, any property other than settled property is treated as beneficially entitled to the property or money. Here, 'general power' means a power or authority enabling the person by whom it is exercisable to appoint or dispose of property as he thinks fit.

14.3.3 **Overseas pensions**
(IHTA 1984, s 153)

In the case of transfers on death only, any pension receivable from a fund set up under the Government of India Act 1935, s 273, or a corresponding fund under Overseas Pensions Act 1973, s 2 and funds relating to various former colonial countries or territories:

(1) constitute property situated outside the UK and are excluded property if the pensioner is domiciled overseas, and

(2) are left out in determining the value of a person's death estate.

In determining the estate's value immediately before death, there is left out of account any pension payable under the regulations or rules relating to any fund vested in Commissioners under s 273 of the 1935 Act or to any fund administered under a scheme made under s 2 of the 1973 Act (and deemed to correspond to an Order in Council under s 273(2) of the 1935 Act).

A pension paid under the authority of a scheme made under s 2 of the 1973 Act which is constituted by the Pensions (India, Pakistan and Burma) Act 1955 or is certified by the Secretary of State to correspond to the Pensions (India, Pakistan and Burma) Act 1955 is treated as if it had been paid by the government of India or of Pakistan (according as the arrangements under which the pension was first paid under the 1955 Act were made with the one or the other Government).

A pension paid out of any fund established in the UK by the government of any country which, at the time when the fund was established, was or formed part of a colony, protectorate, protected state or UK trust territory is, if the fund was established for the sole purpose of providing pensions (whether contributory or not) payable for service under the government, is treated as if it had been paid by the government by which the fund was established.

A pension paid out of the Central African Pension Fund established by the Federation of Rhodesia and Nyasaland (Dissolution) Order in Council 1963, s 24 is treated as if it had been paid by the Government of a territory outside the UK.

So much of any pension paid to or in respect of any person under:

(1) the scheme which under the Overseas Pensions Act 1973, s 2(3) is constituted thereunder by the Overseas Service Act 1958, s 2 or 4(2), or

(2) such other scheme made under the Overseas Pensions Act 1973, s 2 as is certified by the Secretary of State to correspond to s 2 or 4(2)

as is certified by the Secretary of State to be attributable to service under the government of an overseas territory is treated as if it had been paid by the government of that territory.

Here, references to the government of an overseas country or territory which, at the time when the fund was established, was or formed part of a colony, protectorate, protected state or UK trust territory include a government constituted for two or more such countries or territories and any authority established to provide or administer services which are common or relate to matters of common interest to two or more such countries or territories.

If, by reason of the UK government having assumed responsibility for pension, allowance or gratuity payments within the meaning of the Overseas Pensions Act 1973, s 1, the provisions discussed above apply exclusive of so much (if any) of it as is paid by virtue of the application to it of any provisions of the Pensions (Increase) Act 1971 or any enactment repealed thereby, as if it continued to be paid by the government or other body or fund which had responsibility for it before that responsibility was assumed by the UK government.

14.4 ARMED FORCES

14.4.1 Death on active service, etc
(IHTA 1984, s 154)

Subject to certain conditions, no IHT is paid on the death estate of a person who dies whilst on active service. However, the deceased must have been a member of the armed forces, or (not being a member of the armed forces) associated with or accompanied a force on active service against an enemy or on other service of a warlike nature (eg RUC members (ESC F5)). Each case must be certified by the Defence Council or the Secretary of State, stating that he died from a wound inflicted, accident occurring or disease contracted during active service, or from a disease contracted at some previous time hastened by aggravation because of active service.

The death may occur many years after the individual has ceased to be a member of the armed forces (*Barty-King and another v MOD* [1979] STC 218). The fourth Duke of Westminster, who was wounded in action in 1944, died of cancer in 1967. Septicaemia caused by his war wound was noted on the death certificate as a significant condition contributing to his death, 'but not related to the disease or condition causing it'. Exemption from what was then estate duty under FA 1952, s 71 is given for the estate of any person who is certified by the Defence Council to have 'died from a wound inflicted ... when ... the deceased was a member of the armed forces of the Crown ... on active service against an enemy'. The Defence Council rejected the executors' application for a certificate. The High Court held, however, that the executors were entitled to a declaration and that they ought to have been granted a certificate. Although a wound had to be a cause of death, it did not have to be the direct or only cause.

14.4.2 **Visiting forces**
(IHTA 1984, s 155)

Certain property of members of visiting forces is 'excluded property' (under IHTA 1984, s 6(4)):

(1) the emoluments paid by the government of any designated country to a member of a visiting force of that country, not being a British citizen, a British Dependent Territories citizen, a British national (overseas) or a British overseas citizen, and

(2) any tangible movable property the presence of which in the UK is owing solely to the presence in the UK of such a person while serving as a member of the force.

A period during which any such member of a visiting force is in the UK by reason solely of his being such a member is not treated as a period of residence in the UK or as creating a change of his residence or domicile.

References to a visiting force also apply to a civilian component as they apply to the force itself. For the purpose of conferring like benefits on persons attached to any designated allied headquarters, any members of the armed forces of a designated country are, while attached to any such headquarters, deemed to constitute a visiting force of that country; there is a corresponding extension of the class of persons who may be treated as members of a civilian component.

In the case of persons of any category for the time being agreed between the UK government and the other members of the North Atlantic Council, employment by a designated allied headquarters is treated as if it were service as a member of a visiting force of a designated country.

14.5 APSLEY HOUSE AND CHEVENING HOUSE
(IHTA 1984, s 156)

Rights conferred by the Wellington Museum Act 1947, s 3 (Apsley House), and property held on trust under the Chevening Estate Act 1959 (Chevening House) are entirely outside the scope of IHT.

14.6 NON-RESIDENTS' BANK ACCOUNTS
(IHTA 1984, s 157)

In determining for IHT purposes the value of a person's estate immediately before his death there is left out of account the balance on:

(1) any qualifying foreign currency account (ie other than one denominated in sterling) of his with a bank or the Post Office (presumably this now refers to the National Savings Bank), and

(2) any qualifying foreign currency account of the trustees of settled property in which he is beneficially entitled to an interest in possession. This does not apply to settled property if the settlor was UK-domiciled when he made the settlement, or if the trustees are domiciled, resident or ordinarily resident in the UK immediately before the beneficiary's death.

This treatment applies to a person who is non-UK domiciled immediately before his death, and is neither resident nor ordinarily resident there at that time. The question whether a person is resident or ordinarily resident in the UK is determined as for income tax purposes. However, settlement trustees are regarded as not resident or ordinarily resident in the UK unless the settlement's general administration is ordinarily carried on in the UK and the trustees or a majority of them (and, where there is more than one class of trustees, a majority of each class) are resident and ordinarily resident there.

14.7 DOUBLE TAXATION RELIEF

14.7.1 Double taxation conventions
(IHTA 1984, s 158)

An Order in Council may declare that:

(1) arrangements specified in the Order have been made with the government of an overseas territory with a view to affording relief from double taxation against IHT payable under UK law and any tax imposed under the laws of that territory which is of a similar character or is chargeable on or by reference to death or gifts *inter vivos*, and
(2) it is expedient that those arrangements should have effect.

Where such arrangements are in force then, notwithstanding anything in IHTA 1984, they are effective so far as they provide for relief from IHT, or for determining the place where any property is to be treated as situated for IHT purposes.

If it appears to be appropriate, the arrangements specified in an Order in Council may include provisions for the exchange of information necessary for carrying out UK domestic law and the laws of the territory to which the arrangements relate, including in particular provisions about the prevention of fiscal evasion with respect to those taxes. Such arrangements may include provision for relief in cases occurring before the making of the arrangements and provisions as to property which is not itself subject to double taxation.

Where any arrangements have been made, no obligation to secrecy prevents the Revenue from disclosing to any authorised officer of the government with which the arrangements are made such information as is required to be disclosed under the arrangements.

14.7.2 Unilateral relief

Where the Revenue is satisfied that, in an overseas territory, any amount of tax imposed by reason of any disposition or other event is attributable to the value of any property then, if that tax is of a character similar to that of IHT or is chargeable on or by reference to death or gifts *inter vivos*, and any IHT so chargeable is also attributable to the value of that property, a credit is given for that amount ('the overseas tax') against that IHT.

Where the property is situated in the overseas territory and not in the UK, the credit is an amount equal to the overseas tax. Where the property is situated in neither the UK nor the overseas territory, or is situated in both the UK and the overseas territory, the credit is an amount calculated in accordance with the following formula:

$$\frac{A}{A + B} \times C$$

where: A = the amount of the IHT
   B = the overseas tax and
   C = whichever of A and B is the smaller.

Where tax is imposed in two or more overseas territories on property which is situated in neither the UK nor any of those territories, or is situated both in the UK and each of those territories, the formula set out above is applied as if

   B = the aggregate of the overseas tax imposed in each of those territories and

   C = the aggregate of all, except the largest, of A and the overseas tax imposed in each of them.

Where credit is allowed unilaterally or under the terms of a convention against overseas tax imposed in one overseas territory, any credit of overseas tax imposed in another territory is calculated as if the IHT were reduced by the credit allowed. Where, in the case of any overseas territory, credit is allowed against the overseas tax for tax charged in a territory in which the property is situated, the overseas tax is treated for the purposes of those provisions as reduced by the credit.

Here, references to tax imposed in an overseas territory are to tax chargeable under the law of that territory and paid by the person liable to pay it. Where relief can be given both unilaterally and under the terms of a convention, relief is given under whichever provides the greater relief.

14.8 COMPENSATION FOR HOLOCAUST VICTIMS

A Revenue concession gives exemption from IHT for compensation paid by banks on dormant UK bank accounts opened by Holocaust victims and frozen during World War II. Under the 'restore UK' scheme organised by the British Bankers' Association, people who were Holocaust victims, or their beneficiaries, who have moneys restored to them under this scheme receive not only the original capital, but some form of compensation. No tax is payable on any moneys paid out by the banks under this initiative to Holocaust victims or their beneficiaries. This exemption will cover income tax liabilities on any compensation payments as well as death duties in respect of the capital held in the accounts.

Estate duty, capital transfer tax or IHT, as appropriate, is (were it not for this concession) potentially chargeable on UK account balances at death (even if the accountholder had no other UK connection). In many cases, any such liability may turn out to be nil or very small but, given the circumstances lying behind these accounts, a significant effort might be involved in determining the correct tax position. The Government has decided that a blanket tax exemption be given on any compensation paid by the banks in relation to moneys restored under the 'restore UK' scheme.

15

VALUATION

15.1 GENERAL

15.1.1 Market value
(IHTA 1984, s 160)

Valuation of 'whole property'

The general rule is that the value at any time of any property is the price which it might reasonably be expected to fetch if sold in the open market at that time. However, that price is not assumed to be reduced on the ground that the whole property is to be placed on the market at one and the same time.

This basis of valuation was approved in *Duke of Buccleuch and another v CIR* [1967] 1 AC 506, HL, an estate duty case. Here, the Revenue valued a substantial estate by dividing it into 532 'natural units' for valuation purposes. The trustees' view, while accepting that 46 of the units could be sold individually, was that the remaining 486 could only be sold within a reasonable time if they were sold as a whole to an investor or speculator. On that basis the price that such a buyer would pay would be 20 per cent less than the total valuation of the individual units. This contention was rejected by the Lands Tribunal. The House of Lords upheld this decision, holding that the open market value should be found by reference to the aggregate proceeds of sale in a hypothetical market of each individual unit. It was held to be irrelevant that it would have taken a long time to sell the individual units separately, and that delay would have been caused by the need to avoid flooding the market.

The principles set out in *Duke of Buccleuch* were applied in *Lady Fox's Executors v CIR* [1994] STC 360, CA. In this case, at the time of her death, the freeholder of a large estate held a 92.5 per cent interest in a partnership which farmed the land. The Revenue issued a notice of determination claiming IHT on the combined value of the deceased's freehold reversion and her interest in the partnership. This approach was upheld by the Court of Appeal on the basis that the hypothetical sale had to be supposed to have taken the course which would gain the largest price provided that it did not entail 'undue expenditure of time and effort'. Therefore, the freehold reversion and the partnership should be valued as one unit of property.

The basis of valuation of a jointly owned house (as tenants in common in equal shares) was at issue in *Wight and another v CIR* (1982) 264 EG 935. It was agreed that the other co-owner would be the most likely purchaser. The Lands Tribunal held that the value was half the vacant possession value, less a discount to reflect the restricted demand for this type of interest. As it was unlikely that an outside purchaser would be able to obtain an order for sale under the Law of Property Act (LPA) 1925, s 30, the discount should be 15 per cent rather than the 10 per cent used since the decision in *Cust v CIR* (1917) 91 EG 11.

Willett and another (Mrs Benson's Executors) v CIR (1982) 264 EG 257 concerned the value of freehold interest in tenanted agricultural property. The owner of a freehold interest in tenanted agricultural land died in 1977. The Revenue valued the interest for CTT purposes at £45,000. The executors contended that the valuation should be £28,000. The Lands Tribunal held that the valuation should be £39,000, reaffirming the principle that a valuation must assume that property is suitably 'lotted' if it would fetch a better price if sold in that way, applying *Earl of Ellesmere v CIR* [1918] 2 KB 735.

A further and more recent case, *Walton (Walton's Executor) v CIR* [1996] STC 68, CA, reviewed the valuation of partnership interest in a non-assignable agricultural tenancy. The freehold of a farm was held by a father and his two sons as tenants in common in equal shares. The farm was let to a partnership which comprised the father and one of the sons. The father died. It was agreed that the premium for vacant possession was £200,000, and that the value of tenant-right and tenants' improvements, less dilapidations, was £40,000. The Revenue issued a notice of determination, valuing the tenancy at half the vacant possession premium less a 10 per cent discount, giving a value for the 50 per cent part interest of:

$$(£200,000 \times 50 \text{ per cent}) = £100,000 - (£100,000 \times 10 \text{ per cent}) = £90,000,$$

together with the net value of tenant-right and tenants' improvements, which gave a total value of £130,000. The father's half-share was, therefore, valued at £65,000. The executor appealed, contending that the valuation was excessive, as it assumed an immediate purchase by the freeholders; in reality the freeholders would not have been interested in securing the surrender of the tenancy and did not have the funds for such a purchase.

The Lands Tribunal allowed the appeal, holding that the realisation of the vacant possession premium was 'so far from any market expectation as to make a valuation by reference to an apportionment of the vacant possession premium wholly appropriate'. The property was an undivided beneficial interest in the joint tenancy as a partnership asset. That tenancy could only be sold and its value realised if the terms of the partnership agreement permitted it, which they did not. The tenancy's value, as a partnership asset, depended upon the extent to which its terms enhanced the partnership profits by enabling the partners to exploit the partnership assets without paying a full market rent for the farm. The Tribunal held that the value of the entire tenancy, on the basis of a valuation of profit rental and on the assumption that the landlords could not be regarded as a hypothetical purchaser, was approximately £12,600, so that the value of the deceased's share was £6,300. The Court of Appeal upheld the Tribunal decision as one of fact.

Restricted transfers of assets

Any restrictions on the transfer of assets (eg a pre-emption clause in a company's articles in the case of shares) or in any other way affecting the rights attaching to shares must be taken into account, as such restrictions may affect the asset's price (*Salvesen's Trustees v CIR* 1930 SLT 387; *CIR v Crossman and others* [1937] AC 26, HL).

Crossman, an estate duty case, was concerned with the value of unquoted shares in a company whose articles of association imposed restrictions on transfer including a right of pre-emption in favour of existing shareholders. The House of Lords held that the open market value of unquoted shares in the company was not limited to that fixed by the pre-emption clause, but should be estimated at the price obtainable in a hypothetical open market on the terms that the purchaser was registered as holder of the shares and held them subject to the same restrictions as his predecessor.

Valuation of agricultural tenancies

The *Law Society's Gazette*, 18 March 1992 published a summary of a meeting between representatives of the Law Society of England and Wales, the Law Society of Scotland and the Revenue held on 3 February 1992 to discuss the specific issue of valuation of agricultural tenancies. For the purposes of the meeting there was a common acceptance by both Law Societies and the Revenue (including the Valuation Office Agency) that under the existing law, the principles of *Crossman* (above) apply in general to valuation exercises where an asset is subject to restrictions on its disposition. In valuing an agricultural tenancy, there are several special factors which need to be considered:

(1) the benefits attaching to the tenancy (eg residential accommodation, rights of compensation for disturbance, waygoing (Scotland), dilapidations claims, improvements, manurial rights, and the fact that the rent might currently be less than the market rent);

(2) the principle that there should be no automatic presumption that the tenancy's value could be arrived at by a method based upon a standard percentage of the vacant possession premium or value;

(3) the consideration of who might be in the hypothetical market for the tenancy; and

(4) the weight to attach to the various factors relevant in valuing the tenancy, which would be a matter of fact and for negotiation in each case.

In principle it appeared that there was only one area of dispute between the two sides, namely whether the Revenue had been correct to use as a starting point for valuing tenancies a percentage of the land's vacant possession value or the vacant possession premium. The Revenue had difficulty departing from this position since it obviously had a responsibility to both the Exchequer and the government. If it started from a point which was lower than the final value which might be agreed upon, it would be open to the criticism that it had not carried out its duty properly.

It was open to the taxpayer to adduce evidence at an early stage if the landlord's character was to be a factor in determining the value, namely that there was evidence that the landlord was likely to make a bid for vacant possession of the land, or not as the case might be. If the issue had arisen, for example, on a tenant farmer's death within seven years of transferring his tenancy, such evidence could be submitted at the same time as the accounts for the estate were sent in. The Revenue would then be on notice from the outset that the question of a bid by the landlord was a matter that the taxpayer believed was not a factor to take into account.

Valuation of quoted shares

The value of quoted shares while secret takeover negotiations were in progress was the matter under discussion in *Hinchcliffe v Crabtree* [1972] AC 707, HL. A director of a manufacturing company had disposed of some shares in the company during 1965/66, and so it became necessary to ascertain their market value at 6 April 1965. At that date, takeover negotiations were in progress but had not been made public. It was accepted that, had they been public, the quoted price at that date would have been substantially higher than the actual quoted price. The House of Lords held that the mere fact that company directors possessed information which if made public would affect the quoted prices of its shares was not a special circumstance. Only if it could be shown that special circumstances which might affect the share price had been incorrectly withheld could such information be taken into account.

The practice in valuing quoted shares for IHT purposes is to follow the CGT valuation rules (TCGA 1992, s 272(3), (4)). Thus the market value of shares or securities quoted in The Stock Exchange Daily Official List is (except where in consequence of special circumstances prices quoted in that List are by themselves not a proper measure of market value) as follows:

(1) the lower of the two prices shown in the quotations for shares or securities in List on the relevant date plus one-quarter of the difference between those two figures, or

(2) halfway between the highest and lowest prices at which bargains, other than bargains done at special prices, were recorded in the shares or securities for the relevant date.

The amount shown by (1) above is chosen if it is less than the amount under (2), or no such bargains were recorded for the relevant date. The amount at (2) is chosen if it is less than that under (1).

This procedure does not apply to shares or securities for which The Stock Exchange provides a more active market elsewhere. If The Stock Exchange is closed on the relevant date, the market value is ascertained by reference to the latest previous date or earliest subsequent date on which it is open, whichever affords the lower market value.

'Market value' in relation to any rights of unitholders in any unit trust scheme the buying and selling prices of which are published regularly by the scheme's managers means an amount equal to the buying price (ie the lower price) so published on the relevant date, or if none were published on that date, on the latest date before.

Other matters

The Revenue view on the application of these principles for both CGT and IHT purposes with particular reference to the valuation of assets at the date of death were set out in *Tax Bulletin* 16 (April 1995).

Where an asset's value is ascertained for IHT purposes on the owner's death, this is also taken as the beneficiary's acquisition value for CGT purposes (TCGA 1992, s 274). But will the Revenue ascertain the estate assets' value using IHT principles where either the asset is wholly exempt or relieved from IHT or, where no IHT is payable on the deceased's estate, in order to provide a value for any other Revenue purpose, in particular the CGT acquisition value?

An asset's value for IHT purposes is usually the price it would realise if sold in the open market. In certain circumstances, special rules may apply to give a different value. For example, under the related property provisions of IHTA 1984, s 161, property held jointly by husband and wife is treated as a single unit in arriving at the value of their respective interests.

If an asset is wholly exempt or relieved from IHT, neither the deceased's personal representatives nor the Revenue can require that asset's value to be ascertained for IHT purposes.

However, where it is evident that any possible increase or decrease in the value of the estate's chargeable assets, as included in an Inland Revenue Account, will leave the total estate value below the IHT threshold, it is not necessary to ascertain the value of all the individual assets for IHT purposes. In some cases, particularly where the estate is close to the threshold, values may be considered but not necessarily 'ascertained'.

For example, the value included in the Inland Revenue Account for a holding of shares in an unquoted company might appear to the Revenue's Shares Valuation Division (SVD) to be too high. In this situation, as no IHT is at stake, the SVD is unlikely to negotiate an ascertained value for IHT. On the other hand, if the value included seems, on the face of it, too low, the SVD may negotiate an ascertained value if the likely amount of IHT at stake warrants this.

If an asset's value is not ascertained for IHT, the normal rules of TCGA 1992, s 272 apply to determine the beneficiary's CGT acquisition value.

15.1.2 Related property
(IHTA 1984, s 161)

The concept behind the related property provisions is that the aggregate value of fragmented assets could be much less than the value of the whole, undivided, as a unit. Thus, where the value of any property comprised in an estate would be less than the appropriate proportion of the aggregate value of that and any 'related property', the value is taken as the appropriate proportion of the whole value.

The appropriate portion of the aggregate value is such portion thereof as would be attributable to the first-mentioned property's value if that aggregate value were equal to the sums of the values of that and any related property, the value of each property being determined as if it did not form part of that aggregate.

For this purpose, the proportion which the value of a smaller number of shares of any class bears to the value of a greater number is taken to be that which the smaller number bears to the greater; and similarly with stock, debentures and units of any other description of property. Shares are not treated as being of the same class unless they are so treated by the practice of a recognised stock exchange or would be so treated if dealt with on such a stock exchange.

Ascertaining the property value

Related property is an extremely important concept, and is primarily an anti-avoidance provision. Although its most common practical application is likely to be in relation to shares in unquoted companies, it does apply to other property.

The first step is to ascertain the total value of the related property as if held by one notional person. This value is then apportioned among the parties concerned, broadly in proportion to the usual non-related values of each party's assets which were aggregated under the related properties provisions.

Example

Dermot Structures Ltd's shares are held as follows:

Mr Dermot	4,500
Mrs Dermot	3,000
Mr Ellis	2,500
	10,000

It is agreed that the value of a 30 per cent holding is £150 per share, and that the value of a 45 per cent holding is £200 per share.

As Mr and Mrs Dermot are married to each other, their shares are valued as part of a 75 per cent holding, the value of which is agreed at £450 per share. Mr Dermot's shares are thus deemed to be worth 4,500 × £450 = £2,025,000, and not 4,500 × £200 = £900,000.

The practical effect of this concept becomes apparent when considered alongside another basic concept of IHT – the 'loss to donor' principle.

Example

A family company's shares are held and valued as follows:

	Number	£ per share	£ value
Father	4,500	300	1,350,000
Mother	1,000	300	300,000
	5,500	600	1,650,000
Son	4,500	160	720,000
	10,000	1,000	2,370,000

The parents agree to give 1,000 shares to their son, which will give him control of the company. If the father makes the gift, the value transferred is:

Before:	4,500/5,500 × £1,650,000[1] =	1,350,000
Retained:	3,500/4,500 × £720,000[2] =	560,000
IHT value of the gift		790,000

[1] value of 5,500 shares on a majority basis = £300 each
[2] value of 4,500 shares on a minority basis = £160 each

If the mother makes the gift, the value transferred would be:

Before:	1,000/5,500 × £1,650,000 =	300,000
Retained:		Nil
IHT value of the gift		300,000

Example

A family company's shares are held and valued as follows:	
	Number
Father	4,000
Mother	2,500
	6,500
Post-1978 charitable trust	2,000
	8,500
Others	1,500
	10,000

Any disposal by the father or mother would be valued as a proportion of an 85 per cent holding. A disposal by the trust would be valued as a 20 per cent holding (the trust property is related to the shareholdings of the mother and father, but not the other way round).

If the father gave away 2,200 of his shares, his estate would be reduced by the difference in value between 4,000/8,500 of the related property value of 8,500 shares before the transfer and 8,000/4,900 of the related property value of 4,900 shares after the transfer.

The last two examples show how important is the difference between shares held by one person and shares which are aggregated to form a related holding. Suppose that a person holds 55 per cent of a company's shares in his own right with no related property. Suppose further that he disposes of 10 per cent of them. The measure of his loss is the difference between a 55 per cent holding and a 45 per cent holding. If he had held 10 per cent and his wife 45 per cent of the shares, they would be valued as related property as a 55 per cent holding. However, if he then disposes of all his 10 per cent holding, his estate is reduced by the difference between 10/55 of a 55 per cent holding and nil. This gives a much smaller loss than the reduction from a 55 per cent to a 45 per cent holding. The disposal of the balance of 45 per cent would give rise to a loss being the difference between the value of a 45 per cent holding and nil. In this event, the Revenue might seek to apply the 'associated operations' rule under IHTA 1984, s 268.

The second leg of the related property anti-avoidance attack concerns property held by, for example, a charity (ie it was exempt property) having been given by the individual or his spouse within the previous five years. The gift would be exempt, and were it not for this provision, it would have been possible to make such gift which took the combined shareholding of a husband and wife below the control threshold and therefore reducing the loss to the donor on a subsequent gift. Such a manoeuvre is rendered ineffective by this provision, unless a delay of five years is acceptable. It remains open to the Revenue to invoke 'associated operations' under s 268 on the later disposal and ask why control was allowed to 'evaporate'.

15.1.3 Liabilities
(IHTA 1984, s 162)

A liability for which there is a right of reimbursement is taken into account only to the extent that reimbursement cannot reasonably be expected to be obtained. If a liability falls to be discharged after the time at which it is to be taken into account, it must be valued as at that time. However, in determining the value of a person's estate immediately after a transfer of value, his IHT liability is computed without any allowance for the fact that the IHT is not immediately due, and as if any IHT recovered otherwise from the transferor (or in certain cases a spouse under IHTA 1984, s 203) were paid in discharge of a liability for which the transferor had a right of reimbursement.

A charge on any property is taken so far as possible as reducing that property's value. A liability to a non-resident is deducted so far as possible from property outside the UK unless it is to be discharged in the UK, or charged against UK property.

15.1.4 Restriction on freedom to dispose
(IHTA 1984, s 163)

Where, by a contract made at any time, the right to dispose of any property has been excluded or restricted then, in determining the property's value for the purpose of the chargeable transfer happening after that time, the exclusion or restriction is taken into account only to the extent (if any) that consideration in money or money's worth was given for it. However, if the contract was, or was part of associated operations which together were, a chargeable transfer, an allowance is made for the value transferred (calculated as if no IHT is chargeable on it) or for so much of the value transferred as is attributable to the exclusion or restriction

Where the contract was made before 27 March 1974, the above applies only if the first relevant event is a transfer made on death.

15.1.5 Transferor's expenses
(IHTA 1984, s 164)

In determining any value transferred, expenses incurred by the transferor in making the transfer (but not his liability for IHT) are, if borne by him, left out of account. If they are borne by a person benefiting from the transfer, they are treated as reducing the value transferred.

15.1.6 Tax on capital gains
(IHTA 1984, s 165)

Where a chargeable transfer is or includes a disposal of an asset, and on the disposal the transferor realises a capital gain then, if the gain is a chargeable gain, and any CGT charged on the gain is borne by the donee, the CGT amount so borne is treated as reducing the value transferred. This does not apply where the chargeable transfer is made in relation to settled property and the gain accrues to the settlement trustees. But if in such a case any CGT charged on the gain is borne by a person who becomes absolutely entitled to the settled property, the tax amount so borne is treated as reducing the value transferred.

It may be beneficial for a CGT holdover election to be made on gifts of business assets (TCGA 1992, s 165), or on gifts on which IHT is charged (TCGA 1992, s 260). However, such election in the latter case is not available on a PET. IHT paid on a gift should be deducted in the donee's CGT computation.

15.1.7 Creditors' rights
(IHTA 1984, s 166)

In determining the value of a right to receive a sum due under any obligation, it is assumed that it will be duly discharged except to the extent that recovery of the sum is impossible or impracticable other than by any act or omission of the person to whom the sum is due.

15.1.8 Life policies, etc
(IHTA 1984, s 167)

The value of a life policy or annuity contract payable on death is its market value, but not less than the total premiums or other consideration paid under the policy or contract (or any policy or contract for which it was directly or indirectly substituted) less any amount paid by way of partial surrender. The market value cannot be less than the surrender value, but could be greater if there is a substantial deterioration in the life assured's health.

These rules of valuation do not apply in the case of a transfer of value which a person makes on his death, or any other transfer of value which does not result in the policy or contract ceasing to be part of the transferor's estate. Nor do they apply in the case of:

(1) term assurance under which the sum assured becomes payable only if the life assured dies before the expiry of a specified term, and
(2) under which the indemnity period is at least three years, and
(3) the premiums are paid at normal intervals during at least two-thirds of the term at yearly or shorter intervals, and the premiums payable in any one 12-month period are not more than twice the premiums payable in any other such period.

Where the policy is unit-linked, the value of which is published and subject to fluctuation, and the payment of each premium secures the allocation to the policy of a specified number of units, then if the policy-allocated units' value, at the time of the transfer, is less than the aggregate value of those units at the time of allocation, the total premiums paid are reduced by the difference.

These rules apply to transfers by the trustees of no interest in possession trusts (IHTA 1984, ss 58–85, excluding IHTA 1984, s 79 (failure of exemption from ten-yearly charge)).

Where a person pays a life assurance premium for someone else's benefit (eg where the policy is held in trust for another person), this may constitute a transfer of value for IHT purposes. The Revenue takes the view that where the payment of a premium is a transfer of value for capital transfer tax purposes, the amount of the transfer is:

(1) the net amount of the premium after any deduction made under FA 1976, Sched 4, para 5;

(2) the gross premium where the premium is paid without deduction.

(IRPR 17 January 1979.)

15.1.9 Unquoted shares and securities
(IHTA 1984, s 168)

In applying to unquoted shares and securities the basic rule regarding 'market value' mentioned at the beginning of this chapter, a further assumption must be made. It is assumed that in that market there is available to any prospective purchaser all the information which a prudent prospective purchaser might reasonably require if he were proposing to purchase unquoted shares and securities from a willing vendor by private treaty and at arm's length. This provision was added following *Re Lynall Dec'd* (1971) 47 TC 375, HL. However, even now the position is not altogether satisfactory, as the amount of information deemed available to a purchaser of a minority interest is somewhat less than would be available to a purchaser of a majority holding. If the consideration payable is substantial in monetary terms albeit that a minority interest is to be acquired, the purchaser might require rather more information than might otherwise apply (*Clark v Green* [1995] STC SSCD 99). Although relating to a valuation for estate duty purposes, *Duke of Buccleuch v CIR* [1967] 1 AC 506, HL provides a convenient summary:

- market price means the best possible price obtainable on a sale between a willing buyer and a willing seller;
- the condition of the property must be imagined to be conducive to the best possible price;
- all expenses involved in the notional sale are deemed incurred in advance thereof (ie they are taken into account in the valuation).

While there must be a 'willing buyer', this concept excludes an anxious buyer and it must be assumed only that all persons desirous of purchasing can make offers to do so (*CIR v Clay* [1914–15] All ER Rep 882), but evidence of this desirous purchase must be produced.

The determination of the 'market value' of an unquoted company's shares has caused some difficulty over the years. However, *Holt v CIR* (1953) 32 ATC 402, ChD) gives some assistance in solving this problem. It was held that a purchaser of shares in a private company would have a different outlook from a purchaser of shares on The Stock Exchange. He would enquire into the type of trade, its potentiality, its management, other shareholders and the company accounts. In such circumstances, he may pay a price on the basis of a higher dividend yield or a higher capital profit than might be the case for quoted shares. It was also determined in *Holt* that share valuations must not be made with benefit of hindsight and events occurring after the valuation date must, in general, be ignored. However, evidence of actual transactions involving shares in the same company can be taken into account (*Stenhouse's Trustees v CIR* [1992] STC 103, CS).

Any restrictions on the transfer of shares (eg pre-emption clause in articles) or in any other way affecting the rights attaching to shares must be taken into account as such restrictions may affect the shares' price (*Salvesen's Trustees v CIR* 1930 SLT 387; *CIR v Crossman* [1936] 1 All ER 762).

Where the disposal of shares occurs on death or retirement, or in other circumstances where the company is deprived of the services of any key person, the effect that such loss may have upon the shares must be considered.

In valuing unquoted shares, account must be taken of the company's whole history, which will mean an examination of the company balance sheets, records of dividends paid and in particular the prices of share disposals (if any) which have taken place in recent years.

The valuation of shares must take into account a willing buyer and willing seller. Information available to directors cannot be brought into the open market valuation, unless it is information which a prudent purchaser would require, negating the decision in *Re Lynall Dec'd* (above). The effect that an undisclosed possible takeover bid might have on the share valuation was discussed in *Crabtree v Hinchcliffe* (1971) 47 TC 419, HL, where it was held that the non-disclosure of information concerning the possible takeover was not a special circumstance (as defined by statutory law) which could displace the open market price as a measure of market value. Had the information regarding the takeover been finalised before the valuation date, then this would have affected the price, but in this case it had been finalised after that date. However, information which is properly confidential cannot be assumed to be available for disclosure.

It is clear that the question of control must also be considered, as a person acquiring a majority or controlling interest in a company may be prepared to pay more for his shares than if he was merely acquiring a minority interest with no effective control over company activities.

Share valuations for CGT purposes are also negotiated with the SVD.

90+ per cent shareholders

A holder of 90 per cent of a company's ordinary share capital can enforce the sale of the remaining shares (Companies Act 1985, s 428).

75+ per cent shareholders

A holder of more than 75 per cent of a company's ordinary share capital can pass a special resolution. Specifically, he could sell the business as a going concern or pass a resolution to wind up the company. The company would be valued on the basis of realisable value less additional liabilities such as liquidation costs, redundancy, taxation etc. It has been suggested that a discount of 25–30 per cent would be appropriate (*Re Courthorpe* (1928) 7 ATC 538).

50+ per cent shareholders

A holder of more than 50 per cent of a company's ordinary share capital has day-to-day control of the company and can pass an ordinary resolution. Specifically, he can dictate the company's remuneration and dividend policy. The basis of valuation takes account of the company's potential earnings (subject to adjustment for any special factors).

Shared control

If effective (50 per cent or more) control can be obtained by an alliance with another, small shareholder, it would be appropriate to make the valuation on the earnings basis. Where two shareholders each hold 50 per cent there is potential deadlock; the valuation is on a yield basis by reference to the dividends paid on the shares.

Assets and earnings are important only insofar as they demonstrate the company's ability to maintain or increase a dividend. However, many unquoted companies do not pay dividends. The valuation is therefore made on a notional dividend basis, by reference to actual profits, industry norms etc.

Under 50 per cent shareholders

A holder of 25 per cent or more of a company's ordinary share capital has the power to block a special resolution. The valuation would be on a dividend yield basis. In view of the lack of day-to-day control, a marginally higher yield would be appropriate for such a holding.

Under 25 per cent shareholders

A holder of less than 25 per cent of a company's ordinary share capital cannot prevent the passing of a special resolution. The valuation would be on a dividend yield basis. In view of the lack of day-to-day control, a further increase in the yield would be appropriate for such a holding.

A holder of less than 10 per cent of ordinary share capital can be liable to compulsory purchase. Again, an increased yield would be appropriate.

15.1.10 Farm cottages
(IHTA 1984, s 169)

In determining the value of agricultural property which includes cottages occupied by persons employed solely for agricultural purposes in connection with the property, no account is taken of any value attributable to the fact that the cottages are suitable for the residential purposes of persons not so employed.

Expressions used here are as defined for agricultural property relief by IHTA 1984, s 115 (see **9**).

ESC F16 confirms that, on a transfer of agricultural property which includes a cottage occupied by a retired farm employee or their widow(er), the condition concerning occupation for agricultural purposes is regarded as satisfied with respect to the cottage if either the occupier is a statutorily protected tenant, or the occupation is under a lease granted to the farm employee and any surviving spouse for life as part of the employee's employment contract by the landlord for agricultural purposes.

15.1.11 Leases for life, etc
(IHTA 1984, s 170)

Where a lease of property is treated as a settlement (under IHTA 1984, s 43(3)), the value of the lessor's interest in the property is taken to be such part of the value of the property as bears to it the same proportion as the value of the consideration bore, at the time the lease was granted, to what would then have been the value of a full consideration in money or money's worth.

15.2 CHANGES IN PROPERTY'S VALUE AND EXPENSES

15.2.1 Changes occurring on death
(IHTA 1984, s 171)

The value of property in a person's estate immediately before his death must reflect changes in the value of his estate which have occurred by reason of the death and which meet the following condition. A change meets this condition if it is an addition to the property comprised in the estate or an increase or decrease of any property's value so comprised, other than a decrease resulting from an alteration or extinguishment by a close company of its unquoted share or loan capital, or any alteration or extinguishment of any rights attaching thereto (under IHTA 1984, s 98(1)).

The termination on death of any interest or the passing of any interest by survivorship does not meet this condition.

15.2.2 Funeral expenses
(IHTA 1984, s 172)

Reasonable funeral expenses, including the cost of a tombstone and reasonable mourning expenses, are deducted from the estate's value (SP 7/87; ESC F1).

15.2.3 Expenses incurred abroad
(IHTA 1984, s 173)

An allowance against the value of property situated outside the UK of up to 5 per cent is allowed for the added expense of administering or realising that property.

15.2.4 Income tax and unpaid IHT
(IHTA 1984, s 174)

In determining the value of a person's estate immediately before his death, allowance is made for any liability to income tax:

(1) on offshore income gains arising on a disposal which is deemed to occur on death (TA 1988, s 757(3)); and
(2) arising on discounted securities on a transfer which is deemed to occur on death (FA 1996, Sched 13, para 4(2)).

Where, in so determining the value a liability for IHT is taken into account, then if that IHT or any part of it is not in the event paid out of the estate, the estate's value immediately before death is treated as increased by an amount equal to that IHT or so much of it as is not paid.

15.2.5 Liability to make future payments
(IHTA 1984, s 175)

Where in determining the estate value immediately before death a liability to make payments or transfer assets under a disposition (under IHTA 1984, s 262) is taken into account, the liability is computed as if the amount or value of the payments or assets were reduced by the chargeable portion.

15.2.6 Sale of related property after death
(IHTA 1984, s 176)

A special treatment applies where, within three years after death, there is a qualifying sale of any property ('the property concerned') comprised in the estate immediately before death and valued:

(1) as related property (IHTA 1984, s 161), or
(2) in conjunction with property which was also comprised in the estate but has not at any time since the death been vested in the vendors.

If a claim is made for the relief available hereunder, the property concerned's value immediately before death is taken to be what it would have been had it not been determined as related property.

This does not apply unless the price obtained on the sale, with any adjustment needed to take account of any difference in circumstances at the date of both the sale and the death, is less than the value which, apart from this special treatment and IHTA 1984, ss 190–198 (sale of land from deceased's estate), would be the value of the property concerned as related property or in conjunction with other property (see above).

Where the property concerned consists of shares in or securities of a close company, the relief is not available if at any time between the death and the qualifying sale the shares' or securities' value is reduced by more than 5 per cent as a result of an alteration or extinguishment in the company's share or loan capital or in any rights attaching to its shares or securities.

15.2.7 Scottish agricultural leases
(IHTA 1984, s 177)

Where any part of a person's estate immediately before his death is attributable to a tenant's interest in an unexpired portion of a lease for a fixed term of agricultural property in Scotland, then any value associated with any prospect of renewal of the lease by tacit relocation is left out of account. It is a requirement that the deceased must have been tenant of the property in question continuously for a period of at least two years immediately preceding his death or had become tenant by succession. Where the interest of a tenant of agricultural property in Scotland, being an interest which is held by virtue of tacit relocation, and acquired on the death by a new tenant, the value of the interest is left out of account. The value to be left out of account does not include the value of any rights to compensation in respect of tenant's improvements.

15.3 LOSSES ON SALES OF SHARES ETC FROM DECEASED'S ESTATE

Adjustments can be made to take account of losses (compared with probate) realised on quoted shares sold within 12 months of death (IHTA 1984, ss 178–189).

15.3.1 Preliminary

Various terms and definitions (ie 'appropriate person', 'qualifying investments', 'relevant proportion', 'sale value' and 'value on death') are defined in the Glossary at the front of this book. Any reference to investments to which a claim relates is to all qualifying investments which, on the making of the claim, are taken into account in determining the loss on sale.

The deceased's personal representatives and the trustees of a settlement are each treated as a single and continuing body of persons (distinct from the persons who may from time to time be the personal representatives or trustees).

In any case where it is necessary to determine the price at which any investments were purchased or sold or the best consideration that could reasonably have been obtained on the sale of any investments, no account is taken of expenses (whether by way of commission, stamp duty or otherwise) which are incidental to the sale or purchase.

15.3.2 The relief
(IHTA 1984, s 179)

As a prerequisite to a claim being made by the appropriate person it is necessary to calculate the amount by which:

(1) the aggregate values which, otherwise, would be the values for IHT purposes of all the qualifying investments comprised in a person's estate immediately before his death which are sold by the appropriate person within 12 months immediately following the date of death

exceeds

(2) the aggregate values of those investments at the time they were so sold, taking the value of any particular investments for this purpose as the price for which they were sold or, if it is greater, the best consideration which could reasonably have been obtained for them at the time of sale.

In determining the IHT chargeable on death, the value of the investments to which the claim relates is treated as reduced by an amount equal to the loss on sale.

A claim made by the appropriate person must specify the capacity in which he makes the claim, and references to qualifying investments which are sold by him are to investments which, immediately before their sale, were held by him in his capacity to make the claim.

15.3.3 Effect of purchases
(IHTA 1984, s 180)

To prevent the selling of investments to realise a loss and reacquiring them shortly afterwards, an anti-avoidance provision is made. Thus if

(1) a claim is made and
(2) at any time during the period beginning on the date of death and ending two months after the date of the last sale within the 12-month period, the person making the claim purchases any qualifying investments in the same capacity as that in which he made the claim,

the loss on sale of the investments to which the claim relates is reduced by the proportion which the qualifying investments' aggregate purchase prices bears to the aggregate sale values. If the aggregate purchase prices equals or exceeds the aggregate sale values, the loss on sale is extinguished.

Furthermore, no account is taken of any qualifying investments purchased unless they are of the same description as one of the qualifying investments to which the claim relates. Two investments, not being investments in an authorised unit trust or common investment fund, are not treated as of the same description if they are separately listed on a recognised stock exchange, or separately dealt in on the AIM and an investment in one such trust or fund is not treated as of the same description as an investment in another such trust or fund.

15.3.4 Capital receipts
(IHTA 1984, s 181)

If at any time after death (whether during or after the 12-month period immediately following death) the appropriate person receives any capital payment which is attributable to any qualifying investments comprised in the deceased's estate immediately before death, and those investments are sold by him within that period, the price obtained (or the best consideration reasonably obtainable) is increased by the amount of the capital payment. Here, 'capital payment', in relation to any investment, does not include the price paid on the sale of the investment but, subject to that, includes any money or money's worth which does not constitute income for income tax purposes.

If the appropriate person receives or becomes entitled to receive a provisional allotment of company shares or debentures and disposes of his rights, the consideration for disposal purposes is treated as a capital payment attributable to those investments.

15.3.5 Payment of calls
(IHTA 1984, s 182)

If at any time after death (whether during or after the 12-month period) the appropriate person pays an amount under a call for any qualifying investments comprised in the deceased's estate immediately before death, and those investments are sold by him within that period, the value on death of those investments is the aggregate amount so paid and their value as otherwise determined.

15.3.6 Changes in holdings
(IHTA 1984, s 183)

The following procedure applies in any case where, within the 12-month period, there occurs in relation to any qualifying investments comprised in the deceased's estate immediately before death (here referred to as 'the original holding') a transaction to which TCGA 1992, s 127 applies, ie:

(1) a reorganisation under TCGA 1984, s 126(1); or
(2) the conversion of securities under TCGA 1992, s 132; or
(3) the issue by a company of shares or debentures in exchange for another company's shares or debentures in such circumstances that TCGA 1992, s 135 applies; or
(4) the issue by a company of shares or debentures under such an arrangement as is referred to in TCGA 1992, s 136; or
(5) any transaction relating to a unit trust scheme which corresponds to any of the above and to which TCGA 1984, s 78 applies (under TCGA 1992, s 127).

Where this procedure applies, the holding of investments which, as the result of the transaction, constitutes a new holding (under TCGA 1992, s 126(1)) are treated as being the same as the original holding; references below to the new holding are construed accordingly.

If the appropriate person gives, or becomes liable to give, as part of or in connection with the transaction concerned, any consideration for the new holding or any part of it, then, for the purposes set out below, the value on death of the new holding is treated as the aggregate of:

(1) the value on death of the original holding, and
(2) an amount equal to that consideration.

In any other case, the value on death of the new holding is taken to be the same as the value on death of the original holding. For this purpose, there is not treated as consideration given for the new holding or any part of it:

(1) any surrender, cancellation or other alteration of any of the investments comprised in the original holding or of the rights attached thereto, or
(2) any consideration consisting of any application, in paying up the new holding or any part of it, of assets of the company concerned or of any dividend or other distribution declared out of those assets but not made.

If, within the 12-month period, the appropriate person sells any investments comprised in the new holding, the value on death of those investments is determined by the formula:

$$\frac{Vs(H - S)}{(Vs + Vr)}$$

where: Vs = the sale value of the investments,
Vr = the market value at the time of the sale of any investments remaining in the new holding after the sale,
H = the value on death of the new holding, and
S = the value on death of any investments which were originally

comprised in the new holding but have been sold on any previous occasion(s).

For this purpose the market value of any investments at any time means the
value which they would otherwise have for IHT purposes if they were comprised in the estate of a person who died at that time.

15.3.7 Other exchanges
(IHTA 1984, s 184)

If, within the 12-month period, the appropriate person exchanges (with or
without payment by way of equality of exchange) any qualifying investments comprised in the deceased's estate immediately before death, and the
market value of those investments is at the date of exchange greater than
their value on death, then regardless of the nature of the property taken in
exchange, they are treated as having been sold at the date of exchange for a
price equal to that market value.

15.3.8 Acquisition of like investments
(IHTA 1984, s 185)

If, at any time within the 12-month period, the appropriate person sells any
investments which form part of a holding of investments which are all of the
same description and consist of investments:

(1) comprised in the deceased's estate immediately before death, and
(2) acquired by the appropriate person, by purchase or otherwise, after the
death,

the investments so sold are apportioned between those falling within (1) and
those falling within (2) above in the same proportion as, immediately before
the sale, the investments comprised in the holding and falling within (1)
above bore to the investments so comprised and falling within (2) above.

15.3.9 Value of part of a fund
(IHTA 1984, s 186)

In any case where part only of a holding of qualifying investments is comprised in a person's estate, and investments included in that holding are sold
by the appropriate person within the 12-month period, these rules apply as
if the entire holding were comprised in the estate; if a claim is made for
investments referred to in **15.3.8(1)**, the taxable fraction of the value of
those investments, as determined under these rules, is the value of that part
of those investments which is comprised in the estate. Here, 'taxable fraction' means the fraction of which the numerator is the value, as otherwise
determined, of the part of the holding referred to in **15.3.8(1)** and the
denominator is the value, as so determined, of the entire holding.

15.3.10 Cancelled investments
(IHTA 1984, s 186A)

Where any qualifying investments comprised in a person's estate immediately before his death are cancelled within the 12-month period immediately following the date of death without being replaced by other shares or securities, and held, immediately before cancellation, by the appropriate person, they are treated as having been sold by the appropriate person for a nominal consideration (one pound) immediately before cancellation.

15.3.11 Suspended investments
(IHTA 1984, s 186B)

The following rule applies to any qualifying investments comprised in a person's estate immediately before his death for which listing on a recognised stock exchange or dealing on the AIM is suspended at the end of the 12-month period immediately following the date of death ('the relevant period'). Where:

(1) any qualifying investments within this rule are, at the end of the relevant period, held by the appropriate person, and
(2) the value on death of those investments exceeds their value at the end of that period,

they are treated as having been sold by the appropriate person immediately before the end of that period for a price equal to their value at that time.

15.3.12 Attribution of values to specific investments
(IHTA 1984, s 187)

A special rule applies in determining the value for IHT purposes (and, accordingly, the market value for CGT purposes under TCGA 1992, s 274) of any investment (here referred to as a 'specific investment') which is included among the investments to which a claim relates.

In general, the value of a specific investment is its sale value. Subject to the further rules set out below, in a case where the calculation of the loss on sale of the investments to which a claim relates is affected by purchases (IHTA 1984, s 180):

(1) if the value on death of a specific investment exceeds its sale price, the investment's value is the aggregate of its sale value and an amount equal to the relevant proportion of the difference between its sale price and its value on death; and
(2) if the sale price of a specific investment exceeds its value on death, the investment's value is its sale value less an amount equal to the relevant proportion of the difference between its value on death and its sale price.

For these purposes, the sale value of a specific investment for which an amount has been paid under a call is reduced by the amount so paid.

Where the value on death of a new holding (under IHTA 1984, s 183(3)) includes an amount equal to the consideration there referred to, the sale value of any specific investment comprised in the new holding is reduced by an amount which bears to that consideration the like proportion as the value on death of the specific investment sold bears to the value on death of the whole of the new holding.

15.3.13 Limitation of loss on sale

In any case where the loss on sale of any investments for which an amount has been paid in under a call, or where a change in the holding equating the new holding with the original holding, would exceed their value as otherwise determined, their sale value is treated as being of such an amount that the loss on sale would be equal to their determined value.

15.3.14 Date of sale or purchase
(IHTA 1984, s 189)

Where any investments are sold or purchased by the appropriate person, the date on which they are sold or purchased is taken to be the date on which he entered into a contract to sell or purchase them. If the sale or purchase of any investments by the appropriate person results from the exercise (whether by him or by any other person) of an option, then the date on which the investments are sold or purchased is taken to be the date on which the option was granted.

15.4 SALE OF LAND FROM DECEASED'S ESTATE

Actual (higher or lower) sale proceeds can be substituted for probate valuation for land sold within three years of death (IHTA 1984, ss 190–198).

15.4.1 Preliminary
(IHTA 1984, s 190)

Various definitions apply for the purposes of this relief; 'appropriate person', 'interest in land', 'sale price', 'sale value' and 'value on death' are all defined in the Glossary at the front of this work.

For the purposes of this adjustment the deceased's personal representatives and the trustees of a settlement are each treated as a single and continuing body of persons (distinct from the persons who may from time to time be the personal representatives or trustees).

In any case where it is necessary to determine the price at which any interest was purchased or sold, or the best consideration that could reasonably have been obtained on the sale of any interest, no account is taken of expenses (whether by way of commission, stamp duty or otherwise) which are incidental to the sale or purchase.

15.4.2 The relief
(IHTA 1984, s 191)

Where

(1) an interest in land is comprised in a person's estate immediately before his death, and
(2) is sold by the appropriate person within three years immediately following the date of death, and
(3) the appropriate person makes a claim stating the capacity in which he makes it,

the value for IHT purposes of that interest and of any other interest in land comprised in that estate and sold within that period by the person making the claim acting in the same capacity is, subject to the following provisions, its sale value. This does not apply to an interest if its sale value would differ from its value on death by less than the lower of £1,000 and 5 per cent of its value on death. This valuation basis does not apply to an interest if its sale is by a personal representative or trustee to:

(1) a person who, at any time between the death and the sale, has been beneficially entitled to, or to an interest in possession in, property comprising the interest sold, or
(2) the spouse or a child or remoter descendant of such a person, or
(3) trustees of a settlement under which either (1) or (2) has an interest in possession in property comprising the interest sold

or a sale in connection with which the vendor or any of the above persons obtains a right to acquire the interest sold or any other interest in the same land. Here, a person is treated as having in the property comprised in an unadministered estate (under IHTA 1984, s 91(2)) the same interest as he would have if the estate's administration had been completed.

15.4.3 Effect of purchases
(IHTA 1984, s 192)

The following rule applies where a claim is made and, at any time during the period beginning on the date of death and ending four months after the last of the sales made within three years following death, the person making the claim purchases any interests in land in the same capacity as that in which he makes the claim.

If the interests' aggregate purchase prices equals or exceeds the aggregate of the sale prices (as adjusted under IHTA 1984, ss 193–195) of all the interests to which the claim relates, no claim can be made; otherwise, the further adjustment described below applies. In that adjustment 'the appropriate fraction' means the fraction of which:

(1) the numerator is the aggregate of the said purchase prices, and

(2) the denominator is the aggregate of the said sale prices.

Where this further adjustment applies, an addition is made to the sale price of every interest to which the claim relates. Such addition is equal to the appropriate fraction of the difference between the value of the interest on death and its sale price (as adjusted under ss 193–196).

Where the value of an interest on death is less than its sale price (as adjusted under ss 193–196), the further adjustment applies as if it provided for a reduction instead of an increase in the sale price.

15.4.4 Changes between death and sale

Where the conditions set out below are not satisfied in relation to any interest to which the claim relates, an addition is made to the interest's sale price; the addition amount is equal to the difference between:

(1) the value of the interest on death, and

(2) what that value would have been if the circumstances prevailing at the date of the sale and by reason of which the conditions are not satisfied had prevailed immediately before death.

The conditions are that:

(1) the interest was the same in all respects and with the same incidents at the date of both death and sale; and

(2) the land in which the interest subsists was in the same state and with the same incidents at the date of both death and sale.

If after the date of death, but before the date of sale, compensation becomes payable under any enactment to the appropriate person or any other person liable for IHT attributable to the value of the interest because:

(1) of the imposition of a restriction on the use or development of the land in which the interest subsists, or

(2) the interest's value is reduced for any other reason,

the imposition of the restriction or the other cause of the reduction in value is ignored for these purposes, but there is added to the interest's sale price an amount equal to the compensation.

Where the interest's value on death is less than it would have been, the further adjustment applies as if, instead of providing for an addition to be made to the sale price, it provided for that price to be reduced to what it would have been had the change in circumstances not satisfied not occurred.

15.4.5 Leases
(IHTA 1984, s 194)

Where the claim relates to a lessee's interest under a lease the duration of which at the date of death does not exceed 50 years, an addition is made to the interest's sale price; the addition amount is equal to the appropriate fraction of the interest's value on death.

Here, 'the appropriate fraction' means:

$$\frac{P(1) - P(2)}{P(1)}$$

where: $P(1)$ = the percentage that would be derived from the Table in TCGA 1984, Sched 8 for the duration of the lease at the date of the death, and

$P(2)$ = the percentage that would be so derived for the duration of the lease at the date of the sale.

These percentages are derived from the Table in TCGA 1992, Sched 8, para 1 (see Table 15.1).

If the lease's duration is not an exact number of years the percentage to be derived from the above-mentioned Table is for the whole number of years plus one-twelfth of the difference between that and the percentage for the next higher number of years for each odd month, counting an odd 14 days or more as one month.

15.4.6 Valuation by reference to other interests
(IHTA 1984, s 195)

If in determining in relation to a claim any interest's value on death, any other interests, whether in the same or other land, are taken into account. An addition is made to the interest's sale price. The addition amount is equal to the difference between the interest's value on death and the value which would have been the value on death if no other interests had been taken into account.

15.4.7 Sales to beneficiaries etc and exchanges
(IHTA 1984, s 196)

This rule applies where a person who makes a claim, acting in the same capacity as being the claimant:

(1) sells an interest to which the relief would apply but for the exclusion of sales to persons beneficially entitled to an interest in possession, or where there is a right of reacquisition, or

(2) within the three-year period immediately following the death exchanges

Table 15.1

Years	Percentage	Years	Percentage
50 or more	100.000	24	79.622
49	99.657	23	78.055
48	99.989	22	76.399
47	98.902	21	74.635
46	98.490	20	72.770
45	98.059	19	70.791
44	97.595	18	68.697
43	97.107	17	66.470
42	96.593	16	64.116
41	96.041	15	61.617
40	95.457	14	58.971
39	94.842	13	56.167
38	94.189	12	53.191
37	93.497	11	50.038
36	92.761	10	46.695
35	91.981	9	43.154
34	91.156	8	39.399
33	90.280	7	35.414
32	89.354	6	31.195
31	88.371	5	26.722
30	87.330	4	21.983
29	86.226	3	16.959
28	85.053	2	11.629
27	83.816	1	5.983
26	82.496	0	0.000
25	81.100		

(with or without any payment by way of equality of exchange) any interest in land which was comprised in the deceased's estate immediately before his death,

and the interest's sale price, or in the case of an exchange its market value at the date of exchange, exceeds its value on death.

Where this rule applies, an addition is made to the sale price of any interest to which the claim relates; the addition amount, if the claim relates to one interest only, is equal to the excess, and if the claim relates to more than one interest, is equal to the appropriate fraction of that excess.

Here 'the appropriate fraction' in relation to any interest to which the claim relates is the fraction of which:

(1) the numerator is the difference between that interest's value on death and its sale price (as adjusted under IHTA 1984, ss 193–195), and

(2) the denominator is the aggregate of that difference and the corresponding differences for all the other interests to which the claim relates,

and such aggregate is calculated without regard to which is the greater, in the case of any particular interest, of its value on death and its sale price.

15.4.8 Compulsory acquisition more than three years after death
(IHTA 1984, s 197)

If after the end of the three-year period an interest in land is acquired from the appropriate person under a notice to treat served before the death or within that three-year period, by an authority possessing powers of compulsory acquisition, the adjustment applies in relation to the interest as it applies in relation to interests sold within that period. This does not apply in relation to an interest if its sale value would exceed its value on death. The effect of this is that a claim for relief can be made as if there had been an actual sale within the three-year period.

15.4.9 Sales in fourth year after death
(IHTA 1984, s 197A)

Where an interest in land is comprised in a person's estate immediately before his death, and it is sold by the appropriate person in the fourth year immediately following the date of the death, otherwise than to an authority having compulsory purchase powers, the interest is treated as having been sold within the three-year period immediately following death. This does not apply in relation to an interest if its sale value would exceed its value on death.

15.4.10 Date of sale or purchase
(IHTA 1984, s 198)

The date on which an interest in land is sold or purchased by the appropriate person is taken to be the date on which he enters into a contract to sell or purchase it. If the sale or purchase of any interest by the appropriate person results from the exercise (whether by him or by any other person) of an option granted not more than six months earlier, the date on which the interest is sold or purchased is taken to be the date on which the option was granted.

If an interest is acquired from the appropriate person under a notice to treat served by an authority possessing powers of compulsory acquisition, the date on which the interest is sold is taken to be that on which compensation for the acquisition is agreed or otherwise determined (variations on appeal being disregarded for this purpose) or, if earlier, the date when the authority enters on the land in pursuance of its powers.

If an interest in land is acquired from the appropriate person:

(1) in England, Scotland or Wales by virtue of a general vesting declaration

within the meaning of the Compulsory Purchase (Vesting Declarations) Act 1981 or, in Scotland, the Town and Country Planning (Scotland) Act 1972, Sched 24 (IHTA 1984, s 198(4)(a)), or

(2) in Northern Ireland by way of a vesting order,

the date on which it is sold by the appropriate person is taken to be the last day of the period specified in the declaration or, in Northern Ireland, the date on which the vesting order becomes operative.

SETTLEMENTS

16.1 INTRODUCTION

Numerous definitions are given under IHTA 1984, s 43 on the matter of settlements. Definitions for 'settlement', 'settlor', 'trustee', 'reversionary interest' and 'qualifying interest in possession' are given in the Glossary at the front of this book. Further definitions related to settlements are set out below. Settlements with no interest in possession are dealt with in **17**.

16.1.1 Settlement of lease of property

A lease of property:

(1) for a life or lives, or
(2) for a period ascertainable only by reference to a death, or
(3) terminable on, or at a date ascertainable only by reference to, a death

is treated as a settlement and the property as settled property unless the lease was granted for full consideration in money or money's worth. Where a lease not granted as one at a rack rent will at any time become a lease at an increased rent, it is treated as terminable at that time.

16.1.2 Partnership assurance policies

ESC F10 clarifies the treatment of partnership assurance policies. A partnership assurance scheme under which each partner effects a policy on his own life in trust for the other partners is not regarded as a settlement for IHT purposes if the following conditions are fulfilled:

(1) the premiums paid on the policy are not intended to confer gratuitous benefit under IHTA 1984, s 10;
(2) the policy was effected before 15 September 1976 and has not been varied on or after that date (but the exercise of a power of appointment under a 'discretionary' trust policy is not regarded as a variation for this purpose); and
(3) the policy's trusts are governed by English or Scottish law, provided

that in the latter case the policy does not directly or indirectly involve a partnership itself as a separate persona.

16.1.3 Northern Ireland

References to property held in trust for persons include, in Northern Ireland, references to property standing limited to persons and as if the lease did not under the Renewable Leasehold Conversion Act 1849 include a lease in perpetuity (s 1) or a lease under s 37.

16.1.4 Beneficiary occupying dwelling-house as part of trust property

SP 10/79 is concerned with a power for trustees to allow a beneficiary to occupy a dwelling-house. Many wills and settlements contain a clause empowering the trustees to permit a beneficiary to occupy a dwelling-house which forms part of the trust property on such terms as they think fit. The Revenue does not regard the existence of such a power as excluding any interest in possession in the property.

Where there is no such interest in possession, the Revenue does not regard the exercise of power as creating one if the effect is merely to allow non-exclusive occupation, or to create a contractual tenancy for full consideration. The Revenue also takes the view that no interest in possession arises on the creation of a lease for a term or a periodic tenancy for less than full consideration, though this will normally give rise to an exit charge under the no interest in possession rules (under IHTA 1984, s 65(1)(b)). On the other hand, if the power is drawn in terms wide enough to cover the creation of an exclusive or joint right of residence, albeit revocable, for a definite or indefinite period, and is exercised with the intention of providing a particular beneficiary with a permanent home, the Revenue normally regards the exercise as creating an interest in possession. If the trustees in the exercise of their powers grant a lease for life for less than full consideration, this is also regarded as creating an interest in possession (under IHTA 1984, ss 43(3), 50(6)).

A similar view is taken where the power is exercised over property in which another beneficiary had an interest in possession up to the time of the exercise.

16.1.5 More than one settlor
(IHTA 1984, s 44)

Where more than one person is a settlor in relation to a settlement and the circumstances so require, the special rules for settlements apply as if the settled property were comprised in separate settlements.

16.1.6 Interest in possession: Scotland
(IHTA 1984, s 46)

In Scotland, any reference to an interest in possession in settled property is a reference to an interest of any kind under a settlement by virtue of which the person in right of that interest is entitled to the enjoyment of the property, or would be so entitled if the property were capable of enjoyment; this includes an interest of an assignee under an assignation of an interest of any kind (other than a reversionary interest) in property subject to a proper liferent. The person in right of such an interest at any time is deemed to be entitled to a corresponding interest in the whole or any part of the property comprised in the settlement.

16.1.7 Reversionary interest as excluded property
(IHTA 1984, s 48)

A reversionary interest is excluded property, unless it:

(1) was acquired (by the person currently or previously entitled to it) for a consideration in money or money's worth, or
(2) is one to which either the settlor or his spouse is or has been beneficially entitled, or
(3) is an interest expectant on the determination of a lease treated as a settlement.

Reversionary interests acquired for value are not excluded property. This is to prevent a life tenant, who is deemed to be entitled to an entire trust fund, reducing his estate by paying for the reversionary interest, as he would thereby have an absolute interest in the trust fund, which he is already deemed to have, and his estate would be reduced by the cash paid for the reversionary interest.

Where property comprised in a settlement is situated outside the UK, the property (but not a reversionary interest in it) is excluded property unless the settlor was UK-domiciled when the settlement was made. The rule that such property is excluded property if the person beneficially entitled to it is non-UK domiciled applies to a reversionary interest in the property, but does not otherwise apply in relation to the property.

Where FOTRA securities are held by a settlement, they are also excluded property (under IHTA 1984, s 6(2)) if a person neither domiciled nor ordinarily resident in the UK is entitled to a qualifying interest in possession in them, or there is no qualifying interest in possession in them but it is shown that all known persons for whose benefit the settled property or income from it has been or might be applied, or who are or might become beneficially entitled to an interest in possession in it, are persons neither domiciled nor ordinarily resident in the UK. As to the material time for determining whether FOTRA securities constitute excluded property, see *Von Ernst & Cie SA and others v CIR* [1980] STC 111, CA.

Various schemes have attempted to exploit these provisions, but they have either been rendered ineffective by amendments applying after 19 April 1977 (*Von Ernst & Cie SA* above; *Minden Trust (Cayman) Ltd v CIR* [1985] STC 758), or failed (*CIR v Brandenburg* [1982] STC 555, ChD); *Montague Trust (Jersey) Ltd and others v CIR* [1989] STC 477).

Where property ceases to be comprised in one settlement and becomes comprised in another (without any person in the meantime having become entitled to it – and not merely to an interest in possession in it), the property in the second settlement is only excluded property if these requirements are satisfied by both settlements. If the property in both settlements comprises FOTRA securities, and there is no qualifying interest in possession in them, the rule regarding FOTRA securities set out above applies. This does not apply where a reversionary interest in the property expectant on the termination of a qualifying interest in possession subsisting under the first settlement was settled on the trusts of the second settlement before 10 December 1981.

Excluded property is not relevant property for no interest in possession trusts, and is not subject to the special IHT charges for discretionary trusts (IHTA 1984, ss 58–85). However, a reversionary interest is not treated as excluded property for the exit charge and the depreciatory transaction charge, thereby permitting reinvestment in overseas property without crystallising an IHT charge.

The Revenue has confirmed in SP E9 that property is regarded as becoming comprised in a settlement when it, or other property which it represents, is introduced by the settlor.

16.1.8 Excluded property settlements by people domiciled overseas
(IHTA 1984, ss 43, 44, 48)

Tax Bulletin 27 (February 1997) sets out the Revenue's response to the question of how the IHT provisions on excluded property apply to the assets of a settlement made by a non-UK domiciled person where all, or only some, of the settled assets are situated outside the UK when a chargeable event occurs, or a UK-domiciled person has also provided property or funds for the purposes of that settlement.

For persons domiciled abroad, IHT generally applies only to their UK assets; it treats their overseas assets as excluded property (ie not within the charge to IHT (IHTA 1984, s 6(1)). For assets owned outright, it is the owner's domicile at the time of a tax charge that is relevant in deciding whether the assets are excluded property.

Slightly different rules apply to property held in a settlement. An asset is excluded property if it is situated abroad when a chargeable event occurs and if the settlor (defined in IHTA 1984, s 44) was domiciled outside the UK at the time the settlement was made. However, an 'excluded' asset is not always completely irrelevant for the purposes of IHT. So, an excluded asset in a person's estate may still affect the valuation of another asset in the estate (eg an excluded shareholding in an unquoted company may affect the value of a similar holding in the estate which is not excluded). The value of an excluded asset at the time the asset becomes comprised in a settlement may be relevant in determining the rate of any tax charge arising on the settlement under the IHT rules concerning no interest in possession trusts (IHTA 1984, ss 68(5), 66(4), 69(3)).

Domicile is a concept of general law but, in certain circumstances (eg IHTA 1984, s 267), a person with a general law domicile abroad can be treated as having a UK domicile for IHT purposes.

Settlor adds assets to existing settlement

In the light of the definitions of 'settlement' and 'settled property' in IHTA 1984, s 43, the Revenue view is that a settlement in relation to any particular asset is made at the time when that asset is transferred to the settlement trustees to hold on the declared trusts. Thus, assets added to a settlor's own settlement made at an earlier time when the settlor was domiciled abroad are not 'excluded', wherever they may be situated, if the settlor has a UK domicile at the time of making the addition.

In determining the tax treatment of particular assets held in the same settlement it may, therefore, be necessary to consider the settlor's domicile at times other than when the settlement was first made. And if assets added at different times have become mixed, any dealings with the settled fund after the addition(s) may also need to be considered.

Several persons contribute to single settlement

There are rules (IHTA 1984, s 44(2)) which provide that assets contributed to a 'single' settlement by more than one settlor are to be treated as comprised in separate settlements for IHT purposes if 'the circumstances so require'. There is no definition of 'required circumstances' or statutory guidance on how the assets in the single, actual settlement are to be attributed to the deemed separate settlements. However, the provision is similar in terms to FA 1975, Sched 5, para 1(8), which was considered by Chadwick J in *Hatton v CIR* [1992] STC 140. In the light of the decision in that case the Revenue takes the view that:

(1) the determination of the extent to which overseas assets in a settlement are excluded property by reason of the settlor's domicile is a relevant 'required circumstance';

(2) where a clear, or reasonably sensible, attribution of settled property between the contributions made by several settlors is possible, there will be a separate settlement, with its own attributed assets, for each contributor for IHT purposes;

(3) if such an attribution is not feasible, each separate settlement will comprise all the assets of the single, actual settlement.

Trust records

It follows from the above comments that the trustees of a settlement should keep adequate records to enable any necessary attribution of the settled property to be made if either:

(1) the settlor has added further assets to the settlement after it was made; or
(2) two or more persons have contributed funds for the purposes of the settlement.

16.2 INTERESTS IN POSSESSION

16.2.1 What is an 'interest in possession'?

The House of Lords' decision

The House of Lords has provided an authoritative statement on the meaning of 'interest in possession' in *Pearson v CIR* [1980] STC 318, HL. First, there must be a *present right* to the *present enjoyment* of the property. Secondly, the trustees must not have a power to withhold income, and it follows that

(1) a power to accumulate income which would prevent the beneficiary from having an interest in possession (but accumulations held solely for the person having an interest) does not amount to a power to withhold income;
(2) an overriding power of appointment which could be used to defeat a beneficiary's interest does not prevent the beneficiary from being in possession, if it does not affect his right to income which has already arisen (SP E1);
(3) the possibility of an interest's future defeasance does not prevent it from being an interest in possession until the happening of the relevant event; and
(4) a power of revocation does not prevent an interest from being in possession until it is exercised.

The Revenue view on powers of appointment in this context are set out in SP E1.

Thirdly, it is not necessary for the interests of individual beneficiaries to be defined. They can for instance be subject to powers of appointment. In any particular case, the exemption depends on the precise terms of the trust and power concerned, and on the facts to which they apply. In general, however, the official view is that the conditions do not restrict the application of IHTA 1984, s 71 (accumulation and maintenance settlements) to settlements where the individual beneficiaries' interests are defined and indefeasible.

Fourthly, the requirement of s 71 is that one or more persons will, on or before attaining a specified age not exceeding 25, become beneficially entitled to, or to an interest in possession in, the settled property or part of it. It is considered that settled property would meet this condition if at the relevant time it must vest for an interest in possession in some member of an existing class of potential beneficiaries on or before that member attains age 25. The existence of a special power of appointment would not of itself exclude s 71 if neither the exercise nor the release of the power could break the condition. To achieve this effect might, however, require careful drafting.

Fifthly, the inclusion of issue as possible objects of a special power of appointment would exclude a settlement from the benefit of s 71 if the power would allow the trustees to prevent any interest in possession in the settled property from commencing before the beneficiary concerned attained the age specified. It would depend on the precise words of the settlement and the facts to which they had to be applied whether a particular settlement satisfied the conditions of s 71(1). In many cases the rules against perpetuity and accumulations would operate to prevent an effective appointment outside those conditions. However, the application of s 71 is not a matter for a once-and-for-all decision. It is a question that needs to be kept in mind at all times when there is settled property in which no interest in possession subsists.

Finally, a trust which otherwise satisfies the requirement of s 71(1)(a) would not be disqualified by the existence of a power to vary or determine the respective shares of members of the class (even to the extent of excluding some members altogether) provided the power is exercisable only in favour of a person under age 25 who is a member of the class.

SP E1 also gives a number of practical illustrations of the application of s 71. The examples set out below are based on a settlement for the children of X contingently on attaining 25, the trustees being required to accumulate the income so far as it is not applied for the maintenance of X's children.

A – Settlement made on X's marriage who as yet has no children

Section 71 will not apply until a child is born; that event will give rise to a charge for tax under IHTA 1984, s 65.

B – Trustees have power to apply income for benefit of X's unmarried sister

Section 71 does not apply because the condition that no interest in possession subsists in it is not met.

C – X has power to appoint capital not only among his children but also among his remoter issue

Section 71 does not apply (unless the power can be exercised only in favour of persons who would thereby acquire interests in possession on or before attaining age 25). A release of the disqualifying power would give rise to a charge for tax under s 65. Its exercise would give rise to a charge under s 65.

D – Trustees have overriding power of appointment in favour of other persons

Section 71 does not apply (unless the power can be exercised only in favour of persons who would thereby acquire interests in possession on or before attaining age 25). A release of the disqualifying power would give rise to a charge for tax under s 65. Its exercise would give rise to a charge under s 65.

E – Settled property revocably appointed to one of the children contingently on his attaining age 25 and appointment now irrevocable

If the power to revoke prevents s 71 from applying (as it would eg if the property thereby became subject to a power of appointment as at C or D), tax will be chargeable under s 65 when the appointment is made irrevocable.

F – Trust to accumulate income is expressed to be during life of settlor

As the settlor may live beyond the 25th birthday of any of his children, the trust does not satisfy the condition that on a specified date no later than his 25th birthday a child will become beneficially entitled to the property or to an interest in possession therein; hence s 71 does not apply.

It is important to distinguish between 'administrative powers' (eg incurring expenses, payment of taxes), and 'dispositive powers' (eg to dispose of the trust's net income).

Beneficiary's right to income and whether he has interest in possession

Section 31 of the Trustee Act 1925 can affect a beneficiary's right to income, and thus whether he has an interest in possession:

(1) An appointment of income contingent upon the occurrence of the vesting event was intended to carry the right to the intermediate income of the fund (Trustee Act 1925, s 31(1); *Swales and others v CIR* [1984] STC 413, ChD).

(2) Where a settlement provides for infant beneficiaries to become entitled to receive capital at a 'vesting date', s 31 generally operates so as to

confer, on each such beneficiary as he attains his majority, an entitlement to a share of the income. Where s 31 applies to property appointed after the commencement date for the Family Law Reform Act 1969 out of a settlement created before that date, the beneficiary's interest in possession is regarded as arising at age 18 (SP E8).

(3) It is possible for the terms of a settlement to override the Trustee Act 1925, but, in the absence of an express provision, the Act will operate to confer an interest in possession.

Where a beneficiary who is entitled to an interest in possession (the right to receive income) becomes absolutely entitled to the capital, his interest is 'enlarged'. No IHT is payable by the trustees on such an occasion. Where an interest in possession comes to an end during the beneficiary's lifetime, he is generally regarded as having made a PET equal to the value of the settled property in which he had an interest in possession.

Swales and others v CIR (above) was concerned with the effect of the Trustee Act 1925, s 31. In 1970 trustees had appointed income from a trust fund to R absolutely, although complex provisions in the trust prevented R's right to the income from vesting until one of her children became 21 in 1976 (the vesting date). The Revenue issued a determination on the basis that no appointment could come into effect unless and until the vesting event occurred. Accordingly, R's interest under the 1970 appointment took effect only in 1976 when her eldest child attained age 21. The result was that there had been no interest in possession in the fund before that date. Then, on that date, capital distribution equal to the fund's value should be deemed to have been made on that date.

The trustees contended that the appointment to the daughter took effect as an appointment of income in the fund subject to the vesting event occurring and to her then being alive. Consequently the trustees were obliged to pay to her the fund's intermediate income, and that obligation gave the daughter a right to the enjoyment of the income and thus an interest in possession in the fund before the vesting date. Therefore, they argued, there was no capital distribution on the vesting date. The High Court accepted this contention and allowed the appeal, holding that the interest in possession had arisen in 1970 when the trustees had appointed income from a trust fund to R absolutely.

Several cases have been concerned with the existence or otherwise of an interest in possession. In *Moore & Osborne v CIR (in re Trafford's Settlements)* [1984] STC 236, ChD, a settlor directed that income from certain trust funds was to be held upon protective trusts during his life. The trustees were to pay or apply the income to himself or to any wife or children he might have as they in their discretion saw fit. He died in 1978, unmarried and childless. The Revenue issued a determination on the basis that the settlement had created a protected life interest and the settlor had been beneficially entitled to an interest in possession in the trust funds immediately before his death. The High Court held that he was not so entitled, and that the settlement had created an immediate discretionary trust. The fact that the settlor was the sole existing object of the discretionary trust did not give him an interest in possession. The possibility, albeit remote, that another discretionary beneficiary might come into existence prevented him from having an immediate entitlement to trust income as it arose.

In *Gartside v CIR* [1968] AC 553, HL, an estate duty case, the House of Lords held that the beneficiaries of a discretionary trust, not being entitled either individually or collectively to receive any part of the trust's income in any year, did not have interests in possession in the trust fund. It was held that an 'interest in possession' must mean an interest which enables a person to claim now whatever may be the subject of his interest.

In *A-G v Power and another* [1906] 2 IR 272, KB property was held on trust for H, with remainder to his brother if he should die childless before age 21. The trustees were to receive the income arising during H's minority out of which they were to accumulate the surplus on trust for H if he should attain age 21 or, if he should not, for the persons who should ultimately become entitled to the property. H died before reaching 21. The High Court held that he had never become entitled to an interest in possession in the property, as he had never had any entitlement to the income from the property.

Life tenant giving up interest in possession

If a life tenant gives up his interest in possession and the property is thereafter held on discretionary trusts, he is deemed to have made a chargeable transfer, and not a PET.

Example

> Edith, a 90-year-old woman, is the life tenant of a trust which has investments worth £1m. They are, however, low yielding investments and she receives income of only £25,000 per annum.
>
> The value of her life interest (if she could assign it) might be very modest, bearing in mind her age and the level of income. However, if she voluntarily gives up her interest in possession so that another individual becomes entitled to it (or to the trust capital itself), Edith is treated as if she had made a PET of £1m. The trustees are liable to pay the IHT if she dies within the seven-year period.

There is a major distinction between deemed PETs made by life tenants and actual PETs made by individuals in their personal capacity. The 'loss to the donor' principle does not apply where property passes from an interest in possession settlement. The charge is based on the value of the property comprised in the settlement (IHTA 1984, s 52). The same rule applies where a life tenant gives up his interest and there is an immediately chargeable transfer because the settled property is thereafter held on discretionary trusts. However, whereas the settled property is valued without reference to any shares owned by the life tenant personally, the value of any transfer made by him out of his personal shareholding must take into account shares owned by the trust (IHTA 1984, s 49).

Example

> Zorah owns 39 per cent of NDG Ltd in her personal capacity, and the trustees of a settlement in which she has an interest in possession have 13 per cent.
>
> The value of a 52 per cent shareholding in NDG Ltd is £1m. The value of a 39 per cent shareholding is only £500,000 (because of the absence of control). A 13 per cent interest in isolation is worth only £100,000.
>
> If Zorah were to gift 13 per cent of her personal shareholding she would be deemed to make a PET of £500,000 (£1m less the value of the remaining holding by her and the trustees). However, if her interest in possession came to an end the PET would only be £100,000.

A person entitled to benefit when the life tenant's interest in possession ceases has a reversionary interest (see **16.3**), which is normally excluded property.

Example

> Aileen owns a property in her personal capacity which is worth £1m. She is the life tenant of a trust which has investments worth £4m. She also has a reversionary interest under another settlement worth £15m. Aileen's estate would be assessed as follows:
>
> | | £ |
> |---|---|
> | Free estate | 1,000,000 |
> | Settled property with interest in possession | 4,000,000 |
> | | 5,000,000 |

16.2.2 Treatment of interests in possession
(IHTA 1984, s 49)

A person beneficially entitled to an interest in possession is treated as beneficially entitled to the property in which the interest subsists. This does not apply for the purpose of determining the extent of a chargeable transfer where the interest arises following a disposition for a consideration in money or money's worth.

SP E6 sets out the effect for IHT of the exercise by trustees of a power to augment a beneficiary's income out of capital. In the normal case where the beneficiary concerned is life tenant of the settled property, this has no immediate consequences for IHT. The life tenant already has an interest in possession and, under s 49(1), is treated as beneficially entitled to the property. The enlargement of that interest to an absolute interest does not change this position (IHTA 1984, s 53(2)) and it is not affected by the relationship of the beneficiary to the testator.

In the exceptional case where the beneficiary is not the life tenant, or in which there is no subsisting interest in possession, the exercise of the power would give rise to an IHT charge under IHTA 1984, s 52(1), although this may be a PET, or an exit charge under s 65(1)(a). If the life tenant is the surviving spouse of a testator who died before 13 November 1974, exemption might be available under IHTA 1984, Sched 6, para 2.

The exercise of the power would be regarded as distributing the settled property rather than as reducing its value, so that ss 52(3) (charge on termination of interest in possession) and 65(1)(b) (reduction of value of settlement with no interest in possession) would not be in point.

In correspondence dated 12 February 1976, the Revenue set out its understanding of the meaning of the expression. This is that an interest in possession in settled property exists where the person having the interest has the immediate entitlement (subject to any prior claim by the trustees for expenses or other outgoings properly payable out of income) to any income produced by that property as the income arises. However, a discretion or power, in whatever form, which can be exercised after income arises so as to withhold it from that person negates the existence of an interest in possession. For this purpose, a power to accumulate income is regarded as a power to withhold it, unless any accumulations must be held solely for the person having the interest or his personal representatives.

On the other hand, the existence of a mere power of revocation or appointment, the exercise of which would determine the interest wholly or in part (but which, so long as it remains unexercised, does not affect the beneficiary's immediate entitlement to income) does not, in the Revenue view, prevent the interest from being an interest in possession.

16.2.3 Interests in part only
(IHTA 1984, s 50)

Where a person beneficially entitled to an interest in possession is entitled to part only of the property's income (if any), his interest in the underlying property is deemed to be such part only of the property as his share of the income bears to the whole of the income.

Where such a person is entitled to a specified amount of income (or the whole of it less a specified amount) in any period, his interest in the property is such part thereof (or in the whole less such part) as produces that amount of income in that period. If a person were entitled to an annuity, or some other specified amount of income, it would be possible to vary his share of the property by changing the investment policy. This is prevented by imposing limits within which the yield on the trust fund supporting the payment of the income must be deemed to fall. The Treasury prescribes a higher and a lower rate for calculation purposes (the CTT (Settled Property Income Yield) Order 1980 (SI No 1000)):

(1) The *higher prescribed rate* is linked to the FT Actuaries Indices for British Government Stocks ('irredeemables').
(2) The *lower prescribed rate* is linked to the FT Actuaries All-Share Index.
(3) The value of the part of a property which produces a specified amount (or the value of the whole of a property less the value of the part producing that specified amount), is if IHT is chargeable on the value of the part producing the specified amount of income, *not less* than it would be if the property produced income at the *higher prescribed rate* (but such value cannot exceed the value of the whole property), and if IHT is chargeable on the value of the whole of a property less the value of the part producing the specified amount of income, not more than it would be if the property produced income at the *lower prescribed rate*.

This form of calculation is not followed where chargeable transfers are made simultaneously and IHT is chargeable on the value of the part producing the income as well as on the value of the remainder.

Where a person beneficially entitled to an interest in possession is not entitled to any income of the property but is entitled, jointly or in common with other persons, to the property's use and enjoyment, his interest is a fractional share computed by reference to the annual value of his interest compared to the total annual value of all interests in the property. It is not clear how the value of the share of such a person, who also has a small interest in income, is to be calculated.

Where a lease of property is treated as a settlement, the lessee's interest in the property is taken to subsist in the whole of the property less such part of it as corresponds to the proportion which the value of the lessor's interest bears to the total value of the property.

16.2.4 Disposal of interest in possession
(IHTA 1984, s 51)

Where a person beneficially entitled to an interest in possession disposes of his interest, the disposal is not a transfer of value, but is treated as the coming to an end of his interest and IHT is charged accordingly (*Pearson and others v CIR* [1980] STC 318). Where a disposition for the maintenance of the family (IHTA 1984, s 11) is a disposal of an interest in possession, such interest is not thereby treated as coming to an end.

See also below with regard to charges on termination of interest.

16.2.5 **Charge on termination of interest in possession**
(IHTA 1984, s 52)

Where, at any time during the life of a person beneficially entitled to an interest in possession, his interest comes to an end, IHT is charged as if at that time he had made a transfer of value equal to the value of his share of the underlying property.

If the interest comes to an end by being disposed of by such person, and the disposal is for a consideration in money or money's worth, IHT is charged as if the property's value were reduced by the amount of the consideration. But in determining that amount the value of a reversionary interest in the property, or of any interest in other property comprised in the same settlement, is left out of account. This condition is regarded as satisfied where it is a close company that in fact becomes entitled to the property or disposes of the interest (SP E5).

Where a transaction is made between the trustees of a settlement and a person who is, or is connected with:

(1) the person beneficially entitled to an interest in the property, or
(2) a person beneficially entitled to any other interest in that property or to any interest in any other property comprised in the settlement, or
(3) a person for whose benefit any of the settled property may be applied,

and as a result of the transaction, the first-mentioned property's value is less than it would be but for the transaction, a corresponding part of the interest is deemed to come to an end, unless the transaction is such that, were the trustees beneficially entitled to the settled property, it would not be a transfer of value. References here to any property or to an interest in any property include part of any property or interest.

The IHT chargeable on the cessation of part of an interest is charged as if the value of the property (or part) in which the interest subsisted were a corresponding part of the whole. If that value to which or to an interest in which a person becomes beneficially entitled is less than the value on which IHT would otherwise be chargeable, IHT is chargeable on a value equal to the difference.

In a letter to the Law Society (published in the *Law Society's Gazette*, 9 May 1990) the Revenue notified a change of IHT practice relating to the cessation of an interest in possession in settled property. When cessation occurs during the lifetime of the person entitled to it, IHTA 1984, s 52(1) states that the value for IHT purposes is 'equal to the value of the property in which his interest subsisted'. Previously, this value had been determined as a rateable proportion of the aggregate value of that settled property and other property of a similar kind in the person's estate. The Revenue's current view is that, in these circumstances, settled property in which the interest subsisted should be valued in isolation without reference to any similar property. This statement of the Revenue position is made without prejudice to the application in an appropriate case of the *Ramsay* principle or the associated operations provisions (IHTA 1984, s 268).

Exceptions to charge on termination

There are a number of exceptions to the charge on termination of an interest in possession:

(1) No IHT is charged if the settled property is excluded property.
(2) No IHT is charged if the person whose interest in the property ceases becomes, on the same occasion, beneficially entitled to the property or to another interest in possession in the property. This condition is regarded as satisfied where it is a close company that in fact becomes entitled to the property or disposes of the interest (SP E5).
(3) No IHT is charged if the interest comes to an end during the settlor's life and on the same occasion the property in which the interest subsisted reverts to the settlor:
  (a) unless the settlor or his spouse had acquired a reversionary interest in the property for a consideration in money or money's worth; or
  (b) unless a reversionary interest was been transferred into a settlement after 9 March 1981.
(4) No IHT is charged on the occasion when the interest comes to an end:
  (a) where the settlor's spouse or, where the settlor died less than two years earlier, the settlor's widow(er) becomes beneficially entitled to the settled property and is UK-domiciled; or
  (b) unless the settlor, or the spouse or widow(er), had acquired a reversionary interest in the property for a consideration in money or money's worth; or
  (c) unless a reversionary interest was been transferred into a settlement after 9 March 1981.

Note also with regard to (3) and (4) above that a person is treated as acquiring an interest for a consideration in money or money's worth if he becomes entitled to it as a result of transactions which include a disposition for such consideration (whether to him or another) of that interest or of other property.

These rules contain a number of anti-avoidance measures by which indirect and circuitous consideration is traced, in order to establish whether a person has acquired an interest in possession for money or money's worth. Another avoidance was sought to be achieved by creating an interest in property for a short period, the reversionary interest transferred into a settlement as excluded property followed by the interest's IHT-free termination.

16.2.6 Exceptions from charge on death
(IHTA 1984, s 49)

The deceased is deemed to have an absolute beneficial interest in settled property of which he was the life tenant (IHTA 1984, s 49(1)). Where a person is entitled to an interest in possession in settled property which on his death, but during the settlor's life, reverts to the settlor, the settled property's value is left out of account in determining the value of the deceased's estate immediately before his death.

No IHT is charged if on the occasion when the interest comes to an end:

(i) the settlor's spouse, or
(ii) where the settlor died less than two years earlier, the settlor's widow(er)

becomes beneficially entitled to the settled property and is UK-domiciled, the value of the settled property is left out of account when determining the death estate's value.

This rule does not apply if the settlor, or the spouse or widow(er), had acquired a reversionary interest in the property for a consideration in money or money's worth, or if a reversionary interest was been transferred into a settlement after 9 March 1981. Note, also that a person is treated as acquiring an interest for a consideration in money or money's worth if he becomes entitled to it as a result of transactions which include a disposition for such consideration (whether to him or another) of that interest or of other property.

Where it cannot be known which of two or more persons who have died survived the other(s), they are assumed to have died at the same instant.

16.2.7 Special rate of IHT where settled property affected by PETs
(IHTA 1984, ss 54A, 54B)

An anti-avoidance provision prevents the reduction of the IHT charge on transfers to discretionary trusts through the use of short-term interests in possession. In the circumstances described below, this can apply to any chargeable transfer made on the cessation of an interest in possession during the life of the person beneficially entitled to it (referred to as the 'relevant interest'), or on the death of a person beneficially entitled to an interest in possession in settled property (also referred to as the 'relevant interest'). The circumstances are that:

(1) the whole or part of the value transferred is attributable to property in which the relevant interest subsisted and which became settled property in which there subsisted an interest in possession (whether the relevant or any previous interest) on the making by the settlor of a PET at any time after 16 March 1987 and within seven years ending with the date of the chargeable transfer, and

(2) the settlor is alive at the time when the relevant interest comes to an end, and

(3) on the cessation of the relevant interest, any of the property in which that interest subsisted becomes settled property in which there is no qualifying interest in possession (other than property in accumulation and maintenance trusts), and

(4) within six months of the relevant interest ceasing, any of the property in which that interest subsisted has neither become settled property in which a qualifying interest in possession subsists (or which is property in accumulation and maintenance trusts) nor become property to which an individual is beneficially entitled.

In the special rules which are applied, 'the special rate property', in relation to a chargeable transfer, means the property in which the relevant interest subsisted.

Where the special rule applies to a chargeable transfer (the 'relevant transfer'), the IHT chargeable on the value transferred is the greater of the IHT that would have been chargeable apart from this anti-avoidance provision, and the IHT computed as set out below. The special rate of IHT is calculated as the aggregate of:

(1) the IHT that would be chargeable on a notional chargeable transfer as described below; and

(2) so much (if any) of the IHT that would otherwise have been chargeable on the value transferred by the relevant transfer as is attributable to the value of property other than the special rate property.

The notional chargeable transfer postulated above is one:

(1) the value transferred by which is equal to the value transferred by the relevant transfer,

(2) which is made at the time of the relevant transfer by a transferor who has in the preceding seven years made chargeable transfers having an aggregate value equal to the aggregate values transferred by any chargeable transfers made by the settlor in the seven-year period ending with the date of the PET, and

(3) for which the applicable rate is one-half of the normal death rate.

The settlor's death, at any time after a chargeable transfer to which the anti-avoidance provisions apply, cannot increase the IHT chargeable on the value transferred unless, at the time of transfer, the IHT calculated above is greater than the IHT that would otherwise be chargeable.

The death of the person who was beneficially entitled to the relevant interest at any time after a chargeable transfer caught by the anti-avoidance rules cannot increase the IHT chargeable on the value transferred unless, at the time of transfer, the IHT that would otherwise be chargeable is greater than the IHT calculated as above.

If a chargeable transfer caught by the anti-avoidance rules falls to be calculated as above, the IHT on the notional chargeable transfer is IHT attributable to the value of the property in which the relevant interest sub-sisted.

The following rule applies:

(1) during the seven years preceding the date on which a chargeable trans-fer caught by the anti-avoidance provisions (the 'current transfer') is made, there was another chargeable transfer to which that rule applied, and

(2) the person who is for the purposes of the current transfer the settlor who made a PET within seven years preceding the chargeable transfer (whether or not the settlements are the same).

16.2.8 Application of certain exemptions
(IHTA 1984, s 57)

The annual exemption and 'gifts in consideration of marriage' are extended to include references to the termination of interests in possession as a result of which trust property is transferred to the marriage parties absolutely or resettled in trust for them (IHTA 1984, ss 19, 22). This treatment does not apply to a transfer of value unless the transferor gives to the settlement trustees a notice, in prescribed form, and within six months from the trans-fer of value, informing them of the exemption's availability.

The exemption for maintenance funds for historic buildings, etc applies where the value transferred is attributable to property which, immediately after the transfer, remains comprised in a settlement as it applies where property becomes comprised in a settlement by virtue of the transfer (IHTA 1984, s 27).

16.2.9 Relief where property enters maintenance fund
(IHTA 1984, s 57A)

The following rules apply:

(1) a person dies who, immediately before his death, was beneficially enti-tled to an interest in possession in property comprised in a settlement, and

(2) within two years after his death the property becomes held on trusts (whether of that or another settlement) for which a Treasury direction is given, under IHTA 1984, Sched 4, para 1, for that property.

Where these rules are applied, IHT has effect as if the property had, on the death, become subject to the trusts, and

(1) accordingly no disposition or other event occurring between the date of death and the date on which the property becomes subject to the trusts is, so far as it relates to the property, a transfer of value or otherwise

constitutes an occasion for an IHT charge (this does not apply if the disposition by which the property becomes held on the trusts depends on a condition or is defeasible, or the property which becomes held on those trusts is itself an interest in settled property), or

(2) the trustees who hold the property on those trusts have, for a consideration in money or money's worth, acquired an interest under a settlement in which the property was comprised immediately before the death or at any time thereafter; or

(3) the property which becomes held on the trusts does so for a consideration in money or money's worth, or is acquired by the trustees for such a consideration, or has at any time since the death been acquired by any other person for such a consideration.

Where property becomes held on trusts of the kind specified above as the result of proceedings before a court and could not have become so held without such proceedings, the two-year time limit is extended to three years.

If the property's value, when it becomes held on the trusts, is lower than so much of the value transferred on the death as is attributable to the property, this rule applies to the property only to the extent of the lower value.

16.3 REVERSIONARY INTERESTS

16.3.1 Reversionary interest acquired by beneficiary
(IHTA 1984, s 55)

Where a person entitled to an interest (whether or not in possession) in any settled property acquires a reversionary interest expectant (whether immediately or not) on that interest, the reversionary interest is not part of his estate. The exclusion relating to transfers of interest which are not intended to confer any gratuitous benefit (IHTA 1984, s 10) does not apply to a disposition by which a reversionary interest is acquired in these circumstances.

16.3.2 Exclusion of certain exemptions
(IHTA 1984, s 56)

The following exemptions do not apply to property which is given in consideration of the transfer of a reversionary interest if that interest does not form part of the estate of the person acquiring it:

- transfers between spouses (IHTA 1984, s 18);
- gifts to charities (s 23);
- gifts to political parties (s 24);
- gifts to housing associations (s 24A);
- gifts for national purposes (s 25);

- PETs of property subsequently held for national purposes (s 26A); and
- maintenance funds for historic buildings etc (s 27).

Where a person acquires a reversionary interest in any settled property for a consideration in money or money's worth, the exemption for transfers between spouses does not apply to the property when it becomes the property of that person on the termination of the interest on which the reversionary interest is expectant.

The following exemptions do not apply to property if:

(1) the property is an interest in possession and the settlement does not come to an end in relation to that settled property on the making of the transfer of value; or
(2) immediately before the time when it becomes the exempt body's property it is comprised in a settlement and, at or before that time, an interest under the settlement is or has been acquired for a consideration in money or money's worth by that or another exempt body.

For these purposes, a person is treated as acquiring an interest for a consideration in money or money's worth if he becomes entitled to it as a result of transactions which include a disposition for such consideration (whether to him or another) of that interest or of other property. These rules do not apply to a transfer of value if or to the extent that it is a disposition whereby the use of money or other property is allowed by one person to another.

16.4 MISCELLANEOUS MATTERS RELATING TO TRUSTS GENERALLY

16.4.1 Trusts for the benefit of employees
(IHTA 1984, s 86)

Trusts for the benefit of employees must be a trust by which settled property is held, either indefinitely or until the end of a period (whether defined by a date or in some other way) and must not permit any of the settled property to be applied otherwise than for the benefit of:

(1) persons of a class defined by reference to employment in a particular trade or profession, or employment by, or office with, a body carrying on a trade, profession or undertaking, or
(2) persons of a class defined by reference to marriage or relationship to, or dependence on, such persons,
(3) charitable purposes.

Where any class is defined by reference to employment by or office with a particular body, the class must comprise all or most of the persons employed by or holding office with the body concerned, or the trusts on which the settled property is held are those of an approved profit-sharing scheme (under TA 1988, Sched 9).

If the trust meets this description:

(1) the property therein is treated as comprised in one settlement, whether or not it would otherwise fall to be so treated, and

(2) an interest in possession in any part of the settled property is disregarded (except IHTA 1984, s 55 (reversionary interest acquired by beneficiary)) if that part is less than 5 per cent of the whole.

Where any property ceases to be so comprised in a settlement and, either immediately or not more than one month later, the whole of it becomes comprised in another settlement, then if the above conditions again apply to it when it becomes comprised in the second settlement, it is treated as if it had remained comprised in the first.

If the trusts are those of an approved employee share ownership plan (FA 2000, s 47 and Sched 8), no account is taken of any power to appropriate or to acquire shares on behalf of individuals under the plan.

16.4.2 Newspaper trusts
(IHTA 1984, s 87)

In relation to property comprised in a newspaper trust, IHTA 1984, s 86 applies as if newspaper publishing companies were included among persons of a class defined by reference to:

(1) employment in a particular trade or profession, or employment by, or office with, a body carrying on a trade, profession or undertaking, or

(2) marriage or relationship to, or dependence on, such persons.

This applies to a settlement if shares in a newspaper publishing or holding company are the only or principal property comprised in the settlement.

Shares are treated as the principal property comprised in a settlement or the principal asset of a company if the remaining property so comprised or the company's remaining assets are such as may be reasonably required to enable the trustees or the company to secure the operation of the newspaper publishing company concerned.

16.4.3 Protective trusts
(IHTA 1984, s 88)

A special rule applies to settled property (other than property within pre-1978 protective trusts (IHTA 1984, s 73)) which is held on trusts to the like effect as those specified in the Trustee Act 1925, s 33(1)(ii) (which provides for the discretionary trust which follows forfeiture) and which became held on those trusts on the failure or determination before 12 April 1978 of trusts to the like effect as those specified in the Trustee Act 1925, s 33(1)(i) (which specifies the circumstances in which forfeiture occurs).

The failure or determination, before the end of the trust period, of trusts to the s 33(1)(i) like effect is disregarded; the principal beneficiary is treated as beneficially entitled to an interest in possession in any property which is for the time being held on trusts to the s 33(1)(ii) like effect.

16.4.4 Trusts for disabled persons
(IHTA 1984, s 89)

Relief is given to property transferred into settlement and held on trusts:

(1) under which, during the life of a disabled person, there is no interest in possession in the settled property, and
(2) which secure that not less than half of the settled property applied during his life is applied for his benefit.

The disabled person is treated as beneficially entitled to an interest in possession in the settled property.

The trusts on which settled property is held are not disqualified by reason only of the powers conferred on the trustees by the Trustee Act 1925, s 32.

The definition of 'disabled person' when the property was transferred into settlement is as set out in the Glossary at the front of this book.

16.4.5 Trustees' annuities
(IHTA 1984, s 90)

Where, under the terms of a settlement, a trustee is left an annuity as remuneration for his services to the extent that:

(1) it is reasonable in amount, and
(2) he is not deemed to have an interest in possession,

the interest is left out of his death estate, and there is no IHT charge on termination of interest (IHTA 1984, s 52).

16.4.6 Administration period
(IHTA 1984, s 91)

Where a person would have been entitled to an interest in possession in the residue of a deceased person's estate on the completion of the administration period, he is treated as if he had become entitled to an interest in possession in the unadministered estate, and in the property representing ascertained residue, from the earliest from which date which income of the residue would have been attributable to his interest had the residue been ascertained immediately after death.

Where, as between persons interested under a specific disposition, in a general or demonstrative legacy or in an annuity and persons interested in the residue of the estate, any liabilities fall exclusively or primarily upon the property that is the subject of the specific disposition or upon the legacy or annuity, only such part (if any) of those liabilities as falls ultimately upon the residue is treated as charges on residue (TA 1988, s 701(7)).

The reference to the completion of the administration of an estate is construed as TA 1988, ss 695–702.

16.4.7 Survivorship clauses
(IHTA 1984, s 92)

Where the terms of a will etc allow a specified period (known as a *commorientes period*) of up to six months and the beneficiary concerned does not survive for that period, then on his death the other beneficiaries are deemed to have been entitled as from the beginning of the period. This does not affect any distribution or application of property occurring before the dispositions there mentioned take effect.

16.4.8 Disclaimers
(IHTA 1984, s 93)

Where a person becomes entitled to an interest in settled property but disclaims the interest then, provided that the disclaimer is not made for a consideration in money or money's worth, he is treated as if he never had been entitled to the interest.

17

SETTLEMENTS WITH NO INTEREST IN POSSESSION (DISCRETIONARY SETTLEMENTS)

17.1 INTRODUCTION

There are three circumstances in which trustees can be required to pay IHT:

(1) on property leaving the settlement within the first ten years (although there is no charge on property leaving within the first three months) (IHTA 1984, s 65);
(2) on the tenth anniversary and every tenth year thereafter (the 'periodic charge') (IHTA 1984, s 64);
(3) on property leaving the settlement after a periodic charge has arisen (IHTA 1984, s 65)

17.1.1 Relevant property
(IHTA 1984, s 58)

For the purposes of this chapter, 'relevant property' is settled property in which no qualifying interest in possession subsists, other than excluded property and property:

(1) held for charitable purposes only, whether for a limited time or otherwise;
(2) held for the purposes of accumulation and maintenance trusts (IHTA 1984, s 71);
(3) held for the purposes of pre-1978 protective trusts (s 73);
(4) held for the purposes of pre-1981 trusts for disabled persons (s 74);
(5) held for the purposes of trusts for employees (s 86);
(6) held for the purposes of maintenance funds for historic buildings for which a Treasury direction has been given (Sched 4, paras 1, 3);
(7) which is part of or held for the purposes of a pension fund or scheme (s 151); and
(8) comprised in a trade or professional compensation fund.

SP 8/86 sets out the Revenue practice concerning the IHT treatment of discretionary trust income. The Revenue take the view that:

(a) undistributed and unaccumulated income should not be treated as a taxable trust asset, and

(b) for the purpose of determining the rate of charge on accumulated income, the income should be treated as becoming a taxable asset of the trust on the date when the accumulation is made.

17.1.2 Qualifying interest in possession
(IHTA 1984, s 59)

See the Glossary at the front of this book regarding the meaning of 'qualifying interest in possession'; see also **16.2.2** with regard to the Revenue's understanding of the term so far as it is concerned as being an interest in possession in settled property.

17.1.3 Commencement of settlement
(IHTA 1984, s 60)

A settlement is deemed to commence when property first becomes comprised in it.

17.1.4 Ten-year anniversary
(IHTA 1984, s 61)

A ten-year anniversary is the tenth anniversary of the date on which the settlement commenced and anniversaries thereafter at ten-yearly intervals. The ten-year anniversaries of a settlement in which the settlor or his spouse has an initial interest in possession are measured from the date on which the initial settlement was set up, and not the date when the initial settlement is terminated nor when the no interest in possession trust is actually created.

17.1.5 Related settlements
(IHTA 1984, s 62)

Two settlements are treated as related if (and only if) the settlor is the same in each case, and they commenced on the same day. Two settlements are not treated as related if all the property comprised in one or both of them was immediately after the settlement commenced held for charitable purposes only without time limit (defined by a date or otherwise).

17.2 PRINCIPAL CHARGE TO IHT

17.2.1 Charge at ten-year anniversary
(IHTA 1984, s 64)

Where immediately before a ten-year anniversary property comprised in a settlement is relevant property, IHT is charged at the special rate applicable (under IHTA 1984, ss 66, 67). The IHT rate charged ten-yearly depends on whether the settlement commenced after 26 March 1974, or before 27 March 1974.

Where a settlement commenced after 26 March 1974, the rate is determined by reference to the cumulative transfers made:

(1) by the *settlor* in the *seven* years preceding the date on which the settlement commenced, and

(2) by the *settlement* in the *ten* years preceding the anniversary.

Where a settlement commenced before 27 March 1974, the rate is determined by reference to the cumulative transfers made by the *settlement* in the *ten* years preceding the anniversary.

Where a work of art normally kept overseas becomes liable to IHT on the owner's death solely because it is physically situated in the UK at the relevant date, the liability, by concession (ESC F7) is waived if the work was brought into the UK solely for public exhibition, cleaning or restoration. If the work of art is held by a discretionary trust (or is otherwise comprised in settled property in which there is no interest in possession), the charge to tax arising under s 64 is similarly waived.

17.2.2 Charges at other times
(IHTA 1984, s 65)

Exit charges

There is an exit charge where:

(1) the property in a settlement ceases to be relevant property (whether because it ceases to be comprised in the settlement or otherwise), or

(2) the settlement trustees make a disposition as a result of which the value of relevant property comprised in the settlement is reduced.

The amount on which IHT is charged is:

(a) the amount by which the value of relevant property in the settlement is less immediately after the event in question than it would be but for the event, or

(b) where the IHT payable is deducted from relevant property in the settlement immediately after the event, the amount which, after deduction, is equal to the amount on which IHT would otherwise be charged.

The exit charge does not apply:

(1) if the event occurs in a quarter beginning with the day on which the settlement commenced or with a ten-year anniversary;

(2) as a result of a payment:

(a) of costs or expenses (insofar as they are fairly attributable to relevant property), or

(b) which is (or will be) taxed as the income of any person (or would
be income if such person were UK-resident), or in respect of a liability to make such a payment;

(3) if the disposition is such that, were the trustees beneficially entitled to
the settled property, it would not be a transfer of value because it is:

(a) a disposition not intended to confer gratuitous benefit (IHTA
1984, s 10), or

(b) the grant of a tenancy of agricultural property (IHTA 1984, s 16);
or

(4) if property comprised in a settlement ceases to be situated in the UK
and thereby becomes excluded property (IHTA 1984, s 48(3)(a)).

Property is regarded as becoming comprised in a settlement when it, or
other property which it represents, is introduced by the settlor (SP E9).

If the settlor was not domiciled in the UK when the settlement was made,
the exit charge does not apply by reason only that property comprised in the
settlement is invested in 'free of tax' and thereby becomes excluded property (IHTA 1984, ss 6(2), 48(4)(b)). Trustees are treated as making a
disposition if they omit to exercise a right (unless it is shown that the omission was not deliberate). Such disposition is treated as made at the time or
latest time when they could have exercised the right.

SP E6 sets out the effect for IHT of the exercise by trustees of a power to
augment a beneficiary's income out of capital. See **16.2.2** for details.

Beneficiary permitted to occupy dwelling-house

Many wills and settlements contain a clause empowering the trustees to
permit a beneficiary to occupy a dwelling-house which forms part of the
trust property on such terms as they think fit. The Revenue (in SP 10/79)
does not regard the existence of such a power as excluding any interest in
possession in the property.

Where there is no interest in possession in the property, the Revenue
does not regard the exercise of power as creating one if the effect is merely
to allow non-exclusive occupation, or to create a contractual tenancy for
full consideration. The Revenue also takes the view that no interest in possession arises on the creation of a lease for a term or a periodic tenancy for
less than full consideration, though this will normally give rise to an exit
charge under the no interest in possession rules (under IHTA 1984,
s 65(1)(b)). On the other hand, if the power is drawn in terms wide enough
to cover the creation of an exclusive or joint right of residence, albeit revocable, for a definite or indefinite period, and is exercised with the intention
of providing a particular beneficiary with a permanent home, the Revenue
normally regards the exercise as creating an interest in possession. If the
trustees in the exercise of their powers grant a lease for life for less than

full consideration, this is also regarded as creating an interest in possession (under IHTA 1984, ss 43(3), 50(6)).

A similar view is taken where the power is exercised over property in which another beneficiary had an interest in possession up to the time of the exercise.

17.3 RATE OF PRINCIPAL CHARGE

17.3.1 Rate of ten-yearly charge
(IHTA 1984, s 66)

IHT is calculated, using one-half of the death rate, where:

(1) the whole of the relevant property has been comprised in the settlement throughout the ten-year period ending immediately before the ten-year anniversary – three-tenths of the effective rate;

(2) all or part of the relevant property was not relevant property, or was not comprised in the settlement, throughout the ten-year period ending immediately before the ten-year anniversary – three tenths of the effective rate, reduced by one-fortieth for each full quarter before the property became relevant property.

The effective rate is calculated by expressing the IHT chargeable as a percentage of the amount on which IHT is charged on a hypothetical transfer by a hypothetical transferor. The form of the calculation depends upon whether the settlement was set up after 26 March 1974, or before 27 March 1974.

For settlements set up after 26 March 1974, the effective rate is the IHT rate that would be charged on a notional chargeable transfer:

(1) equal to the relevant property's aggregate value immediately before the ten-year anniversary, and the value immediately after it became comprised in the settlement of any property which was not then relevant property and has not subsequently become relevant property while remaining in the settlement, and the value immediately after a related settlement commenced of any property comprised in it; and

(2) made immediately before the ten-year anniversary by a hypothetical transferor who (subject to the adjustment for added property etc) has made chargeable transfers in the preceding seven years equal to the aggregate of:

   (a) the values of chargeable transfers made by the settlor in the seven years ending with the day on which the settlement began; and

   (b) the amounts on which any proportionate charges have been imposed in the ten years before the anniversary concerned; and

(3) on which IHT is charged at one-half of the death rate (IHTA 1984, s 7(2)).

For settlements set up before 27 March 1974, the effective rate is the IHT rate that would be charged on the value of the relevant property:

(1) immediately before the ten-year anniversary, and

(2) made immediately before the ten-year anniversary by a hypothetical transferor who (subject to adjustment for added property etc) has made chargeable transfers in the preceding seven years equal to the aggregate of the amounts on which any proportionate charges have been imposed in the ten years before the anniversary concerned, and

(3) on which IHT is charged at one-half of the death rate (IHTA 1984, s 7(2)).

17.3.2 Added property etc
(IHTA 1984, s 67)

For settlements set up after 26 March 1974 where, after a settlement commenced but before the ten-year anniversary concerned, the settlor makes further chargeable transfers into the settlement which increases the settlement's property's value, the values of chargeable transfers made by the settlor in the seven years ending with the day on which the settlement commenced are replaced by the greater of the two amounts set out below:

(1) the aggregate values of chargeable transfers made by the settlor in the seven years before the settlement commenced, and

(2) (a) the aggregate of the values of chargeable transfers made by the settlor in the seven years before the further chargeable transfers which increased the settlement's property's value, but excluding

   (b) any value attributable to property whose value was taken into account in determining the notional chargeable transfer equal to the aggregate of:

   (i) the value of the relevant property immediately before the ten-year anniversary, and

   (ii) the value immediately after it became comprised in the settlement of any property which was not then relevant property and has not subsequently become relevant property while remaining in the settlement, and

   (iii) the value immediately after a related settlement commenced of any property comprised in it, and

   (iv) the amounts on which any proportionate charges have been imposed in the ten years before the anniversary concerned.

It is immaterial whether the amount of the property in the settlement is increased as a result of the chargeable transfer. Where, however, the amount of the property is not increased, no adjustment is required if the transfer was not primarily intended to increase the value of the settled property, and it did not increase that value immediately after the transfer by more than 5 per cent of its value immediately before the transfer.

Where property comprised in a settlement immediately before the ten-year anniversary charge has within the preceding ten years ceased to be relevant property, then:

(1) if on that occasion IHT was charged by way of a proportionate charge,

(2) the aggregate of notional transfers made immediately before the ten-year anniversary by a hypothetical transferor who (subject to the adjustment for added property etc) has made chargeable transfers in the preceding seven years,

(3) which is equal to the aggregate values of chargeable transfers made by the settlor in the seven years ending with the day on which the settlement commenced (but disregarding transfers made on that day), and the amounts on which any proportionate charges have been imposed in the ten years before the anniversary concerned,

(4) is reduced by the lesser of:

    (a) the amount on which IHT was charged by way of proportionate charge, and

    (b) the value of the relevant property at the ten-year anniversary.

For settlements set up before 27 March 1974, the same basis of calculation is applied, with appropriate modifications.

17.3.3 Property leaving within first ten years
(IHTA 1984, s 68)

The exit charge rate levied before the first ten-year anniversary is the appropriate fraction of the effective rate at which tax would be charged on the value transferred by a notional chargeable transfer, as described below.

The appropriate fraction is three-tenths multiplied by so many fortieths as there are complete quarters in the period beginning with the day on which the settlement commenced and ending with the day before the exit charge. The effective rate is calculated as follows:

(1) compute the IHT payable on a notional transfer equal to the value of the settled property at the time that the settlement was made; and then

(2) divide this figure by the amount of the property put into settlement and multiply by 100 to express as a percentage.

Note with regard to (1) above that the IHT on the notional transfer may not correspond with the IHT actually paid when the settlement was created because BPR (see **8**) and APR (see **9**) cannot be taken into account in arriving at the exit charge rate.

Where the whole or part of the amount on which IHT is charged is attributable to property which was not relevant property or was not comprised in the settlement throughout the period, then in determining the appropriate fraction no quarter which expired before the day on which the property became, or last became, relevant property comprised in the settlement is taken into account, but if that day fell in the same quarter as that in which the period ends, that quarter is counted whether complete or not.

The notional chargeable transfer is one:

(1) the value transferred by which is the amount determined below;
(2) which is made at the time of the exit charge by a hypothetical transferor who has in the period of seven years ending with the exit charge, made chargeable transfers having an aggregate value equal to that of any chargeable transfers made by the settlor in the period of seven years ending with the day on which the settlement commenced, disregarding transfers made on that day;
(3) on which IHT is charged at one-half of the death rate (IHTA 1984, s 7(2)).

The amount referred to in (1) above is an amount equal to the aggregate of the value:

(a) immediately after the settlement commenced, of the property then comprised in it;
(b) immediately after a related settlement commenced, of the property then comprised in it; and
(c) immediately after it became comprised in the settlement, of any property entering after the settlement commenced and before the exit (whether or not it has remained so comprised).

For settlements set up before 27 March 1974, the same basis of calculation is applied, with appropriate modifications.

The exit charge during the first ten years on a discretionary settlement which is below the nil rate band at inception will thus be nil, because the effective rate of IHT is nil.

Example

Brough created a discretionary settlement in July 1996 with property worth £800,000. The IHT payable was £150,000. In September 2000, property worth £200,000 leaves the settlement.

Effective rate of IHT:
$$150,000/800,000 \times 100 = 18.75\%$$

Appropriate fraction: $\dfrac{16 \text{ quarters}}{40 \text{ quarters}}$

Exit charge
$$£200,000 \times 18.75\% \times 16/40 = £15,000$$

If Brough had settled business assets which qualified for 100 per cent BPR, the exit charge would still be calculated on the above basis even though the IHT (if any) actually payable would have been considerably less than £150,000.

Example

> Claudia put £175,000 into a discretionary trust in September 1996, having made no previous chargeable transfers. The trust is terminated in September 2000, when the trust fund is worth £600,000. The notional tax on the trust at inception was nil, so the effective rate will be
>
> 0% of £0
>
> which is, of course, nil.

17.3.4 Rate between ten-year anniversaries
(IHTA 1984, s 69)

The exit charge between ten-year anniversaries is the appropriate fraction of the last ten-yearly charge, ignoring any adjustment where all or part of the relevant property was not relevant property, or was not comprised in the settlement throughout the ten-year period ending immediately before the ten-year anniversary.

If at any time before the exit charge and after the most recent ten-year anniversary property:

(1) has become comprised in the settlement; or
(2) which was comprised in the settlement immediately before the anniversary, but was not then relevant property, has become relevant property,

then, whether or not the property has remained in the settlement or has remained relevant property, the exit charge is the appropriate fraction of the last ten-year charge. This ignores any adjustment where all or part of the relevant property was not relevant property, or was not comprised in the settlement, throughout the ten-year period ending immediately before the ten-year anniversary, and applies provided that immediately before the last ten-year anniversary the property was relevant property and was comprised in the settlement with a value computed as below.

The value of the property which has become comprised in the settlement which was either:

(1) relevant property immediately after it became comprised in the settlement, or
(2) not then relevant property and has not subsequently become relevant property while remaining comprised in the settlement;

is its value immediately after it became comprised in the settlement. In any other case the value to be so attributed is the value of the property when it became (or last became) relevant property.

The appropriate fraction is so many fortieths as there are complete successive quarters in the period beginning with the most recent ten-year anniversary and ending with the exit charge.

17.4 SPECIAL CASES – CHARGES TO IHT

17.4.1 Property leaving temporary charitable trusts
(IHTA 1984, s 70)

A special rule applies to settled property held for charitable purposes only until the end of a period (whether defined by date or in some other way). An IHT charge can arise where:

(1) settled property ceases to be such held for charitable purposes only until the end of a period, otherwise than by an application for charitable purposes; or

(2) the trustees make a disposition (otherwise than by an application of property for charitable purposes) as a result of which the value of settled property held for charitable purposes only until the end of a period is less than it would be but for the disposition.

IHT is not charged, under this rule, on payments (or a liability to make payments):

(1) of costs or expenses (so far as they are fairly attributable to settled property held for charitable purposes only until the end of a period), or

(2) which is (or will be) income of any person for income tax purposes, or would be such income of a non-UK resident person if he were so resident.

IHT is, however, charged if the disposition is such that, were the trustees beneficially entitled to the settled property, it would be a disposition 'not intended to confer gratuitous benefit' (IHTA 1984, s 10) or the grant of an agricultural tenancy for full consideration (IHTA 1984, s 16) and therefore not a transfer of value. The amount on which IHT is hereby charged is:

(1) the amount by which the value of property comprised in the settlement and to which this rule applies is less immediately after the event giving rise to the charge than it would be but for the event, or

(2) where the IHT payable is deducted from settled property held for charitable purposes only until the end of a period immediately after the event, the amount which, after the deduction, is equal to the amount on which IHT would be charged under (1) above.

The IHT rate charged is the aggregate of the following percentages:

(a) 0.25 per cent for each of the first 40 complete successive quarters in the relevant period,

(b) 0.20 per cent for each of the next 40,

(c) 0.15 per cent for each of the next 40,

(d) 0.10 per cent for each of the next 40, and

(e) 0.05 per cent for each of the next 40.

Where the whole or part of the amount on which IHT is charged under this rule is attributable to property which was excluded property at any time during the relevant period then, in determining the IHT rate to be charged on that amount or part, no quarter throughout which that property was excluded property is counted.

In this context 'the relevant period' is the period beginning with the later of

- the day on which the property on which IHT is chargeable became (or last became) settled property held for charitable purposes only until the end of a period, and
- 13 March 1975,

and ending with the day before the event giving rise to the charge. Where the property on which IHT is chargeable:

(a) was relevant property immediately before 10 December 1981, and
(b) became (or last became) property to which this rule applies after 9 December 1981 and before 9 March 1982,

the relevant day is redefined as the day on which the property on which IHT is chargeable became (or last became) settled property held for charitable purposes (only until the end of a period), and was the day on which the property became (or last became) relevant property before 10 December 1981.

Trustees are treated as making a disposition if they omit to exercise a right (unless it is shown that the omission was not deliberate). The disposition is treated as made at the time or latest time when they could have exercised the right.

17.4.2 Accumulation and maintenance settlements
(IHTA 1984, s 71)

An accumulation and maintenance settlement is a special type of discretionary settlement for the benefit of individuals aged under 25 in which there is no interest in possession. These settlements enjoy two privileges: there is no periodic charge every ten years, and no exit charge normally arises when property leaves the trust.

Specifically, an accumulation and maintenance is a settlement where:

(1) there is no interest in possession;
(2) any income not paid out to the beneficiaries for their education, maintenance or other benefit must be accumulated; and
(3) the trust's terms are such that a beneficiary (including an unborn beneficiary) must become entitled to the settled property, or to an interest in possession in it, no later than on attaining age 25.

This last condition is an absolute requirement. The existence of a discretion on the trustees' part to override such an entitlement means that the settlement does not qualify. In *Lord Inglewood and another v CIR* [1983] STC 133, CA, property was, under a 1964 appointment, held on trust for those of B's children who attained age 21 or married under that age, subject to powers of revocation and reappointment, and with interim powers of accumulation and maintenance. B's eldest child became 21 on 5 May 1975, and on 29 March 1976 the trustees released their power of revocation. The trustees appealed against the Revenue's notices of determination, contending that the transfers were within the exemption for accumulation and maintenance trusts. This was rejected by the Court of Appeal, which held that the condition that the beneficiaries 'will ... become beneficially entitled' was not satisfied. There was a power of revocation and reappointment under which the beneficiary's interest could be destroyed at the trustees' absolute discretion and reappointed solely for the benefit of third parties at ages exceeding 25. The word 'will' in 'will ... become entitled to' implies a degree of certainty inconsistent with such a power.

In *Maitland's Trustees v Lord Advocate* 1982 SLT 483, CS, the question under review was whether an accumulation and maintenance settlement had been established. The trustees of a discretionary settlement executed a deed of appointment with the intention of establishing an accumulation and maintenance settlement. The appointment was conditional on the power of accumulation being valid under the Trusts (Scotland) Act 1961. If the accumulations were contrary to Scottish law, the appointment would be void. The Revenue did not accept the deed as establishing an accumulation and maintenance settlement, on the basis that IHTA 1984, s 71(1)(a) was not satisfied. The Court of Session allowed the trustees' appeal, holding that the word 'will' in s 71(1)(a) did not require absolute certainty. The deed was not *ultra vires*, and the fact that the trustees might not safely make any distribution to the primary beneficiaries until the doubt as to the law was resolved did not prevent the settlement from qualifying as an accumulation and maintenance settlement within s 71.

The requirement that the trust's terms must be such that a beneficiary (including an unborn beneficiary) must become entitled to the settled property, or to an interest in possession in it, no later than on attaining age 25 is regarded as being satisfied even if no age is specified in the trust instrument, provided it is clear that a beneficiary will in fact become entitled to the settled property, or to an interest in possession by age 25 (ESC F8).

Exemptions

This rule does not apply to settled property unless either:

(1) no more than 25 years have elapsed since the settlement's commencement or, if it was later, since the time (or latest time) when the above conditions became satisfied with respect to the property, or

(2) all the beneficiaries are or were either:
  (a) grandchildren of a common grandparent, or

(b) children or widow(er)s of such grandchildren who were themselves beneficiaries but died before the time when, had they survived, they would have become entitled to the settled property, or to an interest in possession in it, no later than on attaining age 25.

Note that here a person's children include his illegitimate and adopted children and his stepchildren.

Liability to IHT

There is an IHT charge under these rules where:

(1) settled property ceases to be held in an accumulation and maintenance trust, or
(2) the trustees make a disposition as a result of which the value of settled property held in an accumulation and maintenance trust is less than it would be but for the disposition.

The liability to IHT is otherwise the same as for property held for charitable purposes, as detailed in **17.4.1**; the aggregate percentages listed in that paragraph also apply. The Revenue view on powers of appointment in this context are set out in SP E1 (see **16.2.1**). See also **17.1.1** with regard to SP 8/86.

It is not necessary that the settlement's beneficiaries should become entitled to receive the trust capital at age 25: an entitlement to receive income is sufficient. Also, the requirement that there be an interest in possession at age 25 does not mean that the beneficiaries acquire unrestricted right to income. A settlement would qualify if a beneficiary became entitled to an interest in possession for 12 months on attaining age 25 and the settled property was then held on discretionary trusts (however, in such a case the beneficiary would be deemed to have made a chargeable transfer).

Section 31 of the Trustee Act 1925 may mean that a settlement is an accumulation and maintenance trust. Thus, a settlement which does not exclude the provisions of the Trustee Act and which confers an entitlement to capital which is contingent upon the beneficiary surviving to a vesting date may give rise to an interest in possession on the beneficiary reaching age 18.

When the settlement is created, there must be at least one qualifying beneficiary who is alive. However, the settlement's terms may provide for unborn beneficiaries to participate.

A further provision is designed to prevent the accumulation of income for a long period. The trust deed must provide for interests in possession which must come into being within 25 years of the trust being created; or the class of potential beneficiaries must be so defined that all such beneficiaries have a common grandparent (or are widows or children of deceased beneficiaries who met this requirement).

17.4.3 Employee and 'newspaper' trusts
(IHTA 1984, s 72)

A special rule applies to settled property which is held in an employee trust (under IHTA 1984, s 86) if no qualifying interest in possession subsists in it. There is a charge to IHT:

(1) where settled property ceases to be the property of an employee trust except by a payment out of the settled property; and

(2) where a payment is made out of the settled property for the benefit of the persons described below, or a person connected with such a person; and

(3) if neither of the above apply, where the trustees make a disposition (otherwise than by way of a payment out of the settled property) as a result of which the value of the settled property is less than it would be but for the disposition.

A person falls into the description in (1) above if:

(1) he has directly or indirectly provided any of the settled property otherwise than by additions not exceeding in value £1,000 in any one tax year; or

(2) in a case where the employment is by a close company (under TA 1988, ss 414–417), he is a participator (under TA 1988, s 417(1), (2)) in relation to that company and either:

    (a) is beneficially entitled to, or to rights entitling him to acquire, not less than 5 per cent of, or of any class of the shares comprised in, its issued share capital, or

    (b) would, on a winding-up of the company, be entitled to not less than 5 per cent of its assets; or

(3) he has acquired an interest in the settled property for a consideration in money or money's worth.

Under (3) above, a person is treated as acquiring an interest for a consideration in money or money's worth if he becomes entitled to it as a result of transactions which include a disposition for such consideration (whether to him or another) of that interest or of other property. If the trusts are those of an approved profit-sharing scheme (under TA 1988, Sched 9), IHT is chargeable on a participator in a close company on an appropriation of shares in pursuance of the scheme.

If the trusts are those of an approved employee share ownership plan (FA 2000, s 47 and Sched 8), no account is taken of any power to appropriate or to acquire shares on behalf of individuals under the plan.

The liability to IHT is the same as for property held for charitable purposes, as detailed in **17.4.1**; the aggregate percentages listed in that paragraph also apply. See also generally **16.4.1** and **16.4.2**.

17.4.4 Pre-1978 protective trusts
(IHTA 1984, s 73)

A special rule applies to pre-1978 protective trusts, as discussed at **16.4.3**. The liability to IHT is the same as for property held for charitable purposes, as detailed in **17.4.1**; the aggregate percentages listed in that paragraph also apply.

17.4.5 Pre-1981 trusts for disabled persons
(IHTA 1984, s 74)

A special rule applies to settled property transferred into settlement before 10 March 1981 and held on trusts under which, during the life of a disabled person, no interest in possession in the settled property subsists, and which secure that any of the settled property which is applied during his life is applied only or mainly for his benefit. The liability to IHT is the same as for property held for charitable purposes, as detailed in **17.4.1**; the aggregate percentages listed in that paragraph also apply.

A definition of 'disabled person' for these circumstances is set out in the Glossary at the front of this book.

17.5 SPECIAL CASES – RELIEFS

17.5.1 Property becoming subject to employee trusts
(IHTA 1984, s 75)

Subject to a number of conditions being satisfied, there is no IHT charge (under IHTA 1984, s 65) on company shares or securities which cease to be relevant property on becoming held on trust for the benefit of employees (under s 86(1)). The trust by which settled property is held, either indefinitely or until the end of a period (whether defined by a date or in some other way), must not permit any of the settled property to be applied otherwise than for the benefit of persons of a class defined by reference to:

(1) employment in a particular trade or profession, or employment by, or office with, a body carrying on a trade, profession or undertaking, or
(2) marriage or relationship to, or dependence on, such persons.

The conditions are:

(1) that the persons for whose benefit the trusts permit the settled property to be applied include all or most of the persons employed by or holding office with the company;
(2) that, at the date when the shares or securities cease to be relevant property or at a subsequent date not more than one year thereafter, both the following additional conditions are met:
   (a) the trustees:

    (i) hold more than one-half of the ordinary shares in the company, and

    (ii) have powers of voting on all questions affecting the company as a whole which, if exercised, would constitute a majority of the votes available;

  (b) there are no provisions in any agreement or instrument affecting the company's constitution or management or its shares or securities whereby the voting condition could be altered without the trustees' consent;

  (c) where the company has shares or securities of any class giving powers of voting limited to either or both the question of winding-up the company and/or any question primarily affecting shares or securities of that class, questions affecting the company as a whole comprise all such questions except any in relation to which those powers are capable of being exercised (this does not apply if the trusts permit any of the settled property to be applied at any time (either indefinitely or until the end of a period, whether defined by a date or in some other way)) for the benefit of:

    (i) a person who is a participator in the company; or

    (ii) any other person who is a participator in any close company that has made a disposition whereby property became comprised in the same settlement, being a disposition which would be a transfer of value were it not for the exemption for dispositions by close companies for the benefit of employees (IHTA 1984, s 13); or

    (iii) any other person who has been a participator in the company or such other close company at any time after, or during, the ten years before the transfer of value; or

    (iv) any person who is connected with any such persons;

(3) that the trusts do not permit any of the property to be applied at any time (either indefinitely or until the end of a period whether defined by a date or in some other way (under IHTA 1984, s 86(1)) or later) for the benefit of any of the persons listed in (2)(i)–(iv) above.

The participators in a company referred to here do not include any participator who:

(1) is not beneficially entitled to, or to rights entitling him to acquire, 5 per cent or more of, or of any class of the shares comprised in, its issued share capital, and

(2) on a winding-up of the company would not be entitled to 5 per cent or more of its assets.

In determining whether the trusts permit property to be applied in the manner described above, no account is taken of any power to make a payment which is treated, for income tax purposes, as the income of any person, or would be the income of a non-UK resident person if he were so resident.

17.5.2 **Property becoming held for charitable purposes, etc**
(IHTA 1984, s 76)

IHT is not, in general, charged under the IHT regime for 'no interest in possession' trusts on property which ceases to be relevant property, or ceases to be property held:

(1) for charitable purposes only until the end of a period (whether defined by date or in some other way) (IHTA 1984, s 70),
(2) on accumulation and maintenance trusts (s 71),
(3) by an employee trust (s 72),
(4) in a pre-1978 protective trust (s 73),
(5) in a pre-1981 trust for disabled persons (s 74), or
(6) in a maintenance fund for a historic building etc (Sched 4, para 9),

on becoming property:

(a) held for charitable purposes only without limit of time (defined by a date or otherwise);
(b) of a political party qualifying for exemption (under IHTA 1984, s 24); or
(c) of a national purposes body (under IHTA 1984, Sched 3).

This does not apply to any property if the disposition by which it becomes property of the relevant description is defeasible. For this purpose a disposition which has not been defeated within 12 months after the property becomes property of the relevant description and is not defeasible after that time is treated as not being defeasible, whether or not it was capable of being defeated before that time. Nor does it apply to any property if

(1) it or any part of it may become applicable for purposes other than for a charity, a political party qualifying for exemption or national purposes body; and
(2) at or before the time when it becomes property of the relevant description, an interest under the settlement is or has been acquired for a consideration in money or money's worth by an exempt body otherwise than from a charity, a political party qualifying for exemption or a national purposes body.

A body is treated as acquiring an interest for a consideration in money or money's worth if it becomes entitled to the interest as a result of transactions which include a disposition for such consideration (whether to that body or to another person) of that interest or of other property.

If the amount on which IHT would otherwise be charged on any property exceeds the property's value immediately after it becomes held as described above (less any consideration for its transfer received by the trustees), IHT is charged only on the excess. Here, the reference to the amount on which IHT would be charged is to that on which it would be charged:

(1) assuming (if it is not in fact so) that the IHT is not paid out of settled property, and

(2) apart from IHTA 1984, ss 160–177 (valuation);

and the reference to the amount on which IHT is charged is to the amount on which it would be charged on that assumption and subject to the valuation rules (ss 160–177).

17.6 WORKS OF ART, HISTORIC BUILDINGS, ETC

17.6.1 Maintenance funds for historic buildings etc
(IHTA 1984, s 77, Sched 4)

Treasury directions

Giving of directions

If the conditions set out below are fulfilled in respect of settled property, the Treasury will, on a claim, give a direction in respect of it. The Treasury may give a direction in respect of property proposed to be comprised in a settlement or to be held on particular trusts in any case where, if it were already so comprised or held, the Treasury would be obliged to give the direction. Property comprised in a settlement by a transfer of value made before FA 1982, s 94, and exempt under FA 1976, s 84, is treated as property for which a direction has been given.

Conditions

The conditions are that:

(1) the Treasury is satisfied that:
 (a) the trusts on which the property is held comply with the requirements set out below, and
 (b) the property is of a character and amount appropriate for the purposes of those trusts; and

(2) the trustees:
 (a) are approved by the Treasury;
 (b) include a trust corporation, a solicitor, an accountant (ie a member of an incorporated society of accountants), or a member of such other professional body as the Treasury may allow for the property concerned; and
 (c) are, at the time the direction is given, UK-resident.

Trustees are regarded as UK-resident if:

(1) the trusts' general administration is ordinarily carried on in the UK; and

(2) the trustees or a majority of them (and, where there is more than one class of trustees, a majority of each class) are UK-resident.

Where a trustee is a trust corporation, the question whether the trustee is UK-resident is determined as for corporation tax. A 'trust corporation' is a one for the purposes of the Law of Property Act 1925 or the Administration of Estates (Northern Ireland) Order 1979, Art 9 (IHTA 1984, Sched 4, para 2(3)).

The requirements that the trusts on which the property is held must comply, are that:

(1) none of the property held on the trusts can at any time in the period of six years beginning with the date on which it became so held be applied otherwise than:

    (a) for the maintenance, repair or preservation of, or making provision for public access to, property which is for the time being 'qualifying property', for the maintenance, etc of property held on the trusts or for such improvement of property so held as is reasonable having regard to the trusts' purposes, or for defraying the trustees' expenses in relation to the property so held;

    (b) as respects income not so applied and not accumulated, for the benefit of a national purposes body or of a qualifying charity; and

(2) none of the property can, on ceasing to be held on the trusts at any time in that period or, if the settlor dies in that period, at any time before his death, devolve otherwise than on any such body or charity; and

(3) income arising from property held on the trusts cannot at any time after the end of that period be applied except as mentioned above.

Property is qualifying property if it has been designated as discussed at **4.2(3)–(6)** and

(1) the requisite undertaking has been given with respect to it under IHTA 1984:

    (a) s 30 (conditionally exempt transfers),

    (b) s 32(5)(b) (chargeable events),

    (c) s 32A(6), (8)(b) or (9)(b) (associated properties),

    (d) s 79(3) (exemption from ten-year charge), or

    (e) Sched 5, para 5 (conditional exemption: deaths before 7 April 1976); and

(2) IHT has not (since the last occasion on which such an undertaking was given) become chargeable with respect to it under provisions (b)–(d) above.

If it appears to the Treasury that provision is, or is to be, made by a settlement for the maintenance, etc of any property within the following descriptions it may, on a claim, designate that property, and accept with respect to it an undertaking with regard to the categories listed at **4.2(3)–(6)** that, until the person beneficially entitled to the property dies or the property is disposed of by sale, gift or otherwise, such steps as are agreed between the Treasury and the person giving the undertaking, and are set out in it, will be taken. Matters regarding such undertakings for, eg, the preservation of a property's character, the property's associated objects and land are discussed fully in **4**.

The requirement that none of the property held on the trusts can at any time within six years be used otherwise than for the maintenance, etc of any property, or for the benefit of a national purposes body, or, on the settlor's death, otherwise than for the purposes of such a body does not apply to certain property which:

(1) was previously comprised in another settlement, and
(2) ceased to be comprised in that settlement and became comprised in the current settlement in circumstances such that when the property left the maintenance fund and joined another for an historic building, there was no IHT charge (or, but for there being an amount not so reinvested, there would have been no IHT charge). Income arising from such property held on the trusts cannot be applied except as follows:
  (a) for the maintenance, etc of, or making provision for public access to, property which is for the time being 'qualifying property', for the maintenance, etc of property held on the trusts or for such improvement of property so held as is reasonable having regard to the trusts' purposes, or for defraying the trustees' expenses in relation to the property so held;
  (b) as respects income not so applied and not accumulated, for the benefit of a national purposes body or of a qualifying charity.

This exclusion does not apply if the time when the property comprised in the previous settlement devolved otherwise than on any national purposes body or charity for the purposes referred to above is before the expiration of the six-year period; but in such a case the requirements apply to the current settlement as if for the references to that six-year period there were substituted references to the period beginning with the date on which the property became comprised in the current settlement and ending six years after the date on which it became held on the relevant trusts of the previous settlement (or, where this has already applied in relation to the property, the date on which it became held on the relevant trusts of the first settlement in the series).

Withdrawal

If in the Treasury's opinion the facts concerning any property or its administration cease to warrant the continuance of the effect of a direction, it may withdraw the direction on such grounds, and from such date, as may be specified in a notice to the trustees. The direction ceases to apply accordingly.

Information

The trustees must furnish the Treasury with such accounts and other information relating to the property as the Treasury may reasonably require.

Enforcement of trusts

The trusts on which the property is held are enforceable as suits the Treasury and the Treasury has, as respects the appointment, removal and retirement of trustees, the rights and powers of a beneficiary.

Property leaving maintenance funds

Charge to IHT

Further special rules apply to settled property which is held on trusts which comply with the requirements set out above, and in respect of which a direction has been given by the Treasury.

Subject to further rules set out below, there is a charge to IHT where:

(1) settled property ceases to be property held on trusts and subject to a Treasury direction, otherwise than by use for maintenance etc or by devolving on any national purposes body or charity; or

(2) the trustees make a disposition (otherwise than by use for maintenance etc) or by devolving on any national purposes body or charity, as a result of which the value of settled property applied is less than it would be but for the disposition.

The IHT liability is otherwise as set out at **17.4.1**.

The devolution of property on a national purposes body or charity is not free from IHT charge if, at or before the time of devolution, an interest under the settlement in which the property was comprised immediately before the devolution is or has been acquired for a consideration in money or money's worth by that or another such national purposes body or charity. However any acquisition from another such national purposes body or charity is ignored. A national purposes body or charity is treated as acquiring an interest for a consideration in money or money's worth if it becomes entitled to the interest as a result of transactions which include a disposition for such consideration (whether to that body or charity or to another person) of that interest or of other property.

Exceptions from charge

IHT is not charged in respect of property which, within the permitted period after the occasion on which IHT would be chargeable, becomes comprised in another settlement as a result of an exempt transfer of value to a maintenance fund for an historic building (under IHTA 1984, s 27). 'The permitted period' is 30 days except in a case where the occasion referred to is the death of the settlor, in which case 'the permitted period' is two years. This exception from a charge to IHT does not apply to any property if the person who makes the transfer of value has acquired it for a consideration in money or money's worth. For this a person is treated as acquiring any property for such consideration if he becomes entitled to it as a result of transactions which include a disposition for such consideration (whether to him or another) of that or other property. If the amount on which IHT would otherwise be charged in respect of any property exceeds the property's value immediately after it becomes comprised in the other settlement (less the amount of any consideration for its transfer received by the person who makes the transfer of value) the amount on which IHT is charged is equal to the excess. The reference here to the amount on which IHT would be charged is to the amount on which it would be charged apart from:

(1) IHT due on the amount by which the value of property held for charitable purposes only until the end of a period is less than the amount which, after deducting the IHT, comprised in the settlement is less immediately after the event giving rise to the charge than it would be but for the event, and

(2) IHTA 1984, ss 103–114 (BPR) and IHTA 1984, ss 115–124B (APR).

IHT is not charged on property leaving a maintenance fund for an historic building (under IHTA 1984, Sched 4, para 8) for property which ceases to be held in the maintenance fund on becoming property to which:

(1) the settlor or his spouse is beneficially entitled, or

(2) the settlor's widow(er) is beneficially entitled if the settlor died in the two years preceding the time when it became such property.

The exception from IHT of property leaving a maintenance fund for an historic house does not apply in relation to any property if, at or before the time when it becomes such property, an interest under the settlement in which the property was comprised immediately before it ceased to be property held in a maintenance fund for an historic building is or has been acquired for a consideration in money or money's worth by the person who becomes beneficially entitled. Also, the exception does not apply in respect of property if it was relevant property before it became (or last became) property held in a maintenance fund for an historic building and, on it becoming comprised in such a fund, IHT was not chargeable (under IHTA 1984, s 65).

The exception also does not apply to property if:

(1) before it last became property of a maintenance fund for an historic building it was comprised in another settlement in which it was property in another maintenance fund for an historic building, and

(2) it ceased to be comprised in the other settlement and last became property of a maintenance fund for an historic building by becoming, within the permitted period after the occasion on which IHT would be chargeable, comprised in another settlement as a result of an exempt transfer of value to a maintenance fund for an historic building (under IHTA 1984, s 27) such that there was no IHT charge in respect of it.

The exception from IHT on property leaving a maintenance fund for an historic building etc does not apply unless the person who becomes beneficially entitled to the property is UK-domiciled at the time when he becomes so entitled.

Rates of charge

Where an IHT charge arises on property leaving a maintenance fund for an historic building and

(1) the property in respect of which the IHT is chargeable was relevant property before it left (or last left) a maintenance fund for an historic building, and

(2) on it becoming comprised in such a fund, IHT was not chargeable (under s 65) on its ceasing to be relevant property before becoming (or last becoming) property held in a maintenance fund for an historic building,

the rate at which IHT is charged is the aggregate percentages set out at **17.4.1**. Here, 'the relevant period' is the period beginning with the latest of:

(1) the date of the last ten-year anniversary of the settlement in which the property was comprised before it ceased (or last ceased) to be relevant property, and

(2) the day on which the property became (or last became) relevant property before it ceased (or last ceased) to be such property, and ending with the day before the event giving rise to the charge.

Where the property for which IHT is chargeable has at any time ceased to be and again became property held in a maintenance fund for an historic building in circumstances such that IHT is not charged for property which, within the permitted period after the occasion on which IHT would be chargeable, becomes comprised in another settlement as a result of an exempt transfer of value to a maintenance fund for an historic building (under IHTA 1984, s 27), such that there was no charge to IHT in respect of it, it is treated as having been property held in a maintenance fund for an historic building throughout the period of 30 days or two years (as the case may be).

In other cases where it has ceased to be property held in a maintenance fund for an historic building, the rate at which IHT is charged is the higher of the 'first rate' and the 'second rate'.

The first rate is the aggregate of percentages set out at **17.4.1**. Here, 'the relevant period' is the period beginning with the day on which the property for which the IHT is chargeable became (or first became) property held in a maintenance fund for an historic building, and ending with the day before the event giving rise to the charge.

Any occasion on which property became property held in a maintenance fund for an historic building, and which occurred before an occasion of charge to IHT on the property leaving the fund, is disregarded. The reference here to an occasion of charge to IHT on leaving the fund does not include:

(a) the occasion by reference to which the rate is being determined, or

(b) an occasion which would not otherwise be an occasion of charge.

If the settlor is alive, the second rate is the effective rate at which IHT would be charged, on the chargeable amount, if the amount were the value transferred by a chargeable transfer made by him on the occasion on which the IHT becomes chargeable. The rate (or rates) of IHT so charged in respect of any occasion is (or are) not affected by the settlor's death after that occasion.

If the settlor is dead, the second rate is the effective rate at which IHT would have been charged, on the chargeable amount, had the amount been added to the value transferred on his death and formed the highest part of it.

If the settlor died before 13 March 1975, the second rate is the effective rate at which IHT would have been charged, on the chargeable amount (under the appropriate provision of IHTA 1984, s 7(1) or (2)) if the settlor had died when the event giving rise to an IHT charge on property leaving a maintenance fund for an historic building occurred, the value transferred on his death had been equal to the amount on which estate duty was chargeable when he in fact died, and the chargeable amount had been added to that value and had formed the highest part of it.

Where, in the case of a settlement ('the current settlement'), IHT is chargeable on property leaving a maintenance fund for an historic building which:

(1) was previously comprised in another settlement, and

(2) ceased to be comprised in that settlement and became comprised in the current settlement in circumstances where IHT is not charged in respect of property which, within the permitted period described above,

it is treated as having been property held in a maintenance fund for an historic building throughout the period of 30 days or two years (as the case may be). In such a case, references to a settlor are construed as to the person who was the settlor to the original settlement (or, if the Revenue so determines, the person who was the settlor in relation to the current settlement).

Where, in the case of the current settlement, IHT is chargeable on property leaving a maintenance fund for an historic building which:

(1) was previously comprised at different times in other settlements ('the previous settlements'), and

(2) ceased to be comprised in each of them, and became comprised in another of them or in the current settlement, as a result of an exempt transfer of value to a maintenance fund for an historic building (under IHTA 1984, s 27), such that there was no charge to IHT in respect of it,

references to the settlor are construed as to the person who was the settlor in relation to the previous settlement in which the property was first comprised (or, if the Revenue so determines, any person selected by them who was the settlor in relation to any of the other previous settlements or the current settlement).

A special rule applies if:

(1) in the seven-year period preceding an IHT charge on property leaving a maintenance fund for an historic building (the 'current charge'), there has been another such charge where IHT was charged at the second rate, and

(2) the settlor for the purposes of the current charge is the settlor for the purposes of the other charge (whether or not the settlements are the same and, if the settlor is dead, whether or not he has died since the other charge).

The other charge is referred to as the 'previous charge'. The amount on which IHT was charged on the previous charge (or, if there have been more than one, the aggregate of the amounts on which IHT was charged on each) is, for the purposes of calculating the rate of the current charge if the settlor:

(1) is alive, taken to be the value transferred by a chargeable transfer made by the settlor immediately before the occasion of the current charge, and

(2) is dead, taken to increase the value there mentioned by an amount equal to that amount (or aggregate).

References here to the effective rate are to the rate found by expressing the IHT chargeable as a percentage of the amount on which it is charged.

Maintenance fund following interest in possession

In relation to settled property as described below, the above rules are subject to a number of modifications. These modifications apply to property which became property held by a maintenance fund for an historic building on a transfer of value which was made by a person beneficially entitled to an interest in possession in the property, and which (so far as the value transferred by it was attributable to the property):

(1) was an exempt transfer by virtue of the combined effect of either:
   (a) IHTA 1984, s 27 (maintenance funds for historic buildings) and IHTA 1984, s 57(5) (application of exemption for transfers of value to maintenance funds for historic buildings); or
   (b) IHTA 1984, s 27 (as above) and IHTA 1984, s 57A (relief where property enters a maintenance fund for historic buildings); but
(2) would otherwise have been a chargeable transfer.

The definition of the permitted period is modified so that the reference to the settlor is to either the settlor or the person entitled to the interest in possession. Thus 'the permitted period' is a period of 30 days except in a case where the occasion referred to is the settlor's death (or the person entitled to the interest in possession), in which case the permitted period is two years.

Paragraph 10 of Sched 4 to IHTA 1984 (which deals with exceptions from the charge on property leaving maintenance funds) in its original form does not apply if the person entitled to the interest in possession had died at or before the time when the property became held by a maintenance fund for an historic building. In its revised form, Sched 4, para 10(1) provides that IHT is not charged on property which ceases to be held in a maintenance fund for an historic building:

(1) on becoming property to which the person entitled to the interest in possession is beneficially entitled, or
(2) on becoming property to which:
    (a) that person's spouse is beneficially entitled, or
    (b) that person's widow(er) is beneficially entitled if that person has died in the two years preceding the time when it becomes such property.

Note, however, that this only applies where the spouse or widow(er) would have become beneficially entitled to the property on the termination of the interest in possession had the property not then become property held in a maintenance fund for an historic building.

Paragraph 11 of Sched 4 (IHT rates) does not apply, and Sched 4, para 14 is modified.

The second rate in relation to a person entitled to the interest in possession is the same as for a settlor, as discussed under the heading 'Rates of charge' above. See also under that heading regarding IHT charges in the cases of the current and previous settlements and the special rule, which apply equally to a person entitled to an interest in possession as they do to a settlor.

Property becoming comprised in maintenance funds

IHT is not charged on property leaving a no interest in possession trust (under IHTA 1984, s 65) in respect of property which ceases to be relevant property on becoming property to which a Treasury direction then has effect. This does not apply in relation to any property if, at or before the time when it becomes property subject to a Treasury direction, an interest under the settlement in which it was comprised immediately before it ceased to be relevant property is or has been acquired for a consideration in money or money's worth by the trustees of the settlement in which it becomes comprised on ceasing to be relevant property.

If the amount on which IHT would otherwise be charged on any property exceeds the property's value immediately after it becomes property subject to a Treasury direction (less the amount of any consideration for its transfer received by the trustees of the settlement in which it was comprised immediately before it ceased to be relevant property), the amount on which IHT is charged is equal to the excess.

Here, the references to the amount on which IHT would otherwise be charged are to the amount on which it would be charged apart from:

(1) IHTA 1984, s 65(2)(b) (this is the amount on which IHT is charged where the IHT payable is deducted from relevant property comprised in the settlement immediately after the event, the amount which, after deduction, is equal to the amount by which the value of relevant property comprised in the settlement is less immediately after the event than it would be but for the event (IHTA 1984, Sched 4, para 18(a))), and

(2) IHTA 1984, ss 103–114 (BPR) and IHTA 1984, ss 115–124B (APR) (IHTA 1984, Sched 4, para 18(2)(b)).

The references to the amount on which IHT is charged are to the amount on which it would be charged apart from those provisions.

IHT is not charged on property leaving a no interest in possession trust in respect of property if within the permitted period an individual makes a transfer of value:

(a) which is exempt as a transfer of value to a maintenance fund for an historic building (under IHTA 1984, s 27), and

(b) the value transferred by which is attributable to that property.

Here 'the permitted period' is 30 days beginning with the day on which the property ceases to be relevant property except where it does so on the death of any person, when it is the two-year period beginning with that day.

The IHT charge does not apply if the individual has acquired the property for a consideration in money or money's worth. An individual is treated as acquiring any property for such consideration if he becomes entitled to it as a result of transactions which include a disposition for such consideration (whether to him or another) of that or other property.

If the amount on which IHT would otherwise be charged on any property exceeds the value of the property immediately after the transfer (less the amount of any consideration for its transfer received by the individual), the amount on which IHT is charged is equal to the excess.

17.6.2 Conditionally exempt occasions
(IHTA 1984, s 78)

No IHT charge arises under the no interest in possession regime (other than the ten-year charge under IHTA 1984, s 64) if the transfer of property or other event is an occasion on which IHT is chargeable on which the charge would have been made has been comprised in the settlement throughout the six years ending with the transfer or event, and:

(1) the property is, on a claim, designated by the Treasury (under IHTA 1984, s 31), and

(2) the requisite undertaking is given with respect to the property by such person.

This claim must be made within two years after the date of the transfer or

SETTLEMENT WITH NO INTEREST IN POSSESSION

other event in question or within such longer period as the Revenue may allow.

Where there has been a conditionally exempt occasion in relation to any property, the following provisions apply under IHTA 1984:

(a) s 32 (chargeable events),
(b) s 32A (associated properties),
(c) s 33(1), (3)–(7) (amount of charge following a chargeable event),
(d) s 35(2) (conditional exemption on death before 7 April 1976).

IHT is accordingly chargeable (under s 32 or 32A) as if references to:

(1) a conditionally exempt transfer and to such a transfer of property included respectively a conditionally exempt occasion and to such an occasion in respect of property;
(2) a disposal otherwise than by sale include a transfer of property or other event is an occasion on which IHT is chargeable under the no interest in possession regime (other than the ten-year charge under IHTA 1984 s 64) if the property on which the charge would have been made has been comprised in the settlement throughout the six years ending with the transfer or event;
(3) an undertaking given under IHTA 1984, s 30 include an undertaking given under IHTA 1984, s 78.

The reference in IHTA 1984, s 33(5) (amount of charge on a chargeable event) to the person who made a conditionally exempt transfer applies to a conditionally exempt occasion as the person who is the settlor of the settlement in respect of which the occasion occurred (or if there is more than one such person, whichever of them the Revenue may select).

Where the relevant person under s 33 is the settlor, the rate (or each of the rates) applied, if the relevant person:

(a) is alive, to that amount (under IHTA 1984, s 7(2)) if it were the value transferred by a chargeable transfer made by the relevant person at that time; or
(b) is dead, to that amount (under s 7(1) or (2)) if it had been added to the value transferred on his death and had formed the highest part of that value.

If the occasion occurred before the first ten-year anniversary to fall after the property became comprised in the settlement, the rate is 30 per cent of what it would otherwise be. If the occasion occurred after the first and before the second ten-year anniversary to fall after the property became so comprised, the rate is 60 per cent of what it would otherwise be.

Where the relevant person under IHTA 1984, s 33 is the settlor who died before 13 March 1975, the rate(s) to apply are taken as if the relevant person had died when the chargeable event occurred, the value transferred on his death had been equal to the amount on which estate duty was chargeable when he in fact died, and the chargeable amount had been added to that value and had formed the highest part of it.

Section 34 of IHTA 1984 (reinstatement of transferor's cumulative total) does not apply to a chargeable event on property if its last conditionally exempt transfer has been followed by a conditionally exempt occasion.

17.6.3 Exemption from ten-year charge
(IHTA 1984, s 79)

Where property is comprised in a settlement and there has been a conditionally exempt transfer of the property on or before the occasion on which it became comprised in the settlement, the charge at the ten-year anniversary (IHTA 1984, s 64) does not apply to the property on any ten-year anniversary falling before the first occurrence after the transfer of a chargeable event on the property. The reference here to a conditionally exempt transfer of any property includes a transfer of value in relation to which the value of any property has been left out of account under FA 1975, ss 31–34 and, in relation to such property, the reference to a chargeable event includes a reference to an event on the occurrence of which IHT becomes chargeable under IHTA 1984, Sched 5 (conditional exemption – deaths before 7 April 1976).

Where property is comprised in a settlement and there has been, on or before the occasion on which it became so comprised, a disposal of the property in relation to which TCGA 1992, s 258(4) (CGT relief for works of art etc) had effect, the s 64 charge does not apply to the property on any ten-year anniversary falling before the first occurrence after the disposal of an event on the happening of which the property is treated as sold under s 258(5).

Where property is comprised in a settlement and there has been no such transfer or disposal of the property on or before the occasion on which it became comprised in the settlement, then if:

(1) the property has, on a claim, been designated by the Treasury (under IHTA 1984, s 31),
(2) the requisite undertaking has been given with respect to the property by such person(s) as the Treasury thinks appropriate in the circumstances of the case, and
(3) the property is relevant property,

the s 64 charge does not apply to the property. However, there is IHT on the first occurrence of an event which, if there had been a conditionally exempt transfer of the property when the claim was made and the undertaking had been given (under IHTA 1984, s 30), would be a chargeable event on the property. IHT is not charged on property if, after the occasion and before the occurrence, there has been a conditionally exempt occasion in respect of the property.

The amount on which IHT so charged is an amount equal to the value of the property at the time of the event. The rate at which IHT is charged is the aggregate percentages set out at **17.4.1**.

Here, 'the relevant period' is the period beginning with the latest of:

(a) the day on which the settlement commenced;
(b) the date of the last ten-year anniversary of the settlement to fall before the day on which the property became comprised in the settlement, and
(c) 13 March 1975;

and ending with the day before the event giving rise to the charge.

The following rules apply:

(1) Where the s 64 charge on the ten-year anniversary is disapplied, it does not apply to property on the settlement's first ten-year anniversary to fall after the making of the claim and the giving of the undertaking.
(2) On that anniversary, a charge to IHT is to be made in respect of the settlement under s 64.
(3) The property became comprised in the settlement, and the claim was made and the undertaking was given, within the period of ten years ending with that anniversary.

In calculating the IHT rate to be charged, the value of the consideration given for the property on its becoming comprised in the settlement is treated (under IHTA 1984, s 66(5)(b)) as if it were an amount on which a charge to IHT was imposed in respect of the settlement under IHTA 1984, s 65 (charge at other times) at the time of the property becoming so comprised.

17.6.4 **Variation of undertakings**
(IHTA 1984, s 79A)

An undertaking given under IHTA 1984, s 78 (conditionally exempt occasions) or s 79 (exemption from ten-year charge) may be varied from time to time by agreement between the Revenue and the person bound by the undertaking.

Where a Special Commissioner is satisfied that:

(1) the Revenue has made a proposal for the variation of such an undertaking to the person bound by the undertaking;
(2) that person has failed to agree to the proposed variation within six months after the date on which the proposal was made; and
(3) it is just and reasonable, in all the circumstances, to require the proposed variation to be made;

he may direct that the undertaking is to have effect from a date specified by him as if the proposed variation had been agreed to by the person bound by the undertaking. The date specified by the Special Commissioner must not be less than 60 days after the date of his direction.

A direction so given does not take effect if, before the date specified by the Special Commissioner, a variation different from that to which the direction relates is agreed between the Revenue and the person bound by the undertaking.

17.6.5 Miscellaneous matters relating to no interest in possession trusts

Initial interest of settlor or spouse
(IHTA 1984, s 80)

Where a settlor or his spouse (or widow(er)) is beneficially entitled to an interest in possession in property immediately after it becomes comprised in the settlement, the property is treated as not having become so comprised on that occasion. This does not apply if the occasion occurred before 27 March 1974. However, when the property (or any part of it) becomes held on trusts under which neither spouse is beneficially entitled to an interest in possession, the property is for those purposes treated as becoming comprised in a separate settlement made by that one of them who ceased (or last ceased) to be beneficially entitled to an interest in possession in it.

Property moving between settlements
(IHTA 1984, s 81)

Where property ceases to be comprised in one settlement and becomes comprised in another, unless in the meantime any person becomes beneficially entitled to the property (and not merely to an interest in possession in it), it is treated as remaining comprised in the first settlement. This does not apply where the property ceased to be comprised in the first settlement before 10 December 1981. However, where property ceased to be comprised in one settlement before 10 December 1981 and after 26 March 1974 and, by the same disposition, became comprised in another, it is for the purposes of the rules for no interest in possession settlements treated as remaining comprised in the first settlement. Nor does it apply where a reversionary interest in the property expectant on the termination of a qualifying interest in possession subsisting under the first settlement was settled on the trusts of the other settlement before 10 December 1981.

Excluded property – further rules
(IHTA 1984, s 82)

Under the no interest in possession rules (except IHTA 1984, ss 78, 79) property to which IHTA 1984, s 80 or 81 applies is not be taken to be excluded property (by being property comprised in a settlement and situated outside the UK where the property (but not a reversionary interest in it) is excluded property unless the settlor was UK-domiciled at the time the settlement was made (under IHTA 1984, s 48(3)(a)) unless the further condition outlined below is satisfied. This is in addition to the conditions in s 48(3) that the property is situated outside the UK and that the settlor was not domiciled there when the settlement was made).

Section 65(8) of IHTA 1984 provides that if the settlor of a settlement was not UK-domiciled when the settlement was made, IHT is not charged by reason only that property comprised in the settlement is invested in FOTRA securities (under IHTA 1984, s 6(2)) and thereby becomes excluded property because, although no qualifying interest in possession subsists in them but it is shown that all known persons for whose benefit the settled property or income from it has been or might be applied, or who are or might become beneficially entitled to an interest in possession in it, are persons not ordinarily resident nor domiciled in the UK and beneficially owned by such persons (IHTA 1984, s 48(4)(b)). However, s 65(8) does not apply in relation to property to which IHTA 1984, s 80 or 81 applies unless the condition described below is satisfied. This is in addition to the condition in s 65(8) that the settlor was not UK-domiciled when the settlement was made.

The condition is:

(1) in the case of property to which s 80 applies, that the person who is the settlor in relation to the settlement in which the settlor or his spouse were beneficially entitled to an interest in possession immediately after it became comprised in the settlement was not UK-domiciled when that settlement was made (s 82(3)(a)); and

(2) in the case of property to which s 81(1) or (2) applies, that the person is the settlor in relation to the other settlements.

This condition is more stringent than the normal rules relating to FOTRA securities, and appear to be aimed at the avoidance possibilities as between UK-domiciled and non-domiciled spouses.

Property becoming settled on death
(IHTA 1984, s 83)

Property which becomes comprised in a settlement under a will or on an intestacy is taken for the purposes of the rules for no interest in possession settlements to have become comprised in it on the death of the testator or intestate.

Income applied for charitable purposes
(IHTA 1984, s 84)

For the purposes of the rules for no interest in possession settlements (except IHTA 1984, ss 78 and 79), where the trusts on which settled property is held require part of the property's income to be applied for charitable purposes, a corresponding part of the settled property is regarded as held for charitable purposes.

Credit for annual charges under FA 1975
(IHTA 1984, s 85)

Any IHT charged by FA 1975, Sched 5, para 12(2) and not already allowed as a credit under para 12(3) or FA 1982, s 125 or hereunder is allowed as a credit against IHT chargeable under the no interest in possession rules (except IHTA 1984, s 79 (exemption from ten-year charge)) in respect of the settled property or part concerned.

18

LIABILITY TO IHT

18.1 GENERAL RULES

18.1.1 Dispositions by transferor
(IHTA 1984, s 199)

Persons liable for IHT on value transferred by a chargeable transfer made by a transferor's disposition (including any omission treated as a disposition) are (IHTA 1984, s 3(3)):

(1) the transferor;
(2) any person whose estate value is increased by the transfer;
(3) so far as IHT is attributable to the value of any property, any person in whom the property is vested (whether beneficially or otherwise) at any time after the transfer, or who at any such time is beneficially entitled to an interest in possession in the property;
(4) where by the chargeable transfer any property becomes comprised in a settlement, any person for whose benefit any of the property or income from it is applied.

The persons liable for IHT on the value transferred by a PET (IHTA 1984, s 3A) and for so much of the IHT on the value transferred by any other chargeable transfer made within seven years of the transferor's death as exceeds what it would have been had the transferor died more than seven years after the transfer, are:

(1) the transferor's personal representatives;
(2) any person whose estate value is increased by the transfer;
(3) so far as IHT is attributable to the value of any property, any person in whom the property is vested (whether beneficially or otherwise) at any time after the transfer, or who at any such time is beneficially entitled to an interest in possession in the property;
(4) where by the chargeable transfer any property becomes comprised in a settlement, any person for whose benefit any of the property or income from it is applied.

A purchaser of property and a person deriving title from such a purchaser

213

are not liable for IHT attributable to the property's value unless the property is subject to a Revenue charge.

The following persons may also be liable for IHT:

(1) any person who takes possession of or intermeddles with, or otherwise acts in relation to, property so as to become liable as executor or trustee; and

(2) any person to whom the management of property is entrusted on behalf of a person not of full legal capacity (*CIR v Stype Investments (Jersey) Ltd; Re Clore (dec'd)* [1982] STC 625, CA; *CIR v Stannard* [1984] STC 245, ChD).

'Property' includes any property directly or indirectly representing it.

In correspondence (published in the *Law Society's Gazette*, 13 March 1991) the CTO set out the Revenue practice in regard to the liability of personal representatives for tax on transfers made by the deceased in the seven years before his death. The CTO will not usually pursue for IHT personal representatives who, after making the fullest enquiries that are reasonably practicable in the circumstances to discover lifetime transfers, and having done so in all their powers to make full disclosure of them to the Revenue, have obtained a certificate of discharge and distributed the estate before a chargeable lifetime transfer comes to light.

The interaction of income tax and IHT on assets put into settlements is dealt with in SP 1/82. The income tax rules (TA 1988, ss 660A–694) provide in general terms that the income of a settlement is, for income tax purposes, treated as that of the settlor in all circumstances where the settlor might benefit directly or indirectly from the settlement. If the trustees have power to pay or do in fact pay IHT due on assets which the settlor puts into the settlement, the Revenue has taken the view that the settlor thereby has an interest in the settlement's income or property, and that such income should be treated as his for income tax purposes.

The IHT legislation, however, provides that both the settlor and the trustees are liable for any IHT payable when a settlor puts assets into a settlement. The Revenue has announced that it will not, in these circumstances, treat the income of the settlement as that of the settlor for income tax purposes solely because the trustees have power to pay, or do in fact pay, IHT on assets put into settlements.

18.1.2 Transfer on death
(IHTA 1984, ss 200, 204)

Persons liable for IHT on the value transferred by a chargeable transfer of settled property made on the death of any person are (IHTA 1984, s 4):

(1) the deceased's personal representatives so far as IHT is attributable to the value of property which either was not comprised in a settlement immediately before the death, or was comprised in a settlement immediately

before the death, and consisted of land in the UK which devolved upon or vests in the deceased's personal representatives;

(2) the settlement trustees so far as the IHT is attributable to the value of property which, immediately before the death, was comprised in a settlement;

(3) any person in whom the property is vested (whether beneficially or otherwise) at any time after the death, or who at any such time is beneficially entitled to an interest in possession in the property, so far as the IHT is attributable to the value of any property;

(4) any person for whose benefit any of the property or income from it is applied after the death so far as the IHT is attributable to the value of any property which, immediately before the death, was comprised in a settlement.

A purchaser of property, and a person deriving title from such a purchaser, are not liable for IHT attributable to the property's value unless the property is subject to a Revenue charge.

The following persons may also be liable for IHT:

(1) any person who takes possession of or intermeddles with, or otherwise acts in relation to, property so as to become liable as executor or trustee, and

(2) any person to whom the management of property is entrusted on behalf of a person not of full legal capacity.

'Property' includes any property directly or indirectly representing it.

A person entitled to part only of the income of any property is (notwithstanding IHTA 1984, s 50) deemed to be entitled to an interest in the whole of the property.

A person is not liable for any IHT as a personal representative of a deceased person, except to the extent of the following assets so far as the IHT is attributable:

(1) immediately before the death, to property which was comprised in a settlement and consists of land in the UK, so much of that property as is at any time available in his hands for the payment of IHT, or might have been so available but for his own neglect or default;

(2) to the value of any other property the assets of which he has received as personal representative or might have so received but for his own neglect or default.

A person is not liable for IHT as trustee in relation to any property, except to the extent of so much of:

(1) the property as he has actually received or disposed of or as he has become liable to account for to the persons beneficially entitled to it; and

(2) any other property as is for the time being available in his hands as

trustee for the payment of IHT or might have been so available but for his own neglect or default.

A person not liable as above, but liable for IHT as a person in whom property is vested or as a person entitled to a beneficial interest in possession in any property, is not liable for IHT except to the extent of that property.

A person liable for IHT as a person for whose benefit any settled property (or income therefrom) is applied is not liable for IHT except to the extent of the amount of the property or income reduced because of any income tax borne on it, and because of income tax borne on other property under the anti-avoidance provisions relating to the transfer of the power to enjoy income by the transfer of assets abroad by the amount of that tax (TA 1988, ss 739–740).

Where a person is liable for any IHT otherwise than as:

(1) the transferor or his personal representative; or
(2) a trustee of the settlement;

he is liable only if IHT remains unpaid after it ought to have been paid and, in a case where any part of the value transferred is attributable to the IHT on it, is liable to no greater extent than he would have been had the value transferred been reduced by the IHT remaining unpaid. This does not apply to the excess where the IHT exceeds what it would have been had the transferor died more than seven years after the transfer.

A person liable for any IHT as the transferor's personal representative is liable only to the extent that either:

(1) the IHT remains unpaid 12 months after the end of the month in which the transferor died, or
(2) as a result of the above rules none of the following persons is liable for the IHT:
    (a) any person the value of whose estate is increased by the transfer, or
    (b) so far as IHT is attributable to the value of any property, any person in whom the property is vested (whether beneficially or otherwise) at any time after the transfer, or who at any such time is beneficially entitled to an interest in possession in the property where by the chargeable transfer any property becomes comprised in a settlement, any person for whose benefit any of the property or income from it is applied.

Where the deceased's estate is treated as including property which would not otherwise form part of his estate, a person is liable as a personal representative for IHT attributable to the value of that property only if the IHT remains unpaid 12 months after the end of the month in which the death occurs and, subject to that, only to the extent of the assets coming into his hands (FA 1986, s 102(3)).

The interaction of income tax and IHT on assets put into settlements is dealt with in SP 1/82 (see **18.1.1**).

18.1.3 **Settled property**
(IHTA 1984, s 201)

The persons liable for IHT on the value transferred by a chargeable transfer made under a settlement are:

(1) the settlement trustees;
(2) any person entitled (whether beneficially or not) to an interest in possession in the settled property;
(3) any person for whose benefit any of the settled property or income from it is applied at or after the time of the transfer;
(4) where the transfer is made during the settlor's life and the trustees are not for the time being UK-resident, the settlor, subject to the following exceptions:
    (a) where the chargeable transfer is made within seven years prior to the transferor's death but is not a PET, this does not apply to so much of IHT as exceeds what it would have been had the transferor died more than seven years after the transfer;
    (b) where a settlement is made before 11 December 1974, if the trustees were UK-resident when the settlement was made, but have not been resident there at any time during the period between 10 December 1974 and the time of the transfer;
    (c) in relation to IHT chargeable on the value transferred by a PET which proves to be a chargeable transfer in a case where the settlement was made before 17 March 1987 if the trustees were UK-resident when the settlement was made, but have not been resident there at any time between 16 March 1987 and the transferor's death; and
    (d) where more than one person is a settlor in relation to a settlement and the circumstances so require, there is deemed to be settled property comprised in separate settlements.

Trustees of a settlement are regarded as non-UK resident unless the settlement's general administration is ordinarily carried on in the UK and the trustees or a majority of them are UK-resident. If there is more than one class of trustees, a majority of each class must be so resident.

'Property' includes any property directly or indirectly representing it.

18.1.4 **Close companies**

The persons liable for IHT chargeable under the rules for close company transfers (IHTA 1984, ss 94(1) (charges on participators) and 99(1) (transfers where participators are trustees)) are:

(1) the company making the transfer of value concerned, and
(2) so far as IHT remains unpaid after it ought to have been paid, the persons to whom any amounts have been apportioned and any individual

(whether such a person or not) the value of whose estate is increased by the company's transfer.

A person to whom not more than 5 per cent of the value transferred by the company's transfer is apportioned is not as such liable for any of the IHT. Any other persons to whom any part of that value has been apportioned are liable only for such part of the IHT as corresponds to that part. A person the value of whose estate is increased by the company's transfer is not as such liable for a greater amount than the amount of the increase.

Liability for any IHT arising as a result of close company transfers under ss 94(1) and 99(1) is restricted to those persons who are liable, as above.

The Revenue has clarified the position concerning dividend payments and transfers of assets from a subsidiary company to a parent or sister company as appropriate (SP E15):

(1) whether a disposition is a transfer of value for IHT has to be determined by reference to IHTA 1984, s 10 (dispositions not intended to confer gratuitous benefit),
(2) the Revenue does not treat a transfer of assets between a wholly owned subsidiary and its parent or between two wholly owned subsidiaries as a transfer of value.

18.1.5 Liability of spouse
(IHTA 1984, s 203)

Where:

(1) transferor is liable for any IHT on the value transferred by a chargeable transfer, and
(2) by another transfer of value made by him on or after 27 March 1974 ('the spouse transfer') any property became the property of a person ('the transferee') who at the time of both transfers was his spouse,

the transferee is liable for so much of the IHT as does not exceed the property's market value at the time of the spouse transfer. This rule applies where:

(a) the chargeable transfer is made after the spouse transfer; and
(b) the transferred property either remains the transferee's property at the date of the chargeable transfer or has before that date been sold by the transferee by a qualifying sale; and
(c) the transferred property's market value on the date of the chargeable transfer or of the qualifying sale is lower than its market value at the time of the spouse transfer; and
(d) the transferred property is not tangible moveable property.

'Qualifying sale' is defined in the Glossary at the front of this book.

Shares or securities – capital receipts
(IHTA 1984, s 133, as applied by s 203(4))

See **12.3** in relation to a transferee becoming entitled to capital payment to transferred shares or securities.

Payments of calls
(IHTA 1984, s 134, as applied by s 203(4))

If the transferred property consists of shares or securities and at any time before the relevant date the transferee becomes liable to make a payment under a call in relation to those shares or securities, then for the purposes of the relief for transfers within seven years of death (IHTA 1984, s 203) the shares' market value on the relevant date is (except where otherwise it reflects the liability) reduced by an amount equal to the payment.

Reorganisation of share capital, etc
(IHTA 1984, s 135, as applied by s 203(4))

See **12.5** with regard to transferred property of shares or securities for which before the relevant date there is a transaction under TCGA 1992, s 127 (equation of new shares or securities with original shareholding) or to which TCGA 1992 would apply but for TCGA 1992, s 134 (compensation stock).

Transactions of close companies
(IHTA 1984, s 136 as applied by s 203(4))

See **12.6**, which applies equally to transfers between spouses.

Interests in land
(IHTA 1984, s 137 as applied by s 203(4))

See **12.7** in relation to transferred property which is an interest in land.

Leases
(IHTA 1984, s 138 as applied by s 203(4))

This subject is dealt with under **12.8**, which also gives the appropriate fraction and percentages of sale at the date of death.

Other property
(IHTA 1984, s 139 as applied by s 203(4))

See **12.9** in relation to property which is neither shares, securities nor an interst in land.

Market value
(IHTA 1984, s 140 as applied by s 203(4))

See generally **12.10**.

18.2 SPECIAL CASES

18.2.1 Conditional exemption
(IHTA 1984, s 207)

Where IHT is chargeable under IHTA 1984, s 32 (chargeable events in relation to conditional exemption) on the occurrence of an event which is a chargeable event with respect to any property, the person liable to IHT:

(1) is the person who, at the time the IHT becomes chargeable, if the property were sold, where the Treasury becomes satisfied that at any time an undertaking given with respect to the property (under IHTA 1984, s 30 or 31) has not been observed in a material respect: the failure to observe the undertaking is a chargeable event with respect to the property; or

(2) when the person beneficially entitled to the property dies, is the person who immediately after the death would be entitled to receive (whether for his benefit or not) the proceeds of sale or any income arising from them; or

(3) where IHT is chargeable when the property is disposed of, whether by sale or gift, is the person by whom or for whose benefit the property is disposed of;

(4) where IHT is chargeable (under IHTA 1984, s 32A(3)) (because the Treasury has become satisfied that at any time an undertaking given under s 30 or 32A for the maintenance, repair, preservation, access or keeping of any of the associated properties has not been observed in a material respect, then the failure to observe the undertaking is a chargeable event with respect to the whole of each of the associated properties of which there has been a conditionally exempt transfer), is the person who at the time the IHT becomes chargeable would be entitled to receive (whether for his benefit or not) the proceeds of sale or any income arising from them;

(5) where the person beneficially entitled to the property dies, is the person who at the time the IHT becomes chargeable (under s 32A(4)(a)) would be entitled to receive (whether for his benefit or not) the proceeds of sale or any income arising from them;

(6) where IHT is chargeable (under s 32A(4)(b)) when the property is disposed of, whether by sale or gift, is the person by whom or for whose benefit the property is disposed of.

The persons liable for IHT charged under IHTA 1984, s 79(3) (exemption from ten-yearly charge not to apply on failure of undertakings under IHTA 1984, ss 30 and 31) are:

(a) the settlement trustees, and

(b) any person for whose benefit any of the property or income from it is applied at or after the time of the event giving the charge.

The person liable for IHT chargeable under IHTA 1984, Sched 5, para 1(1), (2) (failure of undertakings under FA 1975, s 31 with respect to objects) or para 3(1), (2) (failure of undertakings under FA 1975, s 34 with respect to buildings and associated property) is the person who, if the property were sold at the time the IHT becomes chargeable, would be entitled to receive (whether for his benefit or not) the proceeds of sale or any income arising from them.

18.2.2 Woodlands
(IHTA 1984, s 208)

The person liable for IHT in relation to a disposal is the person who is entitled to the proceeds of sale or would be so entitled if the disposal were a sale (IHTA 1984, s 126).

18.2.3 Succession in Scotland
(IHTA 1984, s 209)

A person is not liable under IHTA 1984, s 200(1)(a) for IHT attributable to the value of any heritable property in Scotland which is vested in him as executor in the circumstances and for the purposes mentioned in the Succession (Scotland) Act 1964, s 18(1) or (2).

The persons liable for IHT chargeable under IHTA 1984, s 147(4) are the person who claims legitim and any person in whom the property is vested (whether beneficially or otherwise) at any time after the death, or who at any such time is beneficially entitled to an interest in possession in the property, so far as the IHT is attributable to the value of any property.

Section 200(1)(a) does not apply in relation to IHT chargeable under s 147(4), but s 204(1) does apply in relation to the person who claims legitim as it applies in relation to a deceased's personal representatives.

18.2.4 Pension rights, etc
(IHTA 1984, s 210)

Where any IHT chargeable on a transfer of value is attributable to the value of an interest which is, or is a right to, a pension or annuity (IHTA 1984, s 151(2)(a)), and is not an interest resulting (whether by virtue of the instrument establishing the fund or scheme or otherwise) from the application of any benefit provided under the fund or scheme otherwise than by way of a pension or annuity (s 151(2)(b)), the persons liable for IHT do not include the trustees of the scheme or fund but, if the transfer is made on the death of the person entitled to the interest, include his personal representatives.

18.3 BURDEN OF IHT, ETC

18.3.1 Burden of IHT on death
(IHTA 1984, s 211)

Where personal representatives are liable for IHT (and interest thereon) on the value transferred by a chargeable transfer made on death, the IHT and the interest is treated as part of the estate's general testamentary and administration expenses, but only so far as it is attributable to the value of property in the UK which:

(i)   vests in the deceased's personal representatives, and
(ii) was not immediately before the death comprised in a settlement.

This applies subject to any contrary intention shown by the deceased in his will.

Where any amount of IHT (and interest thereon) paid by personal representatives on the value transferred by a chargeable transfer made on death does not fall to be borne as part of such expenses, that amount is, where occasion requires, repaid to them by the person in whom the property to the value of which the IHT and the interest is attributable is vested.

18.3.2 Powers to raise IHT
(IHTA 1984, s 212)

Where a person is liable (otherwise than as transferor and under IHTA 1984, s 203 (liability of spouse)) for IHT (and interest thereon) and to costs properly incurred in respect of IHT attributable to the value of any property, he has power for the purpose of paying the IHT, the interest and to costs so properly incurred, whether or not the property is vested in him, to raise the IHT amount by sale or mortgage of, or a terminable charge on, that property or any part of it.

A person having a limited interest in any property who pays the IHT, the interest thereon and to costs so properly incurred is entitled to the like charge as if the IHT so attributable had been raised by means of a mortgage to him.

Any money held on the trusts of a settlement may be expended in paying the IHT, interest and to costs incurred attributable to the value of any property comprised in the settlement and held on the same trusts.

18.3.3 Refund by instalments
(IHTA 1984, s 213)

Where a person has paid any IHT to the Revenue which is or might at his option have been payable by instalments and he is entitled to recover the whole or part of it from another person, that other person is, unless otherwise agreed between them, entitled to refund the IHT or that part by the same instalments (with the same interest thereon) as those by which it might have been paid to the Revenue.

18.3.4 Certificates of IHT paid
(IHTA 1984, s 214)

On an application to the Revenue by a person who has paid or borne the IHT and interest thereon attributable to the value of any property, being IHT for which he is not ultimately liable, the Revenue grants a certificate specifying the IHT and interest paid and the debts and incumbrances allowed in valuing the property.

Except to the extent of any repayment which may be or became due from the Revenue, such a certificate is conclusive as between any person by whom the IHT specified in the certificate falls to be borne and the person seeking to recover the IHT and interest thereon from him; any repayment of the IHT and interest falling to be made by the Revenue will be duly made to the person producing the certificate.

19

ADMINISTRATION AND COLLECTIONS

19.1 MANAGEMENT
(IHTA 1984, s 215)

IHT is under the care and management of the Board of Inland Revenue.

19.2 ACCOUNTS AND INFORMATION

19.2.1 Delivery of accounts
(IHTA 1984, s 216)

Except as otherwise provided here or by regulations under IHTA 1984, s 256 (the Capital Transfer Tax (Delivery of Accounts) Regulations 1981 (SI No 880)), any person who is liable to IHT (see **18**) must deliver to the Revenue an account specifying to the best of his knowledge and belief all appropriate property and its value.

Where, in the case of the deceased's estate, no grant of representation or confirmation has been obtained in the UK before the expiration of the 12-month period from the end of the month in which the death occurred:

(1) every person in whom any of the property forming part of the estate vests (whether beneficially or otherwise) on or at any time after the death or who at any such time is beneficially entitled to an interest in possession in any such property, and

(2) where any of the property is at any such time comprised in a settlement and there is no person beneficially entitled to an interest in possession in it, every person for whose benefit any of that property (or income from it) is applied at any such time

must deliver to the Revenue an account specifying to the best of his knowledge and belief the appropriate property vested in him, in which he has an interest or which (or income from which) is applicable for his benefit and the value of that property.

Where an account is to be delivered by personal representatives (but not where it is to be delivered by a person who is an executor of the deceased only of settled land in England and Wales), the appropriate property is all property which formed part of the deceased's estate immediately before his death, other than property which would not, apart from FA 1986, s 102(3), form part of his estate; and all property to which was attributable the value transferred by any chargeable transfers made by the deceased within seven years of his death.

If the personal representatives, after making the fullest enquiries that are reasonably practicable in the circumstances, are unable to ascertain the exact value of any particular property, their account is in the first instance sufficient as regards that property if it contains a statement to that effect, a provisional estimate of the value of the property, and an undertaking to deliver a further account of it as soon as its value is ascertained.

The Revenue may from time to time give such general or special directions as it thinks fit for restricting the property to be specified for the above purpose by any class of personal representatives.

Where this does not apply, the appropriate property is any property to the value of which the IHT is or would be attributable.

Except in the case of an account to be delivered by personal representatives, a person is not required to deliver an account:

(1) against any property if a full and proper account of it, specifying its value, has already been delivered to the Revenue by some other person who is:
  (a) or would be liable for the IHT attributable to its value, and
  (b) not or would not be liable with him jointly as trustee;
(2) if he or another such person has satisfied the Revenue that an account will in due course be delivered by the personal representatives.

An account as described above must be delivered:

(1) if by personal representatives, within the 12-month period from the end of the month in which the death occurs or, if such period expires later, the three-month period beginning with the date on which the personal representatives first act as such;
(2) if by a person who is liable under IHTA 1984, s 199(1)(b) (any person the value of whose estate is increased by the transfer), or who is liable under IHTA 1984:
  (a) s 201(1)(b) (any person entitled (whether beneficially or not) to an interest in possession in the settled property),
  (b) s 201(1)(c) (any person for whose benefit any of the settled property or income from it is applied at or after the time of the transfer),
  (c) s 201(1)(d) (where the transfer is made during the settlor's life and the trustees are not for the time being UK-resident, the settlor)
  for IHT on the value transferred by a PET which is made under s 52 (charge on termination of interest in possession) and which proves to be a chargeable transfer, or would be so liable if IHT were chargeable on that value, within 12 months from the end of the month in which the transferor's death occurs;

(3) if by a person who is liable under s 200(1)(c) for IHT on the value transferred by a chargeable transfer made on death, so far as the IHT is attributable to the value of property which, apart from FA 1986, s 102(3) (GWR), would not form part of the deceased's estate, or would be so liable if IHT were chargeable on the value transferred on death, within 12 months from the end of the month in which the death occurs;

(4) where if in the deceased's estate no grant of representation or confirmation has been obtained in the UK within 12 months from the end of the month in which the death occurred:

    (a) every person in whom any of the property forming part of the estate vests (whether beneficially or otherwise) on or at any time after the deceased's death or who at any such time is beneficially entitled to an interest in possession in any such property, and

    (b) where any of the property is at any such time comprised in a settlement and there is no person beneficially entitled to an interest in possession in that property, every person for whose benefit any of that property (or income from it) is applied at any such time,

within three months from the time when he first has reason to believe that he is required to deliver an account;

(5) if by any other person, within 12 months from the end of the month in which the transfer is made or, if this period expires later, within three months beginning with the date on which he first becomes liable for IHT.

A person liable for IHT under IHTA 1984, s 32 (conditional exemption – chargeable events), 32A (conditional exemption – chargeable events: associated properties), 79 (failure of exemption from ten-yearly charge under 'no interest in possession' regime), 126 (charge to tax on disposal of trees or underwood), or Sched 5 (conditional exemption – deaths before 7 April 1976) must deliver an account within six months from the end of the month in which the chargeable event occurs. The IHT account forms are:

- IHT 200/200N, for use where the deceased dies domiciled in the UK;
- IHT 201/201N, for use, in most cases, where the deceased dies domiciled outside the UK; and
- IHT 202/202N, for small estates.

The qualifying condition for the use of the simplified account form IHT 202/202N is restricted to estates where the gross value (before deducting exemptions and reliefs) does not exceed twice the IHT threshold at death. At the threshold levels at time of writing, this means a value of £446,000 or less. Even with this restriction, the simplified form can be used for the overwhelming majority of estates which have to be reported to CTOs. This condition supplements the following existing conditions for the use of the form:

(1) the deceased must have died on or after 18 March 1986 domiciled in the UK;

(2) the estate must comprise only property which has passed under the

deceased's will or intestacy, by nomination, or beneficially by survivorship;

(3) all assets in the estate must be situated in the UK;

(4) the deceased must have made no lifetime transfers chargeable to IHT within seven years of the death; and

(5) the estate's total net value after deducting exemptions and reliefs must not exceed the threshold at death.

19.2.2 Delivery of accounts
(IHTA 1984, s 217)

If a person who has delivered an account (under IHTA 1984, s 216) discovers at any time that it is materially defective by reason of anything contained in or omitted from it he must, within six months of that time, deliver to the Revenue a further account containing such information as may be necessary to remedy it (see further **19.10.3**).

19.2.3 Non-resident trustees
(IHTA 1984, s 218)

Where any person, in the course of a trade or profession carried on by him (except as a barrister), has been concerned with the making of a settlement and knows or has reason to believe that:

(1) the settlor was UK-domiciled, and

(2) the settlement trustees are or will be non-UK resident,

he must, within three months of the making it, make a return to the Revenue stating the names and addresses of the settlor and of the trustees. A person is not required to make such a return in relation to:

(1) any settlement made by will, or

(2) any other settlement, if such a return in relation to that settlement has already been made by another person or if an account has been delivered in relation to it under s 216.

Trustees of a settlement are regarded as non-UK resident unless the settlement's general administration is ordinarily carried on in the UK and the trustees or a majority of them (and, where there is more than one class of trustees, a majority of each class) are for the time being UK-resident.

19.2.4 Power to require information
(IHTA 1984, ss 219, 219A and 219B)

The Revenue may require any person to furnish it within such time, not being less than 30 days, as may be specified in the notice with such information as it may require for the IHT purposes. Such a notice may not be given except with the consent of a Special Commissioner; the

Commissioner is to give his consent only on being satisfied that in all the circumstances the Revenue is justified in proceeding.

A notice relating to IHT may be combined with one relating to income tax.

A barrister or solicitor is not obliged under such a notice to disclose, without his client's consent, any information with respect to which a claim to professional privilege could be maintained. However, a solicitor may be obliged to disclose his client's name and address; if his client is resident outside the UK and carries on a business outside the UK which includes the provision for persons in the UK of services or facilities relating to:

(1) the formation of companies outside the UK,
(2) the making of settlements outside the UK, or
(3) the securing of control over, or the management or administration of, such companies or settlements,

a solicitor may also be obliged to disclose the names and addresses of persons in the UK for whom such services or facilities have been provided in the course of that business.

19.2.5 Inspection of property
(IHTA 1984, s 220)

If the Revenue authorises any person to inspect any property so as to ascertain its value for IHT purposes, the property's custodian or possessor must permit him to inspect it at such reasonable times as the Revenue may consider necessary. If any person wilfully delays or obstructs an inspection he is liable on summary conviction to a fine not exceeding level 1 on the standard scale (under Criminal Justice Act 1982, s 75).

19.3 DETERMINATIONS AND APPEALS

19.3.1 Notices of determination
(IHTA 1984, s 221)

Where it appears to the Revenue that a transfer of value has been made or where a claim under it is made to the Revenue, the Revenue may give notice in writing to any person who appears to it to be the transferor or the claimant or liable for any of the IHT chargeable on the value transferred, stating that it has determined the matters specified in the notice. The matters specified may be all or any of the following:

(1) the transfer date;
(2) the value transferred and the value of any property to which the value transferred is wholly or partly attributable;
(3) the transferor;

(4) the IHT chargeable (if any) and the persons who are liable for the whole or part of it;

(5) the amount of any payment made in excess of the IHT for which a person is liable and the date from which and the rate at which IHT or any repayment of IHT overpaid carries interest; and

(6) any other matter that appears to the Revenue to be relevant for IHT purposes.

A determination for the purposes of a notice of any fact relating to a transfer of value:

(a) is, if that fact has been stated in an account or return and the Revenue is satisfied that the account or return is correct, made by the Revenue in accordance with that account or return, but

(b) may, in any other case, be made by the Revenue to the best of its judgement.

A notice must state the time within and the manner in which an appeal against any determination in it may be made.

Subject to any variation by agreement in writing or on appeal, a determination in such notice is conclusive against the person on whom it is served; if it is served on the transferor and specifies a determination of the value transferred by the transfer, or previous transfers, of value, the determination, so far as relevant to the IHT chargeable in respect of later transfers of value (whether or not made by the transferor) is conclusive also against any other person, subject to any adjustment under IHTA 1984, s 240 or 241.

References here to transfers of value or to the values transferred by them are construed as including:

(1) chargeable events by reference to which IHT is chargeable under IHTA 1984, ss 32 and 32A;

(2) occasions on which IHT is chargeable under IHTA 1984, ss 58–85 ('no interest in possession' regime); and

(3) disposals on which IHT is chargeable under IHTA 1984, s 126 (charge on disposal of trees or underwood).

19.3.2 Appeals against determinations
(IHTA 1984, s 222)

A person on whom a notice of determination has been served may, within 30 days of the service, appeal against such determination by notice in writing given to the Board and specifying the grounds of appeal. Normally, the appeal is to the Special Commissioners, but where:

(1) it is so agreed between the appellant and the Revenue, or

(2) the High Court, on an application made by the appellant, is satisfied that the matters to be decided on the appeal are likely to be substantially confined to questions of law and gives leave for that purpose,

the appeal may be to the High Court. An appeal on any question over the value of land in the UK may be to the appropriate tribunal, ie the Lands Tribunal, the Lands Tribunal for Scotland or the Lands Tribunal for Northern Ireland.

In Scotland, references to the High Court are substituted as to the Court of Session. In Northern Ireland, they are substituted as the Court of Appeal in Northern Ireland.

19.3.3 Appeals out of time
(IHTA 1984, s 223)

An appeal may be brought out of time with the consent of the Revenue or the Special Commissioners. The Revenue must:

(1) give that consent if satisfied, on an application for the purpose, that there was a reasonable excuse for not bringing the appeal within the time limited and that the application was made thereafter without unreasonable delay, and

(2) if not so satisfied, refer the application for determination by the Special Commissioners.

19.3.4 Procedure before Special Commissioners
(IHTA 1984, s 224)

On an appeal before the Special Commissioners, the Commissioners may allow the appellant to put forward any ground of appeal not specified in the notice of appeal and may take it into consideration if satisfied that the omission was not wilful or unreasonable. The Special Commissioners must on an appeal to them confirm the determination appealed against unless they are satisfied that the determination ought to be varied or quashed.

19.3.5 Appeals from Special Commissioners
(IHTA 1984, s 225)

Any party to an appeal, if dissatisfied in point of law with the determination of that appeal by the Special Commissioners, may appeal against that determination to the High Court.

The High Court hears and determines any question of law arising on such appeal and may reverse, affirm or vary the determination appealed against, or remit the matter to the Special Commissioners with the court's opinion on it, or make such other order in relation to the matter as the court thinks fit.

19.3.6 Extension of regulation-making powers
(IHTA 1984, s 225A)

The Lord Chancellor may, with the Lord Advocate's consent, make regulations about the number of Special Commissioners required or permitted to hear, or perform other functions in relation to, appeals or other proceedings under the Taxes Acts. These regulations may:

(1) make different provision for different cases or different circumstances, and

(2) contain such supplementary, incidental, consequential and transitional provisions as the Lord Chancellor thinks appropriate.

Such provision may include amending TMA 1970 or any other Act or instrument made under an Act (TMA 1970, s 46A(3)). Regulations are made by statutory instrument subject to annulment by a resolution of either House of Parliament (IHTA 1970, s 46A(4)).

The Lord Chancellor may also, with the Lord Advocate's consent, make regulations about the practice and procedure to be followed in connection with appeals (TMA 1970, s 56B(1)). The regulations may in particular include provision:

(1) enabling the Commissioners to join as a party to an appeal a person who would not otherwise be a party (TMA 1970, s 56B(2)(a));

(2) for requiring any party to an appeal to provide information and make documents available for inspection by specified persons (s 56B(2)(b));

(3) for requiring persons to attend an appeal hearing to give evidence and produce documents (s 56B(2)(c));

(4) about evidence generally in relation to appeals (s 56B(2)(d));

(5) enabling the Commissioners to review their decisions (s 56B(2)(e));

(6) for the imposition of penalties not exceeding an amount specified in the regulations (s 56B(2)(f)); and

(7) for the determination and recovery of penalties and for appeals against penalties (s 56B(2)(a)).

The 'specified persons' referred to in (2) above are such of the following as may be specified in the regulations:

(1) the Commissioners (s 56B(2A)(a));

(2) any party to the appeal (s 56B(2A)(b)); and

(3) officers of the Revenue (s 56B(2A)(c)).

The regulations may also include provision:

(1) authorising or requiring the Commissioners, in circumstances prescribed in the regulations, to state a case for the opinion of a court (s 56B(3)(a));

(2) for an appeal to lie to a court on a question of law arising from a decision of the Commissioners (s 56B(3)(b));

(3) about the practice and procedure to be followed in connection with cases so stated or such appeals (s 56B(3)(c)).

The regulations may:

(a) make different provision for different cases or different circumstances (s 56B(4)(a)), and
(b) contain such supplementary, incidental, consequential and transitional provision as the Lord Chancellor thinks appropriate (s 56B(4)(b)).

Again, a provision so made may include amending TMA 1970 or any other Act or any instrument made under an Act (s 56B(5)), and regulations made by statutory instrument are subject to annulment by a resolution of either House of Parliament (s 56B(6)).

Regulations made as above may include provision for:

(1) the award by the Special Commissioners of the costs of, or incidental to, appeal hearings before them (s 56C(1)(a)),
(2) the recovery of costs so awarded (s 56C(1)(b)), and
(3) appeals against such awards (s 56C(1)(c)).

Any provision made under (1) above must provide that the Special Commissioners may not award costs against a party to an appeal unless they consider that he has acted wholly unreasonably in connection with the hearing in question (s 56C(2)).

Regulations so made may include provision for the Special Commissioners to publish reports of such of their decisions as they consider appropriate (TMA 1970, s 56D(1)). Any such provision must provide that any report published, other than a report of an appeal that was heard in public, be in a form that so far as possible prevents the identification of any person whose affairs are dealt with in it (s 56D(2)). No obligation of secrecy to which the Special Commissioners are subject prevents their publishing such reports (s 56D(3)).

19.4 PAYMENT

19.4.1 Payment: general rules
(IHTA 1984, s 226)

Except as otherwise provided, IHT on the value transferred by a chargeable transfer is due six months after the end of the month in which the chargeable transfer is made or, where a transfer is made after 5 April and before 1 October in any year otherwise than on death, at the end of April in the next year.

Personal representatives must, on delivery of their account, pay all the IHT for which they are liable and may on delivery also pay any part of the IHT chargeable on the death for which they are not liable, if the persons liable for it request them to make such payment.

So much of the IHT chargeable on the value so transferred made within seven years of the transferor's death as exceeds what it would have been had he died more than seven years after the transfer is due six months after the end of the month in which the death occurs. The IHT chargeable on the value transferred by a PET which proves to be a chargeable transfer is due six months after the end of the month in which the transferor's death occurs.

So much (if any) of the IHT chargeable on the value transferred by a chargeable transfer made under the no interest in possession regime (IHTA 1984, ss 58–85) within the seven-year period ending with the settlor's death as exceeds what it would have been had the settlor died more than seven years after the date of transfer is due six months after the end of the month in which the death occurs.

IHT chargeable under IHTA 1984, ss 32, 32A, 79, 126 and Sched 5 (see **19.2.1**) is due six months after the end of the month in which the event by reason of which it is chargeable occurs.

The Revenue may in the first instance, and without prejudice to the recovery of the remainder of the IHT, accept or demand payment of an amount by reference to the value stated in an account delivered to the Revenue as above.

Nothing here is to be taken to authorise the recovery from, or require the payment by, any person of IHT in excess of his liability as limited by IHTA 1984, s 204.

Where, because of restrictions imposed by a foreign government, executors who intend to transfer to the UK sufficient of the deceased's foreign assets to pay the IHT attributable to them cannot do so immediately, they are given the option of deferring payment until the transfer can be effected. If the amount in sterling that the executors finally succeed in bringing to this country is less than this tax, the balance is waived (ESC F6: Foreign assets).

19.4.2 Payment by instalments – land, shares and businesses
(IHTA 1984, s 227)

Where any of the IHT payable on the value transferred is attributable to the value of qualifying property and:

(1) the transfer is made on death, or
(2) the IHT so attributable is borne by the person benefiting from the transfer, or
(3) the transfer is settled property and the property concerned continues to be comprised in the settlement,

the IHT so attributable may, if the person paying it by notice in writing to the Revenue so elects, be paid by ten equal yearly instalments. This does not apply to:

(1) IHT payable on the value transferred by a PET which proves to be a chargeable transfer, or

(2) additional IHT becoming payable on the value transferred by reason of the transferor's death within seven years of the chargeable transfer, except to the extent that the IHT is attributable to the value of property which satisfies one of the conditions specified below and, in the case of property consisting of unquoted shares or unquoted securities, the shares or securities remained unquoted throughout the period beginning with the date of the chargeable transfer and ending with the transferor's (or, if earlier, the transferee's) death.

Definitions for 'unquoted shares or securities', 'transferee' and 'qualifying property' are given in the Glossary at the front of this book.

The conditions are that:

(1) the property was owned by the transferee throughout the period beginning with the date of the chargeable transfer and ending with the death of the transferor (or, if earlier, the death of the transferee), or
(2) for the purposes of determining the IHT, or additional IHT, due by reason of the death of the transferor, the value of the property is reduced under business property relief (IHTA 1984, ss 103 to 114) or agricultural property relief as applied by IHTA 1984, s 113B or 124B (application to replacement property).

The first of the instalments is payable:

(1) if the chargeable transfer was made on death, six months after the end of the month in which the death occurred, and
(2) in any other case, at the time when the IHT would be due if it were not payable by instalments.

Interest (under IHTA 1984, s 233) on the unpaid portion of the IHT is added to each instalment and paid accordingly, except as otherwise provided under s 234.

Notwithstanding the making of an election, the IHT for the time being unpaid, with interest to the time of payment, may be paid at any time. If at any time (whether before or after the date when the first instalment is payable) the whole or any part of the property is sold, the unpaid IHT (or, in the case of a sale of part, the proportionate part thereof) becomes payable forthwith (or, if the sale precedes the date when the first instalment is payable, on that date), together with any interest accrued under s 233.

Where the IHT is payable on the value transferred by a PET which proves to be a chargeable transfer, this does not apply to any time before the transferor's death.

References above to the sale of property apply where:

(1) the attributable IHT is borne by the person benefiting from the transfer other than where:
 (a) IHT payable on the value transferred by a PET which proves to be a chargeable transfer, or

(b) additional IHT becoming payable on the value transferred by any chargeable transfer by reason of the transferor's death within seven years of the transfer where the transferee dies before the transferor,

as if they included references to any chargeable transfer in which the value transferred is wholly or partly attributable to the value of the property, other than a transfer made on death, and

(2) the transfer is settled property and the property continues to be comprised in the settlement, as references to the property ceasing to be comprised in the settlement.

The sale of an interest or part of it in a business is treated as a sale of part of the business. The payment, under a partnership agreement or otherwise, of a sum in satisfaction of the whole or part of an interest in a business otherwise than on a sale is treated as a sale of the interest or part at the time of payment.

In applying the rules for payment by instalments:

(1) the value of a business or of an interest in a business is taken to be its net value;

(2) a business's net value is the value of the assets used in it (including goodwill) reduced by the aggregate amount of any liabilities incurred for business purposes;

(3) in ascertaining the net value of an interest in a business, no regard is had to assets or liabilities other than those by reference to which the business's net value would have fallen to be ascertained if the IHT had been attributable to the entire business; and

(4) 'business' includes a business carried on in the exercise of a profession or vocation, but does not include a business carried on otherwise than for gain.

19.4.3 Shares to which payment of IHT by instalments applies
(IHTA 1984, s 228)

The payment by instalment rules apply to company shares or securities which:

(1) immediately before the chargeable transfer gave control of the company:
    (a) in the case of a transfer on death, to the deceased,
    (b) in the case of a transfer under the no interest in possession regime, to the trustees, and
    (c) in any other case, to the transferor;

(2) do not fall under (1) above and are unquoted, if the chargeable transfer is made on death and the condition stated below is satisfied;

(3) do not fall under (1) above and are unquoted, if the Revenue is satisfied that the IHT attributable to their value cannot be paid in one sum

235

without undue hardship (assuming, in the case of a chargeable transfer made otherwise than on death, that the shares or securities would be retained by the persons liable to pay the IHT);

(4) do not fall under (1) above and are unquoted, if the conditions stated below are satisfied.

The condition under (2) above is that not less than 20 per cent of so much of the IHT chargeable on the value transferred as is IHT for which the person paying the IHT attributable (under IHTA 1984, s 227(1)) is liable (in the same capacity) consists of IHT attributable to the value of the shares or securities or such other IHT (if any) as may (under s 227) be paid by instalments.

The conditions mentioned in (4) above are that so much of the value transferred (calculated, if the transfer is not made on death, as if no IHT were chargeable on it) as is attributable to the shares exceeds £20,000, and that either:

(a) the shares' nominal value is not less than 10 per cent of the nominal value of all the company's shares at the time of transfer, or

(b) the shares are ordinary shares and their nominal value is not less than 10 per cent of the nominal value of all the company's ordinary shares at that time.

19.4.4 Payment by instalments: woodlands
(IHTA 1984, s 229)

IHT chargeable on the disposal of trees or underwood (under IHTA 1984, s 126) may, if the person paying the IHT by notice in writing to the Revenue so elects, be paid by ten equal yearly instalments, of which the first is payable six months after the end of the month in which the transfer is made.

19.4.5 Acceptance of property in satisfaction of IHT
(IHTA 1984, s 230)

The Revenue may, if it thinks fit and the Secretary of State agrees, on the application of any person liable to pay IHT or interest payable, accept in satisfaction of the whole or any part of it any property in satisfaction of IHT. This applies to any land as may be agreed upon between the Revenue and the person liable to pay IHT, and to any objects which are or have been kept in any building:

(1) if the Revenue has determined to accept or has accepted that building in satisfaction or part satisfaction of IHT, or

(2) if the building or any interest in it belongs to Her Majesty in right of the Crown or of the Duchy of Lancaster, or belongs to the Duchy of Cornwall or belongs to a government department or is held for the purposes of a government department, or

(3) if the building is one of which the Secretary of State is guardian under the Ancient Monuments and Archaeological Areas Act 1979 or of which the Department of the Environment for Northern Ireland is guardian under the Historic Monuments Act (Northern Ireland) 1971, or

(4) if the building belongs to any national purposes body under IHTA 1984, Sched 3,

in any case where it appears to the Secretary of State desirable for the objects to remain associated with the building. This facility also applies to any picture, print, book, manuscript, work of art, scientific object or other thing (or collection or group thereof taken as a whole) which the Secretary of State is satisfied is pre-eminent for its national, scientific, historic or artistic interest.

Here, 'national interest' includes interest within any part of the UK. In determining whether an object or collection or group of objects is pre-eminent, regard must be had to any significant association of the object, collection or group with a particular place.

See further **4.2**.

19.4.6 Powers to transfer property in satisfaction of IHT
(IHTA 1984, s 231)

Where a person has power to sell any property in order to raise money to pay the IHT, he may agree with the Revenue for the property to be accepted in satisfaction of that IHT under IHTA 1984, s 230. Except as regards the nature of the consideration and its receipt and application, any such agreement is subject to the same provisions and treated for all purposes as a sale made in the exercise of this power, and any conveyance or transfer made or purporting to be made to give effect to such an agreement has effect accordingly.

Here, IHT includes interest payable under IHTA 1984, s 233.

Nothing in s 230 affects the rule whereby, on a death before 7 April 1976, the value of an object has been left out of account subject to undertakings given under IHTA 1984, Sched 5, para 5. The acceptance of an object in satisfaction of IHT is not treated as a disposal thereof (Sched 5, para 1(4)).

Nothing in s 230 affects the rule whereby, on a death before 7 April 1976, the sale of any property by private treaty to a national purposes body (under IHTA 1984, Sched 3), or on its being disposed of to such a body otherwise than by sale (Sched 5, para 3(4)(a)), or if it is disposed of otherwise than by sale and the undertaking previously given with respect to it is replaced by a further undertaking (para 3(4)(b)), the acceptance of any property in satisfaction of IHT is not treated as a disposal of the property.

19.4.7 Administration actions
(IHTA 1984, s 232)

Where proceedings are pending in any court for the administration of any property to the value of which any IHT charged on the value transferred is attributable, the court will provide, out of any such property in the court's possession or control, for the payment of any of the IHT so attributable, or interest on it, which remains unpaid.

19.5 INTEREST

19.5.1 Interest on unpaid IHT
(IHTA 1984, s 233; FA 1989, s 178)

IHT charged on the value transferred made after 5 April and before 1 October in any year, and otherwise than on death, which remains unpaid after the end of the period ending with April in the next year, carries interest from the end of that period at the rate then applicable. An amount of IHT charged on the value transferred by any other chargeable transfer which remains unpaid after the end of six months from the end of the month in which the chargeable transfer was made carries interest from that date at the rate then applicable.

IHT chargeable under IHTA 1984, s 32, 32A, 79, 126 or Sched 5 (see **19.2.1**) which remains unpaid after the end of the period of six months beginning with the end of the month in which the event occasioning the charge occurs, carries interest from the end of that period at the rate then applicable.

If the Revenue agrees to accept property in satisfaction of any IHT (under IHTA 1984, s 230) on terms that the value to be attributed to the property is determined as at a date earlier than that on which the property is actually accepted, the terms may provide that the amount of IHT which is satisfied by the acceptance of the property does not carry interest from that date.

Interest on late payment of IHT is not allowed as a deduction in computing any income, profits or losses for any tax purposes.

19.5.2 Interest on instalments
(IHTA 1984, s 234)

Where IHT is payable on the value transferred by a chargeable transfer is payable by instalments under IHTA 1984:

(1) s 227 and is attributable to the value of any shares, securities, business or interest in a business, or to value treated as reduced by APR under IHTA 1984, ss 115–124B, or
(2) s 229, being IHT arising on the disposal of trees or underwood under IHTA 1984, s 126,

interest is added to each instalment from the date at which the instalment is payable. This does not apply to IHT on the value of shares or securities of a company whose business consists wholly or mainly of dealing in securities, stocks or shares, land or buildings, or making or holding investments (not being IHT attributable to value reduced by APR) unless it also falls within either of the following categories:

(1) any company whose business consists wholly or mainly in being a holding company (as defined in the Companies Act 1985, s 736) of one or more companies which are not excluded as above;
(2) any company whose business is wholly that of a market-maker or of a discount house and (in either case) is carried on in the UK.

See further **8.3.2** with regard to such exemptions.

19.5.3 Interest on overpaid IHT
(IHTA 1984, s 235)

Repayment of overpayments of IHT carry interest from the date of payment until the order for repayment is issued. The rate of interest is the same as that which applies to unpaid IHT (see **19.5.1**). Interest on overpayment of IHT is not treated as income for any tax purposes.

If legal personal representatives or trustees require repayment of IHT to a payee other than themselves, they must provide the CTO with their personal written authority to do so (see *Law Society's Gazette*, 18 November 1992).

19.5.4 Special cases
(IHTA 1984, s 236)

The rules charging interest on late payment of IHT apply to the amount by which IHT chargeable on the value transferred by a chargeable transfer made within seven years of the transferor's death exceeds what it would have been had the transferor died more than seven years after such transfer. The rules apply to the amount (if any) by which the IHT chargeable on the value transferred made under the no interest in possession regime (IHTA 1984, ss 58–85) within the seven-year period ending with the settlor's death exceeds what that IHT would have been had the settlor died more than seven years after the transfer date.

IHT over- or underpaid does not carry interest for any period of time before an order is made under IHTA 1984, s 146(1) (Inheritance (Provision for Family and Dependants) Act 1975, s 2), or s 19(1) of the 1975 Act, or the corresponding provision of the Inheritance (Provision for Family and Dependants) (Northern Ireland) Order 1979.

IHT repayable on a claim under IHTA 1984, s 146(2) (following an order under s 10 of the 1975 Act) or under IHTA 1984, s 150 (voidable transfers) carries interest (which is not treated as income for any tax purposes) at the rate applicable under FA 1989, s 178 from the date on which the claim is made.

IHT repayable under IHTA 1984, s 147(2) (renouncement of claim to legitim) carries interest (which is not treated as income for any tax purposes) at the rate applicable under FA 1989, s 178 from the date on which the IHT was paid; IHT charged on value of legitim under s 147(4) carries interest at that rate from the end of the period of six months from the end of the month in which the chargeable transfer was made.

19.6 INLAND REVENUE CHARGE FOR UNPAID IHT

19.6.1 Imposition of charge
(IHTA 1984, s 237)

Unless otherwise provided, while any IHT charged or any interest thereon on the value transferred remains unpaid, a charge for the amount unpaid (known as an 'Inland Revenue charge') is imposed in favour of the Revenue on any property to the value of which the value transferred is wholly or partly attributable. Where the chargeable transfer arises on the making of a settlement or is made under the provisions concerning settled property (IHTA 1984, ss 43–93), the Inland Revenue charge is made on any property comprised in the settlement. In both of these cases, references to any property include any property directly or indirectly representing it.

Where the chargeable transfer is made on death, personal or moveable property situated in the UK which was beneficially owned by the deceased immediately before his death and vests in his personal representatives is not subject to the Inland Revenue charge. For deaths after 8 March 1999, personal property no longer includes leaseholds and undivided shares in land held on trust for sale, whether statutory or not. This extension also applies to IHT charged, after that date, on assets which previously benefited from heritage tax reliefs. In determining whether any property was beneficially owned by the deceased, IHTA 1984, s 49(1) (treatment of person beneficially entitled to an interest in possession in settled property as beneficially entitled to the underlying property) is ignored.

A PET which proves to be a chargeable transfer or an interest in property (of which the value transferred is wholly or partly attributable) which has been disposed of to a purchaser before the transferor's death is not subject to the Inland Revenue charge. However, property which has been otherwise disposed of before the death, and which at the death represents any such property or interest is subject to the charge.

No heritable property situated in Scotland can be subject to an Inland Revenue charge, but where such property is disposed of, any other property which represents it is subject to the charge to which the heritable property would otherwise have been subject.

The Inland Revenue charge imposed on any property takes effect subject to priority for any incumbrance on it which is allowable as a deduction in valuing that property for IHT purposes. Generally, a disposition of property subject to an Inland Revenue charge takes effect subject to that charge.

19.6.2 Effect of purchases
(IHTA 1984, s 238)

Where property which is subject to an Inland Revenue charge, or an interest in such property, is disposed of to a purchaser, then if at 'the time of the disposition':

(1) in the case of land in England and Wales, the charge was not registered as a land charge or, in the case of registered land, was not protected by notice on the register, or

(2) in the case of land in Northern Ireland the title to which is registered under the Land Registration Act (Northern Ireland) 1970, the charge was not entered as a burden on the appropriate register maintained under that Act or was not protected by a caution or inhibition under that Act or, in the case of other land in Northern Ireland, the purchaser had no notice of the facts giving rise to the charge, or

(3) in the case of personal property situated in the UK other than property as described above, and of any property situated outside the UK, the purchaser had no notice of the facts giving rise to the charge, or

(4) in the case of any property, a certificate of discharge had been given by the Revenue (see **19.7**) and the purchaser had no notice of any fact invalidating the certificate,

the property or interest then ceases to be subject to the charge, but the property for the time being representing it remains subject to it.

Where property subject to an Inland Revenue charge, or an interest in it, is disposed of to a purchaser and it does not then cease to be subject to the charge, it ceases to be subject to it at the end of the period of six years beginning with the later of:

(1) the date on which the IHT became due, and

(2) the date on which a full and proper account of the property was first delivered to the Revenue in connection with the chargeable transfer.

Here, 'the time of the disposition' means:

(a) in relation to registered land, the time of registration of the disposition, and

(b) in relation to other property, the time of completion.

19.7 CERTIFICATES OF DISCHARGE

19.7.1 Certificates of discharge
(IHTA 1984, s 239)

Where application is made to the Revenue by a person liable for any IHT on the value transferred by a chargeable transfer attributable to the value of property specified in the application, the Revenue, on being satisfied that the IHT so attributable has been or will be paid, may give a certificate to that effect, and will do so if the chargeable transfer is one made on death, or the transferor has died.

Where IHT is or may be chargeable on the value transferred and:

(1) application is made to the Revenue after two years from the transfer (or, if the Revenue thinks fit to entertain the application, at an earlier time) by a person who is or might be liable for the whole or part of the IHT, and

(2) the applicant delivers to the Revenue, if the transfer is one made on death, a full statement to the best of his knowledge and belief of all property included in the deceased's estate immediately before his death and, in any other case, a full and proper account,

the Revenue may, as the case requires, determine the amount of IHT or determine that no IHT is chargeable. Subject to the payment of any IHT so determined, the Revenue may give a certificate of its determination, and will do so if the transfer of value is one made on death or the transferor has died.

An application in relation to IHT which is or may become chargeable on the value transferred by a PET may not be made before two years from the transferor's death (except where the Revenue thinks fit to entertain the application at an earlier time after the death).

Subject to the additional requirements set out below, a certificate discharges either the property shown in it from the Inland Revenue charge on its acquisition by a purchaser, or all persons from any further claim for IHT on the value transferred, and extinguishes any Inland Revenue charge for that IHT.

A certificate does not protect a person from IHT in case of fraud or failure to disclose material facts and does not affect any further IHT that may afterwards be shown to be payable under the following IHTA 1984 provisions:

- s 93 (disclaimers),
- s 142 (alteration of dispositions taking place on death),
- s 143 (compliance with the testator's request),
- s 144 (distribution of property settled by will), and
- s 145 (redemption of surviving spouse's interest).

Nor does a certificate protect a person from IHT in case of fraud or failure to disclose material facts or affect any further IHT that may afterwards be shown to be payable if any further property is afterwards shown to have been included in the deceased's estate immediately before his death. However, in so far as the certificate shows any IHT to be attributable to the value of any property, it remains valid in favour of a purchaser of that property without notice of any fact invalidating it.

References here to a transfer of value include an occasion on which IHT is chargeable under the no interest in possession regime (apart from IHTA 1984, s 79 (failure of exemption from ten-yearly charge)) or to the amount on which IHT is then chargeable.

19.8 ADJUSTMENTS

19.8.1 Underpayments
(IHTA 1984, s 240)

Where too little IHT has been paid on a chargeable transfer, the IHT under-paid is payable with interest (see **19.5**), whether or not the amount that has been paid was that stated as payable in a notice (see **19.3.1**).

Where IHT attributable to the value of any property is paid in accordance with an Inland Revenue account, and the payment is made and accepted in full satisfaction of the IHT so attributable, no proceedings can be brought for the recovery of any additional IHT so attributable after the end of the six-year period beginning with the later of the date on which the payment (or in the case of IHT paid by instalments, the last payment) was made and accepted, and the date on which the IHT or the last instalment became due. At the end of that period, any liability for the additional IHT and any Inland Revenue charge for that IHT is extinguished.

In any case of fraud, wilful default or neglect by a person liable for the IHT, or in the case of IHT chargeable under the no interest in possession regime, and the person is the settlor in relation to the settlement, the six-year period runs from when the fraud, default or neglect comes to the Revenue's knowledge.

19.8.2 Overpayments
(IHTA 1984, s 241)

If it is proved to the Revenue's satisfaction that too much IHT (and interest thereon) has been paid on the value transferred or on so much of that value as is attributable to any property, the Revenue will repay the excess unless the claim for repayment was made more than six years after the date on which the payment or last payment of the IHT.

19.9 RECOVERY OF IHT
(IHTA 1984, s 242)

The Revenue will not take any legal proceedings for the recovery of any amount of IHT or of interest thereon which is due from any person unless the amount has been agreed in writing between that person and the Board or has been determined and specified in a notice (see **19.3.1**). Where an amount has been so determined and specified but an appeal is pending against the determination, the Revenue will not take any legal proceedings to recover that amount except such part of it as may be agreed in writing or determined and specified in a further notice to be a part not in dispute. This applies to any appeal against a determination (made under IHTA 1984, s 222), but not to any further appeal.

A person on whom a notice of determination has been served may, within 30 days of the service, appeal against any determination specified in it by notice in writing given to the Board and specifying the grounds of appeal. Normally, the appeal is to the Special Commissioners, but may be direct to the High Court (see **19.3.2**).

19.9.1 Scotland: recovery of IHT in Sheriff Court
(IHTA 1984, s 243)

In Scotland, IHT and interest thereon may, without prejudice to any other remedy, and if the amount of the IHT and interest does not exceed the sum for the time being specified in the Sheriff Courts (Scotland) Act 1971, s 35(1)(a), be sued for and recovered in the Sheriff Court.

19.9.2 Right to address court
(IHTA 1984, s 244)

Any officer of the Revenue who is so authorised may address the court in any proceedings in a county court or Sheriff Court for the recovery of IHT or interest thereon.

19.10 PENALTIES

19.10.1 Failure to provide information
(IHTA 1984, ss 245 and 245A)

A person who fails to deliver an account under IHTA 1984, s 216 (delivery of accounts) or s 217 (correction of defective accounts) is liable to a penalty not exceeding £100 and, if the failure continues after the failure has been declared by a court or by the Special Commissioners, to a further penalty not exceeding £60 for each day for which it continues. A further penalty not exceeding £100 may be charged if the account is more than six months late, and no daily penalties have been sought. The total penalty is subject to an overall limit of the tax due.

A person who fails to make a return under IHTA 1984, s 218 (non-resident trusts) to a penalty not exceeding £300 and, if the failure continues after the failure has been declared by a court or by the Special Commissioners, to a further penalty not exceeding £60 for each day for which it continues.

A person who fails to comply with a notice under IHTA 1984, s 219 (power to require information) is liable to a penalty not exceeding £300 and, if the failure continues after the failure has been declared by a court or by the Special Commissioners, to a further penalty not exceeding £60 for each day for which it continues.

A person who fails to comply with a notice under IHTA 1984, s 219A(1) or (4) is liable to a penalty not exceeding £50 and, if the failure continues after the failure has been declared by a court or by the Special Commissioners, to a further penalty not exceeding £30 for each day for which it continues.

The daily penalty is not due if the account is delivered, the return made or provides the information or documents before proceedings in which the failure could be declared are commenced. The penalties do not apply if there is a reasonable excuse for failing to deliver an account provided that it is delivered without unreasonable delay after the excuse has ceased.

19.10.2 Provision of incorrect information
(IHTA 1984, s 247)

If any person liable for any IHT on the value transferred fraudulently or negligently delivers, furnishes or produces to the Revenue any incorrect account, information or document, he is liable:

(1) in the case of fraud, to a penalty not exceeding the aggregate of £3,000 and the difference (see below), and
(2) in the case of negligence, to a penalty not exceeding the aggregate of £1,500 and that difference.

The difference is the amount by which the IHT for which that person is liable exceeds what would be the amount of that IHT if the facts were as shown in the account, information or document.

Any person not liable for IHT on the value transferred who fraudulently or negligently furnishes or produces to the Revenue any incorrect information or document in connection with the transfer is liable to a penalty not exceeding £3,000 for fraud and £1,500 for negligence.

Any person who assists in or induces the delivery, furnishing or production of any account, information or document which he knows to be incorrect is liable to a penalty not exceeding £3,000.

19.10.3 Failure to remedy errors
(IHTA 1984, s 248)

If after any account, information or document has been delivered, furnished or produced by any person without fraud or negligence it comes to his notice that it was materially incorrect, it is treated as having been negligently delivered, furnished or produced unless the error is remedied without unreasonable delay.

If, after any account, etc has been delivered, furnished or produced by any person it comes to the notice of any other person that it contains an error whereby IHT for which that other person is liable has been or might be underpaid, that other person must inform the Revenue of the error. If he fails to do so without unreasonable delay he is liable to a penalty for negligence as set out in **19.10.2**.

19.10.4 Recovery of penalties
(IHTA 1984, s 249)

All proceedings for the recovery of penalties are commenced by the Revenue or, in Scotland, by the Revenue or the Lord Advocate.

Any such proceedings may be commenced either before the Special Commissioners or in the High Court or Court of Session and, if brought in the High Court, are deemed to be civil proceedings by the Crown (under the Crown Proceedings Act 1947, Part II).

Where any such proceedings are brought before the Special Commissioners, an appeal lies from their decision to the High Court or Court of Session by either party on a question of law, and by the defendant (in Scotland, the defender) against the amount of any penalty awarded. In this case, the court may either confirm the decision or reduce or increase the sum awarded.

Proceedings before the Special Commissioners are by way of information in writing made to them, and upon summons issued by them to the defendant (or defender) to appear before them at a time and place stated in the summons. They will hear and determine each case in a summary way.

19.10.5 Time limit for recovery
(IHTA 1984, s 250)

No proceedings for the recovery of a penalty can be brought after the end of the three-year period beginning with the date on which the amount of IHT properly payable was notified by the Revenue to the person or one of the persons liable for the IHT or any part of it. Where the person who has incurred any such penalty has died, any proceedings for its recovery which have been or could have been commenced against him may be continued or commenced against his personal representatives; thus any penalty awarded in such proceedings is a debt due from and payable out of his estate.

19.10.6 Appeals against summary determination of penalties
(IHTA 1984, s 251)

An appeal lies to the High Court or Court of Session against the summary determination by the Special Commissioners of a penalty under the Special Commissioners (Jurisdiction and Procedure) Regulations 1994, reg 24. On such an appeal, the court may either confirm or reverse the Special Commissioners' determination or reduce or increase the sum determined.

19.10.7 Effect of award by Special Commissioners
(IHTA 1984, s 252)

Any penalty awarded by the Special Commissioners is recoverable by the Revenue as a debt due to the Crown.

19.10.8 Mitigation of penalties
(IHTA 1984, s 253)

The Revenue may in its discretion mitigate any penalty, or stay or compound any proceedings for recovery of any penalty, and may also, after judgment, further mitigate or entirely remit the penalty.

19.11 MISCELLANEOUS

19.11.1 Evidence
(IHTA 1984, s 254)

A notice of determination (see **19.3.1**) specifying any determination which can no longer be varied or quashed on appeal is sufficient evidence of the matters determined.

In any proceedings for the recovery of IHT or interest thereon, a certificate by a Revenue officer that the IHT or interest is due, or that to the best of his knowledge and belief it has not been paid, is sufficient evidence that the sum mentioned in the certificate is due or unpaid. A document purporting to be such a certificate is deemed to be so unless the contrary is proved.

19.11.2 Determination of questions on previous view of law
(IHTA 1984, s 255)

Where any payment has been made and accepted in satisfaction of any IHT liability and on a view of the law then generally received or adopted in practice, any question of whether too little or too much has been paid or what was the right amount of IHT payable is determined on the same view, notwithstanding that it appears from a subsequent legal decision or otherwise that the view was or may have been wrong.

19.11.3 Regulations about accounts, etc
(IHTA 1984, s 256)

Regulations about accounts deal with the following matters:

(1) dispensing with the delivery of accounts under IHTA 1984, s 216 in such cases as may be specified in the regulations;
(2) discharging, subject to such restrictions as may be so specified, property from an Inland Revenue charge and persons from further claims for IHT in cases other than those mentioned in IHTA 1984, s 239 (see **19.7.1**);
(3) requiring information to be furnished to the Revenue, in such circumstances as may be so specified, by persons who have not delivered accounts under IHTA 1984, s 216 or who have produced documents other than an account or inventory under arrangements made under the following enactments:
    (a) the Supreme Court Act 1981, s 109(2),
    (b) the proviso to the Probate and Legacy Duties Act 1808, s 42, and
    (c) the Administration of Estates (Northern Ireland) Order 1979, Art 20; and
(4) modifying IHTA 1984, s 264(8) (transfers reported late) in cases where the delivery of an account has been dispensed with under the regulations.

The regulations currently in force are the Inheritance Tax (Delivery of Accounts) Regulations 1981 (SI No 880). There are equivalent regulations applying in Scotland (SI 1981 No 881) and Northern Ireland (SI 1981 No 1441). For the purpose of these regulations 'an excepted estate' is the estate of a person immediately before his death in a case where:

(1) he died after 5 April 2000, domiciled in the UK;
(2) the value of his estate is attributable wholly to property passing under his will or intestacy or under a nomination of an asset taking effect on death or by survivorship in a beneficial joint tenancy;
(3) of that property not more than £50,000 represented value attributable to property which, immediately before that person's death, was situated outside the UK;
(4) he died without having made any chargeable transfers during the seven-year period ending with his death other than specified transfers where the aggregate value transferred did not exceed £75,000; and
(5) the aggregate of the gross value of his estate and of the value transferred by any specified transfers made by him did not exceed £210,000.

Here, 'specified transfers' are chargeable transfers made during the seven-year period ending with that person's death where the value transferred is attributable to cash or to quoted shares or securities. 'The prescribed period' in relation to any person is the period beginning with that person's death and ending 35 days after the making of the first grant of representation in respect of that person in England and Wales (not being a grant limited in duration, in respect of property or to any special purpose). In Scotland, 'the prescribed period' in relation to any person whose estate is an excepted estate is the period beginning with that person's death and ending 60 days after the date on which confirmation to that person's estate was first issued.

Where the deceased made a PET which became chargeable to IHT on his death, his estate cannot be an excepted estate, and likewise if he made a GWR and the reservation subsists at death or ceased within seven years of the death (IRPR 30 June 1989).

Accounts

There is no requirement to deliver an account of the property comprised in an excepted estate, unless the Revenue requests it within the prescribed period. The CTO may seek explanation when the 'excepted estates' procedure is used where one or more of the qualifying conditions does not apply (IRPR 24 February 1993).

If any person who does deliver an account, because it is thought to be an excepted estate, later discovers that the estate is not so, the delivery to the Board within six months of that discovery of an account of the property comprised in that estate will satisfy the requirement to deliver an account.

Discharge of persons and property from tax

Unless, within the prescribed period, the Revenue issues a notice requiring an account of the property comprised in an excepted estate, there can be no claim, after the end of that period, for any IHT on the value transferred by the chargeable transfer made on the deceased's death and attributable to the value of that property and any Inland Revenue charge for that IHT is extinguished. This does not apply in the case of fraud or failure to disclose material facts, nor does it affect any IHT that may be payable if further property is later shown to form part of the estate so that it is not an excepted estate.

Transfers reported late

Where, because it is an excepted estate, no account of a person's estate is required by the Revenue, an account of that estate is deemed to have been delivered on the last day of the prescribed period showing IHT payable as nil.

19.11.4 Form etc of accounts
(IHTA 1984, s 257(1))

All accounts and other documents required for IHT purposes must be in such form and contain such particulars as may be prescribed by the Revenue. This requires either the use of the official form or of an accurate facsimile (SP 2/93).

All accounts to be delivered to the Revenue must be supported by such books, papers and other documents, and verified (whether on oath or otherwise) in such manner, as the Revenue may require. For IHT purposes, an account delivered to a probate registry under arrangements made between the President of the Family Division and the Revenue, or delivered to the Probate and Matrimonial Office in Northern Ireland under arrangements made between the Lord Chancellor and the Revenue, is treated as an account delivered to the Revenue.

19.11.5 Service of documents
(IHTA 1984, s 258)

A notice or other document which is to be served on a person may be delivered to him or left at his usual or last known place of residence, or served by post, addressed to him at his usual or last known place of residence or his place of business or employment.

19.11.6 Inspection of records
(IHTA 1984, s 259)

The Stamp Act 1891, s 16, FA 1946, s 56 and F(No 2)A (Northern Ireland) 1946, s 27 (inspection of public records and records of unit trusts) apply in relation to IHT as they apply in relation to stamp duties.

19.11.7 Inland Revenue Regulation Act 1890
(IHTA 1984, s 260).

Sections 21, 22 and 35 of this Act (proceedings for fines, etc) do not apply in relation to IHT.

19.11.8 Scotland: inventories
(IHTA 1984, s 261)

In Scotland, references to an account required to be delivered to the Revenue by a deceased's personal representatives, however expressed, are construed as such an inventory or additional inventory as is mentioned in Probate and Legacy Duties Act 1808, s 38 which has been duly exhibited as required by that provision.

20

MISCELLANEOUS AND SUPPLEMENTARY IHT MATTERS

20.1 IHT CHARGEABLE IN CERTAIN CASES OF FUTURE PAYMENTS, ETC
(IHTA 1984, s 262)

Where a disposition made for a consideration in money or money's worth is a transfer of value and any payments made or assets transferred by the transferor under disposition are made or transferred more than one year after the disposition is made, IHT (if any) is charged as if:

(1) any payment made or asset transferred under the disposition were made or transferred under a separate disposition made, without consideration, at the time the payment is made or the asset is transferred, and

(2) the amount of the payment made or the value of the asset transferred under each of those separate dispositions were the chargeable portion of the payment or asset.

The chargeable portion of any payment made or any asset transferred at any time is such portion of its value at that time as is found by applying to it the fraction of which:

(a) the numerator is the value actually transferred by the first disposition (calculated as if no IHT were payable on it), and

(b) the denominator is the value, at the time of that disposition, of the aggregate of the payments made or to be made and assets transferred or to be transferred by the transferor under it.

Example

> An individual agrees to sell shares in a family company to a discretionary trust. The consideration is £50,000 in five annual instalments of £10,000 each. (It is assumed that the discounted present value of future payments is, say, £40,000.) The market value of an outright sale is £120,000 and the value transferred is therefore £80,000. When the third instalment is paid, the shares' value has increased to £150,000.

The formula to be applied to this later instalment (ignoring BPR) is:

$$\frac{\text{Value of asset transferred at date of transfer}}{\text{original value transferred (gift element)}} \times \text{total value at time of original gift, ie}$$

$$£150,000/5 \times \frac{£80,000}{£120,000} = £20,000$$

This is the gift element of the third instalment. This amount has to be grossed up in order to calculate the IHT if payable by the individual. However, this is not necessary if the trustees pay the tax.

20.2 ANNUITY PURCHASED IN CONJUNCTION WITH LIFE POLICY
(IHTA 1984, s 263)

Where:

(1) a life insurance policy is issued under an insurance made after 26 March 1974 or is after that date varied or substituted for an earlier policy, and
(2) at the time the insurance is made or at any earlier or later date an annuity on the life of the insured is purchased, and
(3) the benefit of the policy is vested in a person other than the person who purchased the annuity

then, unless it is shown that the purchase of the annuity and the making of the insurance (or the substitution or variation) were not associated operations, the person who purchased the annuity is treated as having made a transfer of value by a disposition made at the time the benefit of the policy became so vested (to the exclusion of any transfer of value which, otherwise, he might have made as a result of the vesting, or of the purchase and the vesting being associated operations). The value transferred is equal to whichever of the following is less:

(1) the aggregate of the value of the consideration given for the annuity, and any premium paid or other consideration given under the policy on or before the transfer, and
(2) the value of the greatest benefit capable of being conferred at any time by the policy, calculated as if that time were the date of transfer.

This applies, with the necessary modifications, where a contract for an annuity payable on a person's death is, after 26 March 1974, made, varied or substituted for or replaced by such a contract or life insurance policy as they apply where a policy is issued, varied or substituted as mentioned above.

SP E4, issued on 5 February 1975, confirms that life assurance policies and annuities are regarded as not being affected by the associated operations rule if, first, the policy was issued on full medical evidence and, secondly, it would have been issued on the same terms if the annuity had not been bought.

20.3 TRANSFERS REPORTED LATE
(IHTA 1984, s 264)

The following apply where a person has made an earlier transfer of value which is:

(1) not notified to the Revenue in an account (under IHTA 1984, s 216) or by information furnished (under s 219) within the 12-month period for the delivery of accounts, and
(2) not discovered until after payment has been accepted by the Revenue in full satisfaction of the IHT on the value transferred by another, later transfer of value made by him.

Where the earlier transfer is made in the ten-year period ending with the date of the later transfer there is charged on the value transferred by the earlier transfer, in addition to any IHT otherwise chargeable on it apart, an amount of IHT equal to the difference (if any) between:

(a) the IHT which, having regard to the earlier transfer, was properly chargeable on the value transferred by the later transfer, and
(b) the payment accepted by the Revenue in full satisfaction of the IHT chargeable on that value.

Any such difference is not chargeable on the value transferred by the later transfer. This does not increase the amount for which interest is payable (under IHTA 1984, s 233) in relation to the earlier transfer for any period falling within six months from the date on which it was discovered.

Where, in the ten-year period ending with the later transfer, there have been two or more earlier transfers, the reference to the earlier transfer is taken as a reference to both or all of those transfers, but the amount of IHT chargeable on each of them is reduced in the proportion which the value transferred by it bears to the aggregate of the values transferred by it and the other(s).

Where the earlier transfers include a settled transfer (ie a transfer for which an amount in full satisfaction of IHT chargeable in relation to it has been paid to and accepted by the Revenue before the discovery of one or more of the other earlier transfers):

(1) no further IHT is chargeable on the settled transfer in consequence of regard being had to the subsequently discovered transfer(s);
(2) the amount so paid and accepted reduces the amount chargeable under on the subsequently discovered transfer(s); and

(3) if there are two or more subsequently discovered transfers, the value transferred by the settled transfer are disregarded in calculating the reduction in the amount of IHT chargeable on each of them.

Where the later transfer is itself an earlier transfer in relation to another later transfer, the references to IHT chargeable on the value transferred by it are to IHT otherwise so chargeable.

Where, otherwise, the earlier transfer would be wholly or partly exempt by reason of some or all of the value transferred by it falling within a limit applicable to an exemption then, if IHT has been accepted as on the basis that the later transfer is partly exempt by reason of part of the value thereby transferred falling within that limit:

(a) IHT is not chargeable on that part of the value transferred by the later transfer, but

(b) a corresponding part of the value transferred by the earlier transfer is treated as falling outside that limit.

The consequences of a transfer of value, not being discovered until after payment has been accepted by the Revenue in full satisfaction of IHT on the value transferred by another, later transfer made by him on or after the day on which he made the earlier transfer apply to a transfer on which no IHT is chargeable because it was within the nil rate band of IHT applicable, are as if payment had been accepted when the transfer was notified in an account (under IHTA 1984, s 216). It is also assumed that the payment is accepted by the Revenue in full satisfaction of the IHT chargeable on that value in relation to that transfer as if the amount of the payment were nil.

A transfer is deemed to be discovered if it is notified to the Revenue in an account or by information furnished after the expiration of the 12-month period for the delivery of accounts. In any other case, a transfer is deemed to be discovered on the date on which the Revenue gives notice of a determination in respect of the transfer.

20.4 CHARGEABLE TRANSFERS AFFECTING MORE THAN ONE PROPERTY
(IHTA 1984, s 265)

Where the value transferred by a chargeable transfer is determined by reference to the values of more than one property, the IHT chargeable on the value transferred is attributed to the respective values in the proportions which they bear to their aggregate. This is subject to IHTA 1984, s 54B(3) (special rate of charge where settled property affected by PET) and to any provision reducing the amount of IHT attributable to the value of any particular property.

20.5 MORE THAN ONE CHARGEABLE TRANSFER ON ONE DAY
(IHTA 1984, s 266)

Where the value transferred by more than one chargeable transfer made by the same person on the same day depends on the order in which the transfers are made, they are treated as made in the order which results in the lowest value chargeable. Subject to this, the rate at which the IHT is charged on such values transferred is the effective rate at which IHT would have been charged had those transfers been a single chargeable transfer of the same total value.

Chargeable transfers under the no interest in possession regime (IHTA 1984, ss 58–85) are, if they relate to the same settlement, treated for these purposes as made by the same person.

20.6 PERSONS TREATED AS UK-DOMICILED
(IHTA 1984, s 267)

A person non-UK domiciled at any time (here referred to as 'the relevant time') is treated as UK-domiciled and not elsewhere at the relevant time if:

(1) he was domiciled in the UK at any time within the last three years; or
(2) if he has been resident in the UK for 17 out of the last 20 tax years.

The deemed domicile rules are ignored where a person has been neither resident nor domiciled in the UK in determining:

(a) whether settled property which became comprised in a settlement before 10 December 1974 is excluded property;
(b) the settlor's domicile for the purposes of the exit charge before the first ten-year anniversary in relation to settled property which became comprised in a no interest in possession trust before 10 December 1974, and
(c) for this purpose, whether the condition that the settlor not be domiciled in the UK.

The normal definition of domicile applies to:

- FOTRA securities (IHTA 1984, ss 6(2), 48(4))
- National Savings products (IHTA 1984, s 6(3)) and
- application of double taxation conventions (IHTA 1984, s 158(6)).

Any question of whether a person is UK-resident in any tax year is determined as for the purposes of income tax (IHTA 1984, s 267(4)).

20.7 ASSOCIATED OPERATIONS
(IHTA 1984, s 268)

The granting of a lease for full consideration in money or money's worth is not taken to be associated with any operation effected more than three years after the grant, and no operation effected on or after 27 March 1974 is taken to be associated with an operation effected before that date.

Where a transfer of value is made by associated operations carried out at different times, it is treated as made at the time of the last of them. However, where any one or more of the earlier operations also constitute a transfer of value made by the same transferor, the value transferred by the earlier operations is treated as reducing the value transferred by all the operations taken together, except to the extent that the transfer constituted by the earlier operations but not that made by all the operations taken together is exempt under IHTA 1984, s 18 (transfers between spouses).

In the debate (*Hansard*, HC Deb, 10 March 1975, Vol 888, col 56) on the original capital transfer tax (now IHT) proposals, the then Chief Secretary to the Treasury, Mr Joel Barnett, explained the reason for IHTA 1984, s 268. It is, he said, reasonable for a husband to share capital with his wife when she has no means of her own. If she chooses to make gifts out of the money she has received from her husband, there is no question of using the associated operation provisions to treat them as gifts made by the husband and taxable as such. In a blatant case, where a transfer by a husband to a wife was made on condition that the wife should at once use the money to make gifts to others, a charge on a gift by the husband might arise under the clause.

He gave some examples of certain circumstances that could mean IHTA 1984, s 268 having to be invoked. There are complex situations involving transactions between husband and wife and others where, for example, a controlling shareholder with a 60 per cent holding in a company wishes to transfer his holding to his son. If he gives half to his son, having first transferred half to his wife, and later his wife transfers her half share to the son, the effect would be to pass a controlling shareholding from father to son. The Revenue would then use the associated operations provisions to ensure that the value of a controlling holding was taxed.

There are ordinary, perfectly innocent transfers between husband and wife. For example, where a husband has money and the wife has none, or vice versa, and the one with the money gives something to the other to enable the spouse to make a gift to a son or a daughter on marriage, that transaction would not be caught by IHTA 1984, s 268.

Suppose that an individual sold an asset to another but left the price outstanding on a loan, part of which was written off each year. The Revenue view (expressed in correspondence) is that the sale of the asset and the writing off of the loans are associated with each other as a single arrangement. Therefore they should be treated as associated operations.

For a general discussion of the application of anti-avoidance legislation and case-law, see guidance note TR588: *Furniss v Dawson*, issued in September 1985 by the Institute of Chartered Accountants in England and Wales (ICAEW), comprising a letter dated 8 July 1985 to the Inland Revenue following a meeting between representatives of the ICAEW, The Law Society and the Inland Revenue, and the reply dated 20 September 1985 from the Board of Inland Revenue.

Macpherson and another v CIR [1988] STC 362, HL deals with associated operations. Here, trustees of a discretionary settlement entered into an agreement with D which meant, in effect, that D would have custody of some valuable trust paintings for 14 years. The agreement was on commercial terms, but nonetheless it reduced the value of the trustees' interest in the paintings. On the following day, the trustees appointed a protected life interest in the paintings, subject to the agreement, to D's son. The Revenue charged what is now IHT on the reduction in value, and the trustees appealed, contending that what is now IHTA 1984, s 10 should be applied because the transactions had not been intended to confer gratuitous benefit. The House of Lords rejected this contention and upheld the charge to tax. They held that the agreement and appointment were 'associated operations' within IHTA 1984, s 268. Together they constituted a transaction intended to confer gratuitous benefit on D's son.

20.8 CONTROL OF COMPANY
(IHTA 1984, s 269)

For certain purposes it is necessary that the shares should give the transferor voting control. This includes shares attributed under the related property rules (IHTA 1984, ss 161, 269(2)). It also includes shares held by trustees of a settlement in which the transferor has an interest in possession.

The control test is based exclusively on voting control, so that even if the donor's shares do not carry a right to the majority of dividends or of any surplus in a winding-up, the test may be satisfied.

See further **8.5** with regard to voting control.

20.9 CONNECTED PERSONS
(IHTA 1984, s 270, TCGA 1992, s 286)

Any question whether a person is connected with another is determined in accordance with the following rules (any provision that one person is connected with another being taken to mean that they are connected with one another under TCGA 1992, s 286(1)).

A person is connected with an individual if that person is the individual's husband or wife, or is a relative, or the husband or wife of a relative, of the individual or of the individual's spouse.

A person, in his capacity as trustee of a settlement, is connected with:

(1) any individual who in relation to the settlement is a settlor;
(2) any person who is connected with such an individual; and
(3) any company which is connected with that settlement.

A company is connected with a settlement if:

(a) it is a close company (or not a close company only because it is not UK-resident) and the participators include the settlement trustees; or
(b) it is controlled (under TA 1988, s 840) by such a company.

Except in relation to acquisitions or disposals of partnership assets under bona fide commercial arrangements, a person is connected with any person with whom he is in partnership, and with the spouse or a relative of any individual with whom he is in partnership.

A company is connected with another company if:

(1) the same person has control of both, or a person has control of one and persons connected with him, or he and persons connected with him, have control of the other; or
(2) a group of two or more persons has control of each company, and the groups either consist of the same, or could be regarded as consisting of the same, persons by treating (in one or more cases) a member of either group as replaced by a person with whom he is connected.

A company is connected with another person if that person has control of it or if that person and persons connected with him together have control of it. Any two or more persons acting together to secure or exercise control of a company are treated in relation to that company as connected with one another and with any person acting on the directions of any of them to secure or exercise control of the company.

Here, 'relative' means brother, sister, ancestor or lineal descendant, uncle, aunt, nephew and niece.

A lease of property for a life or lives, or for a period ascertainable only by reference to a death, or terminable on, or at a date ascertainable only by reference to, a death, is treated as a settlement and the property as settled property (IHTA 1984, s 43(3)):

(a) unless the lease was granted for full consideration in money or money's worth, and
(b) where a lease not granted as one at a rack rent will at any time become a lease at an increased rent, it is treated as terminable at that time.

References to property held in trust for persons include, in Northern Ireland, property standing limited to persons and as if the lease referred to did not include a lease in perpetuity (under the Renewable Leasehold Conversion Act 1849, s 1, or a lease under s 37 of that Act) (IHTA 1984, s 43(5)).

20.10 PROPERTY OF CORPORATIONS SOLE
(IHTA 1984, s 271)

References (except in IHTA 1984, s 59 (qualifying interest in possession)) to property to which a person is beneficially entitled do not include property to which a person is entitled as a corporation sole.

21

CAPITAL GAINS TAX

21.1 CGT BASIC PRINCIPLES

21.1.1 Persons and gains chargeable to CGT, and allowable losses
(TCGA 1992, s 2)

An individual is chargeable to CGT on any chargeable gains accruing to him in a tax year during any part of which he is UK-resident or UK-ordinarily resident. For CGT purposes, 'resident' and 'ordinarily resident' have the same meaning as for income tax (TCGA 1992, s 9(1)). There are also special rules for temporary non-residents (TCGA 1992, s 10A).

Under the rules applying up to 1997/98, CGT was charged on the total amount of chargeable gains accruing to the person chargeable in the tax year, after deducting:

(1) any allowable losses accruing to that person in that tax year, and
(2) so far as they have not already been allowed as a deduction from chargeable gains in any previous tax year, any allowable losses brought forward from a previous tax year.

Except for the special rule applying on death (under TCGA 1992, s 62), an allowable loss in a tax year cannot be carried back against chargeable gains in any earlier tax year. Relief cannot be given more than once for any loss or part of a loss, and is not available at all if and so far as relief has been or may be given under the income tax rules.

Chargeable gains may be treated as accruing to any person in any tax year under any of the following TCGA 1992 provisions:

- s 77 (charge on settlor with an interest in a settlement)
- s 86 (attribution of gains to settlors with interests in non-resident and dual resident settlements)
- s 87 (attribution of gains to beneficiaries) and
- s 89(2) (migrant settlements (read, where applicable, with s 10A (temporary non-residents)).

However, from 1998/99 the application of relief for losses is dealt with in a different manner. In such cases the amount on which an individual is liable to CGT is the aggregate of two amounts:

(1) the amount of other gains remaining after:
  (a) any allowable losses arising in that tax year (including any allowable loss brought back from a later tax year in which the individual concerned dies;
  (b) insofar as they have not been allowed as a deduction in a previous tax year, any allowable losses brought forward from a previous tax year, and
  (c) taper relief (see below);
(2) the amount realised by settlements and included in the settlor's chargeable gains (as above), but giving no relief for losses but allowing taper relief.

21.2 TAPER RELIEF
(TCGA 1992, s 2A)

21.2.1 Overview

For 1998/99 and subsequent tax years, a new form of relief, taper relief, applies (TCGA 1992, s 2A). For 1998/99 and 1999/2000, the effect of the relief is that the amount on which CGT is levied on non-corporate taxpayers is reduced by a percentage that varies according to the length of time (up to ten years) that an asset is held. A different scale of percentages applies to gains on the disposal of business and non-business assets. Also for business assets, there is an extension to the general definition which applies for assets acquired before 17 March 1998. The period for which the asset has been held after 5 April 1998 is notionally extended by a 'bonus' year.

For disposals of business assets made after 5 April 2000 the maximum relief is obtained after four complete years. However, the 'bonus' year given for business assets held on 17 March 1998 is not available for disposals of business assets made after 5 April 2000.

Indexation allowance (TCGA 1992, s 53) is frozen as at April 1998 for expenditure prior to that date, and does not apply at all for later expenditure.

21.2.2 How taper relief is given
(TCGA 1992, s 2A)

Taper relief is given as an adjustment to the amount otherwise chargeable to CGT for the tax year concerned. This is the amount by which a person's chargeable gains for a tax year exceeds the aggregate of any allowable losses arising in that tax year and any unrelieved allowable losses brought forward from earlier tax years (TCGA 1992, s 2(2)). Where there is such an excess, taper relief is available if the excess is or includes the whole or a part of any chargeable gain that is eligible for taper relief. CGT is then chargeable only on a reduced amount which is found by taking the amount otherwise chargeable to CGT and recomputing the reduced amount as follows:

(1) Taper relief is applied to so much of every chargeable gain as eligible for the relief which is represented within the excess.
(2) The reduced amounts of each such gain are then aggregated.
(3) To this aggregate is then added the full amount of any gain, represented in the excess, but not eligible for taper relief.

It is necessary to establish whether the asset on which a chargeable gain has arisen is a business asset or a non-business asset. For a disposal of a business asset a chargeable gain is eligible for taper relief after a qualifying holding period of at least one year. If the gain arises on the disposal of a non-business asset the qualifying holding period must be of at least three years.

Taper relief is then calculated by reference to a table appropriate to business or non-business assets, as the case may be, and is applied on the basis of a percentage of the gain given by the relevant table to business or non-business assets, as the case may be, for the number of whole years in the qualifying holding period of that asset.

The qualifying holding period for an asset is, broadly, the period for which it had been held at the time of its disposal. More specifically, the period starts on 6 April 1998 or on the actual date of acquisition, whichever is later, and ends with the disposal of the asset concerned.

Even if a qualifying period is longer than five or ten years (see **21.2.1**), as the case may be, no further percentage reduction is possible.

Where taper relief applies to the whole or any part of a gain on the disposal of a business or non-business asset, that relief is given by multiplying the amount of the gain or part of a gain by the percentage given by Table 21.1 for the number of whole years in the qualifying holding period of that asset (TCGA 1992, s 2A(4) and (5), as amended by FA 2000, s 65(2)).

The extent to which the whole or any part of a gain on the disposal of a business or non-business asset is treated as represented in the excess referred to above is found by taking the deductions made to give effect to taper, as set against chargeable gains, in such order as results in the largest reduction of the amount otherwise chargeable to CGT. The first step is to identify the extent to which the chargeable gains for the year exceed the current and brought forward losses. The rules allow the individual concerned to allocate the particular gains of the year to the excess (as contrasted with being covered by allowable losses) on the basis which produces the result most favourable to him. Losses carried back from the year of an individual's death for up to three years are treated in the same way as brought forward losses for taper relief purposes. They are deducted before taper relief so that relief only applies to reduce the net gains after allowing the losses brought back.

Table 21.1

Gains on disposals of business assets		Gains on disposals of non-business assets	
Number of whole years in qualifying holding period	*Percentage of gain chargeable*	*Number of whole years in qualifying holding period*	*Percentage of gain chargeable*
–	–	1	87.5
–	–	2	75
3	95	3	50
4	90	4 or more	25
5	85		
6	80		
7	75		
8	70		
9	65		
10 or more	60		

The qualifying holding period of an asset depends on whether it is a business or a non-business asset. There are several possibilities (TCGA 1992, s 2A(8), as inserted by FA 2000, s 65(3)):

(1) For a business asset, the qualifying holding period is the period after 5 April 1998 for which the asset had been held at the time of its disposal.

(2) For a non-business asset, where:
   (a) the time (under TCGA 1992, Sched A1, para 2) when the asset is taken to have been acquired by the person making the disposal is before 17 March 1998, and
   (b) there is no period which (under Sched A1, para 11 (change of activity by the company) or 12 (share subject to value shifting)) does not count for taper relief purposes,
   the qualifying period is that after 5 April 1998 for which the asset has been held at the time of its disposal plus a 'bonus' year.

(3) For any other non-business asset, the qualifying holding period is that after 5 April 1998 for which the asset had been held at the time of its disposal.

Note that where TCGA 1992, Sched A1, para 11 or 12 (see (2)(b) above)) applies (i.e. where the asset is a holding of shares in a non-trading company where there has been either a relevant change in that company's activities or a relevant shift of value involving those shares), there is a double penalty. In addition to a reduction in the qualifying holding period (Sched A1, para 2(4)), the 'bonus year' is also withdrawn. Paragraph 10 of Sched A1 (periods of limited exposure to fluctuations in value) can also reduce the qualifying holding period, but in that case the bonus year is not forfeited.

Where the period after 5 April 1998 for which an asset had been held at the time of its disposal includes any period which (under Sched A1, para 10, 11 or 12) is a period that does not count for taper relief purposes (Sched A1, para 2(4)):

(a) the qualifying holding period of the asset is reduced by the length of the period(s) that do(es) not count; and
(b) the period(s) that do(es) not count is/are:
  (i) left out of account in computing the period of ten years ending with the time of the asset's disposal; and
  (ii) assumed not to be comprised in the asset's relevant period of ownership.

In the context of the Enterprise Investment Scheme, the qualifying holding period of the original shares for taper relief purposes is the period beginning with the date of issue of the original shares and ending with the date of the relevant disposal (TCGA 1992, Sched 5BA, para 3). This is subject to adjustment if there are periods that do not count for taper relief purposes.

TCGA 1992, Sched A1 provides more detailed rules for applying taper relief.

Example 1: Where there is only one asset disposal

Dougal acquired a business asset on 1 August 1998 for £50,000. He sold it on 1 September 2000 for £90,000. It is held as a business asset throughout the whole of that period. He realises a gain of £40,000.

There are two whole years between the dates of acquisition and disposal. The asset has been a business asset throughout the whole of this period, and only 75 per cent of the gain remains chargeable to CGT. In this case there are no losses available for offset arising in the same tax year or brought forward from an earlier tax year. Thus the gain chargeable to CGT (subject to the annual exempt amount) is £30,000.

Example 2 : Where there are losses to take into account

Percival realises gains on two separate assets in the same tax year:

Asset 1: Gain before taper relief is £21,000
The period for which the asset has been held (the taper period) is 3 years.
The asset is held as a business asset throughout.

Asset 2: Gain before taper relief is £15,000
The period for which the asset has been held (the taper period) is 8 years.
The asset is held as a non-business asset throughout.

Asset 3:   Loss (no taper relief available on losses) of £9,000.

The loss is set against the gain which qualifies for the least taper relief so that the maximum taper relief applies against the gain which qualifies for the largest reduction. The loss is therefore set against the gain on Asset 2 as it qualifies for reduction only to 70 per cent of the untapered amount, whereas the gain on Asset 1 will be reduced to 50 per cent. So, of the net gain on Asset 2 of £6,000 (£15,000 – £9,000 losses), 70 per cent is chargeable, i.e. £4,200.

		£	£
Asset 1:	Gain	21,000	
	Taper (business asset): 3 years = 55%		11,550
Asset 2:	Gain	15,000	
	Loss on asset 3	(9,000)	
		6,000	
Taper (non-business asset): 8 years = 70%			4,200
Gains chargeable (subject to annual exempt amount)			15,750

The following points are worth noting:

(1) Indexation ceased to run on 6 April 1998. The new scheme is advantageous to persons whose assets have a comparatively low acquisition cost (eg shares in newly formed companies). In their case the taper relief reduces the amount chargeable to a percentage of the gain. Under indexation, the gain was reduced only by a percentage of the acquisition cost.

(2) For acquisitions after 6 April 1998 the qualifying holding period runs from when the asset is first acquired. This is of considerable importance if the asset's value is disproportionately enhanced by subsequent allowable expenditure.

(3) Losses are not tapered. Care is needed to ensure that sufficient untapered gains or gains qualifying only for a smaller amount of taper relief are realised in a tax year where the taxpayer has allowable losses.

(4) Taper relief does not apply to gains realised by companies (because TCGA 1992, s 2(2) only applies to CGT, and TCGA 1992, s 2A applies only where there are net gains chargeable to CGT).

(5) Indexation continues to apply to companies. Furthermore, indexation continues to apply to the gains of non-resident close companies apportioned to participators under TCGA 1992, s 13.

(6) Changes in the rules for shares and other assets to qualify as business assets took effect for periods of ownership from 6 April 2000. As a

result, some shares and other assets might be treated as non-business assets for periods of ownership up to 5 April 2000 but as business assets after 5 April 2000. The gain on disposal is apportioned between a gain on a business asset and a gain on a non-business asset.

Example

On 6 October 2003, Ambrose sells shares he had owned since before 17 March 1998. He realises a gain of £132,000. Thus there are five whole years in the qualifying holding period which is used for determining taper relief from 6 April 1998 to 6 October 2003. Non-business (but not business) assets qualify for the bonus year.

The relevant period of ownership used for apportionment of gains on business and non-business assets is the period from 6 April 1998 to 6 October 2003. Here, the shares are non-business assets up to 6 April 2000 and, because of the change in the definition of business assets, are business assets from 6 April 2000 to the date of disposal.

The gain on the disposal is divided between the relevant period of ownership that the shares had been non-business assets and business assets respectively. An apportionment of the relevant period of ownership of five years and six months (66 months in total) is made on the following basis:

Two years as a non-business asset = $\frac{24}{66}$ months
Three years and six months as a business asset = $\frac{42}{66}$ months

As a non-business asset = $\frac{24}{66} \times 132,000 =$	£48,000
As a business asset = $\frac{42}{66} \times 132,000 =$	£84,000

The non-business asset gain is entitled to five years' non-business taper relief (plus the bonus year); 80 per cent of the gain is charged to tax. The business asset gain is entitled to five years' business asset taper relief (with no bonus year); 25 per cent of the gain is charged to tax:

	£
Non-business asset gain = £48,000 × 80% =	38,400
Business asset gain = £84,000 × 25% =	21,000
CGT due on	59,400

The position could be improved if Ambrose transferred his shares into an interest in possession trust in his own favour shortly after 6 April 2000. Any gain otherwise arising could be held over by a gift relief hold-over claim (under TCGA 1992, s 165). The asset would have been a business asset throughout the qualifying period of ownership of the trustees. On the subsequent sale on 6 October 2003 the whole of the trustees' gain would relate to business assets and the chargeable gain would be £132,000 × 25% = £33,000. Even though TCGA 1992, s 77 charged that gain on the settlor, there would be a potential reduction in the chargeable amount of £26,400.

21.2.3 Definitions of general application to taper relief rules

Period for which asset held and relevant period of ownership
(TCGA 1992, Sched A1, para 2)

When an asset is disposed of after 5 April 1998, the period of ownership is taken as measured down to the time of its disposal. It is taken as the period for which the asset had been held at the time of its disposal which:

(1) begins with whichever is the later of 6 April 1998 and the time when the asset concerned was acquired by the person making the disposal; and

(2) ends with the time of the disposal on which the gain accrued.

Taper relief is, however, given only for the relevant period of ownership, which is whichever is the shorter of:

(a) the period after 5 April 1998 for which the asset had been held at the time of its disposal; and

(b) the period of ten years then ending.

Certain matters are disregarded in determining whether a person is treated for this purpose as having acquired an asset:

(1) where on the death of a person entitled to an interest in settled property (as against trustees) insofar as it treats the asset concerned as acquired at a date before 6 April 1965 (TCGA 1992, s 73(1)(b));

(2) employee trusts (s 239(2)(b));

(3) gifts to charities (s 257(2)(b)); and

(4) gifts to housing associations (s 259(2)(b)).

Where the period after 5 April 1998 for which an asset had been held at the time of its disposal includes any period which does not count for taper relief purposes, then certain adjustments are required. The periods concerned are:

(a) periods of limited exposure to fluctuations in value (Sched A1, para 10);

(b) periods of share ownership where there has been a change of activity by a company (para 11); and

(c) periods of ownership affected by value shifting (para 12).

The adjustments required are to:

(1) reduce the asset's qualifying holding period by the length of the period, or by the aggregate lengths of such periods;

(2) leave such period(s) concerned out of account in computing the ten-year period ending at the time of the asset's disposal; and

(3) assume that such periods are not comprised in the asset's relevant period of ownership.

These rules are modified in the following circumstances under Sched A1, para 5:

- Options (para 13)
- Assets derived from other assets (para 14)
- Assets transferred between spouses (para 15)
- Postponed gains (para 16)
- Property settled by a company (para 17)
- Assets acquired in the reconstruction of mutual businesses, etc (para 18)
- Ancilliary trust funds (para 19).

Ordinary share capital: 'series' and 'owners'

Any number of companies of which the first directly owns ordinary share capital of the next, and the next directly owns ordinary share capital of the next but one and so on are referred to as 'a series' (see the Glossary at the front of this book for a definition; see also the definition there for 'owned directly or indirectly').

A company in a series which directly owns ordinary share capital of another company in the series is referred to as 'an owner'. Any two companies in a series of which one owns ordinary share capital of the other directly, and not through one or more of the other companies in the series, are referred to as being directly related to one another.

Where every owner in a series owns the whole of the ordinary share capital of the company to which it is directly related, the first owner is deemed to own through an intermediary or a chain of intermediaries the whole of the ordinary share capital of the last owned company.

If one of the owners in a series owns a fraction of the ordinary share capital of the company to which it is directly related, and every other owner in the series owns the whole of the ordinary share capital of the company to which it is directly related, the first owner is deemed to own that fraction of the ordinary share capital of the last owned company through the intermediary or chain of intermediaries.

The first owner is deemed to own through the intermediary or chain of intermediaries such fraction of the ordinary share capital of the last owned company as results from the multiplication of those fractions. The first scenario is where each of two or more of the owners in a series owns a fraction, and every other owner in the series owns the whole, of the ordinary share capital of the body corporate to which it is directly related. The second scenario is where every owner in a series owns a fraction of the ordinary share capital of the company to which it is directly related.

Finally, there are rules to deal with the situation where the first owner in any series owns a fraction of the ordinary share capital of the last owned company in that series through the intermediary or chain of intermediaries, and also owns another fraction or other fractions of the ordinary share capital of the last owned company. Such ownership can be either:

(1) directly, or
(2) through an intermediary or intermediaries which are not members of that series, or
(3) through a chain or chains of intermediaries of which one or some or all are not members of that series, or
(4) in a case where the series consists of more than three companies, through an intermediary or intermediaries which are members of the series, or through a chain or chains of intermediaries consisting of some but not all of the companies of which the chain of intermediaries in the series consists.

In any of these situations, for the purpose of ascertaining the amount of the ordinary share capital of the last owned company owned by the first owner, all those fractions are aggregated and the first owner is deemed to own the sum of those fractions.

Note, however, the exception in Sched A1, para 11 (periods of share ownership not to count where there is a change of activity by the company).

Eligible beneficiary

For a definition of 'eligible beneficiary', see the Glossary at the front of this book.

Where settled property originates from more than one settlor, the taper relief rules are applied as if there were a separate and distinct settlement for the property originating from each settlor (Sched A1, para 20(1)). References here to an eligible beneficiary are construed accordingly.

Settlor
(TCGA 1992, s 79; Sched A1, para 20(2))

A person is a settlor if the settled property consists of or includes property originating from him. Settled property (and property comprised in a settlement) comprises only property originating from that settlor. Property originates from a settlor if it is:

(1) property which that settlor has provided directly or indirectly for the purposes of the settlement,
(2) property representing that property, and
(3) so much of any property which represents both property so provided and other property as, on a just apportionment, represents the property so provided.

Property which a settlor has provided directly or indirectly includes property which has been provided directly or indirectly by another person under reciprocal arrangements with that settlor. However, this does not include property which that settlor has provided directly or indirectly under reciprocal arrangements with another person. Property which represents other property include property which represents accumulated income from that other property.

'Office' and 'employment'
(TCGA 1992, Sched A1, para 22(1))

Broadly, this covers any office or employment the emoluments of which are assessed under Schedule E (TA 1988, s 168(2)).

Qualifying companies

The following rules apply to determine whether a company is a qualifying company.

By reference to an individual
(TCGA 1992, Sched A1, para 6(1))

A company is a qualifying company by reference to an individual at any time when the following conditions were satisfied:

(1) the company is a trading company or the holding company of a trading group, and
(2) one or more of the following conditions is met:
    (a) the company is unlisted,
    (b) the individual is an officer or employee of the company, or of a company having a relevant connection with it, or
    (c) the voting rights in the company are exercisable, as to not less than 5 per cent, by the individual.

Prior to 6 April 2000, the voting rights test was applied as to not less than 25 per cent.

By reference to the trustees of a settlement
(TCGA 1992, Sched A1, para 6(2))

A company is a qualifying company by reference to the trustees of a settlement at any time when:

(1) the company was a trading company or the holding company of a trading group, and
(2) one or more of the following conditions is met:
    (a) the company is unlisted,
    (b) an eligible beneficiary is an officer or employee of the company, or of a company having a relevant connection with it, or
    (c) the voting rights in the company are exercisable, as to not less than 5 per cent, by the trustees.

By reference to the trustees of a settlement
(TCGA 1992, Sched A1, para 6(3))

A company is taken to have been a qualifying company by reference to an individual's personal representatives at any time when:

(1) the company is a trading company or the holding company of a trading group, and
(2) one or more of the following conditions was met:
    (a) the company is unlisted, or
    (b) the voting rights in the company are exercisable, as to not less than 5 per cent, by the personal representatives.

A special rule applies where the disposal is made by an individual who acquired the shares as a legatee (under TCGA 1992, s 64) and at that time the shares were not business assets; by being shares in a qualifying company by reference to him, the shares are nonetheless treated as a business asset if at that time they were held by the deceased's personal representatives.

Unlisted company
(TCGA 1992, Sched A1, para 22(1))

An 'unlisted company' is a company none of whose shares is listed on a recognised stock exchange, and which is not a 51 per cent subsidiary of a company whose shares, or any class of whose shares, is so listed.

Assets provided rather than acquired
(TCGA 1992, Sched A1, para 22(3))

References in the taper relief rules to the acquisition of an asset that was provided, rather than acquired, by the person disposing of it are references to its provision.

Part disposal
(TCGA 1992, Sched A1, para 22(4))

References in the taper relief rules, in relation to a part disposal, to the asset disposed of are references to the asset of which there is a part disposal.

Other definitions

Numerous other definitions are included in the Glossary at the front of this book. These include 'group of companies', 'holding company', 'shares', 'trade', 'trading company', 'trading group' and 'transaction'.

21.3 BUSINESS OR NON-BUSINESS ASSETS

21.3.1 Basic rule
(TCGA 1992, Sched A1, para 3)

The basic rule is that a chargeable gain accruing to any person on the disposal of any asset is a gain on the disposal of a business asset if that asset was such throughout its relevant period of ownership. This is, however, subject to a number of modifications to deal with particular circumstances.

Suppose, for example, that person realises a chargeable gain on the disposal of an asset which has not been a business asset throughout its relevant period of ownership, but that the asset has been a business asset for periods comprising part of that relevant period. In such event, a part of that gain is treated as a gain on the disposal of a business asset. The remainder of the gain is treated as a gain on the disposal of a non-business asset.

The part of the gain treated as a business asset is equivalent, on a time basis, to such part of the relevant period comprised in its relevant period of ownership, being periods throughout which the asset is to be taken to have been a business asset. The balance of such a gain is treated as being one on the disposal of a non-business asset.

A slightly different treatment is applied under the above rules where, on the same disposal, there are gains on both a business asset *and* a non-business asset. The two gains are treated for taper relief as separate gains on separate disposals of separate assets. However, the periods after 5 April 1998 for which each of the assets is treated as having been held at the time of their disposal is the same and is determined without reference to the length of the relevant period of ownership and the periods throughout which an asset is taken to have been a business asset.

Conditions for shares to qualify as business assets
(TCGA 1992, Sched A1, para 4(1)–(5))

There are number of rules which apply in particular circumstances for determining whether a disposal of shares or of an interest in shares in a company (here referred to as the 'relevant company') can be treated as a disposal of the underlying business assets.

Disposal by individual
Where the disposal is made by an individual, the shares are treated as a business asset if, at the time of the disposal, the relevant company is a qualifying company by reference to that individual.

Disposal by settlement trustees
Where the disposal is made by the trustees of a settlement, the shares are

treated as a business asset if, at the time of the disposal, the relevant company is a qualifying company by reference to those trustees.

Disposal by personal representatives

Where the disposal is made by personal representatives, the shares are treated as a business asset if, at the time of the disposal, the relevant company was a qualifying company by reference to the personal representatives.

Disposal by a legatee

A special rule applies where the disposal is made by an individual who acquired the asset as a legatee (under TCGA 1992, s 64) at which time the asset was represented by shares in a company which would, at that time, have been a qualifying company by reference to that individual. In such a case the asset is treated as a business asset at that time if the relevant company was a qualifying company by reference to the personal representatives.

Conditions for other assets to qualify as business assets
(TCGA 1992, Sched A1, para 5(1)–(5))

The following rules apply to determine whether, prior to its disposal, an asset other than shares, or an interest in shares, is a business asset.

Disposals by individuals

For a disposal made by an individual, the asset is treated as a business asset at the time of the disposal if it was being used, wholly or partly, for any one or more of the following purposes at that time:

(1) of a trade carried on by that individual or by a partnership of which he was a member;
(2) of any trade carried on by a company which was a qualifying company by reference to that individual;
(3) of any trade carried on by a company which was a member of a trading group the holding company of which was a qualifying company by reference to that individual;
(4) of any office or employment held by that individual with a person carrying on a trade.

Disposal by settlement trustees

For a disposal made by the trustees of a settlement, the asset is treated as a business asset at the time of the disposal if it was being used, wholly or partly, for any one or more of the following purposes at that time:

(1) of a trade carried on by the settlement trustees;
(2) of a trade carried on by an eligible beneficiary or by a partnership of which an eligible beneficiary was a member;

(3) of any trade carried on by a company which was a qualifying company by reference to the settlement trustees or an eligible beneficiary;

(4) of any trade carried on by a company which was a member of a trading group the holding company of which was a qualifying company by reference to the settlement trustees or an eligible beneficiary;

(5) of any office or employment held by an eligible beneficiary with a person carrying on a trade.

Disposal by personal representatives

For a disposal made by personal representatives, the asset is treated as a business asset at the time of the disposal if it was being used, wholly or partly, for any one or more of the following purposes at that time:

(1) of a trade carried on by the deceased's personal representatives;

(2) of any trade carried on by a company which was a qualifying company by reference to the deceased's personal representatives;

(3) of any trade carried on by a company which was a member of a trading group the holding company of which was a qualifying company by reference to the deceased's personal representatives.

Disposal by a legatee

The same applies as for such disposal set out under 'Conditions for shares to qualify as business assets' above.

21.3.2 Non-qualifying beneficiaries
(TCGA 1992, Sched A1, para 8)

The following applies to a disposal of an asset by the trustees of a settlement where the asset's relevant period of ownership is or includes a period throughout which:

(1) the asset was a business asset by reference to one or more eligible beneficiaries;

(2) the asset would not otherwise have been a business asset; and

(3) there is a non-qualifying part of the relevant income, or there would be if there were any relevant income for that period.

This is referred to as 'a sharing period'.

The period throughout which the asset disposed of is to be taken to have been a business asset is determined as if the relevant fraction of every sharing period were a period throughout which the asset was not a business asset. Here, the 'the relevant fraction', in relation to any sharing period, is that which represents the proportion of relevant income for that period which is, or (if there were such income) would be, a non-qualifying part of that income. Where a sharing period is a period in which such proportion has been different at different times, a separate relevant fraction must be determined for, and applied to, each part of that period for which there is a different proportion. The non-qualifying part of any relevant income for any period is so much of that income for that period as is or would be income to which:

(1) no eligible beneficiary has any entitlement; or
(2) a non-qualifying eligible beneficiary has an entitlement.

A 'non-qualifying eligible beneficiary', in relation to a period, means an eligible beneficiary who is not a beneficiary by reference to whom (if he were the only beneficiary) the asset disposed of would be a business asset throughout that period. 'Relevant income' is income from the part of the settled property comprising the asset disposed of.

21.3.3 Asset used at same time for different purposes
(TCGA 1992, Sched A1, para 9)

A special rule applies to a disposal by any person of an asset where the asset's relevant period of ownership is or includes a 'a mixed-use' period throughout which the asset was:

(1) a business asset by reference to the conditions for other assets to qualify as business assets (TCGA 1992, Sched A1, paras 5(2)–(5)); but
(2) at the same time, being put to a non-qualifying use.

The period throughout which the asset disposed of is to be taken to have been a business asset is determined as if the relevant fraction of every mixed-use period were a period throughout which it was not a business asset. Here, 'the relevant fraction' is that which represents the proportion of the asset's use during that period that was a non-qualifying use.

Where an asset is used at the same time for different purposes and where there are non-qualifying beneficiaries, the rules for non-qualifying beneficiaries set out above take precedence. Further reductions in the period for which the asset disposed of is taken to have been a business asset are made only in respect of the relevant part of any non-qualifying use. In this context, the relevant part of any non-qualifying use is the proportion of that use which is not a use to which a non-qualifying part of any relevant income is attributable.

Where there are non-qualifying beneficiaries, a separate relevant fraction has to be determined for, and applied to, each part of the period for which there is a different proportion or attribution.

'Non-qualifying use', in relation to an asset, means any use of the asset for purposes which are not purposes for which the asset would fall to be treated as a business asset at the time of its use.

21.4 ANTI-AVOIDANCE MEASURES

In order to prevent manipulation of the taper relief rules so as to gain a tax advantage, or to mitigate the effect of the rules, a number of anti-avoidance measures are built into the legislation.

21.4.1 Periods of limited exposure to fluctuations in value not to count
(TCGA 1992, Sched A1, para 10)

A special rule applies where, in the case of any asset disposed of ('the relevant asset'), the period after 5 April 1998 for which that asset had been held at the time of its disposal is or includes a period during which:

(1) the person making the disposal, or
(2) a relevant predecessor of his,

had limited exposure to fluctuations in the asset's value. In such a case, the period during which that person or predecessor had that limited exposure does not count for taper relief purposes.

The times when a person is taken to have had such limited exposure are all the times while he held that asset when a transaction entered into at any time by him, or by a relevant predecessor of his, had the effect that he was not:

(1) exposed, or not exposed to any substantial extent, to the risk of loss from fluctuations in the relevant asset's value; and
(2) able to enjoy, or to enjoy to any substantial extent, any opportunities to benefit from such fluctuations.

The transactions referred to here do not include:

(a) any insurance policy which the person might reasonably have been expected to enter into and which is insurance against the loss of the relevant asset or against damage to it, or against both; or
(b) any transaction having effect in relation to fluctuations in the relevant asset's value so far only as they result from fluctuations in the value of foreign currencies.

A 'relevant predecessor' of a person disposing of an asset is any person other than the person disposing of it who held that asset at a time falling in the period, which is taken to be the whole period for which it had been held at the time of disposal. The relevant predecessor of a person disposing of an asset can also have a relevant predecessor.

When an asset (whether business or non-business) is disposed of after 5 April 1998, the period of ownership is taken as that for which the asset had been held at the time of its disposal:

(1) beginning with the time when the asset concerned was acquired by the person making the disposal (Sched A1, para 2(1)(a)); and

(2) ending with the time of the disposal on which the gain accrued (para 2(1)(b)).

21.4.2 Periods of share ownership not to count where company changes activity
(TCGA 1992, Sched A1, para 11)

A special rule deals with the situation where:

(1) there is a disposal of an asset consisting of close company shares; and
(2) the period beginning with the relevant time, and ending with the time of disposal, includes at least one relevant change of activity involving that company.

Here 'the relevant time' means the beginning of the period after 5 April 1998 for which that asset had been held at the time of its disposal.

So much of the period after 5 April 1998 for which the asset had been held at the time of its disposal as falls before the time, or latest time, in that period when there was a relevant change of activity involving the close company does not count for taper relief purposes.

A relevant change of activity involving the close company is taken to have occurred where:

(1) a close company or any of its 51 per cent subsidiaries has at any time begun to carry on a trade, and
(2) immediately before that time, neither that company nor any of its 51 per cent subsidiaries was carrying on a trade.

A relevant change of activity involving a close company is not taken to have occurred where at the time of disposal, the close company was carrying on a business of holding investments, and there has been any occasion falling within:

(1) the 12-month period ending with that time, or
(2) the 12-month period ending with any earlier time after the relevant time when the close company was not carrying on that business or when the size of that business was small by comparison with its size at the end of that period.

This applies where the relevant change of activity occurs immediately after the latest such occasion before the time of the disposal. For this purpose, the size of any business at any time is determined by assuming it to correspond to the aggregate of the amounts and values given by way of consideration for the assets held at that time for business purposes.

There are rules for determining for these purposes whether a close company is at any time carrying on a business of holding investments and the size at any time of such a business. All the activities of a close company and of all of its 51 per cent subsidiaries are taken together as if they were all being carried on by the close company. The activities that are included in a business of holding investments do not include:

(1) holding shares in a 51 per cent subsidiary of the company holding the shares;
(2) making loans to an associated company or to a participator (under TA 1988, s 417(1)) in the company making the loan or in an associated company; or
(3) placing money on deposit.

A company's carrying on or beginning to carry on a trade that is merely incidental to any non-trading activities carried on by that company or another in the same group of companies is ignored. A business of holding investments also includes a business of making investments.

A company is treated as another's associated company at any time if at that time, or at another time within one year previously:

(1) one of them has had control of the other; or
(2) both have been under the control of the same person or persons.

21.4.3 Periods of share ownership not to count where there is value shifting
(TCGA 1992, Sched A1, para 12)

A special rule applies where:

(1) there is a disposal of an asset consisting of shares (or rights over a company) in a close company; and
(2) at least one relevant shift of value involving that asset has occurred between the relevant time and the time of the disposal.

Here 'the relevant time' is the same as in **21.4.2**. So much of the period after 5 April 1998 for which the asset had been held at the time of its disposal as falls before the time, or latest time, in that period at which there was a relevant shift of value involving that asset does not count for taper relief purposes.

A relevant shift of value involving any asset occurs whenever:

(1) a person having control of a close company exercised his control of that company so that value passed into that asset out of a relevant holding; or
(2) effect was given to any other transaction by virtue of which value passed into that asset out of a relevant holding.

A relevant shift of value involving an asset is disregarded if that shift of value:

(a) is one in which the value passing into that asset out of the relevant holding is insignificant; or

(b) took place at a time when the qualifying holding period for the relevant holding was at least as long as the qualifying holding period for that asset.

The reference here to the qualifying holding period of a holding or other asset at the time when a shift of value takes place is taken to be what, in relation to a disposal at that time of that holding or other asset by the person then entitled to dispose of it, would be taken to have been its qualifying holding period for the purposes of TCGA 1992, s 2A. Thus, the qualifying holding period for an asset broadly refers to the period after 5 April 1998 for which that asset had been held at the time of its disposal. However, this does not apply if:

(1) the time which, under the rules for determining the period for which an asset is held and the relevant period of ownership (TCGA 1992, Sched A1, para 2) is a time when the asset is taken to have been acquired by the person making the disposal before 17 March 1998 (TCGA 1992, s 2A(9)(a)); and

(2) there is no period which in the case of that asset is a period which does not count for taper relief purposes under the rules defining those periods of ownership which do not count where there is a change of activity by the company or under the rules whereby certain periods of share ownership do not count in a case of value shifting (s 2A(9)(b); Sched A1, para 11).

In these cases the period for which the asset has been held after 5 April 1998 is notionally extended by one year (s 2A(8)(b)).

The references here to a relevant holding are construed, in relation to any case in which value has passed out of one asset into another consisting of company shares, as any holding of any shares in that company or in a company under the control of the same person or persons as that company by:

(1) the person who, following the exercise of control or other transaction by virtue of which the value has passed, held the other asset; or

(2) a person connected with him.

21.4.4 Special rule for property settled by company
(TCGA 1992, Sched A1, para 17)

No part of any chargeable gain accruing to the trustees of a settlement on the disposal of any asset is treated as a gain on the disposal of a business asset if:

(1) the settlor (under TA 1988, s 660G(1), (2)) is a company; and

(2) that company has an interest in the settlement at the time of the disposal.

Subject the following points, a company which is a settlor is regarded as having an interest in a settlement if:

(1) any property which may at any time be comprised in the settlement, or any derived property is, or will or may become, payable to or applicable for the benefit of that company or an associated company; or

(2) that company or an associated company enjoys a benefit deriving directly or indirectly from any property which is comprised in the settlement or any derived property.

Here 'derived property' means income from property or any other property directly or indirectly representing proceeds of, or of income from, that property or income therefrom. A company is to be treated as another's associated company at any time if, at that time, or at another time within one year previously:

(1) one of them has had control of the other; or
(2) both have been under the control of the same person or persons.

These rules do not apply unless the settlor or an associated company is within the charge to corporation tax in respect of chargeable gains for the accounting period in which the chargeable gain accrues.

21.5 MISCELLANEOUS SPECIAL RULES

21.5.1 Options
(TCGA 1992, s 144; Sched A1, para 13)

A special rule applies where the grant of an option and the transaction entered into by the grantor in fulfilment of his obligations under the option fall to be treated as one transaction. This rule also applies where the acquisition of an option and the transaction entered into by the person exercising it fall to be treated as one transaction.

The time of the disposal of any asset in pursuance of the transaction is the time when, if the option binds the grantor to sell, the disposal is made in fulfilment of the grantor's obligations under the option. If the option binds the grantor to buy, it is the time when the disposal is made to the grantor in consequence of the exercise of the option.

The time of the acquisition of any asset acquired in pursuance of the option, or in consequence of its exercise, is the time of the exercise of the option.

Any question whether the asset disposed of or acquired was a business asset at any time is determined by reference to the asset to which the option related, and not the option.

21.5.2 Assets derived from other assets
(TCGA 1992, Sched A1, para 14)

A special rule applies, in certain cases, if the value of any asset disposed of is derived (through one or more successive events falling within any of the following categories, but not otherwise) from one or more other assets acquired into the same ownership at a time before the acquisition of the asset disposed of. The categories are where:

(1) assets have merged;
(2) an asset has divided or otherwise changed its nature; or
(3) different rights or interests in or over any asset have been created or extinguished at different times.

The asset disposed of is deemed to have been acquired at the earliest time at which any asset from which its value is derived was acquired into the same ownership.

Any determination of whether the asset disposed of was a business asset at a time when another asset from which its value is derived was in the ownership of the person making the disposal is made as if that other asset were the asset disposed of or, as the case may be, were comprised in it.

21.5.3 Assets transferred between spouses
(TCGA 1992, s 58(1); Sched A1, para 15)

The general rule for transfers between spouses is that if, in any tax year, and in the case of a woman who in that tax year is married and living with her husband, the man disposes of an asset to her, or the wife disposes of an asset to him, both are treated as if the asset was acquired from the one making the disposal on a no gain/no loss basis (ie for a consideration of such amount as would secure that on the disposal neither a gain nor a loss would accrue to the one making the disposal). The taper relief provisions apply where the transferring spouse has disposed of any asset to the transferee spouse by such a disposal.

The rules for determining the period for which an asset is held and the relevant period of ownership (Sched A1, para 2) apply to any subsequent disposal of the asset as if the time when the transferee spouse acquired the asset were the time when the transferring spouse acquired it. If the transferring spouse would be treated as having acquired the asset at a time other than the time when the transferring spouse did acquire it, the reference to the time when the transferring spouse acquired it is read as the time when the transferring spouse is *treated* as having acquired it in a case where:

(1) there has been one or more previous inter-spouse disposals, or
(2) there has not been such a previous disposal, by virtue of any other provision of TCGA 1992, Sched A1.

Where there is a disposal by the transferee spouse, any question whether the asset was a business asset at a time before that disposal is determined as if:

(1) in relation to times when the asset was held by the transferring spouse, the conditions of use by an individual (Sched A1, para 5(2)) are applied

to the individual by whom the disposal is made and also to the transferring spouse; and

(2) the acquisition of the asset as a legatee by the individual by whom the disposal is made (para 5(5)) also includes its acquisition as a legatee by the transferring spouse (para 15(4)(b)).

Where, in the case of any asset, there has been more than one inter-spouse transfer during the period after 5 April 1998 for which the transferee spouse has held it at the time of that spouse's disposal of that asset, this rule is applied as if a reference, in relation to any time, to the transferring spouse were a reference to the individual who was the transferring spouse in relation to the next inter-spouse transfer to have been made after that time.

See also **21.12**.

21.5.4 Postponed gains
(TCGA 1992, Sched A1, para 16)

The following applies where the whole or any part of any gain which would:

(1) (otherwise than under the CGT rules) have accrued on the disposal of any asset, or

(2) have accrued on any disposal assumed under any enactment to have been made at any time

is treated as accruing on or after 6 April 1998 at a time (whether or not the time of a subsequent disposal) which falls after the time of the actual or assumed disposal ('the charged disposal'). The cases in which the whole or part of any such gain would be so treated under TCGA 1992 are:

- Temporary non-residents (s 10A)
- Reorganisations, conversions and reconstructions (s 116(10))
- Compensation stock (s 134)
- Replacement of business assets – new assets are depreciating assets (s 154(2) or (4))
- Enterprise Investment Scheme: reinvestment (Sched 5B)
- Venture capital trusts: deferred charge on reinvestment (Sched 5C) or
- Qualifying indexed securities (FA 1996, Sched 15, para 27).

In relation to the gain (or part of it) treated as accruing after the time of the charged disposal:

(1) references elsewhere in TCGA 1992, Sched A1 to the disposal on which the gain or part accrues are to the charged disposal; and

(2) references here to the asset disposed of by that disposal are to the asset that was or would have been disposed of by the charged disposal.

It therefore follows that the end of the period after 5 April 1998 for which that asset had been held at the time of disposal on which that gain or part accrues is deemed to have been the time of the charged disposal.

In the following circumstances where any gain that is treated, under the specified provisions, as accruing after the time of disposal from which it accrues, references to the disposal on which the gain accrues, to the asset disposed of on that disposal and to the time of that disposal are construed disregarding these provisions:

(a) foreign assets of persons resident or ordinarily resident in the UK, but with foreign domicile (TCGA 1992, s 12(1)), or

(b) foreign assets: delayed remittances (TCGA 1992, s 279(2)).

It is immaterial for these purposes that the time:

(1) of the charged disposal or, as the case may be, of the actual disposal from which the gain accrues was before 6 April 1998; and

(2) at which the charged disposal is treated as accruing is postponed on more than one occasion under any of the enactments listed above.

21.5.5 Assets acquired in reconstruction of mutual businesses etc
(TCGA 1992, Sched A1, para 18)

A special modification of the taper relief rules applies where:

(1) company shares have been issued under any arrangements for the issue of such shares in respect of the interests of the members of a mutual company; and

(2) a person to whom shares were issued under those arrangements falls, under the rules applying to reconstructions or amalgamations involving the issue of securities (TCGA 1992, s 136(3)) to be treated as having exchanged interests of his as a member of the mutual company for shares issued under those arrangements.

In such cases, the rules as to the period for which an asset is held and the relevant period of ownership (Sched A1, para 2) are applied as if the time of that person's acquisition of the shares were the time when they were issued to him. The following apply:

(1) where a registered friendly society has been incorporated under the Friendly Societies Act 1992, and

(2) where there has been a change under Friendly Societies Act 1992, Sched 4 as a result of which a member of the registered society (ie of the society before incorporation, or of a branch of the registered society) has become a member of the incorporated society or of a branch of it (ie of the society after incorporation).

In such event, the rules as to the period for which an asset is held and the relevant period of ownership are applied in relation to the interests and rights in the incorporated society, or the branch of the incorporated society, which that person had immediately after the change, as if the time of their acquisition by him were the time of the change. This applies notwithstanding anything in TCGA 1992, s 217B (rights of members in a registered society equated with rights in an incorporated society).

21.5.6 Ancillary trust funds
(TCGA 1992, Sched A1, para 19)

Use of an asset as part of an ancillary trust fund of a member of Lloyd's:

(1) is not regarded as a use in respect of which the asset is to be treated as a business asset at any time; but
(2) is disregarded in any determination for the purposes of the rules for cases where an asset is used at the same time for different purposes (see above) of whether it was being put to a non-qualifying use at the same time as it was being used for one of the qualifying purposes.

An 'ancillary trust fund' in relation to a member does not include a premiums trust fund of his or his special reserve fund (if any) but, subject to that, means any trust fund required or authorised by the rules of Lloyd's, or required by a members' agent of his (FA 1993, s 184(1)).

21.5.7 General rules for settlements
(TCGA 1992, s 79; Sched A1, para 20)

Where settled property originates from more than one settlor, the taper relief rules are applied as if there were a separate and distinct settlement for the property originating from each settlor. References here to an eligible beneficiary are construed accordingly.

See generally **21.2.3** under 'Settlor'.

21.5.8 General rule for apportionments
(TCGA 1992, Sched A1, para 21)

Any apportionment required under the taper relief rules is made on a just and reasonable basis, and on the assumption that an amount to be apportioned over any period arose or accrued at the same rate throughout such period.

21.6 ANNUAL EXEMPT AMOUNT
(TCGA 1992, s 3)

21.6.1 Individuals

An individual is not chargeable to CGT if his net gains do not exceed the exempt amount for the tax year concerned. Thus, for 2000/01 the first £7,200 of an individual's net gains is exempt from CGT. This is an absolute exemption with no marginal relief.

An individual's taxable amount for any such tax year is the amount for that year on which that individual is chargeable to CGT (under TCGA 1992, s 2) after:

(1) deducting allowable losses of the same tax year and, to the extent not already allowed, of previous years (s 2(2));
(2) applying any reduction for taper relief (s 2A), and
(3) adding any amounts required to be added (by s 2(5)(b)), ie:
    (a) charge on settlor with interest in a settlement;
    (b) attribution of gains to settlors with interests in non-resident or dual resident settlements;
    (c) attribution of gains to beneficiaries; and
    (d) migrant settlements
(in conjunction with the provisions relating to temporary non-residents).

Where the amount of an individual's adjusted net gains for any tax year is equal to or less than the exempt amount for that year, no deduction is made for that tax year for any allowable losses:

(a) brought forward from a previous year; or
(b) carried back from a subsequent tax year in which the individual dies.

Where the amount of an individual's adjusted net gains for any tax year exceeds the exempt amount for the tax year, the deductions made for that tax year for allowable losses is limited to the amount of that excess (thereby leaving an amount of gains equal to the annual exempt amount). Thus, the amount of an individual's adjusted net gains for any tax year is the amount given in his case by:

(1) taking the amount of his gross gains for that tax year (ie the amount from which the deductions for allowable losses of the same tax year and, to the extent not already allowed, for previous tax years would otherwise be deducted); and
(2) deducting only the allowable losses of the current tax year; and
(3) in a tax year in which any amount is brought into account (under s 2(5)(b)) under any of the provisions listed above as an amount of chargeable gains accruing to any person in any tax year, adding whichever is the smaller of the exempt amount for that tax year and the amount falling to be so brought into account.

Example

James realised chargeable gains of £6,400 in 2000/01 and suffered allowable losses of £5,800. Allowable losses brought forward amounted to £2,400. The relief is given as follows:

	£	£
Gains in 2000/01	6,400	
Less: allowable losses in 2000/01	(5,800)	
Net gains in 2000/01		600
Allowable losses brought forward	2,400	
Less: utilised in 2000/01	Nil	Nil
Revised net gains 2000/01		600
Annual exempt amount 2000/01 (part)		600
Allowable losses carried forward	2,400	

Provided that an individual's net gains for 2000/01 do not exceed £7,200 and the total disposal proceeds on all chargeable assets in the tax year do not exceed £14,400, all of that need normally be reported on the annual tax return statement to that effect. However the Inspector has power to call for further information should he require it.

21.6.2 Personal representatives
(TCGA 1992, s 3)

The same reliefs as for an individual apply to a deceased's personal representatives during the tax year in which the death occurs and the following two tax years.

21.6.3 Trusts for disabled persons
(TCGA 1992, Sched 1, para 1)

The annual exemption may be available where property is held on trust, for the lifetime of a mentally disabled person, or of a person receiving attendance allowance or disability living allowance, because of an entitlement to the care component at the middle or higher rate.

A trust qualifies as a trust for the disabled if 50 per cent of the trust property is applied for disabled person's benefit, and either 50 per cent of the trust income is so applied, or its income cannot go to any other person's benefit.

Powers of advancement (eg under the Trustee Act 1925, s 32) do not disqualify the trust. The requirement that income be applied for qualifying purposes during the disabled person's lifetime is satisfied if the income is to be so applied whilst held on protective trusts (eg Trustee Act 1925, s 33).

The special provisions for 'groups' of trusts (see below) also apply, except that the full 2000/01 limit of £7,200 is divided by the number of settlements subject to a minimum exemption of £720 (ie one-tenth of the full exemption) each.

21.6.4 Other trusts
(TCGA 1992, Sched 1, para 2)

A modification of the relief is available for other categories of trusts. This takes the form of exempting an amount equivalent to one-half of the annual exemption available to individuals. Thus, for 2000/01, the first £3,600 of net gains made by trustees in a tax year is exempt. So far as concerns losses, the position is the same for individuals but with a smaller basic exemption.

If the gains realised by a trust created before 7 June 1978 do not exceed £3,600 and the disposal proceeds do not exceed £7,200, the trustees must give full details of the disposals to the Inspector. However, where a person is the settlor of more than one trust created after 6 June 1978, the £3,600 exemption is divided by the number of settlements, with a minimum exemption of £720 (ie one-tenth of the full exemption) each.

Non-resident settlements, charities, pension funds, retirement annuity schemes and sponsored superannuation schemes are ignored for this purpose (TA 1988, ss 69(1), 590–612, 615(3), 624).

Full details of all disposals by the trustees of settlements created after 6 June 1978 must be returned. There is no reduced reporting requirements for trusts created before 7 June 1978.

The CGT rate on gains realised by the trustees of accumulation and discretionary trusts is 'the rate applicable to trusts' which for 2000/01 is 34 per cent (TA 1988, s 686(1)). Where a settlor retains a life interest in settled property any gain realised by the trustees is treated as his gain and taxed accordingly (s 686).

21.7 CGT RATES

21.7.1 Individuals
(TCGA 1992, s 4)

For 2000/01, net gains, after loss reliefs and the annual exempt amount (see **21.6**), realised by individuals are charged to CGT at rates which are equivalent to those which would apply if the gains were treated as the top slice of income. Although for calculation purposes the income tax and CGT systems are integrated, any tax arising on the gains is charged under CGT. There are several alternative calculations which may be applied given various scenarios.

Basic rule

The basic rule, to which there is a number of exceptions, is that the CGT rate on net chargeable gains is equivalent to the 20 per cent savings rate of income tax for the year (TCGA 1992, s 4(1)).

Total income less than the starting rate limit

If, after taking account of personal allowances and any other deductions, an individual has no taxable income, or his total income for the year is less than the starting rate limit (£1,520 for 2000/01), then the amount on which he is chargeable to CGT is at a 10 per cent rate equivalent to the income tax starting rate (TCGA 1992, s 4(1AB)(a), added by FA 2000, s 37(1)). The charge is made on capital gains which, when aggregated with his income, fall within the starting rate band.

The amount on which an individual is chargeable to CGT may exceed the unused part of his starting rate band. In this event, the 10 per cent starting rate applies to the unused part (s 4(1AB)(b), added by FA 2000, s 37(1)).

The unused part of an individual's starting rate band is the amount by which the starting rate limit exceeds his total income (as reduced by any allowances or deductions; s 4(1AC), added by FA 2000, s 37(1)).

Example

The application of the 10 per cent starting rate to CGT benefits an individual who has a relatively low income in excess of his income tax personal allowance, but also has gains over the annual exempt amount. Suppose that Donald has the following income and gains:

Savings income (in excess of income tax personal allowance)	£800
Chargeable gains (in excess of annual exempt amount)	£7,500

2000/01	Income other than savings and dividends £	Savings income other than dividends £	Taxable gains £	CGT £
Net chargeable gains			14,700	
Annual exempt amount			7,200	
CGT due on			7,500	
Starting rate @ 10% £1–1,520	800		720	72
Basic rate @ 22% £1,521–28,400				
Savings rate @ 20% up to £28,400			6,700	1,356
Higher rate @ 40% over £28,400				
	800		7,500	1,428

Income chargeable at the higher rate

If income tax is chargeable at the higher rate or the Schedule F upper rate on any part of an individual's income for a tax year, the CGT rate on his gains for the year is equivalent to the higher rate of 40 per cent (TCGA 1992, s 4(2)).

Income not chargeable at the higher rate

If an individual has no income tax chargeable at the 40 per cent higher rate or the Schedule F upper rate, and even when chargeable gains are aggregated with total income the basic rate limit is not exceeded, the CGT rate applied is equivalent to the 20 per cent savings rate of income tax for the year.

Where, however, an individual has no income tax chargeable at the 40 per cent higher rate or the Schedule F upper rate but the amount on which he is chargeable to CGT, when aggregated with his total income, exceeds the unused part of his basic rate band, the CGT rate on the excess is at the 40 per cent higher rate (TCGA 1992, s 4(3)). The unused part of an individual's basic rate band is the amount by which the basic rate limit exceeds his total income (as reduced by any deductions; s 4(4)). The part within the basic rate band is chargeable to CGT at a rate equivalent to the 20 per cent savings rate of income tax for the year.

Example

Ernest has the following income and gains:

Income other than savings or gains (in excess of personal allowance)	£5,400
Savings income other than dividends	£14,000
Net chargeable gains	£23,200

2000/01	*Income other than savings and dividends* £	*Savings income other than dividends* £	*Taxable gains* £	*CGT* £
Net chargeable gains			23,200	
Annual exempt amount			7,200	
CGT due on			16,000	
Starting rate @ 10% £1–1,520	1,520			

Basic rate @ 22% £1,521–28,400	3,880			
Savings rate @ 20% up to £28,400		14,000	9,000	1,800
Higher rate @ 40% over £28,400			7,000	2,800
	5,400	14,000	16,000	4,600

21.7.2 Trustees and personal representatives

The CGT rate on gains by the trustees of a settlement, or by the personal representatives of a deceased person, is equivalent to the rate applicable to trusts under TA 1988, s 686 which, for 2000/01, is 34 per cent (TCGA 1992, s 4(1AA)).

21.7.3 Settlements
(TCGA 1992, ss 4, 6)

The CGT rate on gains accruing to the trustees of a settlement or to personal representatives is 34 per cent (TA 1988, s 686).

If any income arising under a settlement is treated as the settlor's income (TA 1988, s 683(1) or 684(1)) then, whether or not he is chargeable to tax otherwise than at the lower and basic rates, it is also treated as his income for the purposes of ascertaining the unused part of the lower and basic rate bands. In the calculation of the amount of the basic rate band remaining unused, the following further adjustments may be required.

First, if under TA 1988, s 549(2) (deficiency in final year under a life policy or life annuity contract) a deduction of such an amount is made from total income.

Secondly, suppose that, under TA 1988, s 699(1) (income accruing before death), the estate's residuary income is treated as reduced, and therefore a person's income is reduced for 'excess liability' purposes. The purpose of this adjustment is to give relief where, having already been taken into account for IHT purposes, the income would otherwise also be subject to income tax in the beneficiary's hands. Accordingly, in ascertaining the unused part of the basic rate, his income for the year is reduced by the amount of that reduction.

Thirdly, where under TA 1988, s 547(1)(a) (gains from insurance policies etc) a person's total income for a year of assessment is deemed to include any amount of such gains, the following further adjustments are made:

(1) in ascertaining the amount of the unused part of the basic rate band, his total income includes only 'the appropriate fraction' of the gain (TA 1988, s 550(3));

(2) if relief is given under s 550 and the calculation required by s 550(2)(b) does not involve the higher rate of tax, the ascertainment of the rate of tax applicable to the gain under s 4(2), (3) proceeds as if no income tax were chargeable at the higher rate on his income.

Note that nothing described above is to reduce or increase the amount of a reduction which a person is entitled to make from his total income in relation to personal reliefs (TA 1988, ss 256–278) and which limits any allowance by reference to the level of his total income.

21.8 RESIDENCE STATUS

21.8.1 Residence, including temporary residence
(TCGA 1992, s 9)

Individuals

Individuals are chargeable persons to CGT on any gains which accrue to them in a tax year during which (or part of which) they are resident or ordinarily resident in the UK (TCGA 1992, s 2(1)). For CGT purposes 'resident' and 'ordinarily resident' have the same meaning as for income tax. If there is any dispute over domicile or ordinary residence, the appeals procedure for income tax purposes (TA 1992, s 207) is also applied to CGT.

The territorial sea of the UK and designated areas of the continental shelf are, for CGT purposes, deemed to be part of the UK (TCGA 1992, s 276). A non-resident trading in the UK through a branch or agency may be liable to CGT on gains arising on the disposal of assets situated there and held or used for the purposes of such trade (TCGA 1992, s 10(1)).

Subject to the s 10(1) rules above, an individual who is in the UK only for a temporary purpose, and not with a view or intent to establish residence there, is chargeable to CGT accruing in any tax year if (and only if) the period (or sum of the periods) for which he is so resident there in that tax year exceeds six months. The question of temporary purpose is decided without regard to any living accommodation available in the UK for his use.

Thus, for CGT, an individual is strictly classed as resident or non-resident for the whole of a tax year. The difficulties in the year of commencement or of cessation of residence in the UK is addressed by ESC D2 (see also ESC A11, ESC A78, SP 3/81 and SP 2/91). A person arriving in the UK to take up residence who has not been resident or ordinarily resident there in any of the preceding 36 months is charged only in respect of gains realised after the date of arrival in this country. As a corollary, losses on assets disposed of before arrival in the UK are not allowable. A person leaving the UK for permanent residence abroad, is not chargeable on gains (or eligible for relief on losses) arising on assets disposed of after the date from which they are regarded as non-resident and non-ordinarily resident in the UK. This date is normally that of departure. In general, the status of resident and ordinarily resident are as for income tax as modified by ESC D2.

Trustees, etc

ESC D2 does not apply to trustees of a settlement who commence or cease residence in the UK or to a settlor of a settlement in relation to gains for which he is chargeable under TCGA 1992, s 77 or 86.

So far as concerns trusts generally, the trustees are treated as a single and continuing body, distinct from the persons who are from time to time trustees. The trustees, as a body, are treated as resident or ordinarily resident in the UK unless the trust's administration is carried on outside the UK, and the trustees (or a majority of them) are non-resident or non-ordinarily resident in the UK (TCGA 1992, s 69(1)).

This does not apply to nominees or bare trustees. In these cases it is necessary to look through to the person on whose behalf the nominee holds the asset concerned, or who is absolutely entitled as against the trustee. It is that person's status as resident or ordinarily resident which determines chargeability (s 60(1),(2)). A deceased's personal representatives are similarly treated as a single and continuing body during their administration of the estate (s 65). A trustee in bankruptcy is treated as the debtor's nominee and, if he is acting for an insolvent estate, is deemed to act as a personal representative (s 66(1), (3)).

21.8.2 Temporary non-residents

It will be appreciated that, ultimately, the question of an individual's residence status is one of fact and degree. However, hitherto, it has been accepted that an absence comprising at least three complete tax years gains an individual the status of 'non-resident' or 'non-ordinarily resident' in the UK. Also, an individual whose home and place of business are in one particular place abroad for at least one complete tax year is treated as non-resident for that year. It is probable that he is also treated as non-ordinarily resident (*Reed v Clark* [1985] STC 323; *Levene v CIR* (1928) 13 STC 486). Furthermore, it has also been accepted that an individual who goes abroad for full-time employment is treated as being non-resident and non-ordinarily resident from the date of his departure until that of his return, subject to the condition that his employment and his absence abroad must extend over at least one complete tax year.

These rules have been manipulated by taxpayers seeking to avoid CGT. There have been two main ways in which this was sought to be achieved:

(1) ensuring that disposals of assets occurred during a period when the individual was non-resident; and
(2) distributing capital to a non-resident beneficiary of a non-resident trust, by which the charge under TCGA 1992, s 87 was avoided.

Furthermore (ESC A11; ESC D2) an individual who went to live abroad for at least three complete tax years was not charged on disposals made after his departure but within the same tax year.

Temporary non-residents after 16 March 1998
(TCGA 1992, s 10A)

These manoeuvres are countered, by a new rule, so far as concerns individuals who become non-resident and non-ordinarily resident after 16 March 1998. In short, the method adopted to prevent this form of tax avoidance is to provide that an individual remains in charge to CGT unless he is neither resident nor ordinarily resident for at least five complete tax years. If the individual is non-resident for less than that period, gains and losses accruing to him while he is abroad are deemed to accrue in the tax year of his return.

In the context of the new rule, 'the tax year of departure' is the last tax year before the tax year of return for which the taxpayer satisfied the residence requirements. An 'intervening year' is any tax year which, in a case where the conditions set out below are satisfied, falls between the tax year of departure and the year of return. Also in this context a 'relevant disposal', is a disposal of an asset acquired by the person making the disposal at a time when he was resident or ordinarily resident in the UK. For the purposes of the new rule an individual satisfies the residence requirements for a tax year if that tax year is one during any part of which he is UK-resident or ordinarily resident. Notwithstanding the new rule, it remains open to an individual to claim relief in accordance with any double taxation relief arrangements.

The new rule applies in the case of any individual, subject to the following conditions:

(1) he satisfies the residence requirements for the tax year of his return to the UK;
(2) he did not satisfy the residence requirements for one or more tax years immediately preceding the tax year of his return, but there are earlier tax years for which he did satisfy the residence requirements;
(3) there are fewer than five tax years falling between the tax years of his departure and of his return; and
(4) four out of the seven tax years immediately preceding the tax year of his departure are also tax years for each of which he satisfied the residence requirements.

Subject to the rules set out below and TCGA 1992, s 86A (attribution of gains of settlors in s 10A cases), an individual is chargeable to CGT as if the gains or, as the case may be, losses referred to below accrued to him in the tax year of his return:

(1) All the chargeable gains and losses which (otherwise) would have accrued to him in an intervening tax year.

(2) All the chargeable gains which under TCGA 1992, s 13 (attribution of gains to members of non-resident companies) or s 86 (attribution of gains to settlors with interests in non-resident or dual-resident settlements) would be treated as having accrued to him in an intervening tax year if he had been UK-resident throughout that intervening tax year. This expressly catches gains in offshore trusts attributed to the settlor under s 86 and in offshore companies attributed to participators under s 13. On its general wording, s 87 applies to gains treated as accruing to beneficiaries. Additionally, an individual who falls within s 10A is treated as UK-resident for the s 87 purposes for capital payments made to offshore close companies controlled by UK residents. Were it not for the introduction of new TCGA 1992, s 86A (attribution of gains to settlor in s 10A cases), it would have been possible for gains attributed under s 86 to have been charged also on beneficiaries under s 87.

(3) Any losses which under TCGA 1992, s 13(8) (attribution of losses to members of non-resident companies) would have been allowable in this case in any intervening tax year if he had been UK-resident throughout that intervening tax year. The reference here to losses allowable in an individual's case in an intervening tax year is to only so much of the aggregate losses that would have been available under s 13(8) for reducing gains accruing under s 13 to that individual in that tax year as does not exceed the amount of the gains that would have accrued to him had that tax year been one throughout which he was UK-resident.

The gains and losses which are deemed to accrue to an individual in the tax year of his return do not include any chargeable gains or allowable losses accruing to him in an intervening tax year which have to be brought into account for that tax year under TCGA 1992, s 10 (non-resident with UK branch or agency) or s 16(3) (losses accruing in years when individual neither resident nor ordinarily resident). However, gains and losses which are treated as accruing to an individual in the tax year of his return do not include any gain or loss accruing on the disposal by him of any asset if the following conditions are met:

(1) the asset was acquired by him at a time in the tax year of his departure or any intervening tax year when he was neither resident nor ordinarily resident in the UK;

(2) the asset was so acquired otherwise than by means of a relevant disposal which under TCGA 1992, s 58 (assets acquired from individual's spouse – see further **21.5.3** and **21.12**), s 73 (death of person with

beneficial interest under settlement) or s 258(4) (surrender of works of art etc in satisfaction of IHT liability) is treated as having been a disposal on which neither a gain nor a loss accrued;

(3) the asset is not an interest created by or arising under a settlement; and

(4) the amount or value of the consideration for the acquisition of the asset by him is not required, by reference to any relevant disposal, to be treated as reduced under s 23(4)(b) or (5)(b) (adjustment of acquisition value in certain cases following receipt of compensation or insurance money not treated as a disposal), s 152(1)(b) (reduction of acquisition value by rollover relief on replacement of business assets), s 162(3)(b) (reduction of acquisition value of shares on incorporation of a business) or s 247(2)(b) or (3)(b) (adjustment of acquisition value on receipt of proceeds of compulsory acquisition).

This does not, however, exclude from the gains which are to be treated as accruing to an individual in the tax year of return, where:

(a) any chargeable gain that has accrued or would have accrued on the disposal of any asset is a gain falling (otherwise) to be treated under s 116(10) or (11) (reorganisations, conversions and reconstructions), s 134 (compensation stock) or s 154(2) or (4) (hold-over of gain where proceeds of disposal of business assets are reinvested in depreciating assets) as accruing on the disposal of the whole or any part of another asset; and

(b) that other asset is such an asset, but the first asset is not.

Gains realised in the tax year of departure are assessable as gains of that year, but the time limit for assessment is extended until two years after 31 January next following the year of return. Note also that ESC D2 has been amended so that all gains realised in the tax years of departure from, or arrival in, the UK are taxed for those years (Budget Press Release, 'CGT – temporary non-residence', 17 March 1998).

Example

Perkins has lived in the UK all his life. He leaves the UK on 5 July 1998 on a three-year contract of employment abroad. He returns to the UK and resumes residence there on 5 October 2001. He realises a chargeable gain of £35,000 on 1 September 1998 and a further gain of £90,000 (on shares which he had acquired before he left the UK) on 1 September 2000.

The £35,000 gain is chargeable, under existing legislation, for 1998/99 (the year of his departure). Because he has been UK-resident for the seven years prior to the tax year of his departure he does not qualify for split-year treatment for CGT purposes under the revised ESC D2.

The £90,000 gain is chargeable under s 10A for the tax year of his return to the UK (ie 2001/02). This is because he has been resident outside the UK for less than five full tax years).

Offshore trusts and companies
(TCGA 1992, s 96)

Section 96 deals with payments by and to companies. This now takes account of the introduction of the concept of temporary residence. Thus, for s 96 purposes, an individual is deemed to have been UK-resident at any time in any tax year which in his case is an intervening tax year for s 10A purposes.

If, after the end of any tax year, it appears that any individual is to be treated as having been UK-resident at any time in that tax year, adjustments can be made to the amounts of tax taken to have been chargeable by s 96 on any person, notwithstanding any other time limit for making any claim or assessment (whether by means of an assessment, an amendment of an assessment, a repayment of tax or otherwise).

These new rules apply, in general, in any case in which the tax year of departure is 1998/99 or a subsequent tax year. However, they also apply in any case in which the tax year of departure is the tax year 1997/98 and the taxpayer was resident or ordinarily resident in the UK at a time after 16 March 1998.

21.8.3 Visiting forces, agents-general etc
(TCGA 1992, s 11)

A period during which a member of a visiting force to whom TA 1988, s 323(1) applies is in the UK by reason solely of his being a member of that force is not treated for CGT purposes either as a period of residence in the UK or as creating a change in his residence or domicile.

An agent-general who is resident in the UK is entitled to the same immunity from CGT as that to which the head of a mission so resident is entitled under the Diplomatic Privileges Act 1964.

Any person on the staff of agents-general etc (not being a person employed in any trade, business or other undertaking carried on for the purposes of profit) is entitled to the same immunity from CGT as that to which a member of the staff of a mission is entitled under the 1964 Act.

21.8.4 Foreign assets of persons with foreign domicile
(TCGA 1992, s 12)

Individuals who are resident or ordinarily resident but not domiciled in the UK are chargeable to CGT only on gains arising on the disposal of foreign assets if they are remitted to the UK. It follows that, if a person who is non-UK domiciled incurs a loss on the disposal of a foreign asset, no relief is allowed against that loss.

In addition to amounts actually received in the UK, there are also treated as received in the UK all amounts paid, used or enjoyed in or in any manner or form transmitted or brought to the UK. If sums are applied outside the

UK in payment of debts they may, in certain cases, be treated as received in the UK (TA 1992, s 69(5)–(9)).

21.8.5 Attribution of gains to members of non-resident companies
(TCGA 1992, ss 13, 14)

Chargeable gains realised by certain non-resident companies may be apportioned amongst the shareholders in proportion to their rights in a liquidation of the company. Such companies are those which, although *not* resident in the UK, would be classed as close companies if they *were* resident in the UK.

Participators

Any participator (under TA 1988, s 417(1)) in the company who is resident or ordinarily resident in the UK (and if an individual is also UK-domiciled) is treated as if part of the chargeable gain (*pro rata* to his interest as such participator) had accrued directly to him. A person's interest as a participator comprises all the factors by reference to which he falls to be treated as such, and the extent of such an interest is determined as the proportion of his interests compared with all the participators in the company (including any who are not resident or ordinarily resident) which on a just and reasonable apportionment is represented by that interest.

Where the interest of any person in a company is wholly or partly represented by an interest which he has under any settlement (his 'beneficial interest'), and his beneficial interest is the factor, or one of the factors, by reference to which he would otherwise be treated as having an interest as a participator in that company, the interest as a participator which would be that person's is deemed, to the extent that it is represented by his beneficial interest, to be an interest of the settlement trustees (and not of his).

Any appeal under TMA 1970, s 31 involving any question of the extent, for the purposes of these rules, of a person's interest as a participator in a company is to the Special Commissioners.

No apportionment is made on a person if the amount which would otherwise be apportioned to him is less than 5 per cent of the overall gain.

Participator's CGT liability

Where any amount of CGT is paid by a participator as a result of part of a company's chargeable gain being attributed to him, and an amount of the chargeable gain is distributed (by way of dividend, distribution of capital, or on the company's dissolution) within two years from the time when the chargeable gain accrued to the company, that amount of tax is applied to reduce or extinguish any liability (if any) of that person to income tax or (as the case may be) to any CGT on the distribution. This only applies in so far as the tax concerned has not been reimbursed by the company nor allowed as a deduction in the computation of a gain on a disposal by him of any asset representing his interest as a participator.

In calculating, for these purposes, the amount of income tax or CGT chargeable on any person for any tax year in relation to any chargeable gain or distribution, the following rules apply:

(1) any amount so distributed within the two-year period, and which falls to be treated as income of that person for that tax year, is regarded as forming the highest part of the income on which he is chargeable to tax for the year (TCGA 1992, s 13(7A)(a));

(2) any gain accruing in that tax year on the disposal by that person of any asset representing his interest as a participator is regarded as forming the highest part of the gains on which he is chargeable to tax for that year;

(3) where any amount so distributed within the two-year period falls to be treated as a disposal on which a chargeable gain accrues, that gain is regarded as forming the second highest part of the person's chargeable gains;

(4) any gain treated as accruing to a participator in a non-resident company who is resident or ordinarily resident in the UK (and if he is also UK-domiciled) as part of his chargeable gains (*pro rata* to his interest as a participator) is regarded as the third highest part of his chargeable gains.

So far as they would go to reduce or extinguish chargeable gains accruing, under these rules, to a person in a tax year, the rules apply in relation to a loss accruing to the company on the disposal of an asset in that tax year as they would apply had a gain accrued instead. However, they only so apply in relation to that person; they do not generally apply to a loss accruing to the company.

If a person who is a participator at the time when the chargeable gain accrues to the company is itself a company which is non-UK resident, but which would be a close company if it were UK-resident, the chargeable gain is further apportioned among the participators in the second company *pro rata* to their respective interests as participators. This procedure is followed through any number of companies.

The apportionment procedure also applies to trustees who are participators in a company, or in any company through which a gain is apportioned, if when the gain accrues to the company they are neither resident nor ordinarily resident in the UK.

If any tax payable by any person following an apportionment is paid by the company to which the chargeable gain accrues or, on a sub-apportionment, by any such other company, the amount so paid is not for income tax, CGT or corporation tax purposes regarded as a payment to the person by whom the tax was originally payable.

Exceptions to the charge

The above rules do not apply to a chargeable gain on the disposal of:

(1) tangible property, whether movable or immovable, or a lease of such property, where the property was used, and used only, for the purposes of a trade carried on by the company wholly outside the UK;
(2) currency, or of a debt owed by a bank which is not in sterling and which is represented by a sum standing to the credit of a person in a bank where the currency or debt is or represents money in use for the purposes of a trade carried on by the company wholly outside the UK; and
(3) assets used for a trade carried on through a UK branch or agency of a company which is non-UK resident.

Groups of companies

The apportionment procedures also apply to non-resident groups of companies, none of whose members are UK-resident. In the case of a group where two or more of its members are non-UK resident, the 'non-resident group' comprises only those members of the group who are non-UK resident.

The general definition of a group, as applied for group capital gains purposes, is adopted but with a number of omissions (TCGA 1992, s 170). Except as otherwise provided, the rules set out below apply to determine whether companies form a group and, where they do, which is the principal company of the group. In applying the definition of '75 per cent subsidiary' under TA 1988, s 838, any share capital of a registered industrial and provident society is treated as ordinary share capital. 'Group' and 'subsidiary' are construed with any necessary modifications where applied to a company incorporated under the law of a country outside the UK.

The basic rule is that:

(1) a principal company of the group and all its 75 per cent subsidiaries form a group and, if any of those subsidiaries have 75 per cent subsidiaries, the group includes them and their 75 per cent subsidiaries, and so on, but
(2) a group does not include any company (other than the principal company) that is not an effective 51 per cent subsidiary of that principal company.

A company cannot be the principal company of the group if it is itself a 75 per cent subsidiary of another company.

Where the subsidiary is a 75 per cent subsidiary of another company, but those companies are prevented from being members of the same group, the subsidiary may itself be the principal company of another group unless this rule enables a further company to be the principal company of a group of which the subsidiary would be a member.

A company cannot be a member of more than one group. But where, apart from this rule, a company would be a member of two or more groups (the principal company of each group being referred to below as the 'head of a group'), it is a member only of that group, if any, of which it would be a member under one of the following tests (applying earlier tests in preference to later tests):

(1) it is a member of the group it would be a member of if there were left out of account any amount to which a head of a group is or would be beneficially entitled of any profits available for distribution to equity holders of a head of another group or of any assets of a head of another group available for distribution to its equity holders on a winding-up;

(2) it is a member of the group the head of which is beneficially entitled to a percentage of profits available for distribution to equity holders of the company that is greater than the percentage of those profits to which any other head of a group is so entitled;

(3) it is a member of the group the head of which would be beneficially entitled to a percentage of any assets of the company available for distribution to its equity holders on a winding-up that is greater than the percentage of those assets to which any other head of a group would be so entitled; or

(4) it is a member of the group the head of which owns directly or indirectly a percentage of the company's ordinary share capital that is greater than the percentage of that capital owned directly or indirectly by any other head of a group (interpreting this test as if it were included in TA 1988, s 838(1)(a)).

A company is an effective 51 per cent subsidiary of another company at any time if and only if the parent:

(1) is beneficially entitled to more than 50 per cent of any profits available for distribution to equity holders of the subsidiary; and

(2) would be beneficially entitled to more than 50 per cent of any assets of the subsidiary available for distribution to its equity holders on a winding-up.

Schedule 18 to TA 1988 (group relief: equity holders and profits or assets available for distribution) applies, appropriately amended, in this context.

A group remains the same group so long as the same company remains its principal company, and if at any time the principal company becomes a member of another group, the first group and the other group are regarded as the same, and the question of whether a company has ceased to be a member of a group is determined accordingly.

The passing of a resolution or the making of an order, or any other act, for the winding-up of a member of a group of companies shall not be regarded as the occasion of that or any other company ceasing to be a member of the group.

The following provisions under TCGA 1992 apply in relation to non-resident companies which are members of a non-resident group of companies, as they apply in relation to companies resident in the UK which are members of a group of companies:

- Transfers within a group: general provisions (s 171)
- Transfer of UK branch or agency (s 172)
- Transfers within a group: trading stock (s 173)
- Disposal or acquisition outside a group (s 174)
- Replacement of business assets by members of a group (s 175(1)).

21.8.6 Non-residents: deemed disposals
(TCGA 1992, s 25)

When an asset becomes situated outside the UK and ceases to be a chargeable asset in relation to a person, he is deemed to have disposed of the asset immediately before the time when it became situated outside the UK, and immediately to have reacquired it at its market value at that time. This does not apply where the asset becomes situated outside the UK at the same time as the person ceases to carry on a trade, etc in the UK through a branch or agency, or where it is an exploration or exploitation asset.

Where an asset ceases to be a chargeable asset in relation to a person on his ceasing to carry on a trade in the UK through a branch or agency, he is deemed to have disposed of it immediately before the time when he ceased to so carry on that trade, and immediately to have reacquired it at its market value at that time. This does not apply to a chargeable asset after he ceases to so carry on that trade and before the end of the chargeable period in which he does so.

An asset is at any time a chargeable asset in relation to a person if, were it to be disposed of at that time, any chargeable gains accruing to him on the disposal would be gains for which he would be chargeable to CGT under TCGA 1992, s 10(1).

21.9 TRANSACTIONS DEEMED MADE AT MARKET VALUE
(TCGA 1992, s 17)

The following acquisitions or disposals are deemed to be at market value, and not (if different) for the actual consideration passing (if any), where the acquisition or disposal is otherwise than by way of a bargain made at arm's length (see *Aspden v Hildesley* (1981) 55 TC 609, ChD):

(1) gifts, other than those to which gift relief applies (under TCGA 1992, ss 165 and 260);
(2) transfer into settlement (TCGA 1992, s 70; *Berry v Warnett* (1982) 55 TC 92, HL); and
(3) distribution from a company of its shares.

21.10 CONNECTED PERSONS
(TCGA 1992, s 18)

Special rules apply where the person acquiring an asset and the person disposing of it are 'connected persons'. Notwithstanding the consideration actually given, the transaction is deemed, for computational purposes, to be at such a consideration as would apply between parties negotiating on an arm's length basis (ie at market value).

Where the asset is an option to enter into a sale or other transaction given by the person making the disposal, a loss accruing to the person acquiring the asset is not an allowable loss unless it accrues on a disposal of the option at arm's length to a person who is not connected with him.

Where the asset is subject to any right or restriction enforceable by the person making the disposal, or by a person connected with him, then (where the amount of the consideration for the acquisition is deemed to be equal to the asset's market value), that market value is $(A - B)$, where

A = what the market value would be if not subject to the right or restriction, and
B = the market value of whichever is the less of
    (1) the right, or
    (2) the restriction of the amount by which its extinction would enhance the asset's value to its owner.

However, if the right or restriction is of such a nature that its enforcement would effectively destroy or substantially impair the asset's value without bringing any countervailing advantage either to the person making the disposal or a person connected with him, the restriction is ignored in determining the asset's market value. This also applies in the case of an option or other right to acquire the asset. It may also apply if, in the case of incorporeal property, it is a right to extinguish the asset in the hands of the person giving the consideration by forfeiture, merger or otherwise. However, this does not apply to a right of forfeiture or other right exercisable on breach of a covenant contained in a lease of land or other property. Nor does it apply to any right or restriction under a mortgage or other charge.

A loss on disposal of a chargeable asset to a connected person is allowable only against a chargeable gain arising on a disposal to the same person at a time when they are still connected persons. This does not apply if the disposal is a gift into settlement for which the gift and any income arising therefrom is wholly or primarily for educational or cultural purposes. The potential beneficiaries cannot be a group all or most of whom are connected persons.

Relatives

A person is connected with an individual if he is the individual's spouse, or is a relative, or the spouse of a relative, of his or of his spouse.

Settlements

A person, in his capacity as trustee of a settlement, is connected with:

(1) any individual who in relation to the settlement is a settlor;
(2) any person who is connected with such an individual; and
(3) any company which is connected with that settlement.

The settlor and the trustees are connected persons at the moment when a settlement comes into existence and the first transfer is made into the settlement. Trustees and beneficiaries cease to be connected following the settlor's death (see *Tax Bulletin* 6 (February 1993)).

A company is connected with a settlement if it is:

(1) a close company (or not a close company only because it is non-UK resident) and the participators include the settlement trustees; or
(2) controlled (as defined by TA 1988, s 840) by a close company as above.

21.11 AGGREGATE MARKET VALUATION FOR LINKED TRANSACTIONS
(TCGA 1992, ss 19, 20)

A special rule applies to prevent the CGT avoidance by means of a series of small transactions (say, minority holdings of shares) which are each of low value, but which if sold as a single majority holding would be worth more than their aggregate value. This applies where:

(1) by way of two or more transactions ('material transactions') which form a series of linked transactions, one person disposes of assets to another, or to two or more other persons, with whom he is connected (see **21.10**); and
(2) the original market value of the assets disposed of by any of the material transactions in the series is less than the appropriate portion of the market value of the assets disposed of by all the transactions in the series, valued on the basis of a single disposal comprising all of the assets included in the linked series of material transactions.

Where these two conditions are met, the disposal effected by any of the linked material transactions in the series to which the valuation test applies is deemed to be for a consideration equal to the appropriate portion of the composite single disposal value. Two or more material transactions are linked if they occur within the six-year period ending on the date of the last of them.

This substitution of value does not apply if the disposal is by a material transaction between spouses (TCGA 1992, s 58). This is because the transferee spouse is deemed to have acquired the assets from the transferor spouse on a no gain/no loss basis (s 58(1)). See further **21.12**.

The rule is applied when a second material transaction causes a series of linked transactions to come into being, and whenever, by means of a further material transaction, an existing series is extended. This applies even if, because of the six-year rule, an earlier transaction ceases to form part of the series.

Where there is a series of linked transactions, the original market value of the assets disposed of by each transaction in the series is determined as follows:

(1) if at the time in question the transaction is the most recent in the series, the original market value of the assets disposed of by that transaction is the market value which would otherwise be deemed to be the consideration for that transaction; and

(2) for any other transaction in the series, the original market value of the assets disposed of by that transaction is the value which, prior to the occurrence of the most recent transaction in the series, was or would otherwise have been deemed to be the consideration for the transaction concerned (whether on a previous linked transaction or otherwise).

For any transaction in a series of linked transactions:

(1) the aggregate market value of the assets disposed of by all the transactions in the series means what would have been the market value of all those assets if, considering all the assets together, they had been disposed of by one disposal occurring at the time of the transaction concerned, and

(2) the appropriate portion of the aggregate market value of the assets disposed of by all the transactions in the series is that portion of the aggregate market value which it is reasonable to apportion to those of the assets which were actually disposed of by the transaction concerned.

For these purposes, considering all the assets together includes not only considering them as a group or holding or collection of assets retaining their separate identities, but also (if it gives a higher market value) to considering them as brought together, physically or in law, so as to constitute either a single asset or a number of assets which are distinct from those which were comprised in each of the transactions.

If any of the assets disposed of by all the transactions in a series of linked transactions were acquired after the first of those transactions, then, in the applying the above rules to each of the transactions in the series:

(1) no account is taken of any assets which were acquired after the first transaction, and

(2) the number of assets of which account is taken is limited to the maximum number which were held by the person making the disposal at any time in the period beginning immediately before the first of the transactions in the series and ending immediately before the last.

Where the assets disposed of are securities, the assets disposed of by any of the transactions in a series of linked transactions are identified on a first in/first out basis. 'Securities' in this context include any assets which are of a nature to be dealt in without identifying the particular assets disposed of or acquired.

21.12 HUSBAND AND WIFE
(TCGA 1992, s 58)

Transfers of assets between a husband and wife living together are treated as being made at such a value as gives neither gain nor loss to the transferring spouse, and the transferee spouse acquires the asset at the same value. This does not apply to a transfer to or from trading stock of the other spouse (see also TCGA 1992, s 161). Nor does it apply to disposals between spouses by way of *donatio mortis causa* (gifts in expectation of death). This general rule also applies to transfers in the tax year in which a couple separates, but not thereafter (*Aspen v Hildesley* (1981) 55 TC 609, ChD).

It is not necessary that both partners must be UK-resident (*Gubay v Kington* (1984) 57 TC 601, HL). ESC D2 treats a person as becoming non-resident and non-ordinarily resident from the date of his departure. However, in *ex p Fulford-Dobson* (1987) 60 TC 168, QB, it was held that the Revenue may disapply a concession if it is used for tax avoidance.

21.13 DEATH

21.13.1 No disposal on death
(TCGA 1992, s 62)

On death, there is no disposal under the CGT regime. Assets of which a deceased person was competent to dispose are not deemed to be disposed of by him on his death (whether they pass in accordance with his will, in accordance with the intestacy rules, or otherwise by operation of law).

The assets are, however, deemed to be acquired by the deceased's personal representatives (or legatees) at a consideration equal to their market value at the date of death. Where IHT is chargeable on assets comprised in the deceased's estate on death, and the value of any asset has been ascertained (whether in proceedings or otherwise) for IHT purposes, that value is also taken to be the asset's market value at the date of death for CGT purposes (TCGA 1992, s 274).

The assets of which a deceased person was competent to dispose are the assets of the deceased which (otherwise than in right of a power of appointment or of the testamentary power conferred by statute to dispose of entailed interests) he could, if of full age and capacity, have disposed of by his will. They also include his severable share in any assets to which, immediately before his death, he was beneficially entitled as a joint tenant. This overrides the general law provision whereby assets held by joint tenants would otherwise pass automatically to the surviving joint tenant and not under the deceased's will or intestacy.

In consequence, any latent chargeable gain 'disappears' and the asset passes into the hands of the personal representatives or legatees at probate value, which will be the base for any future disposal of it.

This applies to all of the deceased's assets situated in England and, if he was not domiciled in the UK, that he was domiciled in England at the time of his death. This means that assets which the deceased could have disposed of by his will had he died whilst UK-domiciled, like other assets, have an uplifted base cost.

In the context of CGT the fact of death is, however, of significance, in particular in the following circumstances:

(1) three-year carry-back of losses realised in the tax year of death;
(2) a chargeable gain, or allowable loss, can arise on disposals by personal representatives to third parties;
(3) disposals by personal representatives during the administration period, for whom the full annual exempt amount is available for disposals in the tax year of death and next two tax years (TCGA 1992, s 3(7)); and
(4) legatees acquire estate assets at probate value (s 3(1)).

In Scotland, the completion of an estate's administration is construed as the date at which, after discharging or providing for liabilities to be met out of the estate (including debts, legacies immediately payable, prior rights of a surviving spouse on intestacy and the legal rights of a surviving spouse or children), the free balance held in trust on the residuary legatees' behalf has been ascertained (TA 1988, s 702(a)). There is no statutory definition to show when the administration period of an estate in England and Wales is completed. However, it may be assumed that, following *CIR v Pilkington* (1941) 24 TC 160, CA (on which decision the Scottish law is based), it ends when all debts, specific legacies and liabilities have been provided for. This latter date is also the date as from which a trust provided for by the will is created. If an asset is subsequently discovered after the administration has been completed, the administration period must be re-opened.

There is no CGT disposal if the deceased made a gift by way of *donatio mortis causa* (a gift settled in contemplation of death). The following conditions must be met for a gift to be a *donatio mortis causa*:

(1) it must be made in contemplation of death;
(2) it must be conditional upon the death;

(3) the asset must actually be transferred, or the means of transfer must be available; and

(4) the asset must be capable of being passed as a valid *donatio mortis causa* (this prevents land from being passed in this way, although shares and similar assets can be so transferred (*Duffield v Elwes* (1827) 1 Bli (NS) 497; *Staniland v Willott* (1852) 3 Mac and G 664)).

If the asset is not, in fact, transferred within a reasonable time after death, it reverts to the donor's estate, and therefore falls to be dealt with along with other assets passing because of the death (*Re Craven's Estate, Lloyds Bank Ltd v Cockburn (No 1)* [1937] 1 Ch 423).

So far as relating to the consequences of the death of an heir of an entail in possession of any property in Scotland subject to an entail, whether *sui juris* or not, or of a proper life-renter of any property, these rules also apply. Thus, on the death of any such heir or life-renter the heir of entail next entitled to the entailed property or, as the case may be, the person (if any) who, on the life-renter's death, becomes entitled to possession of the property as fiar is deemed to have acquired all the assets forming part of the property at the date of death at their market value at that date.

21.13.2 Year of death

For CGT purposes the death splits the tax year into two distinct parts. Gains or losses on disposals made in the part year prior to death accrue to the deceased. Gains or losses on disposals to third parties made in the part year after the death accrue to the personal representatives. Annual exempt amounts (under TCGA 1992, s 3) are available for each of such periods.

21.13.3 Losses

As there is no disposal on death, there can be no allowance for latent capital losses. In such event it may be appropriate to transfer the asset concerned to the spouse (see **21.12**), for later disposal, when the full loss amount would be realised. Alternatively, if there are gains against which the loss could be set (see below), the asset could be disposed of prior to death to crystallise the loss. Care is needed to ensure that the disposal is real as it is also provided that no chargeable gain arises if the deceased made a disposal by way of *donatio mortis causa* (notwithstanding TCGA 1992, s 17(1)).

There is special treatment of any allowable losses sustained by the deceased in the tax year in which he dies and which cannot be deducted from chargeable gains accruing in that year. Such losses can be deducted from chargeable gains realised by him in the three preceding tax years. The losses are set against chargeable gains accruing in a later year before those accruing in an earlier year.

21.13.4 Acquisition and disposal by personal representatives
(TCGA 1992, ss 62–65)

The deceased's personal representatives are treated as a single and continuing body of persons (distinct from the persons who may from time to time be the personal representatives). In that capacity, they are treated as having the deceased's residence, ordinary residence and domicile at the date of death. However, except for the annual exempt amount, which personal representatives (acting in that capacity) are entitled to set against net gains on disposals to third parties (TCGA 1992, s 3(7)), and certain other cases where specific relief is available (eg retirement relief under TCGA 1992, ss 163, 164, Sched 6) none of the reliefs available to individuals are available to personal representatives.

The deceased's assets are treated as acquired by the personal representatives at their probate value without any account being taken of any of the deductions made in valuing assets for IHT (eg BPR or APR – see **8** and **9** respectively). Furthermore there is no chargeable gain or allowable loss when the asset is transferred by the personal representatives to the beneficiaries or other legatees, irrespective of when the transfer is actually made (CCAB, June 1967).

When a person acquires an asset as legatee, no chargeable gain accrues to the personal representatives, and the legatee is treated as if the personal representatives' acquisition of the asset had been his acquisition of it. A 'legatee' includes any person taking under a testamentary disposition or on an intestacy or partial intestacy, whether he takes beneficially or as trustee.

In *Bentley v Pike* (1981) 53 TC 590, ChD it was held that sterling is the only permissible unit of currency for computations required to be made under CGT legislation. Specifically, the point at issue was the rate of exchange to be applied on a gain realised abroad. Mrs Bentley inherited a one-sixth share in a property in Berlin from her father. He had died intestate on 31 October 1967, and was resident and domiciled in Israel. Under German law, Mrs Bentley became absolutely entitled to her share of the property on her father's death. Accordingly, this was the date of acquisition under s 62(1)(a). The value of Mrs Bentley's interest in the property at that date was DM132,780. On 6 February 1972, Mrs Bentley and her sister were granted the German equivalent of letters of administration and on 6 July 1972 were entered on the German Land Register as tenants-in-common of their late father's one-third share in the property.

The property was sold on 6 July 1973. Mrs Bentley's share of the net proceeds of sale amounted to DM152,241. The gain on that disposal was computed by reference to the sterling values of the two Deutschmark amounts converted at the rates of exchange ruling at the date of death (31 October 1967) and the date of sale (6 July 1973) respectively. The taxpayers contended that the gain should be calculated by conversion into sterling, at the rate of exchange ruling on the date of sale (6 July 1973), of the difference between the value of the property at the date of death (31 October 1967) and the net proceeds of sale, both amounts being expressed in Deutschmarks. It was, however, held that the gain should be computed by converting the value of Mrs Bentley's interest into sterling at the rate of exchange ruling on the date of acquisition and deducting that sum from the sterling equivalent of the net proceeds of sale converted at the rate of exchange ruling on the date of disposal.

It may be appropriate to agree with a pecuniary legatee that he should take the asset rather than cash, if assets have to be realised giving rise to a gain on which CGT is payable, which would have to be paid by the personal representatives out of the estate. The transfer to the legatee would not give rise to any disposal for CGT. Although the legatee would receive the asset with a base value uplifted to the market value at the date of death, any further uplift is taxable. It is worth noting that an individual legatee is entitled to an annual exempt amount for each tax year. The availability of the annual exempt amount to personal representatives is restricted to the year of death and the next two tax years (TCGA 1992, s 3(7)).

If personal representatives dispose of assets to third parties and thereby realise losses, these are allowable against current or future gains in the same way as for individuals. However, such losses cannot be carried forward for use by legatees. It may be appropriate to agree with a legatee to take an asset which stands below its market value at the date of death in place of cash where the realisation of the asset would give rise to a loss for which no relief can be obtained. If such a legatee subsequently disposes of the asset he could utilise the loss against chargeable gains of the tax year current at the time of the disposal or carry it forward indefinitely.

If a person realises a gain on the disposal of an asset to which he became absolutely entitled as legatee or as against the trustees of settled property, he can deduct, in the computation of the gain accruing to that person on the disposal, any expenditure incurred by him on the transfer of the asset to him by the personal representatives or trustees. Expenditure which is allowable under TCGA 1992, s 38(2) includes the incidental costs, to the person making the disposal, of the acquisition of the asset or of its disposal being expenditure wholly and exclusively incurred by him for the purposes of the acquisition or, as the case may be, the disposal. More specifically, the expenditure is restricted to fees, commission or remuneration paid for the professional services of any surveyor or valuer, auctioneer, accountant, agent or legal adviser and costs of transfer or conveyance (including stamp duty) together with:

(1) in the case of the acquisition of an asset, costs of advertising to find a seller, and

(2) in the case of a disposal, costs of advertising to find a buyer and costs reasonably incurred in making any valuation or apportionment required for the purposes of the computation of the gain, including in particular

expenses reasonably incurred in ascertaining market value where required.

In this particular context, the words appear to be given a broad meaning rather than a strict literal interpretation. Whether expenditure is incurred 'wholly and exclusively', was held, in the House of Lords in *CIR v Richard's Executors* (1971) 46 TC 626, to be a question of law and not of fact, and that a proportionate amount of the fees paid to solicitors for valuing the estate, paying duty, disposing of investments etc was wholly and exclusively incurred by the executors in establishing their title to the assets.

In practice, difficulty may be encountered in establishing this proportion. Accordingly, a scale of expenses allowable under s 38(1)(b), for the costs of establishing title in computing personal representatives' gains or losses on the sale of assets comprised in a deceased's estate, is set out in SP 8/94, and has effect for deaths occurring after 5 April 1993 (see Tables 21.2 and 21.3 below). The Revenue accepts computations based either on this scale or on the actual allowable expenditure incurred.

Table 21.2: Expenditure incurred by personal representatives other than corporate trustees

Gross value of estate	Allowable expenditure
A. Up to £40,000	1.75 per cent of the probate value of the assets sold by the personal representatives.
B. Between £40,001 and £70,000	A fixed amount of £700, to be divided between all the assets of the estate in proportion to the probate values and allowed in those proportions on assets sold by the personal representatives.
C. Between £70,001 and £300,000	1 per cent of the probate value of the assets sold.
D. Between £300,001 and £400,000	A fixed amount of £3,000, to be divided as at B. above.
E. Between £400,001 and £750,000	75 per cent of the probate value of the assets sold.

(The scale does not apply to gross estates exceeding £750,000 where the allowable expenditure is to be negotiated according to the facts of the particular case by the Inspector and the taxpayer.)

Subject to the rules for bare trustees (TCGA 1992, s 60) and any other express provision to the contrary, chargeable gains accruing to the settlement trustees or to the deceased's personal representatives, and CGT chargeable on or in the name of such trustees or personal representatives, is not regarded as accruing to, or chargeable on, any other person; nor shall any trustee or personal representative be regarded as an individual.

Where trustees cease to be UK-resident, and TCGA 1992, s 80 applies, the above rules do not apply to any person who:

(1) ceased to be a trustee of the settlement within 12 months of the time when the trustees of a settlement become neither resident nor ordinarily resident in the UK;

(2) shows that, when he ceased to be a trustee of the settlement, there was no proposal that the trustees might become neither resident nor ordinarily resident in the UK.

Table 21.3: Expenses incurred by corporate trustees

The following scale of allowable expenditure under TCGA 1992, ss 38 and 64(1)(b) applies for expenses incurred by corporate trustees in the administration of estates and trusts.

Transfers of assets to beneficiaries etc
Quoted stocks and shares:

A. One beneficiary	£20 per holding.
B. More than one beneficiary between whom a holding must be divided	£20 per holding to be divided in equal shares between the beneficiaries.
Unquoted shares and other assets	As for quoted stocks and shares, with the addition of any exceptional expenditure.

Actual disposals and acquisitions*

Quoted stocks and shares	The investment fee as charged by the trustee.
Unquoted shares	As for quoted stocks and shares, plus actual valuation costs.
Other assets	The investment fee as charged by the trustee, subject to a maximum of £60, plus actual valuation costs.

Deemed disposals by trustees

Quoted stocks and shares	£6 per holding.
Unquoted shares and other assets	Actual valuation costs.

*Where a comprehensive annual management fee is charged, covering both the cost of administering the trust and the expenses of actual disposals and acquisitions, the investment fee is £0.25 per £100 on the sale or purchase moneys.

In such a case, any CGT which is payable by the migrating trustees (under s 80(2)) cannot be assessed on a former trustee.

It is important to understand that trustees are liable for CGT on disposals which they make in that capacity. This is illustrated in *Prest v Bettinson (as trustee of Gladys Dodd dec'd Residuary Trust)* (1980) 53 TC 437, ChD. In 1963, under her will, Gladys Dodd left her residuary estate, subject to certain annuities, on trust for sale to pay the capital and income equally between five institutions, four of which were charitable. Administration of the estate was said to be completed in 1965. However, the executors/trustees did not execute a written assent to themselves as trustees of certain real property forming part of the trust fund and vested in them as executors. They decided to dispose of some of the real property and pay the proceeds to the five residuary beneficiaries. Assessments were raised on the executors on the gains arising from these disposals. The executors' contention that four-fifths of the gains were exempt since they accrued to charities was rejected because the gains would only have accrued to the charities if they were absolutely entitled as against the trustees. They were not so entitled since the property in question remained charged with the annuities. Accordingly, it was held that the executors or trustees, in whatever capacity, retained full control of the assets until they made their capital distributions to the five residuary beneficiaries. Those beneficiaries could not have directed how the properties were to be dealt with in advance of sale and could not have objected if the trustees, before making the actual distribution, had decided to retain a larger amount as cover for the annuities, or to retain the proceeds of the sales as funds to be set aside under the will to meet the annuities with a view to distributing other assets to the residuary beneficiaries.

Trustees and personal representatives are not, in that capacity, treated as individuals, and thus the remittance basis of assessment to CGT (see TCGA 1992, s 12) is not available.

The Revenue has clarified the position with regard to Qualifying Corporate Bonds (QCBs) held at the time of death (*Tax Bulletin* 5 (November 1992)). Where QCBs are issued in exchange for shares or securities which are not QCBs and TCGA 1992, ss 127–130 (equation of new and old holdings) would otherwise apply, s 116 requires that a computation of the gain that would have arisen if the shares or securities had been sold at their market value be undertaken. The gain is held over and released on a later disposal of the QCBs.

QCBs with a held-over gain may form part of the assets of which the deceased was competent to dispose as at the date of his death. These assets are deemed to be acquired by the personal representatives or other persons on whom they devolve, but are not deemed to be disposed of by the deceased. Therefore, the QCB holder's death does not trigger the release of any held-over gain. In the Revenue's view, the held-over gain is not triggered if the personal representatives dispose of the QCBs, or if they transfer them to the legatees. Nor would the charge be released on a later disposal by the legatees. The held-over gain is wiped out by the death.

The position is different if the share reorganisation to which ss 127–130 would otherwise have applied occurs after the shares and securities have been acquired by the personal representatives. Again, the held-over gain must be computed. If, later, the personal representatives dispose of the QCBs the gain is released in the normal way (s 116(10)(b)). If the personal representatives transfer them to the legatees the gain is not released (s 116(11)). However, the gain will be released on a later disposal of the QCBs by the legatees.

21.14 VARIATIONS

Where within the two-year period after death any of the dispositions (whether effected by will, intestacy or otherwise) of the property of which the deceased was competent to dispose are varied, or the benefit conferred by any of those dispositions is disclaimed, by an instrument in writing made by the persons or any of the persons who benefit or would benefit under the dispositions:

(1) the variation or disclaimer is not a disposal for CGT, and
(2) the variation is deemed to have been effected by the deceased or, as the case may be, the disclaimed benefit is deemed never to have been conferred.

A variation is not valid for this purpose unless the person(s) making the instrument so elect, by notice given to the Revenue within six months after the date of the instrument (or such longer time as the Revenue may in its discretion allow). A variation or disclaimer is not valid if it is made for any consideration in money or money's worth, other than to the extent of consideration consisting of the making of a variation or disclaimer in relation to another of the dispositions. However, a variation is valid irrespective of whether the estate's administration is complete or the property has been distributed in accordance with the original dispositions. It is not important that no-one has taken any benefit under the will or intestacy.

The Revenue confirmed (in *Tax Bulletin* 15 (February 1995)) that, although all the beneficiaries affected by a variation must join in the written election, where one of them dies (the second deceased) before a variation is made that beneficiary's personal representatives may enter into a variation and sign an election. If the variation then reduces the entitlements of the second deceased's beneficiaries then they, as well as the second deceased's legal personal representatives, must agree to the variation. The Revenue requires evidence of the consent of the second deceased's beneficiaries to the variation. If they are not themselves parties to the variation, other written evidence of their consent will be sought.

Great care is needed in framing deeds of variation. In *Russell and another v CIR* [1988] STC 195, ChD it was held that a second deed of variation cannot amend dispositions under an earlier deed. However, it may be possible to obtain a court order for the rectification of errors in the first deed (*Lake v Lake and others* [1989] STC 865, ChD; *Seymour and another v Seymour* (1989) BTC 8043, ChD; *Matthews v Martin and others* (1991) BTC 8048, ChD). In *Schneider and others v CIR* [1993] STC 430, ChD it was agreed that where it was clear that words had been left out of a deed of variation, thereby nullifying its obvious intention, the missing words could nonetheless be read into the deed.

There are similar provisions applying for IHT purposes (see IHTA 1984, s 142), but not for income tax. Any income arising between the date of death and the date of the variation is apportioned to any beneficiary absolutely entitled under the original will or on intestacy. However, a beneficiary whose interest was limited, but which was altered by a variation, never becomes entitled and so no income can be apportioned to him.

It is important to understand that these 'deeming' provisions create a fiction which applies only for the specific provisions of TCGA 1992, s 62 relating to devolution on death. They are not to be applied in any wider context for CGT. Nor do they apply for income tax purposes, or for the underlying property law.

Marshall v Kerr (1994) TC leaflet 3404, HL concerned the extent of the s 62(6) deeming provisions. Mrs Kerr's father had died in 1977 whilst domiciled and ordinarily resident in Jersey, and neither resident nor ordinarily resident in the UK. A one-half share in his residuary estate was left to Mrs Kerr absolutely. By means of a deed of variation made in 1978, Mrs Kerr declared trusts in relation to the fund and its income. The trustee, Regent Trust Co Ltd, was a trust company incorporated in Jersey and resident in Jersey. The administration of the deceased's estate was completed in June 1979.

Mrs Kerr was assessed to CGT for 1983/84 and 1984/85 under what is now TCGA 1992, ss 87–98 on capital payments made to her by the trustees. Those provisions apply only if the settlor was domiciled and resident or ordinarily resident in the UK on the date either when the chargeable gains accrued or of execution of the settlement. This condition would be satisfied if Mrs Kerr was regarded as the settlor, but not if her father was to be regarded as the settlor.

The Special Commissioners allowed Mrs Kerr's appeals, holding that what is now TCGA 1992, s 62(6) applied with the effect that Mrs Kerr's father was regarded as the settlor for the purposes of ss 87–98. However, the Chancery Division held, allowing the Crown's appeal, that Mrs Kerr was to be regarded as the settlor. This was because:

(1) the purpose of s 62(4), (6) is to exclude any difference in value between the date of death and the date of the deed which would otherwise be thought to accrue on anyone who made a deed of variation;

(2) those provisions are fully effective if they mean precisely what they

say: they do not carry over into any further considerations of deeming than they provide;

(3) those provisions do not have any purpose which allows any wider interpretation: in particular there is no reason to apply them in answering the question posed by ss 87–98 whether the settlement was made by a person who was domiciled and resident or ordinarily resident in the UK at the date of either the chargeable gains or of the making of the settlement.

This conclusion was overturned by the Court of Appeal, where it was held *inter alia* that there was nothing in what is now TCGA 1992 as a whole or the deeming provisions of s 62 which required the words of those provisions to be given any meaning other than their normal and natural meaning. A limited purpose for s 62(4), (6) could not be ascertained from the statutory language. No question arose of absurdity or injustice flowing from a literal interpretation. Section 62(4) was not qualified in any way, and the implications of the statutory wording had to be accepted because no prohibition from doing so could be found from the context of s 62. Accordingly the natural implication of s 62(4) was that Mrs Kerr never acquired or disposed of any assets, and she could not, therefore, be a person who made the disposition for ss 87–98 purposes. The final limb of s 62(6) confirmed that for all CGT purposes the variation made by the deed was not a disposal by Mrs Kerr. Thus, in effect, the testator was treated as having made such disposition by his will.

The House of Lords, however, overturned the Court of Appeal decision, and held that Mrs Kerr was regarded as the settlor for ss 87–98 purposes for the following reasons.

The only property which was capable of being settled by Mrs Kerr under the variation was a 'chose in action', being her right to have her father's estate duly administered. The arrangement could not, and did not purport to, settle any specific asset in the deceased's estate. It was only on the later completion of administration of the estate that half of the assets became vested in the trust company as legatee on the trusts of the arrangement.

Further, the first effect of the deeming provision in s 62(6) does not require an assumption that Mrs Kerr did not dispose of any property when she executed the settlement. It required only that that disposition did not give rise to a chargeable event for CGT purposes. The second effect is that, insofar as assets of which the deceased had been competent to dispose of at his death became vested in a beneficiary under a variation, those assets were deemed to have been acquired from the deceased. However, the provision does not require the wiping-out of the process of administering the estate. Nor does it require an assumption that all the assets vested in a beneficiary under a variation are acquired by him at the date of death from the deceased. Nothing in s 62(6) requires an assumption of anything inconsistent with Mrs Kerr being the settlor under the family arrangement.

22

CAPITAL GAINS TAX AND PRIVATE RESIDENCES

22.1 RELIEF ON DISPOSAL OF PRIVATE RESIDENCE
(TCGA 1992, s 222)

22.1.1 Extent of the relief

Relief from CGT applies to a gain realised by an individual attributable to the disposal of, or of an interest in:

(1) a dwelling-house (or part of it) which is, or has at any time in his period of ownership been, his only or main residence, or
(2) land which he has for his own occupation and enjoyment with that residence as its garden or grounds up to the permitted area.

In *Makins v Elson* [1977] STC 46, ChD the question before the High Court was whether a caravan could be looked upon as a dwelling-house. The taxpayer had purchased some land on which to build a house. He lived with his family in a wheeled caravan which was jacked up and resting on bricks on the land, with all utilities installed, while construction took place. However, before the house was complete, he sold the site, along with the caravan. The Revenue assessed him on the gain. He appealed, contending that it was exempt under TCGA 1992, s 222. The court agreed that the gain was within the private residence exemption, and that the caravan was a dwelling-house for the relevant period.

The opposite conclusion was reached in *Moore v Thompson* [1986] STC 170, ChD. In 1973, a husband and wife acquired, with the intention of making it their family home, a farmhouse in need of extensive renovation. In 1975, the husband purchased a caravan, which was parked in the farmhouse's courtyard, and he lived in it while working full-time on the renovation. The caravan had neither electricity nor drinking water. His wife worked with him at weekends and on holidays and, on occasions, she and their children stayed with him in the caravan. The couple separated in 1976, although in 1977 the wife and children stayed for two weeks in the caravan, and thereafter she stayed for short periods in the caravan while carrying out work on the farmhouse. In 1978 she purchased her husband's half share in the farmhouse, and sought to elect that the farmhouse had been her main residence since 1974. The wife sold the farmhouse in 1979 together with the caravan. It was established that she had never lived in the farmhouse as such. The High Court upheld the Revenue's assessment of the gain.

It was confirmed in *Hansard* (21 March 1985) that a houseboat may exceptionally qualify as a private residence, but is normally exempt as tangible movable property which is a wasting asset under TCGA 1992, s 45.

22.1.2 Permitted area

The 'permitted area' is, in general, an area (inclusive of the site of the dwelling-house) of half a hectare (approximately 1¼ acres). However, where the area required for the reasonable enjoyment of the dwelling-house (or part of it) as a residence, having regard to its size and character, is larger than half a hectare, that larger area is the permitted area. Also, where part of the land occupied with a residence is and part is not within the exemption, then (up to the permitted area) that part is taken to be within the exemption which, if the remainder were separately occupied, would be the most suitable for occupation and enjoyment with the residence.

It was found in *Varty v Lynes* [1976] STC 508, ChD that if a house is sold with part of the garden and the rest of the garden is sold later, even though the extent of the land was less than one acre (which was then the unextended 'permitted area'), private residence relief is not due. Here, the taxpayer had meanwhile obtained planning permission for the balance of the garden area, and was able to sell at a substantial profit. The High Court upheld the CGT assessment and held that the test of own occupation and enjoyment related only to the actual moment of disposal of the land, and although the test was met on the first disposal it did not extend to the subsequent disposal.

Comment on the application of this case is found in the *Tax Bulletin*, 12 (August 1994). *Varty* established that no principal private residence relief was due on the sale of a garden where it was sold separately and after the dwelling-house. Certain dicta in that case also suggested that when a dwelling-house and garden were sold together, but after the taxpayer had ceased to occupy the property, the sale of the garden would not qualify for relief. This particular point was not directly in issue in that case, and so was not decided by it, but the case provided grounds for taking that view. For a time, the Revenue did not take this line in cases where house and garden were sold together and not for development. More recent advice suggests that arguments based on those dicta are misconceived and are no longer applied. However, they do apply the decision itself, so that no relief is due on the sale of a garden which takes place after a prior sale of the dwelling-house.

In *Wakeling v Pearce* [1995] SSCD 96, Sp C32, an individual inherited a bungalow and a nearby field in 1969. Although the field was about 30 feet from the bungalow it was separated from it by a cottage in separate ownership. The taxpayer and her family used the field for many years but then sold it, in two plots. Her contention that the field qualified for exemption was upheld. Although the Revenue had rejected the claim on the grounds that the field was not adjacent to the bungalow, the Special Commissioner held that the distance between the bungalow and the field was not sufficient to disqualify the field from qualifying as 'garden or grounds'. It was shown that the field had been used for many years as part of the garden or grounds.

Following this decision, against which the Revenue decided not to appeal because of the particular circumstances, in *Tax Bulletin* 12 (August 1994), the Revenue set out its interpretation of the circumstances in which land is regarded as occupied and enjoyed with a residence as its garden or grounds up to the permitted area.

Longson v Baker (2000) SpC 238, a case before the Special Commissioners, concerned whether the 'permitted area' for which Mr Longson was entitled to relief extended to 7.56 hectares and, in particular, whether the land was required for 'reasonable enjoyment' of a dwelling-house in regard to its size and character.

Mr Longson and his family had lived in a seven-bedroomed house situated on a ½ hectare of land. They stabled about seven horses in stables built in the grounds. As there was insufficient pasture to support the horses, they rented fields from nearby farmers. Mr Longson sold the house and purchased a new property ('the farm') which extended to 7.56 hectares and included a farmhouse, stables and an outhouse. Mr Longson erected a further building which was used as a riding school. In December 1995, following the failure of his marriage, Mr Longson sold his beneficial interest in the farm to his wife. He appealed against CGT assessment for 1995/96 on the basis that 'the permitted area' for which he was entitled to relief as his only or main residence was the whole of the area disposed of, namely 7.56 hectares, as it was 'required for the reasonable enjoyment of' the dwelling-house as a residence. It was agreed that the dwelling-house included not only the farmhouse but the stables and outhouse. The Special Commissioner noted that he was required to look at the dwelling-house and decide what area of land was 'required for the reasonable enjoyment' of the dwelling-house as a residence, having regard to its size and character; it is not possible to take into account the owner's particular requirements. The main dispute concerned the meaning of the word 'require': did it mean 'called for', or was its meaning closer to 'necessary'? The Commissioner's view was that it was not correct that the dwelling-house at the farm *required* an area of land amounting to more than 7.56 hectares in order to ensure its reasonable enjoyment as a residence, having regard to its size and character. At the Longsons' previous property they were able to stable seven horses by using neighbouring fields rented to them by local farmers. Although, that might have been inconvenient for them to have had to shuttle their horses to and from those fields and it was clearly more convenient to have 7.56 hectares available to them when they moved to the farm, such a large area was not necessary or vital when stabling horses at a property. While it might have been desirable or convenient for Mr Longson to have an area of 7.56 hectares to enjoy with the dwelling-house, such an area was not *required* for the reasonable enjoyment of the dwelling-house as a residence having regard to its size and character. The permitted area was therefore the area contended for by the inspector, namely 1.054 hectares, and Mr Longson's appeal was dismissed.

To qualify for private residence relief, the land must meet certain conditions at the date on which it is disposed. The words 'land which he has for his own occupation and enjoyment with that residence as its garden or grounds' make this clear. They contrast with 'which is, or has at any time in his period of ownership been his only or main residence', which applies to a dwelling-house and thus looks both at the present and the past. This difference in interpretation was confirmed in *Varty*. The use of the land other than that at the date of disposal is irrelevant.

The conditions to be met are:

(1) it must be land which the owner has for occupation and enjoyment with the residence;
(2) it must be the garden or grounds of the residence; and
(3) the area of land must not exceed the permitted area.

It is for the Revenue to agree whether land can be regarded as occupied and enjoyed with the residence as its garden or grounds. The determination of what constitutes the permitted area, if over half a hectare, rests with the District Valuer.

In general, the Revenue accepts that land surrounding the residence and in the same ownership is the grounds of the residence, unless it is used for some other purpose. The Revenue would not regard land used for agriculture, commercial woodlands, trade or business as part of the garden or grounds. Land which has been fenced off from the residence to be sold for development is excluded. However, land which has traditionally been part of the grounds but which, at the date of sale, is unused or overgrown is not excluded, nor are paddocks or orchards if there is no significant business use. Included in the definition is land which has a building on it, provided the building is not let or in use for a business, and land which is not used exclusively for recreational purposes. For example, the owner-occupier of a guest-house may allow guests to use the garden. The land would still qualify for relief providing the other conditions are satisfied.

22.1.3 Disposal of physically separated land

Disposal of land which is physically separated from the residence can cause problems. The Revenue does not accept that land is garden or grounds merely if it is in the same ownership as the residence and is used as a garden. However, land which can be shown objectively, on the facts, to be naturally and traditionally the garden, so that it would normally be offered to a prospective purchaser as part of the residence, is accepted. In some villages, it is common for a garden to be across the street from the residence. That separation itself would not be regarded as a reason for denying relief. However, these cases are rare and if land is separated from the residence by other land which is not in the same ownership as the residence, it is usually not part of the garden or grounds. Land bought some distance from the residence owing to an inadequate garden at the residence, and which is cultivated and regarded as part of the garden, does not qualify for relief.

22.1.4 Determination of permitted area

The procedures for determination of the permitted area were reported in detail in the *Tax Bulletin*, 2 (February 1992). When a disposal occurs of land associated with a dwelling-house, and the total holding of land exceeds a half hectare, it may be necessary to determine the size and location of the permitted area. This can involve both the Inspector and the District Valuer. The questions to be answered in such cases are:

(1) Is the land at the date of sale 'garden or grounds'?
(2) What is the size and character of the dwelling-house at the date of sale?
(3) What is the corresponding size of the permitted area?
(4) Where should the permitted area be located?
(5) How should disposal proceeds and acquisition costs be apportioned between the exempt and non-exempt areas?

22.1.5 Extent of 'dwelling-house'

A dwelling-house may include more than one building (*Batey v Wakefield*, below). Whilst the cases to date have been concerned mainly with servants' cottages, the principle can apply to any other outbuildings. The Inspector will therefore try to distinguish between those outbuildings which form part of the entity comprising the dwelling-house, those which are ancillary to the garden or grounds, or in some circumstances those which fall within neither of those categories.

In the first category are buildings close to the main house which serve in its function as a residence, such as garages used for private cars and fuel stores. In the second category are non-commercial greenhouses, gazebos, garden sheds etc. The third category includes, for example, buildings in use for the purposes of a trade or letting. The distinction between these three categories is relevant because:

(1) as well as affecting the dwelling-house's size and character, any building forming part of the entity comprising the dwelling-house is considered for relief by reference to the condition that it is available if it is or has been all or part of the main residence; and

(2) any building merely ancillary to the garden or grounds is considered only by reference to the condition that relief is available if it is or has been all or part of the main residence and stands within the permitted area.

Buildings which fall into neither of these categories do not qualify for any private residence relief.

Not surprisingly there have been a number of cases on this question. In *Batey v Wakefield* [1981] STC 521, CA the issue was whether a bungalow, which was separated from the main residence, was 'part of a dwelling-house'. In this case the taxpayer owned a house in Wiltshire built on 1.1 acres of land. He and his family lived in a London flat during the working week, and returned to the house at weekends. He had elected for the house to be treated as his main residence. For security reasons, a bungalow was built on the land, physically separate from the house and with separate road access, and occupied by a farm labourer who acted as caretaker. Later, the taxpayer lived in the house on a full-time basis, no longer needing a caretaker. The bungalow was sold with 0.2 acres of land. The Court of Appeal held that the bungalow had formed part of his dwelling-house and was exempt. The bungalow had been built to provide services for the benefit of the main house. The occupation by the caretaker amounted to occupation by the taxpayer as part of his residence.

Dicta in this case were disapproved in the Court of Appeal in *Lewis v Rook* [1992] STC 171. The taxpayer had purchased a large house, ten acres of land, and two cottages. One of the cottages, which was 190 yards from her house and had been occupied by a gardener, was sold. The court upheld the assessment. The true test was whether the cottage was within the curtilage of, and appurtenant to, the main property, so as to be part of the entity which, together with the main property, constituted the dwelling-house occupied by the taxpayer as her main residence. Here, the cottage was some 190 yards away from the main building and separated by a large garden.

In contrast, in *Williams v Merrylees* [1987] STC 445, ChD the taxpayer had acquired a small estate comprising a main house with four acres of garden and land and a lodge at the entrance of the estate, about 200 metres from the main house. The house became his main residence and the lodge was occupied by a married couple who were employed as caretaker/gardener and domestic help. The house and lodge were rated together. Later, the taxpayer sold the main house and estate, apart from the lodge and a garden of less than an acre, and went to live in a house which he had previously bought as a holiday home. He retained the lodge and allowed the now widowed caretaker/gardener to live in it. When the caretaker/gardener died, the taxpayer sold the lodge to the purchaser of the main house. On appeal it was held that the lodge was within the private residence exemption from purchase up until the main house was sold. In that period the lodge had been part of the taxpayer's only or main residence and within the curtilage of the property and appurtenant to the main house.

22.1.6 **Curtilage**

These cases show that where there is an identifiable main house, no building can form part of a dwelling-house with the main house unless that building is appurtenant to, and within the curtilage of, the main house. In *Tax Bulletin* 12 (August 1994), it is pointed out that 'curtilage' is defined by the *Shorter Oxford Dictionary* as 'a small court, yard, or piece of ground, attached to a dwelling-house and forming one enclosure with it'. This definition has been adopted by the courts in non-tax cases and emphasis is placed on the smallness of the area comprised in the curtilage. Buildings standing around a courtyard together with the main house are within the curtilage of the main house.

Where more dispersed groups of buildings have a clear relationship with each other, they fall within a single curtilage if they constitute an integral whole. In a Leasehold Reform Act case which was quoted with approval in *Lewis v Rook*, the Court held that

> 'For one corporeal hereditament to fall within the curtilage of another, the former must be so intimately associated with the latter as to lead to the conclusion that the former in truth forms part and parcel of the latter'.

Whether one building is part and parcel of another depends primarily on whether there is a close geographical relationship between them. Furthermore, because the test is to identify an integral whole, a wall or fence separating two buildings normally suffices to establish that they are not within the same curtilage. Similarly, a public road or stretch of tidal water sets a limit to the curtilage of the building. Buildings which are within the curtilage of a main house normally pass automatically on a conveyance of that house without having to be specifically mentioned. There is a distinction between the curtilage of a main house and the curtilage of an estate as a whole and the fact that a whole estate may be contained within a single boundary does not mean that the buildings on the estate should be regarded as within the curtilage of the main house.

The taxpayer lost the appeal in *Markey v Sanders* [1987] STC 256, ChD where the taxpayer's mother had purchased a small country estate of four acres with a main house and outbuildings reached by a 130 metre drive from the main entrance gates. This was sold to her son who owned adjoining land. He built a three-bedroom bungalow by the entrance gates, with a quarter-acre garden, and this was occupied rent-free by a gardener and housekeeper. The bungalow was not separately rated. Later, the whole estate, including the bungalow, was sold to a single purchaser. The contention that the bungalow was within the private residence exemption was rejected.

In *Honour v Norris* [1992] STC 304, ChD the owner of four separate flats, located in separate buildings in the same square, sold one of them. The flat had been used to provide occasional bedroom accommodation for his children and guests and, occasionally, for him and his wife. It was held that the flat was a separate dwelling-house. It could not be regarded as part of a common entity with the flat in which the owner and his wife lived.

22.1.7 Whether land for taxpayer's 'own occupation and enjoyment'

When considering whether land meets the test that it is for the taxpayer's 'own occupation and enjoyment with that residence as its garden or grounds up to the permitted area', the Inspector and the District Valuer only need to consider the relevant questions as at the date of sale. This is because the legislation uses only the present tense. The relevance of this distinction was shown *Varty v Lynes* (see **22.1.2**). However, if the Inspector has to deal with a disposal that also includes part of the dwelling-house he may need details at other dates because the condition requiring 'a dwelling-house or part of [it] which is, or has at any time in his period of ownership been, his only or main residence' is a historic test. Thus, a building that is not part of the dwelling-house at the date of sale but had previously been a part cannot be taken into account in determining the permitted area, although it could still qualify for partial private residence relief.

The Inspector may seek information from the District Valuer before coming to a decision, and the District Valuer may bring to the Inspector's attention material which is relevant but about which the Inspector was not aware. The District Valuer will advise the Inspector on the size and location of the permitted area and on any consequential apportionments.

The District Valuer must decide what is required by the dwelling-house's size and character. This is considered to be an objective test. To be required the land must be needed by each and every occupant of the dwelling-house, not just by a particular occupant who has special needs. There is no direct judicial guidance; the view taken is that the corresponding legislative context makes the compulsory purchase case of *In Re Newhill Compulsory Purchase Order 1937, Payne's Application* [1938] 2 All ER 163 useful guidance. There the judge said:

> '"Required", I think, ... does not mean merely that the occupiers of the house would like to have it, or that they would miss it if they lost it, or that anyone proposing to buy the house would think less of the house without it than he would if it was preserved to it. "Required" means, I suppose, that without it there will be such a substantial deprivation of amenities or convenience that a real injury would be done to the property owner.'

The District Valuer's opinion is based on a comparison of the size of garden and grounds held with other houses in the locality which are of a comparable size and character. An initial review is made, which may not include an inspection of the property. If this supports the taxpayer's claim the District Valuer so informs the Inspector. Otherwise the District Valuer undertakes further work. This includes a sufficient inspection of the property to enable him to take into account the land's attributes. If the Inspector has not yet made an assessment, the opinion formed by the District Valuer at that stage is used as a basis for making an estimated assessment. He then enters into negotiations with the taxpayer's representatives and inspects the property fully.

22.1.8 Disputes over decisions on permitted areas

The Inspector retains responsibility for settling any appeal against a CGT assessment. If the District Valuer cannot reach agreement with the tax-payer, it is for the Inspector to take the matter forward to the Commissioners for a decision.

A dispute may arise about the apportionment of sale proceeds. If the dispute concerns the manner of apportionment (eg that sale proceeds should be apportioned by regard to area rather than by reference to valuations), it is within the Commissioners' jurisdiction. The Commissioners normally consider the point when dealing with the permitted area point. If they find that apportionment should be by reference to valuations then they cannot determine the apportionment dispute. Jurisdiction over such matters lies with the Lands Tribunal.

22.1.9 Nomination and determination of main residence

So far as it is necessary to determine which of two or more residences is an individual's main residence for any period, the individual may conclude that question by nominating the chosen residence and advising the Revenue of it within two years from the beginning of that period. However, this nomination can subsequently be varied by a further notice to the Revenue for any period beginning not earlier than two years before the giving of the further notice. If no nomination is made, the Revenue makes a determination based on the facts.

Griffin v Craig-Harvey [1994] STC 54, ChD concerned the need to lodge a notice of determination of main residence within two years of the acquisition of a second residence. The taxpayer owned a house in Stockwell (in London), and acquired a house in Winchester in August 1985. In July 1986 he sold the house in Stockwell and bought another house in Clapham (also in London). A notification nominating the house in Winchester as his main residence was lodged in January 1988. A year later the house in Winchester was sold realising a capital gain. The Revenue issued a CGT assessment on the basis that the period from August 1985 to June 1986 was not covered by the nomination submitted in January 1988. The basis for this was that the nomination was to determine whether the house in Winchester or the one in Clapham should be deemed to be the main residence.

A nomination deeming whether the house in Stockwell or the one in Winchester had been the taxpayer's main residence should have been lodged within two years of the taxpayer's acquisition of the Winchester house in August 1985. There was no nomination covering the period when the houses in Stockwell and in Winchester were both owned. The election made in January 1988 was a nomination between the house in Clapham and the house in Winchester. The house in Clapham was not acquired until July 1986 and the nomination could not cover any period before that time.

Where an individual has, or is treated as having, more than one residence, but his interest in each of them, or in each of them except one, is such as to have no more than a negligible capital value on the open market (eg a weekly rented flat, or accommodation provided by an employer) the two-year time limit for nominating one of those residences as the individual's main residence for CGT purposes may be extended where the individual was unaware that such a nomination could be made. In such cases, by concession (ESC D21) the nomination may be made within a reasonable time of the individual first becoming aware of the possibility of making a nomination, and the nomination is regarded as effective from the date on which the individual first had more than one residence.

It is the Revenue's view (expressed in *Tax Bulletin* 13 (October 1994)) that occupation of a residence under licence is not a legal or equitable interest in land. It follows that it can be ignored in deciding whether to make a nomination.

If at any time during an individual's period of ownership (after 5 April 1983) of a dwelling-house or part of a dwelling-house he:

(1) resides (under TA, s 356) in job-related living accommodation (s 222(8)(a)), and
(2) intends in due course to occupy the dwelling-house or part of it as his only or main residence (s 222(8)(b)),

the private residence exemption rules apply as if the dwelling-house or part of it were at that time occupied by him as a residence. Job-related accommodation may be occupied under either a service occupancy or a tenancy. Under a service occupancy any rights derive from the service contract and there is no legal or equitable interest in the property which is occupied under licence.

This change of view does not affect the need for a nomination in the majority of cases where an individual owns one property and rents another, since the rented property is normally occupied under a tenancy rather than under a licence.

22.1.10 Married couples

A man and his wife living with him can only have one residence or main residence for both, so long as they live together. Any nomination of a particular residence as the main residence must, if it affects them both, be given jointly.

If an individual has different interests in a residence at different times, the period of ownership is taken to begin from the first acquisition taken into account in arriving at the expenditure which (under TCGA 1992, ss 35–52 (computation of gains: general provisions)) is allowable as a deduction in the computation of the gain. In the case of a man and his wife living with him:

(1) if one disposes of, or of his interest in, the dwelling-house or part of it which is their only or main residence to the other, and in particular if it passes on death to the other as legatee, the other's period of ownership begins with the beginning of the period of ownership of the one making the disposal, but

(2) if the dwelling-house or part of it was not the only or main residence of both throughout the period of ownership of the one making the disposal, account is taken of any part of that period during which it was his only or main residence as if it was also that of the other.

Tax Bulletin 12 (August 1994) states that, when a couple marry and both spouses own a residence, a new two-year period for making an election begins. Where one spouse owns more than one property, and the other owns no property, and there is no change on marriage, the Revenue's view is that a fresh period does not begin as there has been no change in the combination of residences owned by either spouse, and neither spouse needs to become a party to any existing election to which he had not previously been a party. A notice is only required to be given by both spouses where it affects them both. Where only one spouse owns property, only that spouse is affected and he will already have had a two-year period in which to make the election.

Where the spouses jointly own more than one property at marriage but neither separately owns any other property, a new two-year period for making an election would still begin. Although both parties own the same properties as before, and have previously had a two-year period in which to elect, they now have to make a joint election and a new period is required accordingly.

Where a spouse inherits a dwelling-house from the other, he also inherits the other spouse's period of ownership for principal private residence relief purposes. Thus periods of ownership prior to the first spouse's death are taken into account in determining qualifying periods of residence. This may produce results different to those which would be obtained by only looking at the period after the first spouse's death. This can work to the taxpayer's advantage or disadvantage.

By concession (ESC D6), where a married couple separate or are divorced and one partner ceases to occupy the matrimonial home and subsequently as part of a financial settlement disposes of it, or an interest in it, to the other partner the home is regarded as continuing to be a residence of the transferring partner from the date his occupation ceases until the date of transfer, provided that throughout this period it has been the other partner's only or main residence. Thus, where a husband leaves the matrimonial home while still owning it, the usual CGT exemption or relief for an only or main residence would be given on the subsequent transfer to the wife, provided she has continued to live in the house and the husband has not elected that some other house should be treated for CGT purposes as his main residence for this period.

22.1.11 Personal representatives disposing of dwelling-house

ESC D5 provides relief to personal representatives when they dispose of a house which before and after the deceased's death was used as the only or main residence of individuals who, under the will or intestacy, are entitled to the whole or substantially the whole of the proceeds of the house. This is aimed at beneficiaries who have been living in the dwelling-house prior to and at the time of death where there has therefore been continuity of occupation. The intention is that beneficiaries who have lived in the house throughout should not be deprived of relief because their home happened to be sold by the personal representatives rather than by themselves as legatees. This does not extend to beneficiaries for whom the house had not been their only or main residence. To preserve the relief for the resident beneficiaries, the reference to 'substantially the whole' is interpreted as 75 per cent or more.

22.1.12 Beneficiary's disposal of dwelling-house

Where there is a disposal by a beneficiary of an inherited property his period of ownership begins on the date of death. Where the beneficiary does not become resident until a later date, the period prior to taking up occupation does not qualify for relief unless it falls within the final 36-month period prior to disposal (see **22.2**).

22.1.13 Work relocation

ESC D37 deals with the application of the private residence exemption where work is being relocated. In such cases the employer may set up arm's length arrangements under which an employee, who moves home because of the relocation, can sell his home to a relocation company or to the employer and have a right to a share in any later profit made when the relocation company or the employer later sells the home. Such arrangements may also exist where employees are required by their employer to transfer within an organisation and as a result have to move home.

In such circumstances, if the home is fully exempt from CGT, the employee's right to the share in any later profit is also exempt. Some employees' homes may be only partially exempt (eg they may have been used partly for business purposes, or may not have been the main residence throughout an employee's period of ownership). In such cases, a corresponding proportion of any gain relating to the right to later profits will also be exempt. The concession does not apply when the right is held by the employee for more than three years.

Where an employee owns his home jointly with others and moves home in these circumstances, the concession will apply to the other joint holders in the same way as to the employee.

The uncertainty over whether joint owner-occupiers of a property who are not husband and wife were entitled to full private residence relief was dispelled by an article in *Tax Bulletin* 3 (May 1992), and in general the relief is available. Where people jointly own a home, each is considered to have an undivided share in all of the property. Provided it is their only or main residence, relief is available on each owner's share of any gain on disposal in the normal way.

Occasionally property in joint ownership may be divided into separate and identifiable homes, each exclusively occupied. In these cases the legislation does not provide relief for any gain on the part not occupied by each owner. ESC D26 may however enable joint owners to exchange their interests so as to acquire sole ownership of the part each occupies without a charge to CGT. Each individual must undertake to accept for CGT purposes that he is deemed to have acquired the other's interest in the dwelling-house at the original base cost and on the original date on which that joint interest was acquired. A married couple is treated as an individual, so that an exchange of interests which results in a married couple alone becoming joint owners of land or of a dwelling-house meets the terms of the concession.

22.2 AMOUNT OF RELIEF
(TCGA 1992, ss 223, 224)

It is necessary to apportion any gain between periods of occupation and periods of absence. Here, a 'period of absence' is a period during which the dwelling-house or part of it is not the individual's only or main residence and throughout which he had no residence or main residence eligible for relief. However, there are certain periods of absence which can be ignored in this calculation.

22.2.1 Period of ownership

There is a general exemption to the effect that no part of a gain is chargeable if the dwelling-house or part of it has been the individual's only or main residence throughout the period of ownership, or throughout the period of ownership except for all or any part of the last 36 months of that period. If a gain is not covered by this general exemption, a fraction of the gain is not chargeable:

(1) the length of the part(s) of the period of ownership during which the dwelling-house or part of it was the individual's only or main residence, but inclusive of the last 36 months of the period of ownership in any event, divided by
(2) the length of the period of ownership (but not including any period before 31 March 1982).

The following periods are treated as if during such period of absence the dwelling-house or part of it was the individual's only or main residence if both before and after the period there was a time when the dwelling-house was the individual's only or main residence:

(1) a period of absence not exceeding three years (or periods of absence which together did not exceed three years);
(2) any period of absence throughout which the individual worked in an employment or office all the duties of which were performed outside the UK; and in addition
(3) any period of absence not exceeding four years (or periods of absence which together did not exceed four years) throughout which the individual was prevented from residing in the dwelling-house or part of it in consequence of either the situation of his place of work or any condition imposed by his employer requiring him to reside elsewhere, being a condition reasonably imposed to secure the effective performance by the employee of his duties. ESC D3 provides that in the case of a husband and wife who are living together this condition is satisfied as regards one spouse, it is treated as satisfied as regards the other.

In determining how far an individual's gain on the disposal of his residence is exempt, certain periods of absence are treated as periods of residence if he resumes residence there at some time after the absence. By concession (ESC D4) this condition is treated as satisfied where after a period of absence on duties overseas or other absences owing to conditions of employment an individual is unable to resume residence in his previous home because the terms of his employment require him to work elsewhere.

Finally, ESC D49 deals with private residence relief were there is a short delay by an owner-occupier in taking up residence. The concession applies where an individual:

(a) acquires land on which he has a house built, which he then uses as his only or main residence, or
(b) purchases an existing house and, before using it as his only or main residence, arranges for alterations or redecorations or completes the necessary steps for disposing of his previous residence.

In these circumstances, the period before the individual uses the house as his only or main residence is treated as a period in which he so used it, provided that this period is not more than one year. If there are good reasons for this period exceeding one year, which are outside the individual's control, it is extended up to a maximum of two years. Where the individual does not use the house as his only or main residence within the period allowed, no relief is given for the period before it is so used. Where relief is given under this concession it does not affect any relief due on another qualifying property for the same period.

22.2.2 Realisation of gain on disposal of let dwelling-house

Where an individual realises a gain on the disposal of a private residence and the dwelling-house or any part of it is or has at any time in his period of ownership been wholly or partly let by him as residential accommodation, the part of the gain, if any, which otherwise would be a chargeable gain by reason of the letting is only so much of such a gain to the extent, if any, to that it exceeds whichever is the lesser of:

(1) the part of the gain which is not chargeable (this may also apply where a trustee makes a gain and the residence is occupied under the terms of a settlement – see **22.3**); and
(2) £40,000.

SP 14/80 gives an indication to people who let the whole or a part of their homes whether they are likely to be liable to any CGT when they dispose of them.

Where a lodger lives as a member of the owner's family, sharing their living accommodation and taking meals with them, no part of the accommodation is treated as having ceased to be occupied as the owner's main residence, and the exemption is not restricted at all.

The amount of the gain on the let part depends on two matters:

- how much has been let; and
- the length of time during which it was let.

For example, someone occupies the whole of his home (acquired after 6 April 1982) for six years out of his ten-year period of ownership. He lets one-third of it throughout the other four years. The gain on the house as a whole is £30,000. Previously, he would have been exempt from CGT on £26,000 and chargeable on ($\frac{1}{3} \times \frac{4}{10} \times$ £30,000) = £4,000. The special relief applies to the £4,000 (which is less than the two limits referred to above) so that the whole of the gain of £30,000 is now exempt.

Whether the let accommodation is part of the owner's dwelling-house or is itself a separate dwelling-house depends on the facts. The Revenue view of the application of the special relief to the common case where the owner of a house, which was previously occupied as his (or the family) home, lets part as a flat or set of rooms without structural alteration (or with only minor adaptations). For the purposes of the new relief the Board regards this as a letting of part of the owner's dwelling-house, whether or not the tenants have separate washing and cooking facilities. But the relief does not extend to property which, although it may be part of the same building, forms a dwelling-house separate from that which is, or has been, the owner's (eg a fully self-contained flat with its own access from the road).

Owen v Elliott [1990] STC 469, CA concerned a private residence partly used as guest-house. In this case a married couple had carried on a private guest-house business from premises they owned and lived in. Different parts of the premises had been occupied at different times of the year in such a way that every part of the premises had, at some time during their period of ownership, constituted their main residence. The property was sold and it was agreed that one-third of the gain was exempt under the general rules. The Court of Appeal accepted that further relief was due. The phrase 'let by him as residential accommodation' did not, directly or by association, mean premises let which were likely to be occupied as a home. It referred to living accommodation as distinct, for example, from office accommodation. The lettings undertaken here were within the words 'residential accommodation'.

Receipt of 'rent a room relief' (F(No 2)A 1992, s 59, Sched 10) does not normally cause a CGT liability to arise on disposal of main residence.

22.2.3 Disposal of dwelling-house used partially for non-exempt purposes

If a gain accrues from the disposal of a dwelling-house or part of it a part of which is used exclusively for business etc purposes, the gain is apportioned and the exemption for only or main residence applies only to the part of the gain apportioned to the part which is not exclusively used for those purposes. This does not prevent the use of a room occasionally for business purposes. The restriction only applies where there is exclusive business etc use. This test is applied throughout the period of ownership, and does not refer to use only at the date of disposal. Where the restriction applies no relief is due on the part of the dwelling-house used for business etc, even for the last three years of ownership.

22.2.4 Change in substance or use

If there is a change in what is occupied as the individual's residence, whether on account of a reconstruction or conversion of a building or for any other reason, or there have been changes of the use of part of the dwelling-house for the purpose of, for example, a trade, business, profession or vocation, the relief is adjusted in a manner which is just and reasonable.

The approach here is to deal with each case on its merits, and to produce an adjustment which so far as possible reflects

- the extent to which, and
- the length of time over which,

each part of the dwelling-house has been used as part of the residence. It is not normally appropriate to take into account intervening market values when apportioning gains to different periods, since it is clear that time apportionment is the appropriate method.

An example of the application of a 'just and reasonable' allocation is *Green v CIR* [1982] STC 485, CS. The taxpayer sold a mansion house and grounds. The building comprised a central block with 33 rooms, and two wings connected to it by corridors. Some reconstruction and redecoration work had been carried out, during which the taxpayer and various members of his family and others had occupied parts of the central block, while a flat had been made in one of the wings for a gardener. The taxpayer contended that the whole of the gain was within the private residence exemption. The General Commissioners held that the two wings were not part of the residence and that the gain on their sale did not qualify for exemption. So far as concerned the main block, they adjusted the relief for a 'change in what is occupied as the individual's residence', and allowed relief on one-third of the gain. However, the Court of Session held that there were no facts which entitled them to adjust the relief. As a result, the whole of the gain on the sale of the central block and grounds was exempt. Whether the wings were part of the residence was a question of fact and degree for the Commissioners, and their decision was not inconsistent with the evidence. The appeal failed with regard to the gain on the sale of the wings.

22.2.5 Anti-avoidance provisions

To prevent abuse of principal private residence relief there is widely drawn anti-avoidance legislation which applies where:

(1) a dwelling-house is acquired wholly or partly for the purpose of realising a gain from its disposal, or
(2) there is subsequent expenditure on the dwelling-house wholly or partly for the purpose of realising a gain from its disposal.

Where (1) applies, no relief is due on any gain arising from the disposal of that dwelling-house. Where (2) applies no relief is due on any part of the gain attributable to the expenditure.

It is assumed that anyone who buys a dwelling-house is not doing so in the expectation of making a loss on its subsequent disposal; rather he is likely to hope that, in the fullness of time, he will make a gain on its disposal. One house may be chosen over another because its value is more likely to appreciate over time. These cases could be said to fall within (1) but, if the house was genuinely acquired and used as a residence and the conditions for relief are met, relief is not restricted. The anti-avoidance legislation is only applied when the primary purpose of the acquisition was an early disposal at a profit. The same approach is taken when considering whether a restriction of relief is appropriate under (2).

In many cases in which (1) would be applied the transaction of purchase and sale amounts to an adventure in the nature of trade. In these cases the charge to income tax takes priority over the charge to CGT. In some cases subsequent expenditure on the dwelling-house may also be part of an adventure in the nature of trade, giving rise to an income tax charge. The income tax charge again takes priority.

Item (2) is more often applied than (1). It denies relief on the part of a gain which is attributable to particular expenditure. Common circumstances in which it may be applied are:

(a) the acquisition by a leaseholder of a superior interest in the property;
(b) conversion of an undivided dwelling-house into flats; and
(c) barn conversions and other developments of outbuildings or the land attached into a dwelling-house.

There is no indication in the legislation of how this part of the gain should be computed. In practice it implies comparison between the gain which accrues and the gain which would have accrued if the relevant expenditure had not been incurred. In deciding whether a restriction to relief is appropriate under (2), the Revenue ignores cases in which the only relevant expenditure is incurred on obtaining planning permission, or removing restrictive covenants.

In *Goodwin v Curtis* [1998] STC 475, CA the taxpayer and a colleague formed a company and arranged short-term finance to purchase a property which included a farmhouse. When the company exchanged contracts to purchase the property, it also entered into a contract by way of subsale of the farmhouse to the taxpayer. The company completed its purchase of the farmhouse on 7 March 1985 and on 1 April 1985 completed the subsale to the taxpayer. He separated from his wife and took up temporary residence in the farmhouse, living and sleeping at the property seven days a week, and had a telephone connected to the farmhouse. On 11 April 1985 the farmhouse was widely advertised for sale, a sale brochure with photographs and plans was prepared and printed, and on 3 May 1985 the farmhouse was sold for £177,000. On 3 April 1985 the taxpayer completed the purchase of a small cottage to which he moved on completion of the sale of the farmhouse, and which he sold later in the year. In May/June 1985 the taxpayer exchanged contracts for the purchase of a house, which he sold in December 1985. The taxpayer's claim that the gain accruing on the disposal of the farmhouse was exempt was rejected on the ground that it had not been his only or main residence.

In the High Court it was held that the purpose of the exemption of a gain realised on the disposal of a dwelling-house, which had been a person's only or main residence, was to exempt the proceeds of sale of a person's home from liability to CGT. The justification for the exemption was that when a person sold his home, he frequently needed to acquire a new home elsewhere. In order to qualify for the exemption the taxpayer had therefore to provide evidence establishing that his residence at a property showed some degree of permanence, continuity or expectation of continuity.

In this case the taxpayer had decided to sell the farmhouse and had advertised it widely before he had completed the sale to himself, and in view of its size it was wholly unsuitable as the residence of a single man separated from his wife and in financial difficulties. His residence in it between the completion of the sale to him and the completion of the sale by him was intended to be, and was, brief. The conclusion was that the farmhouse had been used by the taxpayer not as an only or main residence within the exemption, but merely as temporary accommodation, and that the proceeds from its disposal were accordingly not exempt from CGT was correct.

An attempt to use this anti-avoidance provision to gain relief for a loss on the sale of a property was unsuccessful in *Jones v Wilcock* [1996] SSCD 389, Sp C92. The taxpayer and his wife purchased a house for more than £120,000. They subsequently incurred considerable expenditure on improvements but, following a general fall in house prices, sold the house for £97,000. The husband had other capital gains in the year of disposal, and claimed that the loss on the house should be set against such gains. The claim was dismissed on the basis that the house had been the couple's private residence, so that the loss was not allowable. An appeal on the basis that the house had been purchased 'wholly or partly for the purpose of realising a gain' was rejected by the Special Commissioner who found that, on the evidence, the couple's purpose in buying the house was to use it as their home.

22.3 PRIVATE RESIDENCE OCCUPIED UNDER TERMS OF SETTLEMENT
(TCGA 1992, s 224)

The exemption of gains on the disposal of only or main residences also applies to a gain accruing to a trustee on a disposal of settled property where, during the period of ownership by a trust, the dwelling-house or part of it is the only or main residence of a person entitled to occupy it under the terms of the settlement. (See further **22.1.11**.)

In *Sansom and another v Peay* [1976] STC 494, ChD the trustees of a discretionary trust had permitted certain beneficiaries to occupy a house subject to the trust as their residence. The house was disposed of and the Revenue raised assessments on the beneficiaries. However, the High Court held that the gain was exempt. So long as the beneficiaries were in occupation with the trustees' permission they were entitled to occupy it. The fact that they had no absolute right under the trust was not conclusive.

22.4 PRIVATE RESIDENCE OCCUPIED BY DEPENDENT RELATIVE BEFORE 6 APRIL 1998
(TCGA 1992, s 226)

Exemption was withdrawn for disposals after 5 April 1988 except where, before 6 April 1988, the dwelling-house was the sole residence of a dependent relative.

23

CAPITAL GAINS TAX SETTLEMENTS

23.1 NOMINEES, BARE TRUSTEES AND FUNDS IN COURT
(TCGA 1992, ss 60, 61)

Where assets are held by a person (often referred to as a bare trustee) as trustee for a person absolutely entitled thereto (or who would be so entitled were he not an infant, or under some legal disability such as lunacy) the assets are treated for CGT purposes as though legal (as opposed to beneficial) ownership thereof had been transferred and any acts of the trustee are treated as done by such persons.

For CGT purposes, an asset is deemed to be held in trust for a person absolutely entitled thereto where such person has the exclusive right to direct how the asset should be dealt with (subject only to the trustees' right to exercise a lien, charge or other right to resort to the asset for payment of duty, taxes or other costs). This rule also applies where two or more persons are, or would be, 'jointly' so entitled. This has been construed, in *Kidson v Macdonald and another* (1973) 49 TC 503, ChD, as meaning 'concurrently' or 'in common' rather than its technical real property law meaning. Megarry J stated, in *Sargaison v Roberts* (1969) 45 TC 612, ChD, that 'where the technicalities of English conveyancing and land law are brought into juxtaposition within a UK taxing Statute, I am encouraged to look at the realities at the expense of the technicalities'.

There are a number of cases in which the meaning of 'absolutely entitled as against the trustee' was the point at issue. In *Tomlinson v Glyn's Executor & Trustee Co Ltd* (1969) 45 TC 600, CA, the beneficiaries were infants. The trust fund was settled in trust for such of K's children as should attain age 21 or marry. The trustees disposed of investments of the trust fund, and were assessed on the gains arising. In the tax years concerned, the beneficiaries were all infants and unmarried. The trustees' contention that the children were assessable under s 60(1) was upheld. Section 60(1) is to be read as stating 'or for any person who would be absolutely entitled against the trustee if he were not under disability and so not able to demand a transfer or give a receipt'.

The matter at issue in *Cochrane's Executors v CIR* (1974) 49 TC 299, CS was whether, when shares were sold to meet a legacy etc, the residuary legatee was 'absolutely entitled'. In this case a testator, domiciled in Scotland, left his estate to his executors in trust, among other things, to convey the residue to his son absolutely. They sold certain shares (eg to pay debts and meet a legacy) and an assessment was raised on the gains on the sales. The executors' contention was that the son (who was non-resident and non-ordinarily resident in the UK) was 'absolutely entitled as against the trustee' to the assets. This line of argument was rejected, because it was up to the executors to decide which assets to realise. The son never had any right to the shares which were sold. His absolute entitlement applied only to the residue.

Crowe v Appleby (1975) 51 TC 457, CA concerned freehold property held, under the terms of a will, on trust to sell and hold the proceeds for the benefit of the testator's five children and their issue. The property was sold and the trustees were assessed on the gain. Two of the children had died, and their shares of the trust fund passed to their children (ie the grandchildren) absolutely. However, the assessment was upheld. This was because the trust fund was comprised in realty. Accordingly, the grandchildren could not direct the trustees on how to deal with their respective shares. As a result, they were not absolutely entitled as against the trustees.

In *Harthan v Mason* (1979) 53 TC 272, ChD, under a will certain properties were vested in Mr Harthan and his sister as trustees for sale as tenants in common. When, eventually, the properties were sold, having been let for several years, a CGT assessment was raised on them. His appeal was on the basis that he was not 'absolutely entitled as against the trustee', and that being so, the disposal was of an interest in a settlement within TCGA 1992, s 76(1). This was not accepted, and the assessment was confirmed.

Transfers of assets between trustees and persons absolutely entitled thereto are ignored (because there is no change in the beneficial ownership of those assets). This is illustrated in *Booth v Ellard* (1980) 53 TC 393, CA where shares were transferred to trustees under a pooling agreement that the original shareholders and their families would retain effective control of the company in the event that it was floated on The Stock Exchange. The original shareholders received the trust income in proportion to the original shares transferred, and could also direct the trustees to exercise votes attaching to the shares or decide whether, for example, to take up a rights issue. In the event that an original shareholder died or wished to sell, the shares would remain in the family. The shareholders collectively had power to end the trust, and although their interests in their shares were subject to restraints, they retained their beneficial interests. Thus they were 'absolutely entitled to their shares as against the trustees'. This falls within TCGA 1992, s 60(1). Accordingly, the transfer of the shares to the trustees was not a chargeable disposal (as beneficial ownership remains in the hands of the original shareholders, despite the transfer of legal ownership to the shares to the trustees).

A somewhat similar conclusion, in a case involving parcels of land, was reached in *Jenkins v Brown, Warrington v Brown and related appeals* (1989) 62 TC 226, ChD. It was held that the execution of a deed of rearrangement distributing settled property to which beneficiaries were 'absolutely entitled to the settled property as against the trustees' was not a disposal for CGT purposes. The quantum of the settlors' beneficial interests was unaffected by the trust.

The position is similar for assets held by a person as nominee for someone else.

The costs of transferring an asset from an estate or settlement to a legatee or beneficiary, whether paid by the trustees or by the legatee or beneficiary, are treated as allowable costs on a subsequent disposal of the asset by the legatee or beneficiary.

Except in the case of a bare trustee, when the assessment is made on the person 'absolutely entitled to the assets as against the trustee', CGT is chargeable in the name of the trustees or personal representatives in that capacity. Such trustees and personal representatives are not treated as individuals, so that the reliefs available specifically to individuals do not apply. As to the application of the basic annual exemption to trusts, etc, see **21.6**.

In certain circumstances, moneys held in court are held by the Accountant General of the Supreme Court of Judicature in England (or of the Supreme Court of Judicature of Northern Ireland) on statutory deposits. Funds in court held in this way are treated as held by him as nominee for the persons entitled thereto, or interested therein, or in some cases for the trustees of such persons.

If the investments are held in a court investment fund the net gain, after CGT, is apportioned amongst those interested therein. The net gain is, however, allowed as an expense (by set-off) in computing a gain on the disposal of an interest in the fund.

Subject to the rules for bare trustees and any other express provision to the contrary, chargeable gains accruing to the trustees of a settlement, and CGT chargeable on or in their name, is not regarded as accruing to, or chargeable on, any other person, nor is any trustee regarded as an individual.

With regard to migrating trustees under TCGA 1992, s 80, see **21.13.4**, after Table 21.3.

Trustees are liable to CGT at 23 per cent (for 1998/99) after applying the appropriate annual exemption (see TCGA 1992, s 3, Sched 1). Note, however, that the CGT rate applying to accumulation and maintenance settlements is 34 per cent (TCGA 1992, s 5). If the settlor or his spouse retains an interest in the assets, any gain thereon is assessed on the settlor and not on the trustees (TCGA 1992, s 77).

23.2 SETTLEMENTS

23.2.1 Settled property
(TCGA 1992, s 68)

Settled property is any property held in trust, but not including property held as nominee or as bare trustee (see above).

23.2.2 Status of trustees
(TCGA 1992, s 69)

Settlement trustees are treated as a single and continuing body of persons, distinct from the persons who from time to time hold the position of trustees, even though there may be changes in the persons so acting. The trustees (as a body) are treated as resident and ordinarily resident in the UK unless the trust's general administration is ordinarily carried on outside the UK and a majority of the trustees are at the time non-resident or non-ordinarily resident therein.

This rule is modified if the trustee is a professional trustee (ie the trustee carries on the business of management of trusts). Suppose that such a trustee so acts, in the course of that business, as trustee of a settlement, where the settlor was not at the time of making the settlement (or at his death in the case of testamentary dispositions or on intestacy) domiciled, resident or ordinarily resident in the UK. In such event the trustee is treated, in relation to that trust, as being non-resident in the UK. If a majority of the trustees are so treated as non-resident, the trust's general administration is treated as carried on outside the UK.

Where part of the property comprised in a settlement is vested in one set of trustees and part in another, they are together treated as a single body of trustees and, if acting separately, are treated as acting on behalf of that single body. This applies in particular where settled land (under the Settled Land Act 1925) is vested in the tenant for life and investments representing capital money are vested in the settlement's trustees. It is also specifically applied on:

(1) a person becoming absolutely entitled to any settled property as against the trustees (TCGA 1992, s 71(1)); and
(2) the termination of a life interest on the death of the person entitled thereto (s 72(1)).

There is a procedure available to the Revenue for recovering CGT assessed on the settlement trustees on a chargeable gain accruing to the trust which is not paid within six months from the date when it becomes payable. This applies if, whether before or after the end of that period, the asset or any part of the proceeds of its sale is transferred by the trustees to a beneficiary who, as against the trustees, is absolutely entitled to it. At any time within two years from the time when the CGT becomes payable, the Revenue may assess and charge such a beneficiary (in the trustees' name) to an equivalent amount of CGT. If only a part of the asset or of the proceeds is transferred, then only a proportionate part of that amount can be charged.

23.2.3 Gifts into settlement
(TCGA 1992, s 70)

A transfer into in settlement, which can be either revocable or irrevocable, is treated as a disposal of the entire property which thereby becomes settled. This can apply even where the donor retains some interest as a beneficiary under, and notwithstanding that he is a trustee of, the settlement. This treatment also extends to transfers, and not merely gifts, into settlement. Thus a sale to a settlement (as in *Berry v Warnett* (1982) 55 TC 92, HL) is within this provision.

23.2.4 Person becoming absolutely entitled
(TCGA 1992, s 71)

When a beneficiary becomes absolutely entitled, as against the trustees, to settled property, there is a deemed disposal of the trust assets at their market value and an acquisition by the beneficiary at the same value. This applies even if the assets are not passed over to the beneficiary. In that case, although the trustees continue to hold the assets, they do so as bare trustees (under s 60(1)).

A remainderman, who becomes absolutely entitled on the death of a life tenant during the administration of an estate, is deemed to take the assets at market value on death in the same way as if he were a legatee (CCAB, June 1997).

There is also a deemed disposal by the trustees where an infant (or other person under a disability) becomes absolutely entitled, as against the trustees, to the settled property (eg by trustees appointment). The consideration for this deemed disposal is an amount equal to the market value of the settled property. However, any gain arising by reference to a deemed disposal on the life tenant's death is exempt.

Two cases, *Hart v Briscoe and others* and *Hoare Trustees v Gardner* (1977) 52 TC 53, ChD, which were heard together, concerned the application of a power of advancement.

Hart v Briscoe

In *Hart v Briscoe* under a settlement and a conveyance, both made by B in 1955, certain assets were held on discretionary trusts. In April 1972, B made a further settlement, and on the same day the assets then subject to the trusts of the 1955 settlement were (in effect) advanced by the 1955 settlement trustees to themselves as trustees of the 1972 settlement. A CGT assessment was made on the basis that the 1955 settlement trustees were deemed under what is now TCGA 1992, s 71(1) to have disposed of and immediately reacquired the assets so advanced.

The trustees contended, on appeal, that the effect of the exercise of a power of advancement was indistinguishable from the effect of the exercise of a special power of appointment and that the 1972 settlement trusts must be read back into the 1955 settlement with the consequence that there was a single settlement. The Crown's contention was that the effect of the exercise of the power of advancement was that the assets advanced ceased to be held on the 1955 settlement trusts and were thenceforth held on the 1972 settlement trusts.

It was held, upholding the Crown's position, that the question whether a disposition which exercises a fiduciary power is to be viewed as a separate settlement, or as part of a single fiduciary arrangement headed by the disposition which created the power, must be answered in the context of the circumstances of the particular case. On the facts of this, the 1955 settlement came to an end in April 1972 in relation to the advanced assets. The advanced assets then ceased altogether to be subject to the 1955 settlement. Whereas, prior to the advance, the assets were subject to a single settlement consisting of the 1955 settlement, thereafter they were subject to a single settlement consisting of the 1972 settlement.

Hoare Trustees v Gardner

In *Hoare Trustees v Gardner*, a fund was held upon certain trusts and the trustees, under a power conferred on them, executed declarations of trust by which certain of the assets forming part of the fund were to be held by themselves on new trusts.

The trustees of the fund, in that capacity, were assessed to CGT for the year 1972/73 on the basis that on the execution of the declarations of trust they were deemed under what is now TCGA 1992, s 71(1) to have disposed of and immediately reacquired the assets subject to the declarations. The trustees' contention was that, as on the execution of the declaration of trust, they did not become beneficially entitled to the assets in question, they did not become 'absolutely' entitled to any settled property and, in any event, they did not acquire the 'exclusive right ... to direct' how the assets should be dealt with within the meaning of what is now s 60(2). For the Crown it was contended that the phrase 'absolutely entitled' is not restricted to absolute beneficial entitlement and that on the execution of the declaration of trust the trustees did have the 'exclusive right ... to direct'.

It was held that the expression 'absolutely entitled' used in the phrase 'absolutely entitled ... as against the trustees' did not mean beneficially entitled; and that s 60(2) did not introduce the requirement that for a person to be 'absolutely entitled' he must be beneficially entitled.

Other case-law

Pilkington v IRC

These cases were distinguished from *Tomlinson v Glyn's Executor & Trustee Co Ltd* ((1969) 45 TC 600 CA) (see **23.1**). However, the dictum of Upjohn LJ in *Pilkington and another v CIR and another* (1962) 40 TC 416, HL was applied. There it was held that trustees are entitled to exercise their power of advancement in favour of a beneficiary by applying money to form a trust, the provisions of which they thought to be for her benefit. For the purpose of the rule against perpetuities, the power of advancement is analogous to a special power of appointment, so that the proposed settlement's trusts must be treated as if contained in a testator's will and some of them were accordingly void as violating the rule.

Stephenson v Barclays Bank Trust

In *Stephenson v Barclays Bank Trust Co Ltd* (1974) 50 TC 374, a testator had died and left his residuary estate upon trust to accumulate the income for 21 years subject to paying annuities therefrom to each of his three daughters during widowhood and then, subject to the annuities, in equal shares for his grandchildren living at his death who should attain age 21. A deed of family arrangement was entered into whereby a fund was appropriated to the annuities, and an amount advanced to the grandchildren to purchase further annuities for the daughters. The balance of the trust fund was transferred to the grandchildren. An assessment was raised on the basis that there had been a notional disposal under what is now TCGA 1992, s 71(1), because the grandchildren had become 'absolutely entitled as against the trustees' at the time of the deed of family arrangement. The annuities could not be treated as 'outgoings' under what is now s 60(2). *Kidson v Macdonald* (1973) 49 TC 503, ChD was applied as to the meaning of 'jointly' (see **23.1**).

Roome and Denne v Edwards

In *Roome and Denne v Edwards* (1981) 54 TC 359, HL, a wife's marriage settlement of 1944 gave her a life interest. After her death, her husband had a protected life interest, and together they had a special power of appointment. In 1955 by deed the wife and husband appointed, under that power, 'the appointed fund' in favour of one of their daughters. Thereafter the appointed fund and the residue of the main 1944 fund were separately administered. Until February 1972 the trustees (then R and A) of both funds were identical.

On 7 February 1972, D replaced A as co-trustee (with R) of the appointed fund. D was never a trustee of the main 1944 fund. As part of a tax-avoidance scheme,

(1) R had valuations made of both funds;

(2) on 28 February 1972 an order was made under the Variation of Trusts Act 1958 approving an arrangement whereby the trusts on which the main fund was held were altered, and that arrangement was brought into effect on 15 March 1972;

(3) on 20 March 1972 all the beneficiaries having interests in the main 1944 fund assigned those interests to two Cayman Islands companies (CRI and Royal Oak) for cash;

(4) on 21 March 1972 R and A were replaced as trustees of the main fund by two non-UK residents;

(5) on 13 April 1972 CRI assigned its interest in the main fund to Royal Oak so that the latter became absolutely entitled to it as against the non-resident trustees.

The Special Commissioners in principle upheld CGT assessments raised on R and D alone, in respect of the occasion of charge arising on 13 April 1972. This was on the basis that both the appointed fund and the main 1944 fund were 'property comprised in a settlement'.

It was held in the House of Lords that the 1955 appointment did not bring into existence a separate settlement. Hence on 13 April 1972, the appointed fund and the main 1944 fund were parts of 'property comprised in a [single] settlement ... vested in [different] sets of trustees', and R and D were thus correctly assessed on the chargeable gain then accruing to the trustees of that single settlement.

The question whether a particular set of facts amounts to 'a settlement' should be approached by asking what a person, with knowledge of the legal context of the word under established doctrine and applying this knowledge in a practical and commonsense manner to those facts, would conclude. If property subject to an original settlement becomes, on the facts, subject to a separate settlement, there must inevitably be a disposal by the trustees of the former to the trustees of the latter, even though they might be the same person.

SP 9/81 was issued on 23 September 1981 following discussions with the Law Society, and set out the Revenue view on the CGT implications of the exercise of a Power of Appointment or Advancement when continuing trusts are declared, in the light of the House of Lords' decision in *Roome and Denne v Edwards*.

Bond v Pickford

Roome and Denne was followed in *Bond v Pickford* (1983) 57 TC 301, CA. The trustees of the main settlement executed Deeds of Allocation whereby the allocated funds were thenceforth to be held on the trusts set out in those Deeds. Those trusts were exhaustive of the beneficial interests in the allocated funds. The trustees were expressed to 'continue' as trustees of the allocated funds and the administrative powers of the main settlement were expressed to 'continue to apply'. The trustees were assessed to CGT on the basis that, on the execution of the Deeds of Allocation, new settlements were created, and they became absolutely entitled to the allocated funds as trustees of the new settlements as against themselves as trustees of the main settlement.

It was held that separate settlements had not been created. On the true construction of all the material documents, the power to allocate was a domestic power being the equivalent of a special (although limited) power of appointment, and its exercise automatically preserved the application of the main settlement's administrative powers and provisions and the enduring retention of the allocated funds by the trustees, as the main settlement trustees.

In deciding whether a separate settlement had been created, it is essential to examine the nature of the power the trustees have purported to exercise. The power to allocate did not empower the trustees to create a new settlement. The relevant distinction between powers is not so much between powers of appointment and powers of advancement as between powers which, either expressly or by necessary implication, permit the trustees to transfer assets out of the settlement, and powers which do not so authorise the trustees.

The Revenue view, as expressed in SP 9/81, has been modified to some extent by the Court of Appeal decision in *Bond v Pickford*, and is set out in SP 7/84.

The consequences of Roome and Denne and Bond v Pickford: deemed disposals

In *Roome and Denne v Edwards* the House of Lords held that where a separate settlement is created there is a deemed disposal of the relevant assets by the old trustees under TCGA 1992, s 71(1). But the judgment emphasised that, in deciding whether a new settlement has been created by the exercise of a Power of Appointment or Advancement, each case must be considered on its own facts, and by applying established legal doctrine to the facts in a practical and commonsense manner. In *Bond v Pickford* the Court of Appeal judgment explained that the consideration of the facts must include examination of the powers which the trustees purported to exercise, and determination of the parties' intention, viewed objectively.

It is now clear that a deemed disposal under s 71(1) cannot arise unless the power exercised by the trustees or the instrument conferring the power, expressly or by necessary implication, confers on the trustees authority to remove assets from the original settlement by subjecting them to the trusts of a different settlement. Such powers (which may be of advancement or appointment) are referred to by the Court of Appeal as 'powers in the wider form'. However, the Board considers that a deemed disposal will not arise when such a power is exercised and trusts are declared in circumstances such that:

(1) the appointment is revocable, or
(2) the trusts declared of the advanced or appointed funds are not exhaustive so that there exists a possibility, at the time when the advancement

or appointment is made, that the funds covered by it will, on the occasion of some event, cease to be held upon such trusts and, once again, come to be held upon the original settlement trusts.

Further, when such a power is exercised the Board considers it unlikely that a deemed disposal will arise when trusts are declared if duties in regard to the appointed assets still fall to the trustees of the original settlement in their capacity as trustees of that settlement, bearing in mind the provision in TCGA 1992, s 69(1) that the trustees of a settlement form a single and continuing body (distinct from the persons who may from time to time be the trustees).

The Revenue accepts that a power of appointment or advancement can be exercised over only part of the settled property and that the above consequences would apply to that part.

Swires v Renton

A more recent case, *Swires v Renton* (1991) 64 TC 315, ChD, shows how these provisions are now applied. By a settlement made in 1954, income was held on a discretionary trust for the settlor's wife, his daughter, her husband and their two sons. Subject to a power to pay or apply capital to or for the benefit of any member of that class 'freed and released from the trusts concerning the same', the capital was held for members of that class living at the expiry of the trust period (which was defined by a royal lives clause).

In 1981 the power to apply capital was exercised by a supplemental deed of appointment. It divided the trust fund into two parts. One part was to be held on trust for the daughter absolutely. The other part was to be held to pay the income to the daughter during her life (or, if shorter, the trust period) and, subject to a power to pay or apply capital to or for her benefit 'freed and discharged from the trusts affecting the same under the settlement and this deed', the capital was to be held for her two sons in equal shares absolutely. Under the appointment, the trustees were given power to disregard the Apportionment Act, and the administrative provisions of the settlement were to continue to apply to the appointed fund as far as they were consistent with the other deed provisions.

The trustee appealed against a CGT assessment for 1981/82 made on the footing that the appointment's effect was to subject the funds to the trusts of a new settlement. It was held that the power of appointment in the 1954 settlement was not exercisable by the trustees only by way of an outright payment or the creation of a new settlement. It gave the trustees the choice of appointing funds to themselves as trustees of a new settlement or of declaring that the funds were to be subject to new trusts within the existing settlement. The language of the deed of appointment rebutted the inference that a new settlement was intended. The description of the appointment as supplemental to the settlement carried little, if any, weight, and the creation of a power to disregard the Apportionment Act was neutral. However, the provision that the administrative and other powers and provisions of the settlement should continue to apply, and the power to appoint capital from the appointed fund 'freed and discharged from the trusts affecting the same under the settlement and this deed', clearly indicated that the trustees contemplated that there would be provisions of the settlement continuing to be applicable to the appointed fund.

Deemed disposals and reacquisitions in practice

In practice (see SP D10), where a life interest in part of settled property terminates, and the part can properly be identified with one or more specific assets, or where within three months of the termination the trustees appropriate specific assets to give effect to the termination, the Revenue accepts that the deemed disposals and reacquisitions under TCGA 1992, ss 71 and 72 apply to those specific assets, and not to any part of the other assets comprised in the settled property. Where the benefit of this practice is claimed the Revenue requires trustees to sign an undertaking, which is binding on the Revenue and the trustees as well as their successors in office, to the effect that the right to compute the gain or loss on any subsequent disposal on any other basis is given up. For this purpose the Revenue is prepared, in particular, to agree with trustees lists of assets properly identifiable with the release of a life interest. This practice applies on any act or event which terminates a life interest, whether voluntarily or involuntarily.

If, when a beneficiary becomes absolutely entitled as against the trustees to settled property, there is a balance of allowable losses (including any allowable loss brought forward to the tax year in which that occasion falls) suffered by the trust and not set against chargeable gains arising in that part of the tax year which falls before that occasion, such losses can be carried forward by the beneficiary and set against his subsequent chargeable gain.

There is an identification requirement here. Thus, on the occasion when such a person becomes absolutely entitled to the settled property, it is only those allowable losses which accrued to the trustee in relation to property which is, or is represented by, the property to which that person so becomes entitled. Such losses are treated as if it were an allowable loss accruing at that time to the person becoming so entitled, instead of to the trustee.

It is a general rule that, where a loss accrues to a person on making a disposal to a connected person, under TCGA 1992, s 18(3) that loss may only be deducted from gains on other disposals by that person to the same connected person. Several questions about the application and interpretation of the rules in TCGA 1992, s 286 arise in cases involving the trustees of settlements and are dealt with in *Tax Bulletin* 6 (February 1993).

The settlor and the trustees are treated as connected at the moment when the settlement comes into existence and the initial property is transferred to the trustees. Section 18(3) applies to a disposal which brings the settlement into existence. It is not restricted to situations where the parties are already connected before the disposal.

The trustees and beneficiaries are, however, not connected after the settlor is dead. If the settlor dies, the connection between the trustees, relatives and the settlor's spouse is broken. Thus, suppose that the beneficiaries of a settlement are the late settlor's children: the trustees are not connected with those beneficiaries, even if one or more of the children are trustees. The basic rule is that the trustees of a settlement are connected with the settlor, and also with any person connected with the settlor (s 286(3)). Under TCGA 1992, s 69(1), the trustees are treated as a single and continuing body distinct from the persons who may be the trustees. Therefore, in determining whether s 286(3) applies, the trustees' identity is disregarded.

The fact that the trustees and beneficiaries are connected does not affect the transfer of losses under TCGA 1992, s 71(2). Prior to 16 June 1999, where a beneficiary became absolutely entitled against the trustees, all the unused losses which had arisen to the trustees in relation to the property to which the beneficiary becomes entitled, including any loss accruing on the deemed disposal to the beneficiary, are transferred to the beneficiary under s 71(2).

For beneficiaries becoming absolutely entitled from 16 June 1999, TCGA 1992, s 71(2) and (2A)–(2D), prohibit the carry-forward of losses, realised on actual disposals by trustees, to beneficiaries on their becoming absolutely entitled as against to the property of the trust. They may use the losses to offset gains realised within the trust under the normal rules. When a beneficiary becomes absolutely entitled to an asset any loss which is thereby deemed to arise thereon must be set first against any gains arising to the trustees, either on the same occasion or earlier in the year. The loss can be carried forward to the beneficiary but can be used by him *only* on the disposal of the same asset, and not against gains realised by him on disposing of any other asset.

23.2.5 Termination of life interest on death of person entitled
(TCGA 1992, s 72)

If a life interest in possession comes to an end (eg on the death of a life tenant of settled property), the trustees are deemed to have disposed of an appropriate part of the trust fund at market value and immediately reacquired it. No chargeable gain accrues on such a disposal. An interest which is a right to part of the income of settled property is treated as an interest in a corresponding part of the settled property.

This rule applies where the person entitled to an interest in possession in all or any part of settled property dies (although the interest does not then terminate) as it applies on the termination of such an interest (under s 72(2)). Likewise, it applies on the death of the person entitled to any annuity payable out of, or charged on, settled property or the income of settled property (s 72(3)). There is a deemed disposal of settled property on a life tenant's death even where his interest is *pur autre vie*, and does not in fact terminate.

Suppose that an entitlement to an annuity is created by a settlement. Some of the settled property is appropriated by the trustees as a fund out of which the annuity is payable. There is no right of recourse to, or to the income of, settled property not so appropriated. In such a case, the settled property so appropriated is, while the annuity is payable, and on the occasion of the death of the person entitled to the annuity, treated as being settled property under a separate settlement (s 72(4)).

If there is an interest in a part of the settled property and, where that is an interest in income, there is no right of recourse to, or to the income of, the remainder of it, the part of in which the interest subsists is, while it subsists, treated as being settled property under a separate settlement (s 72(5)).

The Revenue's understanding of the term 'interest in possession', with particular reference to where such interest is subject to a discretion or power to accumulate the property's income or to divert it elsewhere, is set out in IRPR 12 February 1976. (See further **16.2** for a more detailed analysis of interests in possession.)

An interest in possession in settled property exists where the person having the interest has the immediate entitlement (subject to any prior claim by the trustees for expenses and other outgoings properly payable out of income) to any income produced by that property as the income arises. A discretion or power, in whatever form, which can be exercised after income arises so as to withhold it from that person, negates the existence of an interest in possession. For this purpose a power to accumulate income is regarded as a power to withhold it, unless any accumulations must be held solely for the person having the interest or his personal representatives.

On the other hand, the existence of a mere power of revocation of appointment, the exercise of which would determine the interest wholly or in part (but which, so long as it remains unexercised, does not affect the beneficiaries' immediate entitlement to income) does not in the Revenue's view prevent the interest from being an interest in possession.

It is often difficult, on the termination of an annuity which is regarded as a life interest, to determine the 'corresponding part' of the annuity fund which is deemed to be disposed of. This problem also arises on the death of an annuitant where the termination is treated as of a life interest under TCGA 1992, s 75. Where the rule applies, the 'corresponding part' of the relevant assets is the proportion, up to 100 per cent, which the amount of the annuity bears to the fund's income (or the whole settlement's income on an annuitant's death). For this purpose it is the income of the 12 months up to the annuity's termination, or at the trustees' option the income of the last trust accounts year ending before the termination, that is taken into consideration. There may be difficulties such as widely fluctuating income which need to be looked at specially.

23.2.6 Death of life tenant: exclusion of chargeable gain
(TCGA 1992, s 73)

A special rule applies where, on a person becoming absolutely entitled to any settled property (under s 71(1)), the assets forming part of any settled property are deemed to be disposed of and reacquired by the trustee on the occasion when a person becomes (or would but for a disability become) absolutely entitled thereto as against the trustee. If that occasion is the death of a person entitled to an interest in possession in the settled property:

(1) there is no chargeable gain on the disposal; and
(2) if on the death the property reverts to the disponer, the disposal and acquisition under s 71(1) are deemed to be for such consideration as to secure that neither a gain nor a loss accrues to the trustee. If the trustee first acquired the property prior to 6 April 1965, the disposal and reacquisition are deemed to be at that earlier date.

Where such interest is in part only of such settled property (under s 71), (1) above does not apply, but any chargeable gain accruing on the disposal is reduced by a proportion corresponding to that represented by that part.

An interest which is a right to part of the income of settled property is treated as an interest in a corresponding part of the settled property (s 72(1)).

This rule applies under s 72(2)–(5) as discussed in **23.2.5** above.

23.2.7 Interaction with gift relief
(TCGA 1992, s 74)

Special rules are applied where:

(1) a claim for business asset gift relief is made (under TCGA 1992, s 165), or a claim is made for gift relief on assets subject to IHT (under TCGA 1992, s 260) on the disposal of an asset to a trustee; and
(2) the trustee is deemed to have disposed of the asset, or part of it, on a person becoming absolutely entitled to settled property (under s 71(1)), or the termination of a life interest of a person entitled to an interest in possession in settled property (under s 72(1)(a)).

The rules whereby no chargeable gain arises (ss 72(1)(b), 73(1)(a)) do not apply to the disposal of the asset or part by the trustee. However, any chargeable gain accruing to the trustee on the disposal is restricted to the amount of the held-over gain (under TCGA 1992, s 165 or 260), or a corresponding part of it, on the disposal of the asset to him.

If the rule that there is no chargeable gain on the deemed disposal and reaquisition of settled property has already been disapplied because only part of the settled property is deemed to be disposed of and reacquired (under s 73(2)), the alternative reduction of the chargeable gain accruing on the disposal by a proportion corresponding to that represented by that part is diminished by an amount equal to the proportion there mentioned of the held-over gain (under s 165 or 260).

23.2.8 Disposal of interests in settled property
(TCGA 1992, s 76)

No chargeable gain accrues on the disposal of an interest created by or arising under a settlement (including, in particular, an annuity or life interest, and the reversion to an annuity or life interest) by the person for whose benefit the interest was created by the settlement terms or by any other person except one who acquired, or derives his title from one who acquired, the interest for a consideration in money or money's worth, other than consideration consisting of another interest under the settlement. This does not apply if:

(1) the settlement falls within description set out below; or
(2) the property comprised in the settlement is or includes property deriving directly or indirectly from such a settlement. However, this does not prevent this rule from applying where the disposal in question is in consideration of obtaining settled property that is treated as made an acquired interest (see below).

A settlement falls within this description if there has been a time when the trustees of that settlement:

(1) were non-resident or non-ordinarily resident in the UK; or
(2) were regarded under any double taxation relief arrangements as resident outside the UK.

Except as above, where a person who has acquired an interest in settled property (including in particular the reversion to an annuity or life interest) becomes, as the holder of that interest, absolutely entitled as against the trustee to any settled property, he is treated as disposing of the interest in consideration of obtaining that settled property (but without prejudice to any gain accruing to the trustee on the disposal of that property deemed to be effected by him under s 71(1)).

In *Harthan v Mason* (1979) 53 TC 272, ChD, under a will certain properties were vested in Mr Harthan and his sister as trustees for sale as tenants in common. When, eventually, the properties were sold, having been let for several years, a CGT assessment was raised on them. His appeal, was on the basis that he was not 'absolutely entitled as against the trustee', and that being so the disposal was of an interest in a settlement within TCGA 1992, s 76(1). This was not accepted, and the assessment was confirmed. In *Chinn v Collins* (1980) 54 TC 311, HL (an anti-avoidance case), a central feature of the scheme was the disposal of contingent interests which were exempt under s 76(1)). The scheme was unsuccessful on other grounds.

The exemption to an original beneficiary is not available on the disposal of an interest in settled property where the trustees are non-resident (TCGA 1992, s 85(2)(b)).

23.2.9 Disposal of settled property: deemed disposal of underlying assets
(TCGA 1992, s 76A and Sched 4A)

As noted at **23.2.8**, any gains arising on the disposal of an interest in a UK settlement (as contrasted to its underlying assets) are not generally chargeable to CGT. This prevents a double tax charge arising, one on the sale by the trustees of assets in the trust property, and another on a sale by a beneficiary of an interest in the trust. However, this exemption has been used to sell the underlying assets tax free to third parties. It has also been used by individuals who place assets (which are standing at a gain) in trusts in which they retain an interest that is subsequently sold to a third party.

Furthermore, this exemption has been used to circumvent TCGA 1992, s 71 (as applied from 16 June 1999 – see **23.2.4**) which was intended to prevent the sale of trust losses. This was achieved by placing valuable assets in trust; a contingent interest in the settled property was then created in favour of the settlor, entitling him to acquire the trust property. That interest was then sold to the trustees of another trust which had unused losses. The trustees of the second trust then acquired the assets from the first trust, using gifts hold-over relief, and the assets were then sold by the trustees of the second trust who offset the losses against the gains.

The new rules, described below, counter these tax avoidance devices. Thus, in general terms, where an interest in a settlement in which the settlor has an interest is disposed of for consideration, the assets to which the interest relates are deemed to be disposed of and reacquired by the trustees at their market value. Any resulting gain is chargeable on the settlor under the normal provisions. Gifts hold-over relief cannot be claimed to relieve the gains arising on the disposal.

This rule also applies to any property which formed part of a settlement in which the settlor had an interest at any time in the two previous tax years, or at any time in the period beginning when the contract for the sale of the interest is entered into and ending when the transaction is effectively completed. Action is taken to prevent the tax charge being avoided on property added to the trust during that period.

Effective date
(TCGA 1992, s 76A(3) and Sched 4A, para 1)

The new TCGA 1992 provisions apply to disposals, for consideration, of interests in settled property made or effectively completed after 20 March 2000.

Meaning of 'interest in possession'
(TCGA 1992, Sched 4A, para 2)

'Interest in possession' has a wide meaning and includes, for example, the right to enjoy any benefit arising from the exercise of a power by the trustees in relation to a trust or by anyone in relation to settled property. Specifically, in the new rules an 'interest in settled property' is any interest created by or arising under a settlement. This includes any right to, or in connection with, the enjoyment of a benefit created by or arising directly under a settlement, or arising as a result of the exercise of a discretion or power by the trustees of a settlement, or by any person in relation to settled property.

Meaning of 'for consideration'
(TCGA 1992, Sched 4A, para 3)

Here, a disposal is 'for consideration' if consideration is given or received by any person for, or in connection with, any transaction by which the disposal is effected. In determining whether a disposal is for consideration, any consideration consisting of another interest under the same settlement that has not previously been disposed of is disregarded. 'Consideration' is actual consideration, as opposed to consideration deemed to be given under any TCGA 1992 provision.

Deemed disposal of underlying assets
(TCGA 1992, Sched 4A, paras 4–7)

Where these new rules apply and a number of conditions are met, the trustees of the settlement are treated as disposing of and immediately reacquiring the relevant underlying assets. This treatment is referred to as the 'deemed disposal'.

Under the conditions, which are set out below, 'the relevant tax year' is that in which the disposal of the interest in settled property is made. The deemed disposal of the underlying assets is treated as taking place when the disposal of the interest in settled property is made. There is a special treatment (see Sched 4A, para 13(3)(a)) where the beginning of the disposal and its effective completion fall in different tax years.

Condition as to UK residence of the trustees

This condition is that the trustees of the settlement were either:

(1) UK-resident during the whole or part of the relevant tax year, or
(2) UK-ordinarily resident during that year.

Trustees are not regarded as resident or ordinarily resident in the UK at any time when they are treated as resident in a territory outside the UK under any double taxation treaty. There is a special treatment (under Sched 4A, para 13(3)(b)) where the beginning of the disposal and its effective completion fall in different tax years.

Condition as to UK residence of the settlor

This condition is that, in the relevant tax year, or any of the previous five tax years, a person who is a settlor in relation to the settlement was either:

(1) UK-resident during the whole or part of the year, or
(2) UK-ordinarily resident during the year.

There is a special treatment (under para 13(3)(c)) where the beginning of the disposal and its effective completion fall in different tax years. However, no account is taken of any tax year before 1999/2000

Condition as to settlor interest in the settlement

This condition is that at any time in the relevant period the settlement:

(1) was a settlor-interested settlement, or
(2) comprised property derived, directly or indirectly, from a settlement that at any time in that period was a settlor-interested settlement.

This condition is met if the trust is a 'settlor-interested settlement' (see below) at any time in 'the relevant period' (see below), or if at any time in that period the settled property of the trust includes any property which is directly or indirectly derived from another trust which is itself a settlor-interested settlement at any time in that period. In this latter case it is only necessary for that other trust to have been a settlor-interested settlement at some time during the relevant period.

For this purpose, the relevant period is that:

(1) beginning two years before the beginning of the relevant tax year, and
(2) ending with the date of the disposal of the interest in settled property.

There is a special treatment (under para 13(3)(d)) where the beginning of the disposal and its effective completion fall in different tax years. The relevant period cannot be treated as beginning before 6 April 1999. If the rules for identifying the relevant period (Sched 4A, para 7(2) or 13(3)(d)) would produce that result, the relevant period is treated as beginning on that date.

Here, a settlement is a 'settlor-interested settlement' if anyone who is a settlor in relation to it has an interest in it at any time in the relevant period, or had such an interest at any time in that period prior to becoming a settlor. The rules used to determine whether a settlor has, or had, an interest are essentially the same as those used in TCGA 1992, s 77.

This condition is treated as not met in a tax year in which the settlor dies, and in some cases in a tax year in which the settlor's spouse dies or in which the settlor and spouse cease to be married.

The relevant underlying assets
(TCGA 1992, Sched 4A, para 8)

Some explanation is needed about what is meant by the deemed disposal being a disposal of 'the relevant underlying assets'. In most cases where the interest which triggers the disposal is an interest in the whole of the settled property, the disposal is of the whole or part of each of the assets comprised in the settled property. If, however, the interest is an interest in a defined part of the settled property, the disposal is of the whole or part of each of the assets comprised in that defined part. Thus, where the interest disposed of is a right in relation to a specific fund or other defined part of the settled property, the deemed disposal is of the whole or part of each of the assets comprised in that fund or part.

In either case, the whole of each asset concerned is disposed of unless the interest is an interest in a specific fraction or amount of the income or capital of the settled property, a specific fund or other defined part of the settled property in question. In this case, the deemed disposal is of a corresponding part of each of those assets disposed of. In any other case the deemed disposal is of the whole of each of the assets so comprised.

The above rules are modified (Sched 4A, para 13(4)(a)) where the identity of the underlying assets changes during the period between the beginning of the disposal and its effective completion (para 8(3)). Where part only of an asset is comprised in a specific fund or other defined part of the settled property, that part of the asset is treated as if it were a separate asset (para 8(4)).

Character of deemed disposal
(TCGA 1992, Sched 4A, para 9)

The deemed disposal is taken to be for a consideration equal to the whole or, as the case may be, a corresponding part of the market value of each of the assets concerned, and to be a disposal under a bargain at arm's length. The above rules are modified (see Sched 4A, para 13(4)(b)) where the value of the assets changes during the period between the beginning of the disposal and its effective completion (para 9(2)).

Avoidance of double counting
(TCGA 1992, Sched 4A, para 10)

The following rule prevents a double tax charge arising where the disposal of the interest is not exempt from CGT (or corporation tax on chargeable gains) under TCGA 1992, s 76(1) (disposals of interests in settled property), and the disposal triggers a deemed disposal of the underlying assets. Its effect, broadly, is to maximise the net chargeable gain or, if there is no net gain, minimise the net allowable loss by securing that the provision which would maximise the gain or, as the case may be, minimise the loss has effect and that the other does not.

This is achieved by defining a 'chargeable disposal' for this purpose as one in relation to which TCGA 1992, s 76(1) (disposals of interests in settled property) does not apply.

If there would be a chargeable gain on disposal of the interest in the settlement, then:

(1) if the chargeable gain on disposal would be greater than the net chargeable gain on the deemed disposal, or there would be no net chargeable gain on the deemed disposal, the rules for the deemed disposal of the underlying assets do not apply; and

(2) in any other case, such provisions as to a deemed disposal apply and no chargeable gain is treated as arising on the disposal of the interest in the settlement.

If there would be an allowable loss on the disposal of the interest in the settlement, then:

(1) if there would be a greater net allowable loss on the deemed disposal, the rules for the deemed disposal of the underlying assets do not apply; and

(2) in any other case, such provisions as to a deemed disposal apply.

If there would be neither a chargeable gain nor an allowable loss on the disposal of the interest in the settlement, then:

(1) if there would be a net allowable loss on the deemed disposal, the provisions as to a deemed disposal of the underlying assets do not apply; and

(2) in any other case, such provisions as to a deemed disposal apply.

For these purposes:

(1) there is a net chargeable gain on a deemed disposal if the aggregate of the chargeable gains accruing to the trustees in relation to the assets involved exceeds the aggregate of the allowable losses so accruing; and

(2) there is a net allowable loss on a deemed disposal if the aggregate of the allowable losses accruing to the trustees in respect of the assets involved exceeds the aggregate of the chargeable gains so accruing.

Recovery of tax from person disposing of the interest
(TCGA 1992, Sched 4A, para 11)

The trustees are entitled to recover tax which they have paid as a result of the deemed disposal of the underlying assets of a settlement from the person who disposed of the interest in the settlement. This applies where chargeable gains accrue to the trustees on the deemed disposal and:

(1) tax becomes chargeable on and is paid by the trustees in relation to those gains, or

(2) a person who is a settlor in relation to the settlement recovers from the trustees (under TCGA 1992, s 78) an amount of tax in respect of those gains.

The trustees may require an inspector to give that person a certificate specifying the amount of the gains in question, and the amount of tax that has been paid. Any such certificate is conclusive evidence of the facts stated in it.

Meaning of 'settlor'
(TCGA 1992, s 79(1) and (3)–(5), and Sched 4A, para 12)

A person is a settlor in relation to a settlement if the settled property consists of or includes property originating from him. This comprises:

(1) property which that settlor has provided directly or indirectly for the purposes of the settlement;

(2) property representing that property; and

(3) so much of any property which represents both property so provided and other property as, on a just apportionment, represents the property so provided.

Property which a settlor has provided directly or indirectly includes property so provided directly or indirectly by another person under reciprocal arrangements with that settlor. This does not include property which that settlor has provided directly or indirectly under reciprocal arrangements with another person. Property which represents other property includes property which represents accumulated income from that other property.

Where period between beginning of disposal and effective completion exists
(TCGA 1992, Sched 4A, para 13)

The beginning of the disposal is, in the case of a disposal involving the exercise of an option, when the option is granted, and in any other case of a disposal under a contract, when the contract is entered into. The effective completion of the disposal is the point at which the person acquiring the interest becomes for practical purposes unconditionally entitled to the whole of the intended subject-matter of the disposal.

Where these rules apply and the beginning of the disposal and its effective completion fall in different tax years:

(1) the deemed disposal is treated as taking place in the tax year in which the disposal is effectively completed;

(2) the condition as to the residence of trustees is treated as met if it is met

in four of those tax years or any intervening year;

(3) the condition as to the residence of the settlor is treated as met if it is met in relation to either or both of those tax years or any intervening year; and

(4) the relevant period as to the condition as to the settlor's interest is that beginning two years before the beginning of the first of those tax years, and ending with the effective completion of the disposal.

If the identity or value of the underlying assets changes during the period between the beginning of the disposal and its effective completion, the following provisions apply:

(1) an asset is treated as comprised in the settled property and, where relevant, in any specific fund or other defined part of the settled property to which the deemed disposal relates if it is so comprised at any time in that period; and

(2) the market value of any asset for the purposes of the deemed disposal is taken to be its highest market value at any time during that period.

However, this does not apply to an asset if during that period it is disposed of by the trustees under a bargain at arm's length and is not reacquired.

Exception: maintenance funds for historic buildings
(TCGA 1992, Sched 4A, para 14)

The special rules for the deemed disposal of underlying assets do not apply where an election has been made (under TA 1988, s 691(2)) for income of the settlement to be applied for the maintenance of historic buildings.

23.2.10 Transfers of value by trustees linked with trustee borrowing
(TCGA 1992, ss 76B and 85A, Scheds 4B and 4C)

Two new sets of rules have been introduced with effect for transfers of value where the material time falls after 20 March 2000. As a result a CGT charge arises where trustees make a transfer of value to another person and the transfer is treated as linked with trustee borrowing. TCGA 1992, Sched 4B requires that each chargeable asset which remains part of the settled property after the transfer is deemed to be disposed of and reacquired by the trustees at market value. Schedule 4C attributes gains to beneficiaries where gains accrue to offshore trustees following the Sched 4B rules. Payments or benefits received by beneficiaries of that trust, or any transferee trust, are taken into account in charging the beneficiaries on gains arising on that transfer of value.

These provisions counter an avoidance device, commonly known as a 'flip flop', for extracting gains from a trust tax free using borrowed money. The device has been used to avoid tax in two situations.

First, tax is payable by the settlor of a trust. Where a UK-resident settlor retained an interest in the capital or income of a trust (irrespective of whether it is a resident or non-resident trust), an amount equal to the trustees' capital gains is chargeable on that person. This charge was avoided in the following way. The trustees borrowed money on the security of assets in the trust and advanced the money to another person, usually the trustees of another trust in which the settlor of the first trust had an interest. The settlor then severed his interest in the first trust. In the following tax year the trustees of the first trust sold the assets and used the proceeds to repay the debt. The settlor received his money from the second trust. If the device was successful, the gains could not be charged on the settlor because in the tax year that they were realised the settlor no longer had an interest in the first trust. In the case of a UK trust, the trustees are charged at the rate applicable to trusts (34 per cent) on the gains instead of the settlor being charged at his marginal 40 per cent tax rate.

The second situation was where UK-resident beneficiaries of an offshore trust received capital payments and were chargeable to tax on gains realised by the trustees. In this situation, the borrowing by the trustees and transfer of funds from the trust enabled the beneficiaries to receive capital payments from another trust which has not realised the gains. The purpose of this arrangement was to ensure that the UK beneficiaries paid no tax on the benefits they received from the realised gains.

The rules set out in Sched 4B counter the flip flop by providing that gains on chargeable assets remaining in the trust are crystallised in the hands of trustees. This happens if the trustees transfer value out of the trust when they have outstanding debt and the proceeds from that debt have not been wholly used for normal trust purposes. A 'transfer of value' is, broadly, the transfer or lending of money or any other asset by the trustees to another person. The gains are crystallised because the trustees are deemed to dispose of the whole or part of each of the chargeable assets remaining in the trust after the transfer and to reacquire them immediately at market value. A part of an asset is deemed to be disposed of where the amount of value transferred by the trustees is less than the total value of all the chargeable assets remaining in the trust after the transfer which is not attributable to trustee borrowing. Gifts hold-over relief cannot be claimed to relieve the gains arising on the deemed disposal.

There is, however, no deemed disposal and reacquisition if the proceeds of borrowing are wholly used for normal trust purposes. Trustees apply the proceeds for such purposes if they:

(1) make qualifying payments in respect of ordinary trust assets that are still held by the trustees after the transfer of value is made;

(2) discharge a loan obligation where the proceeds of borrowing have been wholly (or almost wholly) used for normal trust purposes; or

(3) make a payment to meet bona fide current expenses in administering the trust or any of the settled property.

For this purpose, 'ordinary trust assets' are shares, securities, tangible property (whether movable or immovable) and any property used for the purposes of a trade, profession or vocation carried on by the trustees or any beneficiary with an interest in possession in the settled property.

These rules apply to all trusts, except UK trusts in which the settlor does not have an interest. A UK settlor of a trust will be charged in respect of the resulting gains where existing rules provide for it. Further rules set out in Sched 4C charge the gains in the case of a non-resident trust where a UK-resident settlor does not have an interest and gains cannot be charged on the settlor.

UK-resident beneficiaries of offshore trusts who receive certain payments or benefits ('capital payments') from the trustees may be charged to CGT in respect of gains realised by the trustees. The tax due under this charge may be increased by a 'supplementary charge' where there is a delay between the gains arising to the trustees and a payment being made to the beneficiary. These rules are contained in TCGA 1992, ss 87–98.

The new Sched 4C replaces those rules in relation to gains arising under the new Sched 4B. It provides that those who benefit from the transferor settlement or, where funds are transferred to another trust, the transferee settlement, are charged to tax on the gains realised by the transferor trustees on the transfer of value under Sched 4B in appropriate circumstances. Broadly, a charge may arise where:

(1) a UK-resident beneficiary receives a capital payment which exceeds any gains realised by the trustees which fall within the special rules in ss 87–98; and

(2) there is an amount of gains arising under the new Sched 4B in relation to which the settlement from which the capital payment was made is a transferor or transferee settlement.

The Sched 4B rules

General scheme
(TCGA 1992, Sched 4B, para 1)

The rules described below apply where the trustees of a settlement make a transfer of value in a tax year in which the settlement is within TCGA 1992, ss 77, 86 or 87, and under these rules the transfer of value is treated as linked with trustee borrowing. Where these rules apply the trustees are treated as disposing of and immediately reacquiring the whole or a proportion of each of the chargeable assets that continue to form part of the settled property. The new rules apply to any transfers of value in relation to which the material time falls after 20 March 2000.

Transfers of value
(TCGA 1992, Sched 4B, para 2)

The trustees of a settlement make a transfer of value if they:

(1) lend money or any other asset to any person;
(2) transfer an asset to any person and receive either no consideration or a consideration the amount or value of which is less than the market value of the asset transferred; or
(3) issue a security of any description to any person and receive either no consideration or a consideration the amount or value of which is less than the value of the security.

The 'material time', in relation to a transfer of value, is the time when the loan is made, the transfer is effectively completed or the security is issued. The effective completion of a transfer is the point at which the person acquiring the asset becomes, for practical purposes, unconditionally entitled to the whole of the intended subject-matter of the transfer. In the case of a loan, the amount of value transferred is the asset's market value. In the case of a transfer, the amount of value transferred is:

(1) if any part of the asset's value is attributable to trustee borrowing, the asset's market value; or
(2) if no part of the asset's value is attributable to trustee borrowing, the asset's market value reduced by the amount or value of any consideration received for it.

See below for what is meant by the value of an asset being attributable to trustee borrowing.

In the case of the issue of a security, the amount of value transferred is the value of the security reduced by the amount or value of any consideration received by the trustees for it.

The value of an asset is its value immediately before the material time, unless the asset does not exist before that time in which case its value immediately after that time is taken.

Settlements within TCGA 1992, s 77, 86 or 87
(TCGA 1992, Sched 4B, para 3)

Various categories of settlement fall within the scope of Sched 4B. Broadly, they consist in trusts which can fall within the scope of s 77, 86 or 87. These are, in effect, trusts in which a UK settlor has an interest and offshore trusts which have one or more UK beneficiaries.

A settlement is 'within section 77' (charge on settlor with interest in settlement) in a tax year if, assuming that:

(1) there were chargeable gains accruing to the trustees from the disposal of any or all of the settled property, and
(2) after making any deduction for allowable losses of the same year or of

earlier years remaining unrelieved in respect of disposals of the settled property there remains an amount on which the trustees would, disregarding the annual exempt amount, be chargeable to tax for the year in respect of those gains,

chargeable gains would thereunder be treated as accruing to the settlor in that year. A settlement is 'within section 86' in a tax year if, assuming that:

(1) there were chargeable gains accruing to the trustees on disposals of any of the settled property originating from the settlor, and
(2) there is an amount on which the trustees would be chargeable to tax after deducting allowable losses of the same year or of earlier years remaining unrelieved on the assumption that the trustees are resident or ordinarily resident in the UK throughout the year,

chargeable gains would thereunder be treated as accruing to the settlor in that year. A settlement is 'within section 87' in a tax year if, assuming that:

(1) there were trust gains for the year accruing to beneficiaries, and
(2) beneficiaries of the settlement received capital payments from the trustees in that year or had received such payments in an earlier year,

chargeable gains would, under the rules for migrant settlements (see below), be treated as accruing to the beneficiaries in that year.

Trustee borrowing
(TCGA 1992, Sched 4B, para 4)

The circumstances in which, for Sched 4B purposes, the trustees of a settlement are treated as borrowing are set out below. These are not restricted to cases where the trustees are lent money or other assets, but also include cases where an asset is transferred to the trustees and they assume a contractual, as distinct from a fiduciary, obligation to restore or transfer it (or any other asset) to any person. In these rules the term 'loan obligation' includes such obligations. The amount borrowed (here referred to as the 'proceeds' of the borrowing) in any case of this latter sort is the market value of the asset concerned reduced by any consideration received for it.

The trustees of a settlement are treated as borrowing if:

(1) money or any other asset is lent to them; or
(2) an asset is transferred to them and in connection with the transfer the trustees assume a contractual obligation (whether absolute or conditional) to restore or transfer to any person that or any other asset.

The 'proceeds' of the borrowing are taken to be:

(1) in the case of a loan, the asset's market value;
(2) in the case of a transfer, the asset's market value reduced by the amount or value of any consideration received for it.

Here an asset's market value is its market value immediately before the loan is made, or the transfer is effectively completed, unless the asset does not exist before that time in which case it is the market value immediately after that time is taken. The effective completion of a transfer means the point at which the person acquiring the asset becomes for practical purposes unconditionally entitled to the whole of the intended subject-matter of the transfer.

Transfer linked with trustee borrowing
(TCGA 1992, Sched 4B, para 5)

A transfer of value by trustees is treated as linked with trustee borrowing if at the material time there is outstanding trustee borrowing. There is outstanding trustee borrowing at any time to the extent that:

(1) any loan obligation is outstanding; and
(2) there are proceeds of trustee borrowing that have not been either applied for normal trust purposes or taken into account hereunder in relation to an earlier transfer of value.

An amount of trustee borrowing is 'taken into account' in relation to a transfer of value if such transfer is treated as linked with trustee borrowing. The amount so taken into account is that of the value transferred by that transfer of value or, if less, the amount of outstanding trustee borrowing at the material time in relation to that transfer of value.

Application of proceeds of borrowing for normal trust purposes
(TCGA 1992, Sched 4B, para 6)

The circumstances in which the proceeds of trustee borrowing are treated as applied for normal trust purposes are as follows, and not otherwise:

(1) Such proceeds are applied for normal trust purposes if they are applied by the trustees in making a payment in respect of an ordinary trust asset and the following conditions are met:
   (a) the payment is made under a transaction at arm's length or is not more than the payment that would be made if the transaction were at arm's length;
   (b) the asset forms part of the settled property immediately after the material time or, if it does not do so, the alternative condition for assets no longer part of the settled property is met; and
   (c) the sum paid is allowable (under TCGA 1992, s 38) as a deduction in computing a gain accruing to the trustees on a disposal of the asset (or but for s 17 (disposals and acquisitions treated as made at market value) or 39 (exclusion of expenditure by reference to tax on income) would be so deductible).
(2) Such proceeds are applied for normal trust purposes if:
   (a) they are applied by the trustees in wholly or partly discharging a loan obligation of the trustees, and

(b) the whole of the proceeds of the borrowing connected with that obligation (or all but an insignificant amount) have been applied by the trustees for normal trust purposes.

(3) Such proceeds are applied for normal trust purposes if they are applied by the trustees in making payments to meet bona fide current expenses incurred by them in administering the settlement or any of the settled property.

Ordinary trust assets
(TCGA 1992, Sched 4B, para 7)

The following are 'ordinary trust assets' for the purposes of these rules:

(1) shares or securities (TCGA 1992, s 132);
(2) tangible property, whether movable or immovable, or a lease of such property;
(3) property not within (1) or (2) which is used for the purposes of a trade, profession or vocation carried on by the trustees, or by a beneficiary who has an interest in possession in the settled property; and
(4) any right in or over, or any interest in, property of a description within (2) or (3).

Alternative condition for assets no longer part of settled property
(TCGA 1992, Sched 4B, para 8)

The alternative condition under TCGA 1992, s 24(1) in relation to an asset which no longer forms part of the settled property is that:

(1) the asset is treated as having been lost or destroyed or as becoming of negligible value, or
(2) one or more ordinary trust assets which, taken together directly or indirectly, represent the asset form part of the settled property immediately after the material time, or are treated as having been lost or destroyed or as becoming of negligible value.

Normal trust purposes: power to make regulations
(TCGA 1992, Sched 4B, para 9)

The Treasury may introduce regulations as to the circumstances in which the proceeds of trustee borrowing are to be treated for these purposes as applied for normal trust purposes, and these regulations may add to, amend or repeal any of the provisions of Sched 4B, paras 6–8 above, make different provision for different cases, and contain such supplementary, incidental, consequential and transitional provision as the Treasury may think fit.

Deemed transfer of remaining chargeable assets
(TCGA 1992, Sched 4B, para 10)

Where a transfer of value by trustees is treated as linked with trustee borrowing, the trustees are treated for all CGT purposes as having at the material time disposed of, and as having immediately reacquired, the whole or a proportion (see below) of each of the chargeable assets that form part of the settled property immediately after the material time (here referred to as 'the remaining chargeable assets'). The deemed disposal and reacquisition is taken to be for a consideration equal to the whole or, as the case may be, a proportion of the market value of each of those assets, and to be under a bargain at arm's length.

An asset is a chargeable asset if a gain on its disposal by the trustees at the material time would be a chargeable gain. Gifts hold-over relief under TCGA 1992, s 165 or 260 cannot be claimed on such a disposal because its availability is restricted to non-arm's length disposals.

This rule provides for determining whether the deemed disposal and reacquisition is of the whole or a proportion of each of the remaining chargeable assets

Whether deemed disposal is of the whole or a proportion of the assets
(TCGA 1992, Sched 4B, para 11)

If the amount of value transferred is less than that of outstanding trustee borrowing, and is also less than the effective value of the remaining chargeable assets, the deemed disposal and reacquisition is of the proportion of each of the remaining chargeable assets given by:

$$\frac{VT}{EV}$$

where: VT = the amount of value transferred, and
         EV = the effective value of the remaining chargeable assets.

If the amount of value transferred is not less than the amount of outstanding trustee borrowing, but is less than the effective value of the remaining chargeable assets, the deemed disposal and reacquisition is of the proportion of each of the remaining chargeable assets given by:

$$\frac{TB}{EV}$$

where: TB = the amount of outstanding trustee borrowing, and
         EV = the effective value of the remaining chargeable assets.

In any other case the deemed disposal and reacquisition is of the whole of each of the remaining chargeable assets. The effective value of the remaining chargeable assets is the aggregate market value of those assets reduced by so much of that value as is attributable to the trustee.

References here to amounts or values, except in relation to the amount of value transferred, are to amounts or values immediately after the material time.

Value attributable to trustee borrowing
(TCGA 1992, Sched 4B, para 12)

The value of an asset is attributable to trustee borrowing to the extent determined in accordance with the following rules.

Where the asset itself has been borrowed by trustees, the asset's value is attributable to trustee borrowing to the extent that the proceeds of that borrowing have not been applied for normal trust purposes. This is in addition to any extent to which the asset's value may be attributable to trustee borrowing as described here.

The value of any asset is attributable to trustee borrowing to the extent that:

(1) the trustees have applied the proceeds of trustee borrowing in acquiring or enhancing the asset's value, or
(2) the asset represents directly or indirectly an asset the value of which was attributable to the trustees having so applied the proceeds of trustee borrowing.

An amount is applied by the trustees in acquiring or enhancing the value of an asset if it is applied wholly and exclusively by them:

(1) as consideration in money or money's worth for the acquisition of the asset;
(2) for the purpose of enhancing the asset's value in a way that is reflected in the state or nature of the asset;
(3) in establishing, preserving or defending their title to, or to a right over, the asset; or
(4) where the asset is a holding of shares or securities (under TCGA 1992, s 132) that is treated as a single asset, by way of consideration in money or money's worth for additional shares or securities forming part of the same holding.

Trustees are treated as applying the proceeds of borrowing if and to the extent that at the time the expenditure is incurred there is outstanding trustee borrowing.

Assets and transfers
(TCGA 1992, Sched 4B, para 13)

Any reference to an asset includes money expressed in sterling. References to the asset's value or market value are to its amount.

References here to the transfer of an asset include anything that is or is treated as a disposal of the asset for CGT or would be if the above rule applied generally for such purposes. However, such references do not include a transfer of an asset that is created by the part disposal of another asset.

Thus, the normal meaning of 'asset' (under TCGA 1992, s 21) is extended to include money expressed in sterling, and that references to the value or market value of such an asset are to its amount. The 'transfer of an asset' has a very wide meaning and includes anything which is, or is treated as, the 'disposal' of an asset for CGT purposes. In particular, this means that a part disposal of an asset is treated as a transfer of the asset. Where an asset is created by the part disposal of another asset, however, the created asset is not treated as transferred for the purposes of the above rules. Thus, for example, if the trustees of a settlement own a freehold interest in land and grant a leasehold interest in the land to another person, the asset they are treated as transferring to that person for the purposes of the above rules is the freehold interest rather than the leasehold interest.

23.2.11 Transfers of value: attribution of gains to beneficiaries
(TCGA 1992, s 85A and Sched 4C)

New rules deal with the attribution of gains to beneficiaries, which run in parallel with those relating to transfers of value by trustees that are treated as linked with trustee borrowing. The new rules apply to any transfers of value where the material time falls after 20 March 2000.

Introduction
(TCGA 1992, Sched 4C, para 1)

Schedule 4C applies where a chargeable gain or allowable loss has accrued (under TCGA 1992, s 87) to offshore trustees on a transfer of value made by them which falls within the new rules for transfers of value by trustees linked with trustee borrowing (Sched 4B). An offshore trust is one where the trustees are either not resident in the UK or, if they are resident, are treated for the purposes of a double taxation agreement as resident in a territory outside the UK ('treaty non-resident'; ss 87(1) and 88(1)).

Schedule 4C applies to charge beneficiaries on certain gains accruing to offshore trustees following a transfer of value made by them which falls within the new rules regarding trustee borrowing under Sched 4B (see

23.2.10) in place of the general rules for charging beneficiaries in respect of gains realised by offshore trustees, set out in TCGA 1992, ss 86A–95. No account is taken of:

(1) any such chargeable gain or allowable loss in computing the trust gains for a tax year under ss 87–89; or

(b) any chargeable gain or allowable loss to which ss 87–89 apply in computing the Sched 4B trust gains under the Sched 4C rules.

This effectively ringfences Sched 4B trust gains from the general charge on beneficiaries in respect of gains realised by offshore trustees and, also, ringfences other gains realised by the trustees from the charge, under Sched 4C, on beneficiaries for Sched 4B trust gains.

General scheme
(TCGA 1992, Sched 4C, para 2)

The general scheme of these rules is that:

(1) Sched 4B trust gains are attributed to beneficiaries of the transferor settlement, or of any transferee settlement, who have received capital payments from the trustees; and

(2) any allowable loss accruing under Sched 4B may only be set against a chargeable gain so accruing.

Computation of Sched 4B trust gains
(TCGA 1992, Sched 4C, para 3)

Schedule 4B trust gains are computed separately for each transfer of value to which that Schedule applies. The amount of a Sched 4B trust gain is given by the formula:

$$CA - SG - AL$$

where: CA = the chargeable amount computed as set out below;
SG = the amount of any gains attributed to the settlor (see below); and
AL = the amount of any allowable losses that may be deducted (see below).

Briefly, any sums attributed to a settlor and any allowable losses are deducted from the 'chargeable amount' to arrive at the Sched 4B trust gains.

Chargeable amount: non-resident settlement
(TCGA 1992, Sched 4C, para 4)

If the transfer of value is made in a tax year during which the trustees of the transferor settlement are at no time resident or ordinarily resident in the UK the chargeable amount is that on which the trustees would have been chargeable to tax under TCGA 1992, s 2(2) and Sched 4B if they had been UK-resident or ordinarily resident in the year.

Chargeable amount: dual resident settlement
(TCGA 1992, Sched 4C, para 5)

This form of computation is modified if the transfer of value is made in a tax year where:

(1) the trustees of the transferor settlement are UK-resident during any part of the year or UK-ordinarily resident during the year, and
(2) at any time of such residence or ordinary residence they are regarded under any double taxation relief arrangements as resident in a territory outside the UK.

In this event, the chargeable amount is the lesser of:

(1) the amount on which the trustees would be chargeable to tax under TCGA 1992, s 2(2) and Sched 4B on the assumption that the double taxation relief arrangements did not apply, and
(2) the amount on which the trustees would be so chargeable to tax on disposals of protected assets.

In this context, assets are protected assets if they are of a description specified in the double taxation relief arrangements, and were the trustees to dispose of them at any relevant time, the trustees would, under the arrangements, not be liable in the UK to tax on gains accruing to them on the disposal (TCGA 1992, s 88(4)).

Gains attributed to settlor
(TCGA 1992, Sched 4C, para 6)

The chargeable amount in relation to a transfer of value is reduced by the amount of any chargeable gains arising by virtue of that transfer of value that:

(1) are chargeable gains of an amount equal to that on which the trustees would be chargeable to tax for the year under TCGA 1992, s 2(2) if it is assumed that the trustees are UK-resident or ordinarily resident throughout the year; and that the double taxation relief arrangements do not apply. (Note that such gains are treated as forming the highest part of the amount on which the beneficiary concerned is chargeable to

CGT for the year.) In this computation the amount of chargeable gains arising on a transfer of value is treated as accruing to the settlor; any losses which arise otherwise than under Sched 4B are disregarded;

(2) where TCGA 1992, s 10A (special rules for temporary non-residents) applies, are chargeable gains treated thereunder (as it is applied to the attribution of gains to a settlor (see below) as accruing to the settlor in the year of return.

In computing the chargeable amount in relation to a transfer of value, the effect of TCGA 1992, ss 77–79 (charge on settlor with an interest in settlement) are ignored.

Reduction for allowable losses
(TCGA 1992, Sched 4C, para 7)

An allowable loss arising under Sched 4B on a transfer of value by the trustees of a settlement is taken into account to reduce the chargeable amount in relation to another transfer of value by those trustees. Any such allowable loss goes first to reduce chargeable amounts arising from other transfers of value made in the same tax year. If there is more than one chargeable amount and the aggregate amount of the allowable losses is less than the aggregate of the chargeable amounts, each of the chargeable amounts is reduced proportionately.

If in any tax year the aggregate amount of the allowable losses exceeds the aggregate of the chargeable amounts, the excess is carried forward to the next tax year and treated as if it were an allowable loss arising on a transfer of value made in that year.

Any reduction of a chargeable amount required under this rule is made after any deduction under the rule for gains attributed to settlors.

Attribution of gains to beneficiaries
(TCGA 1992, Sched 4C, paras 8 and 9)

Schedule 4B trust gains on a transfer of value are treated as chargeable gains accruing to beneficiaries of the transferor settlement, and of any transferee settlement, by the following rules.

Such trust gains are treated as chargeable gains accruing to beneficiaries who receive capital payments from the trustees in the tax year in which the transfer of value is made, or who have received such payments in any earlier year, to the extent that such payments exceed the amount of any gains attributed to the beneficiaries under TCGA 1992, s 87(4) (attribution of gains to beneficiaries) or 89(2) (attribution of gains to beneficiaries of migrant settlements). This attribution of chargeable gains to beneficiaries is made in proportion to, but cannot exceed, the amounts of the capital payments received by them.

Any Sched 4B trust gains remaining after this rule has been applied in the tax year in which the transfer of value was made is carried forward to the following tax year and treated as if they were gains from a transfer of value made in that year. A capital payment is left out of account:

(1) for the above purposes, to the extent that chargeable gains have, because of it, been treated as accruing to the recipient in an earlier tax year; and

(2) for the purposes of s 87(4) or 89(2), to the extent that chargeable gains have, because of it, been treated as accruing to the recipient as above.

A beneficiary is not charged to tax on chargeable gains treated as above as accruing to him in any year unless he is domiciled in the UK at some time in that year.

For these purposes capital payments received before 21 March 2000, or before the tax year preceding that in which the transfer of value is made, are disregarded.

Residence of trustees from whom capital payment is received
(TCGA 1992, Sched 4C, para 10)

It is immaterial for the above purposes that the trustees of the transferor settlement, or any transferee settlement, are or have at any time been UK-resident or ordinarily resident. A capital payment received by a beneficiary of a settlement from the trustees in a tax year during the whole of which the trustees are UK-resident, or in which the trustees are UK-ordinarily resident, is disregarded for the above purposes if it was made before, but not made in anticipation of, chargeable gains accruing under Sched 4B or of a transfer of value being made to which Sched 4B applies. For this purpose the trustees of a settlement are not regarded as UK-resident or ordinarily resident at any time when they fall to be regarded for the purposes of any double taxation relief arrangements as resident in a territory outside the UK.

Taper relief
(TCGA 1992, Sched 4C, para 11)

Even though Sched 4C requires TCGA 1992, s 2A (taper relief) to be applied in the computation of the amount of Sched 4B trust gains, chargeable gains that are treated as accruing to beneficiaries under TCGA 1992, Sched 4C are not eligible for taper relief.

Attribution of gains to settlor in s 10A cases
(TCGA 1992, Sched 4C, para 12)

The rule described below applies where under TCGA 1992, s 10A (temporary non-residents) an amount of gains arising under Sched 4B in an intervening year, and because of disposals of any of the settled property originating from the settlor, is an amount on which the trustees would be chargeable to tax for the year under TCGA 1992, s 2(2). If it is assumed that the trustees are UK-resident or ordinarily resident throughout the year, or that double taxation relief arrangements do not apply, the amount would (otherwise) be treated as accruing to 'the settlor' in the year of return.

Where this rule applies, only so much (if any) of the Sched 4B trust gains as described above as exceeds the amount charged to beneficiaries falls under the rules for temporary non-residents (s 10A) to be attributed to the settlor for the year of return.

The 'amount charged to beneficiaries' is the total of the amounts on which beneficiaries of the transferor or transferee settlements are charged to tax under Sched 4C by reference to those gains for all the intervening years. Where the property comprised in the transferor settlement has at any time included property not originating from the settlor, only so much (if any) of any capital payment taken into account by way of attribution of gains to beneficiaries as, on a just and reasonable apportionment, is properly referable to property originating from the settlor is taken into account in computing the amount charged to beneficiaries.

Increase in tax payable under Sched 4C
(TCGA 1992, Sched 4C, para 13)

This rule applies where:

(1) a capital payment is made by the trustees of a settlement;
(2) the payment is made in circumstances where there is an attribution of gains to beneficiaries so that chargeable gains are deemed to accrue in relation to the payment; and
(3) a beneficiary is thereby charged to tax on the payment.

The tax payable by the beneficiary on such payment is increased by the amount found below, except that it cannot be increased beyond the amount of the payment. An assessment may charge tax accordingly.

The amount is one equal to the interest that would be yielded if an amount equal to the tax which otherwise would be payable by the beneficiary on the payment carried interest for the chargeable period at a rate of 10 per cent pa (TCGA 1992, s 91(3)).

The chargeable period is that which begins with the later of the two days specified below, and ends with 30 November in the tax year following that in which the capital payment is made. The two days are:

(1) 1 December in the tax year following that in which the transfer of value was made; and
(2) 1 December falling six years before 1 December in the tax year following that in which the capital payment is made.

Interpretation
(TCGA 1992, Sched 4C, para 14)

In Sched 4C, 'transfer of value' has the same meaning as in Sched 4B. References to the time at which a transfer of value was made are to the material time for the purposes of Sched 4B.

In relation to a transfer of value, references to the transferor settlement are to the settlement the trustees of which made the transfer of value; and references to a transferee settlement are to any settlement of which the settled property includes property representing, directly or indirectly, the proceeds of the transfer of value.

References here to beneficiaries of a settlement include persons who have ceased to be beneficiaries by the time the chargeable gains accrue; and include persons who were beneficiaries of the settlement before it ceased to exist, but who were beneficiaries of the settlement at a time in a previous tax year when a capital payment was made to them.

23.2.12 Charge on settlor with interest in settlement
(TCGA 1992, ss 77–79)

The trustees of a settlement are not chargeable to CGT in the following circumstances:

(1) at any time during the year the settlor or his spouse has an interest in the settlement;

(2) chargeable gains accrue to the trustees of a settlement from the disposal of any or all of the settled property; and

(3) after deducting any allowable losses of the same or any earlier tax year (under TCGA 1992, s 2(2)) in relation to disposals of the settled property there remains an amount on which the trustees would, ignoring any annual exempt amount available (s 3 and Sched 1), be chargeable to CGT for the year on those gains.

It will be appreciated that chargeable gains are subject to CGT at income tax rates, with gains of a non-discretionary trust taxed at 24 per cent. The CGT rate on the gains of a discretionary trust is 34 per cent. Were it not for the rules set out in s 77, it would be possible for taxpayers to avoid the 40 per cent CGT rate on their personal gains by having the assets held by trusts of which they or their spouses were the beneficiaries.

For this reason, for trusts where the settlor or his spouse has an interest, chargeable gains of an amount equal to the gains remaining after deducting any allowable losses of the same or any earlier tax year in relation to disposals of the settled property, but ignoring any annual exempt amount available to the trust are treated as accruing to the settlor in that year.

A settlor is regarded as having an interest in a settlement if any property comprised in it, or any derived property is, or will or may become, payable to or applicable for the benefit of the settlor or his spouse in any circumstances whatsoever, or the settlor or his spouse enjoys a benefit deriving directly or indirectly from any property which is comprised in the settlement or any derived property. References here to the settlor's spouse do not include:

(1) a person to whom the settlor is not for the time being married but may later marry, or
(2) a spouse from whom the settlor is separated under court order, or under a separation agreement or in such circumstances that the separation is likely to be permanent, or
(3) the settlor's widow(er).

A settlor is not regarded as having such an interest in a settlement if and so long as none of the property which may at any time be comprised in the settlement, and no derived property, can become payable or applicable except in the event of:

(1) the bankruptcy of some person who is or may become beneficially entitled to the property or any derived property; or
(2) an assignment of or charge on the property or any derived property being made or given by some such person; or
(3) in the case of a marriage settlement, the death of both parties to, and of all or any of the children of, the marriage; or
(4) the death of a child of the settlor who had become beneficially entitled to the property or any derived property at an age not exceeding 25.

Also, a settlor is not regarded as having such an interest in a settlement if and so long as some person is alive and under age 25 during whose life the property or any derived property cannot become so payable or applicable except in the event of that person becoming bankrupt or assigning or charging his interest in that property.

These rules do not apply where the settlor dies during the year. Nor do they apply where the spouse dies, or the settlor and the spouse cease to be married, during the year, in a case where the settlor is regarded as having an interest in the settlement by reason only of the fact that property is, or will or may become, payable to or applicable for his spouse's benefit, or the fact that a benefit is enjoyed by his spouse.

Chargeable gains hereby treated as accruing to the settlor are not eligible for taper relief (under TCGA 1992, s 2A).

These rules do not apply unless the settlor is, and the trustees are, either UK-resident during any part of the tax year or UK-ordinarily resident during the tax year. ESC D2 provides that a person who becomes or ceases to be UK-resident or ordinarily resident in a tax year is normally not liable to CGT on disposals made before he arrives in the UK or after he has left the UK. However, the application of this concession does not apply to a settlement whose trustees commence or cease residence in the UK during a tax year. Nor does it apply to a settlor who ceases or commences residence during a tax year in relation to the gains of a settlement which are chargeable on him.

If any CGT becomes chargeable on and is paid by a person in relation to trust gains treated as accruing to him, he is entitled to recover the tax so paid from the trustees (see **23.3.12**).

In order to ascertain, for this purpose, the amount of CGT chargeable for any tax year on gains treated as accruing to any settlor, those gains are regarded as forming the highest part of the amount on which he is chargeable to CGT for that tax year. However, if such a person also has gains attributed to him from a non-resident trust, those gains are instead regarded as forming the highest part of the amount on which he is chargeable to CGT for that tax year, and gains attributed from a UK-resident trust are regarded as forming the second highest part.

An Inspector may require any person who is or has been a trustee of, a beneficiary under, or a settlor in relation to a settlement to give him, within such time as he may direct (not being less than 28 days), such particulars as he thinks necessary for these purposes. See also **23.3.16**.

The reference to gains accruing to trustees from the disposal of settled property includes gains treated as accruing to them as gains attributed to members of non-resident companies (under TCGA 1992, s 13); the reference to deductions, in respect of disposals of the settled property, for allowable losses includes deductions on account of losses treated under s 13 as accruing to the trustees.

Where the trustees of a settlement have elected that TA 1988, s 691(2) (certain income of maintenance funds for historic buildings not to be income of settlor etc) is to have effect in the case of any settlement or part of it in a tax year, these rules do not apply in relation to the settlement or part for that tax year.

23.2.13 Restriction on set-off of trust losses
(TCGA 1992, s 79A)

Before 21 March 2000 capital losses accruing to trustees could be used to offset their capital gains. Following changes made to TCGA 1992, s 71 in relation to persons becoming absolutely entitled as against the trustees on occasions after 15 June 1999 (see **23.2.4**), trust losses could be used to offset gains arising outside the trust only in very limited circumstances. Schemes were developed to circumvent these rules by enabling individuals with large potential capital gains to buy into trusts with actual or potential losses. The purpose of the schemes was to avoid tax by transferring the relevant assets into the trust using gifts hold-over relief so that the trust losses could then be used to offset the gains arising on the subsequent disposal of the assets so that no tax was paid. To counter these schemes, s 79A, which applies to gains accruing after 20 March 2000, prevents losses accruing to trustees being set against gains on assets that have been transferred into the trust using gifts hold-over relief where the transferor or a connected person has acquired an interest in the trust and any consideration has passed in connection with the acquisition.

Section 79A creates a restriction on the set-off of losses against capital gains arising on the disposal by trustees of assets transferred to them where gains arising on the transfer have been deferred under a claim for gifts relief. The restriction applies where the transferor of the asset or any connected person has purchased an interest in the trust or entered into any arrangement to purchase such an interest. This restriction applies to gains accruing after 20 March 2000 if the conditions described below are met.

The first condition is that, in computing the gain arising to trustees against which losses cannot be allowed, an amount has been deferred on a gifts relief claim on the transfer of an asset to the trust (under TCGA 1992, ss 165 and 260 (see **24**)). Note, however, that the asset being disposed of need not necessarily be the same asset that was transferred. As a result, in computing the gain the allowable expenditure is reduced, directly or indirectly, to the extent of a claim to gifts relief (under ss 165 and 260) on an earlier disposal to the trustees.

The second condition is that the transferor on that earlier disposal, or any person connected with him, has at any time acquired an interest in the settled property, or entered into an arrangement to acquire such an interest.

The third condition is that the transferor of the asset, or a connected person, must have acquired an interest in the trust for consideration, or consideration must have been received by any person in connection with the acquisition.

Where the rule referred to above applies to a chargeable gain, no allowable losses accruing to the trustees (in the year in which the gain accrues or any earlier year) can be set against the gain. This applies to the whole of the chargeable gain (and not just the element deferred as a result of the claim to gifts relief). References here to losses not being allowed to be set against a chargeable gain are to the losses not being allowed as such a deduction to the extent that they include that gain.

Here, an 'interest in settled property' means any interest created by or arising under a settlement (TCGA 1992, Sched 4A, para 2). This includes any right to, or in connection with, the enjoyment of a benefit created by or arising directly under a settlement, or arising as a result of the exercise of a discretion or power by the trustees of a settlement, or by any person in relation to settled property.

In summary, s 79A applies if the following conditions are met:

(1) a chargeable gain accrues to the trustees;
(2) that gain accrued on the disposal of an asset which the trustees acquired under a gift or other disposal eligible for hold-over relief (the hold-over disposal);
(3) the trustees' allowable expenditure is reduced by the gain on the hold-over disposal having in fact been held over;

(4) the person who made the hold-over disposal (the transferor) or any person connected with him, has at some time acquired or arranged to acquire a beneficial interest in the settled property; and

(5) a person has received or become entitled to receive consideration in connection with that transaction.

Where all of these conditions are met, the chargeable gain accruing to the trustees cannot be set against any trust losses, whether current or brought forward. It is made clear that it is the whole gain which cannot be offset and not just the held-over part.

23.3 MIGRATION OF, NON-RESIDENT AND DUAL RESIDENT SETTLEMENTS

23.3.1 Trustees ceasing to be UK-resident
(TCGA 1992, s 80)

The rules set out below apply if the trustees of a settlement become at any time ('the relevant time') neither resident nor ordinarily resident in the UK, and therefore outside the normal scope of CGT. (See generally **21.13.4**, after Table 21.3.)

On becoming neither resident nor ordinarily resident in the UK, the trustees are subjected to an exit charge. This is achieved by deeming them to dispose of the 'defined assets' (see Glossary for definition) immediately before the relevant time, and immediately reacquire them at their market value at that time.

Rollover relief on replacement of business assets (TCGA 1992, s 152) does not apply where the trustees dispose of the old assets before the relevant time, and acquire the new assets after that time. This exclusion is overridden if, at the time when the new assets are acquired, the trustees are carrying on a trade in the UK through a branch or agency, and any new assets are situated in the UK and either used in or for the purposes of the trade or used or held for the purposes of the branch or agency. In this event the assets are eligible for rollover relief.

23.3.2 Death of trustee: special rules
(TCGA 1992, s 81)

A special rule applies where the deemed disposal and reacquisition of defined assets has occurred (under s 80) as a result of a settlement trustee's death, and within six months after the death, the trustees of the settlement become resident and ordinarily resident in the UK. Section 80 then applies as if the defined assets were restricted to such assets (if any) as would otherwise be defined assets, and fall within either of the descriptions set out below:

(1) assets disposed of by the trustees in the period which begins with the death, and ends when the trustees become resident and ordinarily resident in the UK; or

(2) assets of a description specified in any double taxation relief arrangements, which constitute settled property of the settlement at the time immediately after the trustees become resident and ordinarily resident in the UK and, were they to dispose of them at that time, the trustees would, for the purposes of the arrangements, be regarded as not liable in the UK to CGT on gains so accruing to them.

In these circumstances, the deemed disposal and reacquisition of defined assets applies as if the defined assets were restricted to such assets (if any) as would otherwise be defined assets acquired as a result of a disposal for which business asset gift relief is given (under TCGA 1992, s 165), or for which gift relief on assets subject to IHT is given (under TCGA 1992, s 260(3)).

23.3.3 Past trustees: liability for tax
(TCGA 1992, s 82)

There is special treatment where the deemed disposal and reacquisition of defined assets applies (under s 80) as regards any CGT which is payable by migrating trustees (see generally **21.13.4**, after Table 21.3) is not paid within six months from the time when it became payable. The Revenue may, at any time within three years from when the tax amount is finally determined, serve on certain former trustees a notice:

(1) stating particulars of the tax payable, the amount remaining unpaid and the date when it became payable;

(2) stating particulars of any interest payable on the tax, any amount remaining unpaid and the date when it became payable; and

(3) requiring that person to pay the outstanding amount (and any unpaid interest) within 30 days of the service of the notice.

This applies to any person who, at any time within the relevant period (ie 12 months ending with the relevant time), was a trustee of the settlement. However, it does not apply to any such trustee if he ceased to be such trustee before the end of the relevant period, and he shows that, when he ceased to be a trustee, there was no proposal that the trustees might become neither resident nor ordinarily resident in the UK.

Any CGT which a former trustee is required to pay may be recovered from him as if it were tax due and duly demanded of him. He may recover any such amount paid by him from the migrating trustees. However, such a payment is not allowed as a deduction in computing any income, profits or losses for any tax purposes.

23.3.4 Trustees ceasing to be liable to UK tax
(TCGA 1992, s 83)

A further rule applies if settlement trustees, while continuing to be resident and ordinarily resident in the UK, become at any time trustees who, for double taxation relief purposes, are regarded as:

(1) resident in a territory outside the UK, and
(2) not liable in the UK to CGT on gains accruing on disposals of 'relevant assets' (ie assets which are settled property and fall within descriptions specified in the double taxation arrangements).

In such event, the trustees are deemed to dispose of their relevant assets immediately before the time concerned, and immediately reacquire them at their market value at that time.

23.3.5 Acquisition by dual resident trustees
(TCGA 1992, s 84)

Rollover relief on replacement of business assets (under TCGA 1992, s 152) does not apply where:

(1) the new assets are, or the interest in them is, acquired by the settlement trustees;
(2) at the time of acquisition the trustees are resident and ordinarily resident in the UK but, for double taxation relief purposes, are regarded as resident in a territory outside the UK;
(3) the assets are of a description specified in the double taxation arrangements; and
(4) were the trustees to dispose of the assets immediately after acquisition, the trustees would be regarded for double taxation purposes as not liable in the UK to CGT on gains so accruing to them.

23.3.6 Disposal of interests in non-resident settlements
(TCGA 1992, s 85)

Special CGT rules apply to resident trusts which become non-resident. At the time of emigration there is, broadly, a tax charge on unrealised gains and an uplift to market value of beneficiaries' interests in the trust. The purpose of the uplift is to prevent a potential double charge on any increase in value prior to the trustees' migration of both the trust property (which is charged on exit) and a beneficiary's interest in that property (which is charged if the beneficiary later sells the interest when the trust is non-resident).

These rules have been exploited by non-resident trusts (ie those where the trustees are neither UK-resident nor ordinarily resident). Having realised gains which have not been charged to tax on either the settlor or beneficiaries of the trust ('stockpiled gains'), the trusts are brought onshore and then taken offshore again. The gains on the trust property escape a tax charge because they were realised while the trust was offshore. The beneficiary pays little or no tax on the sale of an interest in the trust because of the rule providing for its value to be uplifted on the trust's exit from the UK.

Revisions to TCGA 1992, which apply where the material time falls after 20 March 2000, thwart such schemes by providing that there is no uplift in the value of any beneficial interest in a trust where, after 20 March 2000, the trustees become non-resident at a time when there are stockpiled gains in the trust, or the trust is a 'transferor or transferee trust' which, under the rules introduced by TCGA 1992, ss 76B, 85A and Scheds 4B and 4C, is required to draw on an amount of TCGA 1992, Sched 4B trust gains (see **23.2.10**).

These revisions do not affect the position of emigrating trusts which do not have stockpiled gains and which are not transferor or transferee trusts.

The revised s 85 provides an exception to the special rules giving an uplift in the acquisition cost for CGT purposes of the value of a beneficiary's interest in a trust where a resident trust becomes non-resident. After 20 March 2000, there is no uplift if, at the time of emigration, the trust had any stockpile of gains which has not been attributed to beneficiaries of the trust. Similarly, there is no uplift where there is an amount of gains in relation to which, under Sched 4C, the trust is either a transferor or transferee settlement and those gains have not been attributed to beneficiaries.

Although, in general, there is no chargeable gain when an original beneficiary disposes of an interest under a settlement, unless he acquired, or derives his title from one who acquired, the interest for a consideration in money or money's worth, other than consideration consisting of another interest under the settlement (s 76(1)), this does not apply to a disposal of an interest in settled property if, at the time of the disposal, the trustees are neither resident nor ordinarily resident in the UK.

Also excluded is anyone who acquires such an interest for money or money's worth, and becomes absolutely entitled as against the trustee. Such a person is deemed to have disposed of it at its market value at that time (s 76(2), under s 71(1) or 87). Accordingly there is no need for a further charge. However, the following rule applies where

(1) there is deemed disposal because the trustees of a settlement become non-resident (s 80);
(2) after the relevant time (under s 80(1)) a person disposes of an interest created by or arising under the settlement and the rule (under s 76(1)) that there is no chargeable gain when an original beneficiary disposes of an interest under a settlement does not apply; and
(3) the interest was created for his benefit, or he otherwise acquired it, before the relevant time (under s 80(1)).

In these circumstances, in the calculation of any chargeable gain accruing on the disposal, the person disposing of it is treated as having disposed of it immediately before the relevant time, and immediately reacquired it at its market value at that time. However, this does not apply if a disposal and reacquisition at market value has been deemed to occur at the time when the trustees, although not then ceasing to be resident and ordinarily resident in the UK, ceased to be liable to UK CGT by reason of a double taxation arrangements (under s 83), and the time concerned (ie when as a result of double taxation arrangements the trustees cease to be liable to UK CGT) fell before the time when the interest was created for the benefit of the person disposing of it or when he otherwise acquired it.

Nor does it apply to the disposal of an interest created by or arising under a settlement which has relevant offshore gains at the material time. The material time in this context is any time at which the trustees of a settlement become neither UK-resident nor ordinarily resident. A settlement has relevant offshore gains at any time if, were the tax year to end at that time, there would be an amount of trust gains which (under s 89(2) (migrant settlements) or Sched 4C, para 8(3) (attribution of gains to beneficiaries)) would be available to be treated as chargeable gains accruing to any beneficiaries of the settlement receiving capital payments in the following tax year.

In addition to the rule outlined at (1)–(3) above, a further rule applies where a disposal and reacquisition at market value has been deemed to occur at the time when the trustees, although not then ceasing to be UK-resident or ordinarily resident, ceased to be liable to UK CGT by reason of double taxation arrangements (s 83), and such time fell within the relevant period. The relevant period here is that which begins when the interest was created for the benefit of the person disposing of it or when he otherwise acquired it, and ends with the relevant time (s 80(1)).

In calculating any chargeable gain accruing on the disposal of the interest, the person disposing of it is treated as having done so immediately before the time found as below and immediately reacquired it at its market value at that time. If this latter basis of calculation is applied, the basis of calculation described above cannot also apply. The time referred to here is the time concerned (where there is only one such time) or the earliest time concerned (where there is more than one such time because the deemed disposal on trustees ceasing to be liable to UK tax under double taxation arrangements under s 83 has applied more than once).

The above does not apply to the disposal of an interest created by or arising under a settlement which has relevant offshore gains at the material time. In this context the material time is the time found, as above. A settlement has relevant offshore gains at any time if, were the tax year to end at that time, there would be an amount of trust gains which (under s 89(2) or Sched 4C, para 8(3)) would be available to be treated as chargeable gains accruing to any beneficiaries of the settlement receiving capital payments in the following tax year.

23.3.7 Attribution of gains to settlors with interest in non-resident or dual resident settlements
(TCGA 1992, s 86)

There are special rules which apply where the following conditions are fulfilled as regards a settlement in a particular tax year of assessment:

(1) the settlement is a qualifying settlement in that tax year;
(2) the settlement trustees fulfil one of the residence conditions specified in (a) and (b) below;
(3) a settlor in relation to the settlement is UK-domiciled at some time in that tax year, and is either UK-resident during any part of that tax year or UK-ordinarily resident during the year;
(4) at any time during the tax year the settlor has an interest in the settlement;
(5) because of disposals of any of the settled property originating from the settlor, there is an amount on which the trustees would be chargeable to tax for the year (under s 2(2)) if the assumption set out below is made;
(6) TCGA 1992, Sched 5, para 3, 4 or 5 (exceptions from s 86) does not prevent these special rules from applying.

The residence conditions are that the trustees are:

(a) not resident or ordinarily resident in the UK during any part of the tax year; or
(b) resident in the UK during any part of the year or ordinarily resident in the UK during the year, but at any time of such residence or ordinary residence they fall to be regarded for double taxation relief purposes as resident in a territory outside the UK.

Where the residence condition applies, the assumption as to residence referred to in (5) above is that the trustees are resident or ordinarily resident in the UK throughout the tax year. Such assumption is also that the double taxation relief arrangements do not apply.

Where these special rules apply, chargeable gains of an amount equal to that referred to in (5) above are treated as accruing to the settlor in the year, and those gains are treated as forming the highest part of the amount on which he is chargeable to CGT for the year.

Chargeable gains hereby treated as accruing to the settlor are not eligible for taper relief under s 2A.

23.3.8 Construction of TCGA 1992, s 86(1)(e)
(TCGA 1992, Sched 5, para 1)

With regard to condition regarding the residence assumptions set out above, the construction of this condition under s 86(1)(e) merits further explanation.

In construing TCGA 1992, s 86(1)(e) as regards a particular tax year, the

381

effect of TCGA 1992, s 3 (annual exempt amount) and ss 77–79 (charge on settlor with an interest in settlement) are ignored. Also, any deductions for allowable losses (under s 2(2)) are made for disposals of any of the settled property originating from the settlor. The prohibition on the allowability of losses in a year in which the person concerned is neither resident nor ordinarily resident (s 16(3)) is not taken as preventing losses accruing to trustees in one tax year from being allowed as a deduction from chargeable gains accruing in a later tax year (so far as not previously set against gains).

In a case where:

(1) the trustees are participators in a company in respect of property which originates from the settlor; and

(2) under the rule attributing gains or losses to members of non-resident companies (s 13) gains or losses would be treated as accruing to the trustees in a particular tax year to the extent of so much of their interest as participators as arises from that property if the trustees are assumed resident or ordinarily resident in the UK throughout the tax year, or that double taxation relief arrangements do not apply so as to deem trustees resident outside the UK (s 86(3)),

the gains or losses are taken into account in construing s 86(1)(e) as regards that tax year as if they had accrued on disposals of settled property originating from the settlor.

Where, for a particular tax year, there would otherwise be an amount under s 86(1)(e) and the trustees are deemed to be non-resident under double tax arrangements (under s 86(2)(b)), the following rules apply:

(1) assume that the references in s 86(1)(e), in Sched 5, para 1(2)(a) (deductions for losses) and in para 1(3) (trustees as participators in a non-resident company) to settled property originating from the settlor were to such of it as constitutes protected assets;

(2) assume that the reference, in Sched 5, para 1(3)(a) (trustees as participators in a non-resident company), to shares originating from the settlor were to such of them as constitute protected assets;

(3) find the amount (if any) which would be arrived at under s 86(1)(e) on those assumptions;

(4) if no amount is so found there is deemed to be no amount for the purposes of s 86(1)(e);

(5) if an amount is found under (3) above it must be compared with the amount otherwise arrived at under s 86(1)(e) and the smaller of the two is taken to be the amount arrived at under s 86(1)(e).

For the purposes of this rule assets are protected assets if they are of a description specified in double tax arrangements (s 86(2)(b)), and were the trustees to dispose of them at any relevant time, the trustees would be regarded under those arrangements as not liable in the UK to CGT on gains so accruing to them. The assumption that the trustees are not resident or ordinarily resident in the UK throughout the tax year, or that they are so regarded under double taxation relief arrangements, is ignored. Here a 'relevant time' is any time, in the tax year concerned, when the trustees are regarded for double taxation purposes as resident in a territory outside the UK. If different assets are identified by reference to different relevant times, all of them are protected assets.

The following sub-rules apply in construing s 86(1)(e) as regards a particular tax year ('the year concerned') in a case where the trustees are not resident or ordinarily resident in the UK:

(1) if the conditions in s 86(1) are not fulfilled for the settlement in any tax year falling before the year concerned, no deductions are made for losses accruing before the year concerned;

(2) if such conditions are fulfilled, no deductions are made for losses accruing before that year (or the first of those years) so falling. This does not prevent deductions being made for losses accruing in a tax year in which the conditions in s 86(1)(a)–(d) and (f) are fulfilled as regards the settlement.

In construing s 86(1)(e) as regards a particular tax year, and in relation to a settlement created before 19 March 1991, no account is taken of disposals made before 19 March 1991 (whether in arriving at gains or at losses).

23.3.9 Test whether settlor has interest
(TCGA 1992, Sched 5, para 2)

For the purposes of s 86(1)(d) a settlor has an interest in a settlement if:

(1) any relevant property (ie property originating from the settlor) which is or may at any time be comprised in the settlement is, or will or may become, applicable for the benefit of or payable to a 'defined person' (see the Glossary for a definition) in any circumstances whatever;

(2) any relevant income (ie income originating from the settlor) which arises or may arise under the settlement is, or will or may become, applicable for the benefit of or payable to a defined person in any circumstances whatever; or

(3) any defined person enjoys a benefit directly or indirectly from any relevant property (ie property originating from the settlor) which is comprised in the settlement or any relevant income (ie income originating from the settlor) arising under the settlement.

A settlor does not have an interest in a settlement under (1) or (2) above at any time when none of the property or income can become applicable or payable to a defined person, except in the event of:

(1) the bankruptcy of some person who is or may become beneficially entitled to the property;

(2) any assignment of or charge on the property being made or given by some such person;

(3) in the case of a marriage settlement, the death of both parties to the marriage and of all or any of the children of the marriage; or

(4) the death under the age of 25 or some lower age of some person who would be beneficially entitled to the property on attaining that age.

Nor does he have such an interest in a settlement under (1) or (2) above at any time when some person is alive and under the age of 25 if, during that person's life, none of the property or income can become applicable or payable to a defined person except in the event of that person becoming bankrupt or assigning or charging his interest in the property or income.

23.3.10 Settlements created before 17 March 1998
(TCGA 1992, Sched 5, para 2A)

In determining for the purposes of TCGA 1992, s 86(1)(d) whether the settlor has an interest at any time during any tax year of assessment in a settlement created before 17 March 1998, Sched 5 para 2(3)(da) and (db) (inclusion in defined persons of grandchild of settlor or of his spouse and the spouse of any such grandchild) and the reference thereto in para 2(3)(e) (a company controlled by any such person(s)) are disregarded unless:

(1) that tax year is a tax year in which one of the following four conditions becomes fulfilled as regards the settlement; or

(2) one of those conditions became fulfilled as regards that settlement in any previous tax year ending on or after 5 April 1998.

First condition

After 16 March 1998, property or income is provided directly or indirectly for the purposes of the settlement otherwise than:

(1) under a transaction entered into at arm's length; and

(2) in pursuance of a liability incurred by any person before that date.

For these purposes, where the settlement's expenses relating to administration and taxation for a tax year exceed its income for the year, property or income provided towards meeting those expenses are ignored if the value of the property or income so provided does not exceed the difference between the amount of those expenses and the amount of the settlement's income for that tax year.

The second condition

(1) The trustees become after 16 March 1998 neither resident nor ordinarily resident in the UK, or

(2) the trustees, while continuing to be resident and ordinarily resident in the UK, become after 16 March 1998 trustees who fall to be regarded for double taxation relief purposes as resident in a territory outside the UK.

The third condition

After 16 March 1998, the settlement terms are varied so that any person who is a 'defined person' (see the Glossary for a definition) becomes for the first time a person who will or might benefit from the settlement.

The fourth condition

(1) After 16 March 1998 a person who is a 'defined person' (see the Glossary for a definition) enjoys a benefit from the settlement for the first time, and
(2) the person concerned is not one who (looking only at the settlement terms immediately before 17 March 1998) would be capable of enjoying a benefit from the settlement on or after that date.

In construing s 86(1)(e) as regards any tax year and in relation to a settlement which:

(1) was created before 17 March 1998, and
(2) is a settlement in which the settlor has an interest during that tax year by virtue only of the fulfilment of one of the four conditions above,

no account is taken of disposals made before the relevant day (whether for the purpose of arriving at gains or at losses). Here 'the relevant day' means:

(a) for the tax year 1997/98, 17 March 1998; and
(b) for any other tax year, the 6 April which is the first day of that year.

23.3.11 Exceptions from section 86
(TCGA 1992, Sched 5, paras 3–5)

TCGA 1992, s 86 does not apply if the settlor dies in the year. For the purposes of s 86(1)(d), the settlor has no interest in the settlement at any time in the year except for one of the following reasons:

(1) property is, or will or may become, applicable for the benefit of or payable to any defined person;
(2) income is, or will or may become, applicable for the benefit of or payable to any defined person; or
(3) any defined person enjoys a benefit from property or income.

This also applies where two or all of (1)–(3) above are satisfied by reference to the same person. If this rule applies, s 86 does not apply if the defined person concerned dies in the year. Here, the 'person concerned' is the settlor's spouse, a child of the settlor or of his spouse, the spouse of any such child, a grandchild of the settlor or of his spouse, and the spouse of any such grandchild; s 86 does not apply if the person concerned ceases to be married to the settlor or the child concerned. Here 'child' includes a stepchild and 'grandchild' means a child of a child.

The rule set out below applies where, for the purposes of s 86(1)(d), the settlor has no interest in the settlement at any time in the year except for the reason that there are two or more persons, including his spouse, a child of his or his spouse, or the spouse of a child (or stepchild) of the settlor, or of his spouse, each of whom stands to gain because:

(1) that property is, or will or may become, applicable for his benefit or payable to him;
(2) income is, or will or may become, applicable for his benefit or payable to him;
(3) he enjoys a benefit from property or income;

or two or all of these apply in his case.

If this rule applies, s 86 does not apply if the person concerned dies in the year.

23.3.12 Right of recovery
(TCGA 1992, Sched 5, para 6)

This rule applies where any CGT becomes chargeable on, and is paid by, a person on gains treated as accruing to him in a year (attribution of gains to settlors with interests in non-resident or dual resident settlements under s 86(4)). Such a person is entitled to recover the CGT paid from any person who is a trustee of the settlement. For this purpose he is also entitled to require an Inspector to give him a certificate specifying the amount of the gains concerned, and the amount of CGT paid. Any such certificate is conclusive evidence of the facts stated in it.

SP 5/92 clarifies that the settlor's right to reimbursement (or any payment in reimbursement) of tax paid thereunder is not regarded as creating an interest in a trust for the settlor under TA 1988, ss 660A–694 where the settlor, his spouse and any companies in which they are participators cannot otherwise benefit from the trust (eg where the only beneficiaries are the settlor's children). Similarly, this statutory right to, or payment in, reimbursement is not regarded as bringing the settlor within the provisions of TA 1988, ss 677, 739 and 740, nor as a capital payment for the purposes of TCGA 1992, s 97.

Further, this statutory right is not regarded as a reservation of benefit for IHT purposes; nor is a provision in the trust deed either requiring the trustees to recognise the settlor's right to reimbursement or to reimburse the settlor. But where a settlor does not pursue the statutory right to reimbursement, the failure to exercise this right may give rise to an IHT claim under IHTA 1984, s 3(3), in which case the usual rules for lifetime transfers would apply.

A provision written into a settlement deed requiring the trustees to recognise the settlor's right to reimbursement or to reimburse him is not, of itself, regarded as giving the settlor an interest in the settlement for the purposes of TCGA 1992, Sched 5, nor as bringing into play the above provisions of TA 1988.

23.3.13 Meaning of 'settlor'
(TCGA 1992, Sched 5, para 7)

For the purposes of TCGA 1992, s 86 and Sched 5, a person is a settlor in relation to a settlement if the settled property consists of or includes property originating from him.

23.3.14 Meaning of 'originating'
(TCGA 1992, Sched 5, para 8)

References in TCGA 1992, s 86 and Sched 5 to property originating from a person are to:

(1) property provided by that person;
(2) property representing such property;
(3) so much of any property representing both property provided by that person and other property as, on a just apportionment, can be taken to represent property so falling.

References to income originating from a person are to income from property originating from that person, and income provided by that person.

Where a settlor makes reciprocal arrangements with another person for the provision of property or income:

(1) property or income provided by the other person under the arrangements are treated as provided by the settlor; but
(2) property or income provided by the settlor under the arrangements are treated as provided by the other person (and not by the settlor).

Where property is provided by a qualifying company controlled by one person alone at the time it is provided, that person is taken to provide it. Where property is provided by a qualifying company controlled by two or more persons (taking each one separately) at the time it is provided, those persons are taken to provide the property and each one is taken to provide an equal share of it.

Where property is provided by a qualifying company controlled by two or more persons (taking them together) at the time it is provided, the participators in the company at the time are taken to provide it and each one is taken to provide so much of it as is attributed to him on the basis of a just apportionment. This does not apply where a person would be taken to provide less than one-twentieth of any such property, and he is not be taken to provide any of it. For this purpose a qualifying company is a close company or a company which would be a close company if it were UK-resident.

References to property representing other property include property representing accumulated income from that other property. Property or income is provided by a person if it is provided directly or indirectly by the person.

Whether a company is controlled by person(s) is construed in accordance with TA 1988, s 416. In deciding that question, no rights or powers of (or attributed to) associate(s) of a person are attributed to him under s 416(6) if he is not a participator (under s 417(1)) in the company.

23.3.15 Qualifying settlements, and commencement
(TCGA 1992, Sched 5, para 9)

A settlement created after 18 March 1991 is a qualifying settlement for the tax year in which it is created, and in subsequent tax years.

A settlement created before 19 March 1991 is a qualifying settlement in the tax year 1999/2000, and subsequent tax years. However, where such a settlement is a protected settlement immediately after the beginning of 6 April 1999, that settlement is treated as a qualifying settlement in the tax year 1999/2000 or any subsequent tax year only if:

(1) any of the five conditions set out below becomes fulfilled as regards the settlement in that tax year; or
(2) any of those five conditions became so fulfilled in any previous year of assessment ending after 19 March 1991.

The first condition

Property or income is provided directly or indirectly for the purposes of the settlement otherwise than under:

(1) a transaction entered into at arm's length, and
(2) a liability incurred by any person before that date.

If the settlement's administration and taxation expenses for a tax year exceed its income, property or income provided towards meeting those expenses are ignored if the value of the property or income so provided does not exceed the difference between the amount of those expenses and the amount of the settlement's income.

The application of the charge on the settlor in the case of trusts created before 19 March 1991 is dealt with in SP 5/92. Trusts created before that date, broadly, fall within the new rules only where, on or after 19 March 1991 and subject to certain exclusions, property or income is directly or indirectly provided for the purposes of the trust.

Transactions entered into at arm's length

The first condition is not met where the property or income is provided to the trust under a transaction entered into at arm's length. This applies irrespective of whether the parties to the transaction are connected (under TCGA 1992, s 286).

Solely for the purposes of transactions not entered into at arm's length, a provision in the document governing the transaction for an appropriate adjustment to the consideration where the value agreed by the Revenue differs from the original consideration arrived at by an independent valuer and specified in the sale document is, in general, regarded as falling within the definition of an arm's length transaction. The arm's length value is to be determined in accordance with the principles set out above and will usually correspond to the value for CGT purposes except, for example, where TCGA 1992, s 19 applies (series of linked transactions).

It is also necessary for the contract terms to provide for compensating interest at a commercial rate to be paid in either direction once the arm's length value is determined. For this purpose, the official interest rate (for TA 1988, s 160 purposes) is usually regarded as equivalent to a commercial interest rate, although a different rate may be accepted as so equivalent if the circumstances of a particular case warrant this treatment.

This practice is, however, subject to the consideration passing on sale being realistically based (ie on a third party valuation by a qualified valuer, all the other terms of the transaction being at arm's length and the compensating interest being timeously paid). The position in a particular case depends on all the facts and circumstances.

Close companies

The first condition may be satisfied where property or income is provided to a company in which the trustees are participators. Where, however, the transaction is carried out with the sole object of leaving funds within the company for its own purposes and it can be shown that any indirect benefit to the trust is merely incidental to that object, the transaction is disregarded (eg where another shareholder waives an entitlement to all or part of a dividend; or a director restricts withdrawals of remuneration voted, in order to assist the company's cashflow, and no payments are made, directly or indirectly, to the trustees as a result of this).

Transactions with wholly owned companies

In general, transactions between trustees and companies which they, directly or indirectly, wholly own or between such companies are outside the scope of the first condition and are not treated as capital payments within TCGA 1992, s 97. For this purpose, a company is treated as directly wholly owned by the trustees where the whole of its issued share capital is directly owned by the settlement trustees for the benefit of the beneficiaries of the settlement. A company is treated as indirectly wholly owned by the trustees where the whole of its issued share capital is directly and beneficially owned by a company which is directly wholly owned by the trustees or it is the 100 per cent subsidiary of such a company, or a chain of companies, which is indirectly wholly owned by the trustees. This approach may not, however, be taken where the transaction has been entered into solely or mainly for the purposes of obtaining a UK tax advantage.

Loans made to settlements

Loans made before 19 March 1991 A fixed-period loan made, directly or indirectly, to a relevant settlement prior to 19 March 1991 on non-commercial terms is generally regarded as a provision of property under a liability incurred before that date, provided the loan remains outstanding on the same terms. As such, it is made otherwise than under a liability incurred by any person before that date and the first condition is not met.

There would, however, be a direct or indirect provision of property for the purposes of the settlement where a fixed-period loan falls to be repaid after 18 March 1991 but repayment is not made and so becomes a repayable on demand loan. ESC D41 sets out the position in the case of non-commercial, repayable on demand loans for the purposes of applying the first condition.

A repayable on demand loan which was made, directly or indirectly, to a relevant trust prior to 19 March 1991 on non-commercial terms is, generally, regarded as a provision of property for the purposes of the settlement. Consequently, where after 18 March 1991 a loan has not been repaid or adjusted to commercial terms, the first condition would be met. The condition is not, however, regarded as met where before 31 July 1992 the loan is either:

(1) repaid in full, together with any outstanding interest; or
(2) made subject to fully commercial terms, including a commercial rate of interest payable at least annually for the year ending 5 April 1993 and subsequent years and, in addition, interest at a commercial rate or a sum in lieu thereof has been paid in respect of the year ended 5 April 1992.

Amounts paid under an agreement entered into by the trustees after 5 April 1992 under (2) above are treated as capital payments under TCGA 1992, s 97, made in 1992/93. Where the lender is not a beneficiary of the trust, the payment is not treated as falling within the scope of the fourth condition below. In addition, where such payments are matched, under ss 92–95, to qualifying amounts for 1990/91, s 91(2) does not apply.

Amounts paid under (2) above under an agreement entered into by the trustees before 6 April 1992, or in respect of periods after 5 April 1992, are regarded as interest in the recipient's hands and taxable accordingly.

Loans made after 19 March 1991 A loan made, directly or indirectly, to a relevant settlement after 19 March 1991 on non-commercial terms (eg at a low or nil interest rate) is regarded as a provision of funds for the purposes of the first condition. This is the case whether the loan is for a fixed period or repayable on demand.

Loans made by trustees

The repayment of any loan made, directly or indirectly, to any person by the trustees is not generally regarded as the provision of funds for the purposes of the settlement under the first condition. This does not apply where more is repaid than is due under the original loan terms or, in the case of loans made after 19 March 1991, where the interest charged under those terms exceeds a commercial rate.

Failure to exercise rights to reimbursement

Failure, by any relevant person, to exercise statutory rights to reimbursement (eg under TA 1988, ss 660A–694 (settlements: income tax)) may be regarded as the provision of funds for the purposes of the settlement under the first condition. The settlement could remain outside the terms of the first condition where the exercise of the right to reimbursement is unsuccessful, provided it could be shown that there had been a genuine attempt to enforce that right.

Administrative expenses

A trust may remain outside the scope of the attribution rules (TCGA 1992, Sched 5) where funds are provided to pay certain expenses which exceed the trust income. These expenses are defined as 'expenses relating to administration and taxation'; and could be chargeable either to the trust income or capital. Only sums provided to meet genuine administration expenses fall within the terms of the proviso. Any payments which exceed such expenses are regarded as meeting the first condition and so bringing the trust within the scope of the qualifying settlement attribution rules (Sched 5, para 9).

The following items are not regarded as administration expenses within these terms:

(1) loan interest (other than interest on a loan taken out to meet administration expenses within the terms of the proviso);
(2) the costs of acquiring, enhancing or disposing of an asset;
(3) expenses incurred in connection with a particular trust asset to the extent that such expenditure can be set against income arising from that asset.

For the purpose of the proviso to the first condition, the measure of the gross income from such a source is net of expenses.

'Expenses relating to taxation' in the first condition is regarded as encompassing UK or foreign taxes to which the trustees are liable, along with any interest and penalties due on that tax. It could also include certain costs incurred by the trustees under the trust's terms in obtaining information regarding the beneficiaries' tax liabilities. One example might be where the trustees, in order to ensure they were acting in a beneficiary's best interests, had to ascertain the tax implications for the beneficiary in adopting a particular course of action.

It is only the settlement's administration or taxation expenses which are within the terms of the proviso. Expenses of, for example, a company wholly owned by the trustees fall outside its scope.

An expense on capital account paid out of trust income is not treated as a provision of income by a beneficiary for the purposes of the first condition provided that either:

(1) the trust deed permits payment of capital expenses from income and the beneficiary is entitled only to net income after such payments; or

(2) the trustees borrow money from the income account which is subsequently restored, along with interest over the period of the loan.

The appropriate rate of interest is considered to be that which a Court of Equity would order on the replacement of trust income.

Normally the specific date on which the liability to an administration or taxation expense was incurred determines the year into which it falls for the purpose of applying the proviso to the first condition. Where, however, the expense is incurred for a period rather than on a specific date, the basis of allocating expenses adopted by the trustees in preparing trust accounts or returns is, generally, regarded as acceptable provided that this basis is consistently adopted and is in accordance with conventional trust accounting practice.

Additions to meet the difference between administration and taxation expenses and any income arising to the trust do not have to be made by 5 April in the relevant tax year. There must, however, be a clear connection between the amount added and the computed shortfall. Additions should, therefore, be made as soon as the relevant figures are available.

Income, for the purposes of the proviso to the first condition, is the total income which arises to the trustees in the relevant year, rather than the income which is (or would be if the trust were UK-resident) subject to UK tax. Usually, items of income need to be allocated to the year in which they arise for the purposes of the proviso, but in practice income arising from a trade carried on by the trustees may be apportioned on a time basis, provided that this basis is consistently followed.

Life tenants

A life tenant is not regarded as having provided income or property for the purposes of the settlement merely because there is an administrative delay in paying out the income that has vested in that beneficiary. If, however, the beneficiary directs the trustees to retain this income on the settlement's terms, this is regarded as a provision of funds within the first condition.

Indemnities and guarantees

An indemnity given by the new trustees to retiring trustees is not considered as the provision of funds for the purposes of the settlement under the first condition. Other types of indemnity are considered in light of the facts of a particular case.

The giving of a guarantee is regarded as an indirect provision of funds under the terms of the first condition. Payment of an obligation under a guarantee given before 19 March 1991 is in general regarded as a payment in pursuance of a liability incurred before that date and provided otherwise than under a liability incurred by any person before that date. This may not, however, apply where:

(1) the contingent liability under the guarantee cannot be quantified with a sufficient degree of accuracy (eg where the guarantee is open-ended or the contingency is remote); or
(2) the guarantor does not take reasonable steps to pursue his rights against the debtor.

The second condition

(1) The trustees become on or after 19 March 1991 onwards neither resident nor ordinarily resident in the UK, or
(2) the trustees, while continuing to be resident and ordinarily resident in the UK, become on or after 19 March 1991 trustees who are regarded under any double taxation relief arrangements as resident in a territory outside the UK.

The third condition

The terms of the settlement are varied so that any 'defined person' (see the Glossary for a definition) becomes for the first time a person who will or might benefit from the settlement.

SP 5/92, para 37 explains that, for clarification purposes, this condition deals with ultra vires payments (ie cases where the defined person receives a benefit from the trust for the first time and that person is not a beneficiary under the terms of the trust deed). It may also apply where such a person benefits from a transaction with the settlement carried out, for example, under the trustees' investment powers.

ESC D40 gives clarification of the meaning of 'participator' in this context. Specifically, TCGA 1992, Sched 5, para 8 defines what property originates from the settlor and provides that property put into the trust by certain companies is treated as originating from those who control the company in question. The conditions under which trusts created before 19 March 1991 may fall within the scope of the charge on the settlor, some of which may apply to companies controlled by defined persons, are set out in Sched 5, para 9.

See also **23.3.19** below regarding the charge to UK-resident beneficiaries on certain payments received from non-resident or dual resident settlements.

SP 5/92, para 36 explains that this provision is concerned with situations where the settlement terms are varied by the beneficiaries or a court to admit new beneficiaries within the defined persons without thereby bringing the settlement to an end and creating a new one. For example, where the trust terms include a power to appoint anyone within a specified range to be a beneficiary, exercise of that power after 19 March 1991 will not be regarded as a variation of the settlement.

The fourth condition

(1) On or after 19 March 1991 a person within the list under the fifth condition enjoys a benefit from the settlement for the first time, and
(2) the person concerned is not one who (looking only at the settlement terms immediately before 19 March 1991) would be capable of enjoying a benefit from the settlement on or after that date.

The fifth condition

The settlement ceases to be a protected settlement at any time after 5 April 1999. A settlement is a protected settlement at any time in a tax year if at that time the beneficiaries of that settlement are confined to persons falling within some or all of the following descriptions:

(1) children of a settlor or of his spouse who are under age 18 at that time or who were under that age at the end of the immediately preceding tax year;
(2) unborn children of a settlor, of his spouse, or of his future spouse;
(3) future spouses of any children or future children of a settlor, his spouse or his future spouse;
(4) a settlor's future spouse;
(5) persons outside the defined categories.

For the above purposes, a person is outside the defined categories at any time if, and only if, there is no settlor by reference to whom he is at that time a defined person in relation to the settlement for the purposes of TCGA 1992, Sched 5, para 2(1). Also for the above purposes, a person is a beneficiary of a settlement if:

(1) there are any circumstances whatever in which relevant property which is or may become comprised in the settlement is or will or may become applicable for his benefit or payable to him;
(2) there are any circumstances whatever in which relevant income which arises or may arise under the settlement is or will or may become applicable for his benefit or payable to him;
(3) he enjoys a benefit directly or indirectly from any relevant property comprised in the settlement or any relevant income arising under the settlement.

Here 'relevant property' means property originating from a settlor, and 'relevant income' means income originating from a settlor.

23.3.16 Information
(TCGA 1992, Sched 5, para 10)

An Inspector may by notice require any person who is or has been a trustee of, a beneficiary under, or a settlor in relation to, a settlement to give him within such time as he may direct (which must not be less than 28 days beginning with the day the notice is given) such particulars as he thinks necessary for the purposes of TCGA, s 86 and Sched 5 and which he specifies in the notice.

23.3.17 Attribution of gains to settlor in s 10A cases
(TCGA 1992, s 86A)

This applies in the case of a person who is a settlor where:

(1) under TCGA 1992, s 10A (temporary non-residents), amounts falling within s 86(1)(e) for any intervening tax year(s) would (otherwise) be treated as accruing to the settlor in the tax year of return; and
(2) there is an excess of the relevant chargeable amounts for the non-residence period over the amount of the TCGA 1992, s 87 pool at the end of the tax year of departure.

This subject is dealt with in full at **21.8.2** under 'Temporary non-residents after 16 March 1998'.

23.3.18 Attribution of gains to beneficiaries
(TCGA 1992, s 87)

The following rules apply to a settlement for any tax year during which the trustees are at no time resident or ordinarily resident in the UK.

In this event there is computed, for every tax year to which this condition applies, the amount on which the trustees would have been chargeable to tax (under TCGA 1992, s 2(2)) had they been resident or ordinarily resident in the UK. That amount, together with the corresponding amount for any earlier such year, so far as not already treated (under s 87(4) or 89(2)) as chargeable gains accruing to beneficiaries under the settlement, is referred to here and in ss 89 and 90 as the trust gains for the year. In this calculation, the effect of ss 77–79 (charge on settlor with an interest in a settlement) is ignored.

Where as regards the same settlement and for the same tax year:

(1) chargeable gains, whether of one amount or of two or more amounts, are treated as accruing under the rules for attribution of gains to settlors in non-resident and dual resident trusts (TCGA 1992, s 86(4)); and
(2) an amount has to be computed under s 87(2);

the amount so computed is reduced by the amount, or aggregate amount, of the chargeable gains, which are treated as accruing under the rules for attribution of gains to settlors in non-resident and dual resident trusts.

The trust gains for a year of assessment are treated as chargeable gains accruing in that tax year to beneficiaries of the settlement who receive capital payments from the trustees in that year or have received such payments in any earlier year. This attribution of chargeable gains to beneficiaries is made in proportion to, but cannot exceed, the amounts of the capital payments received by them. A capital payment is left out of account to the extent that chargeable gains have by reason of the payment been treated as accruing to the recipient in an earlier tax year.

Chargeable gains that are treated as accruing to beneficiaries are eligible for taper relief. A beneficiary is not charged to CGT on chargeable gains so treated as accruing to him in any year unless he is UK-domiciled at some time in that year. A settlement arising under a will or intestacy is treated as made by the testator or intestate at the time of his death.

Capital payments received by beneficiaries do not include references to any payment received before 10 March 1981, or any payment received from that date onwards and before 6 April 1984, so far as it represents a chargeable gain which accrued to the trustees before 6 April 1981.

23.3.19 Gains of dual resident settlements
(TCGA 1992, s 88)

The attribution of gains to beneficiaries (under s 87 – see **23.3.18**) also applies to a settlement for any tax year of assessment beginning on or after 6 April 1991 if:

(1) the trustees are UK-resident during any part of the year or UK-ordinarily resident during the year; and
(2) at any time of such residence or ordinary residence they are regarded for double taxation relief purposes as resident in a territory outside the UK.

For every tax year for which there is attribution of gains to beneficiaries, such attribution is applied (s 87(2)) as if the amount to be computed were the assumed chargeable amount; and the corresponding amount for an earlier year is the amount computed otherwise than under, or (as the case may be) the amount computed under, TCGA 1992, s 88. For this purpose the assumed chargeable amount in a tax year is the lesser of:

(1) the amount of gains less allowable losses on which the trustees would be chargeable to CGT for the year (under TCGA 1992, s 2(2)) on the assumption that the double taxation relief arrangements did not apply;
(2) the amount of gains less allowable losses on which, on disposals of protected assets, the trustees would be chargeable to CGT for the year (under s 2(2)) on the assumption that those arrangements do not apply.

Protected assets are as described in **23.3.8**.

In computing the assumed chargeable amount for a particular tax year, the effect of TCGA 1992, ss 77–79 (charge on settlor with interest in settlement) is ignored. For the purposes of s 87, as applied by s 88, capital payments received before 6 April 1991 are disregarded.

23.3.20 Migrant settlements etc
(TCGA 1992, s 89)

Where a period of one or more tax years for which s 87 applies to a settlement ('a non-resident period') succeeds a period of one or more tax years for each of which s 87 does not apply to the settlement ('a resident period'), a capital payment received by a beneficiary in the resident period is disregarded (for s 87 purposes) if it was not made in anticipation of a disposal made by the trustees in the non-resident period.

Where a non-resident period is succeeded by a resident period, and the trust gains for the last year of the non-resident period are not (or not wholly) treated as chargeable gains accruing in that year to beneficiaries, then those trust gains (or the outstanding part of them) are treated as chargeable gains accruing in the first year of the resident period to beneficiaries of the settlement who receive capital payments from the trustees in that year, and so on for the second and subsequent years until the amount treated as accruing to beneficiaries is equal to the amount of the trust gains for the last year of the non-resident period.

This attribution of chargeable gains to beneficiaries is made in proportion to, but cannot exceed, the amounts of the capital payments received by them (s 87(5)). Chargeable gains that are treated as accruing to beneficiaries are eligible for taper relief (s 87(6A)). A beneficiary is not charged to CGT on chargeable gains so treated as accruing to him in any year unless he is UK-domiciled at some time in that year (s 87(7)).

23.3.21 Transfers between settlements
(TCGA 1992, s 90)

If in a tax year for which s 87 (attribution of gains to beneficiaries) or s 89(2) (non-resident period succeeded by a resident period) applies to a settlement ('the transferor settlement') the trustees transfer all or part of the settled property to the trustees of another settlement ('the transferee settlement') then:

(1) if s 87 applies to the transferee settlement for the year, its trust gains for the year are treated as increased by an amount equal to the outstanding trust gains for the year of the transferor settlement or, where part only of the settled property is transferred, to a proportionate part of those trust gains;

(2) if s 89(2) applies to the transferee settlement for the year (otherwise than under (3) below), the trust gains referred to in s 89(2) are treated as increased by the amount mentioned in (1) above;

(3) if neither s 87 nor 89(2) applies to the transferee settlement for the year, s 89(2) is applied to it as if the year were the first of a resident

period succeeding a non-resident period and the trust gains referred to in s 89(2) were equal to the amount mentioned in (1) above.

The reference in (1) above to the outstanding trust gains for the year of the transferor settlement is to the amount of its trust gains for the year so far as they are not treated (under s 87(4)) as chargeable gains accruing to beneficiaries in that year.

Where s 89(2) applies to the transferor settlement for the year, the reference in (1) above to the outstanding trust gains is to the trust gains referred to in s 89(2) so far as not treated as chargeable gains accruing to beneficiaries in that or an earlier year.

This rule does not apply to a transfer so far as it is made for consideration in money or money's worth.

23.3.22 Increase in tax payable under s 87 or 89(2)
(TCGA 1992, ss 91–95)

Where:

(1) a capital payment is made by the trustees of a settlement on or after 6 April 1992;

(2) the payment is made in a tax year of assessment for which s 87 (attribution of gains to beneficiaries) applies to the settlement or in circumstances where s 89(2) (non-resident period succeeded by a resident period) treats chargeable gains as accruing in respect of the payment;

(3) the whole payment is (under ss 92–95) matched with a qualifying amount of the settlement for a tax year falling at some time before that immediately preceding the one in which the payment is made; and

(4) a beneficiary is charged to CGT on the payment under s 87 or 89(2),

the tax payable by the beneficiary on the payment is increased by the amount found as below, except that it cannot be increased beyond the amount of the payment, and an assessment may charge CGT accordingly.

The amount is one equal to the interest that would be yielded if an amount equal to the CGT which would otherwise be payable by the beneficiary on the payment (apart from this section) carried interest for the chargeable period at the rate of 10 per cent per annum. This percentage can be amended at any time by Treasury order to such other percentage as it thinks fit. Such an order may provide that an alteration of the percentage is to have effect for periods beginning on or after a day specified in the order in relation to interest running for chargeable periods beginning before that day (as well as interest running for chargeable periods beginning on or after that day).

The chargeable period is the period which begins with the later of the two days specified below, and ends with 30 November in the tax year following that in which the capital payment is made:

(a) 1 December in the tax year following that for which the qualifying amount in (3) above is the qualifying amount; and

(b) 1 December falling six years before 1 December in the tax year following that in which the capital payment is made.

Qualifying amounts and matching

If s 87 applies to a settlement for 1992/93 or any later tax year, the settlement has a qualifying amount for the year, and that amount is the amount computed for the settlement for the year concerned under s 87(2). The settlement continues to have the same qualifying amount (if any) for 1990/91 or 1991/92 as it had for that year under FA 1991, Sched 17, para 2. Where capital payments are made by the settlement trustees on or after 6 April 1991, and the payments are made in a tax year or years for which s 87 applies to the settlement or in circumstances where s 89(2) treats chargeable gains as accruing in respect of the payments, the payments are matched with qualifying amounts of the settlement for 1990/91 and subsequent tax years (so far as the amounts are not already hereby matched with payments).

For these purposes:

(1) earlier payments are matched with earlier amounts;

(2) payments are carried forward to be matched with future amounts (so far as not matched with past amounts);

(3) a payment which is less than an unmatched amount (or part) is matched to the extent of the payment;

(4) a payment which is more than an unmatched amount (or part) is matched, as to the excess, with other unmatched amounts.

Where part only of a capital payment is taxable, the part which is not taxable is not matched until taxable parts of other capital payments (if any) made in the same tax year are matched. A part of a capital payment is taxable if the part results in chargeable gains accruing under s 87 or 89(2).

Matching: special cases

The rule applies where:

(1) a capital payment is made by the settlement trustees on or after 6 April 1992;

(2) the payment is made in a tax year for which s 87 applies to the settlement, or in circumstances where s 89(2) treats chargeable gains as accruing in respect of the payment; and

(3) a beneficiary is charged to tax in respect of the payment under s 87 or 89(2).

If the whole payment is matched with qualifying amounts of the settlement for different tax years, each falling at some time before that immediately preceding the one in which the payment is made, then:

(1) the capital payment ('the main payment') is treated as being as many payments ('subsidiary payments') as there are qualifying amounts;

(2) a qualifying amount is attributed to each subsidiary payment and each payment is quantified accordingly; and

(3) the CGT on the main payment is divided up and attributed to the subsidiary payments on the basis of a just and reasonable apportionment;

and s 91 (increase in tax payable under s 87 or 89(2)) applies in the case of each subsidiary payment, the qualifying amount attributed to it and the CGT attributed to it. If part of the payment is matched with a qualifying amount of the settlement for a tax year falling at some time before that immediately preceding the one in which the payment is made, or with qualifying amounts of the settlement for different tax years each so falling, then:

(1) only CGT on so much of the payment as is so matched is taken into account, and references below to the CGT are construed accordingly;

(2) the capital payment is divided into two, the first part representing so much as is matched and the second so much as is not;

(3) the second part is ignored; and

(4) the first part is treated as a capital payment, the whole of which is matched with the qualifying amount or amounts mentioned above, and the whole of which is charged to CGT;

and s 91 or ss 91 and 93(1)–(2) apply in the case of the capital payment arrived at hereunder, the qualifying amount or amounts, and the CGT. Sections 91 and 93(1)–(3) apply (with appropriate modifications) where a payment or part of it is to any extent matched with part of an amount (s 93(4)).

Transfers of settled property where qualifying amounts not wholly matched

This rule applies if:

(1) in 1990/91 or a subsequent tax year the trustees of a settlement ('the transferor settlement') transfer all or part of the settled property to the trustees of another settlement ('the transferee settlement'), and

(2) looking at the state of affairs at the end of the tax year in which the transfer is made, there is a qualifying amount of the transferor settlement for a particular tax year ('the year concerned') and the amount is not (or not wholly) matched with capital payments.

If the whole of the settled property is transferred, the transferor settlement's qualifying amount for the year concerned is treated as reduced by so much of it as is not matched, and so much of that amount as is not matched is treated as (or as an addition to) the transferee settlement's qualifying amount for the year concerned. If part of the settled property is transferred:

(1) so much of the transferor settlement's qualifying amount for the year concerned as is not matched is apportioned on such basis as is just and reasonable, part being attributed to the transferred property and part to the property not transferred;

(2) the transferor settlement's qualifying amount for the year concerned is treated as reduced by the part attributed to the transferred property; and

(3) that part is treated as (or as an addition to) the transferee settlement's qualifying amount for the year concerned.

If the transferee settlement did *not* in fact exist in the year concerned, it is treated as having been made at the beginning of that year. If the transferee settlement *did* in fact exist in the year concerned, this rule applies whether or not s 87 applies to the settlement for that or for any year of assessment falling before that year.

Matching after transfer

This rule applies as regards the transferee settlement where TCGA 1992, s 94 (transfers of settled property where qualifying amounts not wholly matched) applies. Matching is made under s 92 by reference to the state of affairs existing immediately before the beginning of the tax year in which the transfer is made, and the transfer does not affect matching so made. Subject to this, payments are matched with amounts in accordance with s 92 and by reference to amounts arrived at under s 94.

23.3.23 Payments by and to companies
(TCGA 1992, s 96)

Where a capital payment is received from a qualifying company which is controlled by the trustees of a settlement at the time it is received, for the purposes of TCGA 1992, ss 87–90 it is treated as received from the trustees. A qualifying company is a close company or a company which would be a close company if it were UK-resident. A company is controlled by the trustees of a settlement if it is controlled by the trustees alone or by the trustees together with a person who (or persons each of whom) is a settlor in relation to the settlement, or is connected with such a person.

Where a capital payment is received from the settlement trustees (or treated as so received by s 96(1)) and it is received by a non-resident qualifying company, the rules set out below apply for the purposes of ss 87–90. A non-resident qualifying company is a company which is non-UK resident and would be a close company if it were so resident.

If the company is controlled by one person alone at the time the payment is received, and that person is then resident or ordinarily resident in the UK, it is treated as a capital payment received by that person. If the company is controlled by two or more persons (taking each one separately) at the time the payment is received, then:

(1) if one of them is then resident or ordinarily resident in the UK, it is treated as a capital payment received by that person;

(2) if two or more of them are then resident or ordinarily resident in the UK ('the residents') it is treated as being as many equal capital payments as there are residents and each of them is treated as receiving one of the payments.

If the company is controlled by two or more persons (taking them together) at the time the payment is received and each of them is then resident or ordinarily resident in the UK:

(1) it is treated as being as many capital payments as there are participators in the company at the time it is received; and

(2) each such participator (whatever his residence or ordinary residence) is treated as receiving one of the payments, quantified on the basis of a just and reasonable apportionment;

but where (under these rules and otherwise) a participator would be treated as receiving less than one-twentieth of the payment actually received by the company, he is not treated as receiving anything under this rule.

These rules are modified where the year of departure is 1998/99 or a subsequent tax year, and in any case in which the tax year of departure is the tax year 1997/98 and the taxpayer was resident or ordinarily resident in the UK at a time in that year on or after 17 March 1998. An individual is deemed to have been UK-resident at any time in any tax year which in his case is an intervening tax year under TCGA 1992, s 10A (temporary non-residents). Note that, in the circumstances described below, the general protection imposing a time limit for making any claim or assessment prevents the making of those adjustments (whether by means of an assessment, an amendment of an assessment, a repayment of tax or otherwise):

(1) it appears, after the end of any tax year, that any individual should be deemed UK-resident at any time in that tax year, and

(2) as a consequence, adjustments are required to the amounts of tax previously taken as chargeable (under s 96) on any person.

23.3.24 Attribution to trustees of gains of non-resident companies

There are special tax rules to combat avoidance of CGT where a UK resident is a participator in an offshore company which is a close company (ie one under the control of five or fewer participators). Broadly, where such a company disposes of an asset (which is not tangible property used in a trade) at a gain, the gain is attributed to participators in proportion to their interest in the company.

However, these rules are being circumvented where assets are held in an offshore company owned by a trust (sometimes through a chain of companies), rather than held directly by the trust. If the offshore company is resident in a country with which the UK has a tax treaty and the treaty provides for gains arising to residents of the other country to be exempt from UK tax, the UK-resident settlor or beneficiaries (or trustees if resident) of the trust cannot under present rules be charged on the gains of the offshore company. In many cases, to take advantage of the exemption valuable assets have being shifted by trustees from tax havens to countries with which the UK has a tax treaty just prior to the sale taking place. This is regarded as an abuse of the tax treaty arrangements, which were never intended to facilitate tax avoidance.

TCGA 1992, s 79B, which applies to gains accruing to offshore companies after 20 March 2000, prevents this abuse by ensuring that tax treaties do not prevent gains of offshore companies being attributed to resident or non-resident trustees as participators of those companies. The effect of this is that the current anti-avoidance legislation that enables gains of certain offshore companies to be charged on UK residents in circumstances where trustees are participators in those companies (either directly or indirectly through a chain of companies) is not prevented from applying by the provisions of double taxation arrangements.

The rule applies where trustees of a settlement are participators (under TA 1988, s 417(1)) in a close company, or in a company that is not UK-resident but would be a close company if it were UK-resident. Where it does apply, nothing in any double taxation relief arrangements prevents a charge to tax arising by the attribution to the trustees (TCGA 1992, s 13), by reason of their participation in the company, of any part of a chargeable gain accruing to a company that is not UK-resident.

Where this rule applies and:

(1) a chargeable gain accrues to a company that is not UK-resident but would be a close company if it were UK-resident, and

(2) all or part of the chargeable gain is treated (under s 13(2)) as accruing to a close company which is not chargeable to corporation tax on the gain by reason of double taxation arrangements, and

(3) had such close company (and any other relevant company) not been UK-resident, all or part of the chargeable gain would have been attributed to the trustees by reason of their participation in the company in which the trustees of the settlement are participators,

s 13(9) (sub-apportionment) is applied as if the close company which is not chargeable to corporation tax on the gain by reason of double taxation arrangements (and any other relevant company) were not UK-resident.

The references here to 'any other relevant company' are to any other company which, if it were not UK-resident, would be a company in relation to sub-apportionment (s 13(9)) applied with the result that all or part of the chargeable gain was attributed to the trustees by sub-apportionment.

23.3.25 Supplementary provisions
(TCGA 1992, s 97)

References to a payment include the transfer of an asset and the conferring of any other benefit, and to any occasion on which settled property becomes property to which a person is absolutely entitled as against the trustee (see TCGA 1992, s 60 and **23.1**).

The fact that the whole or part of a benefit is, under TA 1988, s 740(2)(b) (prevention of avoidance of income tax by transfer of assets abroad: liability of non-transferors), treated as the recipient's income for a tax year after that in which it is received:

(1) does not prevent the benefit or that part of it being treated, under ss 86A–96, as a capital payment in relation to any tax year of assessment earlier than that in which it is treated as his income; but

(2) does preclude its being treated for those purposes as a capital payment in relation to that or any later year of assessment.

'Capital payment' is as defined in the Glossary at the front of this book. For the purposes of ss 86A–96, the amount of a capital payment made by way of loan, and of any other capital payment which is not an outright payment of money, is taken to be equal to the value of the benefit conferred by it.

For the purposes of ss 86A–90 a capital payment is regarded as received by a beneficiary from the trustees of a settlement if:

(1) he receives it from them directly or indirectly; or

(2) it is directly or indirectly applied by them in payment of any debt of his or is otherwise paid or applied for his benefit (s 97(5)(b)); or

(2) it is received by a third person at the beneficiary's direction.

The prohibition on the allowability of losses in a year in which the person concerned is neither resident nor ordinarily resident (TCGA 1992, s 16(3)) is not taken as preventing losses accruing to trustees in a tax year to which TCGA 1992, s 87 (attribution of gains to beneficiaries) applied to the settlement from being allowed as a deduction from chargeable gains accruing in a later tax year (so far as not previously set against gains).

In a case where:

(1) at any time from 19 March 1991 onwards a capital payment is received from the trustees of a settlement, or is treated as so received by s 96(1);

(2) it is received, or treated as received, by a person by s 96(2)–(5) (s 97(8)(b));

(3) at the time it is received or treated as received, the person is not otherwise a beneficiary of the settlement; and

(4) the provisions described below do not prevent this applying;

for the purposes of ss 86A–90 the person is treated as a beneficiary of the settlement as regards events occurring at or after that time.

This does not apply where a capital payment (in (1) above) is made in circumstances where it is otherwise treated as received by a beneficiary. However this exclusion does not apply so as to treat the settlement trustees referred to in s 97(8), or the trustees of any other settlement, as beneficiaries of the settlement referred to in (1) above.

23.3.26 Power to obtain information for ss 87–90 purposes
(TA 1988, s 745; TCGA 1992, s 98)

The Revenue may by notice require any person to furnish within such time as it may direct, not being less than 28 days, with such particulars as it thinks necessary for the purposes of TCGA 1992, ss 87–90. The particulars which a person must furnish as required by such a notice so to do, include:

(1) transactions with respect to which he is or was acting on behalf of others;
(2) transactions which in the Revenue's opinion it is proper that it should investigate notwithstanding that, in the opinion of the person to whom the notice is given, no liability to tax arises thereunder; and
(3) whether the person to whom the notice is given has taken or is taking any part in any transactions of a description specified in the notice, and with a description of that role and those transactions.

However, a solicitor is not deemed to have taken part in a transaction by reason only that he has given professional advice to a client in connection with it, and cannot, in relation to anything done by him on his client's behalf, be compelled except with his client's consent to do more than state that he is or was so acting, and give the name and address of the client. He must also give in the case of anything done by him in connection with:

(1) the transfer of any asset by or to an individual ordinarily resident in the UK to or by a company, or in connection with any associated operation in relation to any such transfer, the names and addresses of the transferor and the transferee or of the persons concerned in the associated operations;
(2) the formation or management of a company, the name and address of the company;
(3) the creation, or with the execution of the trusts, of any settlement by virtue or in consequence of which income becomes payable to a person resident or domiciled outside the UK, the names and addresses of the settlor and of that person.

A bank is not obliged to furnish any particulars of any ordinary banking transactions between the bank and a customer carried out in the ordinary course of banking business, unless the bank has acted or is acting on the customer's behalf in connection with the formation or management of a company or in connection with the creation, or with the execution of the trusts, of any settlement.

'Company' here means a company resident or incorporated outside the UK which is, or if UK-resident would be, a close company, but not a company whose business consists wholly or mainly of the carrying on of a trade or trades.

23.3.27 Settlements with foreign element: information
(TCGA 1992, s 98A and Sched 5A)

This rule applies if:

(1) a settlement was created before 17 March 1998;
(2) a person transfers property to the trustees otherwise than under a transaction entered into at arm's length and otherwise than under a liability by any person before 17 March 1998;
(3) the trustees are not resident or ordinarily resident in the UK at the time the property is transferred; and
(4) the transferor knows, or has reason to believe, that the trustees are not so resident or ordinarily resident.

Before the expiry of the 12-month period beginning with the relevant day (ie the day on which the transfer is made) the transferor must deliver to the Revenue a return which identifies the settlement and specifies the property transferred, the day on which the transfer was made, and the consideration (if any) for the transfer.

This rule applies if a settlement is created on or after 3 May 1994, and at the time it is created the trustees are not resident or ordinarily resident in the UK, or the trustees are resident or ordinarily resident in the UK but are regarded for double taxation relief purposes as resident in a territory outside the UK.

Any person who is a settlor in relation to the settlement at the time it is created, and at that time is UK-domiciled and is either resident or ordinarily resident in the UK must, within three months beginning with the relevant day, deliver to the Revenue a return specifying the particulars set out below:

(1) the day on which the settlement was created;
(2) the name and address of the person delivering the return;
(3) the names and addresses of the persons who are the trustees immediately before the delivery of the return.

The rule below applies if a settlement is created on or after 19 March 1991, and at the time it is created the trustees are not resident or ordinarily resident in the UK, or the trustees are resident or ordinarily resident in the UK but fall to be regarded for double taxation relief purposes as resident in a territory outside the UK.

Any person who:

(1) is a settlor in relation to the settlement at the time it is created;

(2) at that time is non-UK domiciled and is either resident or ordinarily resident in the UK, and

(3) first becomes UK-domiciled and either resident or ordinarily resident in
the UK at a time falling on or after 3 May 1994,

must, within 12 months beginning with the day on which the person first
becomes UK-domiciled and either resident or ordinarily resident in the UK
deliver to the Revenue a return specifying:

(1) the day on which the settlement was created;

(2) the name and address of the person delivering the return;

(3) the names and addresses of the persons who are the trustees immediately before the delivery of the return.

The following also applies:

(1) the trustees of a settlement become at any time on or after 3 May 1994 (the
relevant time) neither resident nor ordinarily resident in the UK, or

(2) the trustees of a settlement, while continuing to be resident and ordinarily resident in the UK, become at the relevant time trustees who fall
to be regarded for double taxation relief purposes as resident in a territory outside the UK.

Any person who was a trustee of the settlement immediately before the relevant time must, within 12 months following the relevant day deliver to the
Revenue a return specifying:

(1) the day on which the settlement was created;

(2) the name and address of each person who is a settlor in relation to the
settlement immediately before the delivery of the return; and

(3) the names and addresses of the persons who are the trustees immediately before the delivery of the return.

Nothing in any of the above rules requires information to be contained in the
return concerned to the extent that (or requires a return to be delivered if):

(1) before the expiry of the period concerned (all) the information has been
provided to the Revenue by any person under the rule concerned or otherwise; or

(2) after the expiry of the period concerned (all) the information is provided
to the Revenue by any person under any provision other than the rule
concerned.

24

CGT HOLD-OVER RELIEF ON GIFTS

24.1 POSITION WHERE 'OLD STYLE' GIFT RELIEF (UNDER FA 1980, S 79) APPLIED
(TCGA 1992, s 67)

Special rules apply where a claim was made for 'old-style' gift relief under FA 1980, s 79, which provided a general relief for gifts, prior to 14 March 1989. Where a disposal on which such a claim has been made is or proves to be a chargeable transfer for IHT purposes, a deduction is allowed, in computing the chargeable gain accruing to the transferee on the asset's disposal. This deduction is the lesser of:

(1) the IHT attributable to the asset's value; and
(2) the amount of the chargeable gain as otherwise computed.

In the case of a disposal which, being a PET (for IHT purposes), subsequently proves to be a chargeable transfer, all necessary adjustments are made, whether by the discharge or repayment of CGT or otherwise.

Where an amount of IHT must be redetermined because of the transferor's death within seven years of making the chargeable transfer, or is otherwise varied after it has been taken into account (or under TCGA 1992, s 79(5)), all necessary adjustments are made, whether by the making of an assessment to CGT or by the discharge or repayment of such tax.

Suppose that a claim for relief has been made on the disposal of an asset to a trustee, and the trustee is deemed to have disposed of the asset, or part of it (under TCGA 1992, s 71(1) or 72(1)(a)). The provisions whereby there is no chargeable gain on the termination of a life interest on the death of the life-tenant (or life-renter) (s 72(1)(b)), or on the death of the life-tenant, so that a person becomes absolutely entitled to the property (s 73(1)(a)) do not apply to the disposal or part by the trustee. However, any chargeable gain accruing to the trustee on the disposal is restricted to the amount of the held-over gain (or a corresponding part of it) on the disposal to him. This does not have effect in a case within s 73(2) (death of person after becoming absolutely entitled to part only of settled property). In such a case the reduction provided for is diminished by an amount equal to the proportion there mentioned of the held-over gain.

A problem can arise if old-style gift relief has been given (under FA 1980, s 79) on a 'relevant disposal' made after 5 April 1981 from trustees (TCGA 1992, s 168(1)(a)) and, prior to the disposal, the transferee becomes neither resident nor ordinarily resident in the UK (s 168(1)(b)); then, a chargeable gain is deemed to arise to him immediately before that time, in an amount equal to the old-style held-over gain on the relevant disposal (s 168(1)).

A transferee is deemed to have disposed of an asset before the time when he becomes neither resident nor ordinarily resident only if he has made a disposal in connection with which the whole of the held-over gain on the relevant disposal was represented by reductions made in accordance with TCGA 1992, s 79(1)(b) (TCGA 1992, s 168(2)). Where he has made a disposal in connection with which part of that gain was so represented, the amount of the chargeable gain deemed to arise to him as described above is correspondingly reduced.

The disposals by the transferee (being an individual) so taken into account do not include any disposal between spouses (under TCGA 1988, s 58). Where any such disposal is made by the transferee, disposals by his spouse are taken into account as if they had been made by him.

This charge arises only if the transferee becomes neither resident nor ordinarily resident within six years after the end of the tax year in which the transfer was made (s 168(4)). Overriding this, however, is the rule that the charge does not arise at all if the transferee (being an individual) becomes neither resident nor ordinarily resident by reason of an employment the duties of which are performed outside the UK (s 168(5)(a)), but becomes resident and ordinarily resident in the UK again within three years and has not meanwhile disposed of the asset (s 168(5)(b)).

A person is taken to have disposed of an asset if he makes a disposal such that all or part of the held-over gain on the disposal would, if he were resident and ordinarily resident in the UK, be represented by a reduction of the deemed costs of acquisition of the asset in the transferee's hands (TCGA 1992, ss 79(1)(b), 260(3)(b)). This does not apply where the transferee is an individual and the disposal is an intra-spouse transfer (s 168(6)).

Any tax arising is due from the transferee; however, if the tax remains unpaid after 12 months, it may be recovered from the transferor (by an assessment in the transferee's name) (s 168(7)). No recovery assessment can be made more than six years after the end of the tax year in which the transfer was made (s 168(8)). A transferor who pays such tax has a right of indemnity as against the transferee (s 168(9)).

Under s 168(10), gains arising on disposals made after a held-over gain has crystallised are computed without reference to the reduction previously made (but clawed back) against the deemed acquisition costs (TCGA 1992, ss 79(1)(b), 260(3)(b)).

24.2 LIFETIME GIFTS OF BUSINESS PROPERTY

24.2.1 Scope
(TCGA 1992, s 165, Sched 7)

A form of hold-over relief can be claimed where a donor makes a disposal otherwise than by an arm's-length bargain. Were it not for this relief the gift of a chargeable asset would give rise to a CGT liability. However, the liability is deferred if the gift is of qualifying business assets and a claim to gifts hold-over relief is made.

Qualifying business assets include assets used in a trade or profession and, for gifts made before 9 November 1999, shares or securities in an unlisted trading company. It was perceived that the relief was being abused where shares or securities, rather than assets used in a trade, were involved. The relief was being exploited in schemes where the main purpose was to avoid a CGT liability on an anticipated sale, rather than simply defer the liability on a bona fide gift. Some of the schemes involved the direct transfer of shares or securities to companies so that a tax exemption or other tax shelter could be taken advantage of. Others employed the relief as part of a complex series of transactions where the sole purpose was to shift gains outside the UK tax jurisdiction. Thus the relief is prohibited in the limited circumstances where shares or securities are transferred by individuals or trustees to companies. The relief continues to be available for all other transfers of business assets, including the transfer of assets used in a trade on the incorporation of a sole trader or partnership business.

Where gifts of business assets hold-over relief is allowed, the donor is treated as making a disposal and the donee as making an acquisition of the asset for a consideration equal to its market value reduced by the gain. If the claim is made the donor is not charged any tax on the held-over gain, but the gain is effectively brought back into charge when the recipient disposes of the asset. The claim must be made jointly by the donor and the donee. However, where the trustees of a settlement are the transferee, the claim is made by the transferor alone.

The assets to which gifts of business assets hold-over relief can apply are:

(1) an asset used for the purposes of a trade, profession or vocation (including, *inter alia*, commercial occupation of woodlands and furnished holiday lettings) carried on by:
   (a) the transferor, or
   (b) his personal company (payment of rent by the company to an individual does not preclude a claim (IR letter 10 November 1981)), or
   (c) a member of a trading group of which the holding company is his personal company, or
   (d) a partnership of which the transferor is a member (whether or not rent is charged (IR letter 23 October 1978; SP D11)); and
(2) shares or securities of a trading company, or of the holding company of

a trading group, where:

(a) the shares or securities are not listed on a recognised stock exchange, or

(b) the trading or holding company is the transferor's personal company.

This form of hold-over relief cannot be claimed in the following instances:

(1) if the gain is already exempt because of retirement relief (TCGA 1992, Sched 6), or

(2) in the case of a disposal of shares or securities, if the transferee is a company or if the gain is already exempt because of retirement relief, on the disposal of shares on the transferor's personal company, or

(3) if the gain arises on the disposal of qualifying corporate bonds, or

(4) if the gift is subject to IHT (even at nil rate or exempt), and relief could be obtained under the rules for gifts upon which IHT is chargeable (TCGA 1992, s 260).

Where a hold-over relief claim is available, the donor is deemed to make a disposal for a consideration equal to the market value of the asset concerned. Likewise the donee is deemed to make an acquisition for the same consideration.

The relief is reduced in certain cases where:

(1) the asset has not been used for business purposes throughout the donor's ownership;

(2) only part of the asset has been used for business purposes throughout the donor's ownership;

(3) in the case of shares, only part of the gain is attributable to underlying business assets;

(4) a gain is partly relieved by retirement relief; or

(5) actual consideration is given of an amount greater than cost, but less than market value.

Where there is actual consideration for a disposal and a claim for hold-over relief is made, and that actual consideration exceeds the sums allowable as a deduction (TCGA 1992, s 38), the held-over gain is the amount by which the unrelieved gain on the disposal exceeds the allowable costs.

If a gift is a chargeable transfer for IHT purposes:

(a) IHT paid is deducted in the computation of the eventual gain on the asset's disposal by the donee;

(b) this deduction cannot exceed the gain and create an allowable loss; and

(c) if the amount of IHT is altered because a PET becomes chargeable, the donee's CGT is recomputed.

In general, hold-over relief claims are admitted by the Revenue without a formal valuation (see SP 8/98 and *Tax Bulletin* 28 (April 1997)) which is postponed until an actual disposal, unless the claim interacts with other reliefs. The relief is modified to apply to agricultural property (see **24.2.4**) and to settled property (see **24.2.5**).

Example

Gregory bought a farm in November 1985 for £800,000, which is now worth £1,300,000. In 2000, Gregory gives his son Harvey the farm. If Gregory and Harvey jointly elect under TCGA 1992, s 165, Gregory is treated as having disposed of the farm at an amount which produces no gain or loss, ie:

	£
Market value of farm	1,300,000
Cost	800,000
Unindexed gain	500,000
Indexation to April 1998 (say)	80,000
Capital gain	420,000
Less hold-over relief	420,000
	Nil

Harvey's acquisition value is taken as £880,000 (the market value less the held-over gain).

Example

Isabel bought a freehold shop in 1989 for £60,000. In 2000, when the shop is worth £250,000, she transfers it to Jenny for £90,000.

Isabel's apparent gain is	£
Actual proceeds	90,000
Cost	60,000
Apparent gain	30,000
Indexation to April 1998 (say)	5,000
	25,000
Isabel's total gain is	
Market value	250,000
Cost	60,000
Gain before indexation	190,000
Indexation to April 1998 (say)	5,000
	185,000

Apparent gain (chargeable now)	25,000
Held-over gain	160,000
Jenny's base value for future disposals is:	
Market value	250,000
Held-over gain	160,000
Base cost	90,000

24.2.2 Transfers to non-residents
(TCGA 1992, s 166)

This form of hold-over relief is not available if the transferee, being an individual, is resident and ordinarily resident in the UK but, being 'dually resident', is treated under a double taxation treaty as resident in another country and thereby not liable to UK CGT. This provision prevents gains being held over where a dual resident individual is treated as resident in a foreign country. It does not prevent hold-over relief on a transfer to a dual resident individual treated as resident in the UK (eg because he has a home in the UK and not in the foreign country).

The following countries have double taxation agreements with the UK which could apply in these circumstances: Canada, France, Germany, Israel, Italy, Spain and the USA.

24.2.3 Gifts to foreign-controlled companies
(TCGA 1992, s 167)

This form of hold-over relief is also not available if the transferee, being a company controlled by a person, or persons, each of whom is resident and ordinarily resident in the UK, is connected with the transferee.

A person who (either alone or with others) controls a company by holding assets thereof and who is resident and ordinarily resident in the UK is treated as non-resident and non-ordinarily resident in the UK if he is treated, under a double taxation treaty, as resident in another country and thereby not liable to UK CGT. (See above for a list of countries with which the UK has agreements.)

24.2.4 Agricultural property
(TCGA 1992, s 165, Sched 7)

The definition of assets is extended to cover transfers of UK agricultural property which would attract IHT APR if the transfer was a chargeable transfer but which would not otherwise be eligible for hold-over relief. Hold-over relief is not available for shares in non-trading companies which own agricultural property (ICAEW TR 854); this is because IHT APR is achieved by attributing the shares' value to the agricultural property – the shares themselves are not agricultural property.

Hold-over relief is available on the full amount of gains on the transfer of agricultural land including 'hope' or 'development' value (*Tax Bulletin* 1 (November 1991)).

24.2.5 Settled property
(TCGA 1992, s 165, Sched 7)

If the trustees of a settlement dispose of an asset otherwise than at arm's length, and a claim is made, hold-over relief is given. Generally, the claim is made by the trustees and the person who acquires the asset. If the trustees of a settlement are also the transferee, the trustees alone make the claim. The assets to which this applies are:

(1) assets used for the purposes of a trade carried on by
    (a) the trustees who are making the disposal; or
    (b) a beneficiary with an interest in possession; and
(2) shares in a trading company or holding company a trading group, where
    (a) the shares are not listed on any stock exchange nor dealt in on AIM
    (b) at least 25 per cent of the voting rights are held by trustees.

There is an extension of the definition of assets to cover transfers of UK agricultural property which for IHT would attract APR if the transfer was a chargeable transfer, but which would not otherwise be eligible for hold-over relief.

24.2.6 Restrictions on relief
(TCGA 1984, s 165, Sched 7)

The relief is reduced in certain cases where:

(1) an asset has not been used for business purposes throughout the transferor's ownership;
(2) only part of an asset has been used for business purposes throughout the transferor's ownership;
(3) in the case of shares, only part of the gain is attributable to underlying business assets; and
(4) a gain is partly relieved by retirement relief.

If an asset has been used for some non-qualifying purpose in the past, only a proportion of the gain can be held-over. The gain reduced by the fraction:

$$\frac{A}{B}$$

where: A = period of non-qualifying use, and
       B = total period of ownership.

This does not apply to property attracting APR for IHT.

Example

Kilroy bought a property in January 1972 for £300,000. In March 1982 it was worth £1,300,000. At first, Kilroy let it as an investment. He then occupied it for business purposes from April 1988 to March 1994. Kilroy gives the property to his son, Laurence, in March 2001, when it was worth £2,800,000. Kilroy's gain is

	£
Market value	2,800,000
1982 value	1,300,000
	1,500,000
Indexation to April 1998 (say)	1,000,000
Gain	500,000

Only a part of the gain can be rolled-over, ie:

$$\frac{6 \text{ years } (1988{-}1994)}{19 \text{ years } (1982{-}2001)} \times £500,000 = £157,895$$

If part of an asset has been used for a non-qualifying purpose throughout the transferor's ownership, only a proportion of the gain can be rolled over. The gain is reduced by the fraction:

$$\frac{A}{B}$$

where: A = part of gain attributed to non-qualifying use, and
B = total gain.

This does not apply to property attracting APR for IHT.

Where shares of a company are transferred, and

(1) the company holds non-qualifying assets, or
(2) in the case of the holding company of a trading group, the group holds non-qualifying assets, and
(3) within the prior 12 months the transferor held 25 per cent of the voting rights, or
(4) the transferor being an individual, the company is a personal company (5 per cent of the voting rights), and
(5) part of the gain is attributable to underlying non-business assets,

the gain is reduced by the fraction:

$$\frac{A}{B}$$

where: A = market value attributed to non-qualifying assets, and

B = market value of all chargeable assets.

Where an asset is or shares are transferred, and

(1) retirement relief is available, and
(2) the held-over gain (reduced as above, if appropriate) exceeds the chargeable gain after retirement relief,

then the held-over gain is reduced by that excess (ie only that part of the gain as does not qualify for retirement relief can be held over.

24.3 GAINS ON WHICH IHT IS CHARGEABLE

24.3.1 Application
(TCGA 1992, ss 260, 261)

A form of hold-over relief may be claimed on the transfer of any asset (not restricted to business assets) where:

(a) an individual or trustees (the transferor) transfers an asset;
(b) an individual or trustees (the transferee) acquires an asset.

The relief applies to disposals not made at arm's length and which are:

(1) chargeable transfers (even if covered by annual exemption) and not PETs (IHTA 1984, ss 2, 3A, 19);
(2) transfers which are exempt transfers for IHT (under IHTA 1984), ie:
    (a) to political parties (s 24);
    (b) to maintenance funds for historic buildings (s 27);
    (c) of designated national interest property (s 30);
    (d) which are eligible for relief on entry to maintenance funds for historic buildings (s 57A);
    (e) which are not subject to IHT on the qualifying beneficiary becoming entitled to trust property, etc (s 71(4));
    (f) of designated property to national purpose bodies (s 78(1)); and
    (g) between maintenance funds for historic buildings (Sched 4, paras 9, 16, 17).

Where hold-over relief is available, the transferor's chargeable gain is reduced by the amount of the held-over gain, and transferee's acquisition cost is reduced by the amount of the gain. Hold-over relief is restricted where there is actual consideration, greater than cost, but less than market value.

As most gifts to individuals, trusts with interests in possession and accumulation and maintenance trusts are PETs, the relief applies mainly to gifts to discretionary trusts. Such trusts are useful to hold-over gains where IHT is covered by the nil rate band. Exit charges from discretionary trusts are usually chargeable transfers and thus appointments of capital are eligible for hold-over. Hold-over is available when a beneficiary becomes entitled to trust property (if income and capital vest simultaneously). Note that the Trustee Act 1925, s 31 gives entitlement to income at age 18 and should be excluded if capital is to vest later.

The relief does not apply on the transfer of gilts or QCBs.

If the gift in question is a chargeable transfer for IHT purposes, IHT paid is deducted in computation of the eventual gain on the asset's disposal. Even on a part disposal all of the IHT can be deducted. This deduction cannot exceed the gain and create an allowable loss. If the amount of IHT is altered because a PET becomes chargeable, the transferee's CGT is recomputed.

Where a gift could qualify either under TCGA 1992, s 165 or 260, the relief under s 260 takes precedence.

Transfers covered by the nil rate band, or by 100 per cent BPR or APR, are chargeable transfers and thus eligible for hold-over.

Hold-over relief may also be available for gifts of non-business assets (unlike TCGA 1992, s 165). This could be relevant where, for example, an individual settles a property which is used by other members of the family for the purposes of a trade carried on in partnership by them. Hold-over relief is not available if the transferee is neither resident nor ordinarily resident in UK. Nor is it available if the transferee, being an individual resident and ordinarily resident in the UK, is treated under a double taxation treaty as resident in another country and thereby not liable to UK CGT.

24.4 RULES OF GENERAL APPLICATION

24.4.1 Beware the disappearing donee
(TCGA 1992, s 168)

Gains held over under TCGA 1992, ss 165 and 260 may be charged on the transferee if he becomes neither resident nor ordinarily resident in the UK unless he has already disposed of the asset (other than by intra-spouse transfer), or to the extent that a held-over gain has been reduced. For transfers to individuals, this charge only arises if the transferee becomes neither resident nor ordinarily resident within six years after the end of the tax year in which the transfer was made.

For transfers to individuals, this charge does not arise if the transferee becomes neither resident nor ordinarily resident by reason of an employment the duties of which are performed outside the UK, provided that he becomes resident and ordinarily resident in the UK again within three years, and has not meanwhile disposed of the asset.

Where gains have been held over on transfers to trustees, a claw-back may arise on the export of the trust whether or not that event occurs within six years.

Any CGT arising is due from the transferee, but if the CGT remains unpaid after 12 months it may be recovered from the transferor. However, a transferee who pays such CGT has a right of indemnity as against the transferee. The Revenue cannot make a recovery assessment more than six years after the end of the tax year in which the transfer was made.

An exit charge may arise on a trust moving outside the ambit of UK CGT if the trustees, whilst continuing to be resident and ordinarily resident in the UK, come to be regarded as resident outside the UK under the terms of any double taxation arrangements, and therefore not liable to UK CGT on the disposal of some or all of the trust assets. The exit charge arises on the deemed disposal and reacquisition of the assets concerned (TCGA 1992, s 83).

Trustees distributing capital (say, out of an accumulation and maintenance trust) should be aware of the possibility that they may be called upon to pay the CGT, should the beneficiary decide to emigrate. Thereafter, it may be difficult to enforce their indemnity. Trustees should therefore consider the following precautions:

(1) Retain sufficient assets to meet the potential liability.
(2) Ask the absolute beneficiary to offer other assets as security.
(3) Obtain an indemnity from the beneficiary or, say, a parent ensuring that this is capable of being pursued anywhere in the world.
(4) Enquire if insurance against the risk is available.
(5) Arrange for the trustees to retire and appoint the beneficiary (and his parents?) as the new trustees. Such appointment of new trustees must be made before the beneficiary attains the vesting age. Provided the 'old' trustees were not aware that the beneficiary was contemplating emigration at the time, then their action in retiring cannot be challenged. The effect of this is that the Revenue thereafter must pursue the trustee(s) incumbent at the vesting date (ie the 'new' trustees and not the 'old' trustee(s)).

24.4.2 Gifts into dual resident trusts

Hold-over relief under either TCGA 1992, s 165 or 260 is also not available on the transfer of an asset to a 'dual resident' trust if:

(1) at the material time, the trustees to whom the disposal is made are treated (under TCGA 1992, s 69) as resident and ordinarily resident in the UK, even though the trust's general administration is carried on outside the UK, and
(2) on a notional disposal of the asset, immediately after the time of the relevant disposal, the trustees are treated under a double taxation treaty as resident outside the UK and thereby not liable to UK CGT.

25

CGT RETIREMENT RELIEF

25.1 INTERPRETATION
(TCGA 1992, Sched 6, paras 1–4)

25.1.1 Definitions

There are a number of definitions which are in general use in relation to retirement relief: those for 'commercial association of companies', 'full-time working officer or employee', 'group of companies', 'holding company', 'personal company', 'trading company' and 'trading group' are given in the Glossary at the front of this book.

With regard to 'full-time working officer or employee', there is no statutory definition of 'full-time', but in a profits tax case involving similar legislation a lady who worked three days per week out of 5½ or 6 days was rather more than a half-time working director for the whole year, but not a full-time working director for more than half the year (*CIR v D Devine & Sons Ltd* (1963) 41 TC 210, NI CA). The Revenue manual suggests that a 'full-time working officer or employee', in relation to one or more companies, is an officer or employee required to devote substantially the whole of his time to the service of the company or companies in question in a managerial or technical capacity (the Revenue suggests at least 75 per cent of the company's full normal working hours where there are other full-time employees). However, in *Palmer v Maloney and another* [1998] STC 425, ChD it was held that a person who devoted 85–90 per cent of his working time to a company and the remainder to his business as a sole trader could not have satisfied this requirement.

A director who has retired from full-time employment, but continues to spend an average of at least ten hours per week in the conduct or management of the company's business, may obtain relief if otherwise qualified. He is entitled to the same measure of retirement relief to which he would have been entitled at the time of his retirement.

Example

> Hamish has been a part-time director for four years since he retired as a full-time working director. He had been a full-time working director for six years. On a disposal now, he is entitled to six-tenths of the maximum relief.

The 'permitted period' is a period of one year, or such longer period as the Revenue may, in any particular case, by notice allow.

With regard to 'personal companies', a question which has arisen is whether voting rights attached to shares held by trustees can be regarded as exercisable by the first named trustee in his capacity as an individual. The Revenue view, expressed in *Tax Bulletin* 20 (December 1995), is that such voting rights cannot be so regarded. There are two specific provisions in particular which point to this conclusion:

(1) TCGA 1992, s 69(1) requires trustees to 'be treated as a single and continuing body of persons (distinct from the persons who may from time to time be the trustees)'.

(2) TCGA 1992, Sched 6, para 1(3) allowed 'voting rights exercisable by trustees of a settlement to be treated as voting rights exercisable by a member of the family of an individual'. This provision was repealed by FA 1993, following the abolition of the 'family company' test. But it still illustrates the basic principle that voting rights are exercisable by the trustees as a body of persons distinct from any individual trustee.

A further question, namely whether voting rights not exercised are 'exercisable', arose in *Hepworth v William Smith Group* [1981] STC 354, ChD. Here, a company had an issued share capital of 100 shares. One share was owned by its principal director, one was owned by his wife, one was owned by another director and 97 were owned by an associated company. However, the associated company had never appointed a representative to exercise the voting rights attaching to those shares. In 1969 the company ceased to trade and the business was transferred to a partnership comprising the principal director and the other director. Subsequently the principal director retired from the partnership. He appealed against an assessment to CGT, contending that the company had qualified as his 'family company' (requiring a 25 per cent holding – now replaced by a 'personal company' requiring a 5 per cent holding) as he had held $33\frac{1}{3}$ of the voting rights actually exercised. The Chancery Division rejected this contention, holding that the company did not qualify as his family company as he had only held 1 per cent of the exercisable voting rights. The fact that the associated company which held 97 per cent of the shares had never exercised its voting rights was not conclusive.

25.1.2 Election against identification of new holding with original holding on a reorganisation

Where, as part of a reorganisation (under TCGA 1992, s 126) there is a disposal of shares or securities of a company and, otherwise, the shares disposed of and the new holding would be treated (under s 127) as the same asset, that rule does not apply if the individual so elects or, in the case of a trustees' disposal, if the trustees and the individual jointly so elect. This election must be given to the Revenue by the first anniversary of the 31 January next following the tax year in which the disposal occurred.

25.1.3 Retirement on grounds of ill-health

An individual who has been concerned in the carrying on of a business is treated as having retired on ill-health grounds if he:

(1) has ceased to be engaged in and, by reason of ill-health, is incapable of engaging in work of the kind which he previously undertook in connection with that business; and
(2) is likely to remain permanently so incapable.

Here, the reference to a person being concerned in the carrying on of a business is to his being so concerned personally or as a member of a partnership carrying on the business.

Tax Bulletin 1 (November 1991) explains that the relevant test for CGT ill-health retirement relief is that claimants have ceased work of the kind which they previously undertook and because of their ill-health they are likely to remain permanently incapable of engaging again in work of the same kind. The Revenue view is that the retirement must be because of the claimant's own ill-health.

Suppose that a partnership business is sold because the ill-health of one partner has forced that partner to retire. Although that partner may satisfy the necessary medical conditions and obtain relief, no other partners are entitled to relief unless they satisfy the necessary medical conditions in their own right.

An individual qualifies for retirement relief if he is retiring early because ill-health makes it impossible for him to continue to carry on the kind of work previously undertaken and he is likely to remain incapable of such work, but he is not precluded from undertaking less demanding work (eg in a consultancy capacity).

The Revenue requires completion of forms CG85 and CG85R by the claimant and his medical practitioner. A medical examination by the Regional Medical Officer may be required (IRPR 16 April 1985).

Retirement relief is not clawed back if a trader's health improves and he is able to resume business activities at the former level. The scope for possible avoidance is limited by the Revenue's right to have a medical examination carried out.

The business which is relevant for these purposes depends upon the nature of the disposal.

Material disposals

A disposal of the whole or part of a business is a material disposal if, throughout a period of at least one year ending with the date of the disposal, the business is owned by the individual making the disposal or:

(1) the business is owned by a company:
    (a) which is a trading company, and
    (b) which is either that individual's personal company or a member of a trading group of which the holding company is that individual's personal company; and
(2) that individual is a full-time working officer or employee of that company or, if that company is a member of a group or commercial association of companies, of one or more companies which are members of the group or association.

A disposal of assets which at the time that the business ceased to be carried on were in use for the purposes of a business is a material disposal if:

(1) throughout a period of at least one year ending with the date on which the business ceased to be carried on either the business was owned by the individual making the disposal or the business is owned by a company as under (1)(a) and (b) above;
(2) that individual is a full-time working officer or employee of that company, as above; and
(3) on or before the date on which the business ceased to be carried on, the individual making the disposal had either attained age 50 or retired on ill-health grounds below that age; and
(4) the date on which the business ceased to be carried on falls within the permitted period before the date of disposal.

Trustees' disposals

The disposal of an asset which at the time that the business ceased to be carried on was in use for the purposes of a business is a trustee disposal if:

(1) throughout a period of at least one year ending not earlier than the beginning of the permitted period before the disposal, the asset was used for the purposes of a business carried on by the qualifying beneficiary; and
(2) on the date of disposal or within the permitted period before that date, the qualifying beneficiary ceased to carry on that business; and
(3) on or before the date of disposal or, if it was earlier, the date on which the qualifying beneficiary ceased to carry on that business, he attained age 50 or retired on ill-health grounds below that age.

Associated disposals

The disposal of an asset which at the time that the business ceased to be carried on was in use for the purposes of a business is an associated disposal if:

(1) it takes place as part of a withdrawal of the individual concerned from participation in the business carried on by a partnership of which he was a member, or by the company which owns the business; and

(2) immediately before the material disposal or, if it was earlier, the cessation of the business, the asset was in use for the purposes of that business; and

(3) during the whole or part of the period in which the asset has been in the ownership of the individual making the disposal the asset has been used for the purposes of:

   (a) the business (whether or not carried on by a partnership or by a company); or

   (b) another business carried on by the individual or by a partnership of which the individual concerned was a member; or

   (c) another business owned by a company:

      (i) which is a trading company, and

      (ii) which is either that individual's personal company or a member of a trading group of which the holding company is that individual's personal company; and

      (iii) that individual is a full-time working officer or employee of that company or, if that company is a member of a group or commercial association of companies, of one or more companies which are members of the group or association.

Employee disposals

In relation to an employee's disposal, a person who has been exercising any office or employment is treated as having retired on ill-health grounds if he:

(a) has ceased to exercise and, by reason of ill-health, is incapable of exercising that office or employment; and

(b) is likely to remain permanently so incapable.

Other matters

In any case where:

(1) the Revenue gives notice under TMA 1970, s 9A(1) or Sched 1A, para 5(1) (notice of intention to enquire into a return or claim or an amendment of a return or claim) to any person, and

(2) the enquiry to any extent relates to the question whether or not a person should be treated as having retired on ill-health grounds,

then the Revenue may, additionally, at the same or at any subsequent time require that person, within not less than 30 days, to produce such evidence relating to the question whether a person should be treated as having retired on ill-health grounds as may reasonably be specified in the notice.

25.2 RELIEF FOR DISPOSALS BY INDIVIDUALS ON RETIREMENT FROM FAMILY BUSINESS

25.2.1 Scope
(TCGA 1992, s 163)

Relief from CGT is given where a material disposal of business assets is made by an individual who, at the time of the disposal, has:

(a) attained age 50, or
(b) retired on ill-health grounds below that age.

The following are treated as the disposal of business assets:

(1) the whole or part of a business, or
(2) one or more assets which, at the time at which a business ceased to be carried on, were in use for the purposes of that business, or
(3) shares or securities of a company (including a capital distribution in respect of shares (per TCGA 1992, s 122)).

If an individual is aged 50 he can qualify for retirement relief even though he does not retire as such. Furthermore, he need not dispose of his entire interest in the business, but must merely ensure that he has made a material disposal.

Example

> David is aged 54 and is an accountant. He sells Robert a 50 per cent interest in the goodwill of the practice for £80,000. David qualifies for retirement relief, even though he retains the other 50 per cent and continues in the practice.

A gain will also qualify for retirement relief on a disposal on a change in profit-sharing ratios combined with a revaluation of partnership assets.

Example

James, who is aged 58, and George are in partnership, sharing profits equally. The firm's balance sheet shows the following assets:

	£
Factory	700,000
Warehouse	200,000
Offices	600,000
	1,500,000
Less: mortgage	(800,000)
	700,000

The assets are revalued to reflect their market value and, at the same time, James's interest is reduced to 30 per cent. A gain arises to James as follows

	£
Surplus on revaluation (say)	400,000
Less: indexation (say)	(80,000)
	320,000
20% thereof	64,000

James's gain will attract retirement relief.

25.2.2 Disposal of whole or part of business

A disposal of the whole or part of a business is a material disposal if, throughout a period of at least one year ending with the date of the disposal, the following conditions are fulfilled at any time if at that time the business is owned:

(1) by the individual making the disposal, or
(2) by a company:
    (a) which is a trading company, and
    (b) which is either that individual's personal company or a member of a trading group of which the holding company is that individual's personal company; and
that individual is a full-time working officer or employee of that company or, if that company is a member of a group or commercial association of companies, of one or more companies which are members of the group or association.

The requirement that there should be a disposal of part of a business has caused difficulties in the case of disposals by partners or sole traders. Does the disposal comprise the whole or part of a *business* or merely *assets* which are used in the business.

Relief was denied on the disposal of 9 acres of agricultural land out of a total holding of 89 acres in *Atkinson v Dancer* [1988] STC 758, ChD. Relief was denied on two disposals of 17 and 18 acres from an agricultural holding of 78 acres in *Mannion v Johnston* [1988] STC 758, ChD. Each of the sales had to be considered separately. The changes caused by each were merely changes of scale. Relief was also denied on the disposal of 5 acres of farmland out of a holding of 35 acres in *McGregor v Adcock* [1977] STC 206, ChD.

Relief was denied in *Pepper v Daffern* [1993] STC 466, ChD. A farmer had owned 113 acres of land, on which he had reared and grazed cattle. He gradually ceased to rear cattle, and sold 83 acres in 1986. In 1987 he obtained planning permission for a covered cattle yard on 0.6 acres, which he sold in 1988. Following the sale, the taxpayer continued cattle grazing on a much reduced scale. Retirement relief was claimed in relation to the sale, but was refused by the Revenue on the ground that the sale of the yard was not a disposal of the whole or part of the business as required by the legislation. The key question was whether the sale of a particular business asset (in this case the cattle yard) amounted to a sale of a part of the farming business or merely one of its assets. It was the prospect of obtaining planning permission for the yard which caused the change in the taxpayer's business, not the sale of the yard which followed. Thus the nature of the business had been changed so that the land in question was no longer required, and so the conditions for obtaining retirement relief were not satisfied.

Relief was allowed in *Jarmin v Rawlings* [1994] STC 1005, ChD where a farmer owned 64 acres together with a milking parlour and yard, and a dairy herd of 34 animals. He sold the parlour and yard in October 1988, and over a period of three months he sold 14 animals. The remaining animals were transferred to another farm owned by his wife. The farmer himself ceased dairy farming and used his land for rearing and finishing store cattle. The milk quota was retained and leased in order to enhance the value of the land on an eventual sale. He claimed retirement relief on the sale of the parlour and yard. The Revenue view was that he had merely sold assets of the business, and not a part of the business. It was held that dairy farming had been 'a separate and distinguishable part of the taxpayer's business', which he had sold and therefore qualified for retirement relief.

In contrast, relief was denied in *Wase v Bourke* [1996] STC 18, ChD. Here, in March 1988 (when he was below the then current age threshold) a dairy farmer sold his entire herd. Then, in February 1989, having passed the age threshold, he sold his milk quota. He claimed retirement relief on the basis that the sale of the milk quota was a 'disposal of the whole or part of a business'. The relief was denied since the milk quota was simply an asset and its disposal was not the disposal of part of a business. The business activity had ceased in March 1988 when the herd was sold. The disposal of the milk quota was merely the disposal of another asset.

In *Barrett v Powell* [1998] STC 283, ChD a tenant farmer surrendered an agricultural tenancy, but continued farming under temporary licence. He had received £120,000 in March 1990 as compensation for surrendering his agricultural tenancy. However, until September 1991, he was allowed to continue to farm the land under a temporary licence. He claimed that the compensation qualified for retirement relief. The Chancery Division held that the compensation was paid for the disposal of an asset, not for the disposal of the whole or part of the farmer's business. Demonstrably, he had been able to continue farming the land under the temporary licence.

It is understood that where farms are concerned, a disposal of half or more of the area being farmed is normally accepted by the Revenue as constituting a sale of part of a business, but that the effect of each disposal on a business must be considered in isolation. The disposal of a dairy herd and milk quota can amount to the disposal of a business (see *Taxation*, 24 June 1993, p 294).

The business must be carried on by the claimant and not by his company (unless the claim relates to the withdrawal by the individual from the business). In *Plumbly and others (Harbour's Personal Representatives) v Spencer* [1997] STC 301, ChD an individual disposed of 163 acres of land which had been used by a trading company of which he was a director and shareholder. The company, which had paid rent to him for the use of the land, qualified as his 'family company'. The personal representatives contended that the sale of the land qualified for retirement relief. Relief was denied because the land was not used for the purposes of a business carried on by him.

The Revenue has confirmed, in correspondence with CCAB, that retirement relief is available for accommodation provided that it is sold within three years after it ceases to be used as furnished holiday accommodation (see CCAB TR 55, 2 July 1984).

It was reported, in a press release dated 19 December 1991 by the Country Landowners Association, that the Revenue had concluded that both parties in a share farming agreement can be considered to be carrying on a farming business for taxation purposes. The Revenue agrees that the landowner in an agreement based on the Country Landowners Association model is regarded as a trading farmer, provided he takes an active part in the share farming venture, at least to the extent of concerning himself with details of farming policy and exercising his right to enter onto his land for some material purpose, even if only for the purposes of inspection and policy-making.

25.2.3 Disposal of one or more assets

A disposal of one or more assets which, at the time a business ceased to be carried on, were in use for the purposes of that business is a material disposal if throughout a period of at least one year ending with the date on which the business ceased to be carried on the following conditions are fulfilled if at that time:

(1) the business is owned by the individual making the disposal, or

(2) the business is owned by a company:
   (a) which is a trading company, and
   (b) which is either that individual's personal company or a member of a trading group of which the holding company is that individual's personal company; and

(3) that individual is a full-time working officer or employee of that company or, if that company is a member of a group or commercial association of companies, of one or more companies which are members of the group or association;

(4) on or before the date on which the business ceased to be carried on, the individual making the disposal had either attained age 50 or retired on ill-health grounds below that age; and

(5) the date on which the business ceased to be carried on falls within the permitted period before the date of disposal.

Relief was allowed in *Marriott v Lane* [1996] STC 704, ChD where an individual owned land and buildings used as an aircraft museum by a company of which he was the controlling director. The museum was closed in October 1988 and a year later, in September 1989, sold to a subsidiary company incorporated to undertake residential development on the site. His appeal against an assessment charging CGT on the disposal was dismissed by the general Commissioners who found that, at the time of the sale, the company had hoped to reopen the museum at different premises. Thus the trade had not ceased and retirement relief was not due. The Chancery Division allowed the taxpayer's appeal against that decision, holding that as the museum had not reopened, the fact that the company had originally hoped to reopen it was inconclusive. If a trade is closed down on a purely temporary basis but that becomes permanent, the date when the trade ceased is the date on which the trade was closed down.

25.2.4 Disposal of company shares or securities

A disposal of shares or securities of a company (including a capital distribution of shares under TCGA 1992, s 122) is a material disposal if, throughout a period of at least one year ending with the operative date (ie generally the date of disposal), the following conditions are fulfilled at any time if at that time:

(1) the individual making the disposal owns the business which, at the date of disposal, is owned by the company or, if the company is the holding company of a trading group, by any member of the group; or

(2) the company is the individual's personal company and is either a trading company or the holding company of a trading group and the individual is a full-time working officer or employee of the company or,

if the company is a member of a group or commercial association of companies, of one or more companies which are members of the group or association.

25.2.5 Company ceasing to be trading company – alternative 'operative date'

In the case of a disposal of shares or securities of a company, where:

(1) within the permitted period before the date of disposal, the company either ceased to be a trading company without continuing to be or becoming a member of a trading group or ceased to be a member of a trading group without continuing to be or becoming a trading company, and

(2) on or before the date of that cessation, the individual making the disposal attained age 50 or retired on ill-health grounds below that age,

then, the operative date becomes the date of the cessation. If, throughout a period which ends on the date of disposal or of cessation, and which begins when the individual concerned ceased to be a full-time working officer or employee of the company as described under (1) above:

(a) the company was his personal company and either a trading company or the holding company of a trading group, and

(b) he was an officer or employee of the company or of one or more members of the group or association and, in that capacity, devoted at least ten hours per week (averaged over the period) to the service of the company or companies in a technical or managerial capacity,

then the operative date becomes that on which the individual ceased to be a full-time working officer or employee. Here, any reference to the disposal of the whole or part of a business by an individual includes the disposal by him of his interest in the assets of a partnership carrying on the business. When a business is carried on by a partnership, the business is treated as owned by each individual who is at that time a member of the partnership.

25.2.6 Retirement relief: date of disposal

Generally, on a sale of assets under a contract, the date of disposal is taken as the date of an unconditional contract, or if the contract is conditional (in particular on the exercise of an option) it is the date on which the condition is satisfied. By concession (ESC D31), the Revenue is prepared to accept the date of completion as the date of disposal where, pending completion, business activities continue beyond the date of unconditional contract. This treatment applies for all purposes of CGT retirement relief where the date of disposal is relevant.

Example

> Kenneth attains age 50 on 28 February 2000 and otherwise qualifies for retirement relief. He enters into a contract on 1 February 2000 to sell his business, with completion on 30 April 2000. For the purposes of retirement relief only, he is treated as if he had disposed of the business on 30 April 2000. The gain is treated as arising in 2000/01. In view of the phasing out of retirement relief, it would not be advantageous to apply the concession, as the disposal would thereby be deemed to occur in 2001/2002 when the limits for retirement relief are further reduced (see **25.3.3**).

25.2.7 Change in nature of business

The availability of retirement relief depends not just on the change in business extent, but also (and more importantly) on the change in business nature. It is thought that relief will be available if the assets disposed of have been used for a completely different activity from the remaining activity no matter how small the disposal in relation to the business as a whole. Thus, if a farmer disposed of his pig unit there would be a disposal of part of his business even though the land involved amounted to only 5 out of 100 acres.

25.3 OPERATION OF THE RELIEF

25.3.1 Disposals on which relief may be given
(TCGA 1992, Sched 6, para 5)

Except for a disposal made by an individual who has attained age 50 (where relief is automatic), retirement relief is given only on the making of a claim by the first anniversary of the 31 January next following the tax year in which the disposal occurred. For a trustees' disposal, the claim must be made jointly by the trustees and the beneficiary.

25.3.2 Gains qualifying for relief
(TCGA 1992, Sched 6, paras 6–12)

For any qualifying disposal, other than one of shares or securities of a company, the gains accruing to the individual or, in the case of a trustees' disposal, the trustees on the disposal of chargeable business assets comprised in the qualifying disposal are aggregated, and only so much of that aggregate as exceeds the amount available for retirement relief is chargeable (but not so as to affect liability on gains accruing on the disposal of assets other than chargeable business assets).

For a qualifying disposal of shares or securities of a trading company which is not a holding company:

(1) the gains which on the disposal accrue to the individual or trustees are aggregated, and

(2) of the appropriate proportion of the aggregated gains, only so much as exceeds the amount available for relief is chargeable (but not so as to affect liability on gains representing the balance of the aggregated gains).

Here, the 'appropriate proportion' is that part of the value of the company's chargeable assets immediately before the end of the qualifying period which is attributable to the whole value of the company's chargeable business assets. In the case of a company which has no chargeable assets, 'the appropriate proportion' is the whole.

For this purpose, every asset is a chargeable asset except one, on the disposal of which by the company immediately before the end of the qualifying period, no gain accruing to the company would be a chargeable gain. This is interpreted as meaning that, on the hypothesis that a gain would accrue on the asset's disposal at the stated time, if that gain would be a chargeable gain then the asset would be a chargeable asset. The important point to be ascertained is not whether a gain (as opposed to a loss) would accrue, but whether a gain accruing in those circumstances would be a chargeable gain. In this context, therefore, it is equally appropriate to say that it is necessary to ascertain whether a loss arising on the disposal would be an allowable loss (Revenue letter 17 October 1978).

The Revenue has confirmed in correspondence (23 November 1978) that a single item of plant or machinery (other than an exempt motor vehicle) with a CGT cost of more than £6,000 and a market value at the relevant date which is less than that cost would be regarded as a chargeable asset whether the market value of that item at the relevant date was more than or less than £6,000 (TCGA 1992, ss 262, 263).

In the case of a qualifying disposal of shares or securities of a holding company:

(1) the gains which on the disposal accrue to the individual or trustees are aggregated, and

(2) of the appropriate proportion of the aggregated gains is chargeable (but not so as to affect liability in respect of gains representing the balance of the aggregated gains).

Here, 'the appropriate proportion' is as described above. For this purpose:

(1) any reference to the trading group's chargeable assets or chargeable business assets is to the chargeable assets or chargeable business assets of every member of the trading group; and

(2) every asset is a chargeable asset except one, on the disposal of which by the member of the group concerned immediately before the end of the qualifying period, no gain accruing to that member would be a chargeable gain (the Revenue correspondence referred to above is also relevant here); and

(3) a holding by one member of the trading group of the ordinary share capital of another such member is not a chargeable asset.

Where the whole of the ordinary share capital of a 51 per cent subsidiary (TA 1988, s 838) of the holding company is not owned directly or indirectly by that company, the value of that subsidiary's chargeable assets and chargeable business assets is reduced by multiplying it by a fraction of which the denominator is the whole of the subsidiary's ordinary share capital and the numerator is the amount of that share capital owned, directly or indirectly, by the holding company.

If, in the case of a trustees' disposal, there is in addition to the qualifying beneficiary at least one other beneficiary who, at the end of the qualifying period, has an interest in possession in the whole of the settled property or in a part of it which consists of or includes the shares, securities or asset which is the subject-matter of the disposal, only the relevant proportion of the gain which accrues to the trustees on the disposal is brought into account and the balance of the gain is, accordingly, a chargeable gain. For this purpose, the relevant proportion is that which, at the end of the qualifying period, the qualifying beneficiary's interest in the income of that part bears to the interests in that income of all the beneficiaries (including the qualifying beneficiary) who then have interests in possession in that part. The reference here to the qualifying beneficiary's interest is to the interest by virtue of which he is the qualifying beneficiary and not to any other interest he may hold in any other capacity.

In the case of an associated disposal, an adjustment is required if:

(1) the asset was in use for the purposes of:
   (a) a business carried on by a partnership of which the individual concerned was a member or by his personal company; or
   (b) another business carried on by the individual or by a partnership of which the individual concerned was a member; or
   (c) another business owned by his personal company and of which he is a full-time working director,
   or only part of the period in which it was in the ownership of the individual making the disposal, or
(2) for any part of the period in which the asset in question was in use for the purposes of such a business, the individual making the disposal was not concerned in the carrying on of that business (whether personally, as a member of a partnership or as a full-time working officer or employee of any company, group of companies, or commercial association of companies), or
(3) for the whole or any part of the period in which the asset in question was in use for the purposes of such a business, its availability for that use was dependent upon the payment of rent (or other consideration given for the asset's use).

In such a case, only such part of the gain which accrues on the disposal as is just and reasonable is brought into account and the balance of the gain is, accordingly, a chargeable gain. In determining how much of a gain it is just and reasonable to bring into account, regard must be had to the length of the period the asset was in use and the extent to which any rent (or other consideration given for its use) paid was less than the amount which would have been payable in the open market.

Retirement relief is not available where:

(1) there is a material disposal of business assets, or a trustees' disposal, which (in either case) is a disposal which the individual or trustees is or are treated as making having received a capital distribution (under TCGA 1992, s 122); and

(2) the capital distribution consists wholly of chargeable business assets of the company or partly of such assets and partly of money or money's worth.

and the capital distribution consists wholly of chargeable business assets. Where the capital distribution consists only partly of chargeable business assets, the aggregate gains accruing on the disposal are reduced by the fraction:

$$\frac{A}{B}$$

where: A = the part of the capital distribution which does not consist of chargeable business assets, and

B = the entire capital distribution.

It is then to that reduced amount of aggregated gains that the appropriate proportion is applied. Any question whether or to what extent a capital distribution consists of chargeable business assets is determined by reference to their status immediately before the end of the qualifying period. In arriving at the aggregate gains:

(1) the respective amounts of the gains are computed as normally under the CGT rules, and

(2) any allowable loss which accrues on the qualifying disposal concerned is deducted,

(3) none of the provisions described affects the computation of the amount of any allowable loss.

For these purposes, a 'chargeable business asset' is an asset (including goodwill, but not including shares or securities or other assets held as investments) which is, or is an interest in, an asset used for the purposes of a trade, profession, vocation, office or employment carried on by:

(1) the individual concerned; or

(2) that individual's personal company; or

(3) a member of a trading group of which the holding company is that individual's personal company; or

(4) a partnership of which the individual concerned is a member.

An asset is not a chargeable business asset if, on its disposal, no gain which might accrue would be a chargeable gain (the Revenue correspondence referred to above is also relevant here). In relation to a trustees' disposal, references to an individual are construed as references to the beneficiary concerned.

A further modification applies if:

(1) a qualifying disposal of shares (whether in a trading company or in a holding company of a trading group) is a disposal which the individual or trustees is or are treated as making on receiving a capital distribution; and

(2) by the first anniversary of 31 January next following the tax year in which the individual or the trustees received the capital distribution, the individual or trustees elect that the modification is to apply.

Where this election is made in relation to a qualifying disposal, any part of the company assets consists, as at the end of the qualifying period, of the proceeds of the sale of an asset sold not more than six months before the end of that period, then retirement relief is available as if:

(1) the asset remained the company's property and was in use for the purposes for which it was used before its sale; and

(2) the asset's proceeds of sale did not form part of the company assets.

25.3.3 Amount available for relief: the basic rule
(TCGA 1992, Sched 6, para 13)

On a qualifying disposal by an individual the amount available for relief is

(1) so much of the gains qualifying for relief as do not exceed the appropriate percentage of £250,000; and

(2) one-half of so much of those gains as exceed the appropriate percentage of £250,000 but do not exceed that percentage of £1m.

The 'appropriate percentage' is a percentage tapered according to the length of the qualifying period which is appropriate to the disposal on a scale rising arithmetically from 10 per cent where that period is precisely one year to 100 per cent where it is ten years. Full retirement relief is thus available only where the individual has been in business for a period of at least ten years ending with the disposal. The relief is not determined by the period of ownership of particular assets.

Trustees' disposals are treated as disposals by the qualifying beneficiary. If, on the same day, there is both a trustees' disposal and a material disposal of business assets by the qualifying beneficiary, the amount available for relief is applied to the beneficiary's own disposal in priority to the trustees' disposal.

Retirement relief is being phased out over the tax years 1999/2000 to 2002/03. The thresholds of £250,000 and £1,000,000 are to be progressively reduced over those tax years as set out below (FA 1998, s 140).

Year	Full relief	Partial relief
1998/99	£250,000	£1,000,000
1999/2000	£200,000	£800,000
2000/01	£150,000	£600,000
2001/02	£100,000	£400,000
2002/03	£50,000	£200,000

Example

Philip, who has been a sole trader since 1994 manufacturing widgets, acquired factory premises in 1998 for £100,000. These are now worth £800,000. Philip sells his business in September 2000, and all of the capital gains realised relate to the premises. He qualifies for retirement relief as follows:

	£	£	£
Capital gain (2000/01) on premises		800,000	
indexation (say)		70,000	
			730,000
Retirement relief:			
6/10 × 150,000		90,000	
6/10 × 600,000	360,000		
less relief at full rate	90,000		
	270,000 × 50%	135,000	
			225,000
Chargeable gain			505,000

25.3.4 Aggregation of earlier business periods
(TCGA 1992, Sched 6, para 14)

If, otherwise, the qualifying period appropriate to a qualifying disposal ('the original qualifying period') would be less than ten years but throughout some period ('the earlier business period') which:

(1) ends not earlier than two years before the beginning of the original qualifying period, and

(2) falls, wholly or partly, within the ten-year period ending at the end of the original qualifying period,

the individual making the disposal or the relevant beneficiary was concerned in the carrying on of another business ('the previous business') then, the length of the qualifying period appropriate to that disposal is redetermined as set out below.

For the purposes of this redetermination, it is assumed that the previous business is the same business as that at retirement and, in the first instance, any time between the end of the earlier business period and the beginning of the original qualifying period is disregarded (so that those two periods are assumed to be one continuous period).

The reference to a person being concerned in the carrying on of a business is to his being so concerned personally or as a member of a partnership or, if the business was owned by a company, as a full-time working officer or employee of that company or subsidiary. The reference to the business at retirement is to that business which, in relation to the qualifying disposal, is

(1) a material disposal where the qualifying disposal is one of business assets;
(2) a trustees' disposal; or
(3) an associated disposal.

An extended qualifying period cannot begin earlier than the beginning of the period of ten years ending with the end of the original qualifying period.

If the earlier business period ended before the beginning of the original qualifying period, any extended qualifying period which would otherwise result is reduced by deducting a period equal to that between the ending of the earlier business period and the beginning of the original qualifying period. Where there is more than one business which qualifies as the previous business and, accordingly, more than one period which qualifies as the earlier business period, this rule is applied first to the business in which the individual was last concerned and is then again applied (as if any extended qualifying period resulting from the first application were the original qualifying period) in relation to the next business, and so on.

The questions whether a disposal is a qualifying disposal and whether the period relating to that disposal is a qualifying period are determined without regard to the requirement that the length of the period be at least one year. However, this rule does not apply if the resulting extended qualifying period would be a period of less than one year.

RI 165, published in February 1997, illustrates when TCGA 1992, Sched 6, para 14 can apply to extend an individual's qualifying period for retirement relief purposes.

Example

Mrs Black worked for seven years as a full-time employee of a large trading company. However, as she held no shares in the company, it was not her 'personal company'. She then resigned and immediately started her own consultancy business. Two years later she sold that business.

Assuming that the sale of the consultancy meets all the retirement relief conditions, her qualifying period is the two years she owned the business.

It has been suggested that the previous period of employment can be counted as an 'earlier business period', so that it can be added on to the later business period to make an extended nine-year qualifying period. The reason for this suggestion is that Mrs Black was 'concerned in the carrying on of a business ... as a full-time working officer or employee', so that the period of employment qualifies as an 'earlier business period'.

However, the Revenue takes the view that this does *not* allow extension of the qualifying period in Mrs Black's circumstances. The length of the qualifying period must be redetermined on certain assumptions. In particular, it must be assumed that the two businesses are the same business. All the qualifying conditions in TCGA 1992, s 163 must be met throughout the extended qualifying period, which is redetermined by reference to that assumed 'same business'.

If the relevant business is owned for some period by a company which is not the individual's personal company, the qualifying conditions are not all met and the qualifying period cannot be extended.

25.3.5 Relief given on earlier disposal
(TCGA 1992, Sched 6, para 15)

In any case where:

(1) an individual makes a qualifying disposal or is the qualifying beneficiary in relation to a trustees' disposal, and
(2) retirement relief has been given on an earlier disposal which was either a qualifying disposal made by the individual or a trustees' disposal for which he was the qualifying beneficiary,

the amount which, otherwise, would be available for relief on the later disposal cannot exceed a limit which is the difference between:

(1) the amount which would be available for relief on the later disposal:
   (a) if the gains qualifying for relief on that disposal were increased by the amount of the underlying gains relieved on the earlier disposal (or the aggregate underlying gains relieved on all the earlier disposals); and
   (b) if the qualifying period appropriate to the later disposal (as redetermined where appropriate) were extended by the addition of a period equal to so much (if any) of the qualifying period

appropriate to the earlier disposal (or to each of the earlier disposals) as does not already fall within the qualifying period appropriate to the later disposal; and

(2) the amount of relief given on the earlier disposal or, as the case may be, the aggregate of the relief so given on all the earlier disposals.

Where there is only one earlier disposal, or where there are two or more such disposals but none of them took place after 5 April 1988, then,

(1) if the earlier disposal took place after 5 April 1988, the amount of the underlying gains relieved on that disposal is the aggregate of:
   (a) so much of the gains qualifying for relief on that disposal as were covered by the full relief band; and
   (b) twice the amount of so much of those gains as were covered by the 50 per cent relief; and

(2) if the earlier disposal took place before 6 April 1988, the amount of the underlying gains retrieved on that (or on each such) disposal is so much of the gains qualifying for relief on that disposal as were, under FA 1985, Sched 20, para 13, not chargeable gains.

Where there are two or more earlier disposals and at least one of them took place after 5 April 1988, then the aggregate amount of the underlying gains relieved on all those disposals is determined as follows:

(1) it is assumed that:
   (a) the amount which resulted from the calculation on the last of those disposals was the amount of the gains qualifying for relief on that disposal which were 'the gains actually relieved';
   (b) the qualifying period appropriate to that disposal (as redetermined where appropriate) was the period extended; and
   (c) the last disposal was the only earlier disposal;

(2) there is then ascertained, on these assumptions,
   (a) how much of the gains actually relieved would not have been chargeable gains (being covered by the full relief); and
   (b) how much of those gains would not have been chargeable gains (being covered by the 50 per cent relief); and

(3) the aggregate amount of the underlying gains relieved on all the earlier disposals is the sum of:
   (a) the amount on which full relief is given; and
   (b) twice the amount of chargeable gains after the 50 per cent relief.

Example

Henry started a business in February 1993. He made a disposal in February 1998 realising a gain of £100,000 and utilised retirement relief based on a five-year qualifying period. In February 2001 he realised a further eligible gain of £400,000. The computation continues as follows.

	£	£	£
Actual gain			400,000
Relief available on aggregate gain:			
Full relief $\frac{7}{10} \times$ £150,000		105,000	
Abated relief based on			
$\frac{7}{10} \times 600,000$	420,000		
Less relief at full rate	105,000		
	315,000 $\times 50\%$	157,500	
Relief available on aggregate gain		262,500	
Relief taken on earlier gain		100,000	
Relief available on second gain			162,500
Chargeable gain			237,500

If the earlier gain had been sufficiently large as to attract 'abated' relief, the calculation is more complicated.

Example

Janet made a disposal in February 1998 and was eligible for retirement relief on a gain of £500,000. At that time she had a five-year qualifying period. In March 2001, she made further eligible gains of £525,000. The computation on the earlier gain is as follows.

	£	£
'Full' relief $\frac{5}{10} \times$ £250,000		125,000
'Abated' relief based on $\frac{5}{10} \times$ £1,000,000 =	500,000	
Less relief at full rate	(125,000)	
	375,000 $\times 50\%$	187,500
Relief available on earlier gain		312,500

On the second gain the computation continues:

	£	£
'Full' relief $\frac{8}{10} \times$ £150,000		120,000
'Abated' relief based on $\frac{8}{10} \times$ £600,000 =	480,000	
Less relief at full rate	(120,000)	
	360,000 $\times 50\%$	180,000
Relief available on aggregate gains		300,000
Relief on earlier gain		312,500
Relief given on second gain		Nil

No further relief is due.

25.3.6 Aggregation of spouse's interest in business
(TCGA 1992, Sched 6, para 16)

In any case where:

(1) an individual makes a material disposal of business assets, and
(2) the disposal's subject-matter (whether business, assets or shares or securities) was acquired, in whole or in part, from that individual's spouse, and
(3) that acquisition was either under the spouse's will or intestacy or by way of lifetime gift and in the year of assessment in which occurred the spouse's death or, as the case may be, the lifetime gift, the individual and his spouse were living together, and
(4) as a result of the acquisition the individual acquired the whole of the interest in the business, assets, shares or securities which, immediately before the acquisition or the spouse's death, were held by the spouse, and
(5) by the first anniversary of the 31 January next following the tax year in which the material disposal occurred, the individual so elects,

the period which, otherwise, would be the qualifying period appropriate to that disposal is extended by assuming that any reference to the individual were either to the individual or his spouse. Where the acquisition was by way of lifetime gift, the amount available for relief on the material disposal, having regard to the extension of the qualifying period, cannot exceed the overall limit. The overall limit is the amount which would have been available for relief on the material disposal if:

(1) the lifetime gift had not occurred; and
(2) the material disposal had been made by the spouse; and
(3) anything done by the individual in relation to the business after the lifetime gift was in fact made had been done by the spouse.

25.4 MAXIMISING CGT RETIREMENT RELIEF

25.4.1 Sole traders

A key question is whether a sole trader's spouse should be admitted into partnership with a view to securing two entitlements to retirement relief. At a minimum, the spouse will need to be a partner for 12 months to obtain a qualifying period. At best, the spouse will have been admitted into partnership ten years before the disposal takes place so that maximum relief is due.

The spouse need not be an equal partner for the whole ten-year period. The spouse would only need to have an interest in the profits of (say) 5 per cent for the qualifying period to commence. The partners should adjust their profit-sharing ratios nearer the time that a disposal will take place.

25.4.2 Wasting assets

Remember that, where a trader has obtained hold-over gains on replacement by purchasing a wasting asset, the gain which has been held-over becomes chargeable on the first of the following events:

(1) the trader disposes of the replacement asset; or
(2) a period (often years) elapses; or
(3) the trader ceases to use the wasting asset for the purposes of his trade.

The Revenue's view is that retirement relief is not available to cover a capital gain which is deemed to accrue in these circumstances. However, the matter is not free from doubt, but the Revenue interpretation is based upon the wording of TCGA 1992, s 154 and on the fact that the gain on the original disposal is deemed to accrue on the asset being sold or taken out of use. A possible way of avoiding this problem is for the trader to incur fresh replacement expenditure before retirement and transfer the held-over gain to a non-wasting asset.

25.4.3 Partners

An individual should ensure that the full relief will be available for privately owned assets. There can be a conflict between satisfying the conditions to obtain income tax relief for loan interest and those necessary to obtain maximum retirement relief. The problem arises because the interest is eligible for relief only if the property is let on a commercial basis and the relief is given only against Schedule A income. One possibility which is suitable for small partnerships is for property to be acquired as a partnership asset. There is no requirement in law that partners should share capital profits in the same proportions as income. A partnership agreement can require individual items of income and expenditure to be credited or debited to particular partners. If, therefore, a partnership agreement provided that any gain or loss on disposal of property should belong to a particular partner, and the interest on the partnership loan taken to acquire it should be debited to him, with a credit corresponding to rent, the overall commercial position is much the same as if he owned it personally. However, the interest would then be a Schedule D Case I expense for the firm and the rent received by him would be treated as an appropriation of profits rather than as Schedule A income.

Another possibility is for the individual to borrow in his personal capacity and then lend the money to the firm which would then acquire the property and hold it on the same terms as mentioned above. Thus, the interest would be allowable without any corresponding restriction of retirement relief.

It is possible to transfer a property already owned by a partner and convert it into a partnership asset. On a subsequent disposal, the retiring partner disposes of an interest in the partnership. It is not relevant that rent was previously charged.

25.4.4 Appreciating assets used privately in the past

Suppose that an individual has occupied a property for non-business use in the past and there is an expectation that the property may eventually acquire development value. Depending upon the present value, it may be worth considering transferring the property into a settlement in which he has an interest in possession. Most of the gain on the transfer to trustees should be covered by hold-over relief. A gain eventually realised by the trustees on the individual's retirement will not then be subject to the restrictions which might apply to the individual.

The position can be improved by a sale and replacement of business assets. Thus where an individual charges rent for the old asset but not for the new one, the restriction does not arise on the sale of the new asset.

Where husband and wife are both partners, the property can be transferred to the other spouse. Provided that the spouse does not charge rent at any time during his period of ownership, the whole of the gain on the property's eventual sale should be eligible for retirement relief.

25.4.5 Shareholders in personal companies

Where a controlling shareholder's spouse is actively involved in the business, he should have 5 per cent of the voting shares as the company can then count as his personal company. Full relief is available provided the company has been the individual's personal company for ten years preceding the disposal. It is not necessary that the individual should have owned all his shares throughout that period. Thus establishing a spouse as a 5 per cent shareholder creates a situation whereby extra gains can be routed through that spouse by share transfers made in the last few years.

The restriction of relief based upon the ratio of chargeable assets over total chargeable assets is normally calculated by reference to the company or group's assets at the time of the disposal. It may be possible to minimise the restriction by selling non-business assets or by replacing investments with exempt assets such as government stocks, etc.

Retirement relief is not available where a liquidator makes distributions *in specie* of chargeable assets used by the company in its business.

25.4.6 Using retirement relief to cover deferred gains

Suppose that a shareholder sells his personal company to a quoted company, taking the payment to him as a mixture of cash and shares. Normally there would be no assessable capital gain on the part of the sale consideration which consists of shares in the quoted company since the gain is deferred until those securities are sold. But the vendor may not have made full use of his retirement relief. When the quoted securities are eventually sold, the gain is assessable with no deduction for retirement relief. However, a vendor can elect for TCGA 1992, s 135 not to apply so that a gain arises on the receipt of quoted securities and can be covered by retirement relief. It is not possible to elect for this treatment to apply only to a proportion of the quoted shares etc taken as consideration.

25.4.7 Avoid wasting retirement relief

Retirement relief is mandatory for individuals (but a claim is required for early retirement on medical grounds). It is not possible to choose not to claim it on a particular occasion. This means that it is as well to make any gifts which can be held over after sales which give rise to capital gains.

25.5 ALTERNATIVES TO RETIREMENT RELIEF

There are other aspects of CGT to be considered, especially in cases where retirement relief is not available or is of only limited benefit.

A possible alternative way of reducing CGT roll-over is relief on replacement of business assets.

Another type of investment which attracts roll-over relief on replacement of business assets, even though the individual's involvement may be limited, is property let as furnished holiday accommodation as this is deemed to be a trade. The property must be situated in the UK, but need not be in a resort area. It must be commercially let as furnished holiday accommodation. It must be available for letting for at least 140 days per annum, and it must actually be let during that period for at least 70 days. The lettings which add up to 70 days must not normally include any period of more than 31 days when the property is occupied by the same person. The individual does not have to take an active part in the property's management; this can be dealt with by agents. An individual who is aged below 50 and in good-health could roll over a gain on the sale of a business against expenditure on properties let as furnished accommodation. Then, a disposal of the properties after he has attained age 50 should attract retirement relief. A younger person might defer CGT by reinvesting in assets used for a trade of leasing.

Where a business is transferred to a company (and certain conditions are met) the company is deemed to acquire the assets at their market value at the transfer date. The gain is then locked into the shares and only becomes payable on the shares' disposal.

A form of roll-over relief is available to individuals and to certain trustees who invest in the shares in unquoted (including AIM issues) qualifying trading companies. This enables them to postpone CGT on the disposal of any asset. Only the gain (not the proceeds) need be reinvested. The reinvestment must be made within a 'window' of one year before and three years after disposal. Reinvestment relief is calculated without regard to retirement relief, and if only a proportion of a gain is eligible, retirement relief is given first against the part of the gain which is not so eligible.

25.6 DIFFERENCES BETWEEN RETIREMENT AND TAPER RELIEFS

Under taper relief, for assets held before 6 April 1998 years of ownership are based on tax years. An acquisition in, say, June 1998 means that taper relief is based on years to June. Taper relief is based on whole years. In comparison, under retirement relief the period of ownership is calculated by reference to the number of months of ownership.

Whilst retirement relief requires the disposal of the whole or part of a business, taper relief can apply to the disposal of a single business asset. Under taper relief, discretionary trusts, and assets used by trustees in a company or a business carried on by them, can qualify for business assets taper relief. Such assets do not qualify for retirement relief. Trustees should now consider whether they could qualify for either retirement relief or business asset taper relief or both.

If discretionary trustees own an asset which is used in an individual's business, neither business asset taper nor retirement relief is available. It should be considered whether there is any scope for bringing the trustees in as partners in the business. This would enable at least business asset taper relief to be claimed.

Alternatively, if retirement relief is also wanted on an eventual disposal of the asset owned by the trust it may be worth considering whether the trust should become an interest in possession trust – provided the life tenant is the individual running the business. Then both retirement and business asset taper reliefs are potentially available.

Where assets have been business assets for only part of the relevant period of ownership or are used partly for business and partly for non-business purposes, apportionment on a time basis is required.

For taper relief, the no gain/no loss rule applies to intra-spouse transfers. Where there is a transfer of an asset between spouses the taper relief on a subsequent disposal is based on the combined ownership period of both spouses. In determining whether an asset is a business asset for taper relief, it is the use made of the asset by the spouse holding it at that time which must be looked at.

Whether to trigger retirement relief before phasing out proceeds further needs to be considered carefully.

26

STAMP DUTY

26.1 GIFTS

Ad valorem duty was charged by F(1909–10)A 1910, s 74 on a conveyance or transfer operating as a voluntary disposition *inter vivos* and calculated according to the value of the property conveyed. However, this charge was abolished by FA 1985, s 82(1).

26.2 TRANSFERS SUBJECT TO MORTGAGE ETC

Certain transfers of mortgaged property are treated as sales for stamp duty purposes even where no money passes (SP 6/90). The charge can arise when the transferee covenants either to pay all or part of the debt or to indemnify the transferor against his liability in respect of it, or when a similar covenant is implied by law and no contrary intention is established. In such cases, the duty payable is 1 per cent of the debt taken over by the transferee.

26.3 SPECIFICALLY EXEMPT INSTRUMENTS

The legislation confers specific exemption from stamp duty upon a number of documents. The most important exemptions are contracts of employment and wills.

26.4 TRUSTS AND TRUSTEES

It is useful to comment briefly on the application of the stamp duty provisions to trusts and to actions by trustees.

26.4.1 On creation

This does not attract ad valorem duty as a voluntary disposition.

26.4.2 On variation

The variation of trusts can involve ad valorem duty when the variation comprises the assignment of a reversionary interest or of a life interest.

All court orders under the Variation of Trusts Act 1958 must be adjudicated.

26.4.3 On revocation

The revocation of a trust attracts 50p fixed duty.

26.4.4 Transfers by trustees

The transfer of property to beneficiaries does not attract ad valorem duty as a voluntary disposition, but almost inevitably will attract conveyance or transfer duty of 50p.

26.4.5 Appointment and retirement of trustees

In the case of all documents dealing with changes in trusteeship, fixed duty of 50p applies. The transfer of property from old to new trustees is not regarded as a voluntary disposition (F(1909–10)A 1910, s 74(6)).

27

QUICK REFERENCE – TAX PLANNING AND POINTS TO WATCH

27.1 AN INTRODUCTION TO IHT

Has full use been made of those transfers which are categorised as not being transfers of value – in particular those which are not intended to confer gratuitous benefit, dispositions for the maintenance of the family, nor conferring retirement benefits (see **1.1.2**)? Bear in mind that IHT is based on the 'loss to donor' principle so that the amount of a chargeable transfer is not the value of the asset of itself, but is measured by the amount of the reduction in the value of the donor's estate. In contrast, the value of a gift, for CGT and stamp duty, is the actual amount of that gift (see **1.1.3**).

Remember that a failure or omission to exercise a right may give rise to a reduction in the value of a person's estate and may therefore give rise to a chargeable transfer (see **1.1.3**).

Most lifetime transfers, if they are not exempt transfers, are likely to be PETs. As such they are treated as being exempt unless the donor dies within seven years, in which case they become chargeable as part of the estate on death. If the amounts are substantial it may be worth taking out term assurance to provide funds to meet any IHT liability arising thereon (see **1.1.4**).

Note the restricted list of liabilities that can be taken into account in arriving at the value of a person's estate and, in particular, the special rules by which loans for which there is a right of reimbursement are ignored unless it is unlikely that reimbursement will, in fact, be obtained. If there is a specific charge on a particular property, that charge reduces the value of that property. If the liability is to a non-resident the deduction is made against property outside the UK, unless the charge is to be discharged in the UK or is taken against UK property (see **1.1.7**).

Where the individual is neither UK-domiciled nor UK-resident, care should be taken in reviewing his investment policy to ensure that full advantage is taken of those forms of investment which, in his circumstances, are classed as excluded property (see **1.1.8**).

Certain categories of property are 'left out of account' or are 'not part of his estate', and it should be borne in mind that such assets are not included in the estate's value (eg certain pension rights – see **1.1.9** and **1.1.10**).

Although dealt with in greater detail elsewhere in this chapter, ensure that maximum use is made by way of lifetime gifts, in transferring assets, of the annual exemption, the exemption for normal expenditure out of income and, if the occasion arises, gifts in consideration of marriage (see **1.1.12**) and for transfers both in lifetime and on death (see **1.1.13**).

Again dealt with in greater detail elsewhere, where an interest in a business or a farm is involved, remember that relief is available on suitably qualifying property at either 100 or 50 per cent, and that this is given as a deduction in arriving at the value to be included in the estate (see **1.1.18**).

Where property is sold shortly after a person's death it may be possible to take account of losses suffered or to substitute the actual proceeds received in place of the probate valuation. The main categories of asset to which this can apply are land, quoted shares and related property (another important concept which is dealt with in greater detail elsewhere in this chapter (see **1.1.19** and **1.1.20**)).

Trust in which there is no interest in possession are liable to IHT under a special regime. It is however worth noting the application (or not) of the various taxable occasions under the no interest in possession regime and the application of many of the main provisions of IHT which also apply to no interest in possession trusts (see **1.1.21**).

As lifetime gifts may be subject to IHT, or be treated as PETs which may become chargeable in the event of death within seven years, it is important to establish just when a gift is 'complete'. The rules applying to various categories of asset should be noted (see **1.2**).

If gifts are made outside the various exemptions available, and the cumulative total of chargeable lifetime transfers exceeds the nil rate band of (from 6 April 1998) £223,000, IHT is charged at one-half of the full rate of 40 per cent (ie 20 per cent). On death it is necessary to bring into account any PETs which fall into the estate on death within seven years, and again IHT is payable if the cumulative total including chargeable lifetime transfers, PETs in date and assets passing by reason of the death exceed £223,000. This is likely to cause additional IHT, previously charged at 20 per cent, to arise because the rate on death is the full 40 per cent rate (see **1.3**).

27.2 DISPOSITIONS THAT ARE NOT TRANSFERS OF VALUE

The various dispositions which are regarded as not giving rise to any transfer of value and which can, therefore, be ignored for IHT purposes give considerable scope for mitigation of IHT.

In connection with dispositions which are not intended to confer gratuitous benefit, one point should be stressed. This concerns partnership interests. It can be taken that the obligations and responsibilities of junior partners can be taken to constitute full consideration, so that the transfer of partnership goodwill does not attract IHT. Being at full consideration, the transfer is clearly not gratuitous (see **2.1**). Note the wide range of persons who qualify as 'family' for the purposes of the exemption of dispositions for the maintenance of the family (see **2.2**).

The most important of the dispositions allowable for income tax or conferring retirement benefits are those falling into the latter category (see **2.3**).

There a number of special rules applying to close companies. Here we are concerned with dispositions of property to the trustees of an employee trust by a close company. This also applies to where the employees concerned are employed by a subsidiary company (see **2.4**).

Great care should be taken with waivers of remuneration and waivers of dividends to ensure that they meet the technical requirements (see **2.5** and **2.6**).

The IHT treatment of farmland is dealt with elsewhere, but it is worth noting here that the grant of a tenancy of agricultural property for full consideration is treated as not being a transfer of value. In this connection note also the extended meaning of agricultural property (see **2.7**)

Would any changes in the distribution of the deceased's estate be beneficial (see **2.8**)? Again these are dealt with elsewhere in this chapter.

27.3 EXEMPT TRANSFERS

There are a number of transfers which are exempt for lifetime gifts only.

The £3,000 annual exemption should not be overlooked. Husband and wife are each entitled to their own annual exemption. Thus over a period of, say, ten years it would be possible for a couple to transfer $(2 \times £3,000 \times 10)$ = £60,000. Also if no gift has been made by either spouse in a particular tax year, it would be possible to use the one year catch-up provision and transfer $(2 \times £3,000 \times 2)$ = £12,000 (see **3.1.1**)

Whilst the annual exemption is an aggregate total per donor, the £250 small gifts exemption is per donee. There is thus no technical overriding limit to the amount which could be transferred (although the limit per donee is obviously a limiting factor in its own right – see **3.1.2**).

Of rather more practical use is the exemption for normal expenditure out of income. There are two primary requirements. First, transfers should be made out of income (while leaving sufficient for the donor's usual standard of living to be maintained). Secondly, payments should be normal (which in this context may be taken to mean regular). A possible use of this exemption could be to provide a donee with funds to enter into a term assurance to provide funds to meet an IHT liability if the donor did not survive for seven years after making a PET. For individuals enjoying substantial incomes it is possible to use this exemption to transfer substantial amounts (see **3.1.3**).

The exemption for gifts in consideration of marriage could mean a happy couple with a full set of parents and grandparents could receive $(4 \times £5,000)$

= £20,000 from the parents and a further (8 × £2,500) = £20,000 from the grandparents. Note that the gifts must be made to the parties to the marriage, or in certain circumstances to trusts for the benefit of children of the marriage and indeed to their spouses. They must also be made before the marriage, perhaps under an enforceable agreement (see **3.1.4**).

Probably one of the most useful exemptions is the unlimited exemption available for intra-spouse transfers. It is important to note the restricted exemption of £55,000 which applies if the transferee (but not the transferor) spouse is non-UK domiciled. Great care is needed to avoid the 'associated operations' rule if onward gifts are contemplated (eg to obtain the benefit of a second set of exemptions, and in particular a second nil rate band). The special valuation rules for related property may also come into play (see **3.2.1**).

Gifts to charities, political parties, housing associations and national purpose bodies, PETs of property subsequently held for national purposes and transfers into maintenance funds for historic buildings all enjoy, subject to conditions, unlimited exemption from IHT (see **3.2.2–3.2.7**).

A gift of shares into an employee trust is an exempt transfer. This is a most useful exemption and can be used to transfer shares out of an individual's estate to a trust. It can provide an IHT-free transfer of company shares to be held for its employees' benefit. This could be a useful way to ensure continuity of a business where there is no obvious succession within the individual's family (see **3.2.8**).

27.4 CONDITIONAL EXEMPTION

A transfer of value comprising an historic house, a work of art or other related assets can be designated as exempt, conditional upon agreeing to certain conditions and entering into appropriate undertakings on such matters as access. If the undertakings are breached, the Treasury may withdraw the conditional exemption with the result that the transfer becomes chargeable and is reinstated in the transferor's cumulative total, which depending upon the value of gifts remaining in charge may give rise to an IHT liability. In order to protect the property which is the primary object of the designation, other associated properties which are deemed necessary for that purpose may also be designated. It is possible for the undertakings to be varied as may from time to time be appropriate (see **4.1–4.8**).

27.5 ALLOCATION OF EXEMPTIONS

On occasion problems of allocation may arise if any of the exemptions described in **27.3** and **27.4** are not wholly exempt. In such event there are specific rules on allocation and modification to those rules if a part of the value transferred is attributable to relevant business property or to the agricultural value of agricultural property (see **5.1–5.6**).

27.6 EXCLUDED PROPERTY

As previously indicated, value transferred by a transfer of value does not take account of any excluded property, nor does a person's estate immediately before his death take account of any excluded property. There are also special rules dealing with excluded property which is settled property with particular reference to no interest in possession trusts.

A primary category is property situated or deemed to be situated (eg by a double tax arrangement) outside the UK. A particular point to watch is the possibility that an individual may be deemed, for IHT purposes, to have acquired UK domicile. There are two situations: first where an individual has been domiciled in the UK at any time during the three prior years; and secondly where an individual has been resident in the UK for 17 out of the last 20 years. Individuals who are non-UK domiciled should avoid direct ownership of UK situs property.

If an individual has a foreign domicile, but is considered likely to acquire a UK domicile, consideration should be given to settling some of those assets before he acquires a UK domicile. Then, so long as the settlement continues to comprise assets situated outside the UK, the settled property remains excluded property. A possible, but less attractive alternative is for the settlor to make a settlement with a life interest for the settlor with remainders over. On the plus side such a transfer is not a transfer of value if it were to be determined that he was UK-domiciled at the time the settlement was made. On the minus side it should be noted that there is a disadvantage if the settlor has an initial interest in possession while the subsequent trusts are discretionary ones. The settled property could then lose its excluded property status on the settlor's death if he was UK-domiciled at the date of his death. Consideration should be given to settling property on an initial discretionary trust followed by his life interest.

As noted above, property in a settlement made by a non-UK domiciled settlor excluded property only if the property has non-UK situs. It may be possible for UK investments to be held by a non-UK registered company. The trust property is then shares in the non-UK registered company which actually holds the UK situs assets. This is not without problems – in particular TA 1988, s 739, which attacks the avoidance of UK income tax by the transfer of assets abroad. It is therefore important not to transfer assets already held in the UK, but rather to invest, or reinvest, funds which are already outside the scope of UK tax.

This sort of arrangement is particularly dangerous if the intention is to retain available accommodation in the UK. The individual may be classed as a shadow director assessed on a benefit-in-kind by way of the additional charge in respect of living accommodation (TA 1988, s 146). Although this benefit charge could be eliminated by liquidating the company, the individual thereafter occupying the accommodation as a beneficiary under of the trust; from an IHT standpoint the property has become UK situs property, and therefore no longer excluded property.

UK-domiciled individuals who are intending to emigrate from the UK should remember that IHT is only avoided if a new domicile is acquired, and cannot be acquired for IHT purposes until at least three years have elapsed.

A useful category of investments for those with non-UK domicile are FOTRA securities, which are issued free of tax if beneficially owned by individuals who are domiciled and ordinarily resident outside the UK, or if held in a trust of which the relevant beneficiaries are domiciled and ordinarily resident abroad. The special IHT domicile provisions do not apply to such securities. FOTRA securities can also be held by an individual entitled to a qualifying interest in possession therein.

Certain overseas pensions, mainly those for civil servants of former colonial territories are classed as excluded property.

Various categories of (mainly) National Savings and similar products are excluded property in the hands of persons domiciled in the Channel Islands or the Isle of Man. The emoluments of members of visiting forces and the chattels of such persons is excluded property. In appropriate circumstances reversionary interests are excluded property.

Finally, as noted above, it is important to determine the situs of assets, as this has a bearing on their categorisation as UK situs or non-UK situs assets, as the case may be. (See **6.1–6.9**.)

27.7 GIFTS WITH RESERVATION

This is a further anti-avoidance provision. What is attacked here is a situation where although a gift has been made the donor has retained, or reserved, a benefit. The effect of this is that such gifts are deemed not to have taken place, and as a result the gifted property is deemed to have remained in the donor's estate. Fortunately there are a number of exceptions, and the Revenue has published a list of *de minimis* exclusions. It is important to distinguish between, on the one hand, a gift with reservation and, on the other, the giving away of part only of the property (eg by creating two or more legal interests in it). The principle is that separate assets are created, and it is one of those interests, in its entirety, that is the subject of the gift, a procedure that is sometimes referred to as a 'Munro carve-out'. On that basis there is no reservation of benefit. This is not without danger, as is illustrated in **7.6**, with particular reference to the *Ingram* case. There are also potential CGT problems. The benefit of the principal private residence exemption is lost on a subsequent sale and the CGT uplift on death is also lost with respect to freehold interest.

If a parent were to transfer one-half of the family residence to a child as tenants in common or joint tenants and both joint owners continue to occupy and share the house with each paying a reasonable proportion of the outgoings, there is no reservation on the basis of mutuality with each joint owner enjoying the share owned by the other. An old estate duty case *A-G v Seccombe* [1911] 2 KB 688 (where it was held that a donor could remain a guest in a house which he has given away without having reserved any benefit, provided that there was no agreement to that effect) is of very doubtful authority; indeed the CTO has cast doubt on it.

A particular area of concern relates to the possible application of the GWR rules to family company shares where the donor continues to be involved in the company as a director. It is important to ensure that remuneration and other benefits do not exceed the market rate that would apply to an unconnected third party, and are not in any way referable to the gift of the shares. If a shareholder/director is giving away his shares as part of a reduction in his involvement with the company and becoming, for example, a consultant with a service agreement, the remuneration and other awards contained in the service agreement must not be referable to the gift of shares. The greatest care must be taken with documentation, separate from the gift of shares, relating to the receipt of income from the company, preferably applying some time before the gift. This also applies where the gift is made into trust. If the trust deed allows the trustees to keep directors' fees, especially if the settlor is the first-named trustee, the GWR rules should not be in point provided the remuneration is at a commercial rate and not linked to the gift.

Similarly, the test of reasonableness and commerciality are applied in the context of partnerships. Thus the transfer of capital account balances from parents in partnership with a son or a daughter can be said to be commercial if they are made at a time when the parents' contribution has decreased and the son or daughter are making a greater contribution to the generation of partnership profits.

Problems can arise in farming partnerships where land is owned outside the partnership. Suppose that a father and his son are in partnership. Suppose further, as is commonly the case, that the land belongs to the father and is farmed by the partnership, rent free, on an informal tenancy basis. A gift of the land to another son who is not a partner, whilst the partnership continues to occupy on a rent-free basis until the father's death, amounts to a reservation of benefit. This is because the father continues to enjoy the land, through the partnership, so that there is a GWR. If the land were let to the partnership on a commercial basis, there would be no GWR.

If a settlor is included in a class of beneficiaries, or if the trustees have discretionary power to add beneficiaries, there is a straightforward GWR. The CGT and income tax consequences must be borne in mind.

The GWR rules extend to the donor/settlor, but not to his spouse. This is on the basis that benefits applied to the settlor's spouse are, in any event, for the benefit of the settlor himself. This line of argument would not run if income distributed at the trustees' discretion were mandated direct to a bank account in the sole name of the other spouse, and that such funds were demonstrably used for personal benefit and not for household expenses.

27.8 BUSINESS PROPERTY RELIEF

27.8.1 Sole traders and partners

There are a number of preliminary considerations:

(1) When should ownership of a business be transferred to the next generation?
(2) Are there children who are too young to take on the responsibility or who may not have any interest in the business itself?
(3) Does the individual himself wish to retain control over the business during his working life?
(4) Is he happy with the prospect of working in a business where the majority ownership is with his children?
(5) Sole traders and partners of an unincorporated business have unlimited personal liability for action taken by their partners. Is the individual comfortable about admitting his children (or other relatives) into partnership?
(6) Are there problems in treating children equally where, for example, one child is engaged on a full-time basis in the business and others are not involved at all?

Some general principles of estate planning can be restated:

(a) The individual should take steps to secure financial security for himself and his wife before making any gifts.
(b) Consideration should be given to the effective use of assurance and pension arrangements to cover the position.
(c) The use of BPR and APR should be maximised and use made of the facility to pay IHT on gifts of land, shares and business interests by instalments. Make sure that no action is taken which puts these very valuable reliefs in jeopardy.
(d) Other things being equal, make gifts sooner rather than later, especially if the business is growing in value.
(e) The individual should draw up his will in the most IHT-efficient way compatible with his wishes on the ultimate destination of his capital.
(f) Consider 'estate freezing' where most of the business's future growth in value can 'bypass' the individual's estate.

(g) Ensure that secured loans are secured on non-business assets if at all possible, as BPR and APR are due only on the net value after deducting any loans secured against the property in question.

(h) Use the annual exempt amount to transfer capital from one partner to another. It is now accepted that the transfer of part of a capital account is an interest in the business and as such is eligible for 100 per cent property relief.

Many partnership deeds include a clause intended to protect the widow(er) and family of a deceased partner. A typical clause states that on the partner's death the firm's accountants are to ascertain the value of his interest according to certain rules, and that the surviving partners must then purchase that interest. Often a partnership deed requires each partner to take out an insurance policy for the benefit of his partners, who can then use the proceeds to buy out the widow(er). These are obviously sensible commercial arrangements. However, they are tantamount to a binding contract for sale. This creates a problem as it is provided that BPR and APR are not available on property which is subject to a contract for sale. This problem can be avoided if one partner grants his partners an option to purchase his share, and the options are worded so that they have to be exercised at market value. The Revenue has confirmed in SP 12/80, that the existence of such options does not jeopardise BPR and APR.

Where a partner owns a property which is used by the firm, 50 per cent BPR is available. However, it might be worth making the property a partnership asset so that 100 per cent BPR is available. The practical problem is reconciling the fact that whilst the individual wishes to ensure 100 per cent BPR, he will also want to ensure that he and his family enjoy the benefit of any capital appreciation. There is, however, no compulsion for partners to share capital profits in the same way as they share income profits. This can be of particular use where the senior partners of a firm wish to retain their interest in the capital appreciation of an asset used in the partnership (eg offices or manufacturing premises), and the junior or incoming partners may not be in a position to fund the purchase of a share in the asset.

BPR is not available where a partner retires and subsequently transfers an asset which he owns personally and which has been used by the firm. This applies even where the transferee is one of the ongoing partners.

There may be occasions where it is better to make a chargeable transfer. This would be so if it is possible that the transferor will not satisfy the requirement for BPR. In such a case it may be better for the gift to take the form of a chargeable transfer rather than a PET.

Example

Nicholas wishes to provide for Andrew. Nicholas is a partner in a firm of accountants, and owns the office building from which the firm practices. He transfers the office block to a discretionary settlement. Suppose the office block is worth £410,000.

	£
Chargeable transfer (value of office block)	510,000
50% BPR	(255,000)
	255,000
Annual exemption	(3,000)
Value of chargeable transfer	252,000
Nil rate band	(223,000)
	29,000
IHT thereon at 20%	5,800

Suppose that Nicholas had made a PET and died in the following year.

	£
Chargeable transfer (value of office block)	510,000
50% BPR	(255,000)
Value of chargeable transfer	255,000
Assume nil rate band utilised on other assets	–
	255,000
IHT thereon at 40%	102,000

Beware that a gift of an asset which is used in the business may not attract BPR where the transferor continues to trade as a sole trader. It is not possible to obtain BPR where individual business assets are transferred. The position is very similar to that for CGT under retirement relief (TCGA 1992, s 163).

Remember that where a business is acquired on a spouse's death, it is possible to take into account the deceased spouse's period of ownership. There is no similar provision where a business passes on a lifetime transfer from a spouse.

BPR is available on PETs only where the donee still holds the property at the date of death. BPR can be lost where business property is given to the trustees of an interest in possession or accumulation and maintenance trust, and during the seven-year period the trustees transfer the properties to the beneficiaries.

Section 3A(3) of IHTA 1984 (potentially exempt transfers), in conjunction with IHTA 1984, ss 71 and 89 which are concerned with gifts into accumulation and maintenance trusts and disabled trusts, requires that the 'transferee' under a PET (namely the trustees) should have owned the asset throughout the period beginning with the donor's transfer and ending with his death. Clearly if the trust is still in being and none of the beneficiaries has become entitled to receive any share of the trust assets, there is no problem. However, if the trustees have appointed any asset to a beneficiary absolutely, BPR is totally lost on that asset. Probably, one can distinguish between the beneficiary who received an absolute interest in the asset and one who merely becomes entitled to an interest in possession. In the latter case, under IHTA 1984, s 49, the beneficiary is to be treated as if he is beneficially entitled to the share of the settled property. For BPR the business property would be treated as part of the beneficiary's estate. Although it cannot be shown that the assets have been owned by the trustees throughout the period from the date of the donor's gift to his death, there is an unpublished concession by the CTO to allow BPR so long as the trustees still hold the property.

It is particularly important to achieve the correct order of gifts where one gift is a chargeable transfer and the other is a PET. The nil rate band is allocated according to which gift actually took place first. Thus, it is generally better for the PET to happen last. Provided the requirements for BPR are satisfied at the transferor's death, the IHT charged on business assets can be paid by instalments over ten years

A foreign-domiciled sole trader should transfer his UK business interests to a foreign-incorporated company since such shares are excluded property. If CGT may be a problem, the IHT situation could still be covered by a transfer of the business to a company incorporated overseas which is centrally managed and controlled in the UK and therefore UK-resident. This would allow CGT hold-over to be claimed (TCGA 1992, s 165). Remember that gains realised by a foreign-domiciled individual settling shares on a trust are chargeable only on the remittance basis and it is not possible to remit a notional or deemed gain such as one arising on a gift into settlement. Then, once put into trust, the shares remain excluded property even if the individual subsequently acquires a UK domicile of choice, or under the 17 out of 20 years rule. Where a foreign-domiciled individual is a partner, there are other aspects to be considered.

27.8.2 Shareholder in a family company

The preliminary considerations outlined in **27.8.1(1)**–**(4)** and **(6)** apply here. See also general principles **27.8.1(a)**–**(g)**.

The practical possibilities of IHT planning are greater for shareholders in companies than for proprietors of unincorporated businesses. When a company has been set up, ownership and management of the business can be separated. It is also easier to achieve a reduction by a sale or gift of a strategic shareholding as may occur where a 51 per cent shareholder reduces his holding in the company to 49 per cent. There is greater scope for estate freezing arrangements.

The constitution of companies or shareholders' agreements often include a provision intended to protect the widow(er) and family of a deceased shareholder. A typical clause states that on a shareholder's death the company's accountants are to ascertain the value of his shares according to certain rules, and that the surviving shareholders must then purchase those shares. Often a shareholders' agreement requires each shareholder to take out an insurance policy for the benefit of fellow shareholders, who can then use the proceeds to buy out the widow(er). However, whilst being sensible commercial arrangements, the issue of binding contract of sale arises, as discussed in **27.8.1**. However, the option to grant fellow shareholders to purchase shares at market value can be utilised (SP 12/80).

There may be some scope for increasing the proportion of an individual's estate which attracts BPR. Many companies are financed by directors' loans and undrawn remuneration. Often there is little practical likelihood that the company's need for working capital will permit it to repay this loan capital. However, such loans do not attract BPR, so it may be beneficial for the individual to convert them into share capital by using the money owing to him to subscribe for shares.

A review of the company's balance sheet will determine whether any unnecessary restriction of BPR arises. For example, a company may hold investments and yet at the same time have significant bank borrowings. Unless there are good commercial reasons against such a strategy, the company should realise the investments and clear the bank loans, thereby avoiding the restriction on the value which attracts BPR and which is based on the fraction:

$$\frac{\text{Company's business assets}}{\text{Company's total assets}}$$

Where the donor makes a PET of unquoted shares which becomes a chargeable transfer because he died within seven years of the transfer, and the shares become quoted shares at some time after the donor's gift, BPR is lost (under IHTA 1984, ss 105(1)(bb) and 113A(1)). Where a donor's shares are unquoted but are likely to become quoted and the donor has a poor life expectancy, consideration should be given to making a chargeable transfer rather than a PET.

Care should be taken to ensure that 50 per cent BPR is not lost on assets owned by controlling shareholders, and the rules on PETs and BPR need to be watched carefully. It could be expensive if an individual reduces his share ownership before he transfers a property which is used by the company.

Example

Charles owns 51 per cent of Fox Ltd. He also owns the shop premises from which the company trades. If he gives away the shop to his son James, and dies within seven years, the PET will attract BPR only if James is a controlling shareholder at the time of Charles's death. Accordingly, Charles gives James his shares in Fox Ltd.

However, the gift of the shop should happen simultaneously as, if there is a few days' delay before the gift is made, the gift will not attract BPR as Charles will no longer be the controlling shareholder.

Example

Edward owns 51 per cent of Teddies Ltd, which are agreed to be worth £500,000.

He has made no previous transfers. He intends to give 17 per cent to each of his three sons but decides to postpone the gift to his youngest son until he reaches age 30. The transfer of value on the gifts to the two older sons is:

	£
Value of 51% shareholding	500,000
Value of 17% shareholding retained (say)	90,000
Loss to donor	410,000
100% BPR	(410,000)
PET	nil

When Edward makes the gift to the youngest son the transfer of value is

	£
Value of 17% shareholding	90,000
50% BPR	(45,000)
PET	45,000

If Edward had already utilised his nil rate band, the younger son could be liable to pay (£45,000 × 20%) = £9,000 IHT. Edward could avoid this by making the gift to his youngest son at the same time as the other transfers but putting the 17 per cent in trust until the son reaches 30.

Under current law (at the time of writing) there is a relatively lenient IHT regime as a legacy of the former Conservative administration. Thus, providing that the conditions for BPR are met, it is possible to transfer qualifying property whether by lifetime transfer or death to obtain 100 per cent BPR, resulting in a nil IHT liability. For some years now, IHT mitigation strategy has revolved around retaining relevant business property (in particular shareholdings in unquoted companies of more than 25 per cent), rather than gifts. This is because for such holdings there is effectively no IHT liability on death and for CGT there is a tax-free uplift in value.

Whether under New Labour, these lenient conditions will remain is an open question. Factors which should now be considered before the March 1999 Budget include:

- What is the donor's age and health? Bear in mind that the saving of IHT on a lifetime transfer will need to be substantial if it is to outweigh the tax-free uplift on death under the CGT rules.
- What previous chargeable transfers has the donor made within the seven years preceding a proposed gift? If previous PETs have been made, the donor's death within seven years thereafter will distort the amount of IHT payable on the current gift.
- Are any of the lifetime exemptions (ie annual exempt amount, normal expenditure out of income, wedding gifts etc) available?

A reasonable estimate should be made of the likely IHT liability in the event that the donor does not survive for seven years after the gift. This may be difficult because of the uncertainties surrounding the valuation of private company shares. Furthermore, BPR and APR may be lost. It should, however, be possible to calculate the maximum liability since the property given is valued as at the date of gift and the IHT rates can never exceed those then in force.

The GWR rules must be borne in mind since, if they apply, the property given is deemed to remain in the donor's estate. It is then valued at the date of his death.

A transferor might consider leaving blocks of shares of, say, 26 per cent separate trusts as this would retain 100 per cent BPR. If trustees are carefully chosen trustees, family control of the shares can be retained.

Where spouses between them own a majority holding, it is usually advisable for the spouse with the smaller shareholding to make the first transfer, taking the combined, related shareholdings down through the 50 per cent valuation threshold. It is only the shares of the spouse who makes the first gift which are charged to IHT on the reduction from control value to minority value; the shares of the other spouse are then charged on a minority value on later transfers.

If a number of exempt (eg to a charity) and non-exempt (eg a chargeable transfer or a PET) gifts are contemplated, it could be advantageous to make a combined exempt and non-exempt gift of the same property rather than two separate transfers on consecutive days.

With the possibility of a modified IHT regime being introduced in the near future, it could be worthwhile considering a 'freezing' operation. This would involve a reorganisation of share capital to divide it into two classes of shares. One class, which would comprise current capital and income rights but with little prospect of growth, would be held by the donor. A newly created class of little current value but which would absorb the future growth would be allocated to the donor's children or appropriate trustees for grandchildren. Note, however, that IHTA 1984, s 98 can deem a reorganisation that amounts to an extinguishment or alteration of the rights attaching to close company shares to be disposition by the participators in the company.

27.9 AGRICULTURAL PROPERTY RELIEF

It is essential, if APR is to be secured, that the various requirements on occupation and ownership are met.

Agricultural property must have been occupied by the transferor, or by a partnership of which he is a member, for agricultural purposes for two years. A replacement farm qualifies for APR provided that the transferor has occupied one or other of the two farms for two out of the last five years. There is also a requirement that the transferor, or a partnership of which he is a member, has owned the agricultural property for seven years. Where there is a replacement, the ownership test must be met, in aggregate, for one or other of the two farms, for seven out of the last ten years.

There are also rules dealing with occupation and ownership by a company. For APR to be available it must be shown that agricultural property has been occupied by a company of which the transferor has control for two years prior to the transfer. The rules described above in relation to replacement property also apply here. APR is also available for shares in a company where agricultural property has been owned by the company for seven years, and occupied whether by the company or by another person for seven years. Again there are rules to allow APR where replacement property has been acquired.

Where a spouse inherits agricultural property, the qualifying period is measured from the deceased spouse's acquisition date. This does not apply to lifetime gifts.

As explained above in relation to BPR, it is essential if APR is to be preserved that the terms of a partnership deed or of a shareholders' agreement creates an option for fellow partners or shareholders to acquire the partnership interest or shares of a deceased partner or shareholder and does not create a binding contract for sale.

Beware that a gift of agricultural property which separates the ownership of land from that of the farmhouse may cause APR to be lost for the farmhouse. In any event APR is only available where the farmhouse is of a character appropriate to farmland in the same occupation and comprised in the same transfer.

As for BPR, a mortgage or charge on agricultural property reduces the value of it for APR purposes. The benefit of BPR is maximised if loans can be set against property not qualifying for APR.

27.10 WOODLANDS RELIEF

In a sense, woodlands relief is not a relief at all, but a deferral of liability. Furthermore, as the value on death of immature woodlands is likely to be somewhat less than the subsequent sale proceeds, which, where an election made, is the basis of the IHT charge. There is some advantage in not being required to pay IHT until there are funds in the form of sale proceeds to pay it. On the other hand, IHT arising on a chargeable transfer of woodlands can be paid by instalments.

27.11 CLOSE COMPANIES

It should not be overlooked that transfers of value made by close companies are deemed to be transfers made by the participators in the company *pro rata* (subject to a *de minimis* exclusion) to their holdings in the company. There are also provisions for tracing ownership through other companies owning shares in the company concerned.

27.12 TRANSFERS WITHIN SEVEN YEARS OF DEATH

If an individual makes a PET, that PET becomes a chargeable transfer on his death within seven years. If it is shown that the property transferred by the PET has decreased, IHT is charged on the reduced amount. There are special rules applying to various categories of assets.

27.13 CHANGES IN DISTRIBUTION OF DECEASED'S ESTATE

This covers a group of provisions by which, in effect, the dispositions made by a person's will or on intestacy can be reorganised or redirected. In effect the will or the rules on intestacy are 'rewritten'. These alterations are not themselves transfers of value and, in general, are backdated so that the revised dispositions are deemed to have taken place as at the date of death. Provisions of similar effect apply for CGT purposes. However, it is not possible to backdate the distribution of income, and for income tax purposes a variation takes effect from the date of the variation.

27.14 MISCELLANEOUS RELIEFS

Note that there is a measure of relief in the form of a reduction of the amount of IHT, ranging from 100 per cent in the first year to 20 per cent in the fifth year, where chargeable transfers have been made within five years before an individual's death, or within five years before a later lifetime transfer.

There are a number of reasons for funding a company pension scheme to the maximum extent:

- to depress profits and result in a lower valuation of shares;
- the death in service cover may fund part of the IHT which would arise on the director's death;
- the individual has secured a right to receive pension income regardless of the company's fortunes which may make him financially independent and therefore able to contemplate making irrevocable gifts of shares in the company;
- securing the maximum widow(er)'s pension means that shares in the company can be passed to the next generation on his death if not during his lifetime.

Death in service life cover can be provided through an approved pension scheme. The maximum amount is four times the individual's final remuneration. This sum may be paid where a director has reached normal retirement date but chooses to continue working and to postpone benefits under the pension scheme. This life cover may also be provided for an individual who has reached normal retirement date and drawn a lump sum. The maximum sum which may be paid is determined by the formula:

Maximum pension which could have been received over five years from retirement date	X
Less pension actually received	Y
Maximum sum which may be paid	Z

The IHT treatment of a lump sum being paid on a director's death depends upon the terms of the scheme. If the lump sum can be paid to any one of a range of potential beneficiaries, it is not part of the deceased's estate and therefore no IHT liability arises. This remains the case even though the trustees may pay out the lump sum in accordance with a 'letter of wishes' completed by the deceased (such a letter is not a legally binding instruction to the pension scheme trustees).

Consider requesting the pension trustees to pay any lump sum into a discretionary trust for the benefit of the surviving spouse and children. The trust deed can be created after death. The spouse can enjoy the income but without the capital forming part of his estate. Capital distributions by the discretionary trustees within three months of the creation of the trust (say to the spouse or children) are not liable to IHT. Alternatively, the pension trustees could limit their liability so that there is no IHT on future distributions of capital provided these are made within the first ten years regardless of the increase in value of the trust fund in that period.

If the terms of the pension scheme trust deed gave the deceased the right to specify the person to whom the lump sum should be paid, such amount forms part of the deceased's estate for IHT purposes. No IHT would be payable if the deceased specified that the lump sum should be paid to the widow(er). The Revenue does not normally approve a pension scheme unless the lump sum is part of the deceased's estate if he is aged over 75 and still in service, although there are circumstances where such a sum can be paid up to age 80 if it is based on a notional retirement at age 75. In addition to the death in service lump sum, an approved pension scheme may also provide a widow(er)'s pension of up to two-thirds of the pension to which the deceased would have been entitled at normal retirement date.

The payment of premiums on a policy effected in trust for the benefit of an individual's family will generally be an exempt transfer because of either the exemption for 'normal annual expenditure out of income' or the £3,000 annual exemption. Where the amount of the death in service cover is adjudged to be insufficient, it may be appropriate for the company to pay additional remuneration so as to enable the director to fund premiums on life policies written in trust. Another possibility where shares are held by trustees is for dividends to be declared to cover such premiums.

Recipients of PETs should consider taking reducing term insurance to cover any liability should the transferor die within the seven-year period.

No liability to IHT arises on benefits payable on a person's death under a normal pension scheme except in the circumstances explained in SP E3 and SP 10/86. Nor does any charge to IHT arise on payments made by the trustees of a superannuation scheme within IHTA 1984, s 151 in the direct exercise of a discretion to pay a lump sum death benefit to any one or more of a member's dependants. It is not considered that pending the exercise of the discretion the benefit should normally be regarded as relevant property comprised in a settlement so as to bring it within the scope of the settled property provisions (IHTA 1984, ss 43–85). However, the protection of IHTA 1984, s 151 would not extend further if the trustees themselves then settled the property so paid.

Benefits are liable to IHT if:

(1) they form part of the freely disposable property passing under the will or intestacy of a deceased person. This applies only if the executors or administrators have a legally enforceable claim to the benefits. If they were payable to them only at the discretion of the trustees of the pension fund or some similar persons they are not liable to IHT; or

(2) the deceased had the power, immediately before the death to nominate or appoint the benefits to any person, including his dependants.

In these cases the benefits should be included in the personal representatives' account which has to be completed when applying for a grant of probate or letters of administration. The IHT (if any) which is assessed on the personal representatives' account has to be paid before the grant can be obtained.

On some events other than the death of a member, information should be given to the appropriate CTO:

(1) the payment of contributions to a scheme which has not been approved for income tax purposes;

(2) the making of an irrevocable nomination or the disposal of a benefit by a member in his lifetime (otherwise than in favour of a spouse) which reduces the value of his estate (eg the surrender of part of the pension or lump sum benefit in exchange for a pension for the life of another);

(3) the decision by a member to postpone the realisation of any of his retirement benefits.

If IHT proves to be payable the CTO will communicate with the persons liable to pay it.

27.15 VALUATION

Perhaps the most important point to be reiterated is the principle that the value transferred by a gift is measured as the difference between the value before and after the gift (ie the amount by which the estate's value has been reduced as a result of the gift). This is often referred to as the 'loss to donor' principle. In contrast the basis of valuation for CGT and stamp duty purposes is the value of what is actually transferred (see **15.1.1**).

Another important principle is that of related property, the concept being that the aggregate value of fragmented assets may be less than the value of the whole undivided unit. Property is related to property in an individual's estate in the following circumstances:

● where it is comprised in the estate of his spouse; and

● where as a result of a transfer by an individual or his spouse the property is, or has been within the preceding five years, the property of a charity or held on trust for charitable purposes, or of one of the exempt bodies.

The most common application is in relation to shares of unquoted companies, but the same principle applies to any kind of property.

In effect the value of related property is ascertained on the basis that all of the related property is held by one notional person. The value of individual holdings is then calculated simply as a proportion of the total value (see **15.1.2**). Only liabilities for which reimbursement can reasonably be expected are taken into account. If a charge is secured on any property the value of that property is reduced (see **15.1.3**).

A restriction on the freedom to dispose of an asset is only taken into account to the extent that consideration was given for it. However, care is needed if the contract was part of 'associated operations' (see **15.1.4**).

Where a chargeable transfer also gives rise to a chargeable gain, any

CGT paid reduces the value of the transfer. This does not apply in relation to settlement gains (see **15.1.6**).

Note the special rules for determining the value of life assurance contracts (see **15.1.8**). Note also the various assumptions that have to be made in the valuation of shares in unquoted companies. Particular stress is laid on the significance of the various control thresholds, and the effect that these have on the value of shares from holdings in excess of the thresholds, compared to the value of shares from holdings below those thresholds (see **15.1.9**).

Account can be taken of various changes occurring on or after death, and allowance can be made for the added expense of administering or realising foreign property. Where income tax liabilities arising on the offshore income gains and on discounted securities has been paid, an adjustment is made where IHT has been included as payable, but later turns out not to have been payable (see **15.2.1–15.2.5**). If related property is sold within three years of a death, the actual sale proceeds, if less than the related property value, are substituted (see **15.2.6**).

Two most valuable reliefs which should not be overlooked also concern subsequent sales of property:

(1) Account can be taken of net losses on all sales of quoted shares (including AIM) (compared with probate) on all such shares sold within 12 months of death (see **15.3**).

(2) Actual (higher or lower sale) proceeds can be substituted for the probate value of land sold within three years of death. Compulsory purchase occurring outside the three-year period is taken into account, provided that the notice to treat was issued within the three-year period. Proceeds from sales otherwise than to compulsory purchase authorities in the fourth year after death can also be taken into account (see **15.4**).

27.16 SETTLEMENTS

The various definitions applying to settlements should be noted (see **16.1**).

27.16.1 Settlements with interests in possession and reversionary interests

The main point to remember when dealing with interests in possession is that they are treated as owned by the person beneficially entitled under a trust to the underlying property. It follows that an IHT charge can arise when an interest in possession comes to an end so that beneficial ownership of the assets passes into new hands. There are, however, a number of exceptions to this general rule. Note also that certain of the exemptions do not apply to interests in possession (see **17.1**).

27.16.2 Settlements with no interest in possession

In contrast to settlements with an interest in possession, a settlement is one with no interest in possession if there is no person who has an interest in possession or a right in reversion to the trust property. Because there is no such person, a special no interest in possession regime applies to property held by such trusts. These are subject to a special ten-yearly IHT charge, calculated using the lifetime rate of IHT at three-tenths of the effective rate of IHT on a notional transfer (see **17.3**).

In addition, an exit charge arises if any property leaves the trust. The amount of the exit charge is based upon the reduction in the value of the trust because of the transfer. The rate of IHT depends upon the date on which the transfer takes place. For property leaving before the first ten-year anniversary, the charge is based on the effective rate of IHT on a notional transfer of the value of settled property at the time the settlement was made. No account is taken of BPR or APR on an exit charge, but it is taken into account for a ten-year charge. Since subsequent exit charges are based upon the last ten-year charge, it may be worth waiting until after the next ten-year charge. The appropriate fraction is multiplied by so many fortieths as there are complete quarters in the period between setting up the settlement and the date of transfer. In arriving at the effective rate of IHT, account is also taken of any transfers made by the settlor in the seven years preceding the settlement's inception. There is no charge on property leaving a settlement within the first quarter after its creation. Note also that there is no increase in the amount of the effective rate even if the value of the property in the settlement has increased substantially (see **17.3.3**). Between ten-year anniversaries the IHT charge is calculated in a similar way, but using the effective rate at the time of the last ten-year anniversary (see **17.3.4**).

There is a special rule that applies to property leaving temporary charitable trusts. This is an anti-avoidance measure aimed at preventing the use of the charitable exemption to obtain an IHT-free transfer of property, followed by a distribution from the settlement at a nil rate. The charge arises on the reduction in value attributed to the property leaving the trust. The rate of IHT charge is reduced progressively as each ten-year anniversary is passed (see **17.4.1**).

An IHT-favoured form of trust is the 'accumulation and maintenance' settlement. The advantage of such settlements is that there is no ten-year charge and no exit charge (usually) when property leaves the trust. Income can be paid out to beneficiaries for their education, maintenance or other benefit, but if not distributed must be accumulated. All of the beneficiaries must be grandchildren of a common grandparent, or the children or widow(er)s of such grandchildren. The settlement must contain a term that a beneficiary must become entitled to the settled property or an interest in possession therein not later than age 25. However, a special charge to IHT arises on property ceasing to be held on accumulation and maintenance trusts (see **17.4.2**).

There are also IHT-favoured regimes for employee trusts, pre-1978 protective trusts, pre-1981 trusts for disabled persons (see **17.4.3–17.4.5**) and for property becoming subject to charitable trusts or for charitable purposes (see **17.5.2**), for maintenance funds for historic buildings etc (see **17.6.1**) and for conditionally exempt transfers (see **17.6.2**).

27.17 LIABILITY TO IHT

It is important to understand upon whom the liability to pay IHT falls. A number of situations are described at **18.2**.

27.18 ADMINISTRATION AND COLLECTION

There is a range of provisions dealing with the administration and collection of IHT. Regulations set out the requirements as to the delivery of an account of a deceased person's estate. This account, usually referred to as the 'Inland Revenue Account', must be submitted to the Revenue, generally within 12 months of the death. There are various forms for use where the deceased was UK-domiciled, where the deceased was non-UK domiciled, and for small estates. If there is any omission or defect in an account it must be corrected within six months of it coming to light. There are also provisions giving the Revenue the right to require information and to inspect property (see **19.2**).

The Revenue has the right to issue a determination of the amount subject to an IHT charge, but there are appeal procedures (see **19.3**).

Payment of IHT arising on a lifetime chargeable transfer must be made within six months from the end of the month in which the transfer occurs or, if the chargeable transfer is made after 5 April but before 1 October in any year, by the end of April in the following year. IHT becoming chargeable because of death within seven years is payable within six months of the death. Where IHT becomes payable because of the failure of an exemption, it falls due six months after the end of the month in which it becomes chargeable (see **19.4.1**).

IHT arising on some chargeable transfers of land, certain shares or securities and businesses may be payable by ten equal annual instalments. The chargeable transfers for which this election can be made are those which arise in the following circumstances:

- the transfer is made on death,
- the attributable IHT is borne by the person benefiting from the transfer, and
- in the case of settled property, where the property continues to held by the settlement.

Each instalment is subject to interest running from the due date of each instalment (see **19.4.2**, **19.4.3** and **19.5.2**).

In appropriate cases, IHT relating to works of art etc may be surrendered in lieu of IHT (see **19.4.4** and **19.4.5**). The Revenue has a charge over property to the value of IHT remaining unpaid (see **19.6**). When all IHT has been paid the Revenue issues a certificate of discharge (see **19.7**). If it should subsequently transpire that too much or too little IHT has been paid, an appropriate adjustment is made (see **19.8**).

There are penalties for failure to provide information, for the provision of incorrect information and for failure to remedy errors (see **19.10**). There are regulations which dispense with the need to submit accounts on estates that do not exceed laid down limits of value for certain types of property and for overall value (see **19.11.3**).

27.19 MISCELLANEOUS AND SUPPLEMENTARY

In some cases IHT is payable on entitlements to receive future consideration (see **20.1**). A potential problem arising on the purchase of an annuity in conjunction with a life policy is highlighted at **20.2**. The procedure to be followed when transfers are reported late is explained at **20.3**. The meaning of 'associated operations', 'control', 'connected persons' and the application of the *Furniss v Dawson* principle are fully discussed in Chapter 19.

27.20 RELATED CGT

Those CGT provisions which are of relevance in the context of estate planning are discussed in Chapter 21. There is discussion of those persons and gains which are subject to CGT in the hands of individuals or trustees (see **21.1**).

A wide-reaching change in the application of CGT to individuals and trustees is the freezing of indexation at April 1998, so far as concerns expenditure prior to that date, and its abolition for expenditure thereafter. In its place there is now taper relief by which the proportion of a gain which is chargeable depends upon the length of the period of ownership. For business assets the tapering is down to 25 per cent for periods of ownership of up to ten years. For non-business assets the first two years do not merit any reduction in the chargeable portion of the gain. Thereafter the gain is tapered down to 60 per cent for periods of ownership in excess of two years up to ten years (see **21.2**). There are rules applying taper relief in a variety of situations to both business and non-business assets (see **21.3**).

A number of anti-avoidance measures are introduced to prevent manipulation of taper relief. The areas concerned are periods of limited exposure to fluctuations in value (see **21.4.1**), periods of share ownership where there is a change of a company's activities (see **21.4.2**), periods of share owner-ship where there is value-shifting (see **21.4.3**), and a special rule which is applied where property is settled by a company (see **21.4.4**). There are also rules to deal with a variety of special situations:

- options (see **21.5.1**);
- further rules for assets derived from other assets (see **21.5.2**);
- assets transferred between spouses (see **21.5.3**);
- postponed gains (see **21.5.4**);
- assets acquired in the reconstruction of mutual businesses (see **21.5.5**);
- ancillary trust funds (see **21.5.6**);
- general rules for settlements (see **21.5.7**); and
- general rule for apportionments (see **21.5.8**).

The application of the annual exempt amount has been amended to accom-modate taper relief (see **21.6**).

The calculation of CGT is explained at **21.7**.

For individuals there is a much longer period of temporary non-resi-dence during which they continue to be subject to CGT on the basis of deemed continuing residence in the UK (see **21.8.2**). Individuals who are resident or ordinarily resident in the UK, but not domiciled there, are only taxable on gains on foreign assets if the proceeds are remitted to the UK (see **21.8.4**). Gains realised by non-resident companies may be attributed to UK-resident members of the company (see **21.8.5**). When an asset becomes situated outside the UK, there is a deemed disposal at that time (see **21.8.6**).

The following transactions are deemed to be made at market value, in place of the actual consideration (if any) passing, or if a disposal is made otherwise than at arm's length (see **21.9**):

- gifts unless covered by gift relief (mainly business assets);
- transfers into settlement;
- distributions from a company in respect of shares therein.

The definition of 'connected persons' which is broadly similar to the defi-nition for IHT is given at **21.10**.

There are rules for linking a series of small transfers out of a large holding of shares in order to prevent manipulation of the valuation rules by making a number of small transactions rather than one large one (see **21.11**).

Transactions between spouses do not, generally, give rise to any CGT lia-bility. The transferee spouse inherits the history of transferred assets (ie base cost date of acquisition etc – see **21.12**).

For CGT there is no disposal on death, but assets are deemed to pass at their probate value. This creates a tax-free uplift. This has a number of consequences which are fully explored at **21.13**.

As for IHT, it is possible to, in effect, rewrite the will or rules on intestacy where a deed of variation is entered into. The effect is that the revised dis-positions are deemed to have been made as at the date of death (see **21.14**).

27.21 CGT AND PRIVATE RESIDENCES

The availability of private residence relief on the disposal of an individual's home is fully explored, as is the availability of the relief where a beneficiary occupies a residence owned by a settlement, in Chapter 22.

27.22 CGT SETTLEMENTS

The rules for nominees, bare trustees and funds in court can be simply stated, as the beneficiary, etc is absolutely entitled as against the trustee, nominee etc and the assets are treated as if any acts by the trustees were actually carried out by the beneficiaries etc (see **23.1**).

There are a number of CGT rules for settlements of general application to all forms of trusts except nominees, bare trusts and funds in court. These include rules for determining the residence status of trustees (see **23.2.2**); making gifts into settlement (see **23.2.3**); persons becoming absolutely entitled as against the trustees (see **23.2.4**); on the termination of a life interest on the death of a person entitled (see **23.2.5**); exclusion of a chargeable gain on the life tenant's death (see **23.2.6**); interaction with gift relief (see **23.2.7**); disposals of interest in settled property (see **23.2.8**); and charges on a settlor with an interest in a settlement (see **23.2.12**).

There is a range of, effectively, anti-avoidance provisions dealing with migrant settlements, non-resident settlements and dual-resident settlements. These include rules dealing with trustees ceasing to be UK-resident (see **23.3.1**); special rules applying on the death of trustees (see **23.3.2**); liability of past trustees for IHT (see **23.3.3**); trustees ceasing to be liable to UK tax under the terms of a double tax arrangement (see **23.3.4**); acquisition by dual resident trustees (see **23.3.5**); disposals of interests in non-resident settlements (see **23.3.6**); attribution of gains to settlors with interests in non- or dual-resident settlements (see **23.3.7**); attributions of gains to sett-lor in temporary non-residence cases (see **23.3.17**); attribution of gains to beneficiaries (see **23.3.18**); gains of dual resident settlements (see **23.3.19**); migrant settlements (see **23.3.20**); transfers between settlements (see **23.3.21**); payments by and to companies (see **23.3.23**) as well as definitions and Revenue power to obtain information.

27.23 CGT HOLD-OVER RELIEF ON GIFTS

Adjustments are needed to deal with gains held over under the general 'old style' gift relief that applied before 14 March 1989 (see **24.1**). There are now two remaining opportunities to hold over gains arising on gifts.:

(1) First where the assets concerned are business property (see **24.2**).

(2) Secondly, disposals that are also occasions of immediate IHT charge, including distributions from discretionary trusts that are chargeable to IHT, but not PETs, gifts to political parties, maintenance funds, etc and beneficiaries under accumulation and maintenance trusts becoming absolutely entitled to capital (see **24.3**).

27.24 CGT RETIREMENT RELIEF

A trigger for an estate planning review is often an impending retirement. Chapter 25 looks at CGT retirement relief.

Over the years the courts have been kept busy reviewing the meaning of various words or phrases used in the legislation. The most significant of these are examined in detail at **25.1.1**.

In a takeover of an unquoted company by a quoted company, consideration is frequently in the form of shares in the purchasing company. As this would not otherwise permit retirement relief, it is possible to elect against the identification of the original shares with the new holding. As a result there is a chargeable gain which is eligible for retirement relief (see **25.1.2**).

In general, relief is available for gains arising on disposals made after the proprietor has reached age 50. However, retirement relief is also available were there is enforced retirement, on medical grounds, below that age (see **25.1.3**).

The relief is available for retirement by a sole trader, and for a partner withdrawing from or reducing his interest in a partnership (see **25.2.1**).

A point which has caused difficulty is that the disposal should comprise the whole or a part of the business. How this has been interpreted by the courts is examined at **25.2.2**.

It is also possible to obtain retirement relief on the disposal of an asset where it is used for the purpose of a trade carried on by a partnership of which the individual was a member, or a company in which he has the requisite shareholding (see **25.2.3**). Retirement relief is available on the disposal of shares in a trading company, or the holding company of a trading group (see **25.2.4** and **25.2.5**).

Retirement relief is also available on employees' disposals, where an employee disposes of assets which he has provided for use in carrying out the duties of his employment (see **25.3.1**). It is available for trustees' disposals where the necessary conditions are satisfied by a beneficiary (see **25.3.2**).

A final category of disposals on which retirement relief can be given comprise associated disposals. These are disposals of assets used by a partnership or company and are associated with a person's retirement from the business, the partnership or company (see **25.3.3**).

The calculation of the relief and the CGT arising thereon is covered, along with a number of special rules regarding the aggregation of earlier business periods, where relief has been given on an earlier disposal but further relief is now due, and aggregation of a spouse's period of ownership of a business (see **25.3.4–25.3.6**).

Possible ways of maximising retirement relief are discussed at **25.4**, and possible alternatives to retirement relief are explored at **25.5**. Finally, as retirement relief is being phased out over a five-year period, the difference between retirement relief and taper relief which has now been introduced are highlighted at **25.6**.

27.25 STAMP DUTY

There is no stamp duty charge on gifts. Liability to stamp duty can arise on certain transactions by or relating to trustees.

27.26 WILLS

It is of vital importance to make the right kind of will. It is not possible to recommend any one particular kind of will, because personal wishes and circumstances are different in every case. However, a number of general points can be made. Although personal factors and not tax considerations should be paramount the aim should be to have a valid and tax efficient will.

If a testator disposes of his estate by way of absolute gifts, the beneficiaries are free to deal with the assets as they choose. If he confers an interest in possession on the surviving spouse with, on her death the capital distributed among children or grandchildren on attaining, say, age 21, life or other limited interest (eg until remarriage) allows the testator to exercise a degree of control over his estate so as to preserve wealth for the benefit of his family.

Frequently the will is a hybrid of the above. Thus as well as creating a life or other limited interest on the surviving spouse, his trustees, are given full unrestricted powers to advance capital and make long-term interest-free loans to the surviving spouse. Thus the trustees have control over the estate, but are able to help the surviving spouse if she should need it. The trustees can also advance or appoint capital to other beneficiaries giving rise to PETs.

A IHT saving can be achieved by utilising the nil rate band available on the first death to make transfers to non-exempt beneficiaries on the first death (eg children). In 2000/01 the saving is worth (£234,000 × 40%) = £93,600. Alternatively, a discretionary settlement could be created by the will with a fund equal to the current nil rate band. Such a settlement could be created with the surviving spouse as a beneficiary without the settled property forming part of the spouse's estate for IHT purposes. This is unsuitable for a house for the spouse to occupy; as such a settlement made by the spouse would be a GWR and remain in the spouse's estate.

An interest in a business (eg shares in a family trading company or a partnership interest) which qualifies for BPR should not be left by will to the surviving spouse. It would make better use of BPR, especially if the 100 per cent rate is available, to make chargeable transfers as specific gifts.

It is normal for wills to contain a survivorship clause providing that a beneficiary only takes a benefit should he survive the testator for a specified period of not more than six months.

A will may direct how any IHT is paid or borne as among his beneficiaries. It is normally assumed that gifts of UK property or legacies payable out of the UK property are free of IHT unless the will otherwise directs. Generally, unless a specific direction is given that a legacy is to bear its own IHT, it is borne by the residuary estate to the detriment of the residuary beneficiaries. If the residuary beneficiary is the deceased's spouse it would be wise to make a specific direction that all legacies (other than *de minimis*) should bear their own IHT.

Finally, as a fallback, there is the possibility of entering into a deed of variation.

LIST OF NATIONAL PURPOSE BODIES EXEMPTED FROM IHT ON GIFTS

The National Gallery

The British Museum

The National Museums of Scotland

The National Museum of Wales

The Ulster Museum

Any other similar national institution which exists wholly or mainly for the purpose of preserving for the public benefit a collection of scientific, historic or artistic interest and which is approved for this purpose by the Treasury

Any museum or art gallery in the UK which exists wholly or mainly for the purpose of preserving for the public benefit a collection of scientific, historic or artistic interest and is maintained by a local authority or university in the UK

Any library the main function of which is to serve the needs of teaching and research at a university in the UK

The Historic Buildings and Monuments Commission for England.

The National Trust for Places of Historic Interest or Natural Beauty

The National Trust for Scotland for Places of Historic Interest or Natural Beauty

The National Art Collections Fund

The Trustees of the National Heritage Memorial Fund

The Friends of the National Libraries

The Historic Churches Preservation Trust

Nature Conservancy Council for England

Scottish Natural Heritage

Countryside Council for Wales

Any local authority

Any Government department (including the National Debt Commissioners).

Any university or university college in the UK

A health service body, as defined in ICTA 1988 s 519A

A Health Authority established under the National Health Service Act 1977 s 8

A Special Health Authority established under the National Health Service Act 1977 s 11

An NHS trust established under the NHS and Community Care Act 1990

A Health Board or Special Health Board, the Common Services Agency for the Scottish Health Service and an NHS trust constituted under the NHS (Scotland) Act 1978 ss 2, 10 and 12A respectively

A State Hospital Management Committee constituted under the Mental Health (Scotland) Act 1984 s 91

The Dental Practice Board

The Scottish Dental Practice Board

The Public Health Laboratory Service Board

A Health and Social Services Board and the Northern Ireland Central Services Agency for the Health and Social Services established under the Health and Personal Social Services (Northern Ireland) Order 1972 Articles 16 and 26 respectively

A special health and social services agency established under the Health and Personal Social Services (Special Agencies) (Northern Ireland) Order 1990

A Health and Social Services trust established under the Health and Personal Social Services (Northern Ireland) Order 1991

INDEX

All references are to paragraph numbers.